Contents

PART TWO: REVIEW SECTION: TIME PERIODS

TIME PERIOD THREE: c. 1815 to c. 1914

TIME PERIOD FOUR: c. 1914 TO PRESENT

PART THREE: MODEL EXAMS

ONLINE

Want more test-taking practice?

Visit *barronsbooks.com/AP/ap-european-hist/* to access
three additional practice tests or scan the QR code below.

*Be sure to have your copy of *AP European History*, 9th edition on
hand to complete the registration process.

As you review the content in this book to work toward earning that 5 on your AP European History Exam, here are five things that you MUST know above everything else:

Barron's Essential 5

1 **Know the important European dynasties and rulers, both autocratic and democratic.** This is a huge subject on the AP exam! There are almost always specific multiple-choice questions on the most important rulers and ruling families and how their power and decisions have a reach through the ages to today.
- ✔ Know the Habsburgs, Romanovs, Valois, Bourbons, Hohenzollerns, Tudors, Stuarts, and Napoleon.
- ✔ Study England and the Netherlands as the first nations to move toward democratic principles.
- ✔ Compare revolutions and the rise of democracy in different nations.
- ✔ Examine the important rulers: monarchical, dictatorial, and democratic.
- ✔ Know the styles of each ruler and the external situations that affected how he or she ruled so that you can make connections within and across the four required time periods.

2 **Know the thematic learning objectives that are required by the College Board and tested on the AP exam.** There are five required objectives that you should consider while reading through this guide. They are:
- ✔ Interaction of Europe and the world
- ✔ Poverty and prosperity
- ✔ Objective knowledge and subjective visions
- ✔ States and other institutions of power
- ✔ Individuals and society
- ✔ National and European identity
- ✔ Examine this in more detail on pages 18–20

3 **Practice preparing for the document-based question.** The DBQ is a hugely important factor in your success on the AP exam. In the weeks leading up to the test, practice at least a few complete DBQ responses. You won't know what the DBQ question is going to be, but you need to concentrate on the thoroughness of your response, your ability to demonstrate point of view in the documents, and provide the amount of detail typical of high-scoring responses. Have your teacher or classmates help with this.
- ✔ Practice your point-of-view commentary on document authors.
- ✔ Show your understanding of the author's purpose, historical context, and audience.
- ✔ Remember to bring in outside information not given in the documents.
- ✔ ANSWER THE QUESTION with a strong thesis and good support. Stay on track and do not go off on a tangent.

4 **Be sure to know the important figures and movements in the twentieth century.** This is essentially a modern history course and knowing the importance of many figures of the last century is key to success on the exam. Figures such as Kaiser Wilhelm II, Otto von Bismarck (not a twentieth-century figure himself, but his machinations toward the end of the nineteenth century had a significant effect on the twentieth century), Winston Churchill, Mohandas Gandhi, Margaret Thatcher, Adolf Hitler, Vladimir Lenin, and Mikhail Gorbachev should be known. Also, movements such as the peace movement, feminism, universal suffrage, fascism, communism, détente, decolonization, and glasnost should be evaluated.
- ✔ The exam is focusing more and more on recent history.
- ✔ The wars of the twentieth century are great fodder for questions.
- ✔ The fights for minority rights are also a big topic for multiple-choice questions.

5 **Know the *Framework*.** You need to be familiar with how you will be assessed on the exam. The College Board has created an *AP European History Curriculum Framework* explaining the course and is available at *http://media.collegeboard.com/digitalServices/pdf/ap/2013advances/ap-european-history-curriculum-framework.pdf*. This framework has specific themes and, more importantly, specific learning objectives that EVERY AP question will be tied to. Read the Framework to know what they will ask.

PART ONE
Introduction

Using This Book

This book is designed primarily to prepare you for the AP European History exam. It provides:

- Systematic methods for studying history
- A guide to the AP European History exam
- Review chapters including sample and practice questions on the various periods of European history
- Two complete model AP exams with answers

TO THE TEACHER AND THE STUDENT

This book can be used as a supplement to classwork and study material, or as a review book to help you refresh your memory on what you learned throughout the year. However you choose to use the book, creating a study plan to suit your needs is simple and easy.

Beginning on page 5 with "Systematic Methods for Studying History," you will first be introduced to the specific historical skills required by the *AP European History Curriculum Framework*:

1. How to utilize chronological reasoning
2. How to improve your skills in comparing and contextualizing historical facts
3. How to craft historical arguments and use historical evidence to support them
4. How to make historical interpretations and synthesize your results into essays and short answers

In addition, this book explains how to frame the big picture; how to read, take notes, and highlight; and how to connect events throughout history using the first four skill sets above and their subsets. These skills are all essential for helping anyone understand history, make sense of it, and retain and interconnect the most relevant bits of information needed to excel on the exam.

The next part of the book is "A Guide to the AP European History Exam" on page 17. Here the basics of the exam are explained. These include:

1. The exam's duration (including duration of each section)
2. The number of questions and types of questions in each section
3. The subject matter
4. The historical time span
5. Sample questions
6. Hints on how to approach questions

Knowing what to expect on test day will reduce any test anxiety you may have—allowing you to perform your best.

Part Two of the book consists of twelve chapters of review of the major historical periods covered on the exam along with sample multiple-choice questions and answers and practice thematic essays. The *AP European History Curriculum Framework* guides the organization of this book as it does the course. The course has been divided into four periods that also reflect the new themes of the course that have been explained in the *AP European History Curriculum Framework*. This book conforms to the *AP European History Curriculum Framework* as much as possible without disturbing the narrative of the historical subjects covered in the framework. This book has been organized into 12 chapters that reflect the *AP European History Curriculum Framework* and thousands of years of historical inquiry. These chapters are organized into the four *Historical Periods* that are now standard for the course with each time period consisting of three chapters. The *Historical Periods* are:

Period 1: c. 1450 to c. 1648
Period 2: c. 1649 to c. 1815
Period 3: c. 1815 to c. 1914
Period 4: c. 1914 to the present

The AP European History course also revolves around **six themes** that you are expected to explore as you gain an understanding of each period over the diverse geography of Europe. Those themes are

1. Interaction of Europe and the World
2. Poverty and Prosperity
3. Objective Knowledge and Subjective Visions
4. States and Other Institutions of Power
5. Individuals and Society
6. National and European Identity

This book will attempt to integrate the themes into a narrative based upon the time periods outlined by the *AP European History Curriculum Framework*. The themes will be explored both within the text and through the sample multiple-choice and essay questions provided for each chapter and in the assessment created for each time period.

Finally, Part Three includes two model AP exams with multiple-choice questions, thematic essays, and document-based questions with suggested answers. You can also access three additional exams online at *barronsbooks.com/AP/ap-european-hist/*

A Suggested Approach for Using This Book

1. Peruse the "Systematic Methods for Studying History" section.
2. Study the "Guide to the AP European History Exam."
3. Read the *Framework* to know what they will ask.

   ■ The College Board has created an *AP European History Curriculum Framework* explaining the course and is available at: *http://media.collegeboard.com/digitalServices/pdf/ap/2013advances/ap-european-history-curriculum-framework.pdf.*
   ■ This framework has specific themes and, more importantly, specific learning objectives that **EVERY AP question** will be tied to.

4. Study any or all of the review chapters and answer the sample and practice questions.
5. Pay special attention to the sample essay questions and explanations; there is a lot of valuable information there.
6. Take and score the model exams in the book and online. Examine the questions you missed and look for any connections that can tell you what areas you need to concentrate on.

To the Teacher

For use of the book as a classroom aid the various review chapters in this book can be used as year-long supplements to sum up or reinforce particular teaching units and homework assignments. The historical review section of each chapter will help your students to make valid, well-supported historical arguments within and across the four time periods. The sample and practice Long-Essay Questions (LEQs), Document-Based Questions (DBQs), Short-Answer Questions, and Multiple-Choice Questions (MCQs) will reinforce the learning.

Part Two, the review section, can be used near the end of the year to pull the course work together and to prepare students for the exam.

It's often helpful for students to study Part One at the beginning of the course to help them to study history and to give them an idea of what the exam will be like. Knowing what they will face is both a motivator and method of organizing the course's information.

To the Student

This book can be used independently of a course in European history or it can be used along with assigned materials to sum up, pull together, clarify, and review. It's best to use it at the beginning of the year and to read *Part One* right away.

That will help you to study better both in and out of class, and it will give you an idea of what's ahead if you decide to take the AP exam. Review the appropriate chapters in *Part Two* right before beginning each topic in class to "frame the picture," and to help fit everything into place. Or go to the appropriate chapter after studying that unit in class in order to pull it all together.

In order to use the book as review and practice for the exam, **don't wait until late April or May**. Instead of getting nervous and wasting energy on test anxiety, put time aside in late March or early April to study the review chapters and to do the sample questions on content you have already covered in class and in homework. Save the model exams for late April or early May, then use these exams and the ones online to check your progress, and to keep practicing the skills that will help you earn a 5 on test day.

SYSTEMATIC METHODS FOR STUDYING HISTORY

What follows are some time-tested methods for studying history. These basic skills will aid you in becoming an involved student in any history course; these suggestions will help you with homework, supplementary reading, and preparation for the AP European History exam. After the basic skills, the historical skills expected of all AP students will be examined.

How to Recognize the Logical Order of History Materials

Most history readings, especially texts, are organized logically; some examples follow:

FACTS SUPPORT A THEME: The Magna Carta, the Puritan Revolution, and the personalities involved help one trace the development of constitutional government in England.

GREAT EVENTS DEFINE AN ERA: The French Revolution colored the political, social, cultural, and diplomatic life of Europe for over a hundred years after it happened.

CAUSE-EFFECT RELATIONSHIPS ARE ASCERTAINED: The outbreak of the First World War in August 1914 was caused by long-term trends, such as militarism, nationalism, and imperialism, which stretched back decades into the nineteenth century.

THE INFLUENCE OF INDIVIDUALS ON AN AGE IS IDENTIFIED: The totalitarian dictatorships of Hitler and Stalin affected the entire planet before and long after the Second World War.

In reading history materials, the object is to focus on this inherent logical order. This can be done by *pre-reading* and by *framing the big picture.*

How to Pre-Read

Before tackling the text itself, be sure to skim the chapter by reading each of the following *in order*:

- ✔ The chapter heading
- ✔ The introductory paragraph
- ✔ Focus questions at the beginning of the chapter
- ✔ Subheadings
- ✔ The concluding paragraph
- ✔ Review questions at chapter's end
- ✔ Assess **bold** print or *italics* within the text

It is better to concentrate on *reading* at this point rather than trying to take notes.

How to "Frame the Big Picture"

During both the *pre-reading* and the *reading* of the text, pose the following questions as a natural way of keeping the mind's eye on the main story, on the *logical order* of the material:

- ✔ What is the theme of the chapter? (What is it about? What is the author trying to prove? How does it fit into the themes elucidated by the *AP European History Curriculum Framework*?)
- ✔ What are the main events? (What happened and what caused them?)
- ✔ Who are the principal personalities? (Who did what, and why?)
- ✔ What are the important results? (New ideas? Significant changes? Power shifts? End of one thing and/or beginning of another?)

Remember: "Don't lose the forest for the trees." These essays are often about putting pieces of little pictures together to make one bigger picture that fully answers the question.

How to Read the Text

Once you have *pre-read* the material and *framed the big picture,* you are ready to attack the text itself. Difficult material deserves a "straight read" before you try to highlight, underline, or take notes; most readings allow you to do both simultaneously as long as you have *pre-read.*

Sample Reading with Underlining, Accompanying Notes, Brief Outline

UNDERLINED PASSAGE

Early nineteenth-century <u>industrialization</u> in England depended upon <u>steam</u> engines made of iron and fueled by coal. Steam-powered <u>textile mills</u> created a <u>factory economy</u> and a new <u>working</u> class. Steam-powered railway <u>trains</u> moved people and products speedily over great distances, <u>concentrating populations</u> into expanded cities and linking the sources of raw materials with the centers of manufacturing. Functional <u>new architectural</u> designs—using structural steel—reflected the practical needs of the new society. <u>Class</u> conflict, brought on by disparities of wealth, extremes of poverty, and the unexpected difficulties of industrialization, raged throughout most of the century.

NOTES

Industrialization, nineteenth-century England

Coal-fueled, iron steam engines powered textile mills = factory economy + new working class.

Speedy steam-powered railroads = expanded cities; linked raw materials + factories.

New steel architecture; class conflict because of income differences & effects of industrialization.

BRIEF OUTLINE

Nineteenth-Century Industrialization in England

I. Steam power, the essential element

   A. Iron engines fueled by coal
   B. Textile factories, new working class
   C. RRs move masses: people, products

II. Effects of industrialization

   A. Expanded cities
   B. New architecture
   C. Class conflict: disparities of wealth

Centuries and Chronology

A consistent problem in studying history is the failure to appreciate that significant trends are often concurrent, that influential people are sometimes contemporaries. For instance, the Reformation and the Age of Exploration shared the sixteenth century, and the personification of absolutism, Louis XIV, reigned while the greatest scientist of the Enlightenment, Isaac Newton, formulated his theories of gravitation.

An excellent method for *connecting* events, trends, and personalities of history is to *identify their century or centuries.* History is not a series of separate strands but rather a fabric of causes, effects, and interwoven influences. Below is an abbreviated list of major figures and events of the centuries covered by the exam:

FIFTEENTH CENTURY (1401–1500) The Renaissance; the fall of Constantinople to the Ottoman Turks; the voyages of Portuguese explorers and Columbus. Contemporaries: Leonardo da Vinci, Suleiman the Magnificent, Gutenberg, Henry the Navigator.

SIXTEENTH CENTURY (1501–1600) The Reformation and Catholic and Counter-Reformations; the Age of Exploration; the growth of national monarchies. Contemporaries: Luther, Henry VIII, Loyola, Holy Roman Emperor Charles V, Copernicus, Elizabeth I, Magellan, Cabral, da Gama, Philip II.

SEVENTEENTH CENTURY (1601–1700) The Age of Colonization; the Commercial Revolution and the rise of capitalism; the rise of modern science; the Thirty Years' War; the Age of Absolutism and the rise of constitutionalism. Contemporaries: Descartes, Galileo, Newton, the Stuart kings and Cromwell, Locke, Richelieu, Drake, Mazarin, the Romanovs, Louis XIV.

EIGHTEENTH CENTURY (1701–1800) The growth of capitalism; the Age of Enlightenment and of Reason; the Age of Benevolent Despotism and of Revolution. Contemporaries: Adam Smith, Voltaire, Rousseau, Frederick the Great, Mary Wollstonecraft, Maria Theresa, Catherine the Great, Louis XVI, George III, Robespierre, George Washington.

NINETEENTH CENTURY (1801–1900) The Age of Napoleon; the Age of Metternich; the Age of Romanticism; the Age of Nationalism and Unification; the Age of "ISMs"; the Age of Imperialism; the Age of Progress; Women's Suffrage; Chartism; Contemporaries: Talleyrand, Metternich, Wordsworth, Goethe, Bismarck, Cavour, Marx, Darwin, Cecil Rhodes, Teddy Roosevelt, Gregor Mendel, Louis Pasteur.

TWENTIETH CENTURY (1901–2000) The Age of Violence; the Age of Technology; the Nuclear Age; the Age of Information; the Age of Anxiety; the Age of Totalitarianism; the Cold War; the European Union; the Age of Democracy. Contemporaries: Kaiser Wilhelm, Clemenceau, Lenin, Wilson, Stalin, Hitler, Gandhi, Churchill, Freud, Einstein, Franklin Roosevelt, Hirohito, Mao, Adenauer, De Gaulle, Thatcher, Gorbachev, Reagan, Yeltsin, Walesa, Havel.

TIP

When studying a historical event, personality, or trend:

1. Determine its century (or centuries).
2. Make up an open-ended chart of the centuries, and make it a habit to place pertinent events, people, and trends in the appropriate time frame.

HISTORICAL SKILLS USED IN ALL AP HISTORY EXAMS

The writers of the AP History exams came together and decided upon a common set of skills that all AP History students should possess. These skills come directly from the *AP European History Curriculum Framework*. These skills have been divided into two categories:

I. AP History Disciplinary Practices
II. AP History Reasoning Skills

The first section focuses more on the skills historians use to "construct and test historical arguments," while the second section of skills focuses more on mental habits often referred to as "thinking historically." Within each skill type there are subsets that you should master. These skills are in many ways similar to the skills required by the Social Studies C-3 framework that was adopted nationally for the subject area. These are in some ways an extension of the skills that all students should be practicing nationally. The skills are divided as follows:

I. AP History Disciplinary Practices

1. Analyzing Historical Evidence
2. Argument Development

II. Making Historical Connections

1. Contextualization
2. Comparison
3. Causation
4. Continuity and Change Over Time (CCOT)

AP HISTORY DISCIPLINARY PRACTICES

Practice 1: Analyzing Historical Evidence

To be successful you will need to be able to examine multiple pieces of evidence in concert with each other, noting contradictions, corroborations, and other relationships among sources to develop and support an argument. It involves the capacity to extract useful information, make supportable inferences, and draw appropriate conclusions from historical evidence, while also noting the context in which the evidence was produced and used, recognizing its limitations and assessing the points of view it reflects. This skill has been further divided into two categories:

1. Analyzing Primary Sources
2. Analyzing Secondary Sources

ANALYZING PRIMARY SOURCES

This practice requires five specific traits. According to the *College Board*, you must be able to:

1. Describe historically relevant information and/or arguments within a source.
2. Explain how a source provides information about the broader historical setting within which it was created.
3. Explain how a source's point of view, purpose, historical situation, and/or audience might affect a source's meaning.
4. Explain the historical significance of a source's point of view, purpose, historical situation, and/or audience.
5. Evaluate a primary source's credibility and/or limitations.

ANALYZING SECONDARY SOURCES

This practice requires six specific traits. According to the *College Board*, you must be able to:

1. Describe the claim or argument of a secondary source, as well as the evidence used.
2. Describe a pattern or trend in quantitative data in non-text-based sources.
3. Explain how a historian's claim or argument is supported with evidence.
4. Explain how a historian's context influences a claim or argument.
5. Analyze patterns and trends in quantitative data in non-text-based sources.
6. Evaluate the effectiveness of a historical claim or argument.

REMEMBER that using historical evidence properly shows many different historical skills in use at the same time. Almost none of the other skills will be demonstrated if you do not use evidence well.

To master Analyzing Historical Evidence, you must be able to:

- Evaluate evidence to explain its relevance to a claim or thesis, providing clear and consistent links between the evidence and the argument.

  - Show that you understand the background of historical evidence with special attention to bias in evidence due to authorial point of view or historical conditions.
  - Evaluate evidence used for validity and reliability.

- Relate diverse historical evidence in a cohesive way to illustrate contradiction, corroboration, qualification, and other types of historical relationships in developing an argument.

  - Show that you know what evidence is relevant by using it creatively and clearly to illustrate the support for or weakness of an argument and to find deeper relationships in historical events and outcomes.
  - This is related to argumentation in that you must use the evidence to make strong, thorough, clear, and concise arguments that are clearly and thoroughly supported with evidence.

Practice 2: Argument Development

To be successful you will need to be able to create an argument and support it using relevant historical evidence. Creating a historical argument includes defining and framing a question about the past and then formulating a claim or argument about that question, often in the form of a thesis. A persuasive historical argument requires a precise and defensible thesis or claim supported by rigorous analysis of relevant and diverse historical evidence. The argument and evidence used should be framed around the application of a specific historical thinking skill (e.g., comparison, causation, or patterns of continuity and change over time). Additionally, argumentation involves the capacity to examine multiple pieces of evidence in concert with each other, noting contradictions, corroborations, and other relationships among sources to develop and support an argument.

This practice requires four specific traits. According to the *College Board* you must be able to:

1. Make a historically defensible claim in the form of an evaluative thesis.
2. Support an argument using specific and relevant evidence.
3. Use historical reasoning to explain relationships among pieces of historical evidence.
4. Consider ways that diverse or alternative evidence could be used to corroborate, qualify, or modify an argument.

REMEMBER that historical argumentation development is the primary skill for the Long-Essay Questions (LEQs), the Short-Answer Questions, and the Document-Based Questions (DBQs). AP readers look for sophisticated arguments that go beyond the traditional interpretations of evidence and show nuanced interpretations supported by specific facts.

To master Historical Argument Development you must be able to:

- Articulate a defensible claim about the past in the form of a clear and compelling thesis that evaluates the relative importance of multiple factors and recognizes disparate, diverse, or contradictory evidence or perspectives.

  - Use the themes of the course to help structure arguments.
  - Write a strong thesis that FULLY answers the question and does not just rearrange the words in the question.
  - Get past traditional historical arguments and be able to argue various viewpoints on others' interpretations of history.
  - Use factual evidence cleverly and remember to interpret it for the reader.
  - Use multiple pieces of evidence (usually three or more) to prove a point.
  - Be able to explain why other interpretations of history have errors.
  - Use only relevant evidence to prevent tangents in your essays.

AP HISTORY REASONING SKILLS

Historical Reasoning Skill 1: Contextualization

You must display the ability to connect historical events and processes to specific circumstances of time and place as well as broader regional, national, or global processes.

To master Contextualization you must be able to:

- Describe an accurate historical context for a specific historical development or process.
- Explain how a relevant context influenced a specific historical development or process.
- Use context to explain the relative historical significance of a specific historical development or process.

  - When taken together, the above skills mean that you should situate historical events, developments, or processes within the broader regional, national, or global context in which they occurred in order to draw conclusions about their relative significance.
  - This one relates to comparison because it aids in comparison by allowing you to place events in context in order to do so.

    - One example would be asking you to explain two different accounts of *Kristallnacht* in Germany: one that was written by a Nazi at the time of the event and one that was written by a Jewish person in the 1970s.

  - Often this is about finding the many ways a fact or figure or event or movement fits into the other things going on at the time.
  - This is about repeating themes in history such as prosperity and poverty, and being able to understand how the six themes of the *AP European History Curriculum Framework* interact to allow you to create a vivid picture of Europe in the past. These themes will be investigated in detail later, but they are:

    - Interaction of Europe and the World
    - Poverty and Prosperity
    - Objective Knowledge and Subjective Visions
    - States and Other Institutions of Power
    - Individual and Society
    - National and European Identity

Historical Reasoning Skill 2: Comparison

You want to display the abilities to identify, compare, and evaluate multiple perspectives on a given historical event in order to draw conclusions about that event. You must also be able to describe, compare, and evaluate multiple historical developments within one society, one or more developments across or between different societies, and in various chronological and geographical contexts. Comparisons help historians understand which factors and characteristics are common and which are different when comparing events or conditions in different places or times. You also need the ability to identify, compare, and evaluate multiple perspectives on a given historical experience.

To master Comparison you must be able to:

- Describe similarities and/or differences between different historical developments or processes.
- Explain relevant similarities and/or differences between specific historical developments and processes.

- Explain the relative historical significance of similarities and/or differences between specific historical developments and processes.
- Compare different historical individuals, events, developments, and/or processes, analyzing both similarities and differences in order to draw historically valid conclusions.

    – For example, what were the similarities and differences between the Dutch, English, and French experiences in gaining constitutional governments?
    – To accomplish this, you must cite specific facts that support your assertions and be sure to present nuanced arguments that show different levels of similarity and difference.

- Comparisons can be made across different time periods, across different geographical locations, and between different historical events or developments within the same time period and/or geographical location.

    – For example, how would a Marxist historian and a political historian differ in perspectives on the French Revolution?
    – Much of studying history is about understanding different perspectives such as how a peasant and a lord would view enclosure differently.

Historical Reasoning Skill 3: Historical Causation

To be successful you will need to be able to identify, analyze, and evaluate the relationships among historical causes and effects, distinguishing between those that are long-term and those that are proximate. Historical thinking also involves the ability to distinguish between causation and correlation. (*This is very difficult; correlations are easier to prove than causations. It is best to fully examine relationships and any data to gather both empirical and anecdotal evidence when making claims of causation.*) It also involves an awareness of contingency, the way that historical events result from a complex variety of factors that come together in unpredictable ways and often have unanticipated consequences.

Debates among historians about the long-term causes of World War I and how the previous decades led to the war provide a good example of the problems of making claims of causation and supporting those claims with strong historical evidence.

REMEMBER that stating that a correlation is discovered, but that there is not enough evidence to make a full claim of causation, is usually a sophisticated enough argument, providing that the correct facts are cited, to get full credit for this skill.

To master Causation you must be able to:

- Explain long- and/or short-term causes and/or effects of an historical event, development, or process.
- Describe causes and/or effects of a specific historical development or process.
- Explain the relationship between causes and effects of a specific historical development or process.
- Explain the difference between primary and secondary causes and between long- and short-term effects.
- Evaluate the relative significance of different causes and/or effects on historical events or processes, distinguishing between causation and correlation and showing an awareness of historical contingency.
- Explain the relative historical significance of different causes and/or effects.

Historical Reasoning Skill 4: Patterns of Continuity and Change Over Time

You must be able to recognize, analyze, and evaluate the dynamics of historical continuity and change over periods of time of varying length, as well as the ability to relate these patterns to larger historical processes or themes. The College Board LOVES this type of question and has for years. It is a great skill to have to be able to say that these factors did not change while these other factors changed over time in the following ways. The key to this skill is to acknowledge that most historical processes are uneven and affect different groups of the population at different rates based upon class, gender, geography, and other factors.

To master Patterns of Continuity and Change Over Time you must be able to:

- Identify patterns of continuity and change over time and explain the significance of such patterns.

  - One example would be an explanation of parenting from the eighteenth to the twentieth centuries. Much changed, such as parental involvement, patterns of work, and levels of education, but much did not, such as parents always being in charge. The changes affected how people interacted with each other at work and socially.

- Explain the relative historical significance of specific historical developments in relation to a larger pattern of continuity and/or change.

- Explain how patterns of continuity and change over time relate to larger historical processes or themes.

  - Example: changes in parental expectations in the twentieth century coincide with improved standards of living and higher educational opportunity.

ADDITIONAL SKILLS NOT REQUIRED BY COLLEGE BOARD

The following skills are no longer required as discrete skills for the AP History courses, but they will add quite a lot to your writing. You are encouraged to understand and utilize these skills in order to master the exam.

Additional Skill 1: Periodization

You must display the abilities to describe, analyze, and evaluate different ways that historians divide history into discrete and definable periods. Historians construct and debate different, sometimes competing, models of periodization; the choice of specific turning points or starting and ending dates might accord a higher value to one narrative, region, or group than to another. To accomplish this periodization, historians identify turning points such as the Thirty-Years' War or the invention of the steam engine, and they recognize that the choice of specific dates accords a higher value to one narrative, region, or group than to another narrative, region, or group. Therefore, historical thinking involves being aware of how the circumstances and contexts of a historian's work might shape his or her choices about periodization.

To master Periodization you must be able to:

- Explain ways that historical events and processes can be organized into discrete, different, and definable historical periods.

  - This is about finding "turning points," which are best defined as moments when several significant changes occurred that had important long-term consequences or key events that create periods.

- One example would be the introduction of the steam engine, which revolutionized life in Europe as it spread through the Continent, leading to industrialization that caused drastic political, social, economic, and military changes.
- Often this is about the terms used by historians to describe eras such as the Age of Enlightenment, or the Industrial Revolution, or the Age of Imperialism.
- Students can always use centuries for periodization if they cannot think of any other way to divide a topic.

- Evaluate whether a particular event or date could or could not be a turning point between different, definable historical periods when considered in terms of particular historical evidence.
- Analyze and evaluate different and/or competing models of periodization.

    - Often you will be asked to argue for or against a particular perspective on history, such as whether World War II began in 1933 or 1937 rather than the traditional 1939.

Additional Skill 2: Synthesis

To be successful you will need to be able to develop an understanding of the past by making meaningful and persuasive historical and/or cross-disciplinary connections between a given historical issue and other historical contexts, periods, themes, or disciplines. Additionally, synthesis may involve applying insights about the past to other historical contexts or circumstances, including the present.

REMEMBER that synthesis is all about creating your own ideas. You need to show that you have the ability to take many different pieces of evidence learned throughout the course and put them together into a cohesive essay or short answer to fully display an understanding of what was asked. The key is often to stay focused and prevent tangents.

To master Synthesis you must be able to:

- Make connections between a given historical issue and related developments in a different historical context, geographical area, period, or era, including the present.
- Make connections between different course themes and/or approaches to history (such as political, economic, social, cultural, or intellectual) for a given historical issue.
- Apply insights about the past to other historical contexts or circumstances, including the present.

    - This is the highest level of historical analysis.
    - Draw conclusions, make claims, and support them with evidence that is clear and nuanced.

Additional Skill 3: Interpretation

To be successful you will need to be able to describe, analyze, and evaluate the different ways historians interpret the past. This includes understanding the various types of questions historians ask, as well as considering how the circumstances and contexts in which individual historians work and write, shape their interpretations of past events and historical evidence. Historical interpretation requires analyzing evidence, reasoning, contexts, and points of view found in both primary and secondary sources.

REMEMBER that creating interpretation is somewhat open-ended, *as long as* assertions are **SUPPORTED** with **SPECIFIC EVIDENCE**.

To master Historical Interpretation you must be able to:

- Analyze diverse historical interpretations.

  - This one, too, goes back to argumentation, in that students must be able to look at multiple interpretations of the same events or a period and analyze them for validity and relevance as well as reliability.
  - Show a mastery of traditional historical arguments and be able to argue various viewpoints on others' interpretation of history.

- Analyze a historian's argument; explain how the argument has been supported through the analysis of relevant historical evidence, and evaluate the argument's effectiveness.

  - Demonstrate an understanding of what historians believe changes over time and place, and that those historians also have biases that must be understood and interpreted as a part of their work.
  - This is about analyzing the evidence as support for the historical argument, so be certain to interpret the evidence clearly as it relates to the argument.

Additional Skill 4: Analyzing Evidence Through Content and Sourcing

To be successful you will need to be able to describe, select, and evaluate relevant evidence about the past from diverse sources (including written documents, works of art, archaeological artifacts, oral traditions, and other primary sources) and draw conclusions about their relevance to different historical issues. A historical analysis of sources focuses on the interplay between the content of a source and the authorship, point of view, purpose, audience, and format or medium of that source, assessing the usefulness, reliability, and limitations of the source as historical evidence. This is one of the tougher skills that the AP History exam requires of you. It demands that you use higher-level thinking to evaluate the different levels of support for a thesis that each piece of evidence presented displays. The key is for you to illustrate the connections between evidence and the thesis to clearly prove or disprove the thesis.

To master Historical Interpretation you must be able to:

- Explain the relevance of the author's point of view, author's purpose, audience, format or medium, and/or historical context, as well as the interaction among these features, to demonstrate understanding of the significance of a primary source.

  - This is the true work of the historian and, as such, it is the true test of a history student.
  - You will always display this skill on the DBQ as well as in other parts of the exam.
  - Point of view and audience are key factors in interpreting any source.
  - The trick here is to present the evidence and then evaluate it relative to the thesis, but also to avoid tangents.
  - Be sure to clearly explain how the evidence supports or contradicts the thesis.

- Evaluate the usefulness, reliability, and/or limitations of a primary source in answering particular historical questions.

  - You will always display this skill on the DBQ as well as in other parts of the exam.
  - Finding flaws in the reliability or limitations in the usefulness of a source is a good way to impress those who score the exam.

A GUIDE TO THE AP EUROPEAN HISTORY EXAM

Section 1: 95 minutes

Part A

- *50–55 Multiple-Choice Questions* will be asked in groups of 2–5 questions based on a common stimulus.

  - 1 point per correct question is awarded for 55 points total
  - Requires analysis of primary and secondary texts, images, graphs, and maps
  - 55 minutes
  - 40% of the Exam

Part B

- *Short-Answer Questions* (3 out of 4 questions with 3 tasks per question must be answered).

  - You will answer 2 required questions and make a choice between 2 other questions
  - 3 points per question
  - 40 minutes
  - 20% of the Exam

Section 2: 100 minutes (15-minute reading period included in the 100 minutes)

Part A

- *Document-Based Question* (*DBQ*): Used to assess your mastery of analyzing written, visual, and quantitative sources as historical evidence and to use that evidence to develop an argument supported by that analysis.

  - One question—55 minutes
  - 5 to 7 documents
  - Question covers years 1600–2001
  - 60 minutes
  - 25% of the Exam

Part B
- *Long-Essay Question*: You must develop an argument and support it with analysis of specific, relevant historical evidence of your choosing.
- You will choose to answer **one** of three provided essay questions.

  - One choice from Period 1, one from Periods 2–3, and one from Periods 3–4
  - 40 minutes
  - 15% of the Exam

Themes

There are six specific themes for this course as of 2016. These themes are required by the College Board and are going to drive instruction throughout each of the four time periods also outlined in the *AP European History Curriculum Framework*. Each of these themes can be observed in each time period. The six themes are

1. Interaction of Europe and the World
2. Poverty and Prosperity
3. Objective Knowledge and Subjective Visions
4. States and Other Institutions of Power
5. Individuals and Society
6. National and European Identity

These themes were designed to foster your understanding of major historical issues and developments, helping you to recognize trends and processes that have emerged over centuries. Each theme is tied to specific learning objectives for each time period, and each theme has overarching questions that you should be able to tackle on exam day. To fully understand the specific learning objectives that EVERY question on the AP exam will be tied to, it is strongly recommended that you download and print the *AP European History Course Outline and Exam Description* available online at: *https://secure-media.collegeboard.org/ digitalServices/pdf/ap/ap-european-history-course-and-exam-description.pdf?ep_ch=PR&ep_ mid=11055781&ep_rid=195344825*

The specific learning objectives for the course can be seen there as well as some sample questions for the AP exam that show how each question is tied to both thematic and period specific learning objectives. Each theme and time period is explained in detail with each learning objective listed.

THEME 1: INTERACTION OF EUROPE AND THE WORLD

This theme is about how Europe changed the world and how the world changed Europe. It traces the history of Europe's interactions starting with the Muslim influence in helping revive knowledge and begin the Renaissance and following that theme through the ages of exploration, imperialism, world wars, decolonization, and into the present. Major economic and cultural themes are expressed here as transatlantic and then global trade rapidly changed Europe and the world and eventually created a global economy, workforce, and cuisine.

The overarching questions for this theme are

- Why have Europeans sought contact and interaction with other parts of the world?
- What political, technological, and intellectual developments enabled European contact and interaction with other parts of the world?
- How have encounters between Europe and the world shaped European culture, politics, and society?
- What effect has contact with Europe had on non-European societies?

THEME 2: POVERTY AND PROSPERITY

This theme is mostly economic and social history but there are many important political and military aspects as well. It examines how at the start of the time period covered in the course, around 1450, global wealth was fairly equally distributed geographically, but how Europe came to dominate international trade until the Second World War. How this new commercial wealth transformed Europe from a mostly agrarian pre-industrial feudal system into eventually socialist democracies that emphasized the elimination of poverty and equality of opportunity was an important trend to watch. The emergence of laissez-faire capitalism, Marxist communism, and socialism must be examined with an eye to business cycles and periods of prosperity such as the 1890s and periods of depression such as the 1930s. How individuals and societies affected and were affected by these changes is the main thrust of this theme.

The overarching questions for this theme are

- How has capitalism developed as an economic system?
- How has the organization of society changed as a result of or in response to the development and spread of capitalism?
- What were the causes and consequences of economic and social inequality?
- How did individuals, groups, and the state respond to economic and social inequality?

THEME 3: OBJECTIVE KNOWLEDGE AND SUBJECTIVE VISIONS

This theme is about methods of acquiring knowledge and how that has changed from 1450 to the present. It examines the philosophical methods of the Renaissance and Reformation thinkers and how thinking evolved during the Enlightenment to include systematic methods of evaluation and inquiry. This theme investigates how knowledge claims gradually moved away from belief in absolute truths to increasingly subjective interpretations of reality. The relationship between the observations and the observer began to be investigated in the nineteenth century, and further developments created "Big Science" that dominated the twentieth century in the fields of science and technology.

The overarching questions for this theme are

- What roles have traditional sources of authority (church and classical antiquity) played in the creation and transmission of knowledge?
- How and why did Europeans come to rely on the scientific method and reason in place of traditional authorities?
- How and why did Europeans come to value subjective interpretations of reality?

THEME 4: STATES AND OTHER INSTITUTIONS OF POWER

This theme is mostly political although, as always, political and economic power are intrinsically linked in so many ways that Richelieu said "finances are the sinews of the state." The rise of states corresponds with the rise of state revenue in order to finance growing armies. The evolution of political power and the rise and fall of absolute monarchies, and the subsequent rise of parliamentary power, popular sovereignty, and the rule of law are examined here. Balance of power diplomacy and the importance of alliance in aiding political power is a strong component of this theme. The rise and fall of totalitarian dictatorships and the tools of government for changing the lives of the citizens in both positive and negative ways are examined. Some examples include the cycle of political history in France in that it was the model of absolutism under Louis XIV, had a bloody republican revolution in 1789–1795, then became the Napoleonic empire at the start of the nineteenth century, only to become a monarchy again in 1815. It went through five republics with periods of empire, occupation, and reestablishment of a republic.

The overarching questions for this theme are

- What forms have European governments taken, and how have these forms changed over time?
- In what ways and why have European governments moved toward or reacted against representative and democratic principles and practices?
- How did civil institutions develop apart from governments, and what effect have they had upon European states?
- How and why did changes in warfare affect diplomacy, the European state system, and the balance of power?
- How did the concept of a balance of power emerge, develop, and eventually become institutionalized?

THEME 5: INDIVIDUALS AND SOCIETY

This theme is mostly social yet it pertains to all of the other economic, political, and technological factors that continually affect the lives of the people of Europe. This is an examination of the evolution of class structure, familial relations, gender roles, ethnic identities, occupational roles, and the rise of consumerism and the welfare state. This is a part of the course that the exam traditionally is very heavy on, and if you can master this theme, you can apply it to all other themes in order to get a strong historical picture of any event.

The overarching questions for this theme are

- What forms have family, class, and social groups taken in European history, and how have they changed over time?
- How and why have tensions arisen between the individual and society over the course of European history?
- How and why has the status of specific groups within society changed over time?

THEME 6: NATIONAL AND EUROPEAN IDENTITY

This theme's main focus is on how and why definitions and perceptions of regional, cultural, national, and European identity have developed and been challenged over time. It examines the inception of nationality coming from early political units that varied in size from the tiny Italian city-states to regions such as Spain. The emergence of powerful monarchs, such as Louis XIV and Peter the Great, used common language and cultural identity to foster a sense of unity in their realms. The creation and dissemination of national symbols and stories will also be a major thrust of this theme. The idea of European well-being that emerged from the Enlightenment will be examined through this lens as well. The power of nationalism that emerged in the nineteenth century, and how it affected the boundaries and stories of Europe and European nations, are also paramount to this theme. The power of nation states during the twentieth century, as well as the rise in European unity at the start of the twenty-first century, are also major thrusts of this theme.

The overarching questions for this theme are

- Where did national identity come from?
- How does national identity affect people's behavior?
- How did leaders use national identity?
- How and why did the concept of European identity emerge, and how did it affect Europe?
- How have people with minority national identities been treated by the majority?
- How did national and European identity affect both world wars and the Cold War and its aftermath?
- How and why does national identity affect European history?

It is also important to note that a strong comprehension of and ability to apply *economic* history can help you with each of the six themes.

Exam Organization

The scope of this course is the history of Europe from the Renaissance (1450) to contemporary times. All four time periods will be covered equally on the exam.

MULTIPLE-CHOICE QUESTIONS (55 QUESTIONS FOR 40% OF EXAM) All multiple-choice questions will be based upon some sort of stimulus provided on the exam. There will be a quote, a chart, a historian's argument, a map, an image, or a cartoon followed by a group of 2–5 questions based upon that stimulus. In general, the questions will go from a lower reasoning level to a higher reasoning level within each group of questions.

SHORT-ANSWER QUESTIONS (FOUR QUESTIONS FOR 20% OF THE EXAM) Four questions will directly address one or more of the thematic learning objectives for the course. You must answer only three of them. You are required to answer two questions from 1600–2001 and can choose to answer one of two questions (one from time periods 1–2 and one from time periods 3–4). Each question will ask you to identify and analyze examples of historical evidence relevant to the source or question. There will be three tasks in each question that are worth one point each.

DOCUMENT-BASED QUESTION (ONE QUESTION FOR 25% OF THE EXAM) This is where the readers want to see your skills with synthesis, analysis, periodization, causation, argumentation, and understanding of continuity and change. You must analyze the documents including written materials, charts, graphs, and cartoons, and use evidence from within those documents and evidence NOT contained in the documents to make a cogent, clear, concise argument that *completely answers all parts of the question*.

LONG-ESSAY QUESTIONS (ONE QUESTION FOR 15% OF THE EXAM) You will be given the choice between three different essay prompts that test the same historical skill, such as periodization, or change and continuity over time. You must select one and develop a strong thesis that addresses all parts of the question. You must further support that thesis with strong historical evidence that can come from both primary and secondary sources that you are familiar with.

Section	Question Type	# of Questions	Timing	Percentage of Total Exam Score
I	Part A: Multiple-choice questions	55 questions	55 minutes	40%
	Part B: Short-answer questions	4 questions Students are required to answer 2 questions from 1600–2001 and can choose to answer 1 of 2 questions (one from time periods 1–2 and one from time periods 3–4.)	40 minutes	20%
II	Part A: Document-based question	1 question	60 minutes includes a 15-minute reading period	25%
	Part B: Long-essay question	1 question chosen from three questions	40 minutes	15%

How the AP European History Exam Is Scored

The AP European History exam is composed of four parts grouped into two sections.

The multiple-choice part is scored with one point given for each correct answer. *There is no penalty for guessing as of May 2011*, so you should answer every question on the exam.

The long essay is given a score from 0 to 6, and the DBQ is scored from 0 to 7, as will be detailed later in this section and throughout the sample essays seen in the book.

To attain your final AP score, the following method should be used:

Multiple-Choice Score × 1.091 = _____

+

Short-Answer Score × 3.334 = _____

+

DBQ Score × 5.357 = _____

+

FRQ Score × 3.75 = _____

Total of all above scores is composite score = _____ (round your score)

To get a final score for the exam, compare your composite score to the chart on page 23.

COMPOSITE SCORE CONVERSION CHART

Score Range	AP Score
104–150	5
91–103	4
79–91	3
69–78	2
0–69	1

SCORES

5 Extremely well qualified, is accepted by most colleges for either course credit or placement into a higher level section.

4 Well qualified, is accepted by many colleges.

3 Qualified, is accepted by some colleges.

2 Possibly qualified, is rarely accepted for either credit or placement.

1 No recommendation, is not accepted anywhere.

The chart above is a sample chart, and the score ranges change annually with each set of exam scores, but it is a good estimation of an average year's test score distribution.

Some colleges require additional documentation about course work.

You may choose to suppress a score on the AP exam once it has been reported to you. You may also cancel the test within a certain time after you have taken it but before the score has been reported.

Multiple-Choice Questions (40% of the Exam)

The multiple-choice section will be composed of approximately 55 questions organized into groups of two to five questions that require you to assess and react to questions based upon a common stimulus such as a primary or secondary source, a historian's argument, or a historical problem. Each set of multiple-choice questions will address one or more of the thematic and time period based learning objectives for the course and will require skills outlined in the AP historical skills mentioned earlier. Although a set may focus on one particular period of European history, the individual questions within that set may ask you to make connections to thematically linked developments in other periods that will also assess your ability with the *change and continuity over time* skill.

Multiple-choice questions will evaluate your ability to analyze the stimulus material in tandem with your knowledge of the historical period being examined. The possible answers for a multiple-choice question will reflect the level of detail present in the required historical developments found in the concept outline for the course. You should be prepared to utilize your knowledge of the forces in history to analyze specific information and situations cited in the stimuli provided.

HINTS FOR TACKLING MULTIPLE-CHOICE QUESTIONS

1. Answer all questions. There is no penalty for incorrect answers.
2. The more incorrect answers you eliminate, the better the odds for guessing.
3. Be methodical. Even on questions you are sure of, put a line through the ENTIRE incorrect answers as they are eliminated.
4. Circle the number of any question you are unsure of so you can return to it if you have the time.
5. Go with your intuition. Your first choice is usually correct, so change an answer only if you are absolutely certain.
6. Underline the key idea in each question.
7. Try reading the answer choices from D back to A.

TYPES OF MULTIPLE-CHOICE QUESTIONS

- ✔ Analysis
- ✔ Quotation
- ✔ Interpretation of a picture, art object, cartoon, or photo
- ✔ Map study
- ✔ Graph or chart

SAMPLE ANALYSIS QUESTIONS

Analysis lends itself to working out the answer with more general understandings or less specific information by considering cause and effect relationships or sorting out the chronology.

Questions 1–2 refer to the map below.

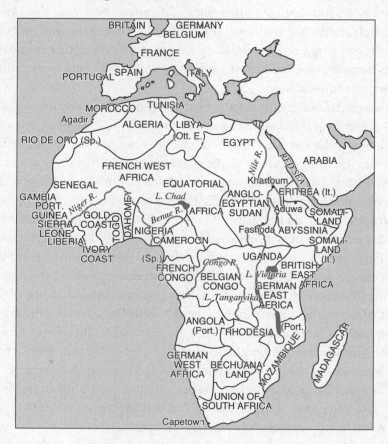

1. Which of the following is the best reason for the creation of the map above?

   (A) It was drawn to reflect the decolonization seen after the Second World War.
   (B) It was drawn to reflect colonial possessions on the eve of the First World War.
   (C) It was drawn to reflect the importance of rivers in the transport of African goods.
   (D) It was drawn to reflect the growing power of the French and the English in East Africa.

2. Which best describes the ways that Europeans used African ethnic divisions to guide them when creating colonies and nations seen above?

   (A) Colonies and nations were created to keep ethnic groups united within Africa.
   (B) Colonies and nations were drawn that did not take any African ethnic divisions into account.
   (C) Colonies and nations were created to intentionally separate ethnic groups and create new colonies of disunited Africans.
   (D) Colonies and nations were created to meet the trade requirements of Europeans, and sizes and boundaries of them depended more upon how big the colonizing nation was.

Answers
   1. **B**
   2. **C**

Comments

Analysis questions let you eliminate some answers if you can figure out that one thing could not be a causation or result of another event or attitude. They make you use general knowledge in a specific way to reason out an answer. Knowing the general time frame of events and developments helps immeasurably. It is worth the trouble and time to try to figure out the answer to this type of question.

Question 1 is a classic analyze the map to see the time period question. If you can determine the sequence of events, you can eliminate certain choices. For example, German West Africa exists so it is before 1918 and after 1905, but Italy does not possess Eritrea or Somalia, so it must be before the 1930s. Additionally the Belgian Congo still exists, so it must be before 1918. Now one must analyze WHY the map was drawn. It seems from the dates given that the only possible choice given was on the eve of the First World War, choice (B). All of the other answers are either before Germany had African colonies or after it lost them. Since the map shows nothing about transportation, and the French and English had little influence in East Africa other than in Egypt, which is not shown on the map, those choices can be easily eliminated.

Question 2 can be answered by determining the reasoning behind the drawing of colonial and eventually national borders in Africa. Here you must analyze which of the choices is MOST correct. Many will have some truth to them, but the best answer is the one that is most complete with nothing inaccurate. In this case, the Europeans did have to take the internal relations of the Africans on the ground into account when drawing borders. They wanted to make their colonies easier to rule so you must reason that because they were trying to rule the Africans, the Europeans would try to keep them disunited, thus eliminating choices (A) and (B). You must also look at the map and reason that the Belgian Congo would not be very big if choice (D) were correct, so that choice can be eliminated. Choice (C) is the correct answer because the Europeans intentionally divided the ethnic groups to keep their populations within each colony fighting with one another rather than with their colonial masters.

SAMPLE QUOTATION QUESTION

Quotation analysis, like most analysis questions, can be done with less specific information than identification requires. Again chronology and cause-effect help in the process of elimination.

"Not only was he accused of imprisoning and torturing or murdering his enemies, but he set into place the whole apparatus of totalitarian repression. He denied basic human rights in pushing forward his policy of industrialization, and the human cost can be measured in the deaths of tens of millions of his own countrymen. His detractors also accuse him of governing according to a 'cult of personality.'"

The individual speaking above is describing the dictator of the Soviet Union through the Second World War and would most likely be which of the following?

    (A)   An ardent Bolshevik who was a member of the Comintern under Stalin
    (B)   An Enlightenment thinker who was looking for a better society
    (C)   A Western writer or academic
    (D)   A member of the cabinet of Leonid Brezhnev who tried to de-Stalinize the Soviet Union

Answer and Comments: **(C)**

Choice (A) is incorrect because leaders of the Communist Party under Stalin did not criticize him in any way.

Choice (B) is out because Stalin lived AFTER the age of Enlightenment and thus none of those great minds could comment on Stalin.

Choice (D) is out because Brezhnev actually re-Stalinized the Soviet Union after Khrushchev tried to reduce cold war tensions there.

Choice (C) makes the most sense because during and even after the Cold War, "Western" (meaning pro-NATO) writers and academics were those most likely to criticize Stalin even up to today.

SAMPLE INTERPRETATION QUESTION

Interpretation can involve identifying the artist, style, subject, or period of a work of art; it may require interpretation of a cartoon, map, photo, or picture.

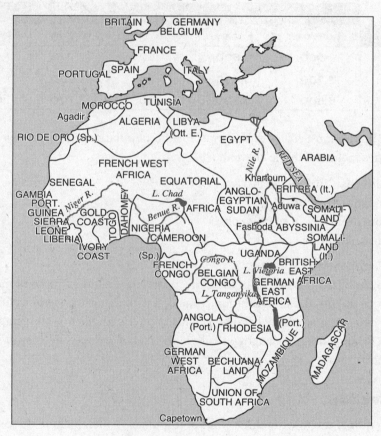

From examining the map above, which of the following was the most important reason for the British to hold Egypt who had built the Suez Canal?

(A) The British needed it to get goods from Africa to Asia.

(B) The British wanted to patrol the Red Sea to make certain that Somali pirates were defeated.

(C) The British wanted to secure trade routes from Asia to Europe to keep growing their trade empire.

(D) The British wanted to take over all French and German colonies in Africa.

Answer and Comments: **(C)**

You must analyze the map to see that the Suez Canal got the British easy access from the Mediterranean to the Red Sea and eventually the Indian Ocean for trade with the entire empire.

Map interpretation questions require use of broad map skills and less general information to work out. They are worth the time and trouble to examine.

SAMPLE CHART QUESTION

Graphs and charts frequently provide all the information necessary in order to answer the question correctly. Graphs are diagrams representing successive changes; charts are information sheets that employ tables or graphs.

Population of Cities in Thousands

Year	Cities				
	London	Paris	Antwerp	Berlin	Moscow
1800	960	600	60	170	250
1850	2,700	1,400	90	500	360
1900	6,500	3,700	280	2,700	1,000

Which would be the most likely explanation for the population change between 1800 and 1900 in the cities included on the chart above?

- (A) Malthusian "unbridled lust"
- (B) Foreign immigration
- (C) Population shift from other cities
- (D) Industrialization

Answer and Comments: **(D)**

The clue to the correct answer is in the early, nearly sevenfold increase of the population of London. Since the Industrial Revolution coincided with a mass movement from the countryside to the cities that also may have been caused by the Enclosure Movement, and since both began in Britain and then caught on later in the rest of Europe, the answer is choice (D), industrialization.

Written Section

This section requires you to write three types of responses, which include three short-answer questions and two essays total: one document-based question (DBQ), and one long-essay question (LEQ). You must respond to the only DBQ prompt presented, but you will be able to choose between three LEQ essay choices that will be similarly structured.

You will be given 60 minutes to answer the DBQ, which includes a 15-minute reading section for the DBQ. You will then be given 40 minutes to write the LEQ.

WRITTEN SECTION SCORING (60% OF THE EXAM TOTAL)

Short-answer questions will each have three specific tasks for one point each. All LEQs are scored on the same rubric out of 6 points. All DBQ questions are scored on the same rubric with a maximum of 7 points. On LEQs a score of 0–2 is pretty poor, a score of 3–4 is adequate, and a score of 5–6 is very good. For the DBQ, a score of 0–3 is pretty poor, a score of 4–5 is adequate, and a score of 6–7 is very good.

SHORT-ANSWER QUESTIONS (20% OF THE EXAM SCORE)

The short-answer section will consist of four questions that require you to use historical thinking skills and content knowledge to respond to a stimulus with a direct, concise response. However, you must only answer three of them. You are required to answer two questions from 1600–2001 and can choose to answer one of two questions (one from time periods 1–2 and one from time periods 3–4). Just like in the multiple-choice section, stimulus material may include: a primary or secondary source, including texts, images, charts, graphs, maps, etc. At least two of the four short-answer questions will include stimulus material. Each short-answer question will directly address one or more of the thematic learning objectives for the course and assess one or more of the nine historical thinking skills. Each short-answer question will ask you to analyze historical developments and/or processes using examples drawn from the concept outline or other examples explored in depth in classroom instruction. The short-answer questions may require you to take a position based on the stimulus material presented, identify a significant cause or effect, or account for differences and similarities in perspectives, historical developments, etc.

Sample Short-Answer Question

"The illiterate is a blind man: Everywhere pitfalls and misfortunes await him." Soviet Poster, 1920.

(A) Briefly analyze how the artwork above reflects artistic trends at the start of the twentieth century.

(B) Based on the poster above and your knowledge of European history, explain TWO aspects of social life under Soviet rule.

This is an art question and a social question. It is a common type of question on the AP exam. To understand how to score the exam, examine the scoring guide below:

SCORING GUIDE

0–3 points (1 point for A and 2 points for B)

(A) ONE point will be given for an analysis of how the poster is typical of the trends of the early twentieth century such as but not limited to: it is related to Art Nouveau or the Belle Epoch, it contains a master narrative, faith in a grand theory is espoused, supports hierarchy and order, concentrates on overall improving society, mass marketing or mass media, centralized knowledge, seriousness of intent and purpose, etc. This can also be juxtaposed with the Dada/surrealist ideas going on contemporarily.

(B) ONE point will be awarded for each aspect of social life in the Soviet Union explained (UP TO TWO POINTS), such as lack of freedom, fear of the state, distrust of others, quotas at work dictated life, long lines for all goods, lack of consumer goods, free medical care, free housing, guaranteed work, assumed equality, gender role relaxation, lack of religion, censored press and other media, governmental control of all aspects of life, etc.

Other types of questions will include those that ask you to analyze arguments between historians; analyze a chart, map, or graph; or respond to some historical generalization such as the Enlightenment was not very enlightened for most people.

Interpreting the Essay Questions

In both the LEQ and the DBQ, it is necessary to understand the way in which the answer is to be presented. In order to do this, you must interpret the *key term or terms* in the question.

EXAMPLES OF KEY TERMS

1. **DEFEND OR REFUTE** (argue for or against a specific statement by framing an essay that uses *factual support*)

   Sample:

   "The Second World War was the inevitable result of a failure of the democracies to confront aggression by totalitarian dictatorships."

   Defend or refute this with factual evidence from the diplomatic history of the 1930s.

2. **ANALYZE** (examine in detail; determine relationships; explain)

   Sample:

   Analyze the ways in which the Protestant Reformation fostered both the growth of capitalism and the rise of modern science.

3. **EVALUATE** (judge the worth of; discuss advantages and disadvantages, pluses and minuses)

   Sample:

   Evaluate both the domestic policies and the foreign involvements of the government of France during the reign of Louis XIV.

4. **TO WHAT EXTENT AND IN WHAT WAYS** (how and how much?)

Sample:

To what extent and in what ways did Napoleon carry out the ideals of the French Revolution?

5. **ASSESS THE VALIDITY** (judge the value of; determine the truth)

Sample:

"The religious wars of the sixteenth and seventeenth centuries were more the result of the territorial ambitions of rival states and the economic interests of competing factions than of doctrinal differences."

Assess the validity of this statement.

6. **CONTRAST AND COMPARE** (show differences and examine for similarities)

Sample:

Contrast and compare the art and architecture of the Renaissance with that of the Romantic period and explain how each reflected the prevailing culture.

7. **EXPLAIN** (offer the meaning, the cause, the reason for; make clear; detail)

Sample:

Explain how the theories of Copernicus, Galileo, Kepler, and Newton affected the religious beliefs and intellectual trends of the seventeenth and eighteenth centuries.

8. **DISCUSS** (consider various points of view; write about; examine)

Sample:

Discuss the accomplishments of the various governments in France during the French Revolution.

9. **DESCRIBE** (tell about; offer an account or a word picture)

Sample:

Describe the lifestyle of noble women in Italy during the Italian Renaissance. Refer to family life, political status, and economic conditions.

Additional sample and practice short-answer and long-essay questions will appear in the review chapters and in the sample exams.

The Long-Essay Question (15% of the Exam)

You will be given a choice between three comparable long-essay options. The long-essay questions are designed to measure your use of historical thinking skills to explain and analyze one or more of the thematic learning objectives for the course. All essays will require the development of a ***thesis*** or argument supported by *analysis* of specific, relevant historical evidence. You must demonstrate in your responses that you have mastered a targeted skill, such as continuity and change over time, comparison, causation, or periodization.

Both long-essay questions on the exam will target the same skill, which varies from year to year, and the tasks required of you will be very similar. The questions will address different chronological periods and topics. Questions will be limited to topics or examples specifically mentioned in the concept outline but framed to allow your answer to include in-depth examples, drawn either from the concept outline or from topics beyond the concept outline discussed in the classroom.

All long-essay questions will be scored on the *long-essay rubric* presented on the next two pages. You should study this rubric closely to know what is expected from your essay responses.

How Will the College Board Score the Free-Response Question?

As Sun Tzu stated in *The Art of War*, "If you know your enemy and you know yourself, you cannot be defeated in one hundred battles." In the case of test preparation, the test and its graders are your "enemy," and understanding the rubrics for the DBQ and the LEQ will help you defeat them. A sample rubric for the sample LEQ is seen below:

AP European History Long-Essay Question (LEQ) Rubric (6 points)

Category	Scoring Method	Helpful Hints
Thesis (0–1 total points)	Responds to the question with an evaluative thesis that makes a historically defensible claim. (1 point)	The thesis MUST consist of one or more sentences located in the introduction or the conclusion of the essay. However, neither the introduction nor conclusion is strictly limited to one paragraph.
Contextualization (0–1 total points)	Describe a broader historical context immediately relevant to the question. (1 point)	This point may be earned by relating the topic of the question to broader historical events, developments, or processes that occur before, during, or after the time frame of the question. This point is NOT awarded for a phrase or reference.
Evidence (0–2 total points)	Provides specific examples of evidence related to the topic of the question. (1 point) OR To earn this point, the thesis must make a claim that responds to the prompt, rather than merely restating or rephrasing the prompt. The thesis must consist of one or more sentences located in one place, either in the introduction or the conclusion. (2 points)	To earn one point, the response must identify specific historical examples of evidence relevant to the topic of the prompt. To earn two points, the response must use specific historical evidence to support an argument in response to the prompt.

Category	Scoring Method	Helpful Hints
Analysis & Reasoning (0–2 total points)	Uses historical reasoning (e.g., comparison, causation, CCOT) to frame or structure an argument that addresses the prompt. (1 point) OR Demonstrates a complex understanding of the historical development that is the focus of the prompt, using evidence to corroborate, qualify, or modify an argument that addresses the question. (2 points)	To earn the first point, the response must demonstrate the use of historical reasoning to frame or structure an argument, although the reasoning might be uneven or imbalanced. To earn the second point, the response must demonstrate a complex understanding. This can be accomplished in a variety of ways, such as: ■ Explaining nuance of an issue by analyzing multiple variables ■ Explaining both similarity and difference, or explaining both continuity and change, or explaining multiple causes, or explaining both causes and effects ■ Explaining relevant and insightful connections within and across periods ■ Confirming the validity of an argument by corroborating multiple perspectives across themes ■ Qualifying or modifying an argument by considering diverse or alternative views or evidence. This understanding must be part of the argument, not merely a phrase or reference.

Interpreting the Long-Essay Rubric

The rubric makes it clear what must be done to score well on the long essay. Here is a checklist to be sure it is clear:

✔ The essay must have a thesis that responds to all parts of the question and makes a claim that can be defended with historical evidence and reasoning. (0–1 total points)

✔ The essay must place the historical argument from the thesis into a broader historical context and explain how that context influenced the topic that the question addresses. (0–1 total points)

✔ The essay must use specific historical examples to support the claim stated in the thesis and make use of historical reasoning skills to explain how the evidence cited inter-relates as well as use that evidence to qualify, moderate, or corroborate the argument from the thesis. (0–2 total points)

✔ The essay must use historical reasoning (e.g. comparison, causation, CCOT) to frame or structure an argument that addresses the prompt and demonstrates a complex understanding of the historical development that is the focus of the prompt, using evidence to corroborate, qualify, or modify an argument that addresses the question. (0–2 total points)

General Advice for Writing Essays

Writing a good essay is like a good speech or a strong lesson in school. There are generally three steps:

1. Tell them what you will tell them or THESIS
2.. Tell it to them or BODY AND SUPPORT.

   Use evidence here to support your ideas. Your evidence can be factual or interpretive; however, both is best, and you must support your thesis with a plethora of evidence.

3. Tell them what you told them, or CONCLUSION.

   Summarize your main points. What was important? Why? Make your final points here. The most important point to remember is to ANSWER THE ENTIRE QUESTION.

Other hints are found below.

HINTS FOR ANSWERING THE LONG-ESSAY QUESTIONS

1. Read both choices before deciding on which one to do.
2. Underline each task in each question and count the tasks. Try to take on the question that has the fewest tasks that can be fully answered.
3. Your primary consideration should be how much you know about the specific subject. This may seem obvious, but it is easy to pass over a question if you are confused about what it asks. Read. Reread those questions that encompass areas you have focused on in class or in your studies.
4. Interpret the key terms. (See pages 30–31.)
5. Make your choice by mentally framing the argument of your essay. (The "argument" is the proof, the statement, the thesis, the core of your essay; and you should follow your intuitions since they flow from what you know most about.)
6. Read the question again and jot down anything that comes to mind.
7. Organize your essay by outlining your argument. Don't fret over format; you are the only one who is going to see or use the outline.
8. Gather facts to support your argument. (If you are not certain of a fact—a date, an event, a cause, a person—don't use it.)
9. Check for consistency. What seems like supporting evidence may actually contradict your assertions.
10. Be certain the thesis addresses all parts of the question and that evidence is strong enough to support that thesis before beginning to write.
11. Now, you are ready to write. Make a clear statement of the intent of your argument in the introduction, a clear summary of your argument in the conclusion.
12. Reread! Rewrite! Delete. Add. "Substance takes precedence over neatness." Don't be afraid to cross out words, sentences, whole paragraphs, whole pages.

How to Write an Essay

It is a lot easier than you think, if you pick the right question, interpret the terms correctly, and follow a few simple procedures. The tricks to picking the right question and interpreting its terms are given in the preceding section.

What then are these "simple" procedures?

The Essence of Your Essay Is the Body

It is here that you do your job of showing "to what extent and in what ways," or of "assessing the validity," or of "contrasting and comparing," or of demonstrating "change and continuity over time," and so on. The introduction simply points out the direction your argument will take and presents a viable thesis that addresses all parts of the question. The conclusion simply summarizes your argument. The key to success in this task is to write a clear, convincing argument that clearly addresses the skill being assessed and that clearly and repetitively ties the evidence to the thesis and explains how the evidence supports the thesis. The best essays will also include counter-arguments to the thesis, or tie the response to additional time periods or movements than those being assessed by the question.

THE SIMPLE PROCEDURES

- ✔ First, ask yourself what the question wants to know.
- ✔ Second, ask yourself what you know about it.
- ✔ Third, ask yourself how you should put it into words.

SAMPLE QUESTION:
To what extent and in what ways did Napoleon's rule continue and expand the ideals of the Enlightenment and the French Revolution?

First, what does the question want to know?
"How and how much did Napoleon, an autocrat, continue and expand the social, political, and economic aims of the Revolution and the pursuit of reason endemic to the Enlightenment?" This is clearly a change and continuity over time essay and, therefore, must address the skills called for in that type of essay. It also wants to know what the ideals of the Enlightenment and French Revolution were, and then requires you to evaluate the extent to which Napoleon continued and expanded those ideals.

Second, ask yourself what you know about it?
Napoleon was a dictator and an emperor and both are generally undemocratic roles while the French Revolution was democratic in nature. He ignored the ideals of thinkers like Montesquieu and Rousseau on allowing the people to have a meaningful voice in government but followed the ideals of Voltaire who called for an *enlightened despot*.

He made domestic reforms in the law, education, and government that furthered democracy. He then spread his Napoleonic Code to the peoples of Europe whom he conquered. However, he was a conqueror, which went directly against the ideals of the Enlightenment. He carried some of the ideals of the Revolution—"liberty, equality, fraternity"—to other countries during his conquests. He had personal reasons for trying to change the *Ancien Régime* or "Old Order." He enforced a meritocracy and rule of law, but also enforced censorship and utilized secret police.

Third, how should you put it into words?

Write about the historical irony: one of history's "bad guys" who was a dictator, conqueror, and vainglorious emperor actually helped to spread liberal ideals throughout Europe along with the rule of law through his Napoleonic Code, and his conquest of Europe and creation of the German Confederation of the Rhine led to the emergence of the most radical of nine-teenth-century European movements—nationalism.

There are two mainstream ways to structure this essay. You could write an introductory thesis paragraph, then one paragraph about the extent to which Napoleon carried out the ideals of the French Revolution, then one about the extent to which he carried out the ideals of the Enlightenment, and then another about how he spread these ideals across Europe. Or there could be a thesis, then one paragraph about each major ideal: liberty, equality, brother-hood, and "Enlightenment ideals" in general. Another advanced method could be to trace Napoleon's narrative as those ideals were carried out chronologically and/or geographically, evaluating Napoleon's progress along the way with a strong thesis either at the start or the end, but preferably *the thesis will be stated at BOTH the beginning and end of every LEQ essay*.

Use the *Simple Procedures* (page 35) to plan the body of every essay.

Use the *Hints for Answering the Long-Essay Questions* (page 34) to do the actual writing.

Use the *AP European History Long-Essay Question Rubric* (pages 32–33) to evaluate your response to every essay that you write for practice.

The Document-Based Essay Question (DBQ) (25% of the Exam Score)

The DBQ is designed to test your ability to analyze documentary materials and use that analy-sis to support a thesis proposed by the prompt. The way the scoring works most years, *the DBQ, if properly done, can often get almost one half of the points needed to attain a score of "3" on the exam*. This section is based upon a skill that can be developed by using documents and the author's points of view in those documents to prove a historical point. Thus, this skill is worth practicing.

The document-based question emphasizes the ability to analyze and synthesize histori-cal evidence, including textual, quantitative, or visual materials. The question also requires you to formulate a thesis and support it with relevant evidence. The five to seven documents accompanying the document-based question are not confined to a single format, may vary in length, and are chosen to illustrate interactions and complexities within the material. The diversity of materials, which may include charts, graphs, cartoons, and works of art alongside written documents, requires you to evaluate different kinds of documents and to utilize a broad spectrum of historical skills. Each DBQ will focus on one targeted skill (such as causa-tion, continuity and change over time, or comparison) that varies from year to year.

The document-based question will typically require you to relate the documents to a his-torical period or theme and, thus, to focus on major periods and issues assessing your abil-ity to incorporate *outside knowledge* related to the question but beyond the specifics of the documents. This ability to place the documents in the historical *context* in which they were produced is essential for your success.

The first key to success on the DBQ is to understand how the question is scored. The readers (people who score the exam) all must use a point-based rubric for grading the DBQ that, if understood, can be used to your advantage. An outline of that rubric follows.

AP European History Document-Based Question Rubric (7 points)

Category	Scoring Method	Helpful Hints
Thesis (0–1 total points)	Responds to the question with an evaluative thesis that makes a historically defensible claim. (1 point)	To earn this point, the thesis must make a claim that responds to the prompt, rather than merely restating or rephrasing the prompt. The thesis must consist of one or more sentences located in one place, either in the introduction or the conclusion.
Contextualization (0–1 total points)	Describe a broader historical context immediately relevant to the question. (1 point)	This point may be earned by relating the topic of the question to broader historical events, developments, or processes that occur before, during, or after the time frame of the question. This point is NOT awarded for a phrase or reference.
Evidence (0–3 total points)	Utilizes content of at least THREE documents to address the topic of the question. (1 point) OR Utilizes the content of at least SIX documents to support an argument about the question. (2 points) AND/OR ↓	**To earn one point**, the response must accurately describe rather than simply quote the content from at least three of the documents. **To earn two points**, the response must accurately describe rather than simply quote the content from at least six documents. In addition, the response must use the content of the documents to support an argument in response to the prompt.
Evidence Beyond the Documents (0–1 total points)	Explains how at least one additional piece of specific evidence beyond those found in the documents relates to an argument about the question. (1 point)	To earn this point, the response must describe the evidence and must use more than a phrase or reference. This additional piece of evidence must be different from the evidence used to earn the point for contextualization.

Category	Scoring Method	Helpful Hints
Analysis & Reasoning (0–2 total points)	For at least THREE documents, explains how or why the document's point of view, purpose, historical situation, and/or audience are relevant to an argument. (1 point)	To earn this point, the response must explain how or why (rather than simply identifying) the document's point of view, purpose, historical situation, or audience is relevant to an argument about the prompt for each of the three documents sourced.
	Demonstrates a complex understanding of the historical development that is the focus of the prompt, using evidence to corroborate, qualify, or modify an argument that addresses the question. (1 point)	A response may demonstrate a complex understanding in a variety of ways, such as: ■ Explaining nuance of an issue by analyzing multiple variables ■ Explaining both similarity and difference, or explaining both continuity and change, or explaining multiple causes, or explaining both cause and effect ■ Explaining relevant and insightful connections within and across periods ■ Confirming the validity of an argument by corroborating multiple perspectives across themes ■ Qualifying or modifying an argument by considering diverse or alternative views or evidence. This understanding must be part of the argument, not merely a phrase or reference.

Scoring Note: If you can write an essay in 40 minutes that completes all of these elements, then you will be very successful on the DBQ.

RULES FOR WRITING THE DBQ

There are a few rules to writing a successful DBQ. If these rules are followed, then the essay will be at the top of the scoring scale.

- ✔ **ANSWER THE QUESTION.** It is amazing how many students do not directly answer the question, but go off on some tangent. Remember to check that the thesis addresses all parts of the question before proving the thesis.
- ✔ **READ THE DOCUMENTS** and write comments on them, including letters to indicate to what group each belongs. If groups are positive or negative reactions, use ±.

- ✔ **CREATE AN OUTLINE** and check that you will prove the thesis with it.
- ✔ **GROUP THE DOCUMENTS** to show they are understood and can be analyzed. There will usually be some way to group the documents to show profession, nationality, class, or some other factor that affects the outlook of the document's author. This will help you gain the points for *Analysis of Evidence*.
- ✔ **INTEGRATE THE USE OF THE DOCUMENTS** smoothly into the overall reasoning of the essay, and do not make it a "laundry list" of documents and points of view. It is important not to accept all documents at face value but to analyze them for *validity*, *origin*, and *purpose* of the author. Use the documents to answer the question and to show understanding and the ability to aptly use them as evidence.
- ✔ **STAY WITHIN THE TIME FRAME** of the question. The question will usually give a specific time frame—do not use anachronistic information.

  - However, REMEMBER that you CAN link the documents or the question to a different time period in order to gain the synthesis point.

- ✔ **FOLLOW GRAMMATICAL CONVENTIONS.** Write an essay with good structure that **follows grammatical conventions**. Use the past tense, avoid clichés and terms like "the people," "history has taught us," "thing," "stuff," and overly simplistic generalizations such as good or bad, and always refer to authors and other historical figures by their last names or royal titles.
- ✔ **READ AND USE THE SOURCE CITATIONS.** The information given in those citations is critical to demonstrating point of view, audience, purpose, nationality, or historical context.
- ✔ **PRESENT POINT OF VIEW.** One strategy that will help in writing a successful DBQ response is to do a good job presenting **point of view**. Remember that the reader will generally attribute persuasive document use, as well as expanded point of view use, to the writer who uses point of view well and often. In reference to the DBQ, point of view is best described as not just saying what an author wrote, but *why* the author wrote it. The focus is on *why* the author would choose to write in the tone chosen, or choose the specific words that were used.

  - If you cannot get to the point of view of the author of the document, REMEMBER to assess at least six documents for either point of view, author's purpose, historical context, and/or audience to be sure to get the point for correct analysis of four documents in that area.
  - Apart from not directly answering the question asked, not demonstrating clear point of view, audience, context, or purpose for the documents is the most common error that students make. If many points of view of many authors are shown, then your DBQ response will likely be a success.

Interpreting the DBQ Essay Rubric

The rubric makes it clear what must be done to score well on the long essay. Here is a checklist to be sure it is clear:

- ✔ Your essay must have a strong thesis that makes a historically defensible claim and responds to all parts of the question. (1 point)
- ✔ Your essay must use evidence from at least SIX documents to support an argument that answers the question completely AND explains the relationships between the evidence

presented, including how the evidence modifies, qualifies, or corroborates the thesis. (1–3 total points)

✔ Your essay must explain how *either* the purpose, point of view, historical situation, and/or audience of the authors of at least FOUR provided documents is relevant to the argument. (1 points)

✔ Your essay must place the answer you provide into a broader historical context that explains how the topic of the essay fits into the time period it comes from. (1 point)

✔ Your essay must cite historical evidence related to the question that is not found in the documents provided in the question. (1 point)

DBQ Organizer

The DBQ organizer below is provided to help you organize your thoughts. There are many boxes to help you think visually. It is strongly recommended that you copy this organizer and use it to practice organizing your DBQs as you work your way through this study guide. The organizer below was included to help you gather the evidence that you will need to write your DBQ essay, so use it your first few times writing, then once you get the hang of it, write without it because you will not have it with you on the day of the exam.

WRITING A DBQ

STEP 1 **THESIS**

Your AP thesis statement should be <u>one to two sentences long</u>. The first sentence should explain your main argument or idea. *Example: Spanish intellectuals were justified in resisting authority when General Francisco Franco seized power because their lives were being threatened.*

Write thesis here:

STEP 2 **DEFEND YOUR THESIS**

Identify THREE more specific examples to back up your argument. These three examples will help to prove that your first sentence is true. It will also make your paper more specific and clear. *Example: More specifically, an illegal seizure of power, imposition of a one-party system, and the disappearance of over 100,000 political dissenters justified the actions of the intellectuals.*

Three examples here:

1.

2.

3.

STEP 3 **THREE TOPIC SENTENCES**

Write your topic sentences. Use the categories that you listed in step 2—defending your thesis—to create topic sentences. You do not need to answer all of the questions below (who, what, when, where) in your topic sentence, but having some of that information in there makes it much clearer.

Category A: *(This should be one of the specific examples from your thesis.)*

Who:

What:

Where:

When:

Why this proves your thesis:

Combine the who, what, where, when, and why above into a topic sentence for your body paragraph:

_____

_____

_____

Category B: *(This should be one of the specific examples from your thesis.)*

Who:

What:

Where:

When:

Why this proves your thesis:

Combine the who, what, where, when, and why above into a topic sentence for your body paragraph:

_____

_____

_____

Category C: *(This should be one of the specific examples from your thesis.)*

Who:

What:

Where:

When:

Why this proves your thesis:

Combine the who, what, where, when, and why above into a topic sentence for your body paragraph:

_____

_____

_____

STEP 4 **INTRODUCTION**

Turn your two-sentence thesis into a one paragraph introduction.

The introduction should be designed to attract the reader's attention and give him/her an idea of the essay's focus. Remember that the readers are reading up to 400 essays daily so you want to attract their attention right away, so that your essay is read more carefully. *Your thesis should be clear and as concise as possible to address all parts of the question, and it should hit the reader as soon as possible.*

1. Create a few sentences explaining your topic in general terms (some background information is usually helpful) that can lead the reader from your opening to your thesis statement. This should include historical context about what was happening in the world and your country.

Background Information:

2. Finish the paragraph with your thesis statement. Here you will present your answer to the research question. Remember to include your main evidence at the end. *Your thesis should be clear and as concise as possible to address all parts of the question.*

Thesis:

STEP 5 **BODY PARAGRAPHS**

List all evidence that you can think of that would support each category. For example: British political policies might include

DBQ Essay Facts and Analysis Chart	
A. *Write topic sentence here.*	1. Evidence here:
	2. Evidence here:
	3. Evidence here:
	4. Evidence here:
B. *Write topic sentence here.*	1. Evidence here:
	2. Evidence here:
	3. Evidence here:
	4. Evidence here:

DBQ Essay Facts and Analysis Chart	
C. *Write topic sentence here.*	1. Evidence here:
	2. Evidence here:
	3. Evidence here:
	4. Evidence here:

STEP 6 ANALYZE PRIMARY SOURCE DOCUMENTS

Applying this analysis to each document will help you interpret it and can be done on the document itself.

Historical Context

- **Causation:** Can you bring connections between the document and historical facts into the open?
- **Chronology:** Can you place the primary source within its appropriate place in the historical narrative or timeline?
- **PRIOR KNOWLEDGE:** What do you know that would help you further understand the primary source?

Audience

- For whom was the source created, and how might this affect the reliability or accuracy of the source?

Purpose

- WHY or FOR WHAT REASON was the source produced at the time it was produced? What was the author's GOAL?

Point of View

- Can you identify an important aspect of WHO the author is, and explain HOW this might have affected what the author wrote?
- Can you identify an influence that shaped the author or source, and EXPLAIN HOW THAT INFLUENCE specifically affected the document's content?
- THE MAIN IDEA: What point is the author trying to convey?

Write one sentence that

- explains **why the source is important in relation to—**

-OR-

- explains **what the source has to do with the DBQ question.**

_____

_____

_____

_____

_____

STEP 7 ADD PRIMARY SOURCE DOCUMENTS TO THE CORRESPONDING CATEGORIES ON YOUR EVIDENCE CHART IN STEP 5

STEP 8 WRITE BODY PARAGRAPHS USING I.Q.C. METHOD

For every document you mention in your essay, be sure to use I (Introduction), Q (Quote or Paraphrase), and C (Commentary Analysis).

I. Introduction for Evidence #1: Briefly explain where/when the source was created to help your reader understand the quotation you will use as evidence. You may want to include the author and date of the quote.

Author:

Date:

Now put it into one complete sentence (example: On August 1st, 1945, Hitler gave a speech about the war.).

Q. Quotation or paraphrase—Evidence #1: A quote or fact that supports your topic sentence

[ ]

C. Commentary Analysis of Evidence #1: Explain how the quote supports your topic sentence and answers the research question. (**At least 2 sentences**) *Use the following commentary analysis words: shows, explains, describes, demonstrates, elucidates, illuminates.*

This shows:

It is important because:

At the end of the analysis you should put the document number in parentheses. (Doc 1)

STEP 9 CONCLUSION

The conclusion of a historical research paper is where you restate your thesis, make connections between your research and the larger world, and give your final thoughts or opinion on your topic.

I. Restate or rephrase the thesis: Remind your reader of your main argument and three supporting claims. Briefly explain how you have used evidence to successfully support your argument.

[ ]

II. Make a larger connection: Make a connection between your historical evidence and another historical figure or era, current global or national events, another academic topic such as literature, or current events.

```


```

III. Why do you care/final thoughts: Here is where you leave your reader with your final ideas about your topic. You can share what you have learned, insights, reflections, and/or further questions that your analysis, research, and exploration have raised.

```


```

Now you are ready to write your essay. Remember to write a minimum of a five-paragraph essay with an introduction, at least three body paragraphs, and a conclusion.

Sample DBQ

TIME:

15 MINUTES TO READ AND MARK DOCUMENTS

40 MINUTES TO WRITE ESSAY

> **Directions:** The following question is based on the accompanying Documents 1–7. This question is designed to test your ability to apply several historical-thinking skills simultaneously, including historical argumentation, use of relevant historical evidence, contextualization, and synthesis. Your response should be based on your analysis of the documents and your knowledge of the topic. The documents have been edited for the purpose of the exercise.

Question 1 is based on the accompanying documents.

In your response you should do the following:

- Respond to the question with an evaluative thesis that makes a historically defensible claim.
- Use Historical Reasoning to explain relationships among the pieces of evidence provided in the response AND how they corroborate, qualify, or modify an argument that addresses the entirety of the question.
- Explain how at LEAST 4 documents' point of view, purpose, historical situation, and/or audience are relevant to the argument.
- Describe a broader historical context immediately relevant to the question.
- Explain how at least one additional piece of specific evidence beyond those found in the documents relates to an argument about the question.

The DBQ is designed to test your ability to read and interpret documents. Show your mastery of this skill by analyzing the content and the point of view and validity of the source's author. Answer the question fully by utilizing your analysis of the documents and the time period discussed to support a well-constructed essay.

1. Analyze how the various responses and reactions to the changes brought on by the advances in methods of production in Great Britain changed from the 1770s through the 1880s.

Source: P. Bairoch International Industrialization Levels from 1750 to 1980 as published in the *Journal of European History,* fall of 1982.

Industrialization Levels in Great Britain from 1750 to 1913
Level per Capita with 100 Being Equal to 1900 Production

Year	Production Level
1750	10
1800	16
1830	25
1860	64
1880	87
1900	100
1913	115

Source: Philosopher and economist, Adam Smith, *An Inquiry into the Nature and Causes of the Wealth of Nations*, 1776.

To take an example, therefore, from a very trifling manufacture, but one in which the division of labour has been very often taken notice of, the trade of a pin-maker: a workman not educated to this business (which the division of labour has rendered a distinct trade), nor acquainted with the use of the machinery employed in it (to the invention of which the same division of labour has probably given occasion), could scarce, perhaps, with his utmost industry, make one pin in a day, and certainly could not make twenty. But in the way in which this business is now carried on, not only the whole work is a peculiar trade, but it is divided into a number of branches, of which the greater part are likewise peculiar trades. One man draws out the wire; another straights it; a third cuts it; a fourth points it; a fifth grinds it at the top for receiving the head; to make the head requires two or three distinct operations; to put it on is a peculiar business; to whiten the pins is another; it is even a trade by itself to put them into the paper; and the important business of making a pin is, in this manner, divided into about eighteen distinct operations, which, in some manufactories, are all performed by distinct hands, though in others the same man will sometimes perform two or three of them. I have seen a small manufactory of this kind, where ten men only were employed, and where some of them consequently performed two or three distinct operations. But though they were very poor, and therefore but indifferently accommodated with the necessary machinery, they could, when they exerted themselves, make among them about twelve pounds of pins in a day. There are in a pound upwards of four thousand pins of a middling size. Those ten persons, therefore, could make among them upwards of forty-eight thousand pins in a day. Each person, therefore, making a tenth part of forty-eight thousand pins, might be considered as making four thousand eight hundred pins in a day. But if they had all wrought separately and independently, and without any of them having been educated to this peculiar business, they certainly could not each of them have made twenty, perhaps not one pin in a day; that is, certainly, not the two hundred and fortieth, perhaps not the four thousand eight hundredth, part of what they are at present capable of performing, in consequence of a proper division and combination of their different operations.

Source: Letter from the Cloth Merchants of Leeds, England, advocating for the introduction of steam-powered looms, 1791.

If then by the Use of Machines, the Manufacture of Cotton, an Article which we import, and are supplied with from other Countries, and which can every where be procured on equal Terms, has met with such amazing Success, may not greater Advantages be reasonably expected from cultivating to the utmost the Manufacture of Wool, the Produce of our own Island, an Article in Demand in all Countries, almost the universal Clothing of Mankind?

In the Manufacture of Woollens, the Scribbling Mill, the Spinning Frame, and the Fly Shuttle, have reduced manual Labour nearly One third, and each of them at its-first Introduction carried an Alarm to the Work People, yet each has contributed to advance the Wages and to increase the Trade, so that if an Attempt was now made to deprive us of the Use of them, there is no Doubt, but every Person engaged in the Business, would exert himself to defend them.

From these Premises, we the undersigned Merchants, think it a Duty we owe to ourselves, to the Town of Leeds, and to the Nation at large, to declare that we will protect and support the free Use of the proposed Improvements in Cloth-Dressing, by every legal Means in our Power; and if after all, contrary to our Expectations, the Introduction of Machinery should for a Time occasion a Scarcity of Work in the Cloth Dressing Trade, we have unanimously agreed to give a Preference to such Workmen as are now settled Inhabitants of this Parish, and who give no Opposition to the present Scheme.

Source: *The People's Petition*, a petition circulated and sent to Parliament, 1838.

Humbly showeth:

That we, your petitioners, dwell in a land whose merchants are noted for their enterprise, whose manufacturers are very skillful, and whose workmen are proverbial for their industry. The land itself is goodly, the soil rich, and the temperature wholesome. It is abundantly furnished with the materials of commerce and trade. It has numerous and convenient harbors in facility of internal communication it exceeds all others. For three and twenty years we have enjoyed a profound peace. Yet with all the elements of national prosperity, and with every disposition and capacity to take advantage of them, we find ourselves overwhelmed with public and private suffering. We are bowed down under a load of taxes, which, notwithstanding, fall greatly short of the wants of our rulers. Our traders are trembling on the verge of bankruptcy, our workmen are starving. Capital brings no profit, and labor no remuneration. The home of the artificer is desolate, and the warehouse of the pawnbroker is full. The workhouse is crowded, and the manufactory is deserted. We have looked on every side; we have searched diligently in order to find out the causes of distress so sore and so long continued. We can discover none in nature or in Providence. . . . The energies of a mighty kingdom have been wasted in building up the power of selfish and ignorant men, and its resources squandered for their aggrandizement. The few have governed for the interest of the few, while the interests of the many have been sottishly neglected, or insolently and tyrannically trampled upon. It was the fond expectation of the friends of the people that a remedy for the greater part, if not for the whole, of their grievances would be found in the Reform Act of 1832. They regarded that act as a wise means to a worthy end, as the machinery of an improved legislation, where the will of the masses would be at length potential. They have been bitterly and basely deceived. The fruit which looked so fair to the eye has turned to dust and ashes when gathered. The Reform Act has effected a transfer of power from one domineering faction to another, and left the people as helpless as before. Our slavery has been exchanged for an apprenticeship to liberty, which has aggravated the painful feelings of our social degradation by adding to them the sickening of still deferred hope. We come before your honorable house to tell you, with all humility, that this state of things must not be permitted to continue That it cannot long continue, without very seriously endangering, the stability of the throne, and the peace of the Kingdom, and that if, by God's help, and all lawful and constitutional appliances, an end can be put to it, we are fully resolved that it shall speedily come to an end.

WE DEMAND UNIVERSAL SUFFRAGE.

The suffrage to be exempt from the corruption of the wealthy, and the violence of the powerful, must be secret.

Source: Philosopher and economist Karl Marx, *The Communist Manifesto*, 1848.

The bourgeois clap-trap about the family and education, about the hallowed co-relation of parents and child, becomes all the more disgusting, the more, by the action of Modern Industry, all the family ties among the proletarians are torn asunder, and their children transformed into simple articles of commerce and instruments of labour.

But you Communists would introduce community of women, screams the bourgeoisie in chorus.

The bourgeois sees his wife a mere instrument of production. He hears that the instruments of production are to be exploited in common, and, naturally, can come to no other conclusion that the lot of being common to all will likewise fall to the women.

He has not even a suspicion that the real point aimed at is to do away with the status of women as mere instruments of production.

For the rest, nothing is more ridiculous than the virtuous indignation of our bourgeois at the community of women which, they pretend, is to be openly and officially established by the Communists. The Communists have no need to introduce community of women; it has existed almost from time immemorial.

Our bourgeois, not content with having wives and daughters of their proletarians at their disposal, not to speak of common prostitutes, take the greatest pleasure in seducing each other's wives.

Bourgeois marriage is, in reality, a system of wives in common and thus, at the most, what the Communists might possibly be reproached with is that they desire to introduce, in substitution for a hypocritically concealed, an openly legalised community of women. For the rest, it is self-evident that the abolition of the present system of production must bring with it the abolition of the community of women springing from that system, i.e., of prostitution both public and private.

Source: British illustration, 1860s.

Source: Thomas Escott, Social and Political Historian, *England: Her People, Polity, and Pursuits*, 1885.

Before the eventful year 1832, most of the places under Government were in the hands of the great families. The Reform Bill admitted an entirely new element into political life; a host of applicants for Parliamentary position at once came forward, and as a consequence the social citadel was carried by persons who had nothing to do with the purely aristocratic section which had hitherto been paramount.

COMMENTS ON THE DBQ

TIP

Before writing your essay, glance at the documents and their authors, and check the question to be certain that your thesis and your essay address all parts of the question!

It is amazing how many DBQ essays do not contain a thesis that directly answers all parts of the question.

This type of question is common for the DBQ because it asks you to describe the *reactions* and *responses* to some event or movement and how they changed over time. There are two tasks to this question. The first task is to identify the *reactions* and *responses* of Europeans to the rise of the Industrial Revolution. The second task is to illustrate how those *reactions* and *responses* **changed over time**. It is clear here that this question is targeting the *continuity and change over time* skill. Different DBQs will assess different skills, but this skill will be a common one as the type of question and the format of the question lead naturally to that type of question.

The first task is accomplished by reading the documents, analyzing the documents and making notes on them, grouping them, and using them to illustrate how Europeans reacted and responded to the new methods of production that were emblematic of the Industrial Revolution.

The second task is made easier because the documents are presented in chronological order. You can choose to have separate paragraphs, illustrating how the reactions and responses changed over time, or to illustrate how responses and reactions changed over time within each paragraph about a separate group of documents.

Do not forget to *demonstrate point of view*, purpose, audience, or at least historical context for many of the documents, which will further help to illustrate the reactions and possibly responses of Europeans to the onset of the Industrial Revolution.

Grouping documents is helpful for success, and there are many ways to group the documents presented in this DBQ. Possible groupings include those who viewed the Industrial Revolution in a positive light, those who viewed the Industrial Revolution in a negative light, the bourgeois bosses and their proponents, workers, and those who observed society, such as historians and artists.

It is best to create a short outline. The structure that is easiest to write quickly includes a thesis that addresses both parts of the question and includes all of the groups you intend to use. The organizer above was included to help you gather the evidence that you will need to write your DBQ essay, so use it your first few times writing, then once you get the hang of it, write without it. Each group identified should have a separate paragraph, with a paragraph on change over time, followed by a concluding paragraph.

DBQ SAMPLE RESPONSE

The evolution in the ways that goods were produced brought profound changes, first to Great Britain, and then to the rest of the world, during the Industrial Revolution, which increased Great Britain's production capabilities (document 1). Reactions and responses to these changes evolved as the era developed and can be understood through the eyes of those who observed society such as historians and artists (documents 2, 5, 6, 7), the bourgeois bosses and their proponents (documents 2 & 3), and the workers and their proponents (documents 4 & 5).

Historians and others who commented on society changed their views on the means of production as the methods and ethos of manufacturing evolved. Adam Smith, the father of economics, was very excited by the increases in productive capacity brought on by the introduction of the division of labor (document 2). As the first British student of economic conditions, he was naturally impressed by the gains made in that field. Karl Marx, the ultimate critic of capitalism, pointed out how this system of economy, and thus of production, exploits women by its very nature (document 5). He was likely to over-exaggerate the flaws of a system that he was condemning to collapse. As the Industrial Revolution progressed, observers started to extol the virtues of the factory system again as can be seen in the drawing showing the general population's acknowledgement of the impressive nature of new machinery (document 6). The illustrator probably is representing modern technology in a positive light to satisfy the patrons of his/her work who are most likely wealthy industrialists who want their machines depicted. By the 1880s, historians like Escott were assessing the changes in the political climate (document 7). As a historian Escott was trying to be unbiased, but was clearly influenced by the Victorian ideals of his times as well as the reform movement he studied. It appears that those who observed these changes professionally were at first in favor, then turned against these changes, and finally came to accept and study these changes.

One group that seemed to be universally in favor of the changes in production was the bourgeois bosses and their proponents. As time progressed, the bosses felt their power grow and demanded more control of their workers and their property. The Leeds wool manufacturers argued that their new methods of production were helping everyone in society, although they did note the fears of the workers (document 3). They were attempting to sway opinion in their direction to allow them to create steam-powered wool looms, so their facts were suspect due to their motives to increase output and thus profit. The community of businessmen continually favored changes in the modes of production over time. Governments and businesses teamed up in both world wars to improve and streamline modes of production and in fact in the First World War, production itself became a method of warfare.

Those who worked or who had worked in the factories seemed to think of the changes brought on by the Industrial Revolution in negative terms despite the fact that these changes had nearly doubled their standard of living by 1850. The People's Charter of 1838 demanded more rights for workers, such as voting, in order to help them address the ills of the factory system (document 4). This charter, which was signed by many workers and politicians of the day, became the basis for the workers' chartist movement that eventually did enlarge the franchise. The petition signers of the petition agreed that there should be a more equitable distribution of power to all citizens, a goal that Escott notes the results of in document 7. Karl Marx was in agreement with the People's Charter, but goes much further and intends to offend the bourgeois class by deriding their gender roles and equating them with class roles (document 5). Marx's forceful dissemination of his ideas would later be used as a justification for a revolution in Russia that attempted to skip the capitalist phase of society as Marx described it, and go directly from monarchy to communism. This is clearly an impossible feat if one believes the majority of Marx's work, which describes an inevitable evolution of society that must go through a capitalist phase to achieve true control of the means of production and distribution by the proletariat. In many ways, the changing attitudes on industrialization and urbanization including those of Karl Marx and others of the era such as Louis Blanc and Marcel Proust led to the communist revolutions first in Russia, then in China, Vietnam, North Korea, and even Cuba.

The responses and reactions of the people living in Great Britain from 1770 through 1880 to the changes in production seem to be based upon their station in life with social observers changing their views to suit the times, employers being in favor of the changes, and workers being against them. However, it is clear that those best able to study those changes were at first in favor of them, became skeptical of them, and later decided to study the social and political effect of the evolution of the means of production from the 1770s through the 1880s.

COMMENTS ON THE SAMPLE ANSWER TO THE DBQ

This is a top notch answer that would receive a **score of 7**. This essay demonstrates insightful use of documents to prove a cogent *thesis that fully addresses all parts of the question*. More importantly, the essay clearly meets all parts of the DBQ rubric (found on pages 37–38) for the following reasons:

1. This essay will be awarded **1 point** for an evaluative thesis that directly addresses all parts of the question and makes a historically defensible claim.
2. This essay will be awarded **1 point** for CONTEXTUALIZATION, because it situates the argument by explaining the broader historical events, developments, or processes immediately relevant to the question.
3. This essay will be awarded **3 points** for EVIDENCE because it utilizes content from at least SIX documents and employs historical reasoning to explain relationships among the pieces of evidence provided in the response AND how they corroborate, qualify, or modify an argument that addresses the entirety of the question. This includes **1 point** for EVIDENCE BEYOND THE DOCUMENTS, because it provides an example or additional piece of specific evidence beyond those found in the documents to support or qualify the argument.
4. This essay will be awarded **1 point** for DOCUMENT ANALYSIS because it explains how more than FOUR documents' point of view, purpose, historical situation, and/or audience is relevant to the argument.

The most important characteristic of this response is the creative use of point of view to demonstrate command of the skill of analyzing historical sources. The use of point of view in Document 5 was creative and historically supportable. The essay also had some panache without using clichés, which may set it apart from other essays the graders read.

* For more information on scoring DBQ essays, turn to "DBQ Rubric" on pages 37–38.

ONLINE

Want more test-taking practice?

Visit *barronsbooks.com/AP/ap-european-hist/* to access three additional practice tests or scan the QR code below.

*Be sure to have your copy of *AP European History*, 9th edition on hand to complete the registration process.

PART TWO
Review Section: Time Periods

For further explanation of the required objectives for this course, which occur both by theme and by time period as separate objectives, it is strongly recommended that you or the teacher reading this book read both the *AP European History Curriculum Framework*, and the Course Outline, both available at the AP European History College Board website.

EXAMINATION OF PERIODIZATION AND REQUIRED TIME PERIODS

The AP European History course has four time periods that are required for study. These time periods are important to understand, for many of the historical skills that will be tested on the exam—such as Periodization, Patterns of Continuity and Change over Time, Contextualization, Causation, and Historical Argumentation—will utilize the periods that are required. The College Board has divided the course themes and key concepts into four chronological periods. These periods divide the years from c. 1450 to the present and provide a chronological framework for the course. *The instructional importance and assessment weighting for each period is equal.*

That does *NOT*, however, mean that each concept and set of events within each time period is equal, and these are very broad time periods that will need to be further divided.

These time periods are:

Period 1: c. 1450 to c. 1648
Period 2: c. 1649 to c. 1815
Period 3: c. 1815 to c. 1914
Period 4: c. 1914 to the present

Each time period has a set of *key concepts* that will be described before each section. The writers of the *AP European History Curriculum Framework* have delineated these time periods based upon major political events. The first time period begins at the start of the course in 1450 or so and ends with the Peace of Westphalia, which reshaped the balance of power in Europe. The second time period ends in 1815 with the defeat of Napoleon and the Congress of Vienna redesigning the map of Europe. The third time period ends with the advent of the First World War. The final time period is the most recent hundred years.

When combined with the new themes in European history seen below, this delineation helps historians organize their ideas around some chronology. These themes are explained in detail in Part One; they are:

1. Interaction of Europe and the World
2. Poverty and Prosperity
3. Objective Knowledge and Subjective Visions
4. States and Other Institutions of Power
5. Individuals and Society
6. National and European Identity

The time periods were created to help organize the facts and movements in historical analysis, but also to help you gain the skill of periodization, which requires you to describe, analyze, and evaluate different ways that historians divide history into discrete and definable periods. Historians construct and debate different, sometimes competing, models of periodization; the choice of specific turning points or starting and ending dates might attribute a higher value to one narrative, region, or group than to another. To help you understand that debate, periodization is discussed throughout this exam preparation guide. It is also important to note that the ability to test the periodization skill was a contributing factor in the decision to make the time periods so large and then to ask you to undertake the task of correct periodization of evidence within and across the specified time periods.

This book also presents periodization that *mostly* agrees with the *AP European History Curriculum Framework*, but *differs on two major points*: the Industrial Revolution and the English struggle for constitutionalism. Because of the timing of the period breaks—which make so much sense from the perspective of a political historian—the history of those two important narratives of European history were bisected by the *Framework*. This book deviates from the *AP European History Curriculum Framework* in that periodization, doing so in order to preserve those two narratives.

Also, because of the complexity of the material as well as because historians have traditionally broken European history into other periods that were shaped by the events of their own times, each time period is broken into several chapters that fit more traditional historical periods, such as the Renaissance or the Reformation. The irony is that the examples used are time periods that overlap the Age of Exploration, which is also often delineated separately, as seen in this book. The logic behind the longer, and more definitive, historical periods makes much sense, but the traditional view is kept for its organizational value in order to preserve some historical narratives that may help with contextualization and periodization in the short-answer, DBQ, and LEQ tasks, and to give you a strong basis of facts and historical interpretations to enable historical argumentation.

Each time period is broken into three chapters. Each chapter ends with 6 to 12 multiple choice questions and answer explanations, and some essay question possibilities with comments on what possible answers would look like.

Each time period ends with an assessment section of about 15 multiple choice questions, some short-answer questions, and two FRQ choices with essay and multiple-choice answer explanations.

Time Period One:
c. 1450 to c. 1648

KEY CONCEPTS AND OVERVIEW

These are the Key Concepts for Time Period 1, according to the *AP European History Curriculum Framework:*

KEY CONCEPT 1.1 The worldview of European intellectuals shifted from one based on ecclesiastical and classical authority to one based primarily on inquiry and observation of the natural world.

KEY CONCEPT 1.2 The struggle for sovereignty within and among states resulted in varying degrees of political centralization.

KEY CONCEPT 1.3 Religious pluralism challenged the concept of a unified Europe.

KEY CONCEPT 1.4 Europeans explored and settled overseas territories, encountering and interacting with indigenous populations.

KEY CONCEPT 1.5 European society and the experiences of everyday life were increasingly shaped by commercial and agricultural capitalism, notwithstanding the persistence of medieval social and economic structures.

TIME PERIOD OVERVIEW

Time Period 1 is about the birth of modern Europe. It examines the beginning of global trade, the acceptance of multiple religious truths, the conflict between divine-right monarchy and parliamentary power, and the importance of the emergence of capitalism as Europe increasingly interacts with the rest of the world. This time period includes the traditional delineations of the following eras:

- The Renaissance
- The Reformation
- The Age of Exploration
- The Age of Absolutism (Old monarchs and emergence of new monarchs up to Louis XIV.)
- The Scientific Revolution (The start of the scientific revolution fits into this time period, i.e., Galileo, but not Newton.)

These traditional delineations do overlap in many ways, and the themes within them, as stated above in the key concepts, can be seen woven through the first three chapters of this book.

The Italian Renaissance and the Northern Renaissance (1450–1550)

1

KEY TERMS/PEOPLE

- → RENAISSANCE
- → CITY-STATES
- → MEDICI FAMILY
- → LEONARDO DA VINCI
- → MICHELANGELO BUONARROTI
- → PETRARCH
- → BOCCACCIO
- → NICCOLO MACHIAVELLI
- → DESIDERIUS ERASMUS
- → LEON BATTISTA ALBERTI
- → LORENZO VALLA
- → THOMAS MORE
- → JOHANN GUTENBERG
- → ALBRECHT DÜRER
- → ELIZABETHAN AGE
- → SECULARISM

- → CHRISTIAN HUMANISM
- → BALDASSARE CASTIGLIONE
- → HUMANISM
- → INDIVIDUALISM
- → DONATELLO
- → FILIPPO BRUNELLESCHI
- → RAPHAEL
- → MANNERISM
- → MANORIALISM
- → OPEN-FIELD SYSTEM
- → CREDIT
- → INTEREST
- → USURY
- → FUGGERS
- → MARSIGLIO FINICIO
- → PICO DELLA MIRANDOLA

OVERVIEW

While the Renaissance was a period of artistic, cultural, and intellectual revival, the term *renaissance*, a rebirth, can be misleading. It implies that the fifteenth and sixteenth centuries marked a distinct awakening for Europeans from the "darkness" of the Middle Ages. Actually, the medieval period gave rise to the basic institutions of Europe: its laws, languages, and economics. The elite culture that developed during the fifteenth century in the city-states of the Italian peninsula not only borrowed from ancient Greece and Rome, but also expressed a new conception of humankind, *individualism*, through innovative art and literature. It was in these independent domains, governed by a merchant class, by despots, or by republicans, that pure *secularism* (a belief that life was more than a preparation for the hereafter) first appeared in the modern world. The name Renaissance was not used until Jules Michelet employed it in the late nineteenth century, which explains why some historians may now see the delineation of the Renaissance as a separate era from the Reformation, the Age of Exploration, the Enlightenment, and the Scientific Revolution as arbitrary. The fall of Constantinople in 1453 to the Ottoman Turks caused many scholars of the Byzantine Empire to relocate in Italy, which helped usher in the Renaissance.

Humanism (a literary and educational movement that was truly modern in that a class of non-clerical writers concerned themselves with secular issues but based their answers to current problems on the wisdom of the ancient Greeks and Romans), rose in Italy in the fourteenth and fifteenth centuries. With their special affinity to classical Greek and Roman culture, schools such as the Florentine Academy emerged based upon studying classical authors such as Homer, Plato, Aristotle, and Cicero. In northern Europe, the "pagan" humanism of the Italian Renaissance was rejected in favor of a blend of religion and classical literature. Christian Humanists, such as Erasmus and Thomas More, tried to recapture the moral force of early Christianity by studying the Greek and Hebrew texts of the Bible and the writings of the Church Fathers.

Whether or not the Renaissance marks the beginning of the modern age, it provided a conception of the role and destiny of humankind vastly different from the ideas of the Middle Ages, and its artistic achievements influenced the culture of all Europe.

Since the Renaissance is defined less by specific events than by individual accomplishments and ideas, the following review focuses on significant personalities, achievements, and concepts. First, though, a few words about the setting for one of the most creative periods in all of human history.

THE ITALIAN RENAISSANCE

The Italian City-States

Italy was not so much a nation as an idea in the fifteenth century. It was an amalgamation of many distinct political entities known as city-states. By the fifteenth century, certain northern Italian towns that had been trade centers of the Roman Empire expanded into independent city-states that ruled wide areas of the surrounding countryside.

"Geography is destiny" proved true for the Italians of the fourteenth and fifteenth centuries. Fragmented as a nation since the fall of Rome, and their land becoming a battleground for the more unified peoples of Europe, Italians took advantage of their proximity to the sea. They applied the energy that springs from being always at the focus of crisis to establish a seagoing trade with the peoples in the eastern Mediterranean. They became the "middlemen" of Europe.

The Major City-States

- The Republic of Florence (considered the cultural center of the Italian Renaissance; often compared to ancient Athens for its utter brilliance over a brief period).
- Republic of Genoa
- Duchy of Milan
- Rome, the Papal States
- Naples, Kingdom of the Two Sicilies
- Venice, Venetian Republic
- Venice, Genoa, and Pisa (in the Republic of Florence) used their strategic locations on the Mediterranean Sea to control the European trade with the Middle East and Asia.

  – Florence, and to a lesser extent Rome, Naples, and Milan, thrived as manufacturing and market centers.

- Bankers from these prosperous cities made profitable loans to the people who shaped European life at the time:

  – Popes and monarchs of Europe financed successful commercial ventures.

    • The economic power of these city-states, combined with Rome as the center of Catholic power, made Italy a center of culture and luxury in Western Europe during the fourteenth and fifteenth centuries.

- As a major cog in trade routes between Europe and Asia, Italian city-states helped to spread ideas from different cultures around the world throughout Europe.

  – The city-states shared Arab mathematics and technology as well as Asian ideas and products with the continent (for a price and a hefty profit).
  – Ideas from many cultures including the revival of ancient Greek and Roman ideas were present.

    - Revived a sense of Italian pride in their past.
    - These factors all contributed to creating a prosperous merchant-centered society that fostered the age of the Renaissance.

  – The powerful middle class of merchants and bankers controlled the governments of the city-states and served as patrons to the artistic geniuses of the times.
  – Their newfound wealth encouraged appreciation of earthly pleasures and diminished dedication to the pious traditions of the Middle Ages.
  – It was not that most were irreligious, but rather that accidents of history and geography presented them with great wealth, far beyond any expectations of the subsistence feudal economy that had ruled Europe for a thousand years.
  – Money was meant to be spent; it just so happened that the more they spent on the beautiful handiwork of the skilled artisans in their cities, the more beautiful things were made for the buying.

- Thus, the Renaissance saw the beginning of the market economy in art, which drew the most talented geniuses to the field in search of profits and fame, setting the stage for other markets to emerge in labor and other resources, for example,

  – Beauty for its own sake, and art for art's sake—values absent from European culture since the end of the ancient world—replaced the medieval notion that art that is not dedicated to God is irreverent.
  – To these people, the world could be changed without the help of God. "Money is power" was becoming true regardless of one's status at birth.
  – *Secularism*, the concept of pursuing the pleasures in this life rather than the promises of the afterlife, was born: the rich nurtured it; the lower classes copied it.

The Medici Family

This was the most famous dynasty of those merchants and bankers who used their vast wealth both to govern the city-states and to patronize illustrious creators in the arts.

- *Giovanni de' Medici* (d. 1429): Merchant and banker of Florence, founder of the dynasty

  – Could be considered one of the world's first modern persons, an ultimate adapter who ignored the Church's prohibitions of lending for interest to provide the necessary funds for a changing world economy.
  – Although his son and great-grandson were the ones who brought glory to the family name by spending the fortune that he established, his originality is reflected in his deeds rather than his ideas, and he is one of the people of Europe whose restless genius molded the modern world.

- *Cosimo de' Medici* (1389–1464): Son of Giovanni who used the family fortune to fill the vacuum of power resulting from the lack of a national monarchy.

- Allied with other powerful families of Florence, he became unofficial ruler of the republic.

- *Lorenzo the Magnificent* (1449–1492): Cosimo's grandson, not only the republic's ruler but a lavish patron of the arts.

    - He personified the Renaissance attitude of living life rather than waiting for its fulfillment after death.

    - His genius was his recognition and support of the creative talent in his city; his luck was to be surrounded by geniuses.

The Medici family ruled the Grand Duchy of Tuscany, of which Florence was the principal city, well into the eighteenth century. Two popes, many cardinals, and two queens of France belonged to the family.

Individualism: A New Conception of Humankind

"Man is the measure of all things." A sense of human power replaced religious awe. Pleasure and accomplishment superseded the medieval dedication to the cloistered life of the clergy. Instead of the disdain for the concerns of this world that the piety of the Middle Ages had fostered, people now valued involvement, a life of activity.

Virtu: Literally, "the quality of being a man"; possible for a woman to express, but expected among aggressive males, the "movers and shakers" of the day; whatever a person's pursuit, in learning, the arts, or even in war, it meant living up to one's highest potential and excelling in all endeavors. The "Renaissance man" was an all-around gentleman, as comfortable with the pen or the brush as with the sword—a lover, poet, painter, conversationalist.

The Arts as an Expression of Individualism

Before the Renaissance, the Church was the greatest patron of the arts. Painters and sculptors labored anonymously to fill the churches and cathedrals of the Middle Ages with figures of the saints—figures that lacked the proportions and animation of real human forms or faces. During the Renaissance, although the Church remained a major patron, the new commercial class and the governments of the city-states also supported the arts. Even though the work was religious in nature, the forms were anatomically proportional, the faces filled with emotion, and the artists reveled in their individuality of style.

- Architecture adapted Greco-Roman symmetry, classical columns, arches, and domes.

    - Architects such as *Filippo Brunelleschi* (1377–1446), famous for Il Duomo (the first dome built since ancient times in Florence), and *Leon Battista Alberti* (1404–1472) studied ancient Roman buildings and used their principles of design to build cathedrals.

- Sculpture once again became freestanding, not designed to fit in niches of churches, and portrayed nude subjects in the Greek tradition in both religious and mythological representations.

    - *Lorenzo Ghiberti* (1378–1455): Sculpted a set of bronze doors for the Florentine baptistery with not only crowds of human figures but the illusion of depth.
    - *Donatello*'s bronze *David* (c. 1440): The first free-standing nude sculpted since Roman times in Europe and a tribute to his teacher, Brunelleschi.

Painting was primarily religious in theme but radically different from medieval art because of the invention of oil paints and because of the illusion of three dimensions created by precise variation of size (perspective). Art was less symbolic, more representational, depicting real people in recognizable settings, and glorifying the beauty of the corporeal world.

- *Giotto* (1267–1337): Painted on walls in Florentine buildings and created the illusions of depth and movement.
- *Masaccio* (1401–1428): Used light and shadow; the adoption of linear perspective, nude figures, and the illusion of perspective.
- *Sandro Botticelli* (1444–1510): Painted themes from classical mythology, such as his *Birth of Venus.*
- *Raphael* (1483–1520): Considered one of the greatest painters of any era; his portraits and Madonnas epitomize the Renaissance style.

The Greatest of the Great

- *Leonardo da Vinci* (1452–1519): Personification of the "Renaissance man"; painter, sculptor, architect, engineer, writer, scientist.

  - The versatility of his genius marks the last time that a single human could command virtually all the realms of knowledge and create masterworks in several areas of competence.
  - His *Mona Lisa* and his *Last Supper* rival any of the world's great paintings for the perfection of their execution and sheer beauty.

- *Michelangelo Buonarroti* (1475–1564): Primarily a sculptor whose *Pietá* (Mary mourning the body of Christ lying across her lap) is often considered the most perfect marble carving.

  - His awesome statues of *Moses* and *David* are unrivaled masterpieces that reflect religiosity and real human emotion.
  - His paintings on the *Sistine Chapel* in Rome, over which he labored for four years, portray biblical and allegorical figures with power, grace, and human clarity.
  - He glorified God by depicting the beauty of His earthly creations.

Humanism

This was a literary and educational movement distinct from the writing of the late Middle Ages in both its subject matter (it dealt with issues of politics and personal concern outside the realm of religion) and in its practitioners (laypeople who considered writing a profession rather than being a pursuit of the clergy). They drew on antiquity, which ironically had been preserved by monks laboriously copying ancient manuscripts. They wrote in Italian rather than Latin, and thereby created the first European vernacular literature.

- The works of the great poet, *Dante* (1265–1321), especially his *Divine Comedy*, along with the speech patterns of Florence influenced the standard form of modern Italian.
- *Petrarch* (1304–1374): Considered the first "modern" writer, he wrote sonnets in Italian, other works in Latin, and used writing to contemplate the ebb and flow of his life and the human condition itself.

  - The irony is that he is most known as a modern writer, but his largest contribution to the era was popularizing the study of the classical writers such as Plato and Cicero.

- *Juan Luis Vives* (1493–1540): A humanist writer who outlined a theory of education based upon the classics that came to define humanism. He was also a strong influence on Montaigne.
- *Marsilio Ficino* (1433–1499): A Catholic priest and an influential philosopher of the Italian humanist movement; he was the first to translate Plato's works into Latin and was named by Cosimo de' Medici as the first heir to the revived Platonic Academy.
- *Boccaccio* (1313–1375): A contemporary of Petrarch and, like him, a Florentine.

    - His most famous work is the *Decameron*, which satirized society and the clergy with entertaining tales that reflected upon the human condition.

- *Leonardo Bruni* (1370–1444): A chancellor of the Republic of Florence in the late fourteenth century, he wrote perhaps the first modern history, an account of the development of Florence, using narrative, drawing on authentic sources, and introducing new historical periods.
- *Baldassare Castiglione* (1478–1529): Offered a manual for the manners of the modern gentleman, *The Book of the Courtier*.

    - A gentleman is trained for polite company, poised and well dressed, skilled in arms and sports, capable of making music and conversation, a reader of the classics, a social mixer who is good humored, lighthearted, and considerate of others' feelings.
    - It was a civilized antidote to the crude social habits of the day, when even the well-born spit on the floor, wiped noses on sleeves, ate without utensils, shrieked, and sulked.

- *Niccolò Machiavelli* (1469–1527): *The Prince* was the first meaningful treatise on political science, an observation of how governments actually rule without moral judgment or exhortation.

    - It is one of the most maligned and misinterpreted books of modern times, called "cynical and ruthless," the "handbook of dictators," and the origin of the concept "The end justifies the means."
    - Machiavelli discovered that successful governments throughout history, whether Italian city-states or national monarchies, acted in their own political interest, making war or keeping the peace, true to their word or deceitful, benevolent or brutal when it was useful.

        - Religion had virtually ceased to influence the process of governing as the rise of the nation-state became the ultimate goal.

    - *The Prince* (1513) offers keen insights and is meant as a guide to the survival of the independent city-states of Italy, which were vulnerable to the predatory powers in the north.

- *Laura Cereta* (1469–1499): A well-known humanist and early feminist, she probably taught moral philosophy at University of Padua, a center of Renaissance learning.

    - Her 1488 *Epistolae familiars* (Familiar Letters) were widely condemned for her criticism of fifteenth-century gender bias.
    - When told by a man that intelligent women were unattractive, she retorted that so were unintelligent men.

THE NORTHERN RENAISSANCE

The Northern Renaissance was the spread of Renaissance ideals from Italy to northern Europe, including what are modern-day Germany, England, Switzerland, France, Belgium, and Holland. This period saw the emergence of market economies in England and the Netherlands, bringing prosperity and artistic renewal to northern Europe. The Northern Renaissance differed from the Italian Renaissance in that the Italian Renaissance was much more secular, whereas religion was emphasized in the north. Social reform through Christian values and an emphasis on reforming all of society through better Christian living were the hallmarks of the Northern Renaissance. Pietism, encompassing more arduous religious devotion of the laity, emerged as an aspect of this line of reasoning.

- *Christian Humanism* also emerged as the thinkers and writers in the north adopted a Renaissance curiosity for knowledge, but based their research on the Hebrew and Greek texts of the Bible, while the Italians had applied their new zeal for knowledge to earlier pagan texts (works from outside the Judeo-Christian ethic were referred to as pagan then, and by historians now) of ancient Greece and Rome.

  - The Northern Renaissance originated in part because of cultural diffusion as northern students went to Italy to study and came back with new ideas and ideals.
  - The thirst for knowledge and the new artistic and engineering techniques of the Italian Renaissance were transferred to northwestern Europe, leading to a Renaissance that was strongest in the Germanic areas and the Low Countries (Holland and Belgium).

Banking

One of the commonalities between the Italian Renaissance and the Northern Renaissance is the importance of rising economies and trade. This was typified by the Medici family in Italy as discussed earlier and the *Fugger* family in the German free imperial city of Augsburg, which peaked in banking power under *Jacob Fugger*. In many ways the Renaissance was an upper-class movement that came about in no small part because of the growing wealth of merchants and bankers. While the Italians were the trendsetters in banking as early as the 1100s, the formalized systems that included banks with offices in multiple cities allowed merchants across Europe to travel without needing to carry gold—now they could withdraw money from offices in many cities, making them less prone to robbery.

As the wealth of the common people grew, so did the banking industry. Christians began to compete with the Jewish money lenders when they found ways around the *usury* ban in Christianity by requiring "insurance" for loans. As banking emerged into a field of finance, many bankers began to offer *credit* so that merchants could borrow money for purchasing wares to sell, then would pay it back to the bankers with interest. Many stronger realms, such as the Ottoman Empire and France, even began to secure the services of a "court Jew" who could attain loans and make loans to citizens at interest to manage the finances of the state. Jewish people were not prevented from loaning money by their religion, as Christians were, so that is why governments chose a Jewish person as their chief banker. These positions later evolved into the modern minister of finance.

The emergence of banking in Northern Europe and Italy coincided with the growth of the Renaissance and its spread of ideas. As merchants who were not nobility gained economic power, they also began to desire political power to match, and much of the political developments of the Renaissance period were tied to the growth of banking.

Germany

Much like Italy, Germany was a collection of principalities that would not be united into a single nation until the late nineteenth century. Often referred to in this text as the Germanic states, Germany consisted of over 300 individual political units during the fifteenth century. At the turn of the sixteenth century, on the eve of the Reformation, Germany was at the heart of European progress. Although politically diverse (the German-speaking world included most of central Europe, Switzerland, and parts of the Netherlands), its economy thrived anyway. Towns sprouted, grew, traded. Banking expanded: the Fuggers and other German families controlled more capital than the Italian bankers and all other Europeans combined.

Science and Technology

The **printing press** was popularized by *Johann Gutenberg* (c. 1400–1468), but Johann Faust and Peter Schoffer also used it around the same time as Gutenberg. The first printing press was actually invented in China, but Gutenberg was the first to make *interchangeable moveable type* from lead molds. The introduction of the printing press in Europe had a massive impact on society because it became easier to spread ideas, propaganda, and stimulate education. Books became cheaper so more people read, which caused a **reading revolution** in society as reading became an individualized activity, rather than one person reading aloud to a group. Now the Bible was printed in many vernacular languages for the laity to read for themselves, which would have a significant social impact. This also helped lead to the advent of the Reformation as many in Europe did not need the Catholic priest to be God's intermediary, and worship became much more individualized.

- *Regiomontanus* (Johann Muller, 1436–1476) and *Nicholas of Cusa* (1401–1464) laid the foundations for modern mathematics and science in the fifteenth century.
- *Martin Behaim* (1459–1507) and *Johannes Schoner* (1477–1547) developed the era's most accurate maps.
- *Nicolaus Copernicus* (1473–1543) upset the time-honored *geocentric view* (that heavenly bodies revolved around the Earth) of astronomy with calculations that offered proof of a *heliocentric* (sun-centered) system.

  - This view contested the Aristotelian model adopted as the official Roman Catholic view of the solar system.
  - This contradiction is a *major milestone in the creation of a divide between religion and science* that began during the period of the Renaissance and continued as a theme throughout European history, helping to mark the Renaissance as the start of the modern era.

- The notion that humankind could understand and control nature evolved from the work of these Germans.

Mysticism

This involved the belief that an individual, alone, unaided by church or sacraments, could commune with God. The mystics, such as *Meister Eckhart* (1260–1328) and *Thomas à Kempis* (1380–1471), author of the inspirational *Imitation of Christ*, pursued religious depth rather than rebellion. They stayed true to the Church, but sought to offer, to the few faithful who could understand, a substance that transcended traditional religiosity.

- *Gerard Groote* (1340–1384): A Dutch lay preacher, he organized the Brothers of the Common Life in the late fourteenth century, a religious organization that stressed personal virtues of Christianity rather than doctrine. Its movement of *modern devotion* preached Christ-like love, tolerance, and humility.
- Both mysticism and the basic religious devotion of many laypeople contrasted, ominously, with the worldliness and smugness of the clergy.
- *Desiderius Erasmus* (1456–1536): "The Christian Gentleman" personified Christian humanism in his philosophic stances known as "the philosophy of Christ."

    - A man of letters, he disdained the Middle Ages, ignored hard philosophy, admired antiquity, and wrote on humanist issues in purified Latin.
    - The ultimate moderate, he championed gradual reform, ridiculed hypocrisy among the powerful, distrusted the fickle opinions of common people, and abhorred violence.
    - Satirized the worldliness of the clergy and was critical of the Catholic emphasis on saints in *The Praise of Folly*.
    - Offered a model of practical Christian behavior in *Handbook of a Christian Knight*.
    - Wrote new Greek and Latin editions of the Bible.
    - Confidant of kings and a critic of Church abuses.
    - Aimed at gentle reform of the Church from within.
    - He was the most famous and influential intellectual individual of his times, and used his writings and his example to preach peace, reason, tolerance, and loving reform.

Artists

- *Albrecht Dürer* (1471–1528): One of the master artists of the era.

    - His self-portraits and woodblock prints, such as *The Four Horsemen of the Apocalypse*, are still revered today.
    - He was a mathematician who was painting landscapes and self-portraits at age thirteen.

- *Peter Brueghel the Elder* (1520–1569): Focused on lives of ordinary people and painted and made prints that depicted them at work and play, which challenged the notion of the Italian Renaissance that art should be focused only on religious and aristocratic subjects.

England

The Renaissance in England coincided with, and was fostered by, the reign of *Elizabeth I* (1558–1603). An era of intense nationalism produced by the resolution of dynastic rivalries and religious turmoil, it gave birth to perhaps the greatest vernacular literature of all time.

- An era of profound economic and cultural growth known as the *Elizabethan Age* prevailed under her reign.
- The dramatist *Christopher Marlowe* (1564–1593).
- Poet *Edmund Spenser* (1552–1599).
- Scientist *Francis Bacon* (1561–1626).

- The greatest writer in English, perhaps in any language, *William Shakespeare* (1564–1616) reflected the influence of the dramatists of the ancient world and also the writers of the Italian Renaissance.

  – He single-handedly set the standard for the English language.

- During the reign of Elizabeth's father, *Henry VIII* (1491–1547), a contemporary of Erasmus, *Sir Thomas More* (1478–1535), had fostered the Erasmian spirit in his *Utopia*, a book that criticized the correctible abuses of various institutions and that offered a blueprint for a perfect society.

  – A devout Roman Catholic, he was beheaded for not supporting the king against the Pope during the English Reformation.

France

After the Hundred Years' War (1337–1453), the monarchy in France was strengthened by a renewal of commerce, which expanded and enriched the middle class. France was also realizing a wave of nationalism during the Renaissance era, possibly in part as a reaction to the Hundred Years' War. Government was centralized because the nobility had been weakened by a century of warfare and the **bourgeoisie** (servant-keeping middle class) provided an ample source of revenue for the royal treasury. Through the late fifteenth and early sixteenth centuries, a succession of strong kings such as *Louis XI, Charles VIII,* and *Louis XII* reduced the power of the nobility, firmed up the structure of the modern nation-state, and brought the middle class into government as advisors.

- *Rabelais* (1494–1553), a priest and a classicist, attacked the failings of French society and the Church in his *Gargantua and Pantagruel*, while advocating rational reform.
- *Montaigne* (1533–1592) invented the format of the essay, which is derived from the French term, *essaier*, meaning to test. His *Essays* preached open-mindedness and rational skepticism and offered an urbane, modern view of life.

Spain

Locked into Catholic orthodoxy by centuries of warfare against the Muslims (Moors), who had conquered much of the Iberian Peninsula, the Spanish reached the height of their expansion in the sixteenth century through exploration and overseas colonization.

Xenophobia and rigidity diluted the impact of Renaissance individualism and humanism. In 1492 (when Aragon and Castille united to form modern Spain), the Jews and Muslims, the core of the nation's educated middle class, were expelled. The expulsion of the Muslims (Moors) and Jewish people led to an intellectual and financial vacuum in Spain. The entire money-lending infrastructure in Spain had been run by the Jewish community, and the loss of this community led to financial chaos for Spain in the late 1500s and into the 1600s. The lack of credit and financial acumen left Spain without a working financial system, which France's Cardinal Richelieu would later term "the sinews of the state." This factor combined with the outlet for Spanish entrepreneurs to settle newly "discovered" lands in the Americas to leave Spain without a merchant class or financial expertise in the mother country.

The century from 1550 to 1650 marks the "Golden Age" of Spanish culture:

- *Miguel de Cervantes* (1547–1616) satirized his society's anachronistic glorification of chivalry and medieval institutions in one of the world's greatest novels, *Don Quixote.*

- *Lope de Vega* (1562–1635) wrote hundreds of dramas.
- *Bartolomé Estaban Murillo* (1617–1682) was one of the great Baroque painters.
- *Doménikos El Greco* (1541–1614) invented his mannerist style that was popular in Spain.
- *Diego Velázquez* (1599–1660) painted magnificent pictures on religious themes.
- *Francisco Suárez* (1548–1617) was a Jesuit priest who wrote widely admired works on philosophy and law.

The Low Countries

There were many societal and artistic achievements made in the Low Countries, which became a center of banking and commerce. This wealthier society placed greater importance on knowledge and art, and thus produced some magnificent artists.

- *Jan van Eyck* (c. 1385–1441) was a Dutch painter of the fifteenth century known as one of the great masters.

  - He was famed for his excellent, and often highly symbolic, oil paintings with meticulous detail that focused on either religious or secular themes.
- *Hieronymus Bosch* (c. 1450–1516) was a Dutch painter of the era who used complex symbolism and explored themes of sin and moral failing.

  - His complex, imaginative, and prevalent use of symbolic figures and obscure iconography was undeniably original and may have been an inspiration for the surrealist movement of the early twentieth century.
- *Rembrandt van Rijn* (1606–1669) was a Dutch master. He is generally considered one of the greatest painters and printmakers.

  - His use of chiaroscuro (dark and light) was powerful and manifested in his many self-portraits and paintings of stormy scenes.
  - He died very poor, as did many Northern Renaissance painters.

RENAISSANCE VIEWS ON GENDER AND ETHNICITY

The Renaissance was a period of loss of status for upper-class and merchant women. The protections on their property and bodies that had been strong during the medieval era were rescinded. Whereas the penalty for rape in the medieval era had been castration, the penalty in the fifteenth century was a fine payable to the father or husband, whosever's "property" had been damaged. Women were banned from many guilds, preventing them from inheriting their husbands' businesses. Few women were allowed into institutions of higher learning, and women were not taken seriously as intellectuals. This makes women like Laura Cereta, Isabella d'Este, and Catherine de' Medici even more impressive.

- Cereta was a prototype feminist and a lecturer at the most advanced university of the day, Padua.
- Isabella d'Este created a court at Mantua that became a center of arts and learning in her day.
- Catherine de' Medici was a power broker, queen, and regent of France as well as the mother of Louis XIII.
- The status of ordinary peasant women was not affected by the Renaissance.

This was also a time of renewed faith in many ways. Those who found that they disagreed with the Roman Catholic Church, which was the only official religion in Western Europe at the time, were often persecuted. Religious conflicts became more and more widespread in the sixteenth century. This era also saw the beginnings of racial bias against black African servants, who were simultaneously seen as exotic symbols of their masters' wealth and prestige and as evil because their dark skin was commonly believed to symbolize evil as portrayed biblically. Consequently, black Africans were not afforded access to the higher levels of European society.

SOCIAL STRUCTURE DURING THE RENAISSANCE

In much of Europe there still existed the medieval social structure of *manorialism*, a system in which the nobility and monarchs held all political power and everyone else had power based upon their income only. Everyone owed some type of tribute to those above them on the social structure. Most areas that experienced the Renaissance had four distinct social classes, in descending order of power: nobility, merchants, tradesmen, and unskilled laborers. It is important to remember that the Renaissance was mostly an urban phenomenon that the majority of people who lived in the countryside knew little of. The nobility was often not as well off economically as the merchant class that was beginning to grow in power at the time. The nobility lived on large estates outside the cities and in most areas acted as the military and as tax collectors. The nobility resented the growing power of the merchant class, while the merchants were driven to gain increasing political power through multiple means, including marrying into noble families. To display this power, the merchants became patrons of the arts. The tradesmen were shop owners and craftsmen. Most of them belonged to *guilds* that regulated their area of trade and provided unity and support for guild members. The guilds set standards within each industry and created rules for apprenticeship and joining the guild as well as limiting competition in each productive industry. The unskilled laborers were by far the majority of society and also by far the lowest rung on the social ladder.

RENAISSANCE POINTS TO REMEMBER

- ✔ It was focused on three ideals: humanism, secularism, and individualism.
- ✔ It occurred primarily in cities because contact with other cultures happened there first.
- ✔ Secularism became more pervasive in the cities and in art, but the Renaissance *did not* abandon interest in religion; in fact, the greatest patron of the arts continued to be the Church.
- ✔ Intellectually, there was a focus on this world rather than on the afterlife, and on description of the world and universe rather than obeying a prescription to religious dogma.
- ✔ The use of the vernacular in literature revolutionized literature and helped national identities solidify.
- ✔ New intellectual ideals gained a following, especially in human experience, manners, politics, and so on; these new subjects were known as "the humane letters," from whence the term "humanism" is derived.
- ✔ For the first time, artists of all types, from painters to authors, became wealthy; it was the birth of new professions that catered to wealthy patrons.
- ✔ The ideal of a "Renaissance man" emerged in the writings of Castiglione and Alberti as someone who is virtuous in every way and has many talents, such as the abilities to sing, compose poetry, dance, and engage in armed combat.

- ✔ Remember that the Renaissance was not a rebirth in law, government, or economic production; in most ways Europe was still medieval.
- ✔ There was some difference in the way that the Renaissance was perceived in northern and southern Europe.

  - Southern Europe was wealthier due to increasing trade with the Arabs and the Byzantines, providing the luxury to spend on arts, learning, and public projects.
  - The fall of Constantinople left the Italians without any means to trade with the Arabs after the Ottoman Turks destroyed the Byzantine Empire.
  - Northern Europe focused more on practical learning, science, and technology. This is one reason why the Reformation began there—that and its distance from Rome, where the wealth and power of the Church were so prevalent. Northern Europeans created many institutions of higher learning, while the Italians and Spanish focused on art and religion, respectively. The north used the precepts of the Renaissance spirit of the individual and took it in a religious direction toward mysticism. This belief holds that the individual soul can commune with God all by itself without the Church, other people, or sacraments.

THE RENAISSANCE CHARACTERS

A brief description of people whose ideas began the modern era.

Masters of the Arts

Giotto di Bondone 1266–1337 Florence Painter	■ Very influential pre-Renaissance painter and a friend of Dante ■ Work notable for its use of realistic scenes from nature
Filippo Brunelleschi 1377–1446 Florence Architect	■ Created *Il Duomo*, the first Italian free-standing dome since antiquity ■ Credited with bringing perspective to Renaissance artists
Donatello (Donato di Niccolò di Betto Bardi) 1386–1466 Florence Sculptor	■ His bronze, *David*, first free-standing bronze statue of a human created in Europe since antiquity
Masaccio (Tommaso di Ser Giovanni di Simone) 1401–1428 Florence Painter	■ Often called "Father of Modern Art," his *Expulsion* and *Holy Trinity* mark advance from medieval to Renaissance painting because of use of anatomy and perspective
Giovanni Bellini 1430–1516 Venice Painter	■ A leading painter of the Venetian school, the master of Giorgione and Titian ■ Known chiefly for his altarpieces and his Madonnas
Sandro Botticelli 1444–1510 Florence Painter	■ Most famous for his *Birth of Venus* ■ Assisted at decorating the Sistine Chapel ■ A follower of Savonarola

Domenico Ghirlandiao 1449–1494 Florence Painter	■ Founder of a school of painting, and was the teacher of Michelangelo
Leonardo da Vinci 1452–1519 Florence painter, sculptor, architect, engineer, and scientist	■ Painter of *The Last Supper, Mona Lisa,* and many other masterpieces ■ An engineer who designed flying machines and tanks ■ A rival of Michelangelo ■ Patrons were Lorenzo the Magnificent and Lodovico Sforza
Michelangelo Buonarroti 1474–1564 Painter, sculptor, architect, and poet	■ His great sculptures: the *Pietá, David,* and *Moses* ■ Famous for painting the ceiling of the Sistine Chapel for Pope Julius II ■ The greatest sculptor of hands ■ Part of the trinity of great fifteenth century artists, including Leonardo and Raphael
Raphael Sanzo 1483–1520 Urbino, Italy Painter	■ Chief architect of St. Peter's Cathedral ■ Master of oil painting in pieces such as *The School of Athens* ■ Part of the trinity of great fifteenth-century artists, including Leonardo da Vinci and Michelangelo
Artemesia Gentileschi (1590–1642) Italian Painter	■ Her father was also a painter whose patrons included King Charles I of England ■ Especially noted for her *Judith* paintings

Masters of Letters

Dante 1265–1321 Florence	■ Author of *Divine Comedy* (about an imaginary journey through Hell, Purgatory, and Heaven) ■ In it he helped define the **vernacular** of what is now the Italian language
Francesco Petrarch 1304–1374 Italian	■ The first great **humanist** thinker and a scholar of Latin ■ Known as the "Father of Humanism" ■ Major works: *Triumphs,* and *On the Solitary Life*
Giovanni Boccaccio 1313–1375 Italian	■ Friend of Petrarch, and a major contributor to the development of classic Italian prose ■ Wrote *Decameron,* a classic bawdy tale of love in all its forms

Leonardo Bruni 1369–1444 Italian humanist	■ His history of Florence noted for a new sense of the need for authentic sources in examining history ■ Translated Plutarch, Demosthenes, Aristotle, and Plato from Greek into Latin
Thomas à Kempis 1380–1471 German ecclesiastic and writer	■ German ecclesiastic and writer. Early religious purist, wrote *Imitation of Christ* ■ His mysticism teaches that the individual soul could commune directly with God in perfect solitude, without sacraments, people, or church
Lorenzo Valla 1406–1457 Italian humanist	■ Leading Italian Renaissance humanist most famous for *On Pleasure,* about the Epicureans
Pico della Mirandola 1463–1494 Italian humanist	■ Leading humanist of the Italian Renaissance and author of *Oration on the Dignity of Man*
Erasmus of Rotterdam 1466–1536 Catholic author and scholar	■ Created new Greek and Latin translations of the New Testament ■ Wrote *The Praise of Folly* and *Handbook of a Christian Knight* ■ Enemy of Martin Luther ■ Ally of Thomas More ■ Wanted reform within the Catholic Church ■ Leader in field of Renaissance learning in northern Europe
Niccolò Machiavelli 1469–1527 Florence	■ *The Prince*, his application for employment with Lorenzo Medici, the most important work on political science for centuries
Baldassare Castiglione 1478–1529 Milan and Urbino	■ Author of *The Book of the Courtier*, the first book of etiquette for nobles
Thomas More 1478–1535 England	■ Author of *Utopia* ■ As lord chancellor of England, opposed Henry VIII's break with the Catholic Church ■ Beheaded for sticking to his principles
Benvenuto Cellini 1500–1571 Florence Sculptor, goldsmith, and author	■ His *Autobiography* an excellent record of life in Renaissance Italy ■ Illustrated why he was the prime exemplar of "virtu" ■ Worked under Michelangelo ■ Patronized by Pope Clement VII
Francois Rabelais (1494–1553) France	■ Priest who attacked the failings of the Church in *Gargantua* and *Pantagruel*

Michel de Montaigne (1533–1592) France	■ Invented the essay ■ Essay derived from the French word for *test*
Miguel de Cervantes (1547–1616) Spain	■ Satirized the chivalry of the Spanish court and the medieval institutions of the state in his *Don Quixote*

Leaders of Religion

Nicholas of Cusa 1401–1464 Rhineland (Germany) Churchman	■ Roman Catholic prelate and philosopher ■ Focused on mystical philosophy ■ Anticipated Copernicus by his belief in the Earth's rotation and its revolution around the Sun
Pope Nicholas V (r. 1447–1455) Italian	■ A great patron of art and literature
Pope Innocent VIII (r. 1484–1492) Italian	■ Declared Henry VII lawful king of England and appointed Torquemada as Grand Inquisitor of Spain
Pope Alexander VI (r. 1492–1503) Spain	■ Bribed his way to the papacy ■ Children were Cesare Borgia and Lucretia Borgia, often at the Vatican when young ■ Gave papal land to his children ■ A great patron of the arts, (especially Bramante, Michelangelo, and Raphael) ■ Ordered execution of Savonarola ■ Purportedly said, "God has given us the papacy. Now let us enjoy it!"
Pope Julius II (r. 1503–1513) Italian	■ Decided to rebuild St. Peter's Basilica ■ Patronized Raphael, Michelangelo, Bramante, and others
Pope Leo X (r. 1513–1521) Italian	■ The second son of Lorenzo the Magnificent ■ Most opulent lifestyle as pope, ate from gold plates and threw them away ■ Failed to realize the importance of the Reformation ■ Issued papal bull excommunicating Luther

Girolamo Savonarola 1452–1498 Ferrara, Italy Dominican monk and church reformer	■ Gave vehement sermons about the corruption of secular life, the ruling class, and the worldliness of the clergy ■ Led Romans to revolt ■ Began the "Bonfires of the Vanities" (into which Sandro Botticelli threw his paintings to be burned) ■ Drove Piero de' Medici from power in Florence ■ Became virtual dictator of the city, preaching a crusade for the establishment of an ideal Christian state ■ Denounced by Pope Alexander VI, lost power in Florence to aristocrats ■ Captured, tried for sedition and heresy, then tortured, hanged, and burned

Scientific Minds

Regiomontanus 1436–1476 Germany Mathematician and scientist	■ Laid foundation for mathematical conception of universe
Nicholas Copernicus 1473–1543 Poland Scientist	■ Revived idea of a heliocentric (sun-centered) solar system from the ancients ■ Shocked Europe when *On the Revolutions of the Celestial Spheres*, published posthumously, but Galileo's support of his ideas later caused a bigger controversy
Johann Gutenberg (1398–1468) Germany	■ Often credited as the first to produce books with movable lead type, c. 1450

Political Leaders

Giovanni de' Medici 1360–1429 Florence	■ Merchant who became wealthy ■ Supporter of smaller guilds and common people ■ Virtual ruler of Florence, 1421–1429 ■ Began banking dynasty
Cosimo de' Medici 1389–1464 Florence	■ Son of Giovanni ■ Banker, patron of the arts ■ "Father of his country"
Lorenzo de' Medici "The Magnificent" 1449–1492, grandson of Giovanni, but not son of Cosimo Florence	■ Major patron of the arts ■ Father of a pope ■ Allegedly immoral and tyrannical ruler

Cesare Borgia 1475–1507 Originally Spanish	■ Son of Pope Alexander VI ■ Conquered much of central Italy, including Urbino ■ Acted with cruelty and treachery ■ Model for Machiavelli's "Prince"
Isabelle d'Este 1474–1539 Marchioness of Mantua	■ Married to Giovanni Gonzaga ■ Outstanding diplomat and patron of learning ■ Turned Mantua into the center of learning and thought

The Renaissance was *a significant artistic movement,* the first of many that occurred throughout European history.

For the AP European History exam, you should be aware of *ALL* artistic movements in Europe from the Renaissance through the modern era. The following chart summarizes the most notable ones.

IMPORTANT ARTISTIC MOVEMENTS IN EUROPEAN HISTORY

Italian Renaissance (1350–1550)

Important Artists: Michelangelo, Raphael, Leonardo Da Vinci, Botticelli, Brunelleschi, Giotto, Donatello, Titian

Composers: Palestrina

Key Writers: Petrarch, Machiavelli

Key Ideas and Writers:

- Individualism, humanism, secularism
- Perspective
- Use of triangles as architecture of art
- Individual portraiture
- Landscapes
- Free-standing human sculptures, nudes

Northern Renaissance (1450–1700)

Important Artists: Albrecht Dürer, Hans Holbein the Elder, Hieronymus Bosch, Pieter Bruegel the Elder, Jan van Eyck, Johannes Vermeer, Rembrandt van Rijn

Composers: Robert Cooper, John Milton, Cornelius Canis

Writers: Cervantes, Thomas Moore, William Shakespeare, Christopher Marlowe, Christine de Pizan

Key Ideas:

- Centralization of power in nation-states
- Reformation
- Focus on common people in art
- More religious than Italian Renaissance

Mannerism (1520–1600)

Important Artists: Giorgione, Tintoretto, El Greco, Velazquez
Composers: Monteverdi
Key Ideas:

- Transition between the end of the Renaissance and the beginning of the Baroque Era
- Art of the Reformation and Counter-Reformation focuses on new ideas and how to express them

Baroque (1550–1750)

Known for over-ornamentation, curved lines, and art that awes the viewer with impressive size and emotional reactions.

Important Artists: Peter Paul Rubens, Nicholas Poussin
Composers: Johann Sebastian Bach, George Frideric Handel
Writers: Descartes, Nicolaus Copernicus, Kepler, Galileo, Newton, Hobbes, Locke, Vesalius, Harvey
Key Ideas:

- The Scientific Revolution and Divine Right Absolutism
- Emergence of classical ballet and theater
- English Civil War

Rococo (1710–1790)

Typified as similar to baroque but more ornamental and less formal.

Important Artists: Thomas Gainsborough, Jean-Honoré Fragonard, Antoine Watteau, Étienne Maurice Falconet
Composers: Wolfgang Amadeus Mozart, Franz Joseph Haydn
Writers: Jean Jacques Rousseau, Denis Diderot, Edmund Burke, Goethe, Montesquieu, Adam Smith, Voltaire
Key Ideas:

- Enlightened despotism
- Enlightenment:
    - Salons
    - *Philosophes*, Encyclopedia

Neoclassicism (1790–1820s)

Revival of styles and spirit of classic antiquity, reflected the Age of Enlightenment and was initially a reaction against the excesses of the Rococo.

Important Artists: Jacques Louis David, Francisco Goya, Jean-Auguste-Dominique Ingres, Jean-Antoine Houdon
Composers: Ludwig van Beethoven, Franz Schubert, Sergei Prokofiev, Igor Stravinsky, Rossini

Key Ideas:

- French Revolution
- Napoleonic Empire
- Nationalism emerges

Romanticism (1820s–1860s)

Evolved as a reaction to neoclassicism and the Industrial Revolution.

Important Artists: Eugene Delacroix, John Constable, Joseph Turner, Théodore Géricault
Composers: Berlioz, Weber, Chopin, Mendelssohn, Liszt, Schumann, J. Strauss, Jr.
Writers: Lord Byron, Alexandre Dumas, Victor Hugo, William Wordsworth, Samuel Taylor Coleridge, John Keats, Mary Wollstonecraft Shelley, Percy Bysshe Shelley, Sir Walter Scott
Key Ideas: Expression of emotional nationalism and heroism; glorifies nature, the past, peasants, and nationalist movements

Realism (late 1850s to 1870s)

An attempt to depict life as it really is, as a reaction to the sentimentalism of Romanticism, showing the grittier side of life with a focus on the "common man."
Important Artists: Camille Corot, Jean-Francois Millet, Honore Daumier, and the Barbizon School of landscape painters. Some works by Edgar Degas and Edouard Manet
Composers: Wagner, Franck, Brahms, Bizet, Verdi, Puccini
Writers: Honore de Balzac, Charles Dickens, Gustave Flaubert, Guy de Maupassant, Henrik Ibsen, Friedrich Nietzsche, Marcel Proust, Emile Zola
Key Ideas:

- Focus on knowledge that can be known, or positivism
- Realpolitik, and a turn away from emotion toward fact, and a rejection of industrial progress
- Shows the ugliness of life for peasants
- Called pornography by critics

Impressionism (1870s–1920s)

Named for Claude Monet's painting "Impression of Sunrise," developed into sub-movements of Post-Impressionism, and Pointillism, which was made famous by Georges Seurat.

Important Artists: Paul Cezanne, Mary Cassat, Edgar Degas, Paul Gauguin, Edouard Manet, Claude Monet, Camille Pissarro, Pierre-Auguste Renoir, Auguste Rodin, George Seurat, Henri de Toulouse-Lautrec, Vincent van Gogh
Composers: Claude Debussy, Gabriel Fauré, Gustav Mahler, Maurice Ravel
Key Ideas:

- New subject matter and a new way of looking at the world
- Everyday life of the middle class became an acceptable subject for high art
- Painting in the outdoors gives new chance to study the play of light. Identifies with "La Belle Epoque"

Modern Art and Post-Modernism, including Futurism, Surrealism, Dada, and Pop Art (20th Century)

Artists are strongly influenced by Sigmund Freud, Albert Einstein, the World Wars, the coming of the Atomic Age, the rise of modern media, and the change in the concept of identity. Art less about sensual pleasure and more about making a statement.

Important Artists: Constantin Brancusi, Georges Braque, Alexander Calder, Marc Chagall, Willem de Kooning, Roy Lichtenstein, Marcel DuChamp, Salvador Dali, Paul Giocometti, Rene Margrite, Henri Matisse, Joan Miro, Aristide Maillol, Henry Moore, Pablo Picasso, Jackson Pollack, Andy Warhol

Composers: Béla Bartók, Alban Berg, George Gershwin, Sergei Prokofiev, Richard Strauss, Igor Stravinsky

Key Ideas:

- Expressionism (introspective into a world of emotional and psychological states)
- Abstractionism (detached examination of life distilling the essence of nature and sense experiences)
- Cubism: Picasso and Braque creating angular impressions of the real world
- Futurism

  – Made fashionable by Fascists

- Surrealism (examined dream fantasies, memory images, and visual paradoxes)
- Dadaism (a revolt against previous classical artistic movements and a response to the horrors of WWI)

  – Nihilistic
  – Challenged polite society; against order and reason

PRACTICE LONG-ESSAY QUESTIONS

These questions are samples of the various types of thematic essays on the exam. (See pages 30–31 for a detailed explanation of each type.) Check over the **generic rubric** (see pages 32–33) before you begin any of these essays and use that rubric to score the essays you write.

Question 1

To what extent and in what ways did the Italian Renaissance result from Italy's geographic advantage in the world trade of the fifteenth century?

COMMENTS ON QUESTION 1

"Geography is destiny," so it is said. And the strategic location of Italy, a peninsula jutting into the Mediterranean, gave it advantages in the world trade of the fifteenth century. This one is a CAUSATION question because it requires you to explain how much the Italian Renaissance was or was not caused by Italian geography. Remember to describe causes AND/OR effects of the Italian Renaissance.

You must explain the reasons for the causes AND/OR effects of the Italian Renaissance and Italian geography. "How and how much" are the questions to answer. The clues are inherent in the geography. With what parts of the world did the Europeans carry on trade at this time? Why did Italy have an advantage? What were the rewards of that advantage? How were those rewards instrumental in fostering history's greatest brief period of creativity? What were the limits on the influence of geography?

To make a strong essay, you must point out how other influences, such as the importance of Crusaders departing from Rome on Venetian and Milanese ships, or of the independence of Padua, must also be examined to create a top-scoring essay.

Question 2

"Although the term *renaissance* is misleading, the modern world began with Renaissance secularism and individualism." Assess the validity of this statement.

COMMENTS ON QUESTION 2

This question is about judging the truth or validity of the given statement. This question is a CHANGE AND CONTINUITY OVER TIME (CCOT) question because it asks how the Renaissance marked a change in how the people lived, earned a living, were ruled, thought about their society, and thought about knowledge. You will need to explain what remained the same after the Renaissance and what changed in all arenas of life, including social, political, intellectual, economic, religious, military, and artistic realms. You should explain how the Renaissance was different from and similar to the Middle Ages, and how it was more or less similar to the periods following the Renaissance, such as the Enlightenment, the Age of Exploration, and so forth.

You must explain the extent to which the Italian Renaissance was different from and similar to developments that preceded AND/OR followed it. This question can be answered by taking either side, but you MUST choose a side and argue for it. The more conventional way would be to argue that individualism and secularism—as they relate to industrialization and the emergence of capitalism and democracy—support the generalization. This answer must be supported with citations from writers and thinkers from the Renaissance and Enlightenment who are more modern.

The other side could argue that terms like *modernity* and *renaissance* are not valid in this context and that citing any era as being caused by another is a dubious argument. Citing the emergence in the nineteenth century of the historical term, "Renaissance," may help here. Either way, the question requires careful thought and planning to answer it.

Question 3

Explain why Machiavelli's *The Prince* is both the first modern treatise in political science and one of the most misinterpreted books of modern times.

COMMENTS ON QUESTION 3

This one seems to call for you to analyze CHANGE AND CONTINUITY OVER TIME because you must analyze the extent to which *The Prince* was different from political thinking that came before it. You should analyze the extent to which Machiavelli's ideas were different from and similar to political thinking that came before *The Prince* was published, and provide a number of specific examples to support the analysis.

You must explain the extent to which *The Prince* was different from and similar to political science developments that preceded AND/OR followed the appearance of the book. You must "examine in detail" the ideas of Machiavelli and the development of political science, and also "determine the relationships" between those ideas. Explain ways that the book has been misinterpreted. Remember, "explain" offers no choice. You must: "make clear," "detail," and "offer meanings, causes, reasons for."

The essence of the book is in the phrase: "The welfare of the state justifies everything." Is this equivalent to arguing that the end justifies the means? It is also important that Machiavelli says a prince must sometimes be bad in order to be a good prince. What was Machiavelli's purpose in writing the book? How did his methods of observation and his arguments make it the first modern treatise in political science? As stated, this essay must also address why and how *The Prince* has been misinterpreted. Would medieval philosophers have thought about the same issues as Machiavelli? If so, what would their arguments be based upon? Use the specific examples that Machiavelli uses and state that he uses historical examples, and then cite other historical individuals who seem to use his ideas but could not have read his book, such as Henry VIII.

Question 4

Compare the Italian Renaissance and the Northern Renaissance.

COMMENTS ON QUESTION 4

This is a COMPARE skill question, so be sure to describe similarities and differences between the Italian Renaissance and the Northern Renaissance. Account for or explain the similarities and differences by providing specific examples and tie them to historical situations, such as the seat of Catholicism being in Rome, far from northern Europe. In showing the differences, consider: how each Renaissance began; which one influenced the other; how their emphases differed; how they interpreted certain ideas differently; and how they expressed their differences. How did their art and literature differ? How did the personalities vary? Who was the "ideal Renaissance man" in Italy, in Northern Europe? What were the qualities of each?

In examining similarities, consider the ideas the Italian and Northern Renaissances had in common, such as "individualism" and "secularism"; look for similarities in their religious commitments, in their artistic and literary techniques and themes, and in their approaches to understanding human life.

Question 5

Analyze how the Northern Renaissance gave rise to two diverse developments: religious mysticism and revival, and science and technology.

COMMENTS ON QUESTION 5

This one is a CAUSATION question because it requires you to decide how the Northern Renaissance brought about increased religious mysticism and a revival of science and technology at the same time. Remember to describe causes AND/OR effects of the Northern Renaissance and explain the extent to which it can be credited (or blamed) for either development.

You must explain the causes AND/OR effects of the Northern Renaissance on intellectual movements. In this case, *analyze* primarily means to "determine the relationships" between the Northern Renaissance and two seemingly different approaches to the human condition: religion and science. How did the study of ancient texts—specifically Hebrew and Greek versions of the Bible and the writings of the early Church Fathers—revitalize religious devotion?

Consider how the concept of "individualism" could encourage the very personal religious experience of mysticism? How did "individualism" and "skepticism" give rise to modern science? Why did the revival of religion and the growth of mysticism occur primarily in Northern Europe? Was Italian religious devotion centered on the arts? Did the papacy have less sway in the North? Why did Northern Europe give birth to modern science? Was the desire to understand and control nature the Northern counterpart to Italian *virtu* or richness of the human spirit? Was it a tradition that began with the mathematician Regiomontanus and evolved into the Copernican formula for a heliocentric universe?

PRACTICE SHORT-ANSWER QUESTIONS

1. Use the image below and your knowledge of European History to answer all parts of the question that follows.

—By Raphael: *pintura.aut.org*, Public Domain, *The Small, Cowper Madonna.*

(A) Briefly explain TWO aspects of Renaissance art that are apparent in the image above.

(B) Briefly explain ONE aspect of Medieval art evident in the image above.

2. Use the passage below and your knowledge of European history to answer all parts of the question that follows.

Petrarch's Letter to Homer
(translated from Latin by James Harvey Robinson)

And now what shall I say about the matter of imitation? When you found yourself soaring so high on the wings of genius you ought to have foreseen that you would always have imitators. You should be glad that your endowments are such that many men long to be like you, although not many can succeed. Why not be glad, you who are sure of holding always the first place, when I, the least of mortals, am more than glad, am in fact puffed up with pride, because I have grown great enough for others—though I scarcely can believe that this is really true—to desire to imitate and copy me? In my case the pride and joy would only increase if among these imitators there should be found some few who were capable of surpassing me. I pray—not to your Apollo, but the true God of Intellect whom I worship, to crown the efforts of all who may deem it worth their while to follow after me, and to grant that they may find it an easy thing to come up with me, and outstrip me too . . . .

It was my intention to speak to you of Virgil, than whom, as Flaccus says, this earth has produced no soul more spotless; and to suggest to you, great master of us both, certain excuses for his conduct . . . . I admit the truth of everything that you say concerning him, but it does not necessarily follow that I lend a sympathetic ear to the charges that you base upon this failure of his to make anywhere any mention of your name, laden and bedecked though he is with your spoils,—mention, you remind me, such as Lucan made, remembering in grateful strains the honor due to Smyrna's bard.

(A) Briefly explain TWO aspects of Renaissance thought that are apparent in the letter above.

(B) Briefly explain ONE aspect of Medieval thought evident in the letter above.

Short-Answer Explanations

1. **0–3 points (2 points for A and 1 point for B)**

   (A) ONE point will be given for EACH of TWO explanations of HOW the painting is representative of Renaissance art. These may include realistic depiction of anatomy, use of perspective, use of light and/or color, the nature depicted in the background, portraiture based upon triangles, attention to details of the face and hands, proportion, or prevalence of nature.

   (B) ONE point will be given for an explanation of HOW the image is still representative of Medieval art. The main thrust here should be that it is still religious art depicting Madonna and child, the most important image in Christendom. The use of blue for the Madonna or the idea that the most important parts of the image are the largest could also be cited for credit.

2. **0–3 points (2 points for A and 1 point for B)**

   (A) ONE point will be given for EACH of TWO explanations of HOW the passage is representative of Renaissance thought. These may include: individualism, revival of Greco-Roman ideas and ideals, focus on intellectualism, pursuit of excellence, the imitation of the styles of other masters, or support of secularism.

   (B) ONE point will be given for an explanation of HOW the passage is still representative of Medieval thought. The main thrust here should be that it is still written in Latin and that it focuses on the ideals supported by the Roman Catholic Church. The nod to the "God of Intellect" can also be used to show that it supports monotheism.

PRACTICE MULTIPLE-CHOICE QUESTIONS

Questions 1 to 3 refer to the following quote from *The Myth of the Renaissance* by Dr. Jeremy Brotton.

The term "Renaissance"—referring to the revolution in cultural and artistic life that took place in Europe in the 15th and 16th centuries—was first applied as late as the 19th century, when the French historian Jules Michelet used it in his *History of France* of 1855. . . .

Michelet's invention of the Renaissance was refined and established by the Swiss historian Jacob Burckhardt, in his book *The Civilization of the Renaissance in Italy* (1860). Like Michelet, Burckhardt believed that the cultural achievements of the period heralded a "rebirth" (the French "renaissance") of the classical Greek and Roman values of literary purity and aesthetic beauty. . . .

Until very recently, this invention of the European Renaissance has remained a powerful and seductive myth, which has ignored much of what was truly revolutionary about this extraordinary period in European history. The problem with the approach of both Michelet and Burckhardt to the Renaissance is that it reflected their own 19th century world, characterized by European imperialism, industrial expansion, the decline of the church, and a romantic vision of the role of the artist in society. Neither of these writers explored how trade, finance, science and exchange with other cultures decisively shaped what they saw as the cultural flowering of the European Renaissance.

1. What is Dr. Brotton's primary argument against the traditional view of the Renaissance as proposed by Michelet and Burckhardt?

   (A) The work of the earlier historians was flawed because they were too focused upon economic causes and effects of the era.

   (B) The work of the earlier historians was flawed because they ignored the importance of trade, finance, and science, and cultural exchange in their analysis of the era.

   (C) The work of the earlier historians was flawed because they were living in the nineteenth century.

   (D) The work of the earlier historians was flawed because they ignored the impact of the arts on the growth of math and sciences.

2. Which of the following was more likely to be emphasized by Burkhardt and Michelet than by Brotton?

   (A) The role of the Roman Catholic Church in promoting the Renaissance and its values

   (B) The importance of the invention of double-entry bookkeeping

   (C) The role of the Fuggers and Medici in creating a commercial environment favorable to the Renaissance

   (D) The role of foreign trade in supporting the cultural diffusion needed for the Renaissance to bloom

3. The Renaissance was a time known for educational and intellectual breakthroughs often attributed to which of the following educational systems?

   (A) The secular system taught at universities in Italy, which ignored all religious traditions
   (B) The individualism taught by artists and their patrons
   (C) The navigational methods of the school of Henry the Navigator
   (D) The focus on Greek and Roman classics required by humanism

Questions 4 to 6 refer to the image below.

David by Michelangelo Buonarroti (1501–1504).

4. Michelangelo's *David* displays which of the following thematic innovations of Renaissance artists?

   (A) The depiction of religious personages
   (B) Accurate human anatomy
   (C) The use of marble as a material
   (D) The portrayal of enigmatic expressions

5. The sculpture of David, above, was placed in front of the new Republic's town hall, the Palazzo della Signoria, in Florence, facing Rome and the pope as a warning against the former power of which of the following families?

(A) The Habsburg family who had dominated politics on the Italian Peninsula and throughout Europe for over a century

(B) The Valois family who had dominated Italy and Germany as a part of their dominance of religious and political life in the 1400s

(C) The Medici family who had dominated Italy through banking

(D) The Fugger family to whom the pope owed huge amounts of money, which eventually led to selling of indulgences

6. Which of the following would explain why the city of Florence commissioned a statue of David rather than another biblical or classical hero?

(A) The story of the righteous underdog who defeated a giant had resonance in the young republic, which wanted to preserve its freedom.

(B) The city of Florence had named David its patron saint and wanted to celebrate him.

(C) The thousands of Florentine Jewish people combined their wealth to sponsor the creation of an Old Testament hero for their city to recognize.

(D) David's purity of actions and thought throughout his story in the Bible made him the perfect representative of the most artistic city of the Italian Renaissance.

Multiple-Choice Explanations

1. **B**
2. **A**
3. **D**
4. **B**
5. **C**
6. **A**

1. **(B)**
(A) is wrong because a big part of Brotton's argument was that the earlier historians ignored the economic growth of the era.
(B) is CORRECT: Brotton says the work of the earlier historians was flawed because they ignored the importance of trade, finance, science, and cultural exchange.
(C) is wrong because B is a clearer summation of why they were wrong, even though Brotton does mention the nineteenth century; B is a MUCH better answer.
(D) is wrong because the impact of the arts on the growth of math and science was not large enough to be a major historical factor.

2. **(A)**

(A) is CORRECT because of the factors listed; this matches best with Michelet and Burkhardt, who ignored economics in large part.

(B) is wrong because Michelet and Burkhardt ignored economics and finance in large part, and double-entry bookkeeping is a form of finance.

(C) is wrong because Michelet and Burkhardt ignored economics and finance in large part, and the Medici and Fuggers were banking families.

(D) is wrong because Michelet and Burkhardt ignored the importance of foreign trade and cultural diffusion into Europe.

3. **(D)**

(A) is wrong because humanism was the educational system of the Renaissance, and universities at the time neither were secular nor ignored traditions.

(B) is wrong because humanism was the educational system of the Renaissance, and while individualism was an important part of modern identity, it was not an educational system.

(C) is wrong because humanism was the educational system of the Renaissance and, although navigational methods taught at Prince Henry's school were important, they were not the educational system for most wealthy youth.

(D) is CORRECT because the educational system of the Renaissance was humanism, which focused on the classical ideas and works of Greece and Rome.

4. **(B)**

(A) is wrong because although David was a biblical story, biblical stories had been the dominant theme of art in Europe for the past 700 years or more.

(B) is CORRECT because accurate and proportionate representations of anatomy were Renaissance "innovations" reintroduced from classical sculpture.

(C) is wrong because in 1500 marble had been used as a material of artists for thousands of years.

(D) is wrong because enigmatic expressions were not a theme of the Renaissance, so B is a *better* answer.

5. **(C)**

(A) is wrong because, although the Habsburgs did dominate Italy, the new Republic of Florence was more fearful of its former rulers, the Medici, whose family included the current pope.

(B) is wrong because, although the Valois did dominate Italy, the new Republic of Florence was more fearful of its former rulers, the Medici, whose family included the current pope.

(C) is CORRECT because the new Republic of Florence was fearful of its former rulers, the Medici, whose family included the current pope.

(D) is wrong because the Fuggers, who dominated Northern European banking, were not involved in internal Italian politics.

6. **(A)**

(A) is CORRECT because David was placed in front of the Palazzo della Signoria facing Rome to celebrate the heroism of the new republic's expulsion of the Medici and as a warning that it takes heroism to preserve freedom.

(B) is wrong because David was not the patron saint of Florence.

(C) is wrong because David was commissioned by all Catholics, and Judaism had nothing to do with its commission or creation.

(D) is wrong because David did not live a pure life according to the Bible, but sent a man to his death in order to marry the man's betrothed.

Protestant Reformation, Catholic- and Counter-Reformations, Wars of Religion (1517–1648)

2

KEY TERMS/PEOPLE

- → REFORMATION
- → SIR THOMAS MORE
- → PEACE OF AUGSBURG
- → INDULGENCES
- → MARTIN LUTHER
- → THE DIET OF WORMS
- → SPANISH INQUISITION
- → JOHN CALVIN
- → URSULINES
- → COUNCIL OF TRENT

- → IGNATIUS OF LOYOLA
- → JESUITS
- → INDEX OF PROHIBITED BOOKS
- → THE THIRTY YEARS' WAR
- → WAR OF THREE HENRYS
- → EDICT OF NANTES
- → CARDINAL RICHELIEU
- → CHARLES V OF SPAIN AND AUSTRIA
- → PHILIP II OF SPAIN

OVERVIEW

This chapter fits 100 percent within the first time period for the course. Historians generally agree that the Protestant Reformation is one of the markers of the beginning of modern Europe and a crucial part in the transformation of Western civilization. What began as an attempt to reform the Roman Catholic Church was co-opted by political forces and resulted in the destruction of the religious unity of Western Europe and the outbreak of bitter wars of religion.

Protestantism was adopted by the growing nation-states of the north as they were about to replace Italy and Spain as leaders of modern Europe; the Inquisition enforced orthodoxy. The Inquisition in Spain was designed to encourage a sense of national unity based on Catholicism. The Muslim Moors and the Jews who had been the educated groups in Spanish society were either driven into exile or forcibly converted. The Inquisition was later adapted in Spain and in Spanish territories to combat Protestantism, and it was imported to Italy for the same purpose. Protestantism, though, dominated most of northern Europe, and the continent suffered devastating disruptions during the wars of the sixteenth and seventeenth centuries.

CAUSES OF THE REFORMATION

1. Corruption of the Roman Catholic Church during the Renaissance; sale of church offices (simony); sale of indulgences; nepotism, absenteeism, decline of morality among the clergy
2. Impact of Renaissance *humanism,* which questioned Church traditions; Humanist "glorification of humanity"

   - Contradicted the Church's emphasis on salvation

3. Prosperity brought the "virtue of poverty" into disrepute and the Church lost the "spirit" of Christ's message and was out of touch with the mass of believers

4. Declining prestige of the papacy:

   ■ *Babylonian Captivity* of the Church in the fourteenth century when popes, subservient to the French king, took up residence in Avignon and lost prestige in the rest of Christendom.

   ■ The *Great Schism* beginning in 1378, when French and anti-French cardinals elected two popes, one of whom lived in Rome, the other in Avignon, and lasting over forty years.

   ■ *Moral decline* of the Renaissance popes bred cynicism. Papal involvement in secular politics fostered contempt.

5. Influence of religious reformers, such as Wycliffe (c. 1330–1384) and John Huss (c. 1372–1415) stressed personal communion with God, which had two effects:

   ■ Diminished the importance of the sacraments
   ■ Weakened the influence of the clergy

6. Resentment of secular rulers over the power of the popes and clergy:

   ■ Monarchs of growing nation-states resisted papal supremacy over national churches.
   ■ Secular rulers also resented vast landholdings of the Church within national boundaries.

7. Resistance to the power of the Holy Roman Emperor, Charles V:

   ■ The princes of the Germanic lands resented the new Holy Roman Emperor
   ■ Charles V (r. 1519–1558), who at age nineteen took the throne along with his vast Habsburg holdings and proclaimed at his coronation, "the empire from of old has had not many masters, but one, and it is our intention to be that master."
   ■ The Holy Roman Emperor had been a symbolic title, and his desire to make it more actual caused resistance to the power of Charles V.
   ■ Protestantism helped the princes do just that.

8. Invention of the **printing press** allowed dissenters to spread their ideas throughout Europe and made the Bible available to the common people. It also meant that a person's ideas and influence in the world would live on long after s/he died. This would become more important as new sects of Christianity challenged the Roman Catholic Church, and those sects were not as easily silenced once the ideas of their leaders were recorded and spread as they had been in the days of Jan Huss.

CHRONOLOGICAL OVERVIEW OF EVENTS, PERSONALITIES, AND IDEAS

1517

Johann Tetzel (c. 1465–1519), a wandering friar, was authorized by *Pope Leo X* to sell *indulgences* (which guaranteed the remission of sins), the proceeds of which would be used to rebuild St. Peter's Church in Rome and to provide funds to local dioceses.

Martin Luther (1483–1546), a Roman Catholic priest, Augustinian monk, and theologian at the University of Wittenburg in Germany, condemned these sales as impious expediencies.

Tormented by obsessions of his own damnation despite a life dedicated to holy service, he came to believe that the traditional means of attaining salvation (*Good works,* such as the sacraments, prayer, and fasting) were inadequate. He supposedly nailed his *95 Theses* to the door of the Wittenburg church (his day's equivalent of calling a press conference), listing the points of his opposition to the indulgences and inviting debate.

1519–1520

When an appeal to Pope Leo X (r. 1513–1521) for reform of this abuse went unanswered, Luther began to formulate the tenets of his beliefs, ideas that he had been mulling over for nearly a decade.

Tenets of Lutheranism as published in a series of tracts:

1. *Salvation by faith alone:* Good works (the sacraments) cannot guarantee salvation but rather are an outward manifestation of the faith that a loving God will grant that salvation. This concept was inspired by Luther's reading, many years earlier, of a passage from Romans 1:17, in which St. Paul says "the just shall live by faith."
2. *The Bible is the ultimate authority:* Neither the Pope nor church councils can define Christian doctrine; every believer should read and interpret the Bible, and the faithful will be divinely guided.
3. *The grace of God brings absolution:* Neither indulgences nor confession can bring forgiveness of sins; the individual is freed of sin only by the grace of God; pilgrimages, veneration of saints, fasts, and worship of relics are useless.
4. *Baptism and communion are the only valid sacraments:* The Roman Catholic Church regarded seven sacraments (baptism; confirmation; Eucharist or communion; matrimony; penance; extreme unction, last rites, or anointing of the sick; holy orders) as outward signs of inner grace. Luther rejected all but baptism and communion. Luther also rejected the Roman Catholic doctrine of *transubstantiation* (the belief that while the bread and wine of the Mass maintain their appearance, they are transformed into the body and blood of Christ). In its place he offered the doctrine of *consubstantiation* (the doctrine that the transformation of the bread and wine was not literal but that God was actually present in more than a symbolic way).
5. *The clergy is not superior to the laity:* Marriage is permitted; Christianity is a "priesthood of all believers"; monasticism should be abolished.
6. *The church should be subordinate to the state:* In the appointment of church officials, the matter of taxing church lands, the organization of the church, and all matters other than the theological, the state is supreme. This appealed to the monarchs and to the German princes who resented papal authority and who coveted the vast landholdings and wealth of the Roman Catholic Church. It would have ramifications for Lutheranism in Germany well into the twentieth century.

1520

Luther publicly burned a *papal bull,* an official proclamation that demanded his recantation, and he was excommunicated by *Pope Leo X.* Holy Roman Emperor *Charles V,* instead of arresting Luther and suppressing Lutheranism, which had a growing appeal in Germany and Scandinavia, honored a political debt to Frederick the Wise, Elector of Saxony, by refusing to outlaw Luther without a hearing.

1521

Luther was called to the Rhineland in Germany to appear before *The Diet of Worms*, a tribunal of the Holy Roman Empire with the power to outlaw, i.e., to condemn to be burned at the stake. Confronted by the sharpest theological debaters of the Roman Catholic Church, Luther contended that only the Bible or reason would convince him. "I neither can nor will I recant anything, since it is neither right nor safe to act against conscience." The Diet outlawed him. "Kidnapped" to safety in Wittenberg by Frederick the Wise, he organized his reformed church and translated the Bible into the vernacular, profoundly influencing the development of the modern German language.

1520s

Lutheranism spread. Preoccupied with wars against the Ottoman Turks and the French, *Charles V*, Holy Roman Emperor, was unable to suppress the growth of Protestantism in northern Europe. In addition to northern Germany, Denmark and its province of Norway, Sweden and its holdings in Finland, and the Eastern Baltic all embraced Lutheranism.

1521

A group of *Anabaptists*, who preached adult baptism and the equality of all Christians, began to spread their ideas in Germanic states and their religious movement began to gain ground.

1522

A league of knights, under the leadership of *Franz von Sickengen*, converted to Lutheranism and attacked the Catholic princes of the Rhineland. They were suppressed, but this clash encouraged most of the German princes to convert. One motive for von Sickengen's followers and the later conversions was the financial gain brought by confiscating Roman Catholic lands.

1524–1526

Luther's theological dissent inspired a variety of radical religious sects to form and to demand social reform based on the early Christian model. Demanding abolition of *manorialism*, the economic and social order of medieval feudalism, German peasants rebelled against the landowners, and Germany was wracked by the *Peasants' War*. Luther supported the princes by publishing *Against the Murderous, Thieving Hordes of Peasants*.

The Anabaptists supported the revolt, and Luther targeted them in some of his most specific chidings. He was appalled by these extremists and others who, he believed, took his ideas too far. The Anabaptists who preached adult total-immersion baptism, and the Millenarians, who expected the imminent return of Christ. He condemned the rebels as "filthy swine" and encouraged the princes to exterminate them.

The radical revolt influenced Luther to demand that his followers obey constituted authority and that, while they read the Bible themselves, they leave its interpretation to knowledgeable ministers. His social and economic conservatism helped check the spread of Lutheranism in southern Germany and elsewhere in Europe.

1529

The Diet of Speyer refused to recognize the right of the German princes to determine the religion of their subjects.

1531

The *League of Schmalkalden* was formed by newly Protestant princes to defend themselves against the emperor. Charles V appealed to the Pope to call a church council that could compromise with the Lutherans and regain their allegiance to the Roman Catholic Church. The Pope, fearing the papacy's loss of power, refused and lost a potential opportunity to reunite Western Christendom.

1530s

The Reformation spread beyond Germany.

1531

In Switzerland, *Huldrych Zwingli* (1484–1531), who established Protestantism in Switzerland, was killed in a nationwide religious civil war. Although his followers accepted most of Luther's reforms, they argued that God's presence during communion is only symbolic. *The Peace of Cappel* allowed each Swiss canton to determine its own religion.

1534

Pope Paul III (r. 1534–1549) assumed office as the first of the "reform popes."

1534

In England, Parliament passed the *Act of Supremacy*, which made *Henry VIII* (r. 1509–1547) and his successors the head of the Anglican Church and its clergy.

- In 1521, when Luther was outlawed by the Holy Roman Empire, Henry VIII had been awarded the title "Defender of the Faith" by Pope Leo X for Henry's tract "Defense of the Seven Sacraments."
- By 1529, Parliament, partly because of Henry's influence, declared the English Church independent of Rome.
  - Parliament cut off revenues to the papacy.
  - Henry, eager to divorce *Catherine of Aragon* in order to marry *Anne Boleyn*, had been denied an annulment for political reasons.
- Catherine was the aunt of Charles V, Holy Roman Emperor.
  - Henry appointed *Thomas Cranmer* as Archbishop of Canterbury in 1533, was granted a divorce by him, and was excommunicated by the Pope.

1534–1539

The English Parliament abolished Roman Catholic monasteries and nunneries, confiscated their lands, and redistributed them to nobles and gentry who supported the newly formed Anglican Church.

1536

In Switzerland, *John Calvin* (1509–1564) published his *Institutes of the Christian Religion* in the Swiss city of Basel. Like Zwingli, he accepted most of Luther's ideas but differed on the role of the state in church affairs.

1. *Predestination:* Calvin argued (from an idea of St. Augustine [354–430]) that since God knows even before birth whether a person is saved or damned, there is nothing anyone can do to win salvation. *The Elect* or *Saints* are a select few saved only by God's love from corrupt humanity and given indications of their status by *conversion* (a mystical encounter with God) or by material prosperity. The latter gave rise to the *Puritan* or *Protestant Ethic*, an incentive to avoid poverty as a sign of damnation, and served to justify the rise of capitalism.
2. *Church government:* Calvin replaced the Catholic hierarchy with a democratic system whereby each individual congregation elected its minister and governed its policies. He disagreed with Luther's claim that the church should be subordinate to the state, and argued that it should actually be a moral force in the affairs of secular government. This stand encouraged *theocracy*, whereby Calvinism became the official religion and intolerant of dissent not only in parts of Switzerland but later in England and the Massachusetts Bay Colony in North America.

1539

In England, Parliament approved the *Statute of the Six Articles.*

1. The seven sacraments were upheld.
2. Catholic theology was maintained against the tenets of both Lutheranism and Calvinism.
3. The authority of the monarch replaced the authority of the pope.

Despite attempts by *Mary I of England* (1516–1558, Henry VIII's daughter by Catherine of Aragon) to reinstitute Catholicism, and the *Puritan Revolution* of the following century, the *Six Articles* helped define the Anglican Church through modern times.

1540s

Calvinism spread: in Scotland the *Presbyterian Church* and in France the *Huguenots* were emerging based upon the ideas of Calvin as his religion spread through the wealthy merchant elite throughout northern Europe. The Counter-Reformation began.

1540

Ignatius Loyola (1491–1556) established the *Jesuits* (Society of Jesus), a holy order that was organized in a military fashion, requiring of its members blind obedience and absolute faith.

The Jesuits swore to suppress Protestantism:

1. They served as advisors to Catholic kings.
2. They suppressed heresy through the Inquisition (clerical courts that tried and convicted religious dissenters who were subject to deportation, torture, or death).
3. They established schools in Catholic nations to indoctrinate the young.
4. They sent missionaries to far corners of the earth to convert "the heathen."
5. The Society of Jesus became the militant arm of the Counter-Reformation.

1541

1. Calvin set up a model theocracy in the Swiss city of Geneva.
2. The Scottish Calvinists (*Presbyterians*) established a national church.
3. The French Calvinists (*Huguenots*) made dramatic gains but were brutally suppressed by the Catholic majority.
4. The English Calvinists (Puritans and Pilgrims—a separatist minority) failed in their revolution in the 1600s but established a colony in New England.

1542

The Jesuits were given control of the Spanish and Italian *Inquisitions*.

- Perhaps tens of thousands were executed on even the suspicion of heresy.
- The *Index of Prohibited Books* was instituted in Catholic countries to keep heretical reading material out of the hands of the faithful.

1545–1563

The Council of Trent responded to the challenge of Protestantism by defining Catholic dogma. Its main pronouncements:

1. Salvation is by both *good works* (such as the veneration of saints and fasts) and *grace*.
2. The seven sacraments are valid, and transubstantiation is reaffirmed.
3. The sources of religious authority are the Bible, the traditions of the Church, and the writings of the Church Fathers. Individuals cannot interpret the Bible without the guidance of the Church, and the only valid version of the Bible is the Vulgate, St. Jerome's Latin translation.
4. Monasticism, with celibacy of the clergy, and the existence of purgatory are reaffirmed.
5. Attempts were made to reform abuses: the principle of indulgences is upheld while its abuses are corrected; bishops are given greater power over clergy in their dioceses; and seminaries are established in each diocese for the training of priests.

1555

The *Peace of Augsburg*, after over two decades of religious strife, allowed the German princes to choose the religion of their subjects, although the choice was limited to either Lutheranism or Catholicism. *Cuius regio, eius religio*: "whose the region, his the religion."

Results of the Protestant Reformation

1. Northern Europe (Scandinavia, England, much of Germany, parts of France, Switzerland, Scotland) adopted Protestantism.
2. The unity of Western Christianity was shattered.
3. Religious wars broke out in Europe for well over a century.
4. The Protestant spirit of individualism encouraged democracy, science, and capitalism.
5. Protestantism, specifically Lutheranism, justified nationalism by making the church subordinate to the state in all but theological matters.

The War of the Three Henrys (1587–1589)

This was partially a religious war and partially a dynastic war. The weak king, Henry III of France, was counseled to root out the Protestant, Huguenot nobility by Henry of Guise.

- The Huguenots in France had gained power among about 10 percent of the nobility.
- When Henry of Navarre married Margaret of Valois, the king's sister, a massacre of Huguenot friends of Henry of Navarre by Roman Catholics known as the St. Bartholomew's Day Massacre erupted initiating this war.
- Henry of Navarre won the war but converted back to Catholicism to rule as Henry IV of France.

  - Issued the Edict of Nantes, allowing Huguenots religious freedom in strongholds.
  - He is reported to have said, "Paris is well worth a mass," before converting back to Catholicism.

The Thirty Years' War (1618–1648)

1. The first continent-wide war in modern history, fought mostly in Germany, it involved the major European powers.
2. It was the culmination of the religious wars of the sixteenth century between Catholics and Protestants.
3. Politically, German princes sought autonomy from the Holy Roman Empire; France sought to limit the power of the Habsburgs who sought to extend power in Germany; Sweden and Denmark hoped to strengthen their hold over the Baltic region.

The Four Phases of the War

- *The Bohemian Phase (1618–1625):*

  - The Czechs, also called Bohemians, who, together with the Slovaks, formed the modern nation of Czechoslovakia after World War I, were largely Calvinist.
  - Fearful that their Catholic king, *Matthias,* would deny their religious preferences, they *defenestrated* (used the old custom of registering dissent by throwing officials out a window) his representatives and briefly installed, as king, a Calvinist, *Frederick V of the Palatinate*, or Elector Palatine.
  - After Matthias's death, *Ferdinand II* became Holy Roman Emperor and King of Bohemia.

    - Supported by troops of the Spanish Habsburgs, he defeated the Bohemians at the *Battle of White Mountain* in 1620.
    - Gave away the lands of the Protestant nobles
    - Enabled the Spanish to consolidate power along the Rhine River

- *The Danish Phase (1625–1630)*

  - *Christian IV of Denmark* (r. 1588–1648), a Lutheran, entered the war to bolster the weakened Protestant position in Germany and to annex German lands for his son.
  - Holy Roman Emperor Ferdinand II (r. 1619–1637) countered by commissioning Albert of Wallenstein to raise a mercenary army, which pillaged and plundered Germany and defeated the Danes in 1626.

- In 1629, the emperor issued *The Edict of Restitution*, which restored all the land to the Roman Catholic Church in states in Germany that had left the Church before the Peace of Augsburg in 1555.
- When Wallenstein disapproved, Ferdinand dismissed him.

- *The Swedish Phase (1625–1630)*

  - *Cardinal Richelieu*, Roman Catholic regent of France, was concerned with the gains made by the Holy Roman Emperor Ferdinand II in Germany.
  - France decided to pursue nationalist interests rather than religious ones as a matter of state policy under *Cardinal Richelieu*.

    - It was good policy to keep the Germanic states divided as France's neighbor.
    - France wanted to weaken the Habsburgs, the ruling house of the Holy Roman Empire.
    - France gained prestige.

  - He offered subsidies to encourage the capable Swedish king *Gustavus Adolphus* (r. 1611–1632) to enter the war.

    - Adolphus, a Lutheran, was eager to help the Protestant cause.
    - After decisive victories over the Habsburg forces, Adolphus was killed.
    - Wallenstein was assassinated for contemplating disloyalty to the emperor.
    - The Protestant states of Germany made a separate peace with the emperor.

- *The Peace of Prague* revoked the Edict of Restitution.
- The Swedes were defeated, but Richelieu was determined to undermine Habsburg power in Germany.
- *The French-International Phase (1635–1648)*

  - France, Holland, and Savoy entered the war in 1635 on the Swedish side.
  - Spain continued to support the Austrian Habsburgs.
  - After a series of victories and reversals on both sides, *Henri Turenne*, a French general, decisively defeated the Spanish at Rocroi.
  - In 1644 peace talks began in Westphalia, Germany.

The Peace of Westphalia, 1648

1. The Peace of Augsburg was reinstated, but Calvinism was added as acceptable for Germany.
2. The Edict of Restitution was revoked, guaranteeing the possession of former Church states to their Protestant holders.
3. Switzerland and Holland were made independent states, freed from the Habsburg dominions.
4. France, Sweden, and Brandenburg (the future Prussia) received various territories.
5. The German princes were made sovereign rulers, severely limiting the power of the Holy Roman Emperor and the influence of the Austrian and Spanish Habsburgs. With over three hundred separate rulers in Germany, national unification was ignored until well into the nineteenth century.

Effects of the Thirty Years' War

1. Germanic states were devastated; the population was reduced in some parts by well over a third. Once a cultural and political leader in Europe, it stagnated, helping to prevent its establishment as a sovereign, united nation for more than two centuries and complicating its relations with the rest of the world into the twentieth century.
2. The age of religious wars ended; the modern age of sovereign states began in Europe, and *Balance of Power* politics prevailed in Europe, whereby nation-states and dynasties went to war to prevent any one power from dominating the continent.
3. The Habsburgs were weakened. The Austrian monarchy lost most of its influence over Germany, ending the possibility of a Europe united under the family. Habsburg Spain was left a second-rate power.
4. The Counter-Reformation was slowed; Protestantism was firmly established in its European strongholds.
5. The Holy Roman Empire ceased to be a viable political structure and the Germanic states would not be unified again until 1871.
6. Calvinism gained acceptance throughout Protestant Europe.
7. Anabaptists were persecuted and disappeared as a religion.

GENDER AND ETHNICITY DURING THE REFORMATION

- Women received mixed blessings from this era.

  - Women did rise in status.

    - Luther and the Protestants preached that there was merit in all work in the eyes of the Eternal including the household work of women.
    - Ministers were allowed to marry, which raised the status of the women who had been their lovers but who now married them considerably, from their previous positions as adulteresses.
    - Women could have more official roles in Protestant religious life than in that of the Roman Catholic Church.
    - Some women became preachers.
    - Women were encouraged to read the Bible themselves, increasing female literacy and intellectual roles in general.

  - On the other hand, there was still considerable misogyny evident in this society.

    - Witch trials were also prevalent at this time.
    - Mostly women were accused of practicing witchcraft and many were burned at the stake after confessions were extracted through torture, or simply without evidence.
    - Nunneries closed in Protestant areas, leaving few options other than marriage or prostitution open to women.
    - Many former nuns were forced into marriage.
    - Women were still denied access to university education.

- This was an age in which minority religion was finding its power.

  - Also an era of zealotry

- Practitioners of many religions were intolerant of those who practiced other faiths.

  - This resulted in the many religious wars of the era.
  - Extermination of the Anabaptists.

- Europeans enslaved and mistreated people of African descent in larger numbers both in Europe and in the colonies.

  - In the colonies, European migrants mistreated, abused, and forced conversion onto native peoples.
  - The European conquistadors and settlers killed tens of millions of Native Americans.
  - Spain and other European powers became rich from the natural bounty of those lands.
  - Slavery and genocide of Africans and indigenous Americans is part of the legacy of this age.

THE BAROQUE PERIOD OF ART

The visual arts began to flourish and become more awe-inspiring; thus, Baroque art was born. The general intent of the *Baroque* period was to create a unity where all forms of art in a single expressive purpose could converge toward a single aim: to engage the viewer physically and emotionally. This art was meant to overpower the viewer and make the viewer feel small in comparison to the art and its subject matter. The term "Baroque" derives from a Portuguese word jewelers used to denote an irregularity in a misshapen or irregular pearl. Baroque therefore literally meant imperfect, grotesque, or absurd. The Baroque era began in the late sixteenth century in Italy and ended in some areas around the early nineteenth century.

- The term also refers to the seventeenth century as a whole and is sometimes used as a general term indicating eccentric or fanciful modes of paintings, architecture, sculpture, dress, or behavior in any period.
- Baroque art spread throughout Western Europe and into Russia and other places in Europe influenced by the court of Louis XIV.
- Also found in Latin America, the English colonies, and northern Europe.

  - Never had the Western world known such active international exchange in the intellectual field.
  - The internationalism was not checked by differences in religious belief.

    - For example, Peter Paul Rubens (1577–1640), a Flemish painter, worked in Italy, France, Spain, and England.
    - Rubens was considered a "European" painter, whereas Jacques-Louis David (1748–1825), a Neoclassical French painter, worked only in France for most of his life.

- Baroque art was an instrument of the *Counter-Reformation*, which took place from 1545 until the end of the Thirty Years' War in 1648.

  - The Catholic Church was losing its followers in rapid numbers due to the rise of Protestantism.

    - Created the *Council of Trent* to set about renovating the Catholic Church.
    - The society at this time was generally illiterate.

- Knowing this, the Catholic Church decided to bring back the wayward Catholics through art.

  - Baroque artists frequently capitalized on the immediacy of these emotional reactions, and spiritual art became an art of sensation.
  - Its effect was not to elevate the spirit but to stagger and overpower the senses.

- Baroque art was larger than life, escaping boundaries and overpowering the viewer.
- It is important to contrast the Baroque style with that of the Calvinist painters of the Dutch Golden Age who concentrated on realistic details in portraits and the interiors of buildings in the works of such artists as Vermeer, Rembrandt, and Hals. Their works were much smaller and more detailed, and attempted to shed insights into slices of life and individual personalities.

  - *Rembrandt Van Rijn's* (1606–1669) innovative portraits and use of light
  - *Johannes Vermeer's* (1632–1675) clear domestic scenes
  - *Franz Hals's* (c. 1582–1666) portraits of wealthy citizens of Antwerp and Amsterdam

Some examples of Baroque painters and their defining characteristics include:

- *Peter Paul Rubens's* (1577–1640) fleshy nudes and overwhelming biblical scenes
- *Michelangelo Merisi da Caravaggio's* (1571–1610) contrast of light and dark
- *Artemisia Gentileschi's* (1593–1652) paintings of dramatic tension and suffering

  - Beyond the realm of the two-dimensional

- *Gian Lorenzo Bernini* (1598–1650) was the greatest sculptor of the era.

In the musical world:

- *Johann Sebastian Bach* (1685–1750) was the ultimate Baroque composer
- *Claudio Monteverdi* (1547–1643) who wrote the oldest opera still performed, *Orfeo*
- *Antonio Vivaldi* (1678–1741) who composed *The Four Seasons*
- *George F. Handel* (1685–1759) whose *Messiah* has become a classic

Eventually, the Baroque style led to the *Rococo* style of art, characterized by elegance, pleasantness, and frivolity. It greatly contrasted the emotional grandeur of the Baroque.

MANY FAITHS CHART

This chart may be helpful in remembering the differences among the many new Christian faiths that emerged from the Protestant Reformation.

The Many Faiths of the Protestant Reformation

	Catholic	Anglican	Lutheran	Calvin	Zurich Protestants	Presbyterian	Anabaptists
Leadership	Pope and religious hierarchy	King and religious hierarchy	Luther	Ministerial government divinely ordained	Zwingli	Knox	No head
Sacraments	Seven	Began with communion, baptism, and penance then became just communion and baptism	Communion, baptism	Communion, baptism	Communion, baptism	Communion, baptism	Lord's supper and baptism
Clergy	Priests: Only clergy may interpret scripture	Married priests	Ministers and priesthood of all believers	Ministers, elders, deacons, congregants	Ministers	Ministers	Ministers including women
How is Salvation Achieved?	Faith and works	Faith and works	Faith: When one is justified, one is forgiven; therefore one can repent fully and do good works.	Faith: Good works may or may not be evidence of justification but wealth is.	Faith: Justification is God's endorsement of the morals of the individual.	Faith	Faith
Role of State	Pope is the Catholic leader of sovereigns.	The sovereign controls the church.	Religious choices are up to the individual who owes obedience to lawful ruler.	Religious organization dominates the state, and in fact is the state, for example, Geneva.	Religion controls the state.		Separation of church and state
Where	Italy, parts of Germany, Ireland, Poland, France, Spain	England	Parts of Germany, Sweden, Norway, Denmark	Holland, France, and Geneva, Switzerland	Zurich, Switzerland	Scotland	Switzerland and NW Germany (Munster) and Netherlands
Eucharist	Transubstantiation		Consubstantiation	Eucharist is just a symbol, not a divine action.	Eucharist is a memorial, not a sacrifice.		
Other	Indulgences, purgatory; abuses: simony, nepotism, pluralism, absenteeism			Predestination, "Protestant ethic and the spirit of capitalism"—19th century historian Max Weber "The Elect"	Focused on rebuilding the community not the individual		

PRACTICE LONG-ESSAY QUESTIONS

The questions that follow are samples of the various types of thematic essays that appear on the AP exam. See pages 30–31 for a detailed explanation of each type. Check over the **generic rubric** (see pages 32–33) before you begin any of these essays and use that rubric to score your essay if you write one.

Question 1

"Calvin's doctrines were a radical departure from those of both the Roman Catholic Church and Lutheranism." Evaluate this statement.

COMMENTS ON QUESTION 1

This one seems to call for you to analyze CHANGE AND CONTINUITY OVER TIME because you must explain the relative historical significance of Calvin's doctrines in relation to the overall Protestant Reformation as well as the overall pattern of European religious history. You should analyze the extent to which Calvin's ideas were different from and similar to the beliefs of Luther and of the Roman Catholic Church, and provide multiple specific examples to support the analysis. To get the second point, the essay must analyze the extent to which the ideas and doctrines of Calvin were different from and similar to developments that preceded AND/OR followed the emergence of Calvinism. This question leaves some room for choice. In evaluating the statement, you may choose to compare the doctrines on *salvation* of each of these Christian sects. In his stand against indulgences, Luther departed from Roman Catholic doctrine and from Church tradition. Calvin argued still another view. The question could be approached through this issue alone.

Another way to attack the question would be through the differing relations of each of these sects to the issues of religion and the state and of church government. A clear contrast can be shown among the three.

Question 2

To what extent was the Reformation caused by long-term political, social, and economic developments?

COMMENTS ON QUESTION 2

This essay question requires that you take a stand on the statement and decide if the Reformation was indeed caused by social, political, and economic developments. This one is a CAUSATION question because it requires you to decide how the Reformation was caused by the other developments. Remember to describe causes AND/OR effects of the Reformation and to state how much each specific development caused the Reformation and how it did not. The essay must explain the reasons for the social, political, and economic causes AND/OR effects of the Protestant Reformation. In this particular question, the crucial term is "caused." Any great historical event is brought about by multiple and complex developments. These are the long-term causes. For instance, corruption among Church officials and the influence of Renaissance ideas are long-term causes of the Reformation. But people and their distinct personalities are often at the center of immediate causation. Immediate causes are actions that precipitate great events. Tetzel's sale of indulgences provoked Luther to issue his *95 Theses*.

Question 3

To what extent was the Protestant emphasis on one's personal relationship with God a logical outgrowth of the Renaissance?

COMMENTS ON QUESTION 3

This one is another CAUSATION question because it requires you to explain to what extent and how the Renaissance CAUSED the Protestant emphasis on a personal relationship with God. Remember to describe causes and effects of an increased personal relationship with God, indicating the degree to which it was caused by the Renaissance. The essay must explain the reasons for the causes AND/OR effects of the Protestant emphasis on a personal relationship with God. The pivotal concept in this statement is "logical outgrowth." Consider its implications before choosing an approach. Does it mean a necessary effect? Or was it the result of one influence among many? In order to answer this, you must be familiar with the Renaissance ideas that emphasized individuality as well as how they differed with notions of the preceding age (the medieval period). These ideas must then be linked as influences for various Protestant theological or social concepts that differed from Roman Catholic views. This is a tough question! It would be easy to fall into the trap of oversimplifying by jumping to conclusions based on a superficial knowledge of complex ideas and doctrines.

PRACTICE SHORT-ANSWER QUESTIONS

1. Use the map below and your knowledge of European History to answer all parts of the following question.

Protestantism in Europe

(A) Briefly explain TWO effects on European politics of the spread of Protestantism during the second half of the sixteenth century as seen in the map above.

(B) Briefly explain ONE effect on the economies of Europe of the spread of Protestantism during the second half of the sixteenth century as seen in the map above.

2. Use the passage below and your knowledge of European History to answer all parts of the following question.

Martin Luther's Address to German Nobility (ca. 1520)

The grace and might of God be with you, Most Serene Majesty, most gracious, well-beloved gentlemen!

It is not out of mere arrogance and perversity that I, an individual poor man, have taken upon me to address your lordships. The distress and misery that oppress all the Christian estates, more especially in Germany, have led not only myself, but everyone else, to cry aloud and to ask for help, and have now forced me too to cry out and to ask if God would give His Spirit to anyone to reach a hand to His wretched people. Councils have often put forward some remedy, but it has adroitly been frustrated, and the evils have become worse, through the cunning of certain men. Their malice and wickedness I will now, by the help of God, expose, so that, being known, they may henceforth cease to be so obstructive and injurious. God has given us a young and noble sovereign, and by this has roused great hopes in many hearts; now it is right that we too should do what we can, and make good use of time and grace.

(A) Briefly explain ONE cause of the conflict referenced by Luther in the above excerpt.

(B) Briefly explain ONE result of the conflict referenced by Luther in the above excerpt.

(C) Briefly identify and describe how ONE country in early modern Europe other than the Germanic states experienced this conflict.

Short-Answer Explanations

1. **0–3 points (2 points for A and 1 point for B)**

   (A) ONE point will be given for EACH of TWO explanations of how the politics of Europe changed due to the spread of Protestantism. The explanations can include the Thirty Years' War, the monarchy of Henry VIII and his descendants, the Protestant Union, the emergence of Sweden as a European power, the Counter-Reformation, the conquest of Belgium by the Habsburgs, the rise of Dutch power, the loss of power and unity caused by the decline of the Catholic Church, or the War of the Three Henrys.

   (B) One point will be given for an explanation of how the European economy changed, including the rise of England and the Netherlands as seafaring powers, the rise of wealth for the common man, the emergence of joint-stock companies and/or stock markets, the enclosure movement, or the loss of financial power for the Roman Catholic Church.

2. **0–3 points (1 point for A, 1 point for B, and 1 point for C)**

   (A) A good response would describe one of several possible causes of the Protestant Reformation, such as: immorality/corruption of the Roman Catholic Church, the selling of indulgences, the Great Schism and the Babylonian Captivity, increased literacy and access to the Bible through the printing press, political frustration with the Holy Roman Emperor, increased wealth of the non-nobility, the rising middle class, the rise of scientific thought that contradicted Roman Catholic teachings, high Church taxes (the tithe), and the ability to spread ideas more easily through printed materials.

   (B) A good response would describe one of several possible results of the Protestant Reformation, such as: the loss of European religious unity, religious wars such as the *Thirty Years' War* or the *War of the Three Henrys*, religion used as a tool to undermine monarchs, removal of the ban on money lending by Christians, the pursuit of wealth being considered permissible by Christianity, and the emergence of new religions such as Lutheranism, Calvinism, and Anglicanism.

   (C) A good response would describe how Protestantism came to other countries in Europe. England's Anglican Church founded by Henry VIII, the French Huguenots struggle in the War of the Three Henrys, Scotland's adoption of Presbyterianism, and Sweden's adoption of Calvinism are the best examples. The rise of Calvinism and Zwingli's emergence in Zurich may also be considered non-Germanic by some, so these may be included.

PRACTICE MULTIPLE-CHOICE QUESTIONS

Questions 1 to 4 refer to the print depicting the Saint Bartholomew's Day Massacre below.

An Account of the Saint Bartholomew's Day Massacre by François Dubois. a Huguenot painter born in northern France. From the Musée Des Beaux-Arts, Lausanne, Switzerland. The Granger Collection, New York.

1. The above picture depicts which two groups engaged in battle?

   (A) The French Huguenots and Catholics
   (B) French and Austrian Soldiers
   (C) Catholics and Anabaptists
   (D) Peasants and nobles

2. The use of propaganda through writing and imagery such as that seen above proliferated during the era of religious conflict in Europe, making which of the following a crucial reason for the success of the Protestant Reformation?

   (A) The widespread use of ballads as a way to share information between towns and villages
   (B) The implementation and proliferation of the printing press
   (C) The political conflict between the Catholic Church and the Germanic princes
   (D) The greatly improved travel network in the Holy Roman Empire

3. The clash depicted above sparked a greater conflict sometimes characterized by historians as a civil war that was ended by which of the following movements toward religious toleration?

(A) Elizabeth I issued her Elizabethan Settlement allowing private worship.
(B) Louis XIV issued the Edict of Fontainebleau allowing many Protestants to worship as they pleased in fortified towns.
(C) Henry of Navarre converted back to Catholicism, became Henry IV of France, and issued the Edict of Nantes allowing many Protestants to worship as they pleased in fortified towns.
(D) The Peace of Westphalia in 1648 allowed Calvinism to be practiced by people in principalities whose leaders chose to follow that religion and its offshoots.

4. Which of the following factors most influenced the image above depicting opposing groups regulating public morals?

(A) The spread of Anabaptist ideas and ideals from Muenster to France causing armed insurrection
(B) The spread of Austrian nationalism throughout the Germanic states and Italy
(C) The spread of Calvinist ideas and ideals from Geneva into France causing religious conflict
(D) The spread of Anglicanism from England causing religious conflict

Questions 5 to 9 refer to the reading below.

"How violently the restless Jesuits and their followers are exerting themselves to undo, by their absurd interpretations and preposterous attacks, the precious and solemnly ratified Religious Peace [of Augsburg] which was drawn up long years ago for many weighty reasons by his Roman Imperial Majesty and all the estates of the empire, is but too clear. Nay, they would completely abolish it and then do away altogether with our true Christian religion, in which we were born and brought up and in which we would live and die. All this is sufficiently proved by the innumerable, violent, and poisonous books which they issue throughout the Roman Empire, directed against the said Religious Peace and its clear provisions, declaring it to be no more than ad interim, a temporary concession of toleration, designed to last only until the conclusion of the Council of Trent; even going so far as to imply that his Imperial Majesty of happy memory had no authority to arrange the peace among the estates of the empire without the consent of the pope...

. . . Moreover, since the nature and character of the Jesuits and their followers are as notorious among Catholics as among Protestants, and since what they have been up to in Sweden, Poland, France, the Netherlands, and, recently, in Italy, is well known, they should be estimated accordingly and precautions taken against their dangerous plots."

—Letter from Protestant Elector of Saxony, 1618

5. The document above was most likely written at the start of which of the following dynastic and religious conflicts?

    (A) The War of the Three Henrys
    (B) The Habsburg-Valois Wars
    (C) The Thirty Years' War
    (D) The Dutch Revolt

6. "[H]is Roman Imperial Majesty" in the document above refers to the Holy Roman Emperor, whose role after the conflict that succeeded the document above can best be described in which of the following ways?

    (A) The Holy Roman Emperor consolidated his control over the Germanic states and ruled them as one single province.
    (B) The Holy Roman Emperor lost power and prestige as the Peace of Westphalia reduced his influence and importance significantly.
    (C) The title of Holy Roman Emperor was abolished at the end of this conflict never to emerge again.
    (D) The Holy Roman Emperor consolidated his control over the Germanic states but was banned from ever being a Habsburg again.

7. Ignatius of Loyola, who founded the Society of Jesus, or the Jesuit order mentioned above, would most likely agree with which of the following statements?

    (A) The Bible is the word of God and its authority is more important than that of the pope.
    (B) The pope is the ultimate authority on Christianity but must be protected from the immorality that infects all humans.
    (C) The pope is pure perfection and if he tells me that the white I see before me is black then I will agree that what I see is black.
    (D) A non-believer or pagan is much worse than a Protestant.

8. The conflict that the Elector of Saxony describes in his letter resulted in which of the following?

    (A) The establishment of several religiously pluralistic and tolerant states within the German-speaking regions
    (B) The weakening of the Holy Roman Empire and the strengthening of smaller sovereign states within its boundaries
    (C) The virtual extinction of all Christian denominations except Lutheranism and Roman Catholicism within the German-speaking regions
    (D) The political unification of most of the German-speaking regions under a Protestant, rather than a Catholic, monarch

9. Which of the following can be safely inferred about the Elector's religious affiliation solely based upon the passage?

    (A) He was an ardent Calvinist.

    (B) He was a somewhat devout Lutheran.

    (C) He was not Roman Catholic.

    (D) He was not a practicing Christian.

Multiple-Choice Explanations

1. **A**	4. **C**	7. **C**
2. **B**	5. **C**	8. **B**
3. **C**	6. **B**	9. **C**

1. **(A)**

(A) is CORRECT because the St. Bartholomew's Day Massacre was between French Catholics and Huguenots that started the War of the Three Henrys in France.

(B) is wrong because soldiers of neither nation are depicted in the image.

(C) is wrong because the Anabaptists were in Muenster and not France and are thus not seen being massacred here.

(D) is wrong because those depicted here in battle are not engaged in a peasant revolt against nobility nor its suppression.

2. **(B)**

(A) is wrong because ballads had been used for years and did not help reformers before Luther such as Hus or Kempis.

(B) is CORRECT because the printing press allowed the spread of propaganda and the Bible itself as well as a proliferation of religious texts on both sides.

(C) is wrong because propaganda was less of an issue in the political battle than the religious one.

(D) is wrong because the roads in the Holy Roman Empire were terrible at the time and not a factor in Luther's success.

3. **(C)**

(A) is wrong because Elizabeth ruled England rather than France where this was depicted.

(B) is wrong because the *Edict of Fontainebleau* actually revoked the *Edict of Nantes* which had allowed religious toleration under Henry IV.

(C) is CORRECT because the *Edict of Nantes*, which had allowed religious toleration under Henry IV, was passed after he converted and became king.

(D) is wrong because this image is about France rather than Germany and it is thus not related to the *Peace of Westphalia*.

4. **(C)**

(A) is wrong because the Anabaptists were destroyed by other religious groups; however, their ideas inspired other groups such as Quakers later, yet did not spread into France, and also because they were pacifists who would not attack others.

(B) is wrong because Austrian nationalism did not spread to Germans and Italians, who resented Austrian rule, and because the depiction is of Huguenots being attacked by Catholics in France.

(C) is CORRECT because the Calvinist ideas came to France where the Huguenots, who were attacked, adopted most of their ideas and ideals from Calvinism.

(D) is wrong because Anglicanism never spread to France in any important way.

5. **(C)**

(A) is wrong because this letter was written in 1618, which is when the Thirty Years' War began, and because it was written by a Germanic prince whose focus would be on the Thirty Years' War rather than the French War of the Three Henrys.

(B) is wrong because this letter was written in 1618, which is when the Thirty Years' War began and it cites the Peace of Augsburg, which ended the Habsburg-Valois Wars in Germany in 1555.

(C) is CORRECT because this letter was written in 1618, which is when the Thirty Years' War began, and it was written by a Germanic prince whose focus would be on the Thirty Years' War.

(D) is wrong because the Dutch revolt was not of importance to the Germanic kingdoms other than as a way to keep Catholic Counter-Reformation forces busy and out of their hair.

6. **(B)**

(A) is wrong because the Thirty Years' War ended in the Peace of Westphalia of 1648 that reduced the power of the Holy Roman Emperor to mostly ceremonial status, allowing France to intervene in Germanic affairs at will, but the title did not disappear until Napoleon conquered the region in 1806.

(B) is CORRECT because the Thirty Years' War ended in the Peace of Westphalia of 1648 that reduced the power of the Holy Roman Emperor to mostly ceremonial status, allowing France to intervene in Germanic affairs at will.

(C) is wrong because the Thirty Years' War ended in the Peace of Westphalia of 1648 that reduced the power of the Holy Roman Emperor to mostly ceremonial status, allowing France to intervene in Germanic affairs at will, but the title did not disappear until Napoleon conquered the region in 1806.

(D) is wrong because the Thirty Years' War ended in the Peace of Westphalia of 1648 that reduced the power of the Holy Roman Emperor to mostly ceremonial status, allowing France to intervene in Germanic affairs at will, but the title did not disappear until Napoleon conquered the region in 1806.

7. **(C)**

(A) is wrong because St. Ignatius of Loyola who started the Jesuits based his order upon fanatical dedication to the pope and saw him as the ultimate authority in everything.

(B) is wrong because St. Ignatius of Loyola who started the Jesuits based his order upon fanatical dedication to the pope and saw him as infallible and thus not in need of protection from immorality.

(C) is CORRECT because St. Ignatius of Loyola who started the Jesuits based his order upon fanatical dedication to the pope and saw him as the ultimate authority in everything and he actually said something very close to that answer.

(D) is wrong because St. Ignatius of Loyola who started the Jesuits saw Protestants as the worst abomination against God for perverting Catholicism and pagans as simple people who did not know better but needed to be educated.

8. **(B)**

(A) is wrong because the Thirty Years' War did not result in the creation of pluralistic and religiously tolerant states in Germany, but in religiously stringent and combative areas.

(B) is CORRECT because the Thirty Years' War resulted in the decline of the Holy Roman Empire and the rise of the power of Germanic states dominated by France.

(C) is wrong because the Peace of Westphalia, which ended the Thirty Years' War, did not result in the removal of all non-Lutheran Christian sects as the Peace of Augsburg had before it.

(D) is wrong because the Thirty Years' War did not result in the unification of the Germanic states at all, but in their disunity, much to the benefit of France.

9. **(C)**

(A) is wrong because the specific religious affiliation of the Elector is not given or inferred other than Protestant. The only thing that the passage makes certain is that he is NOT a Roman Catholic.

(B) is wrong because the specific religious affiliation of the Elector is not given or inferred other than Protestant. The only thing that the passage makes certain is that he is NOT a Roman Catholic.

(C) is CORRECT because the only thing that the passage makes certain is that he is NOT a Roman Catholic.

(D) is wrong because the passage makes it clear that he is a Protestant of some type.

The Growth of European Nation-States and the Birth of Science: Europe in the 1500s and Early 1600s

3

KEY TERMS/PEOPLE

- → PRINCE HENRY THE NAVIGATOR
- → FALL OF CONSTANTINOPLE
- → COLUMBIAN EXCHANGE
- → PETER THE GREAT
- → FREDERICK WILLIAM I OF PRUSSIA
- → FRANCIS I
- → CONCORDAT OF BOLOGNA
- → HENRY II
- → CATHERINE DE' MEDICI
- → HENRY IV
- → EDICT OF NANTES
- → CARDINAL RICHELIEU
- → LOUIS XIV
- → DIVINE RIGHT THEORY OF RULE
- → JEAN-BAPTISTE COLBERT
- → COMMERCIAL REVOLUTION/
  PRICE REVOLUTION
- → HENRY VIII

- → ELIZABETH I
- → THE GLORIOUS REVOLUTION
- → JOHN LOCKE
- → OPEN-FIELD SYSTEM
- → ENCLOSURE MOVEMENT
- → MERCANTILISM
- → ADAM SMITH
- → FRANCIS BACON
- → RENÉ DESCARTES
- → NICOLAUS COPERNICUS
- → GALILEO GALILEI
- → JOHANNES KEPLER
- → DEISM
- → SCIENTIFIC REVOLUTION
- → CROP ROTATION
- → JAMES I
- → CHARLES I
- → CHARLES II

OVERVIEW

By the start of the sixteenth century, centralization of governments had led to the rise of powerful nation-states, to concomitant European exploration of the globe, and to regional wars on the Continent. Spain, following the Portuguese lead, explored the Atlantic and soon surpassed its Iberian neighbor in colonies, wealth, and military power. Gold and silver from the New World helped shift the balance of power from the Mediterranean basin to the Atlantic coast of Europe. The search for wealth helped to usher in an age of scientific discovery that began to reshape European thinking. The wealth from mines in the Spanish colonies created a financial and commercial center in the Netherlands, brought about rampant inflation in Europe, and eventually led to the decline of Spain as a major power.

Feudalism died gradually. The Hundred Years' War (1337–1453), which devastated France and exhausted its nobility, indirectly led to a strong monarchy. Peace encouraged commerce, which gave rise to a taxable middle class that could support a national army independent of the nobility. From the middle of the fifteenth century to the second decade of the sixteenth, the monarchs of France centralized the state, recruited bourgeois administrators into government, and strengthened the army. Through most of the sixteenth century, the foreign adventures of two strong kings and the upheaval caused by the Reformation weakened the monarchy. Under the intelligent guidance of Cardinal Richelieu (1585–1642), prime minister to Louis XIII (r. 1601–1643), the central government brought peace, prosperity, and stability to the realm during the first half of the seventeenth century.

The strong government that developed in France contrasted with the constitutional system that evolved in England. The powers of the English kings had been checked by the nobility as far back as the thirteenth century, with the Magna Carta. The Tudors took the English throne in the fifteenth century as a compromise among the claimants who battled over it in the Wars of the Roses (1455–1487). Having only a tenuous hereditary right to the monarchy, the Tudors were forced to work through Parliament, which gradually represented a greater and greater portion of English society and, therefore, avoided the class distinctions that divided France. The Reformation had its effects on English government: The independence of the Anglican Church from the papacy strengthened the monarchy and Parliament; the Puritan Revolution established the supremacy of Parliament over the king and nurtured the tradition of constitutionalism.

A strong tradition of absolutism developed in Eastern Europe, especially in the rising states of Russia, Prussia, and Austria. Conflicts between the Ottoman Empire and the Austrians emerged over control of southeastern Europe because of Austrian territorial expansion. Social reform was sporadic and largely ineffectual and serfdom was widespread in the region. The Baroque style of architecture was favored by the absolute monarchs of these states as a manifestation of the power and glory of their reigns.

SPECIAL NOTE ON PERIODIZATION

Unlike in the first two chapters of this book, the concepts taught in this chapter do not "neatly" fit into the time period. For example, the struggle for constitutional rule in England runs from the 1640s until at least 1689, when the *Glorious Revolution* resulted in the English Bill of Rights and in William and Mary on the throne. Another prime example is the problem of examining the rise of absolutism without being able to study the crowning glory of Louis XIV and his imitators, such as Peter I of Russia. The "Golden Age" of France was during the reign of the "Sun King," Louis XIV (r. 1643–1715), whose absolutist monarchy dominated all classes in Europe's wealthiest and most populous country, upset the balance of power on the continent, and claimed the "divine right" of rule. Additionally, you are compelled to examine the scientific contributions of very early thinkers such as Copernicus, Kepler, Descartes, and Galileo without being able to examine the ideas of Newton or the great Enlightenment thinkers. In this way you should recognize, in some ways, the arbitrary nature of "periodization." Should we stop at the Glorious Revolution of 1689 or perhaps the defeat of Louis XIV in the War of the Spanish Succession in 1713? The student who truly examines history well will apply this idea of questioning periodization in his/her essays.

EXPLORATION AND COLONIZATION: 1400s TO 1600s

The Portuguese, from the middle to the end of the fifteenth century, supported by their able leader, *Prince Henry the Navigator* (1394–1460), explored the South Atlantic. Explorers from several states on the Atlantic set out on their journeys of discovery. They were spurred by missionary zeal, personal gain, national pride, and Renaissance curiosity, and aided by the development of the magnetic compass, astrolabe, sextant, quadrant, cannons mounted on ships, and more seaworthy craft such as the caravel, galleon, lateen, and carrack, which gave Europeans the ability to sail more confidently across large bodies of water, far from shores. They also created maps called Portolani that ship captains used as charts to find their way at sea. These advances in cartography, navigation, and military power allowed the Europeans to establish overseas colonies and empires in which they created trade networks through both coercion of and negotiation with the native peoples. The Portuguese set up a vast trade network along the African coast, in South America, and in southern and eastern Asia. The Spanish set up an empire in the Americas, the Caribbean, and the Pacific that left them a dominant state on the continent. Shortly after the rise of Spain and Portugal through trade, the English, Dutch, and French began to expand their navigation and create North American colonies to create their own trade networks.

The vast holdings of the Dutch, English, and French in the Caribbean led to significant boosts to the finances of the mother countries as well. The West Indies provided sugar to Europe at a tidy profit to those involved in its trade across the Atlantic Ocean. The distilled form of sugar that became rum also provided revenue streams for the colonial empires in the Caribbean. Additionally, the slave trade, both to the islands from Africa and later from the Islands to America, also enriched the European mother countries. When the Dutch enlarged their trade routes to include Southeast Asia, they turned modern Indonesia into the *Dutch East Indies*, which was incredibly profitable as well and helped the Dutch create the strongest economy in Northern Europe at the time. These islands were also known as the Spice Islands, and the Dutch became rich by bringing such spices as pepper, cinnamon, and anise from Asia to European tables.

- Expeditions led by *Diaz* (1450–1500), *da Gama* (c. 1460–1524), and *Cabral* (1467–1520) explored the coast of Africa and eventually established trading posts in India.

- *Christopher Columbus* (1451–1506), for the Spanish crown to find a direct route to Asia, discovered the Western Hemisphere.

  - Despite opening the "New World," Columbus laid the foundations for Europeans' oppression and exploitation of native peoples.

- *Ferdinand Magellan* (1480–1521)—his expedition circumnavigated the globe for Spain.

- *Cortés* (1485–1547) and *Pizarro* (1475–1541), respectively, conquered the great American empires of the Aztecs and Incas.

  - Gold and silver flowed from the New World mines into the coffers of the Spanish monarchs and to the merchants and manufacturers of the Netherlands.

- These explorers opened up trade routes on three continents for new products that would bring large profits to Europeans for centuries to come. The global exchange of goods, flora, fauna, cultural practices, and disease would prove disastrous for the natives.

  - This exchange of valuable goods and resources from each continent was known as the *Columbian Exchange*.
  - This trade brought European manufactured goods and alcohol to Africa and the Americas, and products such as lumber, fur, gold, sugar, peanuts, beans, potatoes, tobacco, chocolate, vanilla, and corn to Europe.
  - It was the largest redistribution of biological organisms between regions of the globe that the world had ever seen.

- It included diseases, people, and ideas as well as trade in goods and services.
- The Europeans introduced grains, such as wheat, rice, and barley to the New World, along with many other species, such as honey bees, cows, pigs, goats, horses, oxen, multiple types of trees and decorative plants, and many infectious diseases that they spread as they traveled.
- See the map below for more detail.

The Columbian Exchange

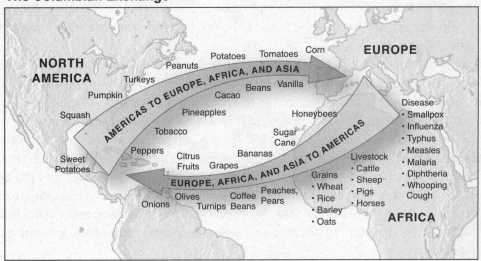

European rule in the Americas resulted in the Spanish and Portuguese raping the land and the people of all resources and wealth.

- Within 50 years, 90 percent of all natives were killed by the germs, guns, steel weapons, and armor that Europeans brought with them.
- Guns and gunpowder, along with horses and armor, gave the Europeans a huge advantage over the natives, who were slaughtered or else surrendered to the military superiority of the Europeans.
- Old methods of agriculture, writing, and worship were forcibly changed; land was taken from natives and distributed to Europeans.
- Although Columbus thought he had sailed to India, explorer *Amerigo Vespucci* realized that Columbus had found two continents previously unknown to Europeans and dubbed them a "Mundus Novus," or "New World."

  - These were later named the "Americas" after Vespucci. Spain reorganized territory in the New World into four viceroyalties:

    • New Spain
    • Peru
    • New Granada
    • La Plata

  - Justice in Spanish territories was enforced by an *audiencia*, a panel of 12 judges with the viceroy as head judge.
  - *Intendants* were local officials, who received authority directly from the crown to enforce laws and impose taxes.

- The *quinto*, a tax on all precious metals found in the New World, was payable to the Spanish king.

    • This tax made up one-quarter of Spain's income during this era.

- Local officials called *corregidores* enforced mercantilist laws banning trade between the Spanish colonies and other European powers

The end result was a huge shift in power, both globally and within the European continent. Millions of indigenous peoples were deprived of life and property while those European nations on the Atlantic saw an unprecedented rise in wealth and power. The indigenous Americans, Africans, and Asians would be dominated by peoples who were of western European ethnicities for over four hundred years in ways that the other cultures of the world still have not fully recovered from. Many cultures were entirely wiped out. This was a major development in the history of Europe's interaction with the rest of the world, which left Europe with much power, but did not endear Europeans to the rest of the world. It set the stage for Europe to become gradually more and more conciliatory with natives of other regions as time progressed from the sixteenth century to modern times.

Meanwhile, economic power in Europe shifted from the Mediterranean basin to the Atlantic coast. The result was competition between European nations for advantages in trade that often led to conflicts between nations over colonial possessions or aspirations. One way that nations engaged in this competition was through adopting *mercantilist policies*.

Mercantilism emerged as a new economic system in which the mother country trades with the colonies, and the colonies are not allowed to trade directly with other nations. It was intended to lessen financial dependence on other European countries.

- The incredible influx of gold and silver in the 1500s led inflation to spread from Spain throughout Europe because the mines at Guanajuarto, Zacatecas, and Potosi in Mexico and Peru flooded the gold and silver markets.

    - The availability of gold in the New World lured many entrepreneurs there, damaging domestic industry in Spain.
    - Slavery, although it had existed since the dawn of time, increased and changed drastically in character—in large part because of exploration.

- Plantation agriculture was practiced by the conquering Europeans in the New World.

    - At first they exploited the natives, who died in the millions as a result of disease and harsh treatment.
    - Soon after, Europeans resorted to importing African slaves, and race would be linked to slavery in the Americas from this point onward.

- Between 1453 and 1865 over 200 million Africans and their descendants were enslaved or killed in the slave trade.

- In 1790 Africans made up about 20 percent of the U.S. population.

- Africans were seen as beastly and were feared for their potent sexuality.

- Many tried to justify slavery by stating that sub-Saharan Africans were subhuman and had no original culture of their own.

The **Commercial Revolution** (1500–1700) helped to bring about and intensify the "Age of Discovery" and exploration. It had its roots in the invention of banking by the Medici in Florence and the Fuggers in Antwerp and Amsterdam, as well as in the tremendous population growth in Europe.

- The huge profits from exploration and shipping, and the high risks associated with these endeavors, spurred the creation of the first joint-stock companies, such as the *Dutch East India Company* in 1602 and the *British East India Company* shortly thereafter.

  - Once companies could sell themselves to investors, stock markets were born, first in the Netherlands, and then they spread.
  - New accounting methods, such as double entry bookkeeping, allowed businesses and nations to assign revenues to specific expenses.
  - New banks, such as the Bank of Amsterdam, emerged as a result of the commercial revolution and the appearance of stock markets.

- The emergence of banking and stock markets led to a rapid revolution in the way the economies of Western Europe worked.

  - Prices rose in part because of the influx of precious metals, rising population, and enclosure, but also because a new wealthy middle class began to emerge.

    - Often called a "price revolution"

  - Further stimulated by the rise of the "putting-out" industry, sometimes known as the domestic system (in which people manufactured goods in their homes for sale to a capitalist who provided raw materials), those with capital to invest found great opportunities for profits, and the new stock markets presented greater opportunities to invest.
  - The putting-out system also meant that more of the common people were paid in money. This led to them spending more and to the emergence of a market economy for the lower classes, which had not consistently existed in Europe before this time. The growth of consumer wealth at the bottom of the social pyramid led those higher up that pyramid to become entrepreneurial and create businesses to cater to them. However, hierarchy and status continued to define social power in both rural and urban settings.
  - Most families continued to derive their livelihoods from agriculture, and the seasons defined lives as did their positions in their villages. Agriculture would become commercialized during the Commercial Revolution, leading to massive social changes during the next two centuries.
  - This combination of factors led to the beginning of the modern capitalist system that is now referred to as the *Commercial Revolution*.
  - Merchants and bankers, a new elite class, were at the top of society in many towns.
  - A new elite class emerged in Spain and its colonies, led by Spanish-speaking gentlemen termed *caballeros* and *hidalgos*.
  - The *gentry*, or landed classes, in England emerged there as the elites.
  - In France, those who gained wealth could buy their way into the untaxed class of the nobility, and such people were termed the *nobility of the robe* as opposed to families that had been noble for centuries and were called the *nobility of the sword*.

The Dutch, the Spanish, and Eastern Europe

Chafing under the oppressive rule of the Spanish Catholic *King Philip II* (r. 1556–1598), the Protestants of the prosperous Low Countries, whose leaders were Calvinist, revolted against Spanish rule in the years 1556 to 1587. The bitter and bloody conflict led to the division of the Low Countries into the mainly Catholic Spanish Netherlands in the south (which eventually became Belgium) and the mainly Protestant United Provinces of the Netherlands in the north (unofficially termed "Holland").

- The defeat in 1588 of Philip II's powerful *Spanish Armada* in its attempt to invade England, an ally of the Netherlands, marked the beginning of the decline of Spain's hegemony in Western Europe.
- The *Thirty Years' War* (1618–1648) began as a religious conflict, evolved into a national struggle for dominance of central Europe, and led to the destruction of vast areas in Germany and the decline of the regional hegemony of the Holy Roman Empire.
- The Austrian Habsburgs confronted the powerful Muslim Ottoman Turks who were attempting to expand their control of Eastern Europe.
- The 1683 attack on Austria by the forces of *Suleiman the Magnificent* was beaten back, and the Austrians eventually gained control of Bohemia, Hungary, and Transylvania.
- Russia and Western Europe experienced radically different paths of development until the eighteenth century.

  - For centuries, the princes of Moscow had been retainers of the Mongol conquerors, and the *czars* (emperors) were able to use their influence with the Mongols to consolidate their power over the Russian people and to establish the hereditary role of czar.
  - Ivan the Terrible (r. 1547–1584) was an autocratic expansionist who limited the power of the nobles (*boyars*), expanded the realm, and solidified the role of czar.
  - A "Time of Troubles" ensued after Ivan's death, marked by civil war because of the lack of an heir.
  - The *Romanov* dynasty was established by the nobles in 1613, and the family ruled with an iron hand, reinstituting serfdom and gaining virtual control over the Russian Orthodox Church.

THE EXPANSION OF EUROPE

(More information is found in Chapter 4.)

- The *open-field system*, used during the Middle Ages, divided the arable land available to a farming community into narrow strips that were assigned to the individual families of the community. Because of a lack of effective fertilizers and ignorance about nitrogen-fixing crops, a large portion of the community's land lay fallow.
- A "mini ice age" had hit Europe at the end of the Medieval era, and the advent of better weather led to more food and a population explosion, which then resulted in a cycle of famine and feast, depending upon harvests.
- For centuries the need for fallow lands had left most of Europe practicing subsistence agriculture by which they survived but created no surplus.
- New ideas, such as crop rotation to nitrogen-providing crops such as clover and turnips, allowed significantly higher output.

- A *price revolution* occurred as a result of the accumulation of capital and the expansion of the free-market economy and the commercialization of agriculture, which enriched the landowners in Western Europe.
- The *Enclosure Movement*, which emerged first in the low countries of Belgium and the Netherlands, and then in England, during the late seventeenth and the eighteenth centuries, fenced off the open fields to enable large landowners to employ crop rotation.

    - Crop rotation was the planting of nitrogen-fixing crops, such as beans and certain grasses, in soil that had been used for other crops.

        • The idea spread with a two-crop rotation near the Mediterranean, and a three-crop rotation in the north.
        • The soil remained fertile and little land lay fallow.

    - Many small or inefficient farmers were displaced, moving to the towns and cities but, ultimately, food production rose dramatically.

        • These small farmers were said to have free-hold tenure on their land.
        • Other farmers paid rent to landowners to farm their land or provided labor services in return for the right to farm on it.
    - The village commons was closed, and villagers lost the ability to graze their own animals there.
    - Landlords' attempts to increase profits by abolishing the traditional rights of peasants led to revolts.

- A greater variety of foods, and the introduction of foods from the New World, specifically the potato, improved general nutrition and contributed, along with the disappearance of the plague, to a dramatic increase in population.

    - Better sanitation, introduction of quarantine methods, and the elimination of the black rat, whose fleas carried the plague microorganisms, eliminated the plague.
    - Except for the development of the smallpox vaccine in the late eighteenth century, the crude and often dangerous medical practices of the day contributed little to the health and longevity of the people.
    - *Mercantilism* was a system developed by various European states to guarantee a favorable balance of trade with other European nations or with their American colonies.

        • By creating an imbalance of exports over imports, the difference was made up in gold or silver payments.
        • Pursued policy to get precious metals from trading partners to pay for the costs of maintaining standing armies and government bureaucracies.

- Populations began to shift from a huge majority of people living and working rurally to many living in cities to pursue commerce and profit, which put stress on the traditional political and social structures of those cities that were not prepared for that growth.

    - This began during the recovery from the Black Plague during the fifteenth century. The inability of many to grow their own food led to a rapid rise in prices, and the price revolution was far more favorable to the wealthy than to those less fortunate.
    - Cities faced many problems, including a loss of the guilds' ability to help govern them, sanitation problems, higher unemployment, poverty, and crime.

- This meant that many cities had to regulate public morals, which religion and guilds had previously rendered unnecessary.
- In rural settings throughout Europe, morals had been preserved through rituals such as the *charivari*, in which the community would come together to give a mock serenade to adulterous couples or those who had otherwise violated mores and norms, such as widows and widowers who remarried too soon. These would be boisterous, loud affairs meant to shame the violators of norms back into following them. In England, the *skimmington* was similar, but it included a parade with effigies of the offenders.

■ The family remained the primary social and economic institution of sixteenth century life. Most households, regardless of whether urban or rural, had clearly defined roles for each family member. The debates raised by the Renaissance and Reformation about women's roles is a theme that crosses all historical time periods in this course.

■ Leisure activities and rituals of the time reflect persistent folk ideas, but some leisure was seen as a challenge to communal norms. They included blood sports, such as bear baiting or bull baiting, the huge Carnival festival that Mardi Gras is a remnant of, and other saints' days. When norms were violated, the violators would be disciplined by their church or town authorities, with such punishments as being put in the stocks, public whipping, or the charivari, a form of public coercion through a mock serenade, intended to get a couple to wed.

THE DEVELOPMENT OF "NATURAL PHILOSOPHY" OR SCIENCE

The idea of studying the universe through scientific experimentation and observation emerged as the ultimate form of gathering knowledge. The great thinkers of the day turned away from their artistic pursuits, which had been so profitable, and began to try to explain the mysteries of the universe or even the multiverse. The term *science* would have to wait until the nineteenth century but, for the time being, during the sixteenth and seventeenth centuries the study of natural phenomena was labeled "natural philosophy."

The Philosophers of Modern Science

Francis Bacon (1561–1626) was an English thinker who advocated the *inductive* or *experimental method*: observation of natural phenomena, accumulating data, experimenting to refine the data; drawing conclusions; formulating principles that are subject to continuing observation and experimentation. He is generally credited as an original empiricist.

René Descartes (1596–1650) was a French philosopher whose *Discourse on Method* (1637) argued that everything that is not validated by observation should be doubted, but that his own existence was proven by the proposition: "I think, therefore I am" *(cogito ergo sum)*. God exists, he argued, because a perfect being would have existence as part of its nature. *Cartesian dualism* divided all existence into the spiritual and the material—the former can be examined only through deductive reasoning; the latter is subject to the experimental method. His goal to reconcile religion with science was short-circuited by the very method of skepticism that subsequent philosophers inherited from his writings. He is generally credited as an original rationalist.

The Revolutionary Thinkers of Science

- *Nicolaus Copernicus* (1473–1543), a Polish astronomer, upset the comfortable assumptions of the *geocentric* (earth-centered) universe of *Ptolemy* (the second century Egyptian) with his *heliocentric* (sun-centered) conception of the universe.

  - Although his work, *Concerning the Revolutions of the Heavenly Bodies*, was not published until after his death, his theories were proven by *Johannes Kepler* (1571–1630), a German who plotted the elliptic orbits of the planets, thereby predicting their movements.
  - *Galileo Galilei* (1564–1642) made telescopic observations that validated Copernican theory, and his spirited advocacy of Copernicus earned him condemnation by the Inquisition.

- The Copernican heliocentric view seemed to contradict the primacy of humanity in God's creation and thereby to deny the teachings of the Church.

  - Supported in Protestant northern Europe, where the Reformation had questioned all orthodoxy.
  - The theory and the scientific method that had formulated it symbolized Europe's new intellectual freedom.
  - The Roman Catholic Church tried to suppress the Copernican revolution by banning writings of the charismatic Galileo and putting him under lifelong house arrest for possible heresy.
  - Galileo had observed the moons of Jupiter as support for Copernicus, which earned him a lasting reputation for rigidity.
  - It took nearly 350 years for the papacy to exonerate Galileo.

- The field of medicine began to advance with the rising practice of human dissection, allowing medical knowledge to grow. New advances in anatomy, the study of human systems such as circulation, and toxicology occurred during this period. The practice of Rome's Greek-born physician and philosopher, Galen, who had healed through adjusting bodily humors, was challenged on many fronts.

  - *Andreas Vasalius* (1514–1564) was the father of modern anatomy. His anatomy book, *De Humani Corporis Fabrica*, revolutionized the study of the human body. He is often credited with the discovery of our skeletal, nervous, and other systems.
  - *Paracelsus* (1493–1541) was a German physician, botanist, and astronomer who invented toxicology. He rejected Galen and wanted to perform medical research based purely on observations in nature rather than by studying what others had written. He served as a physician in the Venetian wars.
  - *William Harvey* (1578–1657) explained the circulatory system in detail for the first time in his work, *On the Motion of the Heart and Blood*.

Results of the Scientific Revolution

- *Deism* emerged from the discovery of the natural sciences as the religious ideal of an era in which God was a kind of cosmic clockmaker who created a perfect universe that He does not have to intervene in.
- *Rationalism:* the conviction that the laws of nature are fathomable by human reason, and that humanity is perfectible—as an assumption and an achievable goal.

- The *Scientific Revolution* of the sixteenth and seventeenth centuries redefined astronomy and physics.
- Less dramatic but still-significant advances took place in *mathematics*, especially with the development of probability and calculus, and in *medicine* through advances in surgery, anatomy, drug therapy, and with the discovery of microorganisms.
- Creation of learned societies dedicated to the advance of science, such as the *French Academy of Sciences* and the *Royal Society of London*.
- The development of science transformed the intellectual life of Europe by convincing people that human reason could understand the secrets of the universe and transform life without the help of organized religion.

The eighteenth century marked the end of the *Age of Religion*, which had governed European thought for over a millennium. Skepticism and rationalism became offshoots of the development of science, which encouraged the growth of secularism.

THE DEVELOPMENT OF ABSOLUTISM IN FRANCE

- *Francis I* (r. 1515–1547), a Valois rival of Holy Roman Emperor Charles V, battled unsuccessfully to weaken the Habsburgs as Europe's most powerful family.

    - Managed to consolidate absolutism in France by instituting the *taille* (a direct tax on land and property).
    - With the *Concordat of Bologna,* he granted the pope the right to collect *annates* (the first year's revenue from Church offices) in return for the power to nominate high officials in the French Church.
    - Effectively nationalized the Church in France and increased the power of the monarchy.

- His successor, *Henry II* (r. 1547–1559), expanded his father's policy and actively persecuted the *Huguenots* (French Calvinists).
- Continued persecution under *Francis II* and *Charles IX* provoked civil war, which was halted by an *edict of toleration* issued by *Catherine de' Medici*, mother of, and regent for, Charles IX.
- The *Massacre of St. Bartholomew's Day* renewed the brutal civil war when Catholic mobs slaughtered Huguenot leaders who had gathered in Paris to celebrate a royal wedding.

    - During the *War of the Three Henrys*, King Henry III was murdered, and Henry of Guise, the Catholic leader, was assassinated.
    - Although the Huguenots were never more than 10 percent of the French population, they wielded great influence since they came from the nobility and the bourgeoisie.

- Persecution, civil war, and dynastic rivalry left *Henry of Navarre*, a Huguenot, as the only legitimate claimant to the French throne.

    - He ascended, after an expedient conversion to Catholicism ("Paris is worth a mass"), as *Henry IV* (r. 1589–1610).
    - Issued the *Edict of Nantes*, a remarkable expression of religious tolerance that guaranteed civil and religious freedom to the Huguenot minority.
    - Finance minister, the *Duke of Sully*, reformed the tax collection system to make it more equitable and efficient, improved transportation, stimulated trade and industry, and fostered prosperity.

- Resulted in an increase in the prestige and power of the monarchy.
- The divine right to rule theory gained ground under the support of philosopher and jurist, Jean Bodin, who wrote in support of indivisible power in the hands of the monarch.

■ After the death of Henry IV, the government suffered from corruption and mismanagement during the regency of *Louis XIII*.

- In 1624, Louis appointed *Cardinal Richelieu* as prime minister, a post he held from 1624 to 1642.
- Richelieu further centralized the government by:

  • Encouraging the commerce and industry that increased the tax base.
  • Strengthening the military.
  • Instituting the *intendant system*, in which bourgeois officials were answerable only to the king who supervised the provinces and diminished the power of the nobility.

■ Richelieu's domestic polices strengthened absolutism in France and prepared the way for its supreme embodiment in the *Sun King, Louis XIV*.

■ *Louis XIV* (r. 1643–1715) was four when he ascended the throne of France.

- His mother was his regent.
- She chose the Italian, *Cardinal Mazarin* (1602–1661), as prime minister.
- Scared by the *Fronde* revolt as a youth.
- His finance minister, Jean-Baptiste Colbert, extended the administrative, financial, military, and religious control of the central state over the French population.
- Like Richelieu, Cardinal Mazarin was a capable administrator, but not a religious man, and he was not even a priest when he was made a cardinal.

THE DEVELOPMENT OF CONSTITUTIONALISM IN ENGLAND

Henry VII (r. 1485–1509), the first of the *Tudor* monarchs, established a strong central government even though many regarded the family as usurpers, invited to the throne as an expedient compromise to end the Wars of the Roses. By regulating trade and internal commerce through monopolies, charters, and licenses, Henry raised revenue from the prosperous middle class. This money enabled him to finance a standing army and keep the nobility in check. The *Court of the Star Chamber* administered central justice and further subdued rebellious nobles. Since the Tudors were beholden to Parliament for inviting them to the throne, Henry and his successors, including his son *Henry VIII* (r. 1509–1547), consulted Parliament on significant issues.

■ Unlike his father, who was levelheaded and tightfisted, *Henry VIII* was an impetuous, extravagant, and passionate man whose temper, ambitions, and appetites were legendary.

- The need to maintain legitimacy by having a male heir led Henry VIII to make the decisions, with Parliament's support, that led to the *English Reformation*. (See pages 99–100.)

- *Edward VI* (r. 1547–1553) assumed the throne upon the death of his father, Henry VIII.

  - Since Edward was only ten and of fragile health, the government was headed by a regent, the *Duke of Somerset*.
  - The basic tenets of the English Reformation were restated, and the *Anglican Book of Common Prayer* was made the basis for all church services.
  - Edward died at the young age of 16.

- *Mary I of England* (r. 1553–1558), the daughter of Henry VIII by his first wife, the Catholic Catherine of Aragon, became queen when Edward died.

  - Unpopular, not only because she was Roman Catholic but because she was married to *Philip II* of Spain.
  - Had to suppress a rebellion against her rule and alliance with Spain.
  - "Bloody Mary" earned her name when she burned hundreds of Protestants at the stake for dissenting against her attempt to reinstitute Catholicism in England.
  - When she died, she was succeeded by her half-sister, *Elizabeth*, Henry's daughter by his second wife, Anne Boleyn.

- *Elizabeth I* (r. 1558–1603), last and greatest of the Tudor monarchs.

  - Elizabeth reigned when the population of England and Wales was between 3 and 4 million, while that of France was over 16 million and that of Spain nearly 9 million.
  - Enriched by its conquests and colonies in the New World, Spain was the predominant power of Europe.
  - England, part of the British Isles, was at the geographic and political fringe of the powerful nations, vying for respect from the major powers, such as France, Russia, and Austria.

    - The Church of England was independent from Rome but close to Roman Catholic theology.
    - Elizabeth's government balanced power between the monarchy and Parliament.
    - England's wealth came from rich arable land and an energetic populace that excelled in commerce and trade.
    - England's social system was unique.

  - The gentry, lesser nobles whose original wealth came from ownership of land, expanded their wealth by entering the world of commerce and by intermarrying with the middle class.
  - There were no glaring distinctions between the upper and middle classes in England, as there were on the Continent, and the interests of nobles, gentry, and bourgeoisie were represented in Parliament.
  - Since the Tudors had been invited to the throne of England to settle the rival claims of the Houses of York and Lancaster during the Wars of the Roses, Elizabeth, her charismatic father, and her capable grandfather had lived under the shadow of being considered "dynastic pretenders":

    - The child of Anne Boleyn, whose marriage to Henry VIII was considered scandalous;
    - The *Virgin Queen* (a euphemism for Elizabeth's having never married, considering her notorious love affairs) had to prove her mettle in the face of the prejudices against her line, her parentage, and her gender;

- Her natural intelligence had been honed by substantial education; her powerful personality had been toughened by living as a family "outcast" at the courts of her father, half-brother, and her half-sister;
- Adored by her people and feared by her enemies, both at home and abroad;
- She reigned for nearly a half-century as one of Europe's greatest monarchs and one of the world's greatest women.

THE ELIZABETHAN AGE

Religion

Upon assuming the throne, Elizabeth repealed Mary's pro-Catholic legislation and reinstated the Acts of Supremacy and Uniformity that had established the English Reformation during her father's reign.

The Thirty-Nine Articles (1563) followed Protestant doctrine and was vague enough to accommodate the majority of the English population, except the *Puritans* (English Calvinists). Puritans believed that the *liturgy* (prescribed ritual) and the *hierarchy* (the order of rank within the organization) needed "purification" from Catholic influence. Militant Puritans challenged royal authority and, while they were suppressed for a time, they grew stronger during the reigns of Elizabeth's successors and would influence the development of constitutionalism.

Diplomacy

When the Netherlands, a Habsburg possession that had adopted Protestantism, revolted against Spanish rule, Elizabeth entered into an alliance with the Dutch in 1577, because both nations had strong traditions of democracy and a Protestant majority among their populations as well as from fear that Holland would provide a base from which Spain could invade England. Both England and Holland sent *privateers* (warships not commissioned by the state, but covertly supported by them) to prey on the Spanish treasure ships from her colonies in the New World.

- Outraged, *Philip II*, Spanish king and Holy Roman Emperor, conspired with English Catholics to overthrow Elizabeth and put her cousin, the Catholic Mary Stuart, queen of the Scots, on the throne.
- In 1587, Elizabeth ordered the execution of Mary for treason, and Philip declared war on England.
- *La Grande y Felicísima Armada*, or "great and most fortunate fleet," of 132 heavily armed warships loaded with troops, was defeated in 1588 by the superior naval tactics of the smaller, more maneuverable English fleet led by *Sir Francis Drake* (1540–1596).
- The superior navigational skills and tactics of the English were aided by winds that drove the Armada into the North Sea, eventually to suffer from severe storms that sank many Spanish ships.
- The failure of the Spanish Armada marked the beginning of the decline of Spanish naval dominance and the rise of the British.

Culture

This was the Golden Age of English Literature, the era of Shakespeare, Spenser, Donne, Marlowe, More, and Francis Bacon, when a brilliant national literature was developed that instilled pride in the uniqueness of English culture.

THE STUART KINGS AND PARLIAMENT (1603–1688)

James I (r. 1603–1625), king of Scotland and son of Mary, Queen of Scots, took the throne upon Elizabeth's death, since she had no direct heirs. A believer in the divine right of kings, James failed to understand the importance of Parliament in governing England. A conference at *Hampton Court* in 1604 failed to reconcile the Puritans, who opposed the Anglican hierarchy as the Church of England. The *Gunpowder Plot*, 1605, was uncovered before disgruntled Catholics (led by Guy Fawkes) objecting to James's enforcement of laws that required participation in Anglican services, could blow up the king and Parliament. The years 1610 to 1611 saw Parliament enmeshed in the issue of its role in financing government.

- The *"Addled" Parliament* met in 1614, so-called by James because it spent its entire session arguing that taxes could be levied only with its consent and that rule was by king and Parliament in conjunction.

  - Dissolving Parliament, James tried to rule without it until England's involvement in the Thirty Years' War necessitated his reconvening it.
  - In 1621, after a rancorous session in which Parliament criticized James's foreign policy, Parliament passed the *Great Protestation*, claiming free speech and authority in conducting governmental affairs. James dissolved the body and arrested its leaders.

- *Charles I* (r. 1625–1649) was, like his father, devoted to the divine right theory and, unlike his father, woefully inept at dealing with Parliament.

  - Embroiled in wars on the Continent, he called for Parliament to vote funds to carry them through.
  - Parliament refused to do so until Charles signed the *Petition of Right*.
  - It guaranteed:

    - Parliament alone can levy taxes.
    - Martial law cannot be declared in peacetime.
    - Soldiers may not be quartered in private homes.
    - Imprisonment required a specific charge.

  - The Bishops' War of 1639–1640, after Archbishop Laud persecuted Puritans and tried to force Anglican worship upon the Presbyterian Scots, led Charles to reconvene Parliament in order to pay war debts from his loss.
  - The *Long Parliament* (1640–1660) demanded the following in return for paying for Charles's defeat:

    - Impeach his top advisers.
    - Allow Parliament to meet every three years without his summons.
    - Promise not to dissolve Parliament without its consent.

- When Charles attempted, in early 1642, to arrest opposition members, Parliament seized control of the army.

  • Charles gathered his forces.
  • The *English Civil War* (1642–1649) began.

THE COURSE OF THE CONFLICT

The Civil War in England was caused by a conflict between the king and the Parliament about where sovereignty lies and what are its limits. In the end, the hostilities would leave Parliament as the sovereign power of England, with the monarch to be reduced to more of a ceremonial role from the 1650s onward. The rising middle class, many of whom were members of Parliament, wanted to gain political power, so this civil war is often viewed by economic historians as a conflict between the monarchy and nobility on one side, and the bourgeoisie on the other. The middle class, the merchants, the major cities, and a small segment of the nobility supported Parliament and were called *Roundheads.* The Anglican clergy, the majority of the nobility, and the peasants backed the king and were referred to as *Royalists* or *Cavaliers.*

1643

The Roundheads allied with Presbyterian Scotland, promising to impose Presbyterianism on England in exchange for military assistance. Charles called on Irish Catholics for help.

1644

Oliver Cromwell (1599–1658), a Puritan leader of Parliament, led his *New Model Army* of Puritans against the Cavaliers at *Marston Moor* and defeated them decisively.

1645

Charles surrendered to the Scots.

1647

The Scots turned Charles over to Parliament, which was led by Cromwell's *Independents,* who favored religious toleration. The Scots turned about and allied with Charles, who promised that he would impose Presbyterianism on the English.

1648

Cromwell defeated the Scots at the *Battle of Preston* and helped purge the Presbyterians from Parliament, thereby creating the *Rump Parliament,* which voted to behead Charles for treason.

1649

With the execution of Charles, England became a republic, the *Commonwealth,* and Cromwell and his army wielded power. In suppressing Irish supporters of the Crown, the Puritans committed terrible atrocities and imposed injustices that would exacerbate the *Irish Question* for centuries.

1653–1660

Cromwell was designated *Lord Protector* by a puppet Parliament and ruled with its support until his death in 1658. His son Richard, a far less capable ruler, was deposed in 1660, and *Charles II* (r. 1661–1685) was proclaimed king.

THE STUART RESTORATION (1660–1688)

The *Cavalier Parliament* (1660–1679) marked the development of the first political parties, the Tory and Whig parties.

- The *Tories*, made up of nobles, gentry, and the Anglicans, were conservatives who supported the monarchy over Parliament and who wanted Anglicanism to be the state religion.
- The *Whigs*, mainly middle class and Puritan, favored Parliament and religious toleration.

  - Since the Tories prevailed in the Cavalier Parliament, Anglicanism was restored by a series of laws that forbade dissenters to worship publicly, required government officials and military personnel to practice Anglicanism, and discriminated against other faiths.
  - The *Whig Parliament*, elected in 1679, was suspicious of Charles II's absolutist and pro-Catholic tendencies and enacted the *Habeas Corpus Act*, which limited royal power by:

    • Enabling judges to demand that prisoners be in court.
    • Requiring just cause for continued imprisonment.
    • Providing for speedy trials.
    • Forbidding *double jeopardy* (being charged for a crime that one had already been acquitted of).

THE GLORIOUS REVOLUTION

The *Glorious Revolution* was actually the culmination of an evolutionary process over centuries which, through historical accident, outright conflict, and painstaking design, increased the power of Parliament over the monarchy. *James II* (r. 1685–1688) was unpopular from the moment he took the throne. A devout Roman Catholic, he appointed Catholic ministers to important posts and gave the appearance of trying to impose Catholicism upon the English.

- In 1688, important nobles invited *William of Orange*, a Hollander, and Mary, the wife of James's oldest child, to rule England conditional upon their granting a bill of rights.
- When *William and Mary* (r. 1688–1704) arrived in England, James fled in exile to France.
- The new monarchs accepted from Parliament, as a condition of their reign, the *Declaration of Rights* (enacted into law as the *Bill of Rights* in 1689).
- The *Habeas Corpus Act*, the *Petition of Right*, and the Bill of Rights have all become part of the *English Constitution*.
- In the centuries that followed, monarchs in England came to reign, while Parliament came to rule.

Although, at the time of the Glorious Revolution, Parliament served the interests of the wellborn or the wealthy, it came to represent "the people" as government came to be viewed as existing and functioning according to *John Locke's* Enlightenment concept of *consent of the governed*. The English, and those who inherited their political traditions, would guarantee individual rights and would create modern democracy.

THE DUTCH REVOLT AND THE GOLDEN AGE OF THE NETHERLANDS

When the Spanish under King Philip II tried to consolidate power in the Low Countries (the 17 provinces of the Netherlands, today's Belgium and the Netherlands), they met stiff resistance. Here, Philip II ignored two of Machiavelli's basic instructions: do not change the religion of newly conquered people and do not raise their taxes. His policies and the policies of his representatives in the Low Countries united both religious and economic powers against his rule.

- The Netherlands was the commercial hub of the developing capitalist world at the time.

    - The people had known a significant degree of self-governance.
    - Philip II tried to tighten the reins by sending his sister, Margaret, who had been personally educated by Ignatius Loyola, there to rule.

        - She introduced the Dutch Inquisition and raised taxes.
        - The Protestants (Calvinists) united with those who resisted the tax hikes and with peasants who suffered from high prices for grain.
        - Protestants began to smash Catholic churches all over Antwerp and the surrounding area.
        - This was mostly a middle-class revolt.
        - The Netherlands had the largest middle class by percentage of population in all of Europe.

    - Philip sent the Duke of Alva with 20,000 troops to pacify the rebellion in 1567.

        - Established the "Council of Blood."
        - Ruthlessly "purified" the Netherlands of Protestant opposition.
        - Added a 10 percent tax to all transactions, crippling the best economy in Europe and under Spain's dominion.
        - Margaret resigned her regency after the Duke of Alva killed 1,500 people on one day in 1568.

- Prince William ("The Silent") of Orange united the 17 provinces against the rule of Spain in 1576.

    - Alexander Farnese, the Duke of Parma, was sent by Philip II to put down the rebellion in 1578 once and for all.
    - A good general with a great plan:

        - He laid siege to one city at a time and avoided pitched battles.
        - Slowly took the ten lower (southernmost) provinces and forced the Protestant forces out of those areas.

- The repercussions of this war were to affect the political and military events in Europe over the next few decades:

    - The ten lower provinces became the Spanish Netherlands and, later, Belgium.

– The seven northern provinces of the Netherlands formed the Union of Utrecht and declared their independence from Spain (1581) as the United Provinces of the Netherlands.

- The Dutch dikes were broken to repel invaders so many times that the tactic hurt the economy by destroying agricultural production.
- The Dutch kept their land free.
- English support of the Dutch Protestants in part led to the Spanish Armada campaign, which the Dutch helped to win by successful early engagements with Spanish forces along their own coast.
- The United Provinces of the Netherlands developed as a commercial powerhouse because of:

  ○ Independence
  ○ Religious tolerance
  ○ The Protestant work ethic

The Golden Age of the Netherlands

The United Provinces of the Netherlands saw a "Golden Age" during the seventeenth century. The Netherlands was a confederation of seven provinces. Each province was autonomous with its leader, a *stadtholder*, who was a representative to a ruling council that ran the confederation. It was the wealthiest and most civilized country in Europe, ruled by an oligarchy of merchants called regents.

- It was the model for Europe of a republican form of government based on economic prosperity.
- Religious tolerance and trading with all religions (always buying and selling in bulk) led to massive profits and prosperity.

  – Amsterdam became the regional center of commerce, replacing Antwerp.
  – Industry shifted from fishing to shipping.
  – The *Dutch East India Company* was formed in 1602.

    • The Dutch were able to corner the maritime shipping market by charging the lowest rates in Europe.

  – They perfected the joint-stock company and created the first stock markets where stocks, or ownership of a part of a company, could be traded.
  – Society was able to share in the profits.
  – In 1630 stock in the East India Company was returning a 35 percent profit annually.
  – Holland had accidentally created the investment industry.

    • Became the center of a bustling new industry.

  – Because of its thriving economy, the Netherlands became "an island of plenty in a sea of want," as the rest of Europe still saw crippling poverty among many of its citizens.

- Dutch economic prosperity brought on a Golden Age of Dutch art that may still be unrivaled to this day.

- Superb artists revolutionized the visual arts by painting detailed domestic interiors, focusing on the lives of commoners, and by providing amazing mathematical detail in their work.

  - *Rembrandt van Rijn*
  - *Johannes Vermeer*
  - *Jan van Eyck*
  - *Albrecht Dürer*

    - Their art captured the emotion and milieu of the lives of the people who lived there as opposed to the overawing prosperity and power of the patron communicated by the Baroque art of such artists as *Peter Paul Rubens*.

> ### ART ANALYSIS TIP
>
> The differences in the patrons was that the Roman Catholic Church and monarchs patronized mostly Baroque art, while mainly Protestant merchants and princelings patronized the art of the "Dutch Masters." This explains the different subject matter, emotional content, and even why the Baroque pieces were much larger than most of the works of the Dutch Masters.

WOMEN DURING THE AGE OF ABSOLUTISM

There were a few female monarchs, such as Elizabeth I and Catherine de' Medici, who showed by example how powerful a woman could be. When Elizabeth I visited her troops, gathered for an expected land battle during the Spanish Armada campaign, her speech was a rousing testament to what a woman can accomplish. Her rule was perhaps one of the greatest periods in the history of her nation and laid the foundation for the creation of the British Empire. Catherine ruled France as regent with the aid of Cardinal Richelieu and used Machiavellian tactics to empower her son and his successors to rule France.

ABSOLUTISM IN THE OTTOMAN EMPIRE

Although Suleiman the Magnificent's push into central Europe came to a halt in Austria in 1529, he was still able to capture Belgrade (Serbia) and nearly half of Eastern Europe, including the Balkan territories, most of Hungary, and part of southern Russia. He collected slaves instead of taxes from the conquered territories.

- Many young male slaves collected from the Christian areas were converted to Islam and trained as soldiers loyal to the Sultan, called *janissaries*.
- The Ottoman Empire practiced some religious toleration, with communities of non-Muslims called *millets* and containing people of the same religious minority, such as Christian or Jewish.

  - Similar to the ghettos that Europeans forced their religious minorities such as Jews or Muslims to live in until the nineteenth and twentieth centuries.

- After Suleiman the Magnificent's death in 1566, the Ottoman Empire began to decline.
- During the late 1600s there was a strong revival of Ottoman power.

- Laid siege to Vienna in 1683.
- Vienna saved from the Turkish attackers by Habsburg and Polish troops.
- Russians and Venetians attacked during the retreat of the Turks.
- The Ottoman Empire's territorial designs on Eastern Europe began to decline again and deteriorated until the late 1800s.
- The Ottoman conflicts with Russia over these areas led them to side with the Central Powers in the First World War.

A GUIDE TO MONARCHS AND THEIR FAMILIES

Many students throughout the years have had trouble keeping historical rulers straight. This chart of national monarchical history is intended to help you with that task.

Rulers in **bold** mean STOP and memorize their names and know why they are important; these people will very likely be on the AP test.

Rulers in italics mean PAUSE and be familiar with who these people are; they may be on the test and rate some attention.

Rulers in regular text mean KEEP GOING. Sure, one might be on the test every ten years as a distraction in one of the last multiple-choice questions, but that is a chance we are willing to take. These names are included mainly for continuity's sake, but most professors do not know who they are and you do not need to either.

Insofar as dates go, keep a ballpark figure of when people reigned, lived, and so on, but memorizing the exact dates is frustrating and not necessary.

Austria

In 1276, Rudolf I of Habsburg became the Duke of Austria; this might be significant, but the test does not start until 1450, so we will begin with Maximilian, the first Habsburg Holy Roman Emperor. On the left is the ruler's given name. The next category is the Anglicized version of the name. Important advisors are listed below the king/queen.

Name (Anglicized)	Reign	Notes
Maximilian I	*(1493–1519)*	
Charles V	**(1519–1556)**	**(Divided up the Habsburg lands)**
Ferdinand I	(1556–1564)	
Maximilian II	(1564–1576)	
Rudolf II	(1576–1612)	
Matthias	(1612–1619)	
Ferdinand II	**(1619–1637)**	**(Started Thirty Years' War)**
Ferdinand III	(1637–1657)	
Leopold I	(1658–1705)	
Joseph I	(1705–1711)	
Charles VI	*(1711–1740)*	*(Pragmatic sanction)*
Maria Theresa	**(1740–1780)**	
Joseph II	*(1780–1790)*	*(Initiated enlightened reforms)*
Leopold II	*(1790–1792)*	*(Reversed reforms of his brother)*
Franz I (Francis)	(1792–1835)	(Declared Emperor of Austria 1806)

Name (Anglicized)	Reign	Notes
Klemens von Metternich (Foreign Minister of Austria)	**(1819–1848)**	**(Congress system)**
Ferdinand I	(1835–1848)	
Franz Josef I (Francis Joseph)	*(1848–1916)*	
Karl (Charles)	(1916–1918)	

Great Britain

The first nation in which a king agreed that his power was limited was also the first country to have the legislative branch execute the monarch legally. By the sixteenth century, the English monarchy was as much about negotiating between powerful parties and religious factions as it was about pomp and circumstance.

Name (Anglicized)	Reign	Notes
Henry VII	*(1485–1509)*	*Tudor*
Henry VIII	**(1509–1547)**	**Tudor**
Edward VI	*(1547–1553)*	*Tudor*
Mary I	*(1553–1558)*	*Tudor "Bloody Mary"*
Elizabeth I	**(1558–1603)**	**Tudor "The Virgin Queen"**
James I	*(1603–1625)*	*Stuart (James VI of Scotland)*
Charles I	**(1625–1649)**	**Stuart (Civil War 1642–1649)**
Oliver Cromwell	**(1649–1658)**	**"Lord Protector" (Dictator)**
Richard Cromwell	(1658–1660)	
Charles II	(1660–1685)	Stuart
James II	(1685–1688)	Stuart
Mary II/William III	**(1689–1702)**	**Stuart/Orange (Glorious Revolution)**
Anne	(1702–1714)	Stuart
George I	*(1714–1727)*	*Hanoverian*
George II	(1727–1760)	Hanoverian
George III	**(1760–1820)**	**Hanoverian**
George IV	(1820–1830)	Hanoverian
William IV	(1830–1837)	Hanoverian
Victoria	**(1837–1901)**	**Saxe-Coburg-Gotha (William's niece)**
Edward VII	(1901–1910)	Saxe-Coburg-Gotha
George V	(1910–1936)	Windsor
Edward VIII	*(1936)*	*Windsor (Abdicated to marry a divorcée)*
George VI	(1936–1952)	Windsor
Elizabeth II	*(1952–)*	*Windsor*

France

The model of absolutism under Louis XIV, this nation was once ruled by Louis's grandfather, who changed religion three times and, in the final conversion, before taking the throne declared: "Paris is worth a mass."

Name (Anglicized)	Reign	Notes
Charles VII	*(1422–1461)*	*Valois*
Louis XI	*(1461–1483)*	*Valois "Spider King"*
Charles VIII	(1483–1498)	Valois
Louis XII	(1498–1515)	Valois-Orléans "Father of the People"
Francis I	(1515–1547)	Valois-Angoulême
Henry II	(1547–1559)	Valois-Angoulême
Francis II	(1559–1560)	Valois-Angoulême
Charles IX	(1560–1574)	Valois-Angoulême
Henry III	*(1574–1589)*	*Valois-Angoulême*
Henry IV of Navarre	**(1589–1610)**	**Bourbon**
Louis XIII	*(1610–1643)*	*Bourbon*
Cardinal Richelieu (Chief Minister and Regent of France)	**(1624–1642)**	
Louis XIV	**(1643–1715)**	**Bourbon "The Sun King"**
Louis XV	(1715–1774)	Bourbon
René de Maupeou (Chancellor)	(1770–1774)	
Louis XVI	*(1774–1792)*	*Bourbon (Executed)*
Louis XVII	(1793–1795)	Bourbon (Jailed throughout "reign")
Legislatures	**(1789–1795)**	**The First Republic**
National Assembly	**(1789–1791)**	
Legislative Assembly	**(1791–1792)**	
National Convention	**(1792–1795)**	**Committee on Public Safety (1793–1794)**
Directory (Directoire)	**(1795–1799)**	**The First Republic**
Napoléon Bonaparte	**(1799–1815)**	**Bonaparte (First Consul until 1804)**
Louis XVIII	*(1814–1824)*	*Bourbon (Monarchy restored)*
Charles X	(1824–1830)	Bourbon
Louis Philippe	*(1830–1848)*	*Bourbon-Orléans "Citizen King"*
François Guizot (Chief Minister)	*(1840–1848)*	
Louis Napoléon	**(1848–1852)**	**Second Republic (President)**
Napoléon III (Louis Napoléon)	**(1852–1870)**	**Second Empire (Emperor)**

Germany

Germany was formed in 1871 as a combination of many different German states, kingdoms, cities, and so on that were dominated by the ruler of Prussia, Wilhelm I of the House of Hohenzollern. Wilhelm traced his lineage from Brandenburg's prince-electors (those who formally approved the successor to the Habsburg throne). The Hohenzollern lineage is outlined here.

Name (Anglicized)	Reign	Notes
Friedrich Wilhelm (Frederick William)	**(1640–1688)**	**"The Great Elector"**
Friedrich I (Frederick)	*(1688–1713)*	*(Crowned King of Prussia in 1701)*
Friedrich Wilhelm I	**(1713–1740)**	**"The Soldier King"**
Friedrich II	**(1740–1786)**	**"Frederick the Great"**

Name (Anglicized)	Reign	Notes
Friedrich Wilhelm II	(1786–1797)	
Friedrich Wilhelm III	(1797–1840)	
Friedrich Wilhelm IV	(1840–1861)	
Wilhelm I (William)	*(1861–1888)*	*(Kaiser of the Second Reich)*
Otto von Bismarck (Chancellor)	**(1862–1890)**	
Friedrich III	(1888)	
Wilhelm II	**(1888–1918)**	**(Kaiser during WWI)**

Russia

Though there were princes of Muscovy before the czar, he is the one credited for forming the modern nation of Russia and, more importantly for us, the earliest czar the test makers would consider putting on the test.

Name (Anglicized)	Reign	Notes
Ivan III	**(1440–1505)**	**"Ivan the Great"**
Vasily III	(1505–1533)	
Ivan IV	**(1533–1584)**	**"Ivan the Terrible"**
Theodore I	(1584–1598)	
Disputed Line of Succession	**(1598–1613)**	**"Time of Troubles"**
Michael	*(1613–1645)*	*Romanov*
Alexis I	(1645–1676)	Romanov
Theodore III	(1676–1682)	Romanov
Ivan V	(1682–1689)	Romanov
Peter I	**(1682–1725)**	**Romanov "Peter the Great"**
Catherine I	(1725–1727)	Romanov
Peter II	(1727–1730)	Romanov
Anna	(1730–1740)	Romanov
Ivan VI	(1740–1741)	Romanov
Elizabeth	(1741–1762)	Romanov
Peter III	(1762)	Romanov
Catherine II	**(1762–1796)**	**Romanov "Catherine the Great"**
Paul I	(1796–1801)	Romanov
Alexander I	*(1801–1825)*	*Romanov*
Nicholas I	(1825–1855)	Romanov
Alexander II	*(1855–1881)*	*Romanov (Reformer)*
Alexander III	(1881–1894)	Romanov
Nicholas II	*(1894–1917)*	*Romanov (Killed by Bolsheviks with his entire family)*
Sergei Witte	*(1892–1903)*	*Minister of Finance*
Peter Stolypin	*(1906–1911)*	*Chief Minister*

Spain

Ferdinand and Isabella were the first king and queen of a unified Spain; hence, we start with them. Each "ruled" their own kingdom, although after 1506 Ferdinand became the regent of Castile as well.

Name (Anglicized)	Reign	Notes
Ferdinand	**(1474–1516)**	**King of Aragon (Joint rule)**
Isabella	**(1474–1504)**	**Queen of Castile (Joint rule)**
Joanna and Philip I	(1504–1506)	Rulers of Castile
Ferdinand	**(1506–1516)**	**Regent of Castile, King of Aragon**
Charles I	**(1516–1556)**	**Habsburg (Charles V of Austria)**
Philip II	**(1556–1598)**	**Habsburg**
Philip III	(1598–1621)	Habsburg
Philip IV	(1621–1665)	Habsburg
Charles II	(1665–1700)	Habsburg
Philip V	*(1700–1746)*	*Bourbon (Great-grandson of Philip IV)*
Ferdinand VI	(1746–1759)	Bourbon
Charles III	(1759–1788)	Bourbon
Charles IV	(1788–1808)	Bourbon
Ferdinand VII	(1808)	Bourbon
Joseph Bonaparte	(1808–1813)	Bonaparte
Ferdinand VII	(1813–1833)	Bourbon (Restored)
Isabella II	(1833–1868)	Bourbon
Francisco Serrano y Domínguez	(1869–1870)	Elected regent
Amadeus	(1870–1873)	Elected regent
Estanislao Figueras	(1873)	First Republic (President)
Francisco Pi y Margall	(1873)	First Republic (President)
Nicolás Salmerón y Alonso	(1873)	First Republic (President)
Emilio Castelar y Ripoll	(1873–1874)	First Republic (Prime Minister)
Alfonso XII	(1874–1885)	Bourbon (King)
Alfonso XIII	(1886–1931)	Bourbon (King)
Niceta Alcalá Zamora	(1931–1936)	Second Republic (President)
Manuel Azaña	(1936–1939)	Second Republic (President)
Francisco Franco	*(1939–1975)*	*Nationalist Government (Chief of State)*
Juan Carlos I	(1975–)	Bourbon (Constitutional monarch)

PRACTICE LONG-ESSAY QUESTIONS

These questions are samples of the various types of thematic essays on the exam. (See pages 30–31 for a detailed explanation of each type.) Check over the **generic rubric** (see pages 32–33) before you begin any of these essays and use that rubric to score your essay if you write one.

Question 1

Compare the development of the nation-state in France and in England from the early sixteenth to the end of the seventeenth centuries.

COMMENTS ON QUESTION 1

This is clearly a COMPARE skill question, so be sure to describe similarities and differences between English and French development as nation-states. Account for or explain why they were so different by providing specific examples of how monarchical power was used differently in each nation. The *contrast* is glaring in that during this period the French developed *absolutism* to its pinnacle while England continued the evolution of *constitutionalism*. "Who did what, when, where, and how" is a convenient formula for tracing the separate developments. Be careful not to get lost in detail. The large scope of the question requires a big-picture perspective.

The comparison of the development of these two very different styles of government is more difficult. "To compare" is to measure for similarities and differences. Were there similarities? Did the monarchs of these two diverse nations have similar traits of personality, similar methods for consolidating power? Were there similar obstacles to overcome, such as the vested interests of the nobility or the need for governmental revenue? Despite the differences between absolutism and constitutionalism, were there common goals: consolidation, centralization of authority, and modernization? Be sure to not just describe the commonalities and differences, but to also analyze the reasons for those similarities and differences, or at least evaluate the historical significance of the emergence of constitutionalism.

Question 2

Analyze the development of absolutism in France (1500–1715).

COMMENTS ON QUESTION 2

This one tests the CHANGE AND CONTINUITY OVER TIME skill. Be sure to describe the level of historical continuity (as in what did not change in political and social life in France from 1500 to 1715) and change (as in what did change in political and social life in France from 1500 to 1715). Explain the reasons for these changes, citing specific examples of what changed, and what parts of French society and political power changed compared to the parts that did not, such as the preservation of the *Ancien Régime* and the monarchy. Examine the roles of the early Valois monarchs in centralizing authority, taking into consideration the religious wars of the sixteenth century, and also the role of Henry IV in restoring national order and royal esteem, examining the profound accomplishments of Richelieu (one of Hollywood's favorite villains), then touring the reign of Louis XIV. Be sure to describe both what has remained unchanged and what has changed, and use specific examples to illustrate and analyze those changes over time.

Question 3

To what extent, and in what ways, did the Puritan Revolution contribute to the supremacy of the English Parliament in 1689?

COMMENTS ON QUESTION 3

This is a difficult question because it requires that you demonstrate how, and how much, a complex set of events contributed to a complex development. This one is a CAUSATION question because it requires you to decide to what extent the Puritan Revolution contributed to (*caused*) the rise to supremacy of Parliament in England in 1689. Remember to describe, through specific examples, the causes AND/OR effects of the emergence of parliamentary power. Explain the reasons for these changes, citing specific examples of what changed and what parts of English political power changed compared to the parts that did not, such as the preservation of the aristocracy and the continuation of the monarchy. An effective approach would be to divide the bigger issue into smaller questions: What was the Puritan Revolution? How did it increase the power of Parliament? How did the Restoration affect Parliament's role? How was the monarchy weakened by the Puritan Revolution? How supreme was the monarchy? Did Puritans do anything that reduced its supremacy? How and why did the Glorious Revolution occur?

Question 4

To what extent did the Tudors bring England into the modern era?

COMMENTS ON QUESTION 4

This one is a CAUSATION question because it requires you to decide to what extent the Tudors brought England into the modern era, or CAUSED England to become modern. Describe causes AND/OR effects of England becoming more modern through specific examples. Be sure to explain the reasons for these changes, citing specific examples of what changed and what parts of English society, economy, political power, military power, and prestige changed under the Tudors compared to the parts that did not. To evaluate this question, the essay must clarify what is meant by "the modern era," examine the Tudor reign, specifically Henry VII, Henry VIII, and Elizabeth I, and demonstrate whether or not the Tudors accomplished a transformation. Be careful about dismissing Henry VIII because of "bad press." Despite his glaring personal failings, abused wives, and gluttony among the most prominent, he strengthened the monarchy and initiated the English Reformation. Elizabeth may be famous for standing up to the superpower of her day, Spain, but the Golden Age of English culture was also during her reign, as was the birth of the commercial revolution and overseas colonization. Her reign set the stage for future British empire building.

Question 5

Explain how the Glorious Revolution of 1688 established a constitutional government in England.

COMMENTS ON QUESTION 5

This one is also a CAUSATION question because it requires you to explain how one event, the Glorious Revolution, resulted in a specific outcome: constitutional government in England. Remember to describe causes AND/OR effects of the Glorious Revolution and to explain them through specific examples. The essay must explain the reasons for the causes AND/OR effects of the Glorious Revolution, such as how the rise of the power of Parliament that resulted in the Glorious Revolution occurred as those in Parliament were gaining economic power and wanted political power to match it. While this requires specific knowledge of events, laws, and effects, the essay should make clear how the abdication of James II, the invitation for William and Mary to take the throne, and the conditions set for this by Parliament laid the foundation for a modern democratic state. How was Parliament's power solidified? How did the Bill of Rights establish rule of law? How did the supremacy of Parliament and those basic rights limit the monarchy?

Question 6

How did transatlantic trade and the Columbian Exchange change lives on both sides of the Atlantic?

COMMENTS ON QUESTION 6

This answer clearly calls for you to analyze CONTINUITY AND CHANGE OVER TIME on both sides of the Atlantic. Be sure to describe the level of historical continuity and change, and analyze specific examples of what changed and what remained the same on both sides of the Atlantic Ocean. Analyze why things changed or stayed the same after the Columbian Exchange began, citing specific examples. The best approach to this question would involve explaining the time period politically, economically, socially, and religiously on both sides of the Atlantic before, during, and after the Age of Exploration and colonialism. The influx of gold and silver in Europe, the outlet for immigration, cheap land, as well as the impact of new foods such as corn and potatoes in Europe must be explored, while the destruction of Native American cultures and the loss of their political, economic, and social power should be explained. The role of religion in exploration should be examined. The question is broad in scope, but needs specific factual references to illustrate the main points.

Question 7

Compare the contributions to the development of modern science of Bacon and Descartes with those of Copernicus and Galileo.

COMMENTS ON QUESTION 7

This task appears to be straightforward since, as the question implies, the roles of Bacon and Descartes in the rise of modern science are similar, and they contrast with those of Copernicus and Galileo. This is a COMPARE skill question, so be sure to describe similarities and differences. Account for or explain them by providing specific examples of how they are similar and different and tie that to historical developments such as the growth of modern science or technology. Bacon and Descartes are "philosophers of science" whose writings helped establish the methodology of science: skepticism, observation, generalization, and experimentation. Copernicus and Galileo, on the other hand, were "genuine" scientists whose theories or experimentation expanded the store of scientific knowledge. Additionally, both Galileo and Copernicus worked in the science of astronomy, and Newton claimed that he owed his accomplishments to the foundational work of Galileo.

The tricky part of this question is to apply the "contrast and comparison" rule to Bacon and Descartes, then to Copernicus and Galileo. Did Bacon's writings contribute differently than Descartes's to the "scientific mind?" Were Copernicus's methods and findings different from those of Galileo? Also contrast and compare each pair to the other.

Question 8

Explain how the replacement of the open-field system by the enclosure movement increased agricultural productivity in eighteenth-century Europe.

COMMENTS ON QUESTION 8

The enclosure movement should be explained as the most important and least-known revolution in European history. This one is also a CAUSATION question because it requires you to explain how one outcome increased agricultural output and resulted from a specific stimulus: the implementation of the enclosure movement. Remember to describe causes AND/OR effects of increased agricultural productivity and to explain them through specific examples. The essay must explain the reasons for these causes AND/OR effects, such as: the ownership of land encouraged people to improve their land through fertilization and irrigation, which increased crop yields. You must describe how the enclosure movement caused increased agricultural productivity, and analyze specific examples that illustrate how the Enclosure Movement did this. You must describe the open-field system and the concept of common lands, focusing on the limitations on land improvement and fallow lands. Explain how the enclosure movement made land improvement, such as irrigation, crop rotation, and fertilization, more practical and widespread. The best essays will also examine how the enclosure movement led to the putting-out system that increased domestic production and disturbed the order of society by moving many farming families from their lands, causing them to find new means of employment.

PRACTICE SHORT-ANSWER QUESTIONS

1. Answer all parts of the question based upon the passage and your knowledge of European History.

Vasco da Gama: *Round Africa to India* (1497)

The inhabitants of this country are tawny-colored. Their food is confined to the flesh of seals, whales and gazelles, and the roots of herbs. They are dressed in skins, and wear sheaths over their virile members. They are armed with poles of olive wood to which a horn, browned in the fire, is attached. Their numerous dogs resemble those of Portugal, and bark like them. The birds of the country, likewise, are the same as in Portugal, and include cormorants, gulls, turtle doves, crested larks, and many others. The climate is healthy and temperate, and produces good herbage. On the day after we had cast anchor, that is to say on Thursday (November 9), we landed with the captain-major, and made captive one of the natives, who was small of stature like Sancho Mexia. This man had been gathering honey in the sandy waste, for in this country the bees deposit their honey at the foot of the mounds around the bushes. He was taken on board the captain-major's ship, and being placed at table he ate of all we ate. On the following day the captain-major had him well dressed and sent ashore.

On the following day (November 10) fourteen or fifteen natives came to where our ship lay. The captain-major landed and showed them a variety of merchandise, with the view of finding out whether such things were to be found in their country. This merchandise included cinnamon, cloves, seed-pearls, gold, and many other things, but it was evident that they had no knowledge whatever of such articles, and they were consequently given round bells and tin rings.

(A) Explain TWO results of European journeys like the one taken by Vasco da Gama and his crew during this period of time.

(B) Explain ONE motivation for journeys like the one taken by Vasco da Gama and his crew during this period of time.

2. Please use the chart below and your knowledge of European History to answer all parts of the following question.

Slave Trading Nations

The number of Africans who were transported to the "New World" between 1520 and 1867 is estimated at 10 million to 15 million persons with 4 million to 6 million additional people perishing on the journey

Carriers

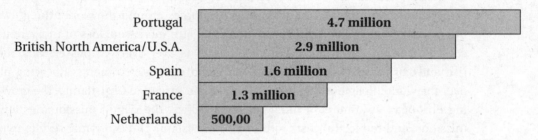

Portugal	4.7 million
British North America/U.S.A.	2.9 million
Spain	1.6 million
France	1.3 million
Netherlands	500,00

(A) Explain TWO results of the European slave trade from Africa to the Americas.

(B) Explain ONE motivation for the European slave trade from Africa to the Americas.

Short-Answer Explanations

1. (A) A good response will include TWO of the results of the era of exploration. They can be social, economic, political, military, or religious results. Social results would include the decimation of the peoples of the Americas; the Columbian Exchange; African slavery in the Americas; the European dominance over the rest of the world for four centuries; the disappearance of many indigenous traditions, languages, legal systems, and lifestyles; European racism against the other peoples of the world; the European diaspora to the Americas and Asia; the intermixing of ethnic groups; and the spread of European languages, laws, and traditions. Political results could include the rise of European colonies around the world, the growing power of non-noble Europeans as their wealth increased, loss of indigenous control over their own lands, European conflicts over overseas possessions, the rise and fall of Spanish power, and European style governments emerging all over the world. Religious results may include the spread of Christianity, the growing European awareness of other religious beliefs, the rise of missionaries and missions, and reduced threats to Europe from Islam. The economic results may include rising European wealth, a higher standard of living in Europe, more social mobility for Europeans, loss of wealth for the other peoples of the world, availability of more goods in Europe, a growing slave trade, merchants rising in status, and growing flows of income into Europe.

    (B) A good explanation will look at ONE of the reasons that Europeans explored the world. These may include pursuit of wealth, curiosity about the rest of the world, the European belief in their superiority over all other peoples of the world, the desire to spread Christianity, the desire for freedom from European rigid class structures and legal codes, and the desire for adventure.

2. (A) A good response will include TWO of the results of the European slave trade. They can be social, economic, or political results. Social results would include the mixing of Africans with Native Americans and Europeans to create offspring of mixed race, the plantation culture emerging in the Americas, the belief that wealthy people in the Americas did not need to do any manual labor, the end of slavery of the indigenous peoples of the Americas, rising racism, religious opposition to slavery, and the long history of subjugating the descendants of Africans in the Americas. Political results could include the rising European influence on African politics, the rising power of Europe globally, wars for trade in the Atlantic and Caribbean, and race-based laws emerging. The economic results may include rising European wealth, a higher standard of living in Europe, a growing slave trade, merchants rising in status, the rising importance of African trade, the emergence of *Triangle Trade*, and flows of income growing in Europe.

    (B) A good explanation will explain ONE reason that Europeans brought African slaves to the Americas. These may include pursuit of wealth, the European belief in their superiority over all other peoples of the world, the writings from people like Bartolome de las Casas against enslaving Native Americans, the massive dying off of the Native Americans (90% within fifty years of Columbus's first voyage), the African resistance to European diseases, African knowledge of European style agriculture, and European racism.

PRACTICE MULTIPLE-CHOICE QUESTIONS

Questions 1 to 3 refer to the following passage.

Moreover, that no one may assume that the Israelites were peculiar in having kings over them who were established by God, note what is said in Ecclesiasticus: "God has given to every people its ruler, and Israel is manifestly reserved to him." He therefore governs all peoples and gives them their kings, although he governed Israel in a more intimate and obvious manner.

It appears from all this that the person of the king is sacred, and that to attack him in any way is sacrilege. . . .

But kings, although their power comes from on high, as has been said, should not regard themselves as masters of that power to use it at their pleasure; . . . they must employ it with fear and self-restraint, as a thing coming from God and of which God will demand an account. "Hear, O kings, and take heed, understand, judges of the earth, lend your ears, ye who hold the peoples under your sway, and delight to see the multitude that surround you. It is God who gives you the power. Your strength comes from the Most High, who will question your works and penetrate the depths of your . . . For God fears not the power of any one, because he made both great and small and he has care for both."

Kings should tremble then as they use the power God has granted them; and let them think how horrible is the sacrilege if they use for evil a power which comes from God.

—Bishop Jacques Benigne Bossuet (1627–1704)
passage from *Politics Derived from Holy Writ*

1. Bishop Jacques Bossuet, in his writing above, lays out the theoretical foundation for which of the following forms of sovereignty?

   (A)   Theocratic aristocracy
   (B)   Divine right of kings
   (C)   Constitutional monarchy
   (D)   Totalitarian control

2. Which of the following political philosophers would be most likely to agree with Bossuet about the proper power structure for a nation's government?

   (A)   Jean-Jacques Rousseau, who wrote *The Social Contract*
   (B)   Baron Montesquieu, who wrote *The Spirit of the Laws*
   (C)   Thomas Hobbes, who wrote *Leviathan*
   (D)   John Locke, who wrote *Two Treatises on Civil Government*

3. The most important governmental innovation of Cardinal Richelieu in France, who was an adherent of the ideas of Bishop Bossuet, was which of the following?

   (A)   The intendant system used to undermine noble power
   (B)   The creation of Versailles as a pleasure palace for the nobility
   (C)   The implementation of the *taille* on all French citizens
   (D)   The requirement that all French nobility study abroad for at least three years

Spanish Gold Exports from the Americas to Seville

Year	Gold Exported (kg)	Silver Exported (kg)
1501–1505	517	0
1536–1540	2,039	12,148
1551–1555	4,707	33,497
1581–1585	1,336	232,208
1611–1615	795	196,820
1641–1645	167	196,820

4. Which of the following can be proven by the chart above?

   (A) Silver imported to Seville slowly built up but peaked near the end of the sixteenth century.
   (B) The value of the silver imported was greater than that of the gold.
   (C) The Spanish purchased many imported goods with this gold and silver.
   (D) The value of the silver leaving Seville was greater than that of the gold.

5. Which of the following is the short-term, medium-term, and long-term results of the influx of precious metals seen in the chart above, in the correct chronological order?

   (A) Inflation, wealth generation, consumer economy
   (B) Wealth generation, market economy, consumer economy
   (C) Wealth generation, consumer economy, market economy
   (D) Market economy, wealth generation, inflation

6. Which of the following was the most important change brought on by the opening and expansion of transatlantic trade?

   (A) The drastic increase of wealth of the Europeans occurred at the expense of the rest of the world.
   (B) The increased political power of Europeans allowed them to dominate the entire world within a century.
   (C) The biological exchange between continents changed life globally.
   (D) The improvements in naval technology allowed Europeans to dominate world commerce and politics.

Multiple-Choice Explanations

1. **B**	3. **A**	5. **B**
2. **C**	4. **A**	6. **C**

1. (B)

(A) is wrong because Bossuet is arguing for a strong king who answers to God, not a government run by religion.

(B) is CORRECT because Bossuet laid the foundations for the divine right of kings theory of government that new monarchs used to consolidate all power within their realms.

(C) is wrong because Bossuet does not support any control other than God on the monarch.

(D) is wrong because Bossuet does not support a form of government that will not appear on the Earth for another almost 400 years when he wrote this.

2. (C)

(A) is wrong because Rousseau would completely disagree with Bossuet, as Rousseau supported rule by a legislature elected by the "general will of the people."

(B) is wrong because Montesquieu advocated dividing government into three branches, while Bossuet prefers all power in the hands of a monarch guided by God.

(C) is CORRECT because Hobbes and Bossuet agree that the alternative to a strong monarch is anarchy.

(D) is wrong because Locke believes in overthrowing tyrants if they do not preserve the natural rights of citizens.

3. (A)

(A) is CORRECT because the French intendant system of tax collectors, army recruiters, and other government bureaucrats took the governing power from the nobility and consolidated it in the hands of the king just as Bossuet advised.

(B) is wrong because, although Louis XIV's use of Versailles increased his power, Versailles was not created by Richelieu and it did not have nearly the impact on true power as the intendants did.

(C) is wrong because Richelieu did not reintroduce the *taille* on everyone because members of the first and second estates were exempt from taxation.

(D) is wrong because there was no requirement for French nobility to study abroad.

4. (A)

(A) is CORRECT because it is the only answer choice that the data given can support without other evidence.

(B) is wrong because it requires you to know the relative values of silver and gold, which are not given.

(C) is wrong because it requires you to know what the Spanish did with all of that gold, which is not given in the chart.

(D) is wrong because it requires you to know the relative values of silver and gold, which are not given.

5. **(B)**

(A) is wrong because inflation occurred after wealth generation, not before it.

(B) is CORRECT because first wealth was generated, creating a market economy, which eventually led the masses to use money and be paid in money, which was a factor that led to a consumer economy along with the desire to emulate the upper classes.

(C) is wrong because a society cannot develop a consumer economy without first creating a market economy.

(D) is wrong because wealth must be present in order to create a market economy.

6. **(C)**

(A) is wrong because, although the rise in European wealth and power changed the world a lot, of the choices given the biological exchange of foods, diseases, textiles, and even medicines had the greatest impact on daily lives of all peoples of the world.

(B) is wrong because, although the rise in European wealth and power changed the world a lot, of the choices given the biological exchange of foods, diseases, textiles, and even medicines has had the greatest impact on daily lives of all peoples of the world.

(C) is CORRECT because the biological exchange of foods, diseases, textiles, and even medicines has had the greatest impact—of perhaps any event in modern world history—on daily lives of all peoples of the world.

(D) is wrong because, although the rise in European naval power changed the world a lot, of the choices given the biological exchange of foods, diseases, textiles, and even medicines has had the greatest impact on daily lives of all peoples.

Time Period One (1450–1648): Practice Assessment

KEY CONCEPTS AND OVERVIEW

KEY CONCEPT 1.1 The worldview of European intellectuals shifted from one based on ecclesiastical and classical authority to one based primarily on inquiry and observation of the natural world.

KEY CONCEPT 1.2 The struggle for sovereignty within and among states resulted in varying degrees of political centralization.

KEY CONCEPT 1.3 Religious pluralism challenged the concept of a unified Europe.

KEY CONCEPT 1.4 Europeans explored and settled overseas territories, encountering and interacting with indigenous populations.

KEY CONCEPT 1.5 European society and the experiences of everyday life were increasingly shaped by commercial and agricultural capitalism, notwithstanding the persistence of medieval social and economic structures.

PRACTICE ASSESSMENT

Each time period concludes with a mini-test consisting of some multiple-choice questions, two short-answer questions, and two essay choices for which you should choose to write at least one answer. This is not so much to simulate an exam, which will have more questions and a Document-Based Question (DBQ), but to help you prepare for the types of questions seen on the exam and to allow you time to practice those skills. DBQs can be found in the Introduction to this book, in the two sample exams at the end of this book, and in the three online exams that accompany this book, which can be found at: *http://barronsbooks.com/AP/ap-european-hist/*. This assessment should take you about two hours. Detailed explanations of all questions follow the assessment.

TIME PERIOD ONE (1450–1648): PRACTICE ASSESSMENT

Section I, Part A

Multiple-Choice Questions (16 Questions)

> **Directions:** Please read the passages and then choose the most correct answer choice for each of the following questions.
>
> As demonstrated in the following examples, question sets will be organized around three to five questions that focus on a primary source, secondary source, or historical issue.

Questions 1 to 3 refer to the following excerpt:

Upon this a question arises: whether it be better to be loved than feared or feared than loved? It may be answered that one should wish to be both, but, because it is difficult to unite them in one person, is much safer to be feared than loved, when, of the two, either must be dispensed with.

Because this is to be asserted in general of men, that they are ungrateful, fickle, false, cowardly, covetous, and as long as you succeed they are yours entirely; they will offer you their blood, property, life and children, as is said above, when the need is far distant; but when it approaches they turn against you. And that prince who, relying entirely on their promises, has neglected other precautions, is ruined. Therefore, a prince, so long as he keeps his subjects united and loyal, ought not to mind the reproach of cruelty.

—Niccolo Machiavelli, *The Prince* (1515)

1. In what way does the passage above challenge the institutional power of the Roman Catholic Church?

   (A) It was a subtle attack on the corrupt leadership and power structure of the Roman Catholic Church.
   (B) It implied that a good leader had to be immoral and go against the teachings of the Roman Catholic Church at times in order to achieve his goals.
   (C) It implied a huge universe with many suns and planets and that the earth was not the center of the universe.
   (D) It portrayed human nature in a negative light, making it seem like humans were evil and beyond redemption.

2. By calling for a strong prince to unify Italy, Machiavelli was the major voice for which of the following movements?

   (A) A revival of the moral principles of the Greeks and Romans, who never confused politics and morality
   (B) A revival of civic humanist culture and a more secular model for political behavior
   (C) A movement toward divine right rule as the only qualification for leadership because of the concept of *realpolitik*
   (D) A movement away from divine right rule of kings in favor of joint rule by three branches of government that would share power

3. Some historians have claimed that Machiavelli's publication of *The Prince* in 1515 marked a turning point in history by stating which of the following?

   (A) A good ruler must strive to be both loved and feared.
   (B) A good ruler must not rely on the strength of mercenaries.
   (C) A good ruler must sometimes do something that is bad to achieve a goal that is good.
   (D) A good ruler must never trust his people but must decide what is best for the state himself.

Questions 4 to 6 refer to the following excerpt.

But I, blameless monk that I was, felt that before God I was a sinner with an extremely troubled conscience. I couldn't be sure that God was appeased by my satisfaction. I did not love, no, rather I hated the just God who punishes sinners. In silence, if I did not blaspheme, then certainly I grumbled vehemently and got angry at God. I said, "Isn't it enough that we miserable sinners, lost for all eternity because of original sin, are oppressed by every kind of calamity through the Ten Commandments? Why does God heap sorrow upon sorrow through the Gospel and through the Gospel threaten us with his justice and his wrath?" . . .

I meditated night and day on those words until at last, by the mercy of God, I paid attention to their context: "The justice of God is revealed in it, as it is written: 'The just person lives by faith.'" I began to understand that in this verse the justice of God is that by which the just person lives by a gift of God, which is by faith. I began to understand that this verse means that the justice of God is revealed through the Gospel, but it is a passive justice, i.e., that by which the merciful God justifies us by faith, as it is written: "The just person lives by faith." All at once I felt that I had been born again and entered into Paradise itself through open gates. Immediately I saw the whole of Scripture in a different light.

—Martin Luther, *The Tower Experience* (1519)

4. The passage above refers to which one of Martin Luther's different answers to age-old questions of faith?

   (A) Salvation is achieved through faith alone.
   (B) A church is the entire community of believers and the leadership of the church.
   (C) All work is sacred in the eyes of God.
   (D) All religious authority resides in the Bible.

5. Luther's explanation of his views on salvation and justification were supported by which of the following trends in literature at the time?

(A) Literature at the time was written in the vernacular.

(B) Satire was becoming prevalent.

(C) Individual literacy was decreasing.

(D) Christian humanism

6. How did the ideas of Luther, explained above, differ from the traditional teachings of the Roman Catholic Church?

(A) The Roman Catholic Church taught that all religious authority was held by the pope and his councils, whereas Luther stated that all authority resides in the Bible.

(B) The Roman Catholic Church taught that only holy warriors' work had merit in God's eyes while Luther stated that all work has merit in God's eyes.

(C) The Roman Catholic Church taught that salvation came from both faith and works, but Luther taught that salvation came from faith alone.

(D) The Roman Catholic Church taught that we are all flawed sinners who must suffer, and Luther taught that a very few were preordained to go to heaven.

Questions 7 to 9 refer to the following table.

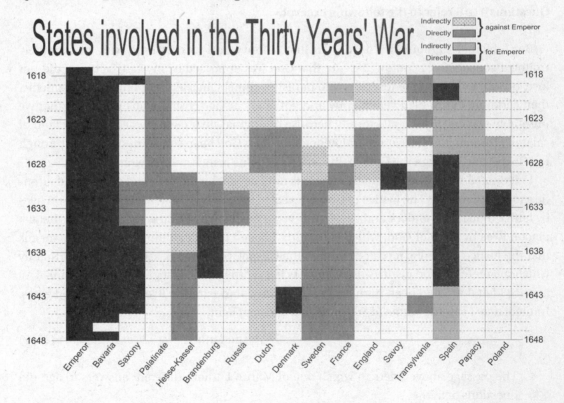

7. Which of the regions in the table above seems least affected by the Thirty Years' War?

(A) Bavaria
(B) Russia
(C) Sweden
(D) France

8. Which of the following trends can be observed in the table above?

(A) Over time, indirect participation increased for countries opposed to the Holy Roman Emperor.
(B) Over time, direct participation decreased for countries opposed to the Holy Roman Emperor.
(C) Direct participation peaked around 1630 for countries opposed to the Holy Roman Emperor.
(D) Over time, participation decreased for countries opposed to the Holy Roman Emperor.

9. The division and change seen in the table illustrate the many factors that helped cause and expand the Thirty Years' War, and are best summarized by which of the following?

(A) Religious conflict, dynastic conflict, power politics in the Holy Roman Empire, and mercantilism
(B) Religious conflict, dynastic conflict, power politics in the Holy Roman Empire, and rising French power
(C) Mercantilism, dynastic conflict, power politics in the Holy Roman Empire, and rising French power
(D) Slave trade, mercantilism, dynastic conflict, and power politics in the Holy Roman Empire

—*Estates General in Palais Bourbon, Paris.* By unidentified artist after a seventeenth century print. Published in *Magasin Pittoresque*, Paris, 1840.

10. Which of the following was most likely the topic of discussion at the meeting depicted above?

    (A) The doctrines of the Roman Catholic Church within France
    (B) The proper weapon to be used when fighting against the English
    (C) The regulations for which classes can wear which type of clothing and furs
    (D) Changing the levels of taxation and the laws within France

11. The meeting depicted in the print above included members of all three estates of the *Ancien Régime* in France but, in the seventeenth century, French political power was beginning to change in which of the following ways?

    (A) New monarchies laid the foundation for the centralized modern state, which witnessed monarchs taking power from the nobility and creating state bureaucracies.
    (B) New monarchies laid the foundation for the centralized modern state, which witnessed these New Monarchs giving greater power to their nobility to control the peasants in France.
    (C) New monarchies laid the foundation for the centralized modern state, which witnessed the rise of parliamentary power and the decline of the divine right monarch.
    (D) New monarchies laid the foundation for the centralized modern state, which witnessed the rise of popular sovereignty.

12. Which of the following paintings would a political historian be most likely to use to contrast this meeting with the famous meetings of the Estates General in 1789?

(A) *Liberty Leading the People* by Eugene Delacroix
(B) *The Tennis Court Oath* by Jacques-Louis David
(C) *The Storming of the Bastille* by Joseph Delaunay
(D) *The Consecration of the Emperor Napoleon and the Coronation of the Empress Josephine* by Jacques-Louis David

Questions 13 to 16 refer to the journal entries below.

October 12, 1492: Here follow the precise words of the Admiral: "As I saw that they were very friendly to us, and perceived that they could be much more easily converted to our holy faith by gentle means than by force, I presented them with some red caps, and strings of beads to wear upon the neck, and many other trifles of small value, wherewith they were much delighted, and became wonderfully attached to us.

October 13, 1492: At daybreak great multitudes of men came to the shore, all young and of fine shapes, very handsome. They were straight-limbed without exception, and not with prominent bellies but handsomely shaped. They came to the ship in canoes, made of a single trunk of a tree, wrought in a wonderful manner considering the country; some of them large enough to contain forty or forty-five men, others of different sizes down to those fitted to hold but a single person. They came loaded with balls of cotton, parrots, javelins, and other things too numerous to mention; these they exchanged for whatever we chose to give them. I was very attentive to them, and strove to learn if they had any gold. Seeing some of them with little bits of this metal hanging at their noses, I gathered from them by signs that by going southward or steering round the island in that direction, there would be found a king who possessed large vessels of gold, and in great quantities."

—*Journal entries from the first transatlantic voyage of Christopher Columbus, 1492*

13. Which of the following seems to be most emphasized by the journal excerpt above?

(A) The attractive healthy bodies and lifestyle of the natives
(B) The religion of the natives being able to be changed
(C) The trade items possible as well as the natives' willingness to trade
(D) The types and numbers of boats that the natives used when approaching

14. Christopher Columbus, who became famous for opening up transatlantic trade and "discovering" the New World, was most stimulated by which of the following motives, according to most historians?

(A) The desire to spread his religion in the world
(B) The desire to accumulate vast wealth through trade
(C) The desire to find spices to bring back to Europe
(D) The desire to become famous by discovering new parts of the world

15. Which of the following shifts in power in Europe occurred after the voyages of Columbus, Cabot, Hudson, Cabral, and others?

    (A) "New monarchs" began to rule the New World directly as a result of exploration.
    (B) The center of economic power in Europe shifted from the Mediterranean to the Atlantic states as a result of exploration.
    (C) The center of religious power shifted from Rome to Spain as a result of exploration.
    (D) The center of political power shifted to Louis XIV as a result of exploration.

16. Which of the following best explains why Columbus praised the natives in this reading but would later write about them very critically?

    (A) Columbus was just meeting them and got a good first impression, but later believed them to be evil.
    (B) In this journal entry, Columbus is trying to aggrandize his discovery, but later he will be explaining his failures as an administrator.
    (C) At first Columbus had many gifts to give to the natives, so they were nice to him, but later he made them work, so their relations soured.
    (D) At first Columbus thought he could get gold from them, but later when he found they had no gold, he had nothing good to say about them.

Section I

Part B: Short-Answer Questions

> **Directions:** Answer both questions completely.

1. Use the passage below and your knowledge of European history to answer all parts of the question that follows.

   The fire broke out in Germany between the states and princes Protestant and the house of Austria. The Catholic cause and the lot of the house of Austria engaged the king of Spain, who was the strongest branch of that stock. King James must needs be drawn in, both by common and particular interest: the religion which he professed and the state of his son-in-law, the Palatine elector, who became the principal part of those wars and the most unfortunate. It was high business to the whole Christian world, and the issue of it had main dependence upon the king of England, being the mightiest prince of the Protestant profession.

   The clouds gather thick in the German sky; jealousies and discontents arise between the Catholics and Lutherans, of the Confession of Augsburg. Both parties draw into confederacies and hold assemblies; the one seeking by the advantage of power to encroach and get ground, the other to stand their ground and hold their own. The potency of the house of Austria, a house devoted to the persecution of the reformed religion, became formidable. The old emperor Mathias declared his cousin, the archduke Ferdinand, to be his adopted son and successor, and caused him to be chosen and crowned king of Bohemia and Hungary.

   —English historian, John Rushworth, writing during the Thirty Years' War

   (A) Briefly identify and describe ONE cause of the conflict discussed in the passage.

   (B) Briefly identify and describe ONE result of the conflict discussed in the passage.

   (C) Briefly identify and describe how one country in early modern Europe, other than the Germanic states, dealt with the type of conflict discussed in the passage.

2. Answer all parts of the question.

   Historians have argued that the Italian Renaissance marked a turning point in Europe's understanding of the world.

   (A) Identify TWO pieces of evidence that support this argument and explain how each piece of evidence does so.

   (B) Identify ONE piece of evidence that undermines this argument and explain how the evidence does so.

Section II: Long-Essay Question

Directions: In this section, you will choose between one of two long-essay questions. The following questions are meant to illustrate an example of a question pairing that might appear in this section of the exam, in which both questions focus on the same historical thinking skill (in this case, comparison) but apply it to different time periods and/or topics.

LONG-ESSAY CHOICES

1. To what extent did the secular humanism of the Italian Renaissance reflect the modern world, while the Christian humanism of the Northern Renaissance compromised between medievalism and modernity?

2. Luther did not ask new questions, but offered new answers to old questions. What were these questions? What were Luther's answers and how did they contradict Roman Catholic answers?

ANSWER EXPLANATIONS

Multiple-Choice Explanations

1. **B**	5. **D**	9. **B**	13. **C**
2. **B**	6. **C**	10. **D**	14. **B**
3. **C**	7. **B**	11. **A**	15. **B**
4. **A**	8. **C**	12. **B**	16. **B**

1. **(B)**
   (A) is wrong because the quote does not directly or subtly criticize the Church leadership or power structure.
   (B) is CORRECT because the major conflict between Church teachings and those of the passage is about whether it is ever permissible to be bad.
   (C) is wrong because this work has nothing to do with the size of the universe.
   (D) is wrong because the Roman Catholic Church also taught that most people were bad and could only be saved through Jesus and the Church.

2. **(B)**
   (A) is wrong because the Greeks and Romans often confused politics with morality.
   (B) is CORRECT because Machiavelli was trying to revive the civic spirit of the Italian people in a secular way that had not been evident there for centuries.
   (C) is wrong because Machiavelli and the excerpt do not support divine right theory.
   (D) is wrong because Machiavelli did not suggest the division of power; Montesquieu did in the 1700s.

3. **(C)**

(A) is wrong because, although Machiavelli did state that, it had been stated many times before, while the advice to be a bad man was new.

(B) is wrong because that advice was also not new or shocking.

(C) is CORRECT because the advice to be a bad man to become a good ruler was revolutionary.

(D) is wrong because the idea of listening to one's subjects is central to Machiavelli's advice on not being hated.

4. **(A)**

(A) is CORRECT because the passage is mostly about salvation by faith alone.

(B) is wrong because the excerpt does not address the community of Christian believers.

(C) is wrong because the passage does not examine the sacred nature of work as much as it is about salvation through faith alone.

(D) is wrong because the passage is not about religious authority.

5. **(D)**

(A) is wrong because although the vernacular was used at the time, that is not the trend that is apparent in this reading.

(B) is wrong because the provided excerpt is not a satire.

(C) is wrong because this time less than one hundred years after the introduction of the printing press saw a RISE in literacy.

(D) is CORRECT because the use of evidence in the Bible to support ideas of changing faith patterns fits in with Christian humanism.

6. **(C)**

(A) is wrong because the passage is not related to religious authority.

(B) is wrong because the passage is not related to what work has merit, and also because the Roman Catholic Church also taught that religious work had merit.

(C) is CORRECT because the passage is about Luther's discovery that the Bible held evidence to support the idea that salvation came from faith alone.

(D) is wrong because Luther did not teach predestination; that was John Calvin's big idea.

7. **(B)**

(A) is wrong because Bavaria was directly involved for most of the war.

(B) is CORRECT because Russia was only indirectly involved for two years and was mostly unaffected.

(C) is wrong because Sweden was directly involved in the war for almost 20 years.

(D) is wrong because France was directly and indirectly involved in the war for over 20 years.

8. **(C)**

(A) is wrong because participation rose then fell for those directly involved in the war.

(B) is wrong because participation rose then fell for those directly involved in the war.

(C) is CORRECT because direct participation peaked around 1630.

(D) is wrong because participation rose then fell for those involved in the war.

9. **(B)**

(A) is wrong because mercantilism was not a major factor in this war.

(B) is CORRECT because religious conflict, dynastic conflict, power politics in the Holy Roman Empire, and rising French power were the major factors in causing and expanding the war.

(C) is wrong because mercantilism was not a major factor in this war.

(D) is wrong because mercantilism and the slave trade were not major factors in this war.

10. **(D)**

(A) is wrong because the Estates General was a French parliament that addressed the taxes and laws of the nation and stayed out of Church affairs.

(B) is wrong because the Estates General was a French parliament that addressed the taxes and laws of the nation and avoided weaponry and military decisions.

(C) is wrong because the Estates General was a French parliament that addressed the taxes and laws of the nation, and clothing regulations were mostly local and were becoming less prevalent at this time.

(D) is CORRECT because this is a meeting of the Estates General, which was the French parliament that approved laws and taxes.

11. **(A)**

(A) is CORRECT because new monarchs were associated with consolidating their own power by undercutting the nobility and building state bureaucracies.

(B) is wrong because during this era new monarchs took power from their nobility rather than gave it to them.

(C) is wrong because during the era of new monarchs parliaments lost power.

(D) is wrong because popular sovereignty did not gain power on a grand stage in Europe until after WWI.

12. **(B)**

(A) is wrong because *Liberty Leading the People* is about the revolutions of 1830 rather than the 1789 revolution, and it is not as political and therefore not as good a match as *The Tennis Court Oath*.

(B) is CORRECT because the analogy of the "Tennis Court Oath" as compared to the staid meeting of the Estates General discussed in the question makes a great political statement about the differences between the times depicted.

(C) is wrong because *The Storming of the Bastille* is not about a political meeting and therefore not as good a match as *The Tennis Court Oath*.

(D) is wrong because *The Consecration of the Emperor Napoleon* is about a coronation rather than a political meeting and therefore not as good a match as *The Tennis Court Oath*.

13. **(C)**

(A) is wrong because although the natives' physical description is given, their willingness to trade was mentioned twice, and the presence of gold was mentioned as a part of that, which is much more of the focus here.

(B) is wrong because although the natives' willingness to convert by kinder means is mentioned, the natives' willingness to trade is mentioned twice, and the presence of gold was mentioned as a part of that, which is much more of the focus here.

(C) is CORRECT because the natives' willingness to trade is mentioned twice and the presence of gold was mentioned as a part of that.

(D) is wrong because although the natives' boats were mentioned, the natives' willingness to trade was mentioned twice, and the presence of gold was mentioned as a part of that, which is much more of the focus here.

14. **(B)**

(A) is wrong because although religion was a guiding force for Columbus, he went to find trade routes from which he wanted to profit, not to find unknown peoples to convert to Roman Catholicism.

(B) is CORRECT because he went to find trade routes to Asia, which he wanted to use to make huge profits from trade.

(C) is wrong because spices were but a means to the ends, which was the wealth gained from trade.

(D) is wrong because he had no expectation to find a new world, but to find Asia.

15. **(B)**

(A) is wrong because although the new monarchs did rise to power during this era, it was not because of exploration in any way.

(B) is CORRECT because while European trade had been centered in the Mediterranean with the Italians making huge profits, it slowed after the Ottomans took Constantinople/Istanbul in 1453, and the Spanish, Portuguese, then later the Dutch and English began to dominate global trade and wealth.

(C) is wrong because religious power in Europe was shattered after the Protestant Reformation, but the center of Roman Catholic power remained in Rome.

(D) is wrong because the reign of Louis XIV was not affected at all by the great explorers.

16. **(B)**

(A) is wrong because it is an oversimplification and is not supported by historical evidence.

(B) is CORRECT because both can be easily explained as his motives for writing both things.

(C) is wrong because Columbus continued to give objects to the natives after he conquered them.

(D) is wrong because Columbus did not write critically about them just because of a lack of gold, but because he was trying to excuse his decimation of the Taino Indians.

Short-Answer Explanations

1. (A)   A good response would explain how two pieces of evidence support the argument that the Italian Renaissance marked a turning point in Europe's understanding of the world, such as: Italian intellectual hallmarks (individualism, humanism, and secularism); new methods of gathering information; increased interaction with the rest of the world; artistic achievement; reorganization of society and governments, such as oli-

garchies and republics; the rise of the merchant elite; the rising importance of wealth; increased emphasis on perfection; and a revival of Greco-Roman political ideas.

(B)   A good response would explain how one piece of evidence undermines the argument that the Italian Renaissance marked a turning point in Europe's understanding of the world, such as: Europe was already increasing trade during the Crusades; these were not new ideas but a revival of old ideas from Greece and Rome; the Renaissance was primarily an artistic movement; the Renaissance affected only the upper classes; the Renaissance era was still a mostly medieval time; religion was able to block the advance of knowledge in Italy, such as with Galileo; and Italy became the center of the Counter-Reformation.

2.   (A)   A good response would describe one of several possible causes of the Thirty Years' War, such as: political conflict in Bohemia, the Germanic states, and other parts of the Austrian Empire; religious conflict between Protestants and Roman Catholics; the use of religion by nobility as a tool of resistance against the Austrian emperor, who was also the Holy Roman Emperor; the emergence of new Protestant sects, such as Calvinists and Presbyterians; the Defenestrations of Prague; and a power struggle between the Bohemian nobility and the Austrian emperor.

(B)   A good response would describe one of several possible results of the Thirty Years' War, such as: French ascendance in international power; the Germanic Princes' ability to choose the religion of their subjects, including Calvinism; the deterioration of the role of the Holy Roman Emperor and the Holy Roman Empire; destruction of Germany and a lost generation of German men; Descartes conceived of analytical geometry as a soldier in this conflict; and German resentment of France will begin to grow.

(C)   A good response would describe one strong example of how a country in early modern Europe, other than Germany, dealt with the conflict between Protestantism and Roman Catholicism, such as: Queen Elizabeth I of England making the Elizabethan Settlement; the French War of the Three Henrys leading to the Edict of Nantes, which was later revoked by Louis XIV; the Dutch, who fought the Spanish invasion with help from England and formed a constitutional government; the English, who had a civil war then restored the Stuarts only to eject them in the Glorious Revolution of 1689; or the Russians, who had the czar preserve the national religion thus avoiding conflict.

Long-Essay Question Sample Answers and Explanations

Question 1

To what extent did the secular humanism of the Italian Renaissance reflect the modern world, while the Christian humanism of the Northern Renaissance compromised between medievalism and modernity?

COMMENTS ON QUESTION 1

Follow the "Simple Procedures" for writing an essay. (See page 35.)

- First, *What does the question want to know?* The best way to approach a question like this one, which is laden with terms and concepts, is to identify each term and concept and then, and only then, determine whether the statement can more easily be defended or refuted.

- Next, decide which skill is being tested. This is a COMPARE skill question, so be sure to describe similarities and differences between the secular humanism of the Italian Renaissance and the Christian humanism of the Northern Renaissance as well as explain how they are similar and different by providing specific examples and tying these to modernity and medievalism.

- Now try to use the themes in the *AP European History Curriculum Framework* such as objective knowledge and subjective visions or individuals and society and skills such as the argumentation skill.

  - What was the Italian Renaissance? Did it occur before or after the Northern Renaissance? Did one influence the other? What did they have in common? How did they differ?
  - What is "secular humanism?" How did it draw on ideas from the ancient world while adapting them to the unique historical circumstances of fifteenth-century Italy?
  - What is "Christian humanism?" How was it influenced by secular humanism and by Christian tradition?
  - What is meant by "medievalism" and "modernity?" Do the attitudes expressed in secular humanism come closer to the attitudes of our world than to those of Christian humanism? Is an idea that "reflects" a future development one of that development's causes?

- Third: *What do you know about it?* Once you have answers to these questions, the choice of whether to defend or refute the statement is actually made for you. If the secular humanism of the Italian Renaissance is significantly different from the Christian humanism of the north, you can measure which more closely reflected the cultural, intellectual, and economical changes that followed, and then you can build a strong case for defense or refutation of the statement.

- Finally: *How would you put it into words?* Remember, since history rarely offers "either/or" simplicities, sometimes the best approach to a "*defend or refute*" question is to argue both sides. Be careful, though, not to make your essay a circle of contradictions. State your defenses and refutations clearly, and let your evidence point to the sophistication of your understanding.

SAMPLE ANSWER

In many ways the secular humanism of the Italian Renaissance began the modern era through an emphasis on finding truths, embracing the beauty of humanity, and the ability of each person to improve himself while the Christian humanism of the Northern Renaissance was a compromise between medievalism and modernity due to its emphasis on Christianity as the root of truth, medieval governmental institutions, and spiritual outlook, but both were tied to the medieval world through their lack of technology and the ability to digest new outlooks.

The Italian Renaissance was a blossoming of knowledge and belief in humanity and its ability to understand and improve the world. The revival of ancient knowledge brought in from growing international trade networks helped cause a flurry of intellectual growth. The Italian interaction with other cultures of the world through trade networks also caused them to question previously held beliefs. The growing wealth gained from this trade made many families wealthier but they still lacked political power. The growing power of the banking families such as the Medici also displayed how economic power could become political power during this period and also led to new ways of examining political power such as Machiavelli's The Prince, which examined how to rule effectively rather than morally and exposed new truths in that realm. Simultaneously, other thinkers such as Michelangelo and Masaccio were revolutionizing painting by examining anatomy and depicting it accurately, thus reviving the ideal of the beauty of humans. Leonardo Da Vinci also expressed this view in works such as the Vitruvian Man, but then expanded upon that by designing flying machines and other technology that reeks of modernity. Just after that, Galileo helped support the claims of Copernicus that the Earth is not the center of the universe, revealing new truths in science. He also explained inertia and began the idea of experimentation, truly ushering in the modern era in that aspect. When all of this is combined with the emphasis on secularism seen by the leaders of this society such as Pope Julius II, or Lorenzo de' Medici, and the growth of the individual as a separate entity as depicted in portraits from the Mona Lisa to Titian's nudes, the idea that the Italian Renaissance began modernity seems clearly supported.

The Northern Renaissance sought to reform human institutions through Christian morality. This attempt at reform seems clearly modern, yet the reliance on Christianity to do so is tied to the medieval era. While Northern Europe did embrace science and experimentation, they clung to a deep religious life that caused many conflicts and much hardship in the region. The Northern Renaissance saw an incredible growth in intellectual pursuits. The spread of the printing press from the Germanic states outward allowed ideas to be exchanged more easily. The skills of the artists in depicting people and interiors such as those of Albrecht Durer and Johannes Vermeer were notable, but the nudes of Italy were absent from this more prudish work. Much of the art echoed that of Van Eyck or Bosch that held moral messages. The work of Kepler and others advanced astronomy which was modern, but much of Northern Europe was still living a feudal life. The wars of religion such as the War of the Three Henrys, and the Thirty Years' War were also somewhat dynastic but also displayed the medieval religious ethic of proselytization. The brutality of these wars also displays medieval tendencies.

In reality both Northern Europe and Italy had barbaric episodes during their Renaissance periods. In Italy, the zealotry of Father Niccolo Savonarola led to the bonfires of the vanities, in which many secular items such as Botticelli's paintings were burned to protest secularism, and eventually led to his being burned on a fire and excommunicated as a reaction against his criticisms of secularism. Later, the Roman Catholic Church condemned Galileo for supporting Copernicus' theories and threatened him with torture which is very medieval. The zealotry of the wars of religion in Northern Europe during the Renaissance there was also clearly medieval as were the actions of some leaders such as Calvin and Cromwell when they gained power in Geneva and England respectively.

While the assertion is mostly true, the fact that Europe was emerging from the medieval era ties both the Northern Renaissance and the Italian Renaissance to Medieval outlooks and actions, but the Italian Renaissance was in the end more modern than anything that had come before it, and the Northern Renaissance did have some modern aspects, and the work of Northern Renaissance thinkers such as Sir Francis Bacon and Renee Descartes eventually led to the most modern idea of the era, the scientific method.

EVALUATE THE SAMPLE ANSWER

Now go back and look at the rubric. It is clear that this essay fulfills all the requirements for a score of 6 on the rubric. The essay answers all parts of the question thoroughly with concrete evidence, at length with a well-balanced essay. The extra concrete support gets this essay a score of 6. The thesis point is certainly earned. The essay definitely describes the similarities and differences between the humanism of Northern Europe and that of Italy and explains the reasons for the similarities and differences, citing specific information by using historical reasoning to explain how evidence is interrelated and qualifies the argument that addresses the entirety of the question, earning all Evidence points and all Analysis and Reasoning points. The essay certainly earns the points for contextualization because it explains how the context of the era and geography influenced the topic of the question.

RATER'S COMMENTS ON THE SAMPLE ANSWER

6—Extremely Well Qualified

This essay is very mature and nuanced and could only be crafted in the time allotted by one who has mastered the subject. It is a good example of what will stand out to a reader, and it clearly answers the question with strong, specific supporting evidence. This is an expertly crafted essay that challenges the generalizations of the period and addresses the vocabulary of the question cogently. It uses numerous references to figures of the time and their ideas to support the thesis. Remember that taking the harder path on a Free Response Question can be very rewarding. The reader will reward the writer's intellectual approach in distinguishing between generalization and fact. Most importantly, this essay makes a thesis that the proposed statement is correct and supports it with strong evidence from many sources.

Question 2

Luther did not ask new questions, but offered new answers to old questions. What were these questions? What were Luther's answers, and how did they contradict Roman Catholic answers?

COMMENTS ON QUESTION 2

- Follow the "Simple Procedures" for writing an essay. (See page 35.)
- First: *What does the question want to know?* List the questions, Luther's answers, and the Roman Catholic Church's answers. Assess the answers for similarities and contradictions.
- Next, you must decide: *Which skill is being tested?* This is a COMPARE skill question, so be sure to describe similarities and differences between the answers offered by Luther and those of the Church, as well as explain reasons for the similarities and differences by providing specific examples of how they are similar and of different interpretations of the Christian faith—tying those differences to other historical developments, such as the reading revolution.
- Third: *What do you know about it?* You need to know that the basic questions are: How is salvation achieved? What are the sacraments? Where does religious authority reside? What is the Church? What kind of miracle occurs during mass? The different answers to these questions must be examined for Luther and for the Roman Catholic Church.
- Finally: *How would you put it into words?* This essay lends itself to easy paragraphs for each of the questions of faith examined. If you write a thesis explaining that Luther's different answers to basic questions of religion led him to challenge the Roman Catholic Church, and then explain each question in its own paragraph, the structure will be strong. You should examine how these different answers were appealing enough to Luther and northern Europe to bring about the Protestant Reformation.

SAMPLE ANSWER

In a time when faith and the Church were the central institutions of society, most people were concerned with salvation. Martin Luther's concern for his own salvation and that of others caused him to come to different conclusions than the Roman Catholic Church on the questions: How is salvation achieved? What are the sacraments?

Where does religious authority reside? What is the church? What kind of miracle occurs during mass? Luther's well-reasoned answers to these age-old questions contradicted the Church. His answers along with the increase in general knowledge and curiosity of the Renaissance and political pressures brought on a revolution in the practice of Christianity.

The Roman Catholic Church had always taught that salvation was achieved through both faith in the Holy Trinity and good works. Luther, who had contradicted his father by becoming a member of the clergy, (thus breaking the commandment to honor thy father), came to the conclusion that eternal salvation could come through faith alone. He believed that unwavering faith would lead one to a life of good work and was enough to achieve salvation. The Church taught that good works, such as donating to the Church or buying indulgences, could achieve salvation for a person. Luther's moral opposition to the practice of indulgences and John Tetzel's sale of them to his students prompted Luther to write his 95 Theses.

Another point that Luther contradicted the Church on was the question of what were the holy sacraments. Luther believed in baptism, the sacrament of the altar, and absolution as being the only acts that were truly sacraments while there are four other Roman Catholic ones according to Luther: confirmation, anointing of the sick, Holy Orders, and matrimony. Luther radically dismissed matrimony as having a less visible link to the Holy Spirit.

The third disagreement between Luther and the Church revolved around where religious authority rests. Luther stated that all religious authority came from the bible, whereas Catholicism taught that religious authority comes from the bible and papal/religious decrees. Luther stated in his debates with Eyck that unless someone would show him a place in the bible that justified papal decrees, he would believe that all religious authority resides in the bible. This contradiction was a major justification for many other Protestant sects which developed shortly after Lutheranism.

The fourth contradiction Luther made with Roman Catholicism was about the definition of the Church. Catholicism teaches that the buildings and the clergy define the Church. Luther defined his church as the community of Christian believers. This community was another important innovation that led many to embrace new forms of Protestantism.

The fifth and final contradiction was the difference between transubstantiation and consubstantiation. Roman Catholicism taught transubstantiation, the act during the Eucharist when the bread and wine become the actual body of Christ, while Luther taught consubstantiation, in which the bread and wine became the spirit of Christ.

Before Luther shared his revolutionary new answers to these important questions of Christian faith, there was a monopoly on religious power in Western Europe. After Martin Luther gained political support of the German princes including Frederick the elector of Saxony, the Roman Catholic Church was no longer the Church, but a church among many on the continent.

EVALUATE THE SAMPLE ANSWER

Now go back and look at the rubric. It is clear that this essay fulfills all the requirements for a score 6 on the rubric. The essay answers all parts of the question thoroughly with concrete evidence, at length, with a well-balanced essay. The thesis is worthy of earning the thesis point. The essay clearly describes the similarities and differences, explains reasons for these similarities and differences, and evaluates the historical significance of these developments. It also uses historical reasoning to explain the relationships between the evidence presented and corroborates the argument with evidence and reasoning, earning both Contextualization points. The essay addresses the question clearly and concisely with specific examples of relevant evidence and utilizes that evidence to effectively substantiate the thesis. The extra concrete support draws on appropriate ideas and methods from different fields of inquiry.

RATER'S COMMENTS ON THE SAMPLE ANSWER

6—Extremely Well Qualified

This answer could certainly have been written in the time allotted, and it answered all parts of a multifaceted question. This essay explained the significance of the conflicts of thought between Luther and the Roman Catholic Church, as well as how these conflicts led to the splintering of the Church in Western Europe. The indignation of Luther with the sale of indulgences is noted, but not emphasized unduly. The essay also does not write about the Protestant Reformation as solely a religious movement, but gives credit to the political and social factors that also played roles in ushering it in.

The essay structure was logical and allowed for a quick, clear progress through a question that requires many tasks. The tasks included stating the questions, answering them for both Luther and Roman Catholicism, and analyzing the conflicts in those questions and the long-term results of those conflicts. The introduction and conclusion of this essay are particularly strong, hitting the reader hard at both the start and end to make an impact.

Although this is a very strong essay, it did not cover any other Protestant faiths or leaders, and could have benefitted from showing the pent-up religious questioning that Luther unleashed. Although it was not required for this essay, some readers may feel more confident giving higher marks to essays that show more historical perspective.

Time Period Two:
c. 1649 to c. 1815

KEY CONCEPTS AND OVERVIEW

KEY CONCEPT 2.1 Different models of political sovereignty affected the relationship among states and between states and individuals.

KEY CONCEPT 2.2 The expansion of European commerce accelerated the growth of a worldwide economic network.

KEY CONCEPT 2.3 The popularization and dissemination of the Scientific Revolution and the application of its methods to political, social, and ethical issues led to an increased, although not unchallenged, emphasis on reason in European culture.

KEY CONCEPT 2.4 The experiences of everyday life were shaped by demographic, environmental, medical, and technological changes.

TIME PERIOD OVERVIEW

This time period examines the further growth of Europe's institutions, power, intellectual progress, and economy to verge on becoming the dominant continent in the world. It examines the expansion of global trade, multiple religious truths being accepted, the conflict between divine right monarchy and parliamentary power, and the importance of the emergence of capitalism as Europe increasingly interacted with the rest of the world. This time period includes the traditional delineations of the following eras:

The Age of Louis XIV
The Enlightenment
Mercantilism and the Rise of Capitalism
The American and French Revolutions
Napoleonic Europe and the Congress of Vienna
The Emergence of Industrialization and Urbanization

These traditional delineations do overlap in many ways, and the themes within them as stated above in the key concepts can be seen woven between the next two chapters of this book. Major challenges to periodization in this time period include the emergence of proto-industrialization or the "putting-out" system and the proliferation of the enclosure movement. These conditions lead to industrialization, which began in this time period with James Watt's invention of the condensing chamber steam engine by 1775, but has its most significant impact during the third time period. As a result, *industrialization*, which crosses time periods, will be covered entirely in Period 2. The constitutional struggles in England and the rise of powerful monarchs like Louis XIV began in Period 1, but will reach their apogee during the second time period. The slow and erratic natures of the spread of the enclosure movement, proto-industrialization, the evolution of monarchical power, and true industrialization pose significant challenges to comprehending competing models of periodization during this second time period.

SPECIAL NOTE ON PERIODIZATION

The third chapter of this section presents a problem to the historian. The AP European History Curriculum Framework presents a split in time periods in 1815, which makes a lot of sense for political history as that is the date of the fall of Napoleon and the rise of the alliance system first put in place by Metternich, which was later altered by Bismarck. However, **the Industrial Revolution does not fit nicely into that division.** While war was raging across the continent, the British were undergoing the start of an industrial revolution that would enable them to gain political and economic power. This revolution continued to occur throughout the nineteenth century and many of its impacts were felt in the decades following 1815.

For that reason, this book will present the Industrial Revolution in **one chapter** in order to preserve the narrative of the historical movement and to encourage you to examine periodization more critically. Historians construct and debate different, sometimes competing, models of periodization; the choice of specific turning points or starting and ending dates might accord a higher value to one narrative, region, or group than to another. If you are to master this skill, then you need to see competing models of periodization. To preserve the continuity of the subject, the Industrial Revolution will be covered entirely in Chapter 6, although much of the content covered is included in Period 3 by the College Board. The chapter will make clear delineations of which material belongs in which time period to help you with the skill of periodization.

Additionally, because the College Board prepares questions on the exam that use one prompt, but come from different time periods, this section will also help you prepare for that outcome better.

The Eighteenth Century: The Expansion of Europe and the Enlightenment

4

KEY TERMS/PEOPLE

→ MERCANTILISM
→ ADAM SMITH
→ FRANCIS BACON
→ RENÉ DESCARTES
→ DISCOURSE ON METHOD
→ NICOLAUS COPERNICUS
→ GALILEO GALILEI
→ ISAAC NEWTON
→ JOHANNES KEPLER
→ SEVEN YEARS' WAR
→ CAPITALISM
→ DEISM
→ SCIENTIFIC REVOLUTION
→ THE ENLIGHTENMENT
→ MADAME GEOFFRIN
→ VOLTAIRE
→ JEAN-JACQUES ROUSSEAU
→ BARON DE MONTESQUIEU

→ DENIS DIDEROT
→ FRANCOIS QUESNAY
→ PHYSIOCRATS
→ MIDDLE PASSAGE
→ TRIANGLE TRADE
→ PLANTATION SYSTEM
→ MARY WOLLSTONECRAFT
→ LOUIS XIV
→ FREDERICK II (THE GREAT)
→ JOSEPH II
→ PHILIP II
→ PETER I (THE GREAT)
→ MARIA THERESA
→ FREDERICK WILLIAM I
→ WAR OF SPANISH SUCCESSION
→ NINE YEARS' WAR
→ CATHERINE II (THE GREAT)

OVERVIEW

An agricultural revolution took place during the later years of the seventeenth century and through the eighteenth century. The traditional "open-field" system, an utterly inefficient method of agricultural production, was replaced by "enclosure," and despite the social cost, productivity increased dramatically. New foods and a disappearance of the plague fostered rapid population growth. An Atlantic economy, built on trade between Europe (primarily England, France, and Holland) and the Americas benefited both Europe and the colonies economically and socially. A series of conflicts over imperial possessions broke out among the leading European competitors during the eighteenth century, culminating in the French and Indian War in North America (the Seven Years' War on the continent) and the American Revolution.

From the end of the fifteenth century to the beginning of the eighteenth, the newly acquired interaction between Europe and the New World and the opening of the Atlantic to exploration and colonization changed the economy of Europe. Mercantilism became the prevailing economic system of the growing nation-states. Inflation, brought about by the stores of gold and silver expropriated from the New World, led to an increase in trade and manufacture that encouraged the growth of early capitalism. As economic activity shifted from the Mediterranean to the Atlantic, the Italian city-states declined as trading middlemen between

Europe and the near and Far East that they had controlled through their interaction with the Byzantine empire and later the Ottomans. Portugal and Spain became the major powers of the sixteenth century—the Netherlands, France, and England of the seventeenth.

The impact of science on the modern world is immeasurable. If the "Greeks had said it all" two thousand years earlier, the Renaissance Europeans rediscovered, evaluated, and elaborated or contradicted the ideas of Aristotle, Ptolemy, and other thinkers. Observation took precedence over tradition. To find out how many teeth a horse had, medieval academics scoured ancient texts to appeal to authority; modern thinkers opened the horse's mouth.

The sixteenth and seventeenth centuries saw the fruition of Renaissance individualism in religion and thought. Luther and the Protestants questioned the traditions of the Catholic Church and rebelled; Copernicus, Galileo, and Newton subjected the theories of Aristotle and Ptolemy to the inductive method and redefined the natural world. The habit of skepticism, which the Renaissance re-introduced and the Reformation strengthened, was science's driving force.

This skepticism gave rise to rationalism, the concept that human reason could uncover the natural laws that govern the universe and humankind itself. Inspired by the revolutionary theories of sixteenth and seventeenth century astronomy and physics, European thinkers ceased to be swayed by medieval superstition, by a belief in miracles, and by blind acceptance of tradition. Rationalism gave rise to the eighteenth century Enlightenment, whose philosophers or *philosophes* argued that humans could discover the immutable laws of the universe through the light of reason, and therefore human progress was inevitable. Critics of the status quo, they commented on the political, economic, and social ills of society and offered designs for the betterment of humanity. Their optimism and impatience aroused the forces for change and contributed to the French Revolution.

THE EXPANSION OF EUROPE

(Abbreviated version also found in Chapter 3.)

The *open-field system*, used during the Middle Ages(400 B.C.E–1450 B.C.E.), divided the arable land available to a farming community into narrow strips, which were designated to the individual families of the community. Due to a lack of chemical fertilizers and ignorance about nitrogen-fixing crops, a large portion of the community's land lay fallow.

- The *Enclosure Movement* in England, during the late seventeenth and the eighteenth centuries, fenced off the open fields to enable large landowners to employ crop rotation.

  - By planting nitrogen-fixing crops, such as beans and certain grasses, in soil that had been used for other crops, the soil remained fertile and little land lay fallow.
  - Many small or inefficient farmers were displaced to the towns and cities, but ultimately, food production rose dramatically.

- This *Agricultural Revolution* included selective breeding of animals, utilization of fertilizer, rotating crops, and generally improving the land for farming.

  - It resulted in huge crop yields and surpluses of food, which freed up labor and allowed population to rise.

- A greater variety of foods and the introduction of foods from the New World, specifically the potato, improved general nutrition and contributed, along with the disappearance of the plague, to a dramatic increase in population.

- Except for the development of the smallpox vaccine in the late eighteenth century, the crude and often dangerous medical practices of the day contributed little to the health and longevity of the people.
- The disappearance of the plague combined with better food production encouraged the emergence of consumerism and leisure activities for the masses such as coffee houses and the theater.
- The Enclosure Movement and increased agricultural production led many to move to cities to look for economic advancement, starting the trend of *urbanization* that continued to build into the twentieth century.

    - This increased urbanization, changed marriage patterns, and led to more illegitimate births toward the end of the eighteenth century.
    - As people became more crowded, they developed a new sense of privacy and built homes and read books that reinforced those ideas.

- Labor and trade in commodities were increasingly freed from traditional restrictions imposed by governments and corporate entities through the advent of market-driven wages and prices.
- *Mercantilism* was a system developed by various European states to guarantee a favorable balance of trade with other European nations or with their American colonies.

    - By creating an imbalance of exports over imports, the difference was made up in gold or silver payments.
    - Mercantilism was pursued as an attempt to get precious metals from indigenous peoples to pay for the costs of maintaining standing armies and government bureaucracies.

- Competition for colonies and for hegemony on the continent culminated in the *Seven Years' War* (1756–1763) fought by Britain and its allies against France and its allies.

    - The Seven Years' War was the first war that the Europeans fought on multiple continents with battles in North America, Europe, and Asia.
    - The British won a decisive battle against the French in India at the *Battle of Plassey* in 1757, which led to British dominance of India until after World War II.
    - The war resulted in the loss of France's North American possessions and in the growing independence of the British North American colonies.

- Mercantilism was largely discredited by the economic liberalism of *Adam Smith*, who argued that free competition, limited government regulation, and individual self-interest expressed through a supply-and-demand market system would foster economic growth.

MERCANTILISM AND THE RISE OF CAPITALISM

The Commercial Revolution

For over 150 years after Columbus "discovered" the Americas for the Europeans, thousands of tons of silver and nearly two hundred tons of gold came to Spain from the riches of the conquered Native Americans and from the mines established by the Spanish colonials. *Inflation,* *"too much money chasing too few goods,"* resulted because while the money supply had vastly increased, productivity had remained stable, giving money reduced purchasing power.

- The *inflation stimulated production*, though, because craftsmen, merchants, and manufacturers could get good prices for their products. The middle class, the bourgeoisie, acquired much of this wealth by trading and manufacturing, and their political influence and social status increased.
- Peasant farmers benefited when their surplus yields could be turned into *cash crops*. The nobility, whose income was based on feudal rents and fees, actually suffered a diminishing standard of living in this inflationary economy.
- The rise in population and the flight of entrepreneurs and industrious people to the New World further exacerbated this inflation as industry in Spain declined and new opportunities for the middle classes to make money emerged.
- The transatlantic slave-labor system expanded in the seventeenth and eighteenth centuries as demand for New World products increased.

  - Examples of this system include the Triangle Trade, Middle Passage, and the plantation system developed by Europeans in their colonies.
  - The Middle Passage was the brutal journey by ship from Africa to the New World that killed as much as 50 percent of the slave cargo.

The Rise of Capitalism

"Capital" is another term for money used as an investment; instead of investing labor, an individual invests capital in some venture in order to make a profit. The bourgeoisie, having accumulated more money than was needed to maintain a subsistence standard of living in seventeenth and eighteenth century society, used money to make money.

- They invested in *chartered companies* that were given a monopoly on trading rights by nations such as Britain and the Netherlands within a certain area.
- *Joint-stock companies* (forerunners of modern corporations), which sold shares of stock publically in order to raise large amounts for various ventures, provided *limited liability* to the shareholders, and offered a profitable return for the original investment.
- In the bourse, a kind of stock exchange, profit made from investment enabled more investment.
- Private banks were able to turn private savings into venture capital that allowed investment in overseas trade and other capitalist ventures such as the first factories.
- New definitions of property rights such as limited liability for owners of stocks and protections against the confiscation of property due to bad stock investments encouraged greater investment.
- Insurance companies emerged to make overseas trade less risky.
- The Bank of England was founded to provide venture capital for English firms.
- The expansion of money created prosperity, advanced science and technology, and supported the growth of the nation-state.
- The rise in wealth led first to the emergence of a market economy and eventually to the emergence of a consumer economy, then a consumer society after World War II.

  - Overseas products such as silk, sugar, tea, tobacco, rum, and coffee led to the emergence of a consumer culture.

Mercantilism

The monarchs of the early modern period needed money to maintain the standing armies that would dominate the powerful nobles of the realm and protect the state against foreign enemies. The Commercial Revolution and the growth of capitalism enriched a sizable segment of the population; personal riches translated into good tax revenues.

Mercantilism prevailed in the seventeenth century and well into the eighteenth century as an economic policy, because it seemed to offer a way for the monarchs of Europe to consolidate their centralized authority.

THE THEORY

- A nation's wealth was measured by the amount of precious metals it had accumulated *(bullionism)* rather than by its productivity.
- Idea is often credited to Jean Baptiste Colbert, the finance minister of Louis XIV.
- A *favorable balance of trade* (exports exceed imports) increases the flow of gold and silver into the national economy, and therefore increases the store of precious metals.
- Overseas colonies supplied the *mother country* with essential raw materials for manufacture and trade.
- Essential industries: manufacturing for the national defense or making a product unique to the nation and valuable in trade were encouraged through subsidies and tax credits.
- The goal of mercantilism is national economic self-sufficiency.

Overseas colonization (old imperialism) was encouraged by the policy of mercantilism.

- Spain and Portugal, following up on the momentum of their early explorations to Asia around the African continent and to the Americas across the Atlantic, monopolized colonization in the sixteenth century.
- By the seventeenth century, the balance had shifted to the Dutch, French, and British, whose internal disorders of the previous century had stabilized and whose inroads in Asia and North America overcame the supremacy of the Spanish and Portuguese.
- The British colonial empire far surpassed that of any other European nation because its colonies attracted proportionately more of its subjects for settlement.

  - Later, a number of them became powerful independent states: the United States, India, Canada, Australia, and a number of other nations in Asia and Africa, but for a time, all of those modern nations were a part of the British empire.

The variety and volume of printed material grew enormously during this period in spite of state and Church censorship. The literate reading public grew exponentially as well, which helped lead to the development of public opinion. Coffeehouses, salons, lending libraries, and new academies of learning helped develop this new reading audience. Some of what they read included *almanacs*, newspapers, other periodicals, pamphlets, and, of course, Denis Diderot's *Encyclopédie*.

THE ENLIGHTENMENT

The towering giant of the Scientific Revolution was an Englishman who wrote, "If I have seen further it is by standing on the shoulders of giants," referring to Galileo (1564–1642) whose work before his made scientific investigation into astral physics possible. If Copernicus (1473–1543) shook the medieval conception of Christianity to its foundations, the work of *Isaac Newton* (1642–1727) not only tested the notion of God's intervention in human affairs, but also established the ascendancy of science in the modern world.

■ Newton demonstrated that natural laws of motion account for the movement of heavenly bodies and earthly objects.

  – These laws are unchangeable and predictable.
  – God's active participation is not needed to explain the operations of the forces of nature, a repudiation of medieval belief.
  – Newton went on to chair the Royal Society of London where his status as the preeminent thinker of his day made England the center of scientific thought for a short while.

■ Newton's work in astronomy and physics convinced European thinkers that human reason, unaided by the tenets and rituals of religion, could uncover the immutable laws of nature.

■ An Englishman, Newton, inspired the Enlightenment; a group of Frenchmen, the *philosophes*, shaped it.

  – The *philosophes*, who were actually literary figures more than academic philosophers, argued that once the natural laws that governed nature and human existence were discovered, society could be organized in accordance with them and progress was inevitable.
  – Leaders of French culture, which dominated Europe, they lauded Newton, borrowed from John Locke, and flooded Europe with radically optimistic notions about how people should live and govern themselves.
  – Ideas created that were to shake the Old Order to pieces and build in its place the democratic, pluralistic, humanistic Western World.

■ While Newton's theories served as the inspiration for the natural law philosophy of the Enlightenment, *John Locke's* political writings translated the natural law assumption into a conception of government.

  – Locke (1632–1704), an Englishman, provided a philosophical apology for the supremacy of Parliament during the Glorious Revolution with his *Two Treatises on Civil Government*.

    • In the *state of nature*, before governments existed, humans lacked protection.
    • Governments, once instituted, replace individual action with the rule of law.
    • However, they rest upon the consent of the governed.
    • The *social contract*, the agreement between a fair government and responsible individuals, is not unconditional.
    • If government oversteps its role in protecting the life, liberty, and property of its citizens, the people have the right to abolish and replace it.

- These conceptions of the *consent of the governed*, the *social contract*, and the *right of revolution* spearheaded the *philosophes'* criticism of the absolutist *ancien régime* or Old Order.

The *Philosophes*

Voltaire (1694–1778) personified the Age of Reason. Born *François Marie Arouet* in Paris at the height of Louis XIV's reign, he lived until two years after the American Declaration of Independence. Although he was more writer than philosopher, he wrote in many formats. As a poet, essayist, dramatist, and, most importantly, as a satirist, his genius for social criticism helped ignite a desire for change and set the stage for the Age of Revolution.

- He preached against injustice and bigotry and for human rights and science.
- *"Ecrasez l'infame"* ("Crush the infamous") was his rallying cry against religious zealotry, governmental abuse, and vestiges of medievalism.
- Imprisoned briefly in the Bastille, he visited England and lived in the court of *Frederick the Great*, (r. 1740–1786) *Enlightened Despot* of Prussia.
- Like most of the Enlightenment thinkers, he was raised as a Christian but came to reject organized religion as corrupt in its leadership, and remote from the urgent message of Jesus.
- He was a staunch advocate of *deism*, the theological offshoot of natural law theory.

    - Believed that prayer and miracles violated the perfect natural order God had created and that the world's evils are caused by man's straying from the natural law.
    - The social reforms that he called for fit the deist notion that human reason alone could uncover the natural law and guide humans to comply with it.

Jean-Jacques Rousseau (1712–1778) is often considered a *philosophe*, a man of the Enlightenment, but he is more accurately the founder of the Romantic Movement. After the excesses of the French Revolution, the Enlightenment's emphasis on the *rule of reason* gave way to a glorification of emotion.

- Despising, intellectually and personally, the rigid and inequitable class structure of the *ancien régime*, he developed the idea of the *noble savage*: that civilization corrupted humankind and that life in the *state of nature* was purer, freer, and more virtuous than "civilized" man.
- The goal of the individual, he argued in his many writings, was to attain full expression of natural instincts by stripping away the artificial restraints of society and returning as far as possible to nature.
- Believed that the goal of a people was to achieve self-determination.

    - A call to the nationalism that the French Revolution awakened all over Europe.

- In *The Social Contract*, he wrote, "Man is born free, and everywhere he is in chains," meaning that property, when regarded as more important than people, causes social injustice.
- The *general will*, a kind of consensus of the majority, he thought should control a nation. This was intended to support a democratic view of government, but because it does not recognize minority viewpoints and since it has no clear way to show itself, it could be used to rationalize extreme nationalism and repression.

- Whatever the flaws in his philosophy, Rousseau is considered one the most influential thinkers of his day.
- His distrust of *civilization* and its institutions led him to criticize rigid educational practices and the strict discipline of children.

  - In his treatise *Emile*, he argued that children have to be understood as individuals and that they need caring from their teachers as well as from their parents.
  - He and other Enlightenment critics helped to change the educational and child-rearing practices of eighteenth-century Europe.

Baron de Montesquieu (1689–1755) in his work, *The Spirit of the Laws*, argued that the powers of government (legislative, executive, and judicial) must be separated in order to avoid despotism. When these functions are divided among various groups or individuals, each *checks and balances* the powers of the others. His theories served as a blueprint for the governmental structure outlined in the U.S. Constitution.

Cesare Beccaria (1738–1794) published his *On Crimes and Punishments* in 1764, which added to Montesquieu's ideas by outlining proportions between crimes and punishments, and arguing against torture. He focused on deterring men from committing crimes.

Denis Diderot (1713–1784) published the writings and popularized the ideas of many of the *philosophes* in his *Encyclopédie*, a collection of political and social critiques rather than a compilation of facts.

Francois Quesnay (1694–1774) led the *physiocrats* whose motto was *laissez-faire*, and who believed that government should remove all restraints to free trade, such as tariffs, so that the natural laws of economics were free to operate for the good of society.

Adam Smith (1727–1790), a Scotsman, refined and expanded the laissez-faire philosophy of the *physiocrats* in his *An Inquiry into the Nature and Causes of the Wealth of Nations*. Published in 1776, the year of the Declaration of Independence, it is the book that defined capitalism. In it, he stated: the economy is governed by natural laws, such as *supply and demand*; in a free economy, competition will induce producers to manufacture most efficiently in order to sell higher-quality, lower-cost goods than competitors; government regulation only interferes with this natural self-governing operation. He also railed against mercantilism as the embodiment of foul government intervention in the economy.

It is important to remember that these new ideas existed alongside the traditional ideas that Europeans had held dear for centuries. Alchemy and astrology continued to appeal to elites and some natural philosophers, in part because they shared with the new science the notion of a predictable and knowable universe. Most peasants and urban folk continued to believe that the cosmos was governed by divine and demonic forces.

Salons were the sites for meetings of the great minds of the day in the houses of the prominent women of the day such as *Madame Geoffrin* (1699–1777) or *Madame Stael* (1766–1817). The *salons* supported a discourse of ideas without the *censorship* that was so prevalent in the writings of the day, and which Voltaire rebelled so strongly against. They also functioned as a means for women to attain an education on the cutting edge of knowledge and thought of the time.

The *coffeehouses* of France and much of Europe at the time served as further meeting places for conversation. Some have theorized that the advent of tea and coffee was a factor that led to the Enlightenment. Caffeine had recently replaced alcohol in daily beverages and people thought with much more clarity and had more energy for thoughtful discourse.

During the Enlightenment, the rational analysis of religious practices led to natural religion and the demand for religious tolerance. Intellectuals, including Voltaire and Diderot, developed new philosophies of deism, skepticism, and atheism. Baron d'Holbach (1723–1789) was the primary proponent of an atheistic world at the time and he disrupted the salons of the day by his insistence on publicly and ardently advocating his belief that God was just an illusion in salons. Religion became increasingly a private rather than a public concern, and by 1800 most forms of Christianity were tolerated by most European governments who also gave civil equality to Jewish people in many cases.

GENDER AND ETHNICITY DURING THE ENLIGHTENMENT

This era saw the emergence of feminist ideas for the first time in earnest. Women like *Mary Wollstonecraft* (1759–1797) and Madame Geoffrin made it clear to society that women could do anything that men could do mentally. The first women graduated from many European universities, and intellectuals discussed openly the idea that women should be equal before the law. The Enlightenment ideals of natural rights and just laws made people reexamine their preconceived notions of gender roles, and women's rights made some grudging progress despite the protests of many men in the field.

The same Enlightenment ideals that made men such as Rousseau and Voltaire question how they treated women had them examine how they treated slaves and the peoples of other nations, too. White men would still be the prominent power in Western society and the other societies of the world that they would dominate, but they began to examine the morality and the consequences of these perspectives during this era through the works of people such as Rousseau (in his novel *Emile*), and others such as Olympe de Gouges (1748–1793). Reform came slowly, with England outlawing slavery in all British holdings first, and France and the United States eventually following the European trend. Religious intolerance also began to be reduced, leading to more social harmony.

GREAT THINKERS OF THE SCIENTIFIC REVOLUTION AND ENLIGHTENMENT

This chart is designed to help you comprehend the ideas that may be tested with specific items or used as evidence in essays about the era.

Copernicus (1473–1534), Poland/East Prussia

He was responsible for spreading the heliocentric (sun centered) theory of the solar system throughout Europe. His *On the Revolutions of the Heavenly Spheres* was published posthumously.

Anton van Leeuwenhoek (1632–1723), Netherlands

He invented and used microscopes to create a basis for modern biological science; his drawings of blood corpuscles, sperm, and bacteria began the science of microbiology.

Michel de Montaigne (1533–1592), France

He was a skeptic and inventor of the essay. He stated that he knew nothing decades before Descartes wrote, "*Cogito ergo sum.*" (I think, therefore I am).

Francis Bacon (1561–1626), England

He is often cited as the codifier of the inductive method. He believed "Knowledge is power," and should be put to practical use.

René Descartes (1596–1650), France

He was an ardent advocate for the deductive method. His *Discourse on the Method* defined two kinds of matter: thinking substance (everything within the mind) and extended substance (the objective world or everything outside the mind). This division of reality is known as Cartesian dualism. He invented analytical geometry and wrote the eternal line, "*Cogito ergo sum*" (I think, therefore I am).

Tycho Brahe (1546–1601), Denmark

This eccentric astronomer collected vast amounts of data and hired a mathematically gifted assistant named Johannes Kepler.

Johannes Kepler (1571–1630), Germany

Brahe's assistant. He discovered three laws of planetary motion that helped Newton later understand gravity, and proved that the orbits of planets are ellipses.

Galileo Galilei (1571–1642), Italy

Perhaps the best example of the Enlightenment emerging from the Renaissance, Galileo was a master of many sciences and tried to know everything he could. His astronomical observations of the moons of Jupiter proved that Earth was not the center of the universe, getting him put under house arrest by the Roman Catholic Church. His experiments with inertia proved that objects of different weights fall at the same rate.

Vesalius (1514–1564), Belgium

His anatomical drawings from dissection of corpses were the first detailed anatomical maps of the human body.

William Harvey (1578–1657), England

He was the author of *On the Movement of the Heart and Blood*, which explained the circulation of the blood through arteries and veins.

Isaac Newton (1642–1727), England

He synthesized Kepler's and Galileo's ideas together in his laws of motion. His definition of physics defined what scientists knew about the universe until Einstein conceived of relativity. He developed calculus to measure and predict curves and trajectories. Newton also explained the laws of universal gravitation. He said he "stood on the shoulders of giants," in deference to Galileo.

Leibnitz (1646–1716), Germany

He invented calculus simultaneously with Newton.

PHILOSOPHES OF THE ENLIGHTENMENT

Bernard de Fontenelle

He was influential in bringing scientific matters to educated people who were not scientists themselves. He also was among the first to think that science contradicted religion, and caused people to think about the nature of religious truth.

Major Works: *Conversations on the Plurality of Worlds*—It is a truly liberal book because it focuses on the concept that humans can make progress, and marvels at the progress already made. It also made scientific progress up to this point available to many people presented on their level of understanding.

Pierre Bayle

Leading skeptic, his conclusion foreshadowing that of Heisenberg was that there is basis for doubt in absolutely everything.

Major Works: *Historical and Critical Dictionary* in 1697 about past religion and persecution

Baruch Spinoza

Equated God and nature and believed in an impersonal mechanical universe. He also denied free will. He was Jewish by birth but became one of the first ardent atheists.

Major Works: *Ethics, Tractatus Theologico-Politicus,* and *Tractatus Politicus*

Denis Diderot

Best known as the editor of the first European *Encyclopédie*, which was supported by Voltaire and Catherine II (the Great) of Russia. He was a writer and member of prominent salons in Paris.

Major Works: *Encyclopédie* or a Systematic Dictionary of the Sciences, Arts and Crafts

Jean-Baptiste le Rond d'Alembert

Famous philosopher, physicist, mathematician, scientist, and writer. Co-edited the *Encyclopédie* with Diderot.

Major Works: *Encyclopédie* or a Systematic Dictionary of the Sciences, Arts and Crafts

Baron de Montesqueiu (Charles-Louis de Secondat)

Defined the theory of separation of powers of the three branches of government. He outlined a system of checks and balances by which a government could be controlled. He also discussed what conditions were favorable to liberty and greatly admired the English balance of power. Satirized European Society as well in *The Persian Letters*. His work helped design most of the governmental systems in the world today.

Major Works: *The Spirit of the Laws, The Persian Letters*

Voltaire (Francois-Marie Arouet)

1. Jailed and had many books censored, but wrote over seventy books.
2. Vehemently tolerant of all religions but was a deist.

3. A biographer summarized his ideas by saying, "I disagree with what you say, but would defend to the death your right to say it."
4. He was a minister to Frederick the Great of Prussia.
5. He did his best work while living with *Madame du Châtelet,* who translated Newton's *Principia Mathematica* and cared for Voltaire with her husband's tacit approval.
6. In 1745, Voltaire was appointed the Royal Historiographer of France. Voltaire believed that monarchy was the best form of government because he did not trust people to rule themselves.

Major Works: *Candide, Zadig, The Maid of Orleans, The Age of Louis XIV*

Thomas Paine

Advocated deism and progress, the idea of an improved society through natural laws. He moved to the British Colonies in America and advocated for American Independence.

Major Works: *The Age of Reason, Common Sense*

Marquis de Condorcet (Marie Jean Caritat)

He was the chairman of the French Academy of Sciences. He stated that human progress would eventually lead to its perfection. There are ten stages of the mind—nine have occurred, the tenth will lead to perfection. He was against gradual, hard-won progress and wanted catastrophic change, much as Karl Marx later would. He committed suicide to avoid the guillotine of the French Revolution.

Major Works: *Progress of the Human Mind, Essay on the Application of Analysis to the Probability of Majority Decisions*

Baron Paul d'Holbach (Paul-Henri Thiry)

He was a staunch atheist who refused to compromise on anything. Known for his financial support of Diderot and Rousseau.

1. People were machines controlled by outside forces.
2. Free will, God, and immortality were myths.
3. Seen as dogmatic and intolerant due to rigid atheism. It broke the unity of the Enlightenment by dividing thinkers.

Major Works: *The System of Nature,* contributed to the *Encyclopédie*

David Hume

Scotsman who emphasized limitations of human reasoning and stated that the human mind is nothing but a bundle of impressions. Later he became dogmatic skeptic who undermined the Enlightenment. He was the best friend of Adam Smith.

Major Works: *A Treatise of Human Nature, Dialogues Concerning Natural Religion*

Jean-Jacques Rousseau

1. He believed rationalism and civilization were destroying rather than liberating the individual.
2. He emphasized nature and passion and influenced the early Romantic Movement.

3. He was surly and paranoid in his later years and had a bowel problem.

4. He was against the culture of the Enlightenment.

5. Believed, the "*general will*" reflects public opinion, and the people (as assessed by the majority of the legislature) displaced the monarch as the holder of sovereign power.

6. *Emile* called for greater love and tenderness toward children, do not use wet nurses, no swaddling—showed the growth of humanitarianism and potential from the Enlightenment.

Major Works: *The Social Contract, Emile*

Immanuel Kant

He argued in 1784 that freedom of the press will result in Enlightenment. He separated science and morality into distinct branches of knowledge. He believed that science could describe natural phenomena of the material world but could not provide a guide for morality.

Major Works: *Critique of Practical Reason, The Metaphysics of Morals*, and *Critique of Judgment*

Mary Wollstonecraft

She was the first true feminist. She was a defender of the Declaration of the Rights of Men. Her daughter was Mary Shelley. She believed marriage was legalized prostitution. She engaged in a public debate with Edmund Burke about the French Revolution, and a private debate with Rousseau on the rights of women.

Major Works: *A Vindication of the Rights of Man, A Vindication of the Rights of Woman, Thoughts on the Education of Daughters*

Olympe de Gouges

Another early feminist, she was the daughter of a baker and rose to run her own salon. She was an abolitionist. She was executed during the Reign of Terror.

Major Works: *Declaration of the Rights of Woman and the Female Citizen*

Adam Smith

He wrote the original statement of capitalist views. It basically created modern economics.

1. It stated that mercantilism was stifling and government regulations and granted privileges made the marketplace not only unfair but also inefficient.

2. He thought free trade would limit government to three duties—defense, civil order, and public institutions.

3. The individual competition in the market led to balance.

4. Believed in the invisible hand of supply and demand to control the marketplace and keep competition free and fair.

5. He was a professor in Scotland, traveled to France with a tutee, and met Quesnay, the first economist there.

6. Explained how division of labor makes work more efficient.

7. Thought profit was stolen from the laborer.

Major Works: *An Inquiry into the Nature and Causes of the Wealth of Nations (1776), Theory of Moral Sentiments*

Madame Geoffrin (Marie Thérèse Rodet Geoffrin)

She was one of the leading Enlightenment personalities. She used her husband's money to host the liveliest salon in France at the time. Her guests included most of the people mentioned above. Other prominent salonnières include Louise de Warens and Julia de Lespinasse. In these salons women were treated like thinking people here and only here in society; it was the only place for a woman to learn about the world and the issues of the day. According to gender theory, women played an important role in organizing salons. She created an independent setting free from censorship where diverse educated people could form their public opinion.

Major Works: Supported the publishing of the *Encyclopédie*

Artistic movements and literature of the era began to reflect the outlook and values of the emerging commercial and bourgeois society as well as new Enlightenment ideals of political power and citizenship. This can be seen in the paintings of the Dutch masters—such as Jan Vermeer, Rembrandt van Rijn, and Frans Hals—who depicted mostly the leaders and servants of bourgeois society in all their glory. The writings of Goethe, Henry Fielding, Jane Austen, and Daniel Defoe also captured similar ideas and ideals of the time.

THE EVOLUTION OF POLITICAL THOUGHT OF HOBBES, LOCKE, AND ROUSSEAU

This chart is designed to compare the ideas of the great political thinkers of the sixteenth, seventeenth, and eighteenth centuries.

	Thomas Hobbes (1588–1679) English	John Locke (1632–1704) English	Jean-Jacques Rousseau (1712–1778) French
State of Nature: What is life like for the uncivilized?	"Life is nasty, brutish and short." Hobbes believed that in a state of nature, might makes right, and that we agree to be governed to protect ourselves from living in a state of nature.	People are born good and corrupted by society. People are created equal not in ability but in rights. All people have the rights to life, liberty, and property.	People are inherently unequal in ability, but this inequality only matters for the corrupted civilized man who deviated from the nobility of savagery.
Natural Law: Defines what the basic human rights are in all societies	The natural law that Hobbes focuses on is survival. He states that in nature every being is so concerned with survival, that any idea of rights includes only what one can physically protect.	All humans are endowed at creation with rights to life, liberty, and property. These are the basic rights that all people have.	Rousseau describes the state of nature as noble, and explains that we only deviate from natural law, in which the needs of each individual are met by the group, because the corrupting force of civilization induces to do so.

	Thomas Hobbes (1588–1679) English	John Locke (1632–1704) English	Jean-Jacques Rousseau (1712–1778) French
Social Contract	People give up some of their rights in order to gain some protection provided by the government.	People give up some of their rights in order to gain some protection provided by the government, but if the government does not do its job, the people must change it.	The social contract is between the people, not the people and the government. Each person gives up all rights to the "general will," which then incorporates every individual through the legislature.
Role of the State	The state prevents people from taking each other's property and killing each other.	The state protects a person's right to life, freedom, and property.	The state enacts the "general will" of the people as expressed through the legislature.
Property	Seen as a limited resource that people compete for.	Ownership of property is among everyone's natural rights.	Property is one of the worst inventions of society; used to manipulate the masses.
Religion	Believed that the state must have only one religion for unity.	Believes in religious toleration by the state.	Abhors organized religion, especially Christianity, but does not reject God.
Favored Form of Government	Absolute monarchy	Any representative government: constitutional monarchy, democracy or republic	Complete consensus based on dictatorship of the "general will"
What Was His Essential Question?	How can society prevent chaos and violence?	How can government protect the citizen and his/her possessions?	How can society combat inequality?

ABSOLUTE MONARCHS OF THE LATE SEVENTEENTH AND EARLY EIGHTEENTH CENTURIES

Louis XIV: The Ideal Monarch Who Domesticated the Nobility

Louis XIV (r. 1643–1715) was four when he ascended the throne of France. His mother was his regent, and she chose Italian *Cardinal Mazarin* (1602–1661) as prime minister.

- Like Richelieu, Mazarin was a capable administrator, and he protected Louis's claim to the throne during the tumultuous *Wars of the Fronde*, which reached their height from 1650 to 1652.
- The *Frondeurs* were nobles who sought to limit the powers of the monarch and to decentralize the government in order to extend their own influence. With the support of the bourgeoisie and the peasants, who had little to gain in a return to the feudal order, Mazarin was able to subdue the *Frondeurs* and their ally, Spain.

- When Mazarin died in 1661, Louis declared himself as his own prime minister.

  - *L'Etat, c'est moi* ("I am the state") became the credo of this most absolutist monarch during the Age of Absolutism.
  - *Bishop Jacques Bossuet* (1607–1704) provided the philosophical justification for the *divine right theory of rule.*
  - He claimed that Louis, like any absolutist monarch, was placed on the throne by God, and therefore owed his authority to no person or group.

- According to feudal tradition, French society was divided into three *Estates*, made up of the various classes.

  - The *First Estate* was the clergy, up to 1 percent of the population.
  - The *Second Estate* was the nobility and comprised 3 to 4 percent of the population.
  - The *Third Estate* included the great bulk of the population: the bourgeoisie or middle classes, the *artisans* and *urban workers*, and the *peasants*.
  - Since France was, as were all European nations at this time, predominantly *agrarian*, 90 percent of its population lived on farms in the countryside.

- Louis XIV reigned over the Golden Age of French culture and influence:

  - With a population of 17 million (about 20 percent of Europe's total), France was the strongest nation on the continent.
  - Its industry and agriculture surpassed that of any other European country.
  - *Jean Baptiste Colbert* (1619–1683), "The Father of French Mercantilism," revitalized trade as Louis's finance minister by abolishing internal tariffs and creating a free trade zone in most of France.

    - He stimulated industry by subsidizing vital manufacturing and by building up the military.
    - He hoped to make France self-sufficient by building a large fleet that would rival that of the English and Dutch and enable the French to acquire an overseas empire.
    - Since even France could not afford both a powerful army and navy, Louis opted for the army.

- The result was the global supremacy of the British, whose navy ruled the seas of the world for over a century over an empire so large that the sun literally did not set on it.
- French became the "universal tongue," spoken by diplomats and in the royal courts of all Europe.

  - Louis patronized artists and especially writers such as *Corneille, Racine* (1639–1699), *Molière* (1622–1673), *de Sévigné, de Saint-Simon* (1607–1693), *La Fontaine, de La Rochefoucauld* (1621–1695).
  - French literature and style (in dress, furniture, architecture) became standards by which all Europeans measured their sophistication.

- France developed Europe's first modern army.

  - Continuation of the military revolution begun by France during the Habsburg-Valois Wars.
  - Artillery, usually supplied by civilian private contractors, was made a part of the army.

– The government, instead of officers, recruited, trained, equipped, and garrisoned troops.
– A chain of command was established, and the army was increased from 100,000 to 400,000, the largest in Europe.

War Was an Instrument of Louis's Foreign Policy

For two thirds of his reign, France was at war.

- *The War of the Devolution* (1667–1668): France's unsuccessful attempt to seize the Spanish Netherlands (Belgium) as part of a feudal claim.
- *The Dutch War* (1672–1678): Revenge for the Dutch role in defeating France in the War of Devolution and an attempt to seek France's "natural boundary in the west," the Rhine River—largely unsuccessful.
- *The Nine Years' War* (1688–1697): Also called the War of the Grand Alliance or the War of the League of Augsburg was a major war of the late seventeenth century.

    – France was opposed by a European-wide coalition, the Grand Alliance, fought primarily on mainland Europe and its surrounding waters.
    – A campaign in colonial North America between French and English settlers and their respective Indian allies, called "King William's War" by the English colonists, was a part of this war.
    – Although France retained Luxembourg, most of Louis's ambitions were frustrated.

- *The War of the Spanish Succession* (1702–1714): Louis threatened to upset the Balance of Power (the theory that no single state should be predominant on the continent) in Europe by laying claim to the Spanish throne for his grandson.

    – The Grand Alliance, which included the major states of Western Europe, fought to prevent this union of the French and Spanish thrones.
    – *The Treaty of Utrecht* (1713–1714): Restored the balance of power by allowing Philip V, Louis's grandson, to remain on the Spanish throne as long as France and Spain were never ruled by the same monarch.

        • Also awarded to the victors were various European and overseas possessions of the Spanish Empire.

Summary of Louis XIV's Reign

Although his reign solidified the central government and marked the high point of absolutism in France, his many wars exhausted the treasury. This left the bourgeoisie and the peasantry with an enormous tax burden since the clergy and nobility were exempted from most taxes. His personal extravagances aggravated the situation: The Royal Palace at *Versailles* cost over $2.3 billion in 2015 U.S. dollars to build, and added to that was the money spent on his elaborate entertainments for the "captive nobility" at court. He defanged the nobles by making participation in court life a social requirement. He suppressed religious dissent, outlawing *Jansenism* (a form of Catholic Calvinism); revoked the *Edict of Nantes*, which had guaranteed toleration for the Huguenots; and made Catholicism mandatory.

Accomplishments of Louis XIV:

- The central government that developed in France from the era of the religious wars to Louis's reign was efficient.
- The power of the nobles was weakened.
- Tax collection was systematized.
- Royal edicts were enforced.
- The bourgeoisie was given a role in the administration.
- The economic system was successful.

  - Agriculture and trade were stimulated.
  - The seeds for revolution were sown in the national debt that had to be paid off by the Third Estate, which bore many responsibilities and enjoyed few privileges.

Prussia

Prussia was an army before it was a nation, it has been said, because its origin was as an outpost of the Holy Roman Empire and its *Hohenzollern* rulers cultivated a superbly trained and well-equipped army drawn from all areas of their domain. Local loyalties were transferred to the army, which then served as the focal point for Prussian nationalism. Brandenburg, an electorate of the Holy Roman Empire, was able to gain a degree of independence as a result of the weakening of the Habsburg rule during the Thirty Years' War.

- The Hohenzollern, Frederick William I (r. 1713–1740), solidified autocratic rule over Brandenburg, Prussia, and the Rhine territories with a strong army and an efficient bureaucracy, and with a policy of weakening the nobles (Junkers) and suppressing the peasants. The Junkers served as elite officers in the army, and absolutist rule was established in Prussia.
- *Frederick William, Elector of Brandenburg* (r. 1640–1688) and his son and grandson, *Frederick I* (r. 1688–1713) and *Frederick William I* (r. 1713–1740) of Prussia, centralized the government and encouraged industry in order to support the state's relatively large standing army.

Russia

Russia became a state in the fifteenth century when the *Duchy of Muscovy*, under *Ivan the Great* (r. 1462–1505), overcame subjugation by the Central Asian *Tartars*. After the *Fall of Constantinople* to the Ottoman Turks in 1453, Russia became not only the inheritor of Byzantine culture and the center of the Orthodox Church, but an empire with Moscow as "the third Rome" and a czar (Caesar) or *tsar* on the throne.

- Under *Basil (Vasily) III* (r. 1505–1533) and the much maligned but very capable *Ivan the Terrible* (1533–1584), expansion and consolidation of the new empire continued in a sporadic fashion with some advances and some reversals.

  - In order to attain soldiers, the empire gave aristocratic landowners, the *Boyars*, control over their peasants, who gradually fell into *serfdom*, a condition of being bound to the land that had ended in virtually all of Western Europe.
  - The Boyars influenced government policy through a council, the *Duma*.

- A theme common in most nations with a monarchy, there was a continuing battle for supremacy between a strong central government and a powerful aristocracy.
- *Peter the Great* (r. 1689–1725), a Romanov and a contemporary of Louis XIV of France, gained vast territories from the Baltic Sea in the north, to the Black Sea in the south, and eastward toward the Pacific Ocean. Probably his greatest contribution was the *Westernization of Russia*.

  - Peter the Great expanded the power of the state and of the czars by establishing a powerful standing army, a civil service, and an educational system to train technicians in the skills developed by western science and technology. He imposed economic burdens, Western ideas, and social restrictions on the peasants to further his power, erected the planned city of St. Petersburg on the Baltic, and built magnificent, ornate baroque palaces, churches, and public buildings to glorify his reign. Russia became one of the major powers of Europe during this period.
  - Although he could not be considered an Enlightened Despot, he recruited hundreds of Western artisans, built a new capital on the Gulf of Finland, *St. Petersburg*, his "window to the West," reformed the government bureaucracy and the Russian Orthodox Church, reorganized and equipped the army with modern weapons, and encouraged commerce and industry.

ENLIGHTENED DESPOTISM

The ideal enlightened despot was a ruler who aimed for the advancement of society by fostering education, aiding the economy, and promoting social justice. Since Voltaire and most of the *philosophes*, and certainly most of Europe's monarchs, believed that the mass of people were incapable of self-government, enlightened despots stayed in power while promoting the good of their people.

In the seventeenth century, *Russia* and *Prussia* rose as powerful states, challenging Poland, the ancient *Habsburg state of Austria*, and the declining empire of the Ottomans. In Prussia and, ironically, in Russia whose culture often lagged decades, even centuries, behind that of the West, enlightened despotism held sway during important periods of the eighteenth century. Such rule helped slow the decline of Austria, whose monarchs still held the title of Holy Roman Emperor. In Western Europe, enlightened despotism manifested itself in Sweden, Spain, and Portugal, but it shone most brilliantly in the East such as in Prussia, Russia, and Austria.

Prussia

Prussian Enlightened Despotism reached fruition during the rule of Frederick I's grandson, *Frederick II* or *Frederick the Great* (r. 1740–1786). "First servant of the state," as he called himself, Frederick the Great was a military genius who made Prussia a major power in Europe, an urbane and educated man who patronized the great Voltaire, a domestic reformer who improved education, codified laws, fostered industry, invited immigration, and extended religious tolerance. Twenty years after he died, although Napoleon was able to defeat his army on the battlefield, they remained the strongest institution within the state; the remnants of the Junker (landowning aristocracy) officer corps rebuilt the army and fostered German Nationalism to create a strong German state.

Russia

Catherine the Great (r. 1762–1796), a German who succeeded to the throne after the murder of her husband, *Czar Peter III* (r. 1762), was a patron of many of the French *philosophes* and considered herself an Enlightened Despot. When a rebellion of the Cossacks, the *Pugachev Rebellion*, gained some ground with the peasantry, Catherine at first tried to dismiss the rebellion; later she took it much more seriously and ended her enlightened reforms. She did continue Peter the Great's work of territorial expansion by annexing both Polish and Ottoman land.

Austria

In Austria, during the eighteenth century, *Maria Theresa* (r. 1740–1780) and her son, *Joseph II* (r. 1780–1790), qualify as genuine Enlightened Despots. *The War of the Austrian Succession* (1740–1748) was fought over the issue of whether or not she could inherit her kingdom, and gave Silesia to Prussia. The *Habsburg Dynasty* had been weakened by the time Maria Theresa inherited the throne under a cloud of counterclaims, and she was determined to strengthen the realm by centralizing the government, promoting commerce, and limiting the power of the nobles. Joseph furthered his mother's reforms by guaranteeing freedom of the press and of religion, reforming the judicial system toward greater equality for all classes, making German the official language for the empire's many ethnic minorities in order to foster centralization, and especially *abolishing serfdom*.

PRACTICE LONG-ESSAY QUESTIONS

These questions are samples of the various types of thematic essays on the exam. (See pages 30–31 for a detailed explanation of each type.) Check over the **generic rubric** (see pages 32–33) before you begin any of these essays and use that rubric to score your essay if you write one.

Question 1

Evaluate the extent to which Newton inspired the Enlightenment, Locke provided the blueprint, and the *philosophes* shaped it.

COMMENTS ON QUESTION 1

This one is a CAUSATION question because it requires you to decide if Newton inspired the Enlightenment, Locke guided it, and the *philosophes* created it. Remember to describe causes AND/OR effects of the Enlightenment and support your analysis of those causes through specific examples. Explain the reason for those causes AND effects with supporting evidence. Remember that assessing the validity of a statement usually means a causation skill is being tested. The goal here is to ascertain how Newtonian physics and astronomy gave rise to "natural law" theory, how Locke applied that theory to the relations between the individual and government, then how the *philosophes* used Newtonian "natural law" and Lockean political theory to shape the Age of Reason. Be careful to define "natural law," to spell out Locke's applications of it in his theory of government, to characterize the Enlightenment that dominated the intellectual life of eighteenth-century Europe, and to show how important *philosophes* such as Voltaire, Montesquieu, Rousseau, Smith, Wollstonecraft, and others influenced the movement. This type of question has at least four parts (Newton's inspiration, Locke's blueprint, shaping by *philosophes*, and the validity of each), and you need to remember to complete all parts of the question.

Question 2

Compare Locke and Rousseau's concept of the social contract.

COMMENTS ON QUESTION 2

The chart on the evolution of political power from this chapter can help to develop an outline for this essay. This is a COMPARE skill question, so be sure to describe similarities and differences between Locke and Rousseau's concepts of the social contract. Account for or explain the reasons for the similarities and differences in them by providing specific examples of how they are similar and different, and tying that to historical developments such as the rise of constitutionalism and democracy. Locke, who lived before the Enlightenment, influenced Rousseau. Rousseau, who dominated the Enlightenment's push for social reform, has been called more of a Romantic than a *philosophe* insofar as he departed from Locke's political theory. The way to "show differences" would be first to "examine similarities" in their concepts of the state of nature and the social contract, then to show how Locke's ideas influenced Rousseau's, and finally to examine how Rousseau departed from Locke. Although this question is straightforward, it requires a thorough understanding of the abstract theories involved.

Question 3

Were the enlightened despots more despotic than enlightened?

COMMENTS ON QUESTION 3

According to the democratic biases of our age, an enlightened despot is a contradiction in terms. For the world of the eighteenth century, mired in the excesses of absolutism, the "enlightened despots" were products of the Age of Reason. This is a COMPARE skill question, so be sure to explain what makes each example despotic or enlightened as well as account for or explain why some enlightened despots were more enlightened than others. Provide specific examples of how the rulers were both despotic and enlightened and different and tying that to historical developments such as the Pugachev Rebellion, or the emancipation of serfs eventually. The essay must explain the reasons for the similarities and differences between an enlightened ruler and a despot. This requires specific references and evaluations of the various monarchs who claimed to be, or have been labeled by history as enlightened despots. Make reference to three or four. Measure their reigns for genuine reform. Did the reforms change the lives of the people? Did they last? Decide whether to defend or refute.

Question 4

Explain how the replacement of the open-field system by the enclosure movement increased agricultural productivity in eighteenth-century Europe.

COMMENTS ON QUESTION 4

This one is a CAUSATION question because it requires you to explain how one event, the replacement of the open-field system by the enclosure movement, resulted in a specific outcome, increased agricultural productivity in eighteenth-century Europe. Remember to describe causes AND/OR effects of enclosure and the agricultural revolution and to support your analysis of those causes through specific examples. The essay must explain the reasons why the enclosure movement increased agricultural activity with specific evidence. The enclosure movement should be explained as the most important and least known revolution in European history. Describe the open-field system and the concept of common lands, focusing on the limitations on land improvement and fallow lands. Explain how the enclosure movement made land improvement, such as irrigation, crop rotation, and fertilization, more practical and widespread. The best essays will also examine how the enclosure movement led to the putting-out system that increased domestic production and disturbed the order of society by moving many farming families from their lands, causing them to find new means of employment.

Question 5

Why did the population of Europe increase dramatically in the 1700s?

COMMENTS ON QUESTION 5

This one is a CAUSATION question because it requires you to explain the causes of the dramatic population increase of the 1700s. Remember to describe causes AND/OR effects of the population increases and to support your analysis of those causes through specific examples. The essay must explain the reasons why the population rose at that time with specific evidence as support. Explain the roles of food production, new foods, and the disappearance of the plague; emphasize that the medical practices of the day played little part in the increase. An increase in the overall standard of living for many of the people in rural Europe at the time due to the emergence of domestic industry may also be mentioned.

PRACTICE SHORT-ANSWER QUESTIONS

1. Please answer all parts of the following question based upon the image below and your knowledge of European History.

—Frontispiece of: "Tabulae Rudolphinae: quibus astronomicae . . ." by Johannes Kepler.

(A) Briefly analyze how the artwork above reflects the artistic trends in the first half of the seventeenth century.

(B) Based on the print and your knowledge of European History, briefly analyze TWO aspects of change that affected Europeans' perceptions during the Enlightenment period.

2. Please use the excerpt from the letter below and your knowledge of European History to answer all parts of the following question.

Letter from Louis XIV to the Town Officers and People of Marseilles

Considering how advantageous it would be to this realm to reestablish its foreign and domestic commerce, . . . we have resolved to establish a council particularly devoted to commerce, to be held every fortnight in our presence, in which all the interests of merchants and the means conducive to the revival of commerce shall be considered and determined upon, as well as all that which concerns manufactures.

We desire, in this present letter, not only to inform you concerning all these things, but to require you, as soon as you have received it, to cause to be assembled all the merchants and traders of your town of Marseilles, and explain to them very particularly our intentions in all matters mentioned above, in order that, being informed of the favorable treatment which we desire to give them, they may be the more desirous of applying themselves to commerce. Let them understand that for everything that concerns the welfare and advantage of the same they are to address themselves to Sieur Colbert. . . .

—Louis XIV

(A) Briefly identify and describe the economic policy for improving the nation's wealth that Louis XIV is promoting in this letter.

(B) Briefly identify and describe ONE positive aspect of the impact of the rule of Louis XIV on France.

(C) Briefly identify and describe how the policy Louis XIV supported was discredited less than a century after his rule.

Short-Answer Explanations

1. (A) ONE point will be given for an analysis of how the image represents the art of the Northern Renaissance. The factors used to support this can include the theme that is secular and scientific, the detailed linear perspective, the appeal to Greco-Roman classicalism, scientific and rational understanding of the world, the emergence of copper engraving as an art form, the rise of book illustrations, and detailed realism.

   (B) TWO points will be awarded, ONE EACH for analysis of change that affected European thought during the period of the scientific revolution and Enlightenment. A change must be more than mentioned, but should be explored for causes and effects to be awarded a point for this question. Some changes to analyze include, but are not limited to: gaining faith in reason and science or religion to solve problems, increasing scientific knowledge alongside increasing moral knowledge, the growth and spread of printed books, the rise of astronomy as an area of study, the decline of religious control of thought, the emerging conflict between religion and science, the rise of deism, the increase in precision of measurement, the fascination with learning the rules of the universe, and focus on gaining knowledge and applying it to social issues.

2. (A) The student must identify mercantilism or bullionism as the economic policies of Louis XIV and Colbert and describe them as policies in which the nation hopes to buy goods and services only from itself, its colonies, and other possessions in order to increase the wealth held within the nation.

   (B) The student may explain any of the following: the rise of French prestige internationally, the growing wealth of the French upper classes, the conquest of the nobility by the intendant system and Versailles, the growth of French military might, France becoming the center of European culture, and the emergence of the Enlightenment after the death of Louis XIV.

   (C) The student must explain how Adam Smith's *The Wealth of Nations* argued against mercantilism and favored free trade in a movement that has remained strong to this day around the world. The rise of free-market economics governed by supply and demand should also be covered.

PRACTICE MULTIPLE-CHOICE QUESTIONS

Questions 1 to 4 refer to the image of a French Stamp from the 1970s below.

1. Which of the following is the best explanation of the popular nickname for Louis XIV as alluded to in the postage stamp above?

    (A) *L'État c'est moi* because Louis XIV was the state of France
    (B) *The Sun King* because all of Europe revolved around Louis XIV
    (C) *The Sun King* because all light in Europe came from Louis XIV
    (D) *The Wig King* because Louis XIV began a trend of wigs being worn across Europe

2. The Versailles palace seen in the background of the stamp was used by Louis XIV in which of the following ways?

    (A) It was a pleasure palace that the nobility flocked to voluntarily to enjoy the grand court of Louis XIV.
    (B) It was built to display the wealth and power of Louis XIV in order to overawe foreign diplomats and officials of the Roman Catholic Church.
    (C) It was a state building constructed to glorify France and to build the pride of the French people.
    (D) It was built as a pleasure prison to control the nobility by requiring their attendance there annually.

3. Which of the following was the greatest weakness of Louis XIV according to many historians, and his probable dying declaration?

    (A) Louis XIV was too focused on controlling his own nobility.
    (B) Louis XIV was a notorious womanizer who ruined many women's lives.
    (C) Louis XIV spent over two thirds of his reign at war and much of it was fruitless.
    (D) Louis XIV was too attached to secular pleasures and was not religious.

4. All of the following are reasons why the French government would choose to issue the stamp above during the 1970s EXCEPT which one?

(A) French nationalism needed rebuilding after defeats in Algeria and French Indochina.
(B) The recent death of Charles de Gaulle left the French in need of a hero.
(C) The social movement in France in the 1970s was building to restore a constitutional monarch.
(D) Nostalgia was building for better times when France was central to world politics.

Questions 5 to 8 refer to the painting below.

Oil by Lemonnier of Madame Geoffrin (1699–1777)
in her salon at Hotel de Rambouillet in Paris.

5. The painting above is a gathering of notable writers and thinkers in order to do which of the following?

(A) Plan a new constitution for their country
(B) Evaluate different paintings being exhibited
(C) Observe the latest fashions in clothing
(D) Discuss important philosophical issues and points of knowledge

6. Which of the following was a direct result of many meetings in France such as the one depicted above?

(A) The general population of France latched onto these ideas and called for democracy after attending such meetings.

(B) The control of the Roman Catholic Church was challenged over the creation and dissemination of knowledge.

(C) The control of France by the nobility was challenged by these gatherings of mostly bourgeois activists who wanted to destroy the social order.

(D) The economy of France was mended, putting off a financial crisis until the final years of Louis XVI.

7. Which of the following statements was most likely to be agreed upon by everyone at a meeting like the one depicted above?

(A) The best form of government is a constitutional monarchy.

(B) The best form of government is a republic with universal suffrage.

(C) Society can be improved through the use of reason.

(D) This is the best of all possible worlds.

8. Madame Geoffrin and her assembled guests were largely responsible for which of the following projects?

(A) The rewriting of the French constitution

(B) The creation of the first European encyclopedia

(C) Writing a satire that examined Dutch society

(D) Creating a collection to match the Library of Alexandria

Multiple-Choice Explanations

1. **B**	3. **C**	5. **D**	7. **C**
2. **D**	4. **C**	6. **B**	8. **B**

1. **(B)**

(A) is wrong because Louis XIV was the Sun King around whom all of Europe revolved, but he did declare that he was the state and is known for that quote.

(B) is CORRECT because Louis XIV was the Sun King around whom all of Europe revolved.

(C) is wrong because Louis XIV was the Sun King around whom all of Europe revolved, not the source of all light.

(D) is wrong because although Louis XIV did prefer and spread his preference for wigs, Louis XIV was the Sun King around whom all of Europe revolved.

2. **(D)**

(A) is wrong because the nobility was forced to come to Versailles by Louis while his government officials called *intendants* administered to governmental affairs throughout the country, reducing the power of the nobility.

(B) is wrong because although Versailles was used to overpower diplomats, its primary use was to control the nobility there while his government officials called *intendants* administered to governmental affairs throughout the country, reducing the power of the nobility.

(C) is wrong because Versailles was built to glorify the monarch, not the state, and because the people resented it rather than taking pride in it.

(D) is CORRECT because the nobility was forced to come to Versailles by Louis while his government officials called *intendants* administered to governmental affairs through-out the country, reducing the power of the nobility.

3. **(C)**

(A) is wrong because although Louis XIV did subjugate his nobility, that was a benefit to his rule. Louis's biggest flaw was his pursuit of war for two thirds of his reign, and his dying declaration is often cited as "I have gone to war too lightly, and pursued it for vanity's sake."

(B) is wrong because although Louis XIV did have many mistresses, Louis's biggest flaw was his pursuit of war for two thirds of his reign, and his dying declaration is often cited as "I have gone to war too lightly, and pursued it for vanity's sake."

(C) is CORRECT because Louis XIV's biggest flaw was his pursuit of war for two thirds of his reign and his dying declaration is often cited as "I have gone to war too lightly, and pursued it for vanity's sake."

(D) is wrong because although Louis XIV was engaged in a pursuit of pleasure he was very religious.

4. **(C)**

(A) is wrong because French nationalism did need rebuilding after these defeats.

(B) is wrong because the French people did need to remember a great French hero with-out a current one present in their nation.

(C) is CORRECT because there was no popular movement to restore a monarchy in France in the 1970s.

(D) is wrong because there was a building nostalgia in France for a time when France mattered more internationally as the Cold War progressed during the 1970s.

5. **(D)**

(A) is wrong because this meeting is a salon in which the enlightened thinkers, or *philosophes*, would discuss the important issues of the day rather than a constitutional convention.

(B) is wrong because this meeting is a salon in which the enlightened thinkers, or *philosophes*, would discuss the important issues of the day rather than an art exhibit.

(C) is wrong because this meeting is a salon in which the enlightened thinkers, or *philosophes*, would discuss the important issues of the day rather than a fashion show.

(D) is CORRECT because this meeting is a salon in which the enlightened thinkers, or *philosophes*, would discuss the important issues of the day.

SPECIAL NOTE

This content is not covered in Chapter 4 or Period 2, but it does model the types of questions that you may encounter on the AP exam in May in which a single prompt may have questions from many time periods, so it is included here.

6. **(B)**

(A) is wrong because salons did not affect the general population at all; they were merely for the social elite to discuss important issues without government or religious censorship.

(B) is CORRECT because the social elites meeting at the salons were able to avoid religious and governmental censorship by speaking their ideas rather than publishing them, and thus were able to shift the control of knowledge and thought away from the Church.

(C) is wrong because salons did not challenge the social order, and because the nobility had already been subjugated in France a century earlier.

(D) is wrong because the economy of France was not fixed at this time, and these meetings had nothing to do with economic planning for France.

7. **(C)**

(A) is wrong because although there would be many constitutional monarchists at a salon, many would disagree with that idea, while they would all agree that reason can be used to improve society.

(B) is wrong because although there would be many republicans at a salon, none would have supported universal suffrage.

(C) is CORRECT because most people at a salon would agree that reason can be used to improve society.

(D) is wrong because many would disagree with Pangloss's assertion in *Candide* because they saw so much that could be done to improve society.

8. **(B)**

(A) is wrong because the salons were discussion groups and they did not try to rewrite the constitution.

(B) is CORRECT because Madame Geoffrin was a major supporter of the Encyclopedia created by Denis Diderot and her guests often wrote articles for it.

(C) is wrong because the salon was not engaged in writing a satire about the Dutch.

(D) is wrong because while they were trying to collect knowledge, they wanted to write their own books rather than collect others.

The French Revolution, Napoleon, and the Congress of Vienna

5

KEY TERMS/PEOPLE

- → ESTATE SYSTEM OR *ANCIEN RÉGIME*
- → NATIONAL ASSEMBLY
- → CONSTITUTION OF 1791
- → DECLARATION OF THE RIGHTS OF MAN AND OF THE CITIZEN
- → MARCH ON VERSAILLES
- → DECLARATION OF PILLNITZ
- → ROBESPIERRE
- → MARAT
- → DANTON
- → BASTILLE
- → CIVIL CONSTITUTION OF THE CLERGY
- → JACOBINS

- → GIRONDINS
- → LIBERAL PHASE
- → RADICAL PHASE
- → CODE NAPOLEON
- → CONCORDAT OF 1801
- → ABOLITION OF PROVINCES AND DIVISION OF FRANCE INTO DEPARTMENTS
- → SECRET POLICE
- → NEPOTISM
- → BOURBONS
- → CONGRESS OF VIENNA
- → WOMEN'S ROLE IN THE REVOLUTION
- → HAITIAN REVOLUTION

OVERVIEW

In 1789, France had a population of about 25 million, a productive economy, rich farmlands, and a culture that dominated the Continent. French was not only the language of diplomacy, but it was the tongue spoken in most of the courts of Europe. France was the center of the eighteenth-century Enlightenment. Despite its wealth and influence, its government was corrupt, inefficient, and in debt, its class structure archaic and unjust, its institutions encrusted with medieval traditionalism. Smoldering class resentments stoked by the ideals and illusions of the Enlightenment, by financial turmoil, and, finally, by famines brought on by bad harvests, erupted in revolution. The Revolution began as a moderate attempt at reform, degenerated into radical bloodletting, then swung back to authoritarianism and a short flirtation with an empire in search of order. Impelled by the ideals of "liberty, equality, fraternity" and by military power, the French Revolution became an international movement that overthrew the feudal structures of the Old Regime in France and shook the foundations of the political and social order in all of Europe.

Napoleon defined an age, 1799 to 1815. His genius for military success created, in less than a decade, a French empire that stretched across the Continent. His gift for administration and reform implemented the ideals of the Revolution. Ambition, growing nationalism throughout Europe, and unexpected events led to his downfall. He lost the cream of his magnificent army in the wasteland of the Russian winter; his campaigns arrayed most of Europe against him when his victories in the field awakened nationalism in the rest of Europe. After his fall in 1815, the "Old Order" tried to restore itself at the Congress of Vienna. A balance of power maintained relative peace for a century, but Europe had entered the Age of "-isms," and powerful new social, economic, and political forces would redefine the Western world.

THE FRENCH REVOLUTION

The Old Regime

A class structure left over from the Middle Ages determined the political and social order of France:

The First Estate (>1 percent), the clergy, despite comprising a tiny fraction of the population, the Roman Catholic Church of France (Gallican Church) owned 20 percent of the land. The clergy and the Church were exempt from taxes.

The Second Estate (2–4 percent), the nobles, owned about 20 percent of the land. They were also exempt from taxes.

The Third Estate (95 percent), the middle class, urban artisans, and peasants. Although France had developed a significant commercial or middle class, the *bourgeoisie*, the mass of the people were peasants who lived on the land.

The Third Estate, especially the peasantry, was subjected to a variety of oppressive taxes:

- taille, a land tax
- tithe, a Church tax equivalent to 10 percent of annual income
- income tax
- poll tax
- salt tax
- local duties paid to the feudal lord

Personal freedom was jeopardized by the *lettre de cachet*, by which the government could imprison anyone without charges or trial. The bourgeoisie was disenchanted by its lack of influence in a system that it disproportionately supported.

Burdened by debts run up by the wars and extravagances of *Louis XIV* (r. 1643–1715), by the corruption and inefficiency of the administration of his successors, and by France's support of the American Revolution, the government of *Louis XVI* (r. 1774–1792) attempted to tax the previously exempt clergy and nobility. A high court of France, the *Parlement of Paris*, ruled that new taxes could not be levied unless approved by the *Estates-General*, the legislative body equivalent to a parliament, which had not met in 175 years, representing the three estates mentioned above.

Timeline: The First or Liberal Stage of the Revolution (1789–1792)

MAY 5, 1789: The Estates-General met in Versailles.

JUNE 13, 1789: Supported by a few members of the First Estate, the Third Estate broke a voting deadlock in the Estates-General by declaring itself the *National Assembly*.

JUNE 20, 1789: After being locked out of their meeting place by the king's troops, members of the National Assembly swore the "Tennis Court Oath" not to disband until they had written a new constitution for France.

JULY 14, 1789: After food riots in the cities, peasant rebellions in the countryside, and the inaction of Louis and his ministers, a Parisian mob stormed the *Bastille*, a fortress that symbolized royal injustice.

AUGUST 4, 1789: The Decrees of this date mark when the National Assembly *abolished feudalism and manorialism*.

AUGUST 26, 1789: The *Declaration of the Rights of Man and the Citizen* was passed. Freedom of speech, thought, and religion were guaranteed, as was due process of law; taxes could be imposed only by consent of the governed; the right to rule was said to belong not just to the king, but to the whole nation.

AUGUST 1789–1790: The "Great Fear" swept through the countryside as the Third Estate rose up against the nobility and destroyed feudal records and noble residences. This movement lent strength to the movement to end feudalism.

OCTOBER 1789: A Paris mob, mostly women, was incited by Jean Paul Marat to *march on Versailles* and force the king to relocate to the *Tuileries*, the royal residence in Paris. The National Assembly also went to Paris and was intimidated by the Parisians.

NOVEMBER 2, 1789: The Assembly *seized Church and monastery lands* for revenue.

1790: *The Civil Constitution of the Clergy* was drafted. Convents and monasteries were abolished; all clergymen were to be paid by the state and elected by all citizens; the clergy was forbidden to accept the authority of the pope. Alienated by this decree, half of the priests of the Gallican Church refused to accept it.

1791: The National (Constituent) Assembly drafted a new constitution that instituted an *elected Legislative Assembly*, which made the king chief executive officer, largely responsible to the Assembly; the latter established voting qualifications for male citizens.

JUNE 14, 1791: The *Le Chapalier Law* was passed banning guilds and the right to strike, which enraged the *sans-culottes*, the poorest people in the city.

JUNE 21, 1791: The *Flight to Varennes* of the royal family in order to raise a counter-revolutionary army was stopped, and the king and queen became prisoners of the Parisian mob.

AUGUST 1791: The *Declaration of Pillnitz* by the king of Austria threatened military action to restore order in France and encouraged the radical revolutionaries who wanted to overthrow the monarchy in defiance of the declaration from foreign aristocrats.

Timeline: The Second or Radical Stage of the Revolution (1792–1795)

APRIL 20, 1792: The Legislative Assembly, the legislature under the new constitution, *declared war on Austria* in response to an ultimatum. The international *Wars of the French Revolution* began.

JULY 25, 1792: The commander of a Prussian army, about to invade France, issued the *Brunswick Manifesto*, threatening the people of Paris if harm came to the king. *Jacobin* (radical republican) leaders aroused the Paris mobs.

AUGUST 10, 1792: The *Tuileries were stormed*, and the king was taken prisoner; the mobs slaughtered over a thousand priests, bourgeoisie, and aristocrats who opposed the radicals' ambitions.

SEPTEMBER 21, 1792: *France was proclaimed a republic*, the first of *five* to come.

1793: An appeal to nationalism inspired the French people to drive back invaders, and the *First Coalition*, an alliance of Austria, Great Britain, Netherlands, Prussia, and Spain, was organized to combat any French advance. Revolutionary armies, raised by mass conscription, sought to bring the changes initiated in France to the rest of Europe.

The *Jacobins*, supported by the Paris mobs, and the *Girondists*, supported by the peasants in the rural areas, battled for control of the *National Convention*, which was the new assembly under the republic.

Maximilien Robespierre (1758–1794), leader of the Jacobins, pushed for the execution of the king, and both Louis XVI and his queen, *Marie Antoinette* (1755–1793), were guillotined in January 1793.

SUMMER 1793: A dictatorial *Committee of Public Safety* launched the "Reign of Terror." Over 20,000 people (nearly 75 percent of them working class and peasants) were executed from the summer of 1793 to that of 1794.

LATE 1793: The *Republic of Virtue* was proclaimed by the Committee of Public Safety in an attempt to de-Christianize France; it largely alienated the Catholic majority of the nation.

1794: When public opinion turned against the excesses of the Reign of Terror, both *Danton* (1759–1794), an original Jacobin, and Robespierre, leader of the Republic of Virtue, were executed by the National Convention.

THE FINAL OR REACTIONARY STAGE OF THE REVOLUTION (1795–1799): The *Thermidorian Reaction*, which was the execution of Robespierre, took place during the month of Thermidor (August 18–September 16) on the new non-Christian calendar, and returned the moderate bourgeois reformers to power.

1795–1799: The *Directory*, a five-member executive, was established by the National Convention to run the government. When a Paris mob threatened the new government, *Napoleon Bonaparte* (r. 1799–1815), a young general who by chance was in Paris at the time, put down the riot and was rewarded with command of the French armies fighting the Austrians in Italy.

Reaction to the French Revolution

While many were inspired by the Revolution's emphasis on equality and human rights, others such as Edmund Burke condemned its violence and disregard for traditional authority.

- Burke's *Reflections on the Revolution in France*, 1793, set the stage for the emergence of conservatism as practiced by Klemens von Metternich after Napoleon's reign.
- Mary Wollstonecraft and others in Great Britain and France rejected Burke's thinking, as exemplified by Wollstonecraft's *Vindication of the Rights of Man*, written in reaction to Burke.

WOMEN'S ROLE IN THE REVOLUTION

Women also played a major role in the French Revolution. In October of 1789, the Revolution was at a turning point. In the midst of a continuing shortage of bread, rumors of counter-revolution spread among the guards and royalty at Versailles. In response, many women (and some men dressed as women) gathered in Paris to march to the royal palace at Versailles to demand an accounting from the king. They marched 12 miles in the rain and were joined by thousands of men. The next day the crowd became rowdy and eventually broke into the royal apartments, killing two of the king's bodyguards. To prevent further bloodshed, Louis agreed to move his family back to Paris.

Women's participation was not confined to rioting and demonstrating. Women started to participate in meetings of political clubs, and a guarantee of women's rights became a topic of discussion during the Revolution. In July of 1790, the Marquis de Condorcet published a newspaper article in support of full political rights for women, which increased the importance of the discussion. He argued that France's women should enjoy equal political rights with men. His ideas were supported by the publication of the *Declaration of the Rights of Woman* by Olympe de Gouges, and the subsequent defense, *Vindication of the Rights of Woman* by Mary Wollstonecraft in 1791.

CAUSE AND EFFECT CHART FOR THE FRENCH REVOLUTION

If you can understand and retain the information on this chart, then you are ready for any question that the AP exam will have about the French Revolution.

---

1. The Estates-General meets for the first time
Cause: The French nation had seen famine and economic collapse. The Estates-General had not met in 175 years, but was convened in order to raise taxes after the Parliament of Paris refused to do so.
Effect: The meeting unified the nobility with the Third Estate and they took the Tennis Court Oath, promising not to leave until they had created a constitution for France.

2. Declaration of the Rights of Man
Cause: The monarchy had consolidated power through the intendant system, and also the failure of crops and the economy. These woes along with the ideas of the Enlightenment and the American Revolution, led to the demand for a French constitution at the Storming of the Bastille, which helped to create it.
Effect: The French Revolution began in earnest with the Great Fear, and the path was cleared for the creation of the National Assembly.

3. The Great Fear
Cause: The pent-up aggression of the Third Estate was unleashed as a reaction to the Declaration of the Rights of Man.
Effect: A chasm developed between the nobility and the peasantry, and factions formed in France about what the new government should look like and how it should act.

4. Formation of the National Assembly
Cause: The disintegration of order in France and the Declaration led to the formation of the National Assembly, or Constituent Assembly, in order to make a constitution and rule the country.
Effect: They created a constitution that allowed for election of a legislative assembly with the king at the helm. The king then tried to escape with his family.

5. Attempted escape of Louis XVI and family
Cause: The revolutionary mood in France made them fear more for their lives than for their titles and possessions.
Effect: This further cemented national sentiment against the royal family and was a factor in their later execution.

6. The Legislative Assembly declares war on Austria
Cause: The Declaration of Pillnitz saw Austria try to intervene in French affairs by pursuing military action to protect the monarchy.
Effect: The *sans-culottes* and the radicals came together with support building all over France against foreign invasion.

7. Radicals and *sans-culottes* gain power
Cause: The pendulum of change had been held to the right for so long that it swung far in the other direction. Pent-up aggression from the Third Estate led to the most demagogical leaders gaining power: *Marat*, *Danton*, and *Robespierre*.
Effect: Revolutionary zeal swept the common people of France. Society was turned upside down, and the Reign of Terror would eventually result.

8. The National Convention is formed
Cause: The new constitution, which created the First Republic, called for a National Assembly to be formed.
Effect: This body was very politically biased with the radical Jacobin Party in power. The modern-day terms, Right and Left for Conservative and Liberal, come from the seating arrangement in this body.

9. The Jacobin Club gains prominence
Cause: The radical mood of Paris and the overwhelming support of the poor and the peasants led the radical Jacobin Party to gain power. The powerful demagogues mentioned in box 7 and France's military needs also contributed.
Effect: The Revolution went through a second stage that was more radical and sometimes known as the *Reign of Terror*.

10. Execution of King Louis XVI
Cause: The radical turn of the Revolution: the king's alliance with Austria, and his life of excess and poor national management, led to his execution.
Effect: The other nations of Europe condemned France, and the Revolution turned more radical as it became clear that no one who opposed the Revolution was safe in France.

> **11. Committee of Public Safety oversees Reign of Terror**
> **Cause:** The radical mood of Paris, the rise of radicals, and the execution of the king combined to lead the Third Estate to kill over 20,000, most of whom were in the Third Estate. Anyone associated with nobility was in danger and many innocents were executed at the guillotine.
> **Effect:** Many abroad opposed the Revolution, and the Terror soon convinced many French that the Revolution had gone too far.

> **12. End of the Reign of Terror and Rise of the Directory**
> **Cause:** The leadership of the Committee turned on each other and, by 1794, Marat, Robespierre, and Danton were dead, the last two killed as enemies of the Revolution. The radical phase ran its course and the people wanted stability.
> **Effect:** France was ruled by moderates, and many of the *sans-culottes* felt abandoned by the Revolution.

> **13. Napoleon rises to power**
> **Cause:** There was definitely a power vacuum, and the nation was looking for a strong leader to emerge, which Napoleon did in style. He was a brilliant general and a lesser noble who was not a part of the establishment, but who understood power very well.
> **Effect:** Napoleon took over France and conquered most of Europe. He instituted reforms of the law and instituted freedom of religion across the Continent. He also unified Italy and Germany for the first time (in centuries for Italy). His legacy was a reorganization of European power at the Congress of Vienna after his defeat.

Summary of Social Change During the French Revolution

In many ways, the onslaught of the French Revolution was an example of Europeans attempting to use rational and empirical thought to challenge traditional values and ideals. It was a spread of the ideas on constitutionalism of John Locke from Great Britain to the Continent. At the same time, religion was becoming increasingly a matter of private rather than public concern. The increased population made possible by the agricultural revolution caused strains on social and political norms. The disappearance of the plague and the introduction of a smallpox vaccine significantly reduced death rates as well. The consumer revolution explained in the previous chapter led to higher expectations of political freedom as well. New consumer goods from abroad, such as porcelain, tobacco, sugar, and tea, also changed society. Other consumer goods, such as mirrors, printed art, and linens, also became more abundant as consumer society emerged.

NAPOLEON

In 1799, after spectacular victories against the Austrians and later against British armies in Egypt, Napoleon overthrew the Directory in a coup d'état and formed a new government, the *Consulate*, made up of three consuls, with Napoleon as head consul.

Napoleon's Domestic Reforms

Even as emperor, Napoleon was committed to many of the ideals of the French Revolution. He was an outsider to Paris, raised on Corsica (which had only recently become French), without wealth or connections, which makes his meteoric rise even more noteworthy. Napoleon reached the heights he did because the Revolution opened society to men of ability. His reforms assured the dissolution of the Old Regime by establishing egalitarianism in government, before the law, and in educational opportunity.

- *The Concordat of 1801*, in which the papacy renounced claims over Church property seized during the Revolution and Napoleon was allowed to nominate bishops.

    - In return, those priests who had resisted the Civil Constitutions of the clergy would replace those who had sworn an oath to the state.
    - Since the pope gave up claims to Church lands, those citizens who had acquired them pledged loyalty to Napoleon's government.

- With the *Code Napoleon*, 1804, Napoleon replaced varied and inequitable medieval law with a uniform legal system.

    - Became a model for codes of law in many European countries.

- In 1808, instituted a *state-supported educational system* with rigorous standards and made available to the masses.
- Created a *merit system* to recruit and reward those in government, despite the fact that he practiced flagrant *nepotism* by placing his relatives on the thrones of nations he conquered.
- Lowered the taxes on farmers.
- Guaranteed that the redistributed Church lands remained in the hands of their new owners, who were mostly peasant farmers.
- Created an *independent peasantry* that would become the backbone of French democracy.

Napoleon's Conquests and Defeats

Napoleon's aim was to unite Europe under France's leadership. In a decade, he was able to conquer vastly more territory and to influence the destinies of more nations than the Sun King, Louis XIV, had in his sixty and more years' reign. His very success convinced the peoples he conquered or battled with that their future lay in national unity, and the force of nationalism eventually led to his downfall and shaped the destiny of Europe well into the twentieth century. Napoleon's *new military tactics* allowed him to exert direct or indirect control over much of the European continent, spreading the ideals of the French Revolution across Europe. These tactics included: the use of "light" artillery; forcing a pitched battle from the front and then sending a cavalry charge from behind; and the use of professional ambulance corps and a professional supply system.

Italy: In 1797, his victories led to a northern Italian republic, the *Cisalpine*, and to several satellites in central and southern Italy under French control.

- By 1809, he controlled virtually all of Italy, abolishing feudalism and reforming the social, political, and economic structures.
- Practiced nepotism by placing family members on many European thrones.

- Revolutionary ideals inspired a slave revolt led by Toussaint l'Overture in the French colony of Saint Domingue, which became the independent nation of Haiti in 1804 despite Napoleon sending troops to put down the rebellion. This was his first defeat.
- He decided against *national* unity for the Italians, who had been divided into competing city-states and kingdoms during the Middle Ages, because unity might pose a threat to French dominance of the region.

Germany: After soundly defeating the two most powerful and influential German states, Austria and Prussia, Napoleon reorganized Germany:

- Consolidated many of the nearly 300 independent political entities (among these consolidations was the *Confederation of the Rhine*).
- Abolished feudalism and carried out reforms.
- Awakened German nationalism.

The Continental System

The Continental System: Through a series of shifting alliances, the British had consistently opposed the upset of the European balance of power brought about by French victories on the Continent, and Napoleon decided to engage in economic warfare rather than launch an actual invasion of the island.

- Unable to overcome British supremacy at sea and invade, Napoleon decided to starve Britain out by closing the ports of the Continent to British commerce.
- He coerced Russia, then a temporary ally of the French, his defeated enemy, Prussia, neutral Denmark and Portugal, and French satellite, Spain, all to adhere to the boycott.
- This policy was a complete failure and caused inflation and dissent in his empire, contributing to his downfall.

Spain: When Napoleon tried to tighten his control over Spain by replacing the Spanish king with one of his own brothers, the Spanish waged a costly *guerrilla war* that was aided by the British under one of their ablest commanders, the *Duke of Wellington* (1769–1852).

Russia: Napoleon *invaded Russia* in June of 1812, when the Russians withdrew from the Continental System that was preventing Russia from trading with Great Britain and causing Russian economic hardship.

- Napoleon assembled more than 600,000 of his best soldiers and marched into Russia, only to be met by *scorched earth* tactics rather than pitched battle.

  – The Russians destroyed all materials that could be foraged for Napoleon's army and only attacked in skirmishes at strategically advantageous points.

- Napoleon's army took Moscow, but due to the city being burned, his stretched supply lines, and the oncoming winter, he retreated.
- He returned from Russia with only about 22,000 soldiers.
- This devastated Napoleon's army and diminished his image.

The Collapse of the Napoleonic Empire

Napoleon's empire was in disarray after his defeat in Russia. The other powers he had defeated saw his vulnerability and unified to attack him.

- Lost 500,000 of his 600,000-man Grand Army in Russia.
- Riots in Italy against his rule.
- British invasion of southern France by Wellington's army.
- Napoleon was defeated by the combined forces of Russia, Prussia, and Austria in October 1813 at the *Battle of Leipzig*, also known as the *Battle of Nations*.

  - *Napoleon abdicated* as emperor on April 4, 1814.
  - The *Bourbons* were restored to the throne of France in the person of *Louis XVIII* (r. 1814–1824).
  - Napoleon was exiled to the island of *Elba* in the Mediterranean.
  - France surrendered all territory gained since the international wars of the French Revolution began in 1792.
  - King Louis created a legislature that represented only the upper classes.
  - The restoration, however, maintained most of Napoleon's reforms such as the Code Napoleon, the concordat with the Pope, and the abolition of feudalism.

THE CONGRESS OF VIENNA (SEPTEMBER 1814–JUNE 1815)

Representatives of the major powers of Europe, including France, met to redraw territorial lines and to restore, as far as was possible, the social and political order that existed before the Revolution and Napoleon. The *rule of legitimacy* was one primary goal: to return the "rightful" rulers of Europe to their thrones was one; a return to a balance of power that would guarantee peace was the other.

The August assemblage consisted of *Klemens von Metternich* (1773–1859), chancellor of Austria; Viscount *Castlereagh* (1769–1822), foreign minister of Great Britain; *Czar Alexander of Russia* (r. 1801–1825); *Prince Hardenberg* of Prussia; and *Charles Maurice de Talleyrand* (1754–1838), foreign minister of France.

- Metternich, Castlereagh, and Talleyrand constituted the first "Big 3" in European history.

The Settlement

To prevent her future expansion, France was surrounded by a number of strong states:

1. A newly united Holland and Belgium, called the Kingdom of the Netherlands.
2. A Prussian satellite area on the Rhine.
3. Austrian buffer states in Northern Italy.
4. In Germany, Napoleon's reorganization remained, and the 300 originally independent states were reduced to 39.
5. The Habsburg Holy Roman Empire was not reestablished.

The 100 Days

The Hundred Days began on March 1, 1815, when Napoleon managed to escape from his exile in Elba and made it to the south of France with a small honor guard of less than 100 men, marching, to popular acclaim, into Paris.

- He raised an army.
- Defeated a Prussian army in Belgium.
- Was defeated on June 18 at *Waterloo*, in Belgium, by the Duke of Wellington and Prussian general Gebhard von Blücher.
- Imprisoned on the island of *St. Helena* in the South Atlantic, and died there on May 5, 1821.

The Concert of Europe was created in November 1815 by a coalition known as the *Quadruple Alliance*: Great Britain, Prussia, Russia, and Austria.

- Its aim was to maintain the status quo that the Congress of Vienna had established, upholding the territorial boundaries and shoring up the monarchies of Europe against the spread of revolutionary ideas, such as *republicanism* (that the people should elect their rulers).
- The *Holy Alliance* of Austria, Prussia, and Russia was formed to prevent the dual economic and political revolutions from occurring anywhere in Europe.
- In effect the members of this alliance pledged to send their armies to any area intent on destroying monarchies and the status quo. The Holy Alliance, the Concert of Europe, and the Quadruple Alliance were effective in the short term at preventing republican and economic revolutions in Poland, Italy, and Spain, as well as contributing to the failure of the Decembrists in Russia.
- Belgium did gain independence in 1830.
- In 1848, all bets were off when most of Europe erupted into short-lived revolution, and Metternich fled to England.

Even though the Quadruple Alliance did not last for long, the balance of power created by the Congress of Vienna prevented a general war for a hundred years.

Criticism of Napoleon

Napoleon was criticized by his contemporaries and by historians for many of his practices. He curtailed the freedoms of his own people through *police censorship, limitation of women's rights,* and his use of his *secret police* to spy on his own people. He also used nepotism to appoint family members to positions of rule, and ignited nationalism across the Continent in reaction to his conquests. He was egotistical to the point that he designed his own tomb so that those who wished to view him must bow to him.

PRACTICE LONG-ESSAY QUESTIONS

These questions are samples of the various types of thematic essays on the exam. (See pages 30–31 for a detailed explanation of each type.) Check over the **generic rubric** (see pages 32–33) before you begin any of these essays and use that rubric to score your essay if you write one.

Question 1

Compare the stages of the French Revolution.

COMMENTS ON QUESTION 1

This is a COMPARE skill question, so be sure to describe similarities and differences between each stage of the French Revolution (moderate, radical, and reactionary), as well as account for or explain the reasons for the similarities and differences between each phase by providing specific examples of how they are similar and different and tying that to the overall course of the Revolution or the bigger fight for individual rights and sovereignty through specific evidence. The "differences" part of this question is easy, since the various stages of the Revolution have significant differences: the groups, personalities, and methods are glaringly different in each. The tough part of this question is to detail what the stages had in common, what their similarities were. Each had a form of government, a type of leadership, a constitution, a legislative body, and its own goals. Sort them out and stress their similarities.

Question 2

Analyze the way the attempt of Louis XVI to raise taxes to pay off the debts of his government precipitated the French Revolution.

COMMENTS ON QUESTION 2

This one is a CAUSATION question because it requires you to explain how one factor, Louis's attempt to raise taxes, resulted in a specific outcome, the French Revolution. Remember to describe causes AND/OR effects of the French Revolution and to support your analysis of those causes with specific details. The essay must explain the reasons why Louis's attempts to pay off his huge debts resulted in the French Revolution—citing specific evidence as support. To answer this question, the essay must apply all the meanings of the term "analyze." It must "determine the relationship" between the Revolution and Louis's attempt to raise taxes. The assembling of the Estates-General for the first time in almost 175 years started the chain of events. You must "examine" the sequence of events "in detail." Class factionalism in the Estates-General led to the creation of the National Assembly. And you must "explain" why this particular attempt to raise taxes was significantly different from previous attempts. Louis wanted to tax the First and Second Estates, which had been exempt since the Middle Ages.

Question 3

To what extent did Napoleon's successes in battle awaken the nationalistic forces that defeated him?

COMMENTS ON QUESTION 3

This one is also a CAUSATION question because it requires you to explain how one factor, Napoleon's successes in battle, resulted in a specific outcome, awakening nationalistic forces that defeated him. Remember to describe causes AND/OR effects of Napoleon's defeat, supporting your analysis of those causes with specific details. To get the second point, the essay must explain reasons for Napoleon's military success awakening the forces that defeated him—citing specific evidence as support. The strategy is simple: Show how his victories over specific states led to increased nationalism both there and back in France. Napoleon's installation of relatives as heads of state, his weakening of Habsburg power, and his addiction to winning victories should also be mentioned. Perhaps the most important factor to cite is that Napoleon united Germany and Italy, for the most part, a feat that the Germans and Italians themselves had failed to accomplish.

Question 4

To what extent and in what ways did the Congress of Vienna restore the Old Order in Europe?

COMMENTS ON QUESTION 4

It clearly calls for you to analyze CONTINUITY AND CHANGE OVER TIME. Be sure to describe the level of historical continuity (as in what did not change from the Old Order after the Congress of Vienna redrew the map of Europe), and change (as in how did national security, international diplomacy, and national character change as a result of Napoleon's defeat). Explain the reasons why European diplomacy and the balance of power were altered—citing specific evidence as support. Here the essay must "examine in detail" as well as "determine relationships." "How and how much" did the Congress restore the Old Order? What had the Old Order been? How had the Revolution and Napoleon's campaigning changed it? What provisions of the Congress dealt with it? What was the overall result, both immediately and in the long term?

PRACTICE SHORT-ANSWER QUESTIONS

1. Please use the passages below and your knowledge of European History to answer all parts of the following question.

Source 1

Napoleon was synonymous with the history of Europe for almost two decades. His influence on events was so immense that he was adored and feared by the people he ruled and those whom he conquered. He brought a set of legal codes with him to all of the territory he controlled. His reach was immense, as was his desire for order and logic. France under Napoleon was at its zenith of international power and has declined ever since his fall. Also, Napoleon is indirectly responsible for the emergence of many of the current nations of Europe, such as Germany and the Czech Republic. He was a figure so grand and so spectacular that King Louis Philippe brought his remains back from St. Helena, where he died, to be entombed at Les Invalides, where the tradition of bowing to the tomb is a homage that onlookers must perform to see the tomb, a perfect epitaph.

—Historian Burke Arielle

Source 2

Napoleon may have been a dominating figure in European history, but he was a flash in the pan compared to the reigns of figures like Otto von Bismarck or Louis XIV. He had to work to ensure his own legacy after his imprisonment on St. Helena by writing about his own posterity. He may have been good for France for a short while, but his actions led to the creation of European nationalism and sowed the seeds for France's greatest defeats. He himself designed his own tomb so that all viewers would have to bow down to him in order to see his grave.

—Historian Jessica Gillespie

(A) Based on **Source 1**, briefly analyze the positive aspects of the reign of Napoleon for the European continent.

(B) Based on **Source 2**, briefly analyze the negative aspects of the reign of Napoleon for the European continent.

(C) What role did international trade play in the rise and fall of Napoleon?

2. Please use the following legislation and your knowledge of European history to answer all parts of the question that follows.

ARTICLE I. The National Assembly hereby completely abolishes the feudal system. It decrees that, among the existing rights and dues, both feudal and *censuel*, all those originating in or representing real or personal serfdom shall be abolished without indemnification. All other dues are declared redeemable, the terms and mode of redemption to be fixed by the National Assembly. Those of the said dues which are not extinguished by this decree shall continue to be collected until indemnification shall take place.

II. The exclusive right to maintain pigeon houses and dovecotes is abolished. The pigeons shall be confined during the seasons fixed by the community. During such periods they shall be looked upon as game, and every one shall have the right to kill them upon his own land.

III. The exclusive right to hunt and to maintain uninclosed warrens is likewise abolished, and every landowner shall have the right to kill, or to have destroyed on his own land, all kinds of game, observing, however, such police regulations as may be established with a view to the safety of the public.

—National Assembly

(A) Briefly explain ONE economic development that led to the changes asked for in the piece of legislation above.

(B) Briefly explain ONE political result of the ideas in the legislative document above.

(C) Briefly explain ONE social change brought on as a result of the ideas in the legislation above.

Short-Answer Explanations

1. (A) You should explain the unity Napoleon brought to Europe as well as the freedoms he guaranteed to the peoples of Europe in his *Napoleonic Code.* The rise of France to controlling most of Europe should also be noted. Other aspects that may be taken into account include his military genius; his ability, through charisma, to make people believe in him; his saving of many ideals of the French Revolution; his keen political mind; and the patriotism he expanded in France and later throughout the Continent as a reaction to his conquest of the Continent.

   (B) You should begin with his huge ego and shortsightedness. You may then explain how his legacy was bad for France by citing how his legacy led to many tragedies for France and for Europe, including the Franco-Prussian War, the two world wars, the growth on nationalism as a force, the continued subjugation of women, nepotism, and trade wars.

   (C) This part must examine the Continental System and how Napoleon attempted to prevent the rest of Europe from trading with Britain. It should also explain that Napoleon invaded Russia, his costliest and most foolish military maneuver, to enforce the Continental System when Russia began to trade with Britain. Partial credit can be given for an explanation of the Battle of Trafalgar and how the British exerted their dominance of the sea after that point in history for over a century, enriching them at the expense of the rest of the Continent.

2. (A) You should explain the conditions under the *Ancien Régime* that divided France into three estates with privileges based upon the family one was born into. The growth of the commercial revolution and economic prosperity for some should be examined as a cause for the people wanting more political freedom. The bankruptcy of France and the famine of 1787–1789 within the country could also be used as economic explanations of the worsening conditions for the emerging middle and lower classes in France.

   (B) You should explain one of the political results of the French Revolution, ranging from the rise of Robespierre to the rise of Napoleon and to the creation of the National Convention, to the battle for power between the Girondins and Jacobins, and to the Great Panic and the Reign of Terror. The rise of France as an international military power again may also be mentioned as a political result.

   (C) You should discuss the complete transformation of French society, with former street urchins such as the *sans-culottes* gaining power, to the death of over 20,000 in the Reign of Terror, to revolutionary colors becoming fashionable and adults calling each other "citizen," to the long tradition from 1789 to the present of French people engaging in protests against their governments or other institutions, to the rise of the middle class, and to the ideals of equality, brotherhood, and freedom being adopted (liberty, equality, fraternity).

PRACTICE MULTIPLE-CHOICE QUESTIONS

Questions 1 to 3 refer to the following excerpt from "*What is the Third Estate?*" by Emmanuel Joseph Sieyès in 1789.

Who then shall dare to say that the Third Estate has not within itself all that is necessary for the formation of a complete nation? It is the strong and robust man who has one arm still shackled. If the privileged order should be abolished, the nation would be nothing less, but something more. Therefore, what is the Third Estate? Everything; but an everything shackled and oppressed. What would it be without the privileged order? Everything, but an everything free and flourishing. Nothing can succeed without it; everything would be infinitely better without the others.

It is not sufficient to show that privileged persons, far from being useful to the nation, cannot but enfeeble and injure it; it is necessary to prove further that the noble order does not enter at all into the social organization; that it may indeed be a burden upon the nation.

1. The assertion made by Sieyès above—that the Third Estate is everything—is best supported by which of the following?

   (A) The Third Estate included over 95 percent of the French population.
   (B) The Third Estate was the most powerful political body in France at the start of 1789.
   (C) The Third Estate was unified and equal within their own estate.
   (D) The Third Estate was supporting a foreign invasion of France.

2. Which of the following best describes the role of *"What is the Third Estate"* in the French Revolution?

   (A) It was a rallying cry for the nobility who used it to get foreign aid.
   (B) It steadied the soldiers as they prepared to meet the Austrians in battle.
   (C) It was a catalyst that helped get the people of France ready to revolt against their king.
   (D) It refuted the logic of the Enlightenment and embraced raw emotion instead.

3. The reform of the French Revolution that was most consistent from the Revolution onward was which of the following?

   (A) Increased participation of the people in shaping the direction of France.
   (B) The Roman Catholic Church lost all power within France.
   (C) A constitutional monarchy was created.
   (D) The hereditary privileges of the nobility were abolished.

Questions 4 to 6 refer to the following chart of the deaths during the Reign of Terror in France from March 1793 to August 1794.

Social Class	Number Killed	Percentage of People Executed	Percentage of Population
None Given		1%	
Clergy (First Estate)	920	7%	0.5%
Nobility (Second Estate)	1,158	8%	1.5%
Middle Class	3,452	25%	4%
Working Class	4,399	31%	8%
Peasants/Farmers	3,961	28%	86%

4. Which of the following groups saw the highest percentage of its members executed during the Reign of Terror?

(A) The working class
(B) The middle class
(C) The clergy
(D) The nobility

5. Who or which of the following did NOT help control governmental power in France during the Reign of Terror?

(A) Napoleon Bonaparte
(B) Maximillian Robespierre
(C) Georges Danton
(D) The Committee of Public Safety

6. The immediate cause of the outbreak of revolution in 1789 was which of the following?

(A) Grinding poverty among all classes of society
(B) Government oppression
(C) The ideas of the *philosophes*
(D) The government's financial crisis

Multiple-Choice Explanations

1. **A**   3. **D**   5. **A**
2. **C**   4. **C**   6. **D**

1. **(A)**

(A) is CORRECT because the fact that the Third Estate was 95 percent of France supports the idea that the Third Estate is everything and would be better without the nobility and the clergy.

(B) is wrong because the Third Estate had very little political power in 1789 until the French Revolution began in July.

(C) is wrong because the Third Estate was stratified and divided between many social levels of people.

(D) is wrong because the Third Estate never supported foreign invasion of France.

2. **(C)**

(A) is wrong because the nobility were not helped in any way by this document, and did not use it to get aid.

(B) is wrong because it was written before the Revolution to incite the people to revolt against an unfair feudal system, and did nothing to help soldiers prepare to meet Austrians in battle.

(C) is CORRECT because it was written before the Revolution to incite the people to revolt against an unfair feudal system.

(D) is wrong because it relied on the logic of the Enlightenment to argue that France needed a new social structure.

3. **(D)**

(A) is wrong because the participation of the people in politics increased and decreased over the next century, depending upon who was ruling France.

(B) is wrong because the Roman Catholic Church in France did lose influence, then regained it, and then lost it again.

(C) is wrong because the constitutional monarchy in France appeared and then disappeared, then reappeared, and then disappeared.

(D) is CORRECT because after feudal privileges were suspended they were never reinstated.

4. **(C)**

(A) is wrong because the clergy at just ½ of 1% of the population made up 7% of the executed, making their death rate 14% of the total per 1% of population while the working class saw a death rate of about 4% per 1% of population.

(B) is wrong because the clergy at just ½ of 1% made up 7% of the executed, making their death rate 14% of the total per 1% of population while the middle class saw a death rate of about 6.25% per 1% of population.

(C) is CORRECT because the clergy at just ½ of 1% made up 7% of the executed, making their death rate 14% of the total per 1% of population.

(D) is wrong because the clergy, at just ½ of 1%, made up 7% of the executed, making their death rate 14% of the total per 1% of population while the nobility saw a death rate of about 5.3% per 1% of population.

5. **(A)**

(A) is CORRECT because Napoleon did not hold power until after overthrowing the Directory in a coup d'état in 1799.

(B) is wrong because Robespierre did hold political power during the Reign of Terror.

(C) is wrong because Danton did hold political power during the Reign of Terror.

(D) is wrong because the Committee of Public Safety was the sole holder of all political power during the Reign of Terror.

6. **(D)**

(A) is wrong because although there was poverty, there always had been poverty in France so it was nothing new.

(B) is wrong because government oppression, while present, did not lead directly to the Revolution.

(C) is wrong because, although the ideas of the *philosophes* were long-term causes of the Revolution, the meeting of the Estates-General and the events that followed were caused directly by a financial crisis in France.

(D) is CORRECT because the meeting of the Estates-General and the events that followed were caused directly by a financial crisis in France.

Industrialization Reshapes Europe

6

KEY TERMS/PEOPLE

→ CAPITALISM
→ INDUSTRIAL REVOLUTION
→ MEDIEVAL COMMON LANDS
→ PROLETARIAT
→ CHILD LABOR LAWS
→ FACTORY ACT OF 1833
→ MINES ACT OF 1842
→ TEN HOURS ACT OF 1847
→ JEREMY BENTHAM
→ JOHN STUART MILL

→ BOURGEOISIE
→ CLASS CONSCIOUSNESS
→ UTILITARIANISM
→ THOMAS MALTHUS
→ DAVID RICARDO
→ COMTE DE SAINT-SIMON
→ KARL MARX
→ JAMES WATT
→ ADAM SMITH
→ SOCIALISM

SPECIAL NOTE ON PERIODIZATION

The subject of the Industrial Revolution was split between time periods by the new framework for European History. To preserve the continuity of the subject, the Industrial Revolution will be covered entirely in Chapter 6, although much of the content covered is included in Period 3 by the College Board. This chapter will make clear delineations of which material belongs in which time period to help you with the skill of Periodization.

Periodization is done based upon many different markers in history. One historian may use political markers such as the Peace of Westphalia, while another may choose economic ones, such as the opening of transatlantic trade and the Columbian Exchange. The *AP European History Curriculum Framework* uses the political markers of the Peace of Westphalia, the Congress of Vienna, and the outbreak of World War One. Unfortunately, social and economic movements do not always fit into the same delineations as political history. The largest problem for the traditional historian in periodization posed by the framework is contained in this chapter. The author believes that it is more important to preserve the narrative of industrialization than to alter the narrative to fit the framework. Therefore, special attention will be given to the periodization outlined in the *AP European History Curriculum Framework* in this chapter to help avoid confusion and to give you ideas about how to display the skill of periodization in your essay. The *AP European History Curriculum Framework* was written to emphasize the use of historical thinking rather than memorization of facts. The authors believe that by offering an alternate sense of periodization compared to that framework, they will enhance your understanding of that skill and of the many different markers that can be used with periodization.

Great Britain had begun industrialization by the 1790s and saw industrial output soar and demographics change mightily before the end of the Napoleonic Wars in 1815, when Period 2 ends according to the *AP European History Curriculum Framework*, but the Industrial Revolution was just getting into full swing at that point. As yet, parts of Europe had not even seen enclosure or an agricultural revolution, much less an industrial one, so the slow cultural diffusion of enclosure and then industrialization, as well as the fact that its implementation came with bursts and lulls, make fitting this chapter into the framework a challenge. The issues of *urbanization* and the growth of *consumerism* are of particular concern as they occur over both time periods. This chapter addresses the following Key Concepts from the *AP European History Curriculum Framework*:

KEY CONCEPTS AND OVERVIEW

KEY CONCEPT 2.4 The experiences of everyday life were shaped by demographic, environmental, medical, and technological changes.

KEY CONCEPT 3.1 The Industrial Revolution spread from Great Britain to the Continent, where the state played a greater role in promoting industry.

KEY CONCEPT 3.2 The experiences of everyday life were shaped by industrialization, depending on the level of industrial development in a particular location.

KEY CONCEPT 3.3 Political revolutions and the complications resulting from industrialization triggered a range of ideological, governmental, and collective responses.

OVERVIEW

The Industrial Revolution fostered into existence by the growth of commerce, the development of capitalism, the introduction of improved technology, and the unique political climate in Britain during the eighteenth century changed life in Western Europe in the 1800s more profoundly than had the French Revolution. The landowning aristocracy, which had its origins in the early Middle Ages and whose decline had begun with the growth of a commercial and professional middle class, lost more wealth and political power with the inception of a spectacularly wealthy capitalist class. The lives of the mass of Europeans shifted from the farm to the factory, from the predictable rhythms of a rural existence to the grinding and impersonal poverty of the industrial cities. Along with the capitalists, a new *proletariat*, or working class, was created, and a whole new set of social and economic doctrines sought to explain their rights and better their lives. The family was reshaped, concepts of time were changed, and trade unions and other organizations promoting social welfare were created. The European balance of power was shifted multiple times by industrial production as first the United Kingdom, then Germany, dominated industrial output and thus gained international power. Because industrialization can also create the capability to reshape the world, industrialization became a national project with ramifications for those who advanced the slowest or the most quickly. Added to the "isms" that grew out of the French Revolution— such as republicanism, conservatism, and nationalism—were *socialism* and *Marxism*. By the last third of the nineteenth century, an "Age of Progress," a technological revolution, had altered the Western world and was to lead the way into the woes and wonders of the twentieth century.

THE INDUSTRIAL REVOLUTION

Industrialization was never really a "revolution" or a violent, drastic change but, rather, industrialization has been a continuous and usually gradual process throughout human existence, from the use of the first stone tools to the development of high technology. The so-called *Industrial Revolution* was a period of rapid development, roughly between *1780 and 1830*, during which new forms of energy from coal and other fossil fuels powered machines rather than muscles, water, or wind. The advent of the steam engine allowed massive amounts of energy to be exerted by machinery, such as the water frame and power looms, that appeared in large factories, where most textile workers began to work. This contrasted markedly with pre-industrial society where textiles were made in cottages from thread spun on wheels and fabric was woven on human-powered looms.

Industrialization began in Britain in the second half of the eighteenth century and moved to France, Holland, Belgium, and the United States in the second decade of the nineteenth. It began in Germany, Austria, and Italy in the middle of the nineteenth, then arrived in Eastern Europe and Russia at the end of the century and in parts of Asia and Africa well into the twentieth. It carries on today as new technologies continue to reshape society.

The Agricultural Revolution in Britain

After the Glorious Revolution of 1688, British landowning aristocrats dominated Parliament and passed the *Enclosure Acts*, which fenced off the *medieval common lands*. The *Enclosure Movement* is the least understood and possibly most important change that happened to legal rights in Europe during its history. It took centuries to complete and radically changed the relationships people had with the land, production, and each other.

- The *Enclosure Movement* put into place the last of the four needed ingredients for capitalism: **land**, **labor**, **capital**, and **markets** (entrepreneurs and technology).
- Allowed the struggle for money to be based on factors other than just birth and luck.
- Opportunities for advancement were there for anyone who had a profitable idea and a work ethic.
- The modern economy began.
- The struggle between capital and labor became a true battle.

RESULTS OF THE ENCLOSURE MOVEMENT

- Large landowners became prosperous; they invested in technology, meaning machinery, breeding, improved planting methods. Crop yields and livestock production soared.
- Surplus production enabled agriculture to support a larger population in the cities.
- The population of Britain doubled during the eighteenth century.
- Small farmers who were displaced by the Enclosure Movement moved to the cities and made up the growing force of factory workers (the *industrial proletariat*).

Demographic Changes Altered Lifestyles

The population explosion of the sixteenth century resulted in both food shortages and food gluts throughout Europe during the seventeenth and eighteenth centuries, resulting in mortality disasters. The European marriage pattern, which limited family size, became the most important check on population levels, although some couples also adopted birth-control practices to limit family size. By the middle of the 1750s, better weather, improvements in transportation, new crops and agricultural practices, less epidemic disease, and advances in medicine and hygiene meant a reduction of, or end of, the cycle of feast and famine. By the start of the nineteenth century, reductions in child mortality and increases in life expectancy led to the emergence of new attitudes toward children and families.

- Economic motivations for marriage, while still important for all classes, diminished as the middle-class notion of companionate marriage began to be adopted by the working classes.
- This demographic revolution, along with the rise in prosperity, produced advances in the general standard of living that allowed cultural and intellectual growth for the masses.

  - Greater prosperity was associated with increasing literacy, education, and richer cultural lives.

    - Growth of publishing and libraries.
    - Founding of schools.
    - Establishment of orchestras, theaters, and museums.

  - As the nineteenth century began, it was clear that a large percentage of Europeans were better fed and healthier, lived longer, and were more secure and comfortable in their material well-being than at any previous time in history.
  - This relative prosperity was offset by increasing numbers of the poor throughout Europe.

    - Poor depended upon charitable resources.
    - Distressed government officials and local communities.

- A *consumer revolution* changed the lives of the European people as it spread from the Dutch and British, first to Western Europe, then more slowly southward and toward the East.

  - Consumers demanded new items such as porcelain, mirrors, manufactured cotton goods, and even printed art.
  - New leisure venues, such as taverns and opera houses, attracted these emerging consumers.
  - Blood sports and betting also common entertainments for the working classes.

- Family patterns and ideas about privacy began to change:

  - Explosion of illegitimate births between 1750 and 1850 throughout Europe.

    - Labor became more mobile and social punishments for moral infractions were no longer easy to enforce.
    - Infant and child mortality decreased, and commercial wealth increased; families could dedicate more space and resources to children and child-rearing, as well as to private life and comfort.

Urbanization

Perhaps the most important change that took place during the nineteenth century era of industrialization was the huge migration from the rural village to the relative anonymity and fast pace of the cities. A trend that took centuries to spread throughout Europe, and one that is still occurring in parts of the world today, *urbanization* is a change that has reshaped human existence.

- Communal values were eroded when families that did not know each other migrated from villages to the big cities.
- At first, there were areas in cities with concentrations of many poor people, which led to a greater awareness of poverty, crime, prostitution, and other social problems, causing many to want better policing of those living on the margins of society.
- Cities experienced overcrowding and filthy living conditions.
- Rural areas suffered labor shortages and weakened communities.
- Social activists brought the problems of the poor to light.
- Cities were redesigned with urban planning and zoning.
- Labor unions were established.
- Governments responded to the problems of urbanization.

The last four fit into Period 3.

Technological Advances

Inventions of new machines and improvement of production processes throughout the eighteenth century made large-scale production possible in *textile manufacturing* and *coal mining*. The *steam engine* revolutionized transportation.

THE SCARCITY OF ENERGY

By the eighteenth century, most of Britain's forests were gone, and its supply of wood for fuel nearly depleted. The British were importing wood from Russia. *Coal*, plentiful, but traditionally shunned as a fuel because of its pollution of the air, gradually replaced wood as both a fuel and for industrial processes. Most British coal was mined near the coasts.

- The most profitable energy source humans had yet found, producing a calorie extraction ratio to yield result, at worst, 1 : 27 and possibly 1 : 200.

  - This meant that for every calorie invested in mining they got 27–200 calories of energy back.
  - Fossil fuels became the way for Europe to power a way to reshape the world.

- Mines kept filling with water, so pumps were needed to empty them.

  - The early *steam engines*, such as Thomas Newcomen's clumsy contraption, a maze of rods and leather straps, used heat from burning coal to boil water that made steam power to set the engine in motion; they were employed as pumps in mines.
  - *James Watt* in 1763 saw the problems of the earlier engines, such as those of Newcomen and Thomas Savery (that they lacked a condensing chamber), and created an improved steam engine that became a great success in Britain.

    - Revolutionized every mode of production and transportation, starting with mining, then the textile industry, and culminating in the railroad industry.

The mastery of coal, then oil and natural gas, gave Western Europeans the power to dominate the world and to improve the lives of workers, who could now accomplish much more with machines powered by fuel than by using animals, water, and wind.

TEXTILES

The story of the textile industry mirrors that of industrialization. In many ways, the textile industry was the first to be industrialized, so it is often tied to the teaching of this unit. Second, everyone needs clothes, so making them more quickly and less expensively allowed for huge profits and generated a consumer market and a feeling of consumerism. What follows is a list of important events in the development of the textile industry that are often asked about on the exam:

- The *fly shuttle* (John Kay, 1733) cut manpower needs on the looms in half.
- The *spinning jenny* (James Hargreaves, 1764) mechanized the spinning wheel.
- The *water frame* (Richard Arkwright, 1769) improved thread spinning.
- Use of the *steam engine* (Arkwright, 1780s) powered the looms and required factory production of textiles instead of domestic industry.
- The *cotton gin* (Eli Whitney, American, 1793) separated seed from raw cotton fiber and increased the supply of cotton, which was spun into thread and then woven into cloth.

COAL

- *Steam pump* (Thomas Newcomen, 1702) rid coal mines of water seepage.
- *Condensing chamber steam engine* (James Watt, 1763).
- Plentiful coal boosted iron production and gave rise to *heavy industry* (the manufacture of machinery and materials used in production).

TRANSPORTATION AND COMMUNICATION

New efficient methods of transportation and other innovations created new industries, improved the distribution of goods, increased consumerism, and enhanced the quality of life.

- The *steamboat* (Robert Fulton, American, 1807).

> **Marker**
> From this point until the "Theories on Economics" section, everything covered is in Period 3, but some of it is called for in both periods.

- *The railroad steam locomotive* (George Stephenson's *Rocket*, 1829).

  - Both the *steamboat and steam locomotive* enhanced an already-efficient system of river transportation that had been expanded in the eighteenth century by a network of canals.
  - The canals meant that transportation was cheap and easy for most of the nation, leading to trade networks and higher demand for goods as well as for higher transportability of resources.
  - Together they opened new sources of raw materials and new markets for manufactured goods, and they made it possible to locate factories in population centers.
  - The railroad building boom, from 1830 to 1850, brought about massive social and economic changes in Britain's largely agrarian economy.
  - The ease of transport encouraged rural workers to move to the cities.
  - The lower costs of shipping goods in bulk fostered expanding markets.
  - The railroad was a culminating invention of the Industrial Revolution because it utilized steel and a steam engine, and was so massive that it induced many workers to learn the skills needed for an industrial society.

- It also allowed the creation of *mass marketing* through the use of catalogs.
- Refrigerated rail cars added much to the ability to feed the world cheaply.
- Led to the ability to more easily gather raw materials.
- Led to the advent of trolleys, streetcars, and eventually subways, which opened the cities to new designs.

■ New technologies and means of communication and transportation—including railroads—resulted in more fully integrated national economies, a higher level of urbanization, and a truly global economic network.

- Streetcars and trolleys revolutionized the cities and allowed their redesign.
- Bicycles allowed the common person some freedom of transportation at an affordable price.
- Automobiles, and eventually airplanes, would complete the transportation network by the advent of the First World War in 1914.

■ Communication advanced notably with the invention, first of the telegraph, then the radio and telephone.

OIL

By the end of the nineteenth century, the refinement of petroleum allowed its use as a fuel for the newly developed *internal combustion engines* that propelled automobiles, locomotives, and even ships, and also for heating and industrial processes.

Britain Was First in Industrialization

Great Britain was the first nation to industrialize for many reasons, not the least of which was the availability of coal, the energy source that powered the first Industrial Revolution. The Continent did not see industrialization until after the end of the Napoleonic Wars, which ravaged the Continent for the first 15 years of the nineteenth century. Why was Britain the first nation to industrialize?

■ Stable governments and government institutions supported business.
■ Availability of coal, iron ore, and a shortage of wood.
■ High levels of economic freedom.
■ Economic institutions and human capital were available there.
■ No wars at home.
■ Enclosure made land, labor, markets, and entrepreneurship available.
■ The British government supported industrialization with financial rewards for inventors.
■ Britain already had a strong network of canals and roads.
■ Private businessmen created many of the inventions and networks needed to industrialize.

After the British industrialized, they tried to keep their methods of production a secret, and banned engineers from foreign travel. However, after the defeat of Napoleon, industrialization spread to Europe through people such as Fritz Harkort, who made steam engines in Germany. The Continent slowly caught up to Britain after she invited the world to see her wonders at the Great Exposition of 1851, held in the *Crystal Palace*, London, an exhibition venue built for the exposition. The British gave financial awards to inventors and did everything possible to promote industry within the British realm.

The Nations on the Continent Followed Later

PRUSSIA: The state became a leader of a unified Germany, which rapidly industrialized with strong government leadership and some industrial leaders.

- The *Zollverein*, or the Prussian-led trade union of German states, allowed them to unify their efforts at industrialization.
- *Friedrich List* was a writer and philosopher who

  - Believed manufacturing was the primary means of increasing people's well-being and relieving poverty, hence it is the duty of the government to improve industry;
  - Wrote *National System of Political Economy*;
  - Conceived of and advocated for the *Zollverein*, or German customs union, created in 1834.

- For the first time, goods were allowed to move within German states without tariffs.
- Still-high protective tariffs on foreign goods (from outside the *Zollverein*).
- Helped to develop growing German nationalism.
- Fritz Harkort got ideas for machinery from Britain.

  - Known as the "Watt of Germany," he borrowed materials and hired foreign workers to build steam engines in Germany.
  - Roads too bad to deliver them fully assembled.

FRANCE: The state led a slower industrialization with less dislocation of traditional methods of production in order to try to prevent societal upheaval. The government supported banks, canals, and a national railroad.

SOUTHERN AND EASTERN EUROPE: A combination of factors, including lack of resources, feudal traditions, geography, the persistence of serfdom in some areas, and lack of government sponsorship accounted for eastern and southern Europe's lag in industrial development.

Results of the Industrial Revolution

- The most significant result was the *increased production and availability of manufactured goods.*

  - Material prosperity increased because there were cheaper high-quality goods.
  - Increased consumption led to more jobs.

- Factory workers lived in poverty on low wages.

  - Housing was in dismal tenements.
  - For the first half of the nineteenth century, entire families, including children from age five up, worked 14 hours a day under unsafe and unhealthy conditions.
  - Crowded slums were worsened by the absence of public services in cities that had expanded too rapidly.
  - Although these living conditions did not differ much from those under which people had lived for centuries on farms, the *concentration of the population* made them more unhealthy.
  - This visibility of poverty in the cities led thinkers to ponder the causes of poverty and prompted the institutions of society to push for its alleviation.

    - The *Sadler Commission* in Great Britain helped initiate legislation to improve working conditions in factories.

- *Urbanization* was one of the Industrial Revolution's most important socioeconomic effects.

  – Working-class injustices, gender exploitation, and standard-of-living issues became the nineteenth century's great social and political dilemmas.
  – Literally tens of millions of people moved from the countryside to the city as the factory system replaced the domestic system.
  – The family structure changed greatly in that productive work was taken out of the home and to the factory, and children were separated from their families and rural settings.
  – Gender roles changed.

    • Women's work was seen as less valuable and was increasingly associated with domestic duties.
    • Men were separated from wives and children, leaving home to go to work or working in different factories.

- By the end of the century, wages and the quality of life for the working class improved because of laws restricting the labor of children and women, creating social welfare programs, and promoting improved diet and the use of birth control.

  – The many reform laws that restricted the labor of women and children included:

    • The Factory Act of 1833
    • The Mines Act of 1842
    • The Ten Hours Act of 1847

- The Industrial Revolution may have prevented a large-scale human tragedy by increasing production, but the filthy conditions of crowded city life and the grinding poverty of the cities led many reformers, such as *Edwin Chadwick*, to call for changes.

Effects on Class and Gender

Two new overall classes developed as a result of the Industrial Revolution: *industrialists/capitalists* and *factory workers*. However, the reality was that there were many levels of class distinction within each of these overall classifications of class and, thus, class distinctions became more important at the time.

- There was a huge divide between the *bourgeoisie*, the servant-keeping middle class, and the *proletariat*, or working class.
- The division of labor by gender was much more pronounced among the upper classes, where women were homemakers, than in the lower classes, where women often had to work outside the home.
- The gap between wealthy and working classes remained enormous.

  – 5 percent of British households received 33 percent of all income.
  – 20 percent of households made 50–60 percent of British income.
  – 80 percent of the population shared 40 percent of the income.
  – The competitive nature of the markets led many of the factory owners to offer low wages for long hours, to create poor and unsafe working conditions, and to employ child labor.

- The rigid discipline of factory work contrasted with the rural pace of farm work that most of the laborers had been accustomed to.
- Not until the mid-nineteenth century did the standard of living improve for the average industrial worker.
- *Child labor laws* were enacted after the first three decades of the nineteenth century to limit the number of hours children could be required to work.
- A gender division of labor emerged.

  - Men became the main breadwinners, while married women tended to stay home to raise the children.
  - Jobs available to women were "dead-end" and poorly paid.
  - The early attempts of workers to organize were met with hostility from industrialists and anti-union regulations from governments, and had very limited success.

■ Class diversity was remarkable, even within the traditional classes.

- The upper class was created when the newly wealthy industrialists intermarried with the fading nobility to create a new top notch in European society.
- The middle class, or *bourgeoisie*, saw huge diversity:
  - Tended to own homes;
  - Usually made about $10,000/year while the poor made $400;
  - Spent 25 percent on food and 25 percent on servants;
  - Victorian behavior pattern emerged as the norm.

■ Drinking, gambling, and sex condemned as vices.
■ Hypocritically ignored in private.
■ Age becomes one of the most sexually repressed yet privately perverted.

- Included industrialists, bankers, white-collar workers, bureaucrats, shopkeepers, business owners, and technical workers.
- The lower class or *proletariat*, which also had huge diversity, totaled about 80 percent of the population,

  - Top of the lower classes tried to emulate the upper classes' Victorian behavior;
  - Many different levels of lower classes with Labor aristocracy or those who could hire and fire at the top;
  - Skilled workers, such as plumbers or masons, were next;
  - Semi-skilled laborers, such as carpenter's assistants;
  - Day laborers did jobs for a day's pay, such as loading ships;
  - Domestic servants were low on the level of working class workers, but were relatively well paid, and many young women spent time as domestic servants.

Leisure Time

Leisure time centered increasingly on the family or small groups, concurrent with the development of activities and spaces to use that time. Some of the activities included:

■ Enjoying the parks.
■ Attending sporting events.
■ Going to the beach.

- Shopping in department stores.
- Visiting museums.
- Attending operas and the theater.

Reforms Began in the Cities

The rapid growth of cities during the Industrial Revolution necessitated urban reform to improve conditions that had existed for centuries: poor sanitation and other services, overcrowded housing, and inadequate transportation. Influenced by *Jeremy Bentham* (1748–1832), whose philosophy of *utilitarianism* emphasized "the greatest good for the greatest number," city planners and urban reformers redesigned the many European cities and initiated a public health movement to improve urban life for all classes.

- The Chadwick Report of 1842 indicated that British citizens were living in filthy, unsanitary conditions that were spreading disease.

  - Calculated that installing sewage and water systems in British cities would be less expensive than exporting the filth by other means.
  - Cholera epidemic broke out after its release, supporting its conclusions.
  - Cholera used to create the Public Health Act of 1848.

- Paris redesigned between 1853 and 1870 by Georges Haussmann.

  - First urban planning in Europe.
  - Slums destroyed.
  - Public transportation created.
  - Zoning laws passed.

    - Shopping districts at street level with housing above.
    - Large townhomes.
    - Many large roundabouts.
    - Parks and open spaces added.

  - Sewage and water systems added.
  - Soon followed by electricity.
  - Broad avenues to prevent revolutionary barricades.
  - Other cities such as Vienna followed the French example.

- Standard of living improved for most Europeans from the middle of the nineteenth century and into the early twentieth.
- Disparities in wealth between the classes led to conflict between them.

  - Encouraged the growth of political radicalism.
  - Hierarchies of wealth and status existed among both the middle and working classes.

- Relegation of women to menial jobs or to child raising fostered a women's rights movement.

  - First wave of *feminism* emerged.
  - Goals included gender equality in opportunity, and legal and voting rights.

THEORIES OF ECONOMICS

The competing economic theories below mostly emerged during Period 2, but were hotly contested during Period 3, so you must be familiar with all of the theories and theorists below. In reality, all of them, except for the *Comte de Saint-Simon*, Louis Blanc, and Karl Marx did most of their work during Period 2.

■ *Adam Smith* (see page 188) can be considered the first modern economist.

  – His *Wealth of Nations* has been called the "Bible of capitalism" and is the foundation for *classical* or laissez-faire economics, which opposed the regulations imposed by mercantilism by arguing that certain natural laws, such as *supply and demand*, govern an economy and should be free to operate.
  – People follow their own "enlightened self-interest," without the interference of government in the economy.
  – This private initiative will result in benefits to all in society.

■ *Thomas Malthus* (1766–1834) was the first of the classical economists to try to explain why the mass of people did not benefit from the operation of the "natural laws" of economics.

  – Poverty existed, he said, because the *population increased at a geometric rate while the food supply increased arithmetically*.
  – Believed that poverty was a divine punishment for humankind's lust.

■ *David Ricardo* (1772–1823) introduced the *Iron Law of Wages*: the natural wage is that which maintains a worker's subsistence.

  – When labor is in demand, the wage will increase, the worker will prosper, the size of families will increase, and the general population will grow.
  – The result will be more workers competing for fewer jobs and inevitable starvation.
  – Believed government attempts to change this only led to greater suffering.

■ *Utopian Socialists* rejected the *dismal science* of the classical economists and sought solutions to the plight of the masses.

  – *Robert Owen* (1771–1858): a Scottish textile manufacturer whose humane working conditions—shorter workday, decent housing, and free education—served as a model for capitalists who wanted to make a profit without exploiting workers.
  – The *Comte de Saint-Simon* (1760–1825): one of the early French founders of *socialism*.

    • Helped define the movement by advocating *public ownership of factories*.
    • Wanted a professional managerial corps to run factories: the *technocrats*.
    • Coined the slogan, "From each according to his ability, to each according to his need," an idealistic but vague proposal for a *planned economy*.

  – *Louis Blanc* (1811–1882): had a more practical approach than other early French utopian socialists.

    • Urged workers to fight for universal suffrage and to overthrow the state peacefully.
    • Believed the government should set up workshops and factories to guarantee full employment.
    • Ideas had an opportunity to be tested when he briefly became a leader of France after the Revolution of 1848.

- *Karl Marx* (1818–1883): the primary proponent of the "class struggle" model of history.

  - His *Communist Manifesto,* written with *Friedrich Engels* (1820–1895) during the revolutions of 1848, called for radical solutions to the dilemma of mass poverty in the industrialized world.
  - *Das Kapital,* the first volume of which was published in 1867, offers a complete analysis of capitalism and an explanation of communism.

Marx's Theories

Hegelian dialectic (so named after the German philosopher Georg Hegel): In every historical period a prevailing ideal, *thesis,* conflicts with an opposing ideal, *antithesis,* and results in a new ideal, *synthesis.* This becomes the thesis of the next period and the process continues.

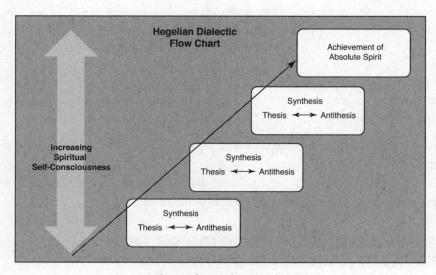

Chart of Hegelian Dialectic

Dialectical materialism: Marx adapted the Hegelian dialectic to argue that society is a reflection of economics. History progresses from agrarian communalism to slaveholding, feudalism, bourgeois commercialism, capitalism, socialism and, finally, to *communism* (a classless society in which the workers own the means of production and government is unnecessary). Marx saw this as an inevitable process, and that led him to believe more strongly in his predictions.

The chart and the explanation below it on the following page should help you understand Marx's theories on capitalism, communism, and the coming revolution.

Class struggle: The *dominant class* in every society, whether they are slaveholders, feudal lords, or capitalists, is a thesis with an antithesis, such as slaves, serfs, or workers, respectively, who will overthrow the old order.

Inevitable revolution: This is the result of the capitalists' increasing profits gained by lowering the workers' wages for labor to the point that the proletariat cannot afford to consume the products of manufacture (*surplus-value theory*). Economic depression occurs and lays hardship on the working class until it carries out a revolution. A *dictatorship of the proletariat* will establish a socialist government to wipe out capitalism.

Dialectical Materialism Flow Chart

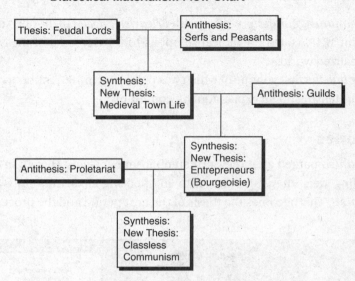

Communism: The *"withering away of the state"* will follow, whereby private property will cease to exist and economic exploitation will stop, ending crime, vice, and injustice; democracy will prevail on a local level; *Utopia* (a perfect society) will result.

- *Anarchists,* such as Mikhail Bakunin and Georges Sorel, asserted that all forms of governmental authority were unnecessary and should be overthrown and replaced with a society based on voluntary cooperation—and they went even further than Marx and Engels in their message about the corrupt nature of society.

THE TECHNOLOGICAL REVOLUTION OR THE SECOND INDUSTRIAL REVOLUTION

Around the last third of the nineteenth century, the application of science to industry brought about a radical change in the way Europeans lived. During the Second Industrial Revolution (c. 1870–1914), more areas of Europe experienced an increase in industrial activity, and industrial processes increased in scale and complexity.

- Mechanization and the factory system became the predominant modes of production by 1914.
- *Mass production* lowered the cost of goods and made them available to the general public; consumer goods became part of the mass market.
- Smaller companies merged and consolidated until whole industries were dominated by *big business.*
- High wages in the cities caused a *population shift* from the countryside.
- Electricity and the internal combustion engine not only increased productivity but improved the quality of life.
- New industries emerged, adding to the new consumerism of the era:

  – The chemical industry
  – The electricity industry
  – Leisure travel, professional sports
  – The automobile industry

- New means of communication, such as the telegraph and telephone, changed business and culture.
- New forms of transportation changed everything from business to migration and marriage patterns.
- Increased consumerism changed leisure and home life including the spread of:
  - Advertising
  - Department stores
  - Catalogs

INVENTORS OF THE INDUSTRIAL REVOLUTION

1708	Jethro Tull's mechanical seed drill made cultivation in rows widespread as it was more efficient and allowed easier weeding.
1712	Thomas Newcomen built the first commercially successful steam engine. It kept deep coal mines clear of water. It was the first significant industrial use of fossil fuels and marked the first major power source invented since wind, water, and animal power were used.
1733	John Kay invented the flying shuttle, which improved weaving significantly.
1761	James Brindley's Bridgewater Canal opened. Barges carried coal from Worsley to Manchester.
1765	James Hargreaves invented the spinning jenny, automating thread spinning for the first time.
1769	Arkwright's water frame allowed much more efficient spinning of thread.
1775	James Watt created the first efficient steam engine with a condensing chamber.
1779	The first steam-powered mill used Crompton's "mule" and Hargreaves' and Arkwright's machines, fully automating the weaving process.
1787	Cartwright built a power loom.
1792	William Murdock (James Watt's assistant) lit his home with coal gas.
1793	Eli Whitney developed the cotton gin, increasing the efficiency of cotton as a source of raw material for textiles.
1801	Robert Trevithick demonstrated his steam locomotive.
1807	Robert Fulton built the *Clermont,* the first successful steamboat.
1826–42	Marc Brunel built the first underwater tunnel—under the Thames.
1830	The Liverpool and Manchester Railway began the first regular commercial rail service.
1831	Michael Faraday discovered electromagnetic current, making possible generators and electric engines.
1834	Charles Babbage created the analytic engine, the first ancestor of the computer.
1837	Samuel F. B. Morse developed the telegraph and Morse Code.
1838	Daguerre perfected the Daguerrotype, an early form of photography.
1849	Monier developed reinforced concrete.
1850	Gasoline was refined for the first time.
1851	Singer invented the first practical sewing machine.
1854	Bessemer invented the steel converter, which revolutionized the production of steel.

1858	First transatlantic cable completed.
	Cathode rays discovered.
1867	Alfred Nobel created dynamite, the first high explosive that could be safely handled.
1876	Alexander Graham Bell invented the telephone.
1877	Thomas Alva Edison invented the phonograph.
1879	Edison invented the incandescent lamp.
1883	The first skyscraper (ten stories) was built in Chicago and the Brooklyn Bridge opened; this large suspension bridge was a triumph of engineering.
1884	Maxim invented the machine gun, making possible mass slaughter and beginning the mechanization of warfare.
1885	Benz developed the first internal-combustion automobile engine.
1889	The Eiffel Tower was built for the World Exposition in Paris.
1896	Marconi patented the wireless telegraph.
1901	Marconi transmitted the first transatlantic radio message (from Cape Cod, Massachusetts).

PRACTICE LONG-ESSAY QUESTIONS

These questions are samples of the various types of thematic essays on the exam. (See pages 30–31 for a detailed explanation of each type.) Check over the **generic rubric** (see pages 32–33) before you begin any of these essays, and use that rubric to score your essay if you write one.

Question 1

Analyze how the opening of Atlantic commerce sparked the rise of capitalism.

COMMENTS ON QUESTION 1

This question is testing the CAUSATION skill because it wants to know how one factor, the opening of Atlantic trade, sparked another outcome: the rise of capitalism. Remember to describe causes AND/OR effects of the rise of capitalism and to support your analysis of those causes and effects through specific examples. Explain the reasons why the opening of Atlantic trade sparked the rise of capitalism with specific evidence to support claims made. The essay must clearly indicate multiple ways that capitalism's rise was caused by the opening of transatlantic trade. This question requires all the applications of analysis: examining in detail, determining relationships, explaining. A special emphasis should be on determining the relationships between the new intercontinental trade and the growth of capitalism. How could the Atlantic discoveries and colonization of the New World have encouraged the growth of capitalism in Europe? There were strong and complex relationships between the colonization of the New World and the growth of capitalism, including the development of international banking, stock markets, and nationally chartered companies, as well as the taking of risk to make profits. New markets, new products (such as tobacco, vanilla, and cocoa), new territory, and new opportunities spurred entrepreneurship seen in men like Cortez and Pizarro and those who accompanied them. Abundant resources from the New World, including precious metals, led to exploitation by merchants, giving them huge profits. Along with the resulting creation of the first merchant class and the development of surplus wealth, capitalism developed through these methods. The emergence of mercantilism and Adam Smith's theory of *laissez-faire capitalism* as an antidote to mercantilism should also be discussed. The essay could also focus on inflation caused by the gold flow into Europe and the emigration of skilled entrepreneurial artisans and merchants to the New World. There is a lot of supporting evidence that can be used in this essay.

Question 2

Analyze the extent to which industrialization changed human interaction with the environment and other people.

COMMENTS ON QUESTION 2

This question is asking you to use the CHANGE AND CONTINUITY OVER TIME skill because you must analyze the extent to which the Industrial Revolution changed human interactions with each other and the environment. This is asking what changed and what remained the same. Remember to explain the European economy in 1750 and in 1850, and provide specific examples of how things changed after the opening of transatlantic trade. Your essay must explain the extent to which human interaction with the environment and other people was changed after industrialization began. This essay is asking you to decide how much industrialization changed life on many levels.

Approach this first by considering what life was like both before and after industrialization. Once a list is created of the things that are similar both before (a long list, including where people lived, relationship to time/seasons, family life and structure, types of jobs done, standard of living, education, political representation, and more) and after (a short list, including class distinctions still existing, difficulty in rising up in class, war, taxes, and differences between city and rural life). Then write a thesis that offers specific answers to the question from your list. Support your answer with many facts. Be certain to explain why it was different from what came before or why it was the same. Be clear and assume nothing about what the reader will link together on his/her own.

Question 3

Explain why it was no accident that the Industrial Revolution started in late eighteenth-century Britain.

COMMENTS ON QUESTION 3

This one is a CAUSATION question because it requires you to explain how one environment—eighteenth-century Britain—resulted in a specific outcome, the Industrial Revolution. Describe causes AND/OR effects of the Industrial Revolution occurring in Britain and support your analysis of those causes and effects with specific examples. The essay must explain the reasons that the environment of Britain fostered the advent of the Industrial Revolution. It is necessary to examine why fertile farm fields nurtured the development of industrialization in Britain from 1780 to 1830. You must identify the links in the causal chain: the supremacy of Parliament after 1688, the Enclosure Movement, the Agricultural Revolution, the growth of towns, the improvement of technology, available capital and land, stable government, lack of foreign invasion, transportation networks, existing cottage industry, and the abundance of coal.

Question 4

To what extent did the Industrial Revolution diminish the quality of life of the common person in Europe?

COMMENTS ON QUESTION 4

This question is also testing the CAUSATION skill because it requires you to evaluate the extent to which one thing, the Industrial Revolution, resulted in a specific outcome: diminished the quality of life of the common person in Europe. Remember to describe causes AND/OR effects of the Industrial Revolution on the lives of common Europeans and to support your analysis of those causes and effects with specific examples. The essay must explain the reasons for the changes in the quality of life at the time. Use facts to argue for or against. This essay question is very open-ended, and the appropriate response is to write an essay that says both, depending upon what era the question is asked. It is clear that the quality of life for the average Briton was reduced from 1750 to 1850. However, the quality of life for the British and the entire world began to improve after 1850 and continues to do so today, mostly due to the wonders of industrialization. Therefore, the miserable labor and living conditions of the early nineteenth century, as well as the reforms of the later part of that century and how living improved, each deserve a paragraph. A strong thesis needs to explain why the statement is both supported and refuted, depending upon what vantage point one uses.

PRACTICE SHORT-ANSWER QUESTIONS

1. Please answer all parts of the question that follows based upon your knowledge of European History. Historians have argued that urbanization changed the age-old relations between families, the land, production, and the government.

   (A) Identify TWO pieces of evidence that support this argument and explain HOW that evidence supports the argument.

   (B) Identify TWO pieces of evidence that refute this argument and explain HOW that evidence supports the argument.

2. Use the image and passage below to answer all parts of the question that follows.

Source 1

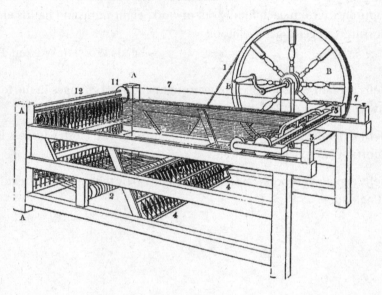

By Andrew Ure, Peter Lund Simmonds, H. G. Bohn, 1861.

Source 2

The number of Scribbling-Machines extending about seventeen miles south-west of LEEDS, exceed all belief, being no less than one hundred and seventy! and as each machine will do as much work in twelve hours, as ten men can in that time do by hand, (speaking within bounds) and they working night-and day, one machine will do as much work in one day as would otherwise employ twenty men.

As we do not mean to assert anything but what we can prove to be true, we allow four men to be employed at each machine twelve hours, working night and day, will take eight men in twenty-four hours; so that, upon a moderate computation twelve men are thrown out of employ for every single machine used in scribbling; and as it may be supposed the number of machines in all the other quarters together, nearly equal those in the South-West, a full four thousand men are left to shift for a living how they can, and must of course fall to the Parish, if not timely relieved. Allowing one boy to be a bound apprentice from each family out of work, eight thousand hands are deprived of the opportunity of getting a livelihood.

—Leeds Woollen Workers Petition, 1786

(A) Briefly explain ONE social change brought about by changes in the textile industry between 1770 and 1815.

(B) Briefly explain one reason that creating more woolen cloth with less labor became important after 1750.

(C) Briefly explain one political change brought on by the increase in textile production in England.

Short-Answer Explanations

1. (A) You may cite many trends of change, from growing illegitimacy to wage workers, loss of agricultural jobs, putting out changing to factory work, new regulations on the poor, foundling homes, changing gender roles, increasing literacy, increased political activity of the lower classes, reductions in church attendance, tenement living, increased pollution and sewage problems, increased education, the new laws regulating work hours and conditions, and the Chartist movement, explaining how each piece of evidence was a change from life previous to the start of the nineteenth century.

   (B) You may cite many pieces of information, from the poor still having a small political voice to many one-wage families, the remaining rural workers, the ongoing importance of agriculture, the class system that was not very different from manorialism, and the rise of conservative ideas, explaining how each piece of evidence proves that life was similar to life previous to the start of the nineteenth century.

2. (A) You should FULLY EXPLAIN one of the following: changes in gender roles, less interaction between the genders, creation of factories, changing family lives due to work outside of the home, changes in class identity, the emergence of the capitalist class, destruction of guilds, the end of domestic industry, increased urbanization, drop in price of clothes leading to fashion emerging, or landholders gaining wealth.

   (B) This answer revolves around the Enclosure Movement coming to full fruition around 1700 in England. The increase in wool from the sheep that replaced peasants on many estates meant that it had to be turned into cloth. Another approach could be to explain the domestic industry in wool, and how the weavers of cloth needed many spinners before the spinning jenny. You could also explain that the increased production led England to be a dominant force in international trade as it had a ready export to sell.

   (C) You should FULLY EXPLAIN one of the following: the rise of England on the international stage as trade increased in importance, the new regulations affecting child labor and women at work, the Chartist movement, the Poor Laws, or the banning of unions.

PRACTICE MULTIPLE-CHOICE QUESTIONS

These questions are representative of the various types that appear on the AP exam.

Questions 1 to 3 refer to the chart below.

Population Estimates in the Millions		
Selected Nations in Europe	1800	1900
BRITAIN	9	33
GERMANY	25	56
ITALY	17	34
FRANCE	27	39

1. The chart above provides population estimates for selected European countries in the years 1800 and 1900. Which of the following is the most valid interpretation of the statistics?

   (A) The population doubled in each of the countries identified.
   (B) The population of Italy and Germany doubled because of national unification.
   (C) The population growth reflects the degree to which each of the nations industrialized.
   (D) The population of Britain grew at a faster rate than any of the nations identified.

2. Which of the following played the LEAST significant role in creating the demographic change noted in the chart?

   (A) Transatlantic trade brought many immigrants from the Americas, Asia, and Africa.
   (B) The Agricultural Revolution increased food production.
   (C) The Black Plague disappeared, and a vaccination for smallpox was developed.
   (D) Transatlantic trade brought many new foods to all parts of the world, increasing output and thus population.

3. Scholarly statistical studies of the condition of the British working class indicate that during the nineteenth century which of the following was true?

   (A) Their standard of living improved from the beginning of industrialization.
   (B) Incidences of infanticide increased throughout the nineteenth century.
   (C) Improvement in the standard of living did not come until the period after 1830.
   (D) Only skilled workers enjoyed improvements in their standard of living.

Questions 4 to 6 refer to the print below.

—A woodcut print of the Krupp steelworks in Essen, Germany.

4. The illustration above shows the industrialization of Germany, including the bucolic surrounding area, indicating that this piece belongs in which of the following artistic movements?

   (A) Naturalism
   (B) Romanticism
   (C) Neoclassicism
   (D) Impressionism

5. The mass production of this woodblock print was most likely done for which of the following reasons?

   (A) The owner of the factory wanted a copy to put in his office.
   (B) The capitalists who built factories wanted pictures of their competitors' factories.
   (C) The workers at the factories could now afford to put art in their houses.
   (D) The town council required it of the artist if he wanted to live there.

6. The greatest change workers faced with the shift from cottage industry to the factory work depicted above was which of the following?

   (A) A new tempo and discipline
   (B) Harder work
   (C) The destruction of family-unit labor
   (D) Lower wages

Multiple-Choice Explanations

| 1. **D** | 3. **C** | 5. **C** |
| 2. **A** | 4. **B** | 6. **A** |

1. **(D)**

   (A) is wrong because the population of France did not double.

   (B) is wrong because the chart does not indicate WHY the population increased, and it may be due to an agricultural revolution there.

   (C) is wrong because France industrialized more than Italy during this period, but did not see its population grow as much as Italy.

   (D) is CORRECT because the chart clearly shows the population of Britain grew faster than any other nation.

2. **(A)**

   (A) is CORRECT because migration into Europe did not affect the population growth nearly as much as the other factors listed.

   (B) is wrong because migration into Europe did not affect the population growth nearly as much as the surplus of food created by the Agricultural Revolution did.

   (C) is wrong because migration into Europe did not affect the population growth nearly as much as the conquest of these diseases did.

   (D) is wrong because migration into Europe did not affect the population growth nearly as much as the surplus of food created by the new foods such as corn and the potato did.

3. **(C)**

   (A) is wrong because the standard of living for workers actually got worse at the start of the Industrial Revolution, but improved after about 1830.

   (B) is wrong because infanticide started to rise at the start of the century but was reduced as the century came to a close.

   (C) is CORRECT because the standard of living for workers actually got worse at the start of the Industrial Revolution, but improved after about 1830 or 1850, depending upon which statistics are used.

   (D) is wrong because the standard of living for all workers actually improved after about 1830.

4. **(B)**

   (A) is wrong because the print does not show the depiction of nature as supreme that the naturalists sought.

   (B) is CORRECT because the portrayal of industry as polluting pristine nature is a hallmark of Romantic art of all genres.

   (C) is wrong because there is no reference to Greco-Roman themes or architecture seen in neoclassical works.

   (D) is wrong because the details are too clear to be impressionist.

5. **(C)**

(A) is wrong because if the owner just wanted one copy, a painting would have been commissioned.

(B) is wrong because the print has none of the details that a capitalist would need to spy on a rival.

(C) is CORRECT because the new consumer market meant that the artist could create and sell many copies of his work.

(D) is wrong because there is no record of town councils requiring such tasks of citizens without payment.

6. **(A)**

(A) is CORRECT because adjusting to the tempo set by the company clock rather than that set by nature, as well as the discipline of the boss in a factory rather than the freedom of putting out work or farming, was very challenging.

(B) is wrong because the work was in many ways easier but more tedious in many cases.

(C) is wrong because at first families came to work together in factories, then the tempo and discipline there required them to leave.

(D) is wrong because factory workers earned higher wages than cottage workers.

Time Period Two (1649–1815): Practice Assessment

KEY CONCEPTS AND OVERVIEW

KEY CONCEPT 2.1 Different models of political sovereignty affected the relationship among states and between states and individuals.

KEY CONCEPT 2.2 The expansion of European commerce accelerated the growth of a worldwide economic network.

KEY CONCEPT 2.3 The popularization and dissemination of the Scientific Revolution and the application of its methods to political, social, and ethical issues led to an increased, although not unchallenged, emphasis on Reason in European culture.

KEY CONCEPT 2.4 The experiences of everyday life were shaped by demographic, environmental, medical, and technological changes.

SPECIAL NOTE ON PERIODIZATION

To preserve the continuity of the subject, the Industrial Revolution was covered entirely in Chapter 6, although much of the content covered is included in Period 3 by the College Board. With that in mind the following Key Concepts are also addressed to some extent in Chapters 7 and 8.

KEY CONCEPT 3.1 The Industrial Revolution spread from Great Britain to the Continent, where the state played a greater role in promoting industry.

KEY CONCEPT 3.2 The experiences of everyday life were shaped by industrialization, depending on the level of industrial development in a particular location.

KEY CONCEPT 3.3 Political revolutions and complications resulting from industrialization triggered a range of ideological, governmental, and collective responses.

PRACTICE ASSESSMENT

Each time period concludes with a mini-test consisting of some multiple-choice questions, two short-answer questions, and two essay choices for which you should choose to write at least one answer. This is not so much to simulate an exam, which will have more questions and a document-based question (DBQ), but to help you prepare for the types of questions seen on the exam and to allow you time to practice those skills. The DBQs can be found in the Introduction to this book, in the two sample exams at the end of this book, and in the online exams that accompany this book that can be found at: *http://barronsbooks.com/AP/ap-european-hist/*. This assessment should take you about two hours. Detailed explanations of all questions follow the assessment.

TIME PERIOD TWO (1649–1815): PRACTICE ASSESSMENT

Section I, Part A

Multiple-Choice Questions (16 Questions)

> **Directions:** Please read the passages and then choose the most correct answer choice for each of the following questions. As demonstrated in the following examples, question sets will be organized around three to five questions that focus on a primary source, a secondary source, or a historical issue.

Questions 1 to 3 refer to the following woodblock print.

—Peter I (1672–1725), Czar of Russia, 1682–1725. Contemporary Russian cartoon.

1. The depiction of Peter I of Russia above, a rare surviving piece from the time critical of the czar, is specifically criticizing which of the following?

    (A) The beard tax that Peter imposed on all men
    (B) The dress of the boyars at the time
    (C) The dentistry of Peter I who would extract teeth from subjects
    (D) The relationship between Peter I and the clergy

2. Which of the following was the group most likely to support the publication of the print seen above, and why would they support it?

   (A) The peasants had it published because they wanted to maintain their traditional habits and dress.
   (B) The thriving middle class in Russia had it published to display their newfound influence over the czar.
   (C) The boyar nobility had it published to encourage the commoners to join them in thwarting the growing power of the czar.
   (D) The Duma that was created by Peter to be Russia's legislative body published this cartoon to show that they were not simply controlled by the czar.

3. Which of the following was the most important reason that Peter the Great thought he needed to change the ethnic and cultural identities of the Russian people as depicted in the cartoon above?

   (A) Russian beards were making it easy for criminals to hide in plain sight.
   (B) Russia was seen by the rest of Europe as too masculine and domineering.
   (C) Russia was a backward country that needed to be forced to Westernize and modernize.
   (D) Russia needed to industrialize and modernize by following the Ottoman model for domination.

Questions 4 to 6 refer to the following excerpt from Jean-Jacques Rousseau's *A Dissertation on the Origin and Foundation of the Inequality of Mankind*, written in 1755.

Before the invention of signs to represent riches, wealth could hardly consist in anything but lands and cattle, the only real possessions men can have. But, when inheritances so increased in number and extent as to occupy the whole of the land, and to border on one another, one man could aggrandize himself only at the expense of another; at the same time the supernumeraries, who had been too weak or too indolent to make such acquisitions, and had grown poor without sustaining any loss, because, while they saw everything change around them, they remained still the same, were obliged to receive their subsistence, or steal it, from the rich; and this soon bred, according to their different characters, dominion and slavery, or violence and rapine. The wealthy, on their part, had no sooner begun to taste the pleasure of command, than they disdained all others, and, using their old slaves to acquire new, thought of nothing but subduing and enslaving their neighbors; like ravenous wolves, which; having once tasted human flesh, despise every other food and thenceforth seek only men to devour.

4. The new models of government that were created by Locke and Rousseau were based upon which of the following?

   (A) The divine right theory of Jacques Bossuet
   (B) The theory of gravity explained by Sir Isaac Newton
   (C) The concept of popular sovereignty based upon universal suffrage
   (D) The theory that we are all born with natural rights

5. Which of the following groups did Rousseau believe was not worthy of the natural rights that he adamantly supported for others?

(A) American Indians
(B) Africans
(C) women
(D) peasant men

6. Jean-Jacques Rousseau was the last great thinker of the Enlightenment because he challenged which of the following beliefs of most Enlightenment thinkers?

(A) All problems can be solved through the exclusive use of reasoning.
(B) All problems can be solved through emotional knowledge.
(C) All problems can be solved with enough money.
(D) Society does not need fixing as this is the best of all possible worlds.

Questions 7 to 10 refer to the image below.

—*Napoleon Crowning Josephine Empress of France* by Jacques Louis David

7. Napoleon Bonaparte, who crowned himself Emperor of France and then crowned his Empress, above, can be best described as which of the following?

(A) A bloodthirsty conqueror
(B) A divine right monarch
(C) An enlightened despot
(D) An autocratic dictator

8. Which of the following policies of Napoleon was most often used by his opponents to cast him in a negative role?

   (A) The Concordat of 1801
   (B) His use of nepotism in government
   (C) His use of the merit system in government
   (D) His Code Napoleon

9. Napoleon helped make the French Revolution an international movement in the regions he conquered by pursuing which of the following policies?

   (A) Imposing a universal currency based on the French franc
   (B) The brutal suppression of guerrilla resistance
   (C) Abolishing feudalism and manorialism
   (D) Encouraging French as the universal language

10. Jacques Louis David, who painted many portraits of Napoleon, including the one above, was a premier example of which of the following artistic movements?

    (A) Romanticism
    (B) Baroque
    (C) Realism
    (D) Neoclassicism

Questions 11 to 13 refer to the quote from Adam Smith's *Wealth of Nations* below.

No society can surely be flourishing and happy of which by far the greater part of the numbers are poor and miserable. . . .

It is not from the benevolence of the butcher, the brewer, or the baker that we expect our dinner, but from their regard to their own self-interest. We address ourselves not to their humanity but to their self-love, and never talk to them of our own necessities, but of their advantages. . . .

Nobody ever saw a dog make a fair and deliberate exchange of one bone for another with another dog. Nobody ever saw one animal by its gestures and natural cries signify to another, this is mine, that yours; I am willing to give this for that . . .

But man has almost constant occasion for the help of his brethren, and it is in vain for him to expect it from their benevolence only. He will be more likely to prevail if he can interest their self-love in his favor, and show them that it is for their own advantage to do for him what he requires of them. Whoever offers to another a bargain of any kind, proposes to do this. Give me that which I want, and you shall have this which you want, is the meaning of every such offer; and it is in this manner that we obtain from one another the far greater part of those good offices which we stand in need of.

11. Adam Smith challenged the mercantilist theory of the time by inventing laissez-faire capitalism as described above, which calls for which of the following?

   (A) Selfishness and greed should be ignored by all market participants.
   (B) Unrestricted free trade should be encouraged with very little regulation.
   (C) Government intervention to make certain that the best companies succeed.
   (D) International trade should be pursued in the interests of entire nations.

12. Although he was distrustful of them and their motives, Adam Smith has become the hero of which of the following?

   (A) Governmental regulators
   (B) Average consumers
   (C) Capitalist businessmen
   (D) Small shopkeepers

13. Smith's theories, which created the modern field of economics, were based in large part on the political arguments of which of the following thinkers who wrote before him?

   (A) John Locke
   (B) Baron Montesquieu
   (C) Jean-Jacques Rousseau
   (D) Hobbes

Questions 14 to 16 refer to the following excerpt from the *Declaration of the Rights of Man and of the Citizen* of 1789.

1. Men are born and remain free and equal in rights. Social distinctions may be founded only upon the general good.
2. The aim of all political association is the preservation of the natural and imprescriptible rights of man. These rights are liberty, property, security, and resistance to oppression.
3. The principle of all sovereignty resides essentially in the nation. No body nor individual may exercise any authority which does not proceed directly from the nation.
4. Liberty consists in the freedom to do everything which injures no one else; hence the exercise of the natural rights of each man has no limits except those which assure to the other members of the society the enjoyment of the same rights. These limits can only be determined by law.
5. Law can only prohibit such actions as are hurtful to society. Nothing may be prevented which is not forbidden by law, and no one may be forced to do anything not provided for by law.
6. Law is the expression of the general will. Every citizen has a right to participate personally, or through his representative, in its foundation. It must be the same for all, whether it protects or punishes. All citizens, being equal in the eyes of the law, are equally eligible to all dignities and to all public positions and occupations, according to their abilities, and without distinction except that of their virtues and talents.

14. The document above was written during which of the following phases of the French Revolution?

   (A) The monarchical phase
   (B) The moderate phase
   (C) The radical phase
   (D) The reactionary phase

15. Which of the following documents does NOT serve the same function as the *Declaration of the Rights of Man and the Citizen*?

   (A) *Magna Carta*
   (B) American *Bill of Rights*
   (C) English *Bill of Rights*
   (D) American *Declaration of Independence*

16. Which of the following French *philosophes* had his/her ideas included most clearly in this excerpt from the *Declaration of the Rights of Man and of the Citizen*?

   (A) Jean-Jacques Rousseau
   (B) Montesquieu
   (C) Adam Smith
   (D) Voltaire

Section I

Part B: Short-Answer Questions

> **Directions:** Answer both questions completely.

1. Use the passage below and your knowledge of European History to answer all parts of the question that follows.

> So we end as we began, by perceiving that it was the philosophers and the theologians, not the warriors and diplomats, who were fighting the crucial battle of the eighteenth century, and that we were justified in calling that period the Age of Voltaire. "The philosophers of different nations," said Condorcet, "embracing in their meditations the entire interests of mankind[,] . . . formed a firm and united phalanx against every description of error and every species of tyranny." It was by no means a united phalanx; we shall see Rousseau leaving the ranks, and Kant striving to reconcile philosophy and religion. But it was truly a struggle for the soul of man, and the results are with us today.
>
> —Historian and writer Will Durant, from *The Age of Voltaire*

(A) Provide one piece of evidence that supports Durant's assertion at the end of the passage.

(B) Provide one piece of evidence that undermines Durant's assertion at the end of the passage.

(C) Identify one example of the influence of the Enlightenment in the twentieth century, and analyze the extent to which it has changed political, social, or economic life.

2. Use the passages below by two opposing thinkers of the late 1700s and your knowledge of European History to answer all parts of the question that follows.

Rousseau:	"The education of women should be always relative to men. To please, to be useful to us, to make us love them, to render [make] our lives easy and agreeable; these are the duties of women at all times, and what they should be taught in infancy."
Wollstonecraft:	"Woman was not created merely to be the solace of man. . . . On this error has all the false system been erected, which robs dignity."
Rousseau:	"Girls must be subject all their lives to the most constant and severe restraint[,] . . . that they may the more readily learn to submit to the will of others. . . . But is it not just that she should partake of the suffering which arise from those evils [woman] hath caused us?"
Wollstonecraft:	"How can a woman believe that she was made to submit to man—a being like herself, her equal?"
Rousseau:	"Women ought to have but little liberty: they are apt to indulge [involve] themselves excessively in what little is allowed them. Girls are far more transported [carried away] by their diversions than are boys."
Wollstonecraft:	"Slaves and mobs have always indulged themselves in excesses when once they broke loose from authority. The bent bow recoils with violence, when the hand is suddenly relaxed that forcibly held it."
Rousseau:	"Boys love sports and noise and activity: to whip the top, to beat the drum, to drag about their little carts; girls on the other hand are fond of things of show and ornament—trinkets, mirrors, dolls."
Wollstonecraft:	"Little girls are forced to sit still and play with trinkets. Who can say whether they are fond of them or not?"

Sources: *Emile*, by Jean-Jacques Rousseau, 1762; and *A Vindication of the Rights of Woman*, by Mary Wollstonecraft, 1792.

(A) Explain the major inconsistency between Rousseau's views on the rights of men and women.

(B) List one other thinker or work contemporary to Wollstonecraft who challenged Rousseau's views on women.

(C) Name and explain the importance of one twentieth century advocate for women's rights.

Section II: Long-Essay Question

Directions: In this section, you will choose between one of two long-essay questions. The following questions are meant to illustrate an example of a question pairing that might appear in this section of the exam, in which both questions focus on the same historical thinking skill (in this case, CHANGE AND CONTINUITY OVER TIME (CCOT)) but apply it to different time periods and/or topics.

LONG-ESSAY CHOICES

1. Machiavelli suggested that a ruler should behave both like a fox and a lion, and be both loved and feared. Analyze the policies of THREE of the following monarchs, indicating the degree to which they followed Machiavelli's advice, and how the application of that advice evolved as absolutism progressed.

   Peter I of Russia
   Louis XIV of France
   Charles II of Spain
   Joseph II of Austria
   Catherine II of Russia

2. To what extent and in what ways was the light of Adam Smith's economic optimism dimmed by the "dismal science" of Thomas Malthus and David Ricardo?

ANSWER EXPLANATIONS

Multiple-Choice Explanations

1. **A**	5. **C**	9. **C**	13. **A**
2. **C**	6. **A**	10. **D**	14. **B**
3. **C**	7. **C**	11. **B**	15. **D**
4. **D**	8. **B**	12. **C**	16. **A**

1. **(A)**

(A) is CORRECT because this is a cartoon protesting the beard tax imposed by Peter I.

(B) is wrong because the cartoon is criticizing the czar, not the nobility.

(C) is wrong because although Peter was a dentist and pulled teeth, that is not alluded to in this cartoon.

(D) is wrong because the cartoon has nothing to do with the clergy.

2. **(C)**

(A) is wrong because the peasants could not publish anything in Russia at the time and were more concerned with daily living than big ideas.

(B) is wrong because Russia had no thriving middle class at the time and did not get one until the 1990s.

(C) is CORRECT because the nobility still resents the increased power of the czar, which Ivan IV enforced and Peter I extended, and they railed against the czar. This could have been published with support of the nobles.

(D) is wrong because although Russians needed to modernize, they would not follow the antiquated Ottoman model of doing so.

3. **(C)**

(A) is wrong because beards did not help criminals hide, and that had nothing to do with the cartoon.

(B) is wrong because Russian masculinity was not the issue; its backwardness was.

(C) is CORRECT because Peter I was trying to Westernize and modernize his country through the beard tax, building St. Petersburg, and other actions such as making the boyar youth study abroad.

(D) is wrong because the Ottomans were as backward as the Russians, if not more so.

4. **(D)**

(A) is wrong because Rousseau did not support divine right monarchy.

(B) is wrong because Rousseau based his governmental plan not on the laws of gravity, but on the concept of natural rights.

(C) is wrong because Rousseau never supported suffrage for women, whom he thought did not deserve rights.

(D) is CORRECT because Rousseau based his governmental plan on the concept of natural rights as explained by John Locke.

5. **(C)**

(A) is wrong because Rousseau believed in the concept of the noble savage as embodied by the American Indian, who was unspoiled by society and therefore preserved all of his natural rights.

(B) is wrong because Rousseau believed in the concept of the noble savage (which Africans qualified as at the time), who was unspoiled by society and therefore preserved all of his natural rights.

(C) is CORRECT because Rousseau was a well-known misogynist.

(D) is wrong because Rousseau believed that all men should have their political voices heard as a part of the *general will* of the people.

6. **(A)**

(A) is CORRECT because Rousseau emphasized the emotional part of knowledge and began to reject pure Reason, which helped usher in the Romantic era as a result.

(B) is wrong because most Enlightenment thinkers emphasized Reason over emotion.

(C) is wrong because Rousseau showed disdain for wealth, and no great thinker argued for just throwing money at problems.

(D) is wrong because the *philosophes* of the Enlightenment were focused upon fixing the problems that they identified within their societies, and they believed that through Reason they could fix them and improve the world.

7. **(C)**

(A) is wrong because, while Napoleon did conquer most of Europe, he used conquest as a political tool and was more of an enlightened despot than just a conqueror because he imposed reforms on conquered territories that helped modernize them.

(B) is wrong because Napoleon never claimed to rule by divine right and crowned himself rather than have the pope, who was in attendance, crown him emperor.

(C) is CORRECT because, although Napoleon did rule with complete authority as emperor of France, he used his power to implement a meritocracy and the Napoleonic Code, while he engaged in state-building and expansion as had the other enlightened despots before him.

(D) is wrong because, while Napoleon did exercise significant power, his own code of laws limited his power and that of the government.

8. **(B)**

(A) is wrong because the Concordat of 1801 was a reconciliation between the Catholic Church and France and included returning church lands seized in the Revolution (a radical policy that many of Napoleon's opponents had supported).

(B) is CORRECT because by putting his relatives, mainly siblings, on the thrones of European states he had conquered, he often inspired nationalistic uprisings.

(C) is wrong because the meritocracy that he used in government was almost universally praised as an enlightened reform.

(D) is wrong because his Napoleonic Code was a set of enlightened laws that he spread to the areas he conquered—laws that included the abolition of feudalism and manorialism as well as the establishment of rights for male citizens—and was hugely popular.

9. **(C)**

   (A) is wrong because Napoleon did not establish a single currency for the areas that he conquered.

   (B) is wrong because Napoleon's suppression of guerilla fighters in Spain hurt his reputation as a spreader of the ideals of the French Revolution.

   (C) is CORRECT because Napoleon was adored by common people across Europe for abolishing feudalism and dues paid to the local manor in order to be allowed to farm.

   (D) is wrong because French was already the international language, thanks to the court of Louis XIV.

10. **(D)**

    (A) is wrong because David was a neoclassical artist, not a romantic one (as exemplified by Turner or Constable who painted, respectively, fierce storms and bucolic scenes of harmony).

    (B) is wrong because David was a neoclassical artist, not a baroque one (as exemplified by Rubens, who painted huge, awe-inspiring, often Biblical scenes).

    (C) is wrong because David was a neoclassical artist, not a realist one (as exemplified by Jean-François Millet or Diego Velázquez, who painted scenes that attempted to capture realistic slices of real life).

    (D) is CORRECT because David was a neoclassical artist, who depicted a rejection of the emotion of the Baroque era and used portraits to show a stark patriotism.

11. **(B)**

    (A) is wrong because Smith thought that selfishness should be exploited to make society run properly.

    (B) is CORRECT because Smith's laissez-faire capitalism was defined by a lack of government regulation and the support of free trade.

    (C) is wrong because Smith wrote directly against most government intervention.

    (D) is wrong because Smith wrote that nations should stay out of trade and that when they exerted their interests, they unbalanced trade.

12. **(C)**

    (A) is wrong because Smith argued for the elimination of many government regulators and therefore would not be their hero.

    (B) is wrong because Smith favored consumers in his writings, but he had become a hero of the capitalist class as he seemed to support the raw pursuit of profits.

    (C) is CORRECT because Smith had become a hero of the capitalist class as he seemed to support the raw pursuit of profits.

    (D) is wrong because Smith favored small shopkeepers, but he had not been as celebrated by them as he had by capitalists.

13. **(A)**

    (A) is CORRECT because John Locke's ideas that government needs to preserve liberty were central to Smith's ideas that government should not interfere with business, as it was in effect interfering in people's liberty to seek profits and bargains.

    (B) is wrong because Montesquieu advocated dividing government into three branches, which had no bearing on Smith's arguments.

(C) is wrong because Rousseau and Smith were contemporaries, and Smith was much closer to Locke and the *philosophes* such as Voltaire than he was to Rousseau.

(D) is wrong because Hobbes argued for absolute monarchy, which Smith's laissez-faire capitalism clearly rejected.

14. **(B)**

(A) is wrong because there was no monarchical phase of the French Revolution; monarchy existed before the Revolution.

(B) is CORRECT because this document was created during the moderate phase of the Revolution, when a constitutional monarchy was the goal.

(C) is wrong because the radical phase of the Revolution occurred after the failure of the Constitution of 1791, when the Committee of Public Safety and Robespierre were in control of the government.

(D) is wrong because the later Directory and, finally, the empire were the reactionary phases of the Revolution.

15. **(D)**

(A) is wrong because both the Magna Carta and the *Declaration of the Rights of Man and of the Citizen* serve as lists of the rights of the citizens of a nation.

(B) is wrong because both the American Bill of Rights and the *Declaration of the Rights of Man and of the Citizen* serve as lists of the rights of the citizens of a nation.

(C) is wrong because both the English Bill of Rights and the *Declaration of the Rights of Man and of the Citizen* serve as lists of the rights of the citizens of a nation.

(D) is CORRECT because the Declaration of Independence did not give Americans any specific rights, while the *Declaration of the Rights of Man and of the Citizen* served as a list of the rights of the citizens of France.

16. **(A)**

(A) is CORRECT because the concept of the general will as expressed in Rousseau's *Social Contract* is evident in this excerpt.

(B) is wrong because the ideas of Montesquieu on the separation of powers of government are less evident than are the ideas of Rousseau.

(C) is wrong because the ideas of Smith deal mostly with economic freedom and are not as clearly evident here as are the ideas of Rousseau.

(D) is wrong because the ideas of Voltaire are not expressed here at all, as Voltaire was wary of the masses and did not believe in true equality.

Short-Answer Explanations

1. (A) A good answer will give one piece of evidence to support the idea that the Enlightenment was a struggle for the soul of man, and that the results remain with us today, such as, but not limited to: individual freedoms; struggle between Church and science; use of Reason to improve society; rewriting legal codes; creating social sciences such as economics and sociology; or the contributions science has made to bettering daily life.

(B) A good answer will give one piece of evidence to refute the idea that the Enlightenment was a struggle for the soul of man, and that the results remain with us today, such as, but not limited to: the Enlightenment was not a struggle, but an evolution; the Enlightenment was more an extension of the Renaissance or Scientific Revolution than a stand-alone movement; most Enlightenment governments failed in Europe in the 1800s; and stating that the struggle has ended.

(C) A good answer will present one way that Enlightenment thought has influenced the twentieth century, such as: the emergence of representative governments, governments with three branches, laissez-faire capitalist systems, rule of law, equality of opportunity, and the supremacy of science; AND explain how much the cited legacy has changed society.

2. (A) A good answer will explain how Rousseau was inconsistent in that he wanted men to all be free, but felt that women should be subordinate to men.

(B) A good answer will list Olympe de Gouges, Marquis de Condorcet, Leibnitz, or Smith.

(C) A good answer will list any of many advocates, from Emmeline Pankhurst to Millicent Fawcett to Simone de Beauvoir to Gloria Steinem to Betty Friedan, and explain the importance of the woman chosen.

Long-Essay Question Sample Answers and Explanations

Question 1

Machiavelli suggested that a ruler should behave both like a fox and a lion and be both loved and feared. Analyze the policies of THREE of the following monarchs, indicating the degree to which they followed Machiavelli's advice and how the application of that advice evolved as absolutism progressed.

Peter I of Russia
Louis XIV of France
Charles II of Spain
Joseph II of Austria
Catherine II of Russia

COMMENTS ON QUESTION 1

Follow the "Simple Procedures" for writing an essay. (See page 35.)

- First: *What type of question is it?* This one tests the CHANGE AND CONTINUITY OVER TIME skill. Be sure to describe the level of historical continuity (as in what did not change and how the art of ruling stayed essentially the same) and change (as in how monarchs gained more personal power as the nobility was subjugated across Europe), and to analyze specific examples of what changed and how sovereignty advanced compared to the parts that did not, such as the growing power of the bureaucracy. This essay must also explain the reasons for CHANGE AND CONTINUITY OVER TIME, supporting claims with specific evidence.
- Second: *What does the question want to know?* Which rulers would Machiavelli have praised or criticized and why? How did monarchical rule change over time? Is it better to write about those he would have praised, criticized, or both?

- Third: *What do you know about it?* Define Machiavellian principles and ideas and decide which monarchs would be good to use. Use the rulers that best support the argument through facts. Machiavelli wanted strong rulers who knew when to take advice and when to give orders. He admired those who seemed virtuous but would do anything for the best of the nation. Machiavelli said to never make the people hate the ruler or take their religion, land, or women. He also distrusted mercenaries. One of the most important tasks here is to choose which rulers to examine. The rulers chosen will determine the structure of the essay.

- Finally: *How would you put it into words?* This essay lends itself to easy paragraphs for each of the rulers examined. If you write a thesis explaining that different rulers followed Machiavelli's advice to different degrees, but those who followed it most closely were most successful, and then use one paragraph for each monarch discussed, being sure to go chronologically and to show how the ideas of absolute rule changed over time, the essay will be logically ordered.

SAMPLE ANSWER

Machiavelli's The Prince revolutionized political thought or at least outlined a revolution in political thought that was occurring at the time in the actions of the "new monarchs," such as Henry VII and Louis XI, in governing with the best interests of the state as the only measure of the goodness of any action. His little treatise, sent to the Medici family in hopes of regaining favor, outlined how a ruler should act in order to rule effectively. Peter I (the Great) of Russia followed his advice well, as did Catherine II (the Great) of Russia, but Charles II was unable to follow the advice of Machiavelli, and thus lost his realm to the Bourbon family, illustrating how the implementation of Machiavellian principles by rulers has steadily gained importance as time has progressed.

Peter I was both loved and feared, but rarely hated. He was able to subjugate the nobility and consolidate power after the Strelski revolt by building St. Petersburg, and sending them abroad for schooling. Machiavelli would have praised his reliance on Russian troops during the Great Northern War. His use and treatment of advisors would have gained praise from Machiavelli as he listened to them at his own will. Peter acted as both a fox by using St. Petersburg and wars to subjugate his nobility and a lion because he put down the Strelski revolt and won the Great Northern War to get a port city in St. Petersburg. However, Peter was not an efficient administrator, and was not able to refrain from the property of his citizens, and thus was not a completely Machiavellian ruler.

Catherine the Great ruled Russia a century after Peter the Great had. She further implemented Machiavellian principles strongly after she had to put down the Pugachev Rebellion that had occurred when she had tried to ignore Machiavelli, and change her people's customs. She learned to use others to accomplish her ends early with the Orlov brothers orchestrating a palace coup to put her on the throne. She used war powerfully as a tool of the state and employed only Russian soldiers. By the time of her death, she had followed almost every tenet of Machiavelli's advice and was thus known as a great ruler of Russia even though she was born a Prussian princess. Her reign saw the pinnacle of Machiavellian principles in Russia with her controlling the nobility, the serfs, and the military through both love and fear. She was able to increase the size of her realm, control her people, improve education in Russia, and make Russia a feared international power because of her use of Machiavelli's advice.

Charles II of Spain was simply not able to follow the advice of Machiavelli; his vast realm ended up falling into the hands of the Bourbon family after the War of the Spanish Succession due to his ineffectual rule. Charles did not learn to talk until age four and he could not walk until age eight. He was born with significant physical, mental, and emotional disabilities that meant that he could not follow any advice on ruling. Without a strong monarch, his realm began to fall apart and was finally conquered just as Machiavelli would predict from a leader who was neither loved nor feared, nor a fox, nor a lion.

While the Russians, Peter I and Catherine II, followed Machiavelli's advice, their realms prospered, and prospered more the more that Machiavelli's advice was followed, but Charles II was unable to follow the advice of Machiavelli and his realm was lost. While monarchs had existed in Europe for millennia, the "New Monarchs" evolved to rule more effectively as they employed Machiavelli's advice more.

To this day, the advice of Machiavelli is used or ignored by leaders to their benefit or peril. His work influenced European leaders throughout history and helped create the realpolitik of Bismarck and Cavour and set the stage for ruthless rulers such as Stalin, Hitler, and Mao.

EVALUATE THE SAMPLE ANSWER

Now go back and look at the rubric. It is clear that this essay fulfills all of the requirements for a score 6 on the rubric. The essay answers all parts of the question thoroughly with concrete evidence, at length, with a well-balanced essay. The thesis is appropriate and earns the thesis point. The essay presents strong evidence and reasoning that explains the relationships among the evidence presented and corroborates an argument about how good rulers should behave, which addresses all parts of the question. That should be good enough to earn both Evidence points. The argument certainly addresses the topic with specific, relevant examples and utilizes specific evidence to substantiate the thesis fully and effectively. That should earn both Analysis and Reasoning points. The relation to the inception of realpolitik and the rise of dictators at the end explains how relevant historical context influenced the topic on Machiavellian behavior, gaining the Contextualization point.

RATER'S COMMENTS ON THE SAMPLE ANSWER

6—Extremely Well Qualified

This is an answer that could certainly have been written in the time allotted, and it answered all parts of a multifaceted question. This essay explained very well what Machiavelli meant by "fox" and "lion" and by "loved and feared." It also explained the extent to which each of the three rulers cited were able to follow Machiavelli's advice. The extra advice included helped gain the Synthesis point, but could have been clearer, and tying it to another time period by stating that *The Prince* was still used by politicians today would have been much easier. The CHANGE AND CONTINUITY OVER TIME was a bit weak, but the concluding sentence did a lot to save the essay. This essay was asking students to do a whole lot, and it does meet the requirements, but it is not too pretty, just functional.

Question 2

To what extent and in what ways was the light of Adam Smith's economic optimism dimmed by the "dismal science" of Thomas Malthus and David Ricardo?

COMMENTS ON QUESTION 2

Follow the "Simple Procedures" for writing an essay. (See page 35.)

- First: *What type of question is it?* This one tests the CHANGE AND CONTINUITY OVER TIME skill. Be sure to describe the level of historical continuity (as in what did not change and how interpretations of economic realities stayed essentially the same) and change (as in how Malthus and Ricardo found reasons for eternal misery in their analysis compared to Smith's rosy picture of perfect self-interest), and to analyze specific examples of what changed and how economic understanding advanced compared to how Smith still prevailed. The essay must explain reasons for the CHANGE AND CONTINUITY OVER TIME citing specific evidence as support.
- Second: *What does the question want to know?* How and how much was Smith's "natural law" theory of the operation of an economy altered by the pessimistic views of Malthus and Ricardo? This is the crux of the question.
- Third: *What do you know about it?* Smith was considered an Enlightenment philosopher, a theoretician for the inevitable human progress that the age had projected. Malthus and Ricardo observed the mass misery that the Industrial Revolution and laissez-faire economics had created and, while accepting Smith's basic theory, they sought explanations for its failure in practice.
- Finally: *How would you put it into words?* Show how and how much Malthus and Ricardo created the "dismal science" of economics while still accepting the basic principles of Smith's "natural law" model of the economy.

Adam Smith published his Wealth of Nations in 1776, at the peak of the Enlightenment and during the heyday of governmental mercantilist regulation of European economies. Describing the small business economy of the British "nation of shopkeepers," Smith applied the prevailing natural law theory to the operation of economies. According to Smith, an individual's "enlightened self-interest," if left alone (borrowing the laissez-faire economics of the French physiocrats), will allow the operation of the natural laws of economics.

Whenever a government interferes with one of these laws, such as that of "supply and demand," it creates more problems than are solved. In a free and unregulated economy, each producer will try to lower the cost of production by using the most advanced technology, by making the best use of materials, and by using efficient labor. In that way, the product can be sold cheaper than a competitor's, and the profit will be higher. Also, producers will turn out higher-quality goods to try to surpass those of their competitors.

Smith's natural laws of economics fit the progressive, optimistic view of human society that saturated the thinking of the Age of Enlightenment. Following Isaac Newton's momentous discoveries that universal and unchangeable laws govern the planets and all earthly motion, Enlightenment philosophes sought "natural laws" to govern everything from political morality to economics.

By the time the Industrial Revolution had taken hold of the British economy, during the first two decades of the nineteenth century, Smith's laissez-faire economics had not delivered the general prosperity he had promised. Poverty blighted the new industrial cities of England and Scotland. Men, women, and young children labored long hours for subsistence wages at tedious, dangerous, unhealthy work. Poverty had been the rule among the rural population of small farmers, but it had become unavoidably visible in the crowded, dirty slums of the cities.

Malthus, a clergyman, argued that people were poor because the population had outrun food production. Food increased at an arithmetic rate while population increased at a geometric rate. He thought that war, famine, and disease were divine punishments for humankind's lust.

Ricardo offered a less cosmic but equally despairing view of why poverty is inevitable. His Iron Law of Wages stated that while workers are usually paid a subsistence wage (enough to keep them and their family alive), when labor is in great demand the wages will exceed the "natural wage." Workers prosper; prosperity leads to bigger families; a larger population causes an overabundance of workers; wages drop; workers and their families starve.

During the Age of Reason, Smith's natural laws of economics promised general prosperity. He was reacting against the arbitrary regulation of economics by modern monarchs seduced by the bullionism of mercantilist theory, and he was following the optimistic assumptions of the Enlightenment. Observing the abuses of industrialization, Malthus and Ricardo tried to salvage classical economics by explaining how poverty could exist in an unregulated economy. Once they had offered their theories, they felt no obligation to alleviate the economic and social ills they had pronounced to be unavoidable. That they left to the socialists and Marxists who would follow them.

EVALUATE THE SAMPLE ANSWER

3—Now go back and look at the rubric. It is clear that this essay looks to be pretty weak on the rubric. The essay has a weak thesis that is not found until the final paragraph, but the essay does get the thesis point. The support for evidence and reasoning is only tangential support, so it gets only 1 point for providing specific examples of evidence related to the topic of the question. While continuity and change over time is described, it is not analyzed, and reasons for it are not explained through specific examples. It does describe the Age of Reason as a broader historical context immediately relevant to the question, so it also gets one Contextualization point.

RATER'S COMMENTS ON THE SAMPLE ANSWER

3—Not qualified

This essay is included to show you what NOT to do. This essay mostly goes off on tangents and does not answer the question thoroughly or clearly. By taking time to explain Adam Smith before stating a thesis, this essay risks losing the reader, who may miss the thesis in the conclusion. Its fractured nature and tangential approach lacks structure and clarity. The thesis only being present in the conclusion certainly hurts the essay. This essay is well written and factual, but it does not cohesively create an answer to the question asked. To review, the question was to determine *to what extent* Smith's science was altered by Malthus and Ricardo, who, in contrast, have both been discredited as time has passed, while Smith's ideas live on as the framework of the modern economy. If anything, Adam Smith is more pertinent in 2018 than he was in 1776, and certainly more so than Malthus or Ricardo; this was not examined at all. Because this essay question is testing the CHANGE AND CONTINUITY OVER TIME skill, the answer must use that idea as the backbone of the essay, which is clearly missing here. This essay examined the ideas of all three men, but it did not draw conclusions about how Malthus and Ricardo changed the study of economics, or how it stayed the same. Remember, do not just write everything you know about a subject, but rather create a cohesive answer with a strong thesis that answers the question.

Time Period Three:
c. 1815 to c. 1914

KEY CONCEPTS AND OVERVIEW

KEY CONCEPT 3.1 The Industrial Revolution spread from Great Britain to the Continent, where the state played a greater role in promoting industry.

KEY CONCEPT 3.2 The experiences of everyday life were shaped by industrialization, depending on the level of industrial development in a particular location.

KEY CONCEPT 3.3 Political revolutions and the comlications resulting from industrialization triggered a range of ideological, governmental, and collective responses.

KEY CONCEPT 3.4 European states struggled to maintain international stability in an age of nationalism and revolutions.

KEY CONCEPT 3.5 A variety of motives and methods led to the intensification of European global control and increased tensions among the Great Powers.

KEY CONCEPT 3.6 European ideas and culture expressed a tension between objectivity and scientific realism, on one hand, and subjectivity and individual expression, on the other.

TIME PERIOD OVERVIEW

This time period is about the industrialization of Continental Europe, the growth of nationalism, modernization, urbanization, the spread of imperialism, conflicts between competing economic and political theories, the birth of existentialism, and the struggles to replace absolute monarchies with constitutional governments that gave citizens a voice in politics across the Continent. This chapter examines how the industrialization of Europe led to urbanization and social problems that in turn led to changes in government and in people's expectations of their governments. The fragile stability of the European balance of power will be examined in detail through the assessment of many alliance systems of the era. The European dominance of the rest of the world will be assessed from many perspectives. This time period includes the traditional delineations of the following eras:

The Industrial Revolution
The Age of Metternich (1815–1848)
Nationalism
Imperialism

These traditional delineations do overlap in many ways, and the themes within them, as stated above in the key concepts, can be seen woven through the next three chapters of this book.

> **SPECIAL NOTE ON PERIODIZATION**
>
> As stated in Chapter 6 and in the preface to time Period 2, the subject of the Industrial Revolution was split between time periods by the new framework for European History. To preserve the continuity of the subject, the Industrial Revolution was covered entirely in Chapter 6, which is contained in the Period 2 section of this book.

The Growth and Suppression of Democracy: From the Age of Metternich to the First World War (1815–1914)

7

KEY TERMS/PEOPLE

- → GREAT REFORM BILL
- → CHARTIST MOVEMENT
- → REVOLUTIONS OF 1848
- → AGE OF METTERNICH
- → NAPOLEON III/LOUIS NAPOLEON
- → CRIMEAN WAR
- → GREEK WAR OF INDEPENDENCE
- → POLISH REBELLION
- → DECEMBRIST REVOLT IN RUSSIA

- → JULY REVOLUTION IN FRANCE
- → GIUSEPPE MAZZINI
- → *ZOLLVEREIN*
- → EMANCIPATION OF RUSSIAN SERFS
- → CARLSBAD DECREES/DIET
- → PRAGUE CONFERENCE
- → COMPROMISE OF 1867
- → PAN-SLAVIC MOVEMENT

OVERVIEW

The period from the fall of Napoleon in 1815 to the Revolutions of 1848 is often referred to by historians as the "Age of Metternich." Klemens von Metternich (1773–1859) personified the spirit of reaction that followed a quarter-century of revolution and war. Chancellor of Habsburg Austria and one of the chief participants at the Congress of Vienna, Metternich and others who shared his desire to preserve monarchy and the status quo designed a Continental balance of power all over Europe that would for the most part preserve the peace for a century (until the First World War) but was challenged in 1848 and seemed it would burst at the seams. Metternich was a tall, handsome man whose charm worked equally well on his fellow diplomats and on the elegant ladies of Vienna. He was the prototype of conservatism in leadership style for European ministers. He spoke five languages fluently, thought of himself as a European, not as a citizen of any single country, and once said "Europe has for a long time held for me the significance of a fatherland." Early in his career, Metternich linked himself to the Habsburgs and became Austria's foreign minister, an office he held for 39 years. Because of his immense influence on European politics, these years are often called the Age of Metternich. He felt liberals were imposing their views on society, mostly motivated by their nationalist self-determination ideals—a position that threatened Austria because of its diverse and large population.

During the Age of Metternich, two great nations developed the basis for modern constitutional democracy. Britain continued its democratization through the perpetuation of the unique and stabilizing evolutionary process that represented the interests in government of more and more of its populace. France, on the other hand, experienced destabilizing see-saw battles between reaction and radicalism. Volatile business cycles in the last quarter of the nineteenth century led corporations and governments to try to manage the market through monopolies, banking practices, and tariffs. The processes continued through the nineteenth century and into the early twentieth until the British and the Germans (along with brave examples set by the Scandinavian nations) had established the foundations for modern welfare states by the 1930s.

Three nations that played important roles in the nineteenth and early twentieth centuries—Germany, Austria, and Russia—suppressed the democratic urges of significant elements of their populations. In Germany, the move toward unification of the varied and independent states fell out of the hands of the constitutionalists and into those of Prussian militarists. In Austria, the Germanic Habsburg rulers continued to suppress the move toward autonomy of the polyglot nationalities that made up the empire. In Russia, sporadic attempts at reform and modernization were consumed by the ruling class's obsession with "Autocracy, Orthodoxy, and Nationalism."

THE GROWTH OF DEMOCRACY

Britain

The ideals and promises of the French Revolution and a growing but poverty-stricken working class shook the foundations of stability in Europe's greatest emerging democracy. Parliament, after the end of the Napoleonic Wars in 1815, represented the interests of aristocrats and the wealthy.

- The *Corn Laws of 1815* effectively raised prices at a time when Europe was war torn because importation of foreign grain was prohibited until the price rose above 80 shillings per quarter-ton, benefiting the land owners who ran Parliament.

  - This resulted in many riots and political unrest as food prices rose for the poor.
  - The Corn Laws were repealed in 1846 in large part because of the actions of the Anti-Corn Law League, which convinced Prime Minister Robert Peel and some of his Tory party (the conservative party) members to do what was "right for Britain rather than their personal interests." Free import of grain was again allowed.
  - By the 1820s, though, new and younger leaders of the Tories implemented reforms such as restructuring the penal code, providing for a modern police force, allowing membership in labor unions, and granting Catholics basic civil rights.

- By 1830, when abortive revolutions had broken out all over the Continent, the *House of Commons*, the lower chamber of Parliament, had not been reapportioned since 1688.

  - Many of the boroughs that elected representatives to Parliament in fact no longer existed, while large and growing industrial cities had no representation at all.
  - *The Great Reform Bill*, 1832, abolished the *rotten boroughs*, expanded the electorate, and empowered the industrial middle class.

- The *Chartist movement*, representing demands by radical working-class activists, sought an array of reforms from 1838 into the late 1840s.

  - It advocated universal male suffrage, a secret voting ballot, "one man, one vote" representation in Parliament, abolition of property qualifications for public office, and public education for all classes.
  - Although its program failed during the decade of its existence, all of its features were eventually incorporated into British society.

- When the discontent of the working class on the Continent exploded during the *Revolutions of 1848,* the British proletariat was able to trust in its government's capacity to make gradual reforms.
- In 1866, *Whig* (liberal party) prime minister, *William E. Gladstone* (1807–1898), attempted to expand voter eligibility, but was defeated in Parliament.
- A new government under Tory (conservative) *Benjamin Disraeli* (1804–1881) turned the tables on the Whig reformers by getting the *Second Reform Bill,* 1867, through Parliament.

  - It not only doubled the size of the electorate, but it gave the vote to many industrial workers.
  - When Disraeli's party lost the general election in 1868 (the head of the party that wins the most seats in a parliamentary election forms a government and becomes prime minister), Gladstone returned to power and enacted sweeping reforms.

- *Labor unions were legalized;* the *secret ballot* was introduced.
- *Free public education* was offered to working-class children.
- The Third Reform Bill of 1885 largely granted universal male suffrage.
- In the decade immediately before the start of the First World War, Britain laid the foundations for its *social welfare state*: government institutions and laws that guarantee all citizens a decent standard of living.

  - The right of unions to strike was put into law.
  - Government insurance was provided for those injured on the job.
  - Unemployment insurance and old-age pensions were enacted.
  - A compulsory school-attendance law went into effect.

France

During the *Age of Metternich* (the period of reaction after the 1815 Congress of Vienna, which ended with the Continent-wide Revolutions of 1848), France was ruled by Bourbon reactionaries and a "bourgeois" king whose watered-down constitutions excluded the expanding proletariat from representation. After the upheavals of 1848, a self-styled emperor, a relative of Napoleon, took the French throne.

- When Bourbon *Louis XVIII* (r. 1814–1824), a brother of the guillotined Louis XVI, was restored to the throne in 1814, he issued a constitution but gave power to only a small class of landowners and rich bourgeois.
- Absolutist pretenses were continued with his successor and younger brother, *Charles X* (r. 1824–1830), whose repressive measures led to rioting in Paris and the abdication of Charles in the summer of 1830, a year when abortive insurrections broke out all over Europe.

  - Charles's abdication caused a rift between radicals, who wanted to establish a republic, and bourgeoisie, who wanted the stability of a monarchy.
  - Through the intercession of the Marquis de Lafayette, hero of the American Revolution, Louis Phillipe (r. 1830–1848), an aristocrat, became the *"bourgeoisie king"* by agreeing to honor the Constitution of 1814. His reign empowered the bourgeoisie but left the proletariat unrepresented.

- Known as the *July Revolution*, this insurrection in 1830 included the Three Glorious Days of July 27–29 in which students were massacred and the bourgeois king was placed upon the throne, resulting in no gains for the movement. This vain revolution was glorified in great French works such as *Liberty Leading the People* by Eugene Delacroix.

- Rampant corruption in the government of Louis Phillipe incited republican and socialist protests, which erupted in violence and led to his abdication in February 1848, another year that saw mostly abortive insurrections all over Europe.

  - The *Chamber of Deputies*, the lower house of the two-chamber French legislature that was created in 1814 by Louis XVIII's constitution, was pressured by Parisian mobs to *proclaim a republic* and to name a provisional government that would rule temporarily until a Constituent Assembly could be elected to draft a new constitution.
  - When the provinces—the countryside outside the large cities—elected a largely conservative Constituent Assembly, conflicts between the government and socialist and radical workers erupted into bloody class battles on the streets of Paris by early summer 1848.

- The June Days Uprising was an uprising staged by the workers of France in response to plans to close the National Workshops, created by the Second Republic to provide work and a source of income for the unemployed. The National Guard, led by General Louis Eugène Cavaignac, was called out to quell the protests and over 10,000 people were either killed or injured, while 4,000 more were deported to Algeria.

  - Frightened by the threat of a radical takeover, the Constituent Assembly brutally suppressed the riots, then established the *single-chambered Legislative Assembly* and *a strong president*, both to be elected by *universal male suffrage*.

- *Louis Napoleon Bonaparte* (r. 1848–1870), Napoleon's nephew, was elected president of the *Second Republic* (the First Republic had been established in 1792, during the French Revolution).

  - He dedicated his presidency to law and order, to the eradication of socialism and radicalism, and to the interests of the conservative classes: the Church, the army, property-owners, and business.
  - Through a political ploy, he was able to discredit many members of the Legislative Assembly, win a landslide re-election, and proclaim himself in 1852 as Emperor *Napoleon III* of the *Second French Empire*. (His uncle, Napoleon Bonaparte, had crowned himself Emperor in 1804.)
  - While the Second Empire was not an absolutist government, it was an autocracy.
  - Napoleon III controlled finances and initiated legislation.
  - He was immensely popular in the early years of his reign because of his internal improvements such as highway, canal, and railroad construction, and because of his subsidies to industry and his stimulation of the economy.
  - The bourgeoisie was grateful for the general prosperity; the proletariat was appreciative of employment and the right to organize unions.
  - During the *Liberal Empire* (1860–1870), he eased censorship and granted amnesty to political prisoners.
  - Foreign affairs were his downfall.

- The *Crimean War* (1853–1856), in which the French and British went to war to prevent the Russians from establishing dominance over the Black Sea possessions of the Ottomans, was costly on all sides.

- The *Franco-Prussian War*, which helped unify Germany, was a disaster for the French and Napoleon III. The Germans crushed the French and laid siege to Paris, forcing a humiliating defeat upon the French that would contribute to the destabilization of Western Europe during the twentieth century.

- The French defeat in this war ended the Second Empire and began the Third Republic. Controlled by monarchists and the bourgeoisie, the new National Assembly brutally suppressed a radical socialist counter-government, the *Paris Commune*.

- In 1875, the assembly voted to set up a *Chamber of Deputies*, elected by universal male suffrage, a *Senate*, indirectly elected, a ceremonial president, elected by the whole legislature, and a premier, directly responsible to the Chamber of Deputies.

- From the establishment of the Third Republic in 1871 to the beginning of the First World War in 1914, *the French government fell dozens of times.* The governments were inherently unstable because there were so many political parties (in a *multiparty system* unlike the British or American two-party systems) that none could win a clear majority in the Legislative Assembly, and the coalitions fell apart during many a crisis.

- The *Dreyfus Affair* (1894–1906), in which a Jewish army captain was falsely accused of spying by anti-republican conservatives, was one instance of the political infighting that often paralyzed the government.

- The multiparty system of France seemed to carry democracy to excess but, by the First World War, France had universal male suffrage and had instituted a *social welfare system* similar to that in Britain.

By the early part of the twentieth century, Britain and France had evolved into two of the world's three most powerful democracies, the United States being the third. The old liberalism of laissez-faire government had been replaced by a new liberalism that supported the extension of suffrage and the improvement of living conditions for all citizens.

THE SUPPRESSION OF DEMOCRACY

Germany Through the Age of Metternich (1815–1848)

The Congress of Vienna had set up a *Germanic Confederation* of the 39 independent German states that existed after the fall of Napoleon, which destroyed the Holy Roman Empire once and for all.

- Radical student organizations, *Burschenschafts*, which were dedicated to the creation of a unified Germany that would be governed by constitutional principles, organized a national convention in 1817, and, in 1819, attempted the assassination of reactionary politicians.

- In 1819, Metternich issued the infamous Carlsbad Decrees, which were anti-subversive laws designed to get the liberals out of Austria, its press, and the universities.

  - He had a state secret police and attempted to control what was published and what was discussed at universities. The Carlsbad Diet drove liberalism and nationalism underground.

- Although the reactionary forces in Germany quickly put down the *Revolutions of 1830*, Prussia set up an economic union of 17 German states, the *Zollverein*, which eliminated internal tariffs and set the tone for greater union.

The Age of Metternich Ended in the Revolutions of 1848

- Every nation in Europe save the most advanced, Britain, and the least advanced, Russia, experienced revolutions.
- This year saw Metternich flee Austria during the Continent-wide uprisings.
- Proved what Mary Wollstonecraft had said in reference to the oppression of women: "The bow that is bent twice as far snaps back twice as hard."
- The revolutions ended in failure for the most part because the political conditions after the revolutions were unchanged from what they had been before the revolutions for the most part.
- The Prussian king, Frederick William IV (r. 1840–1861), reacted to the *Revolutions of 1848* by calling a nominal legislative assembly rather than using military force.

    - In 1850, he granted a constitution that established a House of Representatives elected by universal male suffrage but controlled by the wealthiest classes.
    - The Frankfurt Assembly, an extralegal convention not to be confused with the king's Legislative Assembly, met from May 1848 to May 1849 and *established the nature of the future union of Germany.*
    - Advocates of a *Greater Germany* (*Grossdeutsch*) wanted to include Austria and to have a Habsburg emperor rule over the union.
    - Supporters of a *Lesser Germany* (*Kleindeutsch*) wanted to exclude Austria and to have Prussia lead the union.

- The debate was resolved when Austria backed away from the proposed union. When the Frankfurt Assembly offered Frederick William the crown of a united Germany with Austria excluded, he declined by saying that he would accept it only from the German princes themselves.
- The failure of the Frankfurt Assembly to implement its design for a democratic union (it had framed a kind of bill of rights) left the job of German unification to Prussian militarism and *Bismarck's policy of "Blood and Iron."* (German politics until the First World War will be considered in a later chapter.)

THE REVOLUTIONS OF 1848

France

Causes	Length of Time	Protagonists	Events	Results
The economic changes in Britain as well as the expansion of the franchise there led to social pressures in France. Political demonstration was outlawed so people held political banquets instead, which were outlawed. Also the oppression of Louis Napoleon and his repressive minister, Guizot, pushed the people to the breaking point because of censorship and restriction of freedoms when 52 demonstrators were killed by soldiers.	1847–1848	Louis Blanc, Pierre Proudhon, Louis Cavaignac, Alphonse de Lamartine, Napoleon III	Louis Philippe fled to Britain, and Guizot resigned as barricades emerged across Paris. The Second Republic was formed in 1848 based upon universal male suffrage. A class struggle ensued between rich and poor, rural and urban. The urban workers tried a Marxist experiment that failed.	Napoleon III reigned after winning elections in landslides. He dismissed the National Assembly and ruled with more power and control than Louis Philippe had held.

German States

Causes	Length of Time	Protagonists	Events	Results
The news of the revolutions in France spread throughout Europe, and the people of the 39 Germanic states began to demand rights.	February 1848–May 1848	The French leaders and the bourgeoisie of Germany, Richard Wagner.	The people of Baden demanded the first German Bill of Rights in February of 1848. Soon a crowd threatened the palace in Berlin and after an incident in which demonstrators were killed, King William Frederick IV demonstrated support for the revolutionaries and promised to reorganize his government. King Ludwig abdicated in Bavaria, and Saxony also saw calls for reform.	The king still reigned and Bismarck would soon come to power with Wilhelm I and unite the western German states into modern Germany through almost dictatorial rule.

Habsburg Empire

Causes	Length of Time	Protagonists	Events	Results
This multiethnic empire had been held together with force by and Metternich's political machinations.	Feb. 1848–Aug. 1849	Many listed in other columns.	The empire burst asunder.	The Habsburg Empire was returned to its former state of a multiethnic empire.
In 1848, Continental Europe was mostly France, Germany, Russia, and the Habsburg Empire or former Habsburg Empire.			Austria, with the help of arch-conservative Russian czar, Nicholas I, was able to reassemble a weakened empire.	Croats, Slovaks, Germans, Austrians, Poles, Magyars, Serbs, Ruthenians, Italians, and Czechs.
The Habsburg Empire was in decline and was not held together well.				The Habsburg Empire was returned to its former state of a multiethnic empire.
The different ethnic groups all attempted to gain autonomy in 1848 as the idea of nationalism seemed to sweep the continent.				The central authority had been further weakened, and the empire would only last until 1918.
In this year the Communist Manifesto was published in German.				

Hungary

Causes	Length of Time	Protagonists	Events	Results
Ethnic oppression by the Austrian Habsburgs burst the Austrian Empire asunder in 1848. The Hungarian parliament had been called in 1825 to address financial matters. A bloodless revolution occurred in March of 1848, led by a governor and a prime minister.		Louis Kossuth and Louis Bathyany	The Hungarians took advantage of the general revolutions throughout the Habsburg Empire and got Austria to grant them autonomy. Once Austria beat down the other revolutions, the new emperor, Franz Josef I, decided to crush Hungary. With help from Russia, the Hungarians were defeated in a failed war for independence.	The Habsburg Empire was returned to its former state of a multiethnic empire of Croats, Slovaks, Germans, Austrians, Poles, Magyars, Serbs, Ruthenians, Italians, and Czechs. The Hungarians practiced passive resistance against the Habsburgs.

Italian States

Causes	Length of Time	Protagonists	Events	Results
Giuseppe Mazzini	March 1848–May 1849	Giuseppe Mazzini, Giuseppe Garibaldi	The revolutions resulted in Venetian and Roman republics. The Austrians marched through Piedmont and southward into Italy, conquering most of Italy by May of 1849.	Almost 1,000 people were killed by the Austrians as they regained power throughout the peninsula.

Poland

Causes	Length of Time	Protagonists	Events	Results
The Prussians armed Polish prisoners and encouraged them to return to Poland with Revolutionary and anti-Russian motives.	March 1848–June 1848	Jerzy Zdrada, Frederick William IV, Natalis Sulerzyski, and Seweryn Elzanowski	The Prussians supported a Polish revolution to weaken the Russians. The Poles did not trust the Prussians, but needed them. The Poles and Prussians ended up in armed conflict, which the Prussians won.	The Poles learned that they could not bargain with the Germanic states to gain statehood. They focused on economic growth rather than political growth.

Austria from the Age of Metternich to the First World War (1815–1914)

The Revolutions of 1830 hardly touched the reactionary government of Austria under Metternich. However, the ethnic mix that made up the Austrian Empire: Germans, Hungarians, Slavs, Czechs, Italians, Serbs, Croats, and many others helped bring about revolution in 1848.

- When Paris erupted in rebellion in March of 1848, *Louis Kossuth*, a Hungarian nationalist, aroused separatist sentiment in the *Hungarian Diet* (a national assembly legal in the empire).

  - Rioting broke out in Vienna.
  - Prince Metternich, then chancellor, fled the country, and the Hungarians, the Czechs, and three Northern Italian provinces of the empire declared autonomy.
  - The empire collapsed temporarily.
  - The Prague Conference, called by the Czechs in response to the all-German Frankfurt Conference.

- Developed the notion of Austroslavism, by which the Slavic groups within the empire would remain part of the empire.
- Set up autonomous national governments in ethnic regions.

  - Before the idea could be adopted, a series of victories by Austrian armies restored Habsburg authority over the various nationalities that had declared independence.

- *Franz Joseph* (r. 1848–1916) replaced *Emperor Ferdinand I,* and conservative forces within the government centralized power and suppressed all opposition.

  - The Revolutions of 1848 failed in Austria largely because the empire's ethnic minorities squabbled among themselves rather than make a united front against imperial Habsburg forces.

- The defeat of Austria in the Austro-Prussian War of 1866 (to be considered in a subsequent chapter) led to some governmental reform.
- The Compromise of 1867 set up a constitutional government with limited suffrage, granted the Hungarians internal autonomy, and created a *dual monarchy,* the *Austro-Hungarian Empire.*

  - Exclusion of the Slavic minorities from a voice in government encouraged the *Pan-Slavic movement* to seek independence for ethnic minorities.
  - It was an important cause of the First World War.

Russia from the End of the Napoleonic Wars to the First World War (1815–1914)

Alexander I (r. 1801–1825) began his reign by extending the reforms of Catherine the Great, by modernizing the functioning of his government, and by offering greater freedom to Jews within his empire. Napoleon's invasion of Russia in 1812 turned this disposition about until, by 1820, Alexander had ordered statewide censorship and the adherence of all his subjects to the Russian Orthodox Church.

- When Alexander died, a confusion of succession (his two brothers, *Constantine* and *Nicholas,* were in line) led to the *Decembrist Revolt* of army officers in December 1825, in the capital of St. Petersburg.

  - They supported the candidacy of Constantine, who they believed would modernize the nation and offer a constitution.

- *Nicholas I* (r. 1825–1855) attained the throne after crushing the revolt, and his reign continued Alexander's autocratic policies.

  - He was creator of the infamous *Third Section*, the secret police who prevented the spread of revolutionary or Western ideas. "Orthodoxy, Autocracy, Nationality" was the rallying cry of his reaction.
  - Intellectuals in Russia developed two opposing camps during this period:

    - *Slavophiles,* who believed that Russian village (the mir) culture was superior to that of the West; and
    - *Westernizers,* who wanted to extend the "genius of Russian culture" by industrializing and setting up a constitutional government.

- *Alexander II* (r. 1855–1881) began his reign as a reformer and ended it as a conservative.

  - His *Emancipation Proclamation* of 1861 *ended serfdom*, the Medieval institution largely abolished in the rest of Europe, under which peasants were bound to the land and virtually owned by the aristocratic landowners.
  - His murder at the hands of a militant faction of the *Narodniks,* a socialist group who wanted Russia to return to some mythical ideal of village life, increased repression under his successors, who turned to "Autocracy, Orthodoxy, and Nationality."

- By the 1890s, Russia had undertaken *industrialization* in order to remain a world power.

  - At the beginning of the First World War, 25 million of its population of 140 million were city dwellers.
  - The *Trans-Siberian Railroad* linked European and Asiatic Russia.
  - The members of the growing proletariat were largely employed in state-owned factories that exploited and abused them.

PRACTICE LONG-ESSAY QUESTIONS

These questions are samples of the various types of thematic essays on the exam. (See pages 30–31 for a detailed explanation of each type.) Check over the **generic rubric** (see pages 32–33) before you begin any of these essays and use that rubric to score your essay if you write one.

Question 1

To what extent and in what ways did the failure of the German constitutionalists lead to the Prussian militarists unifying Germany?

COMMENTS ON QUESTION 1

This one is a CAUSATION question because it requires you to explain how one event, the failure of the constitutionalists to unify Germany, resulted in a specific outcome: the Prussian militarists dominating German unification. Remember to describe causes AND/OR effects of German unification, and to support your analysis of those causes and effects with specific evidence. The essay must also explain how the failure of the constitutionalists led Germany to be united later by Bismarck and the Prussian militarists, and cite specific evidence as support. There is little room for choice in this question, since it requires that you show "how and how much" of German unification was the result of a failure of the forces of democracy to take the lead, thereby leaving it to the militarists in Prussia. Refer to specifics in the breakdown of the leadership of constitutional forces, in the assumption of leadership by Prussia, and in the militaristic nature of Prussian leadership.

Question 2

To what extent did Austria's suppression of Slavic autonomy within the empire create more dissolution than unity?

COMMENTS ON QUESTION 2

This one is a CAUSATION question because it requires you to explain to what extent one factor, Austrian suppression of a Slavic minority within the empire, resulted in a specific outcome: the dissolution of unity within the empire. Remember to describe causes AND/OR effects of the dissolution of the Austrian Empire, and to support your analysis of those causes and effects with specific evidence. The essay must explain the reasons that suppression of the Slavic minority did or did not result in the dissolution of the empire. In this case—because of the crucial phrase "more dissolution than unity"—the argument must show that one or the other was true.

As is often the case, the question itself shows the direction of the best possible argument: that dissolution was the result of Austria's policy toward its Slavic minorities. Back this up with both previous and future actions and evaluations of the strength of the Austrian Empire over time. Then tie the result to the causation, the attempt to suppress the Slavs, and decide to what extent it was the cause of the weakening of the empire.

Question 3

Compare the growth and suppression of democracy in nineteenth-century Europe.

COMMENTS ON QUESTION 3

This is a COMPARE skill question, so be sure to describe similarities and differences between how democracy simultaneously grew and was crushed during the era, as well as account for or explain them by providing specific examples of how they could suppress democracy, and by tying the trends in political voices being heard to historical developments such as the rise of conservatism. This is a double effort: to "show differences" and to "examine similarities." Democracy did not grow easily in the states where it was ultimately successful, nor did it flounder completely in those where it was suppressed. This is a broad question that requires more than a comparison of only two states.

PRACTICE SHORT-ANSWER QUESTIONS

1. Historians have often referred to the period of European History between 1815 and 1848 as the Age of Metternich.

   (A) Provide TWO pieces of information that support this characterization of the period and explain how they support it.

   (B) Provide ONE piece of information that refutes this characterization of the period and explain how the information refutes it.

2. Please use the image and the passage below to answer all parts of the following question.

Source 1

The reception of Queen Victoria by Napoleon III at St. Cloud, August 18, 1855.

Source 2

James Russell Lowell, *On Democracy*

But is it democracies alone that fall into these errors? I, who have seen it proposed to erect a statue to Hudson, the railway king, and have heard Louis Napoleon hailed as the savior of society by men who certainly had no democratic associations or leanings, am not ready to think so. But democracies have likewise their finer instincts. I have also seen the wisest statesman and most pregnant speaker of our generation, a man of humble birth and ungainly manners, of little culture beyond what his own genius supplied, become more absolute in power than any monarch of modern times through the reverence of his countrymen for his honesty, his wisdom, his sincerity, his faith in God and man, and the nobly humane simplicity of his character.

   (A) Explain one accomplishment of Louis Napoleon.

   (B) Assess the form of government in France when Louis Napoleon took power in 1848.

   (C) Assess the form of government used by Louis Napoleon by the end of his reign in 1870.

Short-Answer Explanations

1. (A) You should cite TWO of the following and EXPLAIN HOW each supports the characterization of the time period as the Age of Metternich: rise of conservatism, Austria's central role in European politics at the time, Metternich's redesign of Europe after the Congress of Vienna to create the Concert of Europe, Metternich's role at the Congress of Vienna, the Holy Alliance, or Austria's dominance over the other Germanic states.

   (B) You should cite ONE of the following and EXPLAIN HOW it refutes the characterization of the period as the Age of Metternich: the rise of the United Kingdom as a European power, the collapse of the Concert of Europe, the Revolutions of 1830 and 1848, the decline of the Austrian Empire, the lack of Austrian international trade, the concurrent rise of democracy in much of Europe (UK and France), and Metternich fleeing to London in 1848.

2. (A) You may fully explain any ONE of the following: eradication of radicalism in France, banning socialism in France, creating the Second French Empire, improving France's infrastructure, bringing prosperity to the French bourgeoisie.

   (B) You must indicate that Louis Napoleon was elected by a popular vote and ran a democratic state when he was first elected president.

   (C) You must explain the rise of the Second French Empire and the fact that Napoleon III was an emperor by the end of his rule in 1870. You should also mention that this was an autocratic government, and that Napoleon III was able to hold most power by himself.

PRACTICE MULTIPLE-CHOICE QUESTIONS

Questions 1 to 4 refer to the writing of historian Jonathan Sperber in his *The European Revolutions 1848–1851* below.

Rather darker is another version of the 1848 revolutions that views them primarily as farce, a revolution made by the revolutionaries who were at best incompetent dilettantes, and at worst cowards and blowhards who stole away from the scene when going got rough. This version features the story of the Parisian revolutionary observing from his window a demonstrating crowd go by, springing up from his chair, and rushing out, proclaiming 'I am their leader; I must follow them.' Another typical victim of the retrospective contempt is the Frankfurt National Assembly, the all-German parliament.

The third and probably most substantial of the historians' versions of 1848 directs attention to the failure of the revolutions of that year to establish new regimes, pointing out that after a shorter or longer interval, usually shorter, the authorities overthrown at the onset of the revolutions were returned to power.

1. Which of the following viewpoints is Sperber most likely to support according to the excerpt above?

   (A) The Revolutions of 1848 had no impact on European political evolution.
   (B) The Revolutions of 1848 were failures mostly because of poor leadership.
   (C) The Revolutions of 1848 ended with mostly the same people in power as when they had begun.
   (D) The Revolutions of 1848 changed Eastern Europe more than Western Europe.

2. Which of the following was destroyed as a result of the Revolutions of 1848?

   (A) The Concert of Europe
   (B) The European alliance system
   (C) The belief that liberal republics could be formed
   (D) The legacy of Klemens von Metternich

3. Which of the following countries did NOT experience a revolution in 1848 for the reason given in the answer?

   (A) Britain, because it was experiencing an industrial revolution already
   (B) Britain, because it had already become a mostly capitalist democracy
   (C) France, because the French Revolution made the French less likely to revolt in the future
   (D) Italy, because the independent states began to work together to eliminate poverty there

4. Which of the following utopian socialists got the opportunity to test out his ideas in France during the revolutions of 1848?

   (A) Henri de Saint-Simon
   (B) Louis Blanc
   (C) Charles Fourier
   (D) Louis Kossuth

Questions 5 to 7 refer to the image below.

—Troops storming a barricade in the Donesgasse in Frankfurt, Germany, in 1848. The Granger Collection (0009086).

5. The Revolutions of 1848 were most often led by those below who were which of the following?

   (A) Aristocrats tired of losing their privileges
   (B) Military leaders fed up with inefficient leaders
   (C) Liberal bourgeois gentlemen dedicated to romantic ideals
   (D) The poorest citizens who had nothing to lose

6. The original goal of the Frankfurt Assembly (1848–1849) was which of the following?

   (A) Design and implement a constitutional government for a unified Germany
   (B) Consolidate Germany under Austrian Habsburg leadership
   (C) Unify the northern states of Germany under Prussia
   (D) Create a united Germany for Germans only

7. The overall results of the Revolutions of 1848 can best be described as which of the following?

   (A) Overthrew the governments of France, Germany, and Russia
   (B) Dissipated the nationalistic urges of the peoples of Eastern Europe
   (C) Marked the decline of the political influence of the proletariat
   (D) Gave rise to communism and realpolitik

Multiple-Choice Explanations

1. **C**	3. **B**	5. **C**	7. **D**
2. **A**	4. **B**	6. **A**	

1. **(C)**

(A) is wrong because the Revolutions of 1848 changed European society and awakened a desire for popular sovereignty.

(B) is wrong because Sperber is arguing that the most substantial version is the one that returned old leaders to their original posts, not the view that poor leaders ruined it.

(C) is CORRECT because Sperber is arguing that the most substantial version is the one that returned old leaders to their original posts.

(D) is wrong because 1848 affected Western Europe much more than Eastern Europe which was controlled mostly by Russia, Austria, and the Ottomans.

2. **(A)**

(A) is CORRECT because the Concert of Europe disintegrated when Metternich fled in 1848.

(B) is wrong because the European Alliance system was revived by Bismarck and played a large role in Europe through the First World War.

(C) is wrong because many still believed in liberal republics after 1848, but they would not become a reality in most of Europe until after the First World War.

(D) is wrong because Metternich's legacy as the prototype conservative lives on after 1848.

3. **(B)**

(A) is wrong because most of Europe was in the middle of an industrial revolution when they had revolts in 1848, so that does not explain why Britain was spared.

(B) is CORRECT: Britain was spared a revolution because it was already politically and economically more advanced than the rest of Europe.

(C) is wrong because France began the 1848 Revolutions.

(D) is wrong because Italy did experience revolutions in 1848.

4. **(B)**

(A) is wrong because Saint-Simon was already dead in 1848 (he died in 1825).

(B) is CORRECT because Louis Blanc was helping rule France for a short time in 1848 and tried national workshops and other socialist methods to try to help France recover.

(C) is wrong because Fourier was already dead by 1848 (he died in 1837).

(D) is wrong because Louis Kossuth was a Hungarian leader in 1848 and had little to do with France.

5. **(C)**

(A) is wrong because the aristocracy was not taking to the streets to try to regain privileges they had lost, as the time of their authority had passed.

(B) is wrong because the military leaders were in the minority in the revolts that were mostly led by romantically minded liberal bourgeois young men who thought they could fix the world.

(C) is CORRECT because the Revolutions were led mostly by romantically minded liberal bourgeois young men who thought they could fix the world.

(D) is wrong because the poor citizens were followers rather than leaders.

6. **(A)**

(A) is CORRECT because the Frankfurt Assembly was created to design and implement a German constitution for all Germanic states. The Assembly offered the Crown to Wilhelm of Prussia, but he refused.

(B) is wrong because there was never a plan to unify Austria and Prussia at the Frankfurt Assembly.

(C) is wrong because the plan was to unify all German states.

(D) is wrong because Germans did not take part in ethnic cleansing in the 1800s.

7. **(D)**

(A) is wrong because Russia did not even have an uprising in 1848.

(B) is wrong because nationalism remained strong in Eastern Europe after 1848 and would be an immediate cause of the First World War.

(C) is wrong because the proletariat would continue to gain strength well into the twentieth century.

(D) is CORRECT because the ideas of *realpolitik* and *communism* will be used after this point to change European society.

The Ideologies of the 19th Century: Liberalism, Conservatism, Nationalism, and Culture

8

KEY TERMS/PEOPLE

→ UNIFICATION

→ OTTO VON BISMARCK

→ KAISER WILHELM I

→ AUSTRO-PRUSSIAN WAR
   (SEVEN WEEKS' WAR)

→ FRANCO-PRUSSIAN WAR

→ GUISEPPE MAZZINI

→ GUISEPPE GARIBALDI

→ CAMILLO DI CAVOUR

→ VICTOR EMMANUEL II

→ LIBERALISM

→ PAN-SLAVISM

→ SOCIALISM

→ ROMANTICISM

→ MEIJI RESTORATION

→ THEODORE HERZL

→ REALISM

→ IMPRESSIONISM

→ SERGEI WITTE

→ PETER STOLYPIN

OVERVIEW

The period following the French Revolution and the Napoleonic Wars, known as the Age of Metternich, saw the rise of powerful ideologies, some of which were legacies of the French Revolution, and some of which were responses to the political, economic, and social upheavals of the previous decades. Nationalism was both the most promising and the most destructive of these. Nationalism was the prime motive for the unification of Italy and of Germany; it was a force that redefined political boundaries and loyalties and that encouraged claims of national or racial superiority.

Liberalism, socialism, and romanticism profoundly influenced the politics, economics, and culture of the first half of the nineteenth century. *Realism* defined the literature of the latter half of the century, *impressionism* brought the artist's personal visual experience to painting, and *Social Darwinism* and positivism provided scientific models for politics and the arts.

One decade, 1861 to 1871, saw the triumph of the large nation-state as Europe's primary political unit. Italy and Germany consolidated; Austria and Hungary formed autonomous but united states; Russia centralized governmental control.

The nation-state is founded upon a sense of nationalism: a common identity; a specific geographic area; a common language, history, destiny, culture, ethnicity, or religion. It is a consciousness of belonging and of the differences between one's own people and all others on this planet.

The French Revolution and Napoleon's military successes inspired the drive to national unity throughout Europe. Nationalism promised power, the mystical connection that the Romantic Movement glorified, and autonomy from the remote leadership of amorphous, arbitrarily controlled, and administered multinational empires. France and England were the two most powerful nation-states before 1861; Italy became united as a kingdom in 1861;

Germany formed a new empire in 1871. War played a crucial role in both Italy's and Germany's unifications.

The idealism of the Revolutions of 1848 had failed to realize the nationalist aspirations of the Italians or the Germans. If the Italian and German peoples, traditionally separated into small independent states, were ready for unification, it still took the "power politics" (*realpolitik*) of two determined men to bring about unity: Camillo di Cavour, Sardinian prime minister, and Otto von Bismarck, Prussian chancellor. They used the might and prestige of their states to bring smaller independent entities together to create the modern nation-states of Italy and Germany. After 1871, the balance of power in Europe was changed in a way that would last well into the twentieth century.

THE AGE OF NATIONALISM

After 1848, nationalism became more prevalent in Europe and around the world. A new breed of conservative leaders—including Napoleon III, Cavour, and Bismarck—co-opted the agenda of nationalists for the purposes of creating or strengthening the state. The supremacy of the nation-state was gaining ground in organizing the political, social, economic, and cultural activities of a group. Ethnic identities were central to the development of nationalism, which should not be confused with patriotism, or with the level of support for a nation-state.

- *Napoleon III* was the nephew of *the Napoleon* (Napoleon I) who, despite defeat, exile, and death, was considered by the French to be one of their greatest leaders.

  - Louis Napoleon was elected president of France by a landslide in 1848, largely because of his illustrious name.
  - Between 1852, when he had proclaimed a Second Empire, and 1870, after France's ignominious defeat in the Franco-Prussian War, he made many improvements:

    - Restored the economy.
    - Laid the foundations for democratic reforms.
    - Renewed the national pride of the French people.

- The creation of the dual monarchy of Austria-Hungary, which recognized the political power of the largest ethnic minority, was an attempt to stabilize the state of Austria into the Austro-Hungarian Empire, by reconfiguring national unity.
- The Civil War (1861–1865) in the United States resulted in a more solid union and in a more powerful federal government, setting an example for Europe.
- After defeat at the hands of the French and English in the *Crimean War* (1853–1856), Russia modernized and industrialized and initiated a program of limited reforms to solidify czarist control over the multinational peoples of Russia's vast reaches.
- Japan, in response to Western incursions in the 1850s and 1860s, developed a modern military, an industrial economy, and a centralized government under Emperor Meiji, whose ancestors had been mere figureheads, in what became known as the *Meiji Restoration.*
- In Russia, autocratic leaders pushed through a program of reform and modernization, which gave rise to revolutionary movements (and eventually to the Revolution of 1905), and included: the economic reforms of Czar Alexander II, who emancipated the serfs in 1861; Sergei Witte's economic reforms and attempted industrialization; and the attempted but failed reforms of Peter Stolypin.
- Many nations would be formed in Europe between 1860 and 1914.

- *Pan-Slavism* emerged as a force calling for Russia to protect other majority Slavic nations.
- Anti-Semitism emerged as a form of nationalist hatred against neighbors within their nation.

    - As a result, *Theodore Herzl* conceived of the idea of *Zionism*, or establishing a Jewish homeland in Israel, a concept that picked up energy through the nineteenth century and became a reality after the end of the Second World War and the "Holocaust."

THE UNIFICATION OF ITALY

Italy Before Unification

FOUR SEPARATE STATES

- *The Kingdom of Naples* ("Two Sicilies") was made up of the island of Sicily and the southern half of the Italian Peninsula.
- The *Papal States* comprised the middle of the peninsula.
- *Lombardy–Venetia*, industrialized provinces in the North, were ruled by Austria, as were Tuscany, Lucca, Modena, and Parma.
- *The Kingdom of Sardinia* (Piedmont–Sardinia) was made up of the island of Sardinia and the northwestern provinces of Nice, Savoy, and Piedmont.

    - Sardinia was a constitutional monarchy ruled by *Victor Emmanuel II* (r. 1849–1878).
    - Only independent state in Italy.
    - *Camillo di Cavour* (1810–1861) became prime minister of the parliament instituted during the Revolutions of 1848.

        - Rejected the romantic nationalism of *Giuseppe Mazzini* (1805–1872), who had argued in his *Duties of Man* that the nation was a divine device and an extended family.
        - Decided that Italy could be unified only through force, and that Sardinia would have to lead the battle.
        - In order to gain the support of liberals throughout Italy, Cavour reformed the government of his state by:

            - Weakening the influence of the papacy;
            - Investing in public works, such as railroads and harbor improvements;
            - Abolishing internal tariffs;
            - Encouraging the growth of industry;
            - Emancipating the peasantry from the vestiges of manorialism;
            - Making the Sardinian government a model of progressive constitutionalism.

Cavour's "Power Politics"

After the Crimean War ended in 1856, Cavour, who had brought Sardinia into the war on the side of France in order to attain the favor of France in future situations, petitioned Emperor Napoleon III to support Sardinia in a projected war with Austria, which controlled many Italian provinces.

- Plombieres: In 1858, Cavour persuaded Napoleon III to send a supporting army into Italy in the event that Sardinia could maneuver Austria into a war.
- Napoleon, who wanted to weaken the Austrians, was promised the French-speaking provinces of Nice and Savoy in return for allowing the Sardinians to annex Northern Italy.
- April 1859: *Austria declared war on Sardinia*, and the French came to Cavour's aid.

   - After a series of victories by the combined Sardinian–French forces, Napoleon suddenly pulled out of the war because of criticisms at home and threats from the Prussians.
   - The Austrians kept Venice.
   - Lombardy went to the Sardinians.
   - Several of the northern duchies under Austrian domination declared independence and carried out plebiscites for union with Sardinia by 1860.
   - *Giuseppe Garibaldi* (1807–1882), an ardent nationalist, invaded Sicily in 1860 with the encouragement of Cavour.

      - His thousand-man *Red Shirts* used popular support to defeat a Bourbon ruler's force that was ten times that number.
      - Within months, Garibaldi had subdued Sicily and Naples.
      - The Two Sicilies (Kingdom of Naples) joined Sardinia, and in *March 1861 the Kingdom of Italy was proclaimed*, with Victor Emmanuel II on the throne.

Final Unification

By 1870, the last holdouts of the kingdom of Lombardy–Venetia and the Papal States, despite opposition from the pope, had been incorporated into the growing nation of Italy. *Italia Irredenta* ("Italy unredeemed"—Italian areas still under Austrian control) remained "unliberated," but Italy had been united and was a constitutional monarchy. Democracy was diluted by the small percentage of the male population that had suffrage and by the dominance, in Southern Italy, of the landowners. There would be a divide between the wealthier and more industrialized Northern Italy and the southern more agrarian and less prosperous region.

THE UNIFICATION OF GERMANY

Germany Before Unification

In the two decades or so before German unification took place, the population, productivity, and wealth of the German states increased many times over. The *Zollverein* (customs union) had opened most of the states to a mutually advantageous trade, and Germany became a single economic unit. Prussia, with its booming industry, powerful army, militaristic Junkers (landowning aristocrats), and expansionist ambitions led the states of Northern Germany in a face-off with Austria. The Habsburgs of Austria (rulers of a multinational empire held together by tradition and raw power and the prime influence among the divided states of Germany) had long feared a Germany united by the Hohenzollerns of Prussia. After the Frankfurt Assembly failed to unify the independent German states in 1848, however, the Prussian *Hohenzollern* kings determined to achieve it by force.

Bismarck's Realpolitik

When the Prussian parliament refused to approve military expenditures in 1862, *King Wilhelm I* (r. 1861–1888) appointed Otto von Bismarck (1815–1898), a prominent and conservative Junker, as chancellor. He trampled the parliament by collecting illegal taxes, ignoring its protests, enlarging the army, and, in the process, killing democracy in Prussia.

■ *"Blood and Iron,"* he insisted, would solve the issues of his day and unite Germany.
■ Achieved after Prussia won three wars:

  – *The War Against Denmark*, 1864, allied Prussia, Austria, and the other German states in an *all-German war* against Denmark, which had hoped to annex the neighboring province of *Schleswig*.

    • Denmark was quickly defeated and, after some prodding by Bismarck, Prussia and Austria fell out over who should get the spoils of war.

  – The *Austro-Prussian War* (*Seven Weeks' War*), 1866, broke out when the issues of the war with Denmark remained unresolved.
  – Although the Austrians enlisted the help of most of the other German states, the superior arms, training, and leadership of the Prussian Army defeated them in seven weeks: why it is sometimes called the Seven Weeks' War.

    • Hoping to gain Austria's support in the inevitable struggle with France, which had become alarmed by Prussia's swift victories, Bismarck made the surrender terms lenient.

■ Bismarck established the *North German Confederation* in 1867 to replace the loose union of the *German Confederation* that Napoleon had set up and that the Congress of Vienna had confirmed.

  – Twenty-one Germanic states of northern Europe united under the leadership of the Prussian king, with a two-house legislature:

    • The *Reichstag*, or lower house, to represent all the people and to be elected by universal male suffrage.
    • The *Bundesrat*, or upper house, was created to represent the former nobility.

■ The *Franco-Prussian War* of 1870 broke out after a dynastic dispute over the Spanish throne led to a flurry of diplomatic exchanges between Prussia and France.

  – Bismarck deliberately altered the wording of the *Ems Dispatch*, an account of the German king's meeting with the French ambassador over the issue, and made the inflammatory revision public.
  – Napoleon III, bowing to public opinion and bad advice, declared war on Prussia in July 1870.
  – By September, the Prussian army had defeated the French in battle, taken the emperor prisoner, and begun a four-month siege of Paris.
  – The *Treaty of Frankfurt*, May 1871, gave *Alsace-Lorraine* to Germany and imposed a punishing *indemnity*, both of which the defeated French people were to resent for generations to come.

    • This treaty's harshness would lead the French to demand punishing terms for Germany in the *Treaty of Versailles* after the First World War.
    • Alsace-Lorraine would go back to France after the First World War.

Unification

Four southern German states—Baden, Bavaria, Hesse, and Württemberg—that did not already belong to the North German Confederation, joined after the flush of Prussian victory, and *the German Empire was born* in January 1871. The Prussian king became emperor, or *Kaiser*.

The Empire Under Kaiser Wilhelm I and Bismarck

Although the lower house of the imperial legislature, the *Reichstag*, was elected by universal male suffrage, it had little real power because the chancellor and his ministers were responsible to the Kaiser rather than to the legislature.

- Democracy in Germany took a backseat to autocracy.
- Bismarck's *Kulturkampf* (cultural struggle) was his repression of the so-called subversive elements in the empire, such as the Roman Catholic Church and socialists.
- Reversing his original attacks on the Catholic Center Party by the late 1870s, he turned to the socialist "menace," represented by the growing Social Democratic Party.
- When his official measures backfired, and the party grew even more popular, he pulled the rug out from under it by *sponsoring a series of social reforms*.

    - Workmen's compensation, old-age pensions, and medical protection created one of the world's most advanced social-welfare systems.
    - He took away any reason for the liberals to complain, and consolidated his power.

- When *Kaiser Wilhelm II* (r. 1888–1918) assumed the throne in 1888, he brought with him the archaic notion of *divine right* of rule and a deep resentment of Bismarck's personal power.

    - In 1890, he *dismissed Bismarck* and up until his abdication at the close of the First World War in 1918, he dominated his chancellors.
    - His arrogance, ambition, and ineptitude in the early 1900s upset the balance of power and drove Europe toward world war.

RESULTS OF NATIONALISM

Nationalism became a very important force in world and European politics during the last half of the nineteenth century. It became one of the major causes of the First World War. That is why this chart is located here, even though many of the people listed lived during the twentieth century. National identities became increasingly important, and national autonomy for each ethnic group, in the form of national self-determination, became an ardent desire for many historically oppressed ethnic groups, just as it became an important justification for unification of Italy and Germany. The identity of a "we versus them," discussed by Johan Gottfried Herder as part of his concept of the *volk* (folk of one nation), also explains much of the war and hardship of the twentieth century. Many of the worst conflicts in the world today still focus on this concept of one nation or ethnic group being better than or having more right to a land than any other nation or group. Nationalism also led to more popularly elected governments because of nationalist revolutions and unifications.

MODERN LEADERS OF ASSORTED EUROPEAN COUNTRIES, OR "MUSICAL CHAIRS"

From the early 1800s, the parliamentary system began to come into vogue across the Continent, although in a lurching manner. However, suffice it to say that the parliamentary system these countries adopted usually had several parties and coalition governments. Rarely would one party gain enough votes to form its own government, leading to the creation of coalition governments composed of several parties with different agendas. Party loyalties shifted frequently and sometimes without an apparent cause. When one party decided to withdraw from the government (often for personal and seemingly ridiculous reasons), new elections would have to be held. Thus, there are many changes in European leadership to keep track of:

- Rulers in **bold** mean STOP and memorize their names and know why they are important; these individuals will very likely be on the AP test.
- Rulers in *italics* mean PAUSE and be familiar with who they are; they may be on the test and rate some attention.
- Rulers in regular text mean KEEP GOING. Sure, one might be on the test every ten years as a distractor in one of the last multiple-choice questions, but that is a chance we are willing to take. These names are included mainly for continuity's sake, but most professors do not know who they are and you do not need to either.
- Insofar as dates go, keep a ballpark figure of when people reigned, lived, and so on, but memorizing the exact dates is frustrating and not necessary.

France

The French have changed rulers as often as some people change clothes. The variety of rulers has been mostly unimportant, but a few French leaders after 1871 may indeed pop up on the exam.

Name	Duration in Office	Which Government?
Louis Adolphe Thiers	*1871–1873*	*Third Republic (President)*
Marie E. P. M. de MacMahon	1873–1879	Third Republic (President)
François P. J. Grévy	1879–1887	Third Republic (President)
Sadi Carnot	1887–1894	Third Republic (President)
Jean Casimir-Périer	1894–1895	Third Republic (President)
François Félix Faure	1895–1899	Third Republic (President)
Émile Loubet	1899–1906	Third Republic (President)
Clement Armand Fallières	1906–1913	Third Republic (President)
Raymond Poincaré	**1913–1920**	**Third Republic (President)**
Paul E. L. Deschanel	1920–1920	Third Republic (President)
Alexandre Millerand	1920–1924	Third Republic (President)
Gaston Doumergue	1924–1931	Third Republic (President)
Paul Doumer	1931–1932	Third Republic (President) Assassinated
Albert Lebrun	1932–1940	Third Republic (President)
Henri Philippe Pétain	*1940–1944*	*Vichy Government (Chief of State)*

Name	Duration in Office	Which Government?
Charles de Gaulle	**1944–1946**	**Provisional Government (President)**
Félix Gouin	1946	Provisional Government (President)
Georges Bidaul	1946–1947	Provisional Government (President)
Vincent Auriol	1947–1954	Fourth Republic (President)
René Coty	1954–1959	Fourth Republic (President)
Charles de Gaulle	**1959–1969**	**Fifth Republic (President)**
Georges Pompidou	1969–1974	Fifth Republic (President)
Valéry Giscard d'Estaing	1974–1981	Fifth Republic (President)
François Mitterrand	1981–1995	Fifth Republic (President)
Jacques Chirac	*1995–2007*	*Fifth Republic (President)*
Nicolas Sarkozy	2007–2012	Fifth Republic (President)
François Hollande	2012–2017	Fifth Republic (President)
Emmanuel Macron	2017–	Fifth Republic (President)

Germany

The German nation came into existence in 1871 but did not gain democratic rule until after World War I. This is a list of German chancellors and the governments they represented.

Name	Duration in Office	Which German Government?
Friedrich Ebert	1919–1925	Weimar Republic
Paul von Hindenburg	1925–1934	Weimar Republic
Adolf Hitler	**1934–1945**	**Third Reich**
Karl Doenitz	1945–1945	Third Reich
Konrad Adenauer	**1949–1963**	**West Germany**
Ludwig Erhard	1963–1966	West Germany
Kurt Georg Kiesinger	1966–1969	West Germany
Willy Brandt	**1969–1974**	**West Germany**
Helmut Schmidt	1974–1982	West Germany
Helmut Kohl	**1982–1990**	**West Germany**
Wilhelm Pieck	1949–1960	East Germany
Walter Ulbricht	1960–1973	East Germany
Willi Stoph	1973–1976	East Germany
Erich Honecker	*1976–1989*	*East Germany*
Egon Krenz	1989	East Germany
Manfred Gerlach	1989–1990	East Germany
Sabine Bergman-Pohl	1990	East Germany
Helmut Kohl	*1991–1998*	*Germany*
Gerhard Schröder	1998–2005	Germany
Angela Merkel	**2005–**	**Germany**

United Kingdom

Though the cabinet system was begun under Charles II, the position of a prime minister answerable to Parliament did not really develop until Robert Walpole.

The British party system developed around the time of the American Revolution. The *Tories* were the *conservative* party while the *Whigs* were the more *progressive* party. Eventually these evolved, respectively, into the Conservative (old Tory) and Liberal (old Whig) parties. The Liberal Party went on to become the Labour Party. During times of national emergencies (the First World War, the Second World War, and the Falkland Islands War), the two parties would "overcome their differences" and form coalition governments, which usually broke apart once peace was in sight.

Listed below are all of the British prime ministers since Walpole.

Name	Duration in Office	Notes
William Pitt the Younger	*1783–1801*	*Tory*
Henry Addington	1801–1804	Tory (Later, Viscount Sidmouth)
William Pitt the Younger	*1804–1806*	*Tory*
Baron Grenville	*1806–1807*	*Whig*
Duke of Portland	1807–1809	Tory
Spencer Perceval	1809–1812	Tory
Earl of Liverpool	1812–1827	Tory
George Canning	1827	Tory
Viscount Goderich	1827–1828	Tory (Later, Earl of Ripon)
Duke of Wellington	*1828–1830*	*Tory (Led British troops in defeat of Napoleon at Waterloo)*
Earl Grey	1830–1834	Whig
Viscount Melbourne	1834	Whig
Sir Robert Peel	*1834–1835*	*Tory*
Viscount Melbourne	1835–1841	Whig
Sir Robert Peel	*1841–1846*	*Conservative*
Lord John Russell	1846–1852	Whig (Later Earl of Russell)
Earl of Derby	1852	Conservative
Earl of Aberdeen	1852–1855	Liberal/Conservative
Viscount Palmerston	*1855–1858*	*Liberal*
Earl of Derby	1858–1859	Conservative
Viscount Palmerston	*1859–1865*	*Liberal*
Earl Russell	1865–1866	Liberal
Earl of Derby	1866–1868	Conservative
Benjamin Disraeli	**1868**	**Conservative**
William Gladstone	**1868–1874**	**Liberal**
Benjamin Disraeli	**1874–1880**	**Conservative**
William Gladstone	**1880–1885**	**Liberal**
Marquess of Salisbury	1885–1886	Conservative
William Gladstone	**1886**	**Liberal**
Marquess of Salisbury	1886–1892	Conservative
William Gladstone	**1892–1894**	**Liberal**
Earl of Rosebery	1894–1895	Liberal

Name	Duration in Office	Notes
Marquess of Salisbury	1895–1902	Conservative
Arthur Balfour	*1902–1905*	*Conservative*
Sir Henry Campbell-Bannerman	1905–1908	Liberal
Herbert Asquith	*1908–1916*	*Liberal*
David Lloyd George	**1916–1922**	**Coalition**
Andrew Bonar Law	1922–1923	Conservative
Stanley Baldwin	*1923–1924*	*Conservative*
Ramsay MacDonald	*1924*	*Labour*
Stanley Baldwin	*1924–1929*	*Conservative*
Ramsay MacDonald	*1929–1931*	*Labour*
Ramsay MacDonald	*1931–1935*	*National*
Stanley Baldwin	*1935–1937*	*National*
Neville Chamberlain	**1937–1940**	**National**
Winston Churchill	**1940–1945**	**Coalition**
Clement Attlee	**1945–1951**	**Labour**
Sir Winston Churchill	**1951–1955**	**Conservative**
Sir Anthony Eden	*1955–1957*	*Conservative*
Harold Macmillan	1957–1963	Conservative
Sir Alec Douglas-Home	1963–1964	Conservative
Harold Wilson	1964–1970	Conservative
Edward Heath	1970–1974	Conservative
Harold Wilson	1974–1976	Labour
James Callaghan	1976–1979	Labour
Margaret Thatcher	**1979–1990**	**Conservative**
John Major	1990–1997	Conservative
Tony Blair	1997–2007	Labour
Gordon Brown	2007–2010	Labour
David Cameron	2010–2016	Conservative
Theresa May	2016–	Conservative

Russia

This "democracy" was born out of the Revolution of 1905 and has seen a series of either ineffectual or oppressive rulers hold the top elected post in the nation since that time.

Name (Anglicized)	Reign	Notes
Prince Georgi Lvov	1917	Provisional Government
Alexander Kerensky	*1917*	*Provisional Government*
Vladimir Ilyich Lenin	**1917–1924**	**Union of Soviet Socialist Republics**
Joseph Stalin	**1924–1953**	**Union of Soviet Socialist Republics**
Georgi M. Malenkov	1953–1955	Union of Soviet Socialist Republics
Nikolai A. Bulganin	1955–1958	Union of Soviet Socialist Republics
Nikita S. Khrushchev	**1958–1964**	**Union of Soviet Socialist Republics**
Leonid I. Brezhnev	*1964–1982*	*Union of Soviet Socialist Republics*
Yuri V. Andropov	1982–1984	Union of Soviet Socialist Republics
Konstantin U. Chernenko	1984–1985	Union of Soviet Socialist Republics
Mikhail S. Gorbachev	**1985–1991**	**Union of Soviet Socialist Republics**
Boris Yeltsin	*1991–1999*	*President of Russian Republic*
Vladimir Putin	2000–2008	President of Russian Republic
Alexander Medvedev	2008–2011	President of Russian Republic
Vladimir Putin	*2011–*	*President of Russian Republic*

> At this point you may have noticed that Austria has been omitted. There is a simple reason for this: after 1917 (and some would argue after 1848), the country ceased to be important to international politics.

UNIFICATION OF ITALY AND GERMANY CHART

Year	Italy	Germany
1848	■ Revolutions erupted throughout Europe after the French Revolt. ■ They were quickly put down after an unsuccessful revolt. ■ *Giuseppe Garibaldi* fled back to Uruguay with other expatriates. ■ Victor Emmanuel ruled Piedmont–Sardinia after the Austrians repressed the revolts.	■ Frederick William IV refused to accept the crown of a united Germany "from the gutter" when the Frankfurt Assembly offered it to him. ■ The revolutions in Germany led to Frederick William IV reorganizing the government and promising to be more attuned to the people.
1852	■ *Count Camillo Benso di Cavour* became prime minister of Piedmont–Sardinia.	
1859	■ The French saved Piedmont–Sardinia from Austrian invasion. ■ The French then betrayed them in a separate peace, which infuriated many Italians. ■ Tuscany, Modena, Parma, and Romagna all vote to join Piedmont–Sardinia.	
1860	■ *Giuseppe Garibaldi* and his 1,000 *Red Shirts* invaded Sicily and started to move northward up the peninsula. ■ He wanted to establish a *republic.* ■ Victor Emmanuel and Cavour wanted a monarchy. ■ Garibaldi was met with overwhelming support from the people who joined his forces. ■ He met Cavour outside the Papal States, and a deal was made to create a *constitutional monarchy* in Italy.	
1861	■ All of Italy, save Rome and Venice, became part of a unified Italian Peninsula with a parliament.	■ Wilhelm I became the King of Prussia. ■ Named **Otto von Bismarck** his chief minister.
1864		■ Prussia defeated Denmark in the battle of Schleswig-Holstein.
1861–1866		■ Bismarck engaged in a constitutional struggle with the Prussian parliament. ■ He utilized his *gap strategy* to ensure monarchical privilege.
1866	■ Venice joined Italy in 1866 after Austria's defeat in the *Seven Weeks' War.*	■ Prussia defeated Austria in the *Seven Weeks' War.* ■ Demonstrated Prussia was most powerful Germanic military.
1867		■ Bismarck organized the North German Confederation of the 21 northern, mostly Protestant, German states.
1870	■ Rome was added to Italy when French troops left during the Franco-Prussian War. ■ The entire Italian Peninsula was united into one nation for the first time since the fall of Rome.	■ Bismarck manufactured causes for a war with France as a means of uniting the German states against a common enemy. ■ The Franco-Prussian war was a rout in which the Parisians were besieged and shelled. ■ All of the German states united behind Wilhelm I and Bismarck.
1871		■ Wilhelm I was declared the first *Kaiser* of Germany, and Bismarck was named chancellor.

IDEOLOGY AND CULTURE

Liberalism

Classical *liberalism*, an offshoot of the ideals of liberty and equality of the French Revolution, set as its political goals legal equality, freedom of the press, nationalism, freedom of assembly and of speech, and above all, representative government. Reacting to monarchial absolutism and to the reactionary repression (as represented by the policies of Austria's Prince Metternich, whose conservative attempt to roll back the ideals of the French Revolution amounted to a crusade against liberalism), the liberalism of the early nineteenth century generally opposed government intervention.

- *Laissez-faire*, a form of economic liberalism and a principle espoused most convincingly by Adam Smith, argued for a free market system unfettered by government regulations.

  - While this concept fostered economic growth, the theories of economists Thomas Malthus and David Ricardo (see Chapter 6) were often used to back up the predatory business practices of early capitalists and industrialists, which can be supported by Smith as well.

- After the first few decades of the nineteenth century, liberalism was espoused mostly by the middle class and tended to ignore the rights and aspirations of the working class.

Socialism

Early *socialism* was a reaction to the gross inequities created by the Industrial Revolution. The exploitation of workers by the early capitalists convinced the *utopian socialists* (see Chapter 6) that one of the best remedies for this was to have governments intervene in the economy.

- Their program included government control of property, economic equality for all, and government economic planning.

  - *Charles Fourier* (1772–1837), a Frenchman, described a scheme for a utopian community based on a socialist idea.
  - His countryman, *Louis Blanc*, pushed a program for the democratic takeover of the state by workers to guarantee full employment.

- The impracticality of their programs relegated the early *utopian socialists* to a minor political role, and modern socialism was largely shaped by the theories of Karl Marx. (See Chapter 6.)

Anarchists

Anarchists stated that all forms of government were oppressive and, therefore, the best government was none at all. They ignored the ideas of Thomas Hobbes and went even further than Marx against the current forms of government. They believed that society should be based upon voluntary associations of people.

- Popular in Russia.
- Main proponents: Mikhail Bakunin and Georges Sorel.

Romanticism

Romanticism, a glorification of the emotional component of human nature, was a reaction to the rationalism and restraint of the Enlightenment. The excesses of the French Revolution and the destructiveness of the Napoleonic Wars eroded faith in the "inevitable perfectibility" of humankind through Reason.

- Romantic artists, composers, and writers shared a world view:

  - Willingness to express the deepest and most turbulent emotions.
  - Fervent belief in personal freedom.
  - Awe of nature.
  - Reverence for history.

SOME REPRESENTATIVE FIGURES

William Wordsworth (1770–1850): English, a poet who glorified the beauty and solemnity of nature.

Victor Hugo (1802–1885): French, a poet and dramatist best remembered for his vibrant novels, such as *The Hunchback of Notre Dame*, which explored the darker side of the human experience.

John Constable (1776–1837), an English painter who said: "Nature is spirit visible." He painted bucolic scenes that attempted to cast rural life in an idyllic fashion, typifying the emotional examination of nature and history seen in this artistic movement.

George Sand (1804–1876): French, a countess who took a man's name as her pen name. She wrote modern, autobiographical, emotionally revealing novels about unconventional love.

Ludwig van Beethoven (1770–1827): German, his musical genius is expressed in virtually every musical form of his day, from songs to symphonies, and his evolution as a romantic is evident in the course of his composing. The symphonic music of his later period makes full use of the expanded orchestra, a romantic innovation that added three times as many instruments as the classical orchestra known to Mozart, and expressed the profound emotionality of romantic music.

Realism

Realist and materialist themes and attitudes influenced art and literature as painters and writers depicted the lives of ordinary people and drew attention to social problems. *Realism*, the literary movement that had replaced literary romanticism by the middle of the nineteenth century, portrayed a kind of *determinism*, the belief that human nature and human destiny are formed by heredity and environment, and that human behavior is governed by natural laws that preclude free will.

- Writers devoted their work to a depiction of everyday life, especially of the working class and especially of its more unsavory aspects.
- Focused on the here and now.

- Often shocked readers with their objective depictions of life in the cities, the slums, and the factories.

  - Frenchmen *Emile Zola* (1840–1902), *Honoré de Balzac* (1799–1850), and *Gustave Flaubert* (1821–1880).
  - Englishwoman *George Eliot* (Mary Ann Evans) (1819–1880).
  - Russians *Fyodor Dostoyevsky* and *Leo Tolstoy*.
  - The popular *Charles Dickens* was also a well-known realist author.
  - Spurning the romantic obsession with distant times and distant places.

Impressionism

The popularization of photography in the nineteenth century encouraged a group of artists, the *impressionists,* to avoid realistic depiction (better served by photography) and to capture, instead, the transitory feeling of a scene, the personal "impression."

- Most famous in France, but spread like the Renaissance around the world.

  - *Pierre-Auguste Renoir* (1841–1919)
  - *Claude Monet* (1840–1926)
  - *Edouard Manet (1832–1883)*
  - *Edgar Degas* (1834–1917)
  - *Mary Cassatt* (1844–1926)

Feminism

Feminists such as Flora Tristan began to push for women's political rights, economic rights, and better working conditions.

- In 1858 Barbara Bodichon set up the *English Women's Journal.*

  - Organ for discussing employment and equality issues directly concerning women and the reform of laws pertaining to the genders.

- The Women's Social and Political Union (WSPU) was founded in Manchester in October 1903 by Emmeline Pankhurst.

  - Her sister, Christabel, once disrupted a speech by Winston Churchill in order to make a statement about women's lack of rights.

- Women fought for suffrage and other citizenship rights that they did not get until after the First World War.

Science

After the first few decades of the nineteenth century, and directly as a result of the technological requirements of the Industrial Revolution, "pure" scientific discoveries found application in explaining how the machinery and techniques of industrial processes worked.

- Physicists were able to formulate principles of *thermodynamics* applicable to a variety of technological systems, such as the operation of engines, which converted heat into motion.

- The theories of biology were used by researchers, such as *Louis Pasteur* (1822–1895), to preserve food and to improve medical procedures.
- A burgeoning chemical industry provided a variety of new products from medicines to synthetic dyes.
- The generation of electricity created whole new industries in transportation and lighting.
- *Charles Darwin* (1809–1882) was not the first theorist to formulate the concept of evolution, but his meticulous research and voluminous specimens added weight to his idea that life evolved in its myriad forms from a common ancestor, through the process of a *struggle for survival.*

    - The mechanism that aided this was the development of anomalies in a given species, which would actually aid in the survival of that species.
    - His insight predates the development of the science of *genetics.*
    - For instance, when the only foliage available for grazing was on high trees, the mutant long-neck giraffe would outlive and out-propagate his short-neck cousins; thus, his characteristics would be more successfully passed on to later generations.
    - Darwin's theory had a powerful effect on the intellectual life of Europe.
    - It was used by skeptics to attack the biblical account of creation and religion itself.
    - *Herbert Spencer* (1820–1903) used Darwin's theories to argue that history and human society reflect a struggle for supremacy resulting in the *survival of the fittest:*

        - The rich, the rulers, the powerful nations are "fit"; the poor, the downtrodden masses, the world's colonies are "weak."
        - This *Social Darwinism* appealed to those in power and to racists and imperialists of every stripe.

- *Friedrich Nietzsche* (1844–1900), a German philosopher and contemporary of Darwin, argued that Christianity presented a "slave morality" that fettered the creativity of great individuals, the *ubermench* (superman), who must free himself from conventionality and redefine life and morality.

PRACTICE LONG-ESSAY QUESTIONS

These questions are samples of the various types of thematic essays on the exam. (See pages 30–31 for a detailed explanation of each type.) Check over the **generic rubric** (see pages 32–33) before you begin any of these essays and use that rubric to score your essay if you write one.

Question 1

To what extent was Italian unification the result of the strong personal wills and tenacity of Mazzini, Cavour, and Garibaldi?

COMMENTS ON QUESTION 1

This question is testing the CAUSATION skill because it requires you to evaluate whether two things—the personal wills and tenacity of Garibaldi, Cavour, and Mazzini—resulted in a specific outcome: the unification of Italy. Remember to describe causes AND/OR effects of the Italian unification, and to support your analysis of those causes and effects with specific evidence. The essay must explain how these three men brought about Italian unification—be sure to support those claims with specific evidence. Mazzini has been called the "heart" of Italian unification, Cavour the "brain," and Garibaldi the "sword." How and how much did Mazzini's proselytizing of the glories of mystical union prepare the Italian people and the world for the realpolitik of Cavour? How and how much did Garibaldi's flamboyant appeal and adventures in the Two Sicilies enable Cavour to complete unification? What compromises and other events led to complete unification of the Italian Peninsula?

Question 2

Explain how nationalism was a liberal ideal during the Napoleonic era and the Age of Metternich, but became a conservative ideal by the time the First World War broke out in 1914.

COMMENTS ON QUESTION 2

This question is asking you to use the CHANGE AND CONTINUITY OVER TIME skill in that you must analyze how the view of nationalism changed over time from a force that leaders had to contend with to a force that leaders used to build national unity and identity. Be sure to describe the extent to which the view of nationalism in 1814 was different from, and similar to, the way it was viewed in 1914, and provide multiple specific examples to support the analysis. Your essay must explain the extent to which nationalism changed from a liberal idea to a conservative one, with specific supporting evidence. This essay is asking you to decide how nationalism transformed from a concept associated with liberalism to one associated with conservatism. This essay must first examine the nationalist reactions to Napoleon's domination of Europe, perhaps focusing on Spain and the Confederation of the Rhine, but also on Russia and Austria. The multiethnic nature of many European empires, such as the Russian and the Austrian, especially must be addressed as must the conservatism of Metternich. The revolutions of the 1820s, 1830, and 1848 must also be addressed as liberal nationalist movements that mostly failed (except for Greece), and how Cavour, Bismarck, and others co-opted nationalism as a conservative tool to unite nations through "blood and iron" must be explained. Later uses of nationalism, such as the Berlin Conference, will add a lot to this essay. Overall, the essay needs to explain how nationalism was at first a change favored by liberals, and that the idea was used by conservatives to unify new nations and hold older empires together until the First World War.

Question 3

To what extent did Bismarck's use of war result in German unification?

COMMENTS ON QUESTION 3

This question is testing the CAUSATION skill because it requires you to evaluate whether one factor, Bismarck's use of war, resulted in a specific outcome: the unification of Germany. Remember to describe causes AND/OR effects of German unification, and support your analysis of those causes and effects with specific evidence. This essay should explain the reasons that Bismarck's use of war resulted in the unification of Germany, citing specific evidence as support. "Examine in detail" how the war for Schleswig-Holstein (the All-German War), the Seven Weeks' War, and the Franco-Prussian War were used by Bismarck to effect unification. This was a process of distinct stages: War with Denmark aroused a sense of German nationalism and set Austria up for the fall; the Seven Weeks' War aligned most Germanic states with the loser, Austria, and against the winner, Prussia, but generous terms achieved the establishment of the North German Confederation; finally, victory over France, which had historically dominated the Germanic states, inspired a patriotic yearning for union that created the German Empire.

Question 4

What were the differences between the political situations in Italy from 1820 to 1850 and from the 1850s through 1871 that allowed Piedmont-Sardinia to take the lead in Italian unification?

COMMENTS ON QUESTION 4

This is a COMPARE skill question, so be sure to describe similarities and differences between the political situations in Italy during the specified periods as well as account for or explain them by providing specific examples of how they are similar and different and tying that to historical developments. The Revolutions of 1848 were the kinds of failures that whetted the appetite for greater success and that pointed the way toward unification led from above rather than from the masses. Power politics grew out of the frustrations of the erstwhile reformers. Piedmont was the logical leader of unification because it was the only independent state in Italy with any economic prosperity. Most of the North was under the yoke of Austria; central Italy was controlled by the traditionalistic politics of the papacy; and the South was under-developed and under the sway of anachronistic manorialism. When Cavour reformed and strengthened Piedmont, he was making the most of its opportunities. The lack of a strong state in Italy that could have led a unification movement in the earlier part of the century was part of the reason for the failure of the revolutions of the 1820s and 1848. The disunity of the plans and leaders calling for Italian leadership before 1850, such as Garibaldi, Mazzini, and Gioberti, also contributed to the failure of this political movement until Cavour's leadership emerged.

PRACTICE SHORT-ANSWER QUESTIONS

1. Please use the excerpt below and your knowledge of European History to fully answer all parts of the question that follows.

Liberalism Evaluated

The social problem of the future we considered to be, how to unite the greatest individual liberty of action, with a common ownership in the raw material of the globe, and an equal participation of all in the benefits of combined labor. We had not the presumption to suppose that we could already foresee by what precise form of institutions these objects could most effectually be attained, or at how near or how distant a period they would become practicable. We saw clearly that to render any such social transformation either possible or desirable, an equivalent change of character must take place both in the uncultivated herd who now compose the laboring masses, and in the immense majority of their employers. Both these classes must learn by practice to labor and combine for generous, or at all events for public and social purposes, and not, as hitherto, solely for narrowly interested ones. But the capacity to do this has always existed in mankind, and is not, nor is ever likely to be, extinct. Education, habit, and the cultivation of the sentiments, will make a common man dig or weave for his country, as readily as fight for his country.

—John Stuart Mill, 1873

(A) Briefly explain TWO of the social changes that European society was going through as liberalism emerged.

(B) Briefly explain the political philosophy that emerged to counteract liberalism in the late nineteenth century.

2. Please use the image below and your knowledge of European History to answer all parts of the following question.

Water Lilies and Japanese Bridge

—Claude Monet 1897–1899.

(A) Briefly analyze how the artwork above reflects artistic trends of the late nineteenth century.

(B) Briefly analyze TWO aspects of change that affected Europeans' perceptions during the late nineteenth century.

Short-Answer Explanations

1. (A) You should look at the changes brought on by the Industrial Revolution and Enclosure Movements that tore European society asunder by the mid-nineteenth century. You may include any TWO of the following: increased urbanization, changing gender roles, changing work schedules, the emergence of laissez-faire capitalism, the redesign of cities, the sanitation movement, the rise of public education, changing leisure activities, the decline in illegitimacy rates in the nineteenth century, increased personal liberties, the loss of communal lands and therefore communal life, or the end of the putting-out system.

   (B) Here, you should identify *conservatism* as the response to *liberalism* and explain its characteristics and impact, including: rising governmental power, rising nationalism, rebound of religious devotion, supporting the bourgeoisie over the workers, growing militarism, and the reemergence of traditional family roles.

2. (A) You should identify the artistic trend as *impressionism* and identify how it is a reflection of that movement. You should identify Monet as the man who coined the term impressionism and explain the style as one that moved away from a realistic depiction of the world to a more blurred impression of a scene in action. Impressionism should be noted as a momentous break from tradition in European painting. You should identify the change in the look of these paintings as brought about by a change in methodology: applying paint in small touches of pure color rather than broader strokes, and painting out of doors to catch a fleeting impression of color and light. You should explain that impressionist art is a style in which the artist captures the image of an object as someone would see it if they just caught a glimpse of it, and that the artists liked to capture their images without detail but with bold colors.

   (B) You should discuss the rise of science and technology, including the invention of the camera, as motivations to create this new style of art. You should also look at the emergence of romanticism as a change in the sentiment of society that harkened to the simpler life before industrialization. Other aspects you may explore as changes that brought on impressionism are the changing gender roles, class divisions, uses of leisure time, changing professions, changing modes of production, and changing political ideologies from liberalism to conservatism.

PRACTICE MULTIPLE-CHOICE QUESTIONS

Questions 1 to 4 refer to the map of Italian city-states below.

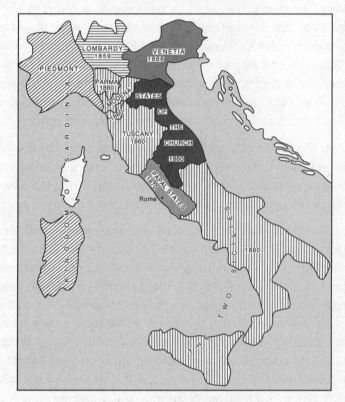

Map showing the unification of Italy.

1. Which of the Italian city-states on the map above was the dominant power in a united Italy after 1861?

   (A) Modena
   (B) Parma
   (C) Piedmont-Sardinia
   (D) Kingdom of the Two Sicilies

2. Which of the following gave up his dream of a united republic of Italy in order to preserve the movement for Italian unification?

   (A) Count Camillo Benso di Cavour
   (B) Giuseppe Garibaldi
   (C) Giuseppe Mazzini
   (D) Victor Emmanuel II

3. Which province shown on the map above was gained by the Kingdom of Italy in return for its support of Prussia in the Seven Weeks' War against Austria?

   (A) Parma
   (B) The states of the Church
   (C) The Papal States
   (D) Venetia

4. The new nations of Italy and Germany disrupted which of the following the most?

   (A) Balance of power
   (B) European alliances
   (C) Global commerce
   (D) The industrialization of the world

Questions 5 to 7 refer to the passage by Prussian chancellor, Otto von Bismarck.

We had to avoid wounding Austria too severely; we had to avoid leaving behind in her any unnecessary bitterness of feeling or desire for revenge; we ought rather to reserve the possibility of becoming friends again with our adversary of the moment, and in any case to regard the Austrian state as a piece on the European chessboard and the renewal of friendly relations as a move open to us. If Austria were severely injured, she would become the ally of France and of every other opponent of ours; she would even sacrifice her anti-Russian interests for the sake of revenge on Prussia.

On the other hand, I could not see any guarantee for us in the future of the countries constituting the Austrian monarchy, in case the latter were split up by risings of the Hungarians and Slavs or made permanently dependent on those peoples. What would be substituted for that portion of Europe which the Austrian state had hitherto occupied from Tyrol to Bukowina?

Source: Otto von Bismarck, *Memoirs*

5. Which of the following changes in the nationalist movements is documented by the passage above?

   (A) Nationalism was supported by liberals and radicals.
   (B) Nationalism was most supported by conservatives.
   (C) The nationalist agenda was co-opted for the purposes of creating or strengthening the state.
   (D) Prussian leaders arrested nationalists who threatened their monopoly on control.

6. Which of the following tactics was NOT employed by Bismarck in his attempt to unify Germany?

   (A) Industrialized warfare and weaponry
   (B) Motorized infantry
   (C) Diplomatic negotiations
   (D) Manipulation of foreign affairs

7. What was the clearest Prussian goal in Bismarck's alliance system?

   (A) To create a fully inclusive German confederation
   (B) To isolate France from the rest of Europe
   (C) To control Russian trade and expansion
   (D) To defeat the British navy

Multiple-Choice Explanations

1. **C**   3. **D**   5. **C**   7. **B**
2. **B**   4. **A**   6. **B**

1. **(C)**

   (A) is wrong because Modena was a small, weak state, while Piedmont–Sardinia would dominate the new Italian state, which was ruled by the king of Piedmont–Sardinia, Victor Emmanuel II.

   (B) is wrong because Parma was a small, weak state while Piedmont–Sardinia would dominate the new Italian state that was ruled by the king of Piedmont–Sardinia, Victor Emmanuel II.

   (C) is CORRECT because Piedmont–Sardinia would dominate the new Italian state that was ruled by the king of Piedmont–Sardinia, Victor Emmanuel II.

   (D) is wrong because the Kingdom of the Two Sicilies was a poorer, more agrarian area that was dominated by Piedmont–Sardinia, and Italy was ruled by the king of Piedmont–Sardinia, Victor Emmanuel II.

2. **(B)**

   (A) is wrong because Cavour realized his dream of a united Italy under his king, Victor Emmanuel II.

   (B) is CORRECT because Garibaldi and his Red Shirts invaded Sicily, then southern Italy, and fought all the way to the Papal States, where Garibaldi agreed to give up an Italian republic in order to attain a united nation with a constitutional monarchy.

   (C) is wrong because Mazzini was gone from Italy by 1860 and played only an inspirational role in the unification of Italy.

   (D) is wrong because Victor Emmanuel gave up very little and became the first king of a united Italy.

3. **(D)**

   (A) is wrong because the Seven Weeks' War ended in 1866 when Venice was given to Italy and Parma was already allied with Piedmont–Sardinia.

   (B) is wrong because the States of the Church were fictional

   (C) is wrong because the Papal States were the last to join Italy in 1871, well after the Seven Weeks' War.

   (D) is CORRECT because Venetia was ceded to Italy as a reward for its support of Prussia during the Seven Weeks' War.

4. **(A)**

   (A) is CORRECT because the entire global balance of power was disrupted by the unification of Italy and Germany.

   (B) is wrong because the balance of power was disrupted more than the alliances were as a result of these new nations being formed.

   (C) is wrong because the balance of power was hurt by this change, but global trade was not.

   (D) is wrong because the balance of power was disrupted more than the industrialization of the world as a result of these new nations being formed.

5. **(C)**

(A) is wrong because liberals and radicals had always been the main supporters of nationalism, but what changed was that the conservative Prussian leaders co-opted nationalism for their own purposes.

(B) is wrong because the passage makes it clear that conservative Austria would be ruined by nationalism.

(C) is CORRECT because what changed was that the conservative Prussian leaders co-opted nationalism for their own purposes.

(D) is wrong because Prussia had been the most friendly regime to nationalism in Western Europe since 1848.

6. **(B)**

(A) is wrong because Bismarck relied heavily upon industrialized warfare and weaponry such as the first cartridge rifles to fight the three wars that unified Germany.

(B) is CORRECT because motorized infantry did not exist during the end of the nineteenth century, but was introduced in the First World War.

(C) is wrong because Bismarck relied heavily upon diplomatic negotiations to unify Germany.

(D) is wrong because Bismarck relied heavily upon manipulation of foreign affairs such as the Ems Telegram incident to unify Germany.

7. **(B)**

(A) is wrong because Bismarck did not rely heavily upon the alliances to unify his nation, and really became a player in the alliance system after Germany unified, but he used his alliances to attempt to isolate France, particularly from Great Britain.

(B) is CORRECT because Bismarck used his alliances to attempt to isolate France, particularly from Great Britain.

(C) is wrong because Bismarck did not interfere with Russian trade in any major way.

(D) is wrong because Bismarck knew better than to try to take on the British navy.

Imperialism and the Causes of the First World War (1870–1914)

9

KEY TERMS/PEOPLE

- → SURPLUS CAPITAL
- → "WHITE MAN'S BURDEN"
- → SOCIAL DARWINISM
- → SEPOY MUTINY
- → OPEN DOOR POLICY
- → SUEZ CANAL
- → THE BOXER REBELLION
- → MEIJI RESTORATION
- → ZULU RESISTANCE
- → OPIUM WARS
- → RUSSO-JAPANESE WAR
- → COLONIALISM
- → BERLIN CONFERENCE
- → MOHANDAS K. GANDHI
- → FRENCH-ALGERIAN WAR
- → BRITISH EAST INDIA COMPANY
- → DUTCH EAST INDIA COMPANY

- → CONGRESS OF BERLIN
- → PABLO PICASSO
- → MAX PLANCK
- → MARIE CURIE
- → FRIEDRICH NIETZSCHE
- → QUININE
- → LOUIS PASTEUR/GERM THEORY
- → ANTISEPTICS
- → ANESTHESIA
- → GEORGES SOREL
- → HENRI BERGSON DUAL ALLIANCE
- → ALGECIRAS CONFERENCE
- → MILITARISM
- → BALKAN CRISIS
- → PAN-SLAVISM
- → BALKAN WARS
- → MOROCCAN CRISIS

OVERVIEW

A contemporary definition of imperialism is any instance of a more-powerful nation or group of nations acting, or being perceived to be acting, at the expense of a lesser power, usually when the more powerful nation dominates militarily or economically. Imperialism is therefore used not only to describe overt empire-building policies—such as those of the Roman Empire, the Spanish, or the British—but was also used controversially and/or disparagingly; for example, most of Europe referred to Napoleon's actions as imperialistic. The colonial power may rule the colony politically or exploit it economically or impose its culture upon it. During the so-called old imperialism of the sixteenth through eighteenth centuries, the Europeans did not acquire overseas territories (with the exception of the Americas, where the death of 90 percent of the native population allowed establishment of colonies), as much as they set up trading stations. They largely respected and frequently cooperated with the local rulers in India, China, Japan, the Spice Islands (Indonesia), and the other geographic areas where a flourishing trade developed between locals and European coastal trading centers.

The new imperialism that began in the 1870s colonized Asia and Africa by using military force to take control of local governments, by exploiting the local economies for the raw materials required by Europe's growing industry, and by imposing Western values to benefit the "backward" colonies. Most of Asia's rich and ancient cultures were either carved up into economic "spheres of influence" or colonized outright; virtually all of Africa was taken over by only six European nations; and Latin America was dominated by the United States.

CAUSES OF IMPERIALISM

1. The Search for *Markets* and for *Raw Materials*

The rapidly industrializing and competing nations of Europe produced more manufactured goods than their own populations could consume and, since a favorable balance of trade was not possible for all European nations, colonies promised potential markets.

- In the long run, since the non-Europeans lacked purchasing power, the promise of markets far outweighed the reality.
- Studies of foreign trade from 1870 to 1914 show that the best consumers of manufactured goods were other industrialized nations rather than undeveloped colonies.
- As the income level of Western workers rose, so did the profitability of investing surplus capital into domestic ventures.
- Colonies were needed as sources of raw materials to supply newly industrialized Western society.
- They argued that unless their more advanced technologies and business methods were applied to the mining and processing of these materials, not enough would be supplied to the voracious factories.
- They claimed that they had to set up colonies in order to maintain the stability that would protect their investments.

2. Missionaries

A burst of religious revivalism during the mid-nineteenth century in Western Europe and the United States led to development of worldwide missions to convert the people of Asia and Africa to Christianity.

- On rare occasions missionaries were attacked or endangered by locals.
- Religion was used as an excuse to erase cultures and take wealth and power.
- Many medical and technological improvements were made in some colonies (mostly British ones).

3. Military and Naval Bases

Once trade developed, the home (or mother) countries felt compelled to establish a chain of naval bases to protect their overseas interests and military outposts to stake claims and maintain order. European national rivalries and strategic concerns fostered imperial expansion and competition for colonies.

- This process tended to feed on itself since a competition to acquire colonies developed among the industrialized nations.
- They claimed to want to maintain the international balance of power.
- This was more about international prestige.
- This led to increased tensions when the "haves" (like the British Empire, which had acquired colonies for two or more centuries) clashed with the "have-nots" (like the

Germans and Italians, whose late-blooming national unity gave them a slow start in the race).

4. Ideology

Europeans justified imperialism through an ideology of cultural and racial superiority. The so-called "*White Man's Burden*" was a form of racist paternalism that preached that the "superior" Westerners had an obligation to bring their culture to "uncivilized" peoples in other parts of the world.

- *Social Darwinism*, a half-baked philosophical application of Darwin's theory of natural selection, bolstered the idea that some races or peoples were more fit for survival than others and therefore designed by nature for rule.
- Imperial adventures and adventurers appealed to the masses in the industrialized countries who felt part of some great crusade to improve people whose lot was even worse than theirs.
- Imperialism won votes; politicians coddled the voters.

5. Industrial and Technological Developments

Industrial and technological developments (the Second Industrial Revolution) facilitated European control of global empires.

- Advanced weaponry such as the machine gun, the breech-loading rifle, and other gunpowder weapons allowed the Europeans to dominate the natives of all regions and conquer them quickly.
- Advances in communication such as the radio, telegraph, and telephone allowed Europeans to coordinate their efforts to dominate the rest of the world.
- Advances in medicine such as *quinine, anesthesia, antiseptics, public health projects*, and *Louis Pasteur's germ theory* supported European control of Africa and Asia by preserving European lives.

REGIONS

Africa

- **Egypt:** after winning autonomy within the Ottoman Empire in the mid-nineteenth century, became a British protectorate in the 1880s.
- The British had invested in the Suez Canal, a vital link to India and Asia. To maintain stability in the region, they helped Egypt take control of the Sudan and set up an Anglo-Egyptian administration for both areas.
- Wealthy industrialist Cecil Rhodes planned to build a railroad that crossed the African continent, but he did not build it.
- South Africa became an important colony to the British, who fought the Afrikaners in the two *Boer Wars*. Superior British weaponry helped defeat the Afrikaners and also the Zulus.
- The DeBeers family profited by taking natural resources from the north and south of the continent, but they did little to develop the people or any sustainable industry.

Algeria, **Tunisia**, and most of **Morocco** fell into French hands right before the First World War, and **Libya**, once part of the decrepit Ottoman Empire, was taken by the Italians.

- Africa *south of the Sahara* was terra incognita until the 1870s, when Belgian, German, and French explorers began to lay claims.
- Scottish medical missionary David Livingstone was the first white man to do humanitarian and religious work in south and central Africa.
- He was writing a regular column for London papers and failed to report; his worried readers thought he must be dead.
- In 1871, after six years of no word from Livingstone, American journalist Henry M. Stanley found him in a remote part of East Africa. Stanley's newspaper reports created greater European interest in Africa.
- *King Leopold II of Belgium* sought the aid of Stanley to dominate the **Congo** region. Leopold ruled the **Congo** in a brutal and exploitive fashion and became an example of cruel imperialist masters, ruling with whips and threats.
  - The Belgian Congo—Congo Free State—was over seventy times the size of Belgium and was ruled privately by King Leopold until 1908.
  - Reports of abuses there resulted in the Congo being taken over by a Belgian administration, dominated by the Roman Catholic Church, until independence in 1960.

The **Berlin Conference** of 1885, sponsored by Bismarck to prevent disputes among the imperialists, set up rules that diminished squabbles and encouraged the partition of the entire African continent among the major European powers.

Asia

India: In 1857, the *Sepoy Mutiny* in India became the best-known aspect of a wider rebellion of native troops against their British and Indian commanders. The Hindu and Muslim troops objected to disrespectful treatment, and to their bullets being wrapped in animal fat, which was offensive to their faiths.

- The rebellion was put down, but the British East India Company was relieved of its rule over India, and British government administration of the Indian subcontinent began.
- Over the next 90 or more years the Indian people struggled with British rule until the British finally left after the Second World War.

By the mid-1880s the British also took control of Burma, the Malay Peninsula, and North Borneo.

- The British did not interfere with the basic social structure of these colonies.
- They introduced educational reforms and technological advances, especially to India, that smoothed the way for eventual independence.
- Of all the colonial powers, the British proved to be most enlightened.

Other Colonial Holdings

- The Dutch expanded their hold over the *Dutch East Indies* (the islands of Indonesia).
- The French seized Indochina (Vietnam, Cambodia, and Laos).
- The Germans had small African holdings and occupied islands in the Pacific.
- The Russians set up a sphere of influence (an area under the economic and military control of one imperial power) in Persia (Iran).

China, with its teeming population, vast land area, and incredibly rich and ancient culture, was carved up into spheres of influence by the Western powers after the Opium Wars of the 1840s and 1850s.

- "Extraterritoriality" made Westerners there subject to their home country's laws rather than China's.
- Exclusive trading rights and limited governing powers were given to the Western nations.
- The Chinese were forced to cede outlying regions of historical Chinese influence, such as Siberia and part of Manchuria, and Korea, to the Russians and the Japanese, by the late 1800s.
- The Taiping Rebellion from 1850 to 1864 cost 15–20 million lives and resulted in the Qing dynasty being weakened further by seeking American and British help to end the rebellion.
- The Open Door Policy, implemented by the United States in 1899 in order to open Chinese commerce to imperial latecomers like itself, urged the Europeans to allow free trade within China while respecting its territorial integrity.
- The *Boxer Rebellion*, a patriotic uprising by Chinese nationalists against Western encroachment, was put down by the imperial powers in 1900.

  - Since the Dowager Empress, who had seized control of the government, had supported the Boxers, the Manchu dynasty fell into decline until it was overthrown in 1911.

- Sun Yat-sen set up a republic dedicated to modernizing China through three principles:

  - Nationalism, democracy, livelihood.

Japan was the only major Asian power to resist being swallowed up by the imperialists.

- Mid-sixteenth-century Portuguese traders had opened the insular Japanese to commerce and Christianity, both of which were suppressed by the shogun (Medieval military ruler).
- U.S. warships, under the command of Commodore Matthew Perry, reopened the islands in 1853 and, unlike China and India, the Japanese rapidly modernized.
- The rule of the shogun was replaced by that of a powerful emperor, Meiji.
- Feudalism was abolished; industry fostered; a central government installed; and education and the military reformed.
- Japan engaged in a modernization movement in which it sent people abroad to learn from other cultures; they came back and rebuilt Japan rapidly, known as the *Meiji Restoration*.
- Japan became so Westernized, while maintaining its basic social structure, that it jumped on the imperialist bandwagon by going to war with China in 1898 and winning Korea.
- Japan shocked the West by decisively defeating the Russians in 1905, during the *Russo-Japanese War*.

The Philippines were taken over by the United States following the *Spanish-American War* of 1898, which America ostensibly fought to "liberate" the colonies of Spain from Spain, the yoke of their colonial master.

■ The United States was victorious and gained control of **Cuba**, **Puerto Rico**, **Guam**, and **the Philippines.**

– When the United States claimed the Philippines as an American territory in January 1899, a revolt of the Filipino people followed within a month.

– The rebellion was brutally suppressed but lasted several years, with the deaths of 35,000 Filipino fighters and as many as 200,000 civilians.

– The United States had turned from champion of the oppressed to oppressor within a few months.

■ Between actions in Japan, China, Hawaii, and the possessions gained from the Spanish-American War, the United States had entered its own era of being an imperialist power.

THE END OF COLONIALISM

SPECIAL NOTE ON PERIODIZATION

Much of this information is included, although it is part of Period 4, in order to preserve the narrative of imperialism and to help you see the connections across periods that will help you understand how to apply the skill of Periodization on the exam.

Traditional imperialist acquisitions ended before the First World War, when virtually the entire non-Western world was divided among the Western powers.

Colonialism: the control of overseas colonies by imperialist powers, and the idea that Europeans and Americans were superior in culture to the rest of the world and therefore were helping to "civilize" the peoples they conquered, while making a tidy profit. It was shaken by the First World War and collapsed in the decades following World War II.

■ Long-term causes for colonialism's fall were many and included the importance of the hypocrisy of people who wanted to rule themselves with liberty and democracy, but who still ruled colonies whose citizens had no voice in government. Also, the economic and political realities of a post–World War II world as explained below helped cause the end of official colonialism:

– *Westernized educational systems* preached the ideals of democracy and awakened nationalistic yearnings among the colonials.

– The concept of *self-determination* espoused by the Allies after the First World War.

– The example and ideals of the *Russian Revolution* and the anti-imperialist *dogma of Communism.*

– The *decline of Europe* in the decades after the Second World War.

– The *example of Japan's resistance* to Western domination after the Meiji Restoration.

The British Empire

- India, the "jewel in the crown" of the British Empire, attained independence in 1948.

  - Decades of *nonviolent resistance*, led by *Mohandas K. Gandhi*, known as Mahatma, helped prepare the populace for self-rule.
  - Bloody clashes between Hindus and Muslims marred the move to independence.
  - The subcontinent was partitioned by mutual agreement of the British and leaders of India into mainly Hindu India and mainly Muslim Pakistan.

- Britain's colonies in Southeast Asia—Ceylon (Sri Lanka), Burma (Myanmar), Malaya (Malaysia)—and its colonies in Africa attained independence in the two decades after the Second World War.
- Most joined the British *Commonwealth of Nations*, a loose political grouping that offered economic advantages.
- When the former British mandate, Palestine, was created as a Jewish state in 1948, long-standing rivalries between Westernized Jewish settlers and Muslim Arabs developed into a volatile and ongoing conflict.

  - Wars between Israel and neighboring Arab countries broke out in 1948, 1956, 1967, and 1973.
  - Nationalization of the Suez Canal, a waterway vital to British trade, by charismatic Egyptian leader Gamal Abdel Nasser provoked war in 1956 between Egypt and allies Britain, France, and Israel.
  - The area continues to be one of the world's most unstable.

The Dutch Empire

Early in the Second World War, the Japanese drove the Dutch out of the *Dutch East Indies* (originally called the *Spice Islands* by the Europeans, but called *Indonesia* after independence).

- When the Dutch tried to resume control after the war, nationalists under the leadership of *Sukarno* (an eventual dictator until his overthrow in 1966) fought a bloody war of resistance and attained total independence in 1954.

The French Empire

After the Second World War, the French colonies in Indochina (Vietnam, Cambodia, and Laos) tried, like the Dutch in Indonesia, to take back the possessions they had been driven from by the Japanese.

- After a costly seven-year guerrilla war, nationalists under Communist *Ho Chi Minh* (1890–1969) attained independence from France in 1954.

  - The Geneva Accords recognized the independence of Vietnam, Cambodia, and Laos, and provisionally partitioned Vietnam into northern and southern sectors until nationwide elections would determine leadership.
  - The agreement broke down into full-scale civil war between the Communist-led North Vietnam and the pro-capitalist South Vietnam.
  - By the mid-1960s the United States had sent massive military forces to aid the south.

- In North Africa, Morocco and Tunisia were granted independence by the French in 1956.

- *Algeria*, considered by many French to be an integral part of France, was not granted independence.

  - The bitter *French-Algerian War* led to independence in 1962 and the mass exodus of French settlers.
  - This war drained the French of resources and of their belief in the ability of their forces to win any major conflict in the developing world.

African Independence

In sub-Saharan Africa independence came suddenly, from the late 1950s through the 1960s.

- The process was painful and costly in some places.
- In the former Belgian Congo (Democratic Republic of the Congo) a legacy of violence and corruption was left by the Belgians who made few infrastructure improvements to their colony.

  - A horrific genocide between the ethnic groups in Rwanda and Burundi (Tutsi and Hutu) occurred as a direct result of Belgian racial policies that enabled the minority Tutsis to rule the majority Hutus.

- Because the Europeans had ignored tribal loyalties when drawing up imperial boundaries, the newly independent states often lacked a unified heritage.
- Former British colonies were best prepared for self-rule, since the British had gradually transferred administration to locals and had built the best infrastructure such as roads, railroads, and telecommunication lines.

Impact of the End of Imperialism

The collapse of the European colonial empires was one of the modern world's most revolutionary and sudden developments.

- Within two decades after the Second World War, the European colonies, encompassing more than 25 percent of the Earth's population, had disappeared,
- Most of the newly independent states, though, still do not enjoy genuine freedom and democratic rule.
- While they often started out with democratic institutions, poverty, ethnic conflicts, and inexperience in self-rule often led to military dictatorship or one-party rule.
- Freedom from foreign rule did not guarantee political freedom.
- Many new nations became pawns of the United States and the Soviet Union during the Cold War.
- The end of imperialism and its messy outcome still causes problems in the world today such as the conflicts in Sudan and Syria as well as the conflict in the Middle East.
- Although imperialism exploited and abused its colonial peoples, it provided them with the technological, industrial, and cultural achievements of the West and linked all the world's peoples.

Modern Thought and Art Emerge

Imperial encounters with non-European peoples influenced the styles and subject matter of artists and writers and provoked debate over the acquisition of colonies. A new relativism in values and the loss of confidence in the objectivity of knowledge led to modernism in intellectual and cultural life. Philosophy, science, the arts, and literature contributed to this crisis of confidence and conscience, but also offered new models to explain and portray humanity.

PHILOSOPHY

- *Friedrich Nietzsche* (1844–1900), a German, attributed the decline of Western civilization to the *slave morality* of Christian ethics.
- *Henri Bergson* (1859–1941), a French thinker, argued that intuition and experience are just as powerful as science and reason for understanding the human condition.
- *Soren Kierkegaard* (1813–1855), a Dane, established the foundations of *existentialism*, a philosophical school, popularized by *Jean-Paul Sartre* after the Second World War, that emphasized individual responsibility and the capability for giving meaning to a meaningless universe.

PSYCHOLOGY

- *Sigmund Freud* (1850–1939), an Austrian, portrayed human behavior as the interplay of powerful irrational and *unconscious* forces.
  - The *id* was the driving force of the personality, a reservoir of sexual and aggressive drives.
  - The *ego* attempts to satisfy the desires of the id rationally and negotiates between the id and the superego.
  - The *superego*, in the unconscious mind like the id, presented conflicting parental and social values that clashed with the selfish drives of the id.
  - Individual lives and civilization itself were fragile balancing acts to keep these unconscious and potentially destructive forces in balance.

PHYSICS

- The work of *Max Planck* (1858–1947), a German, demonstrated that atoms were not the basic building blocks of the universe.
- *Marie Curie* and her husband discovered radioactivity, and that proved that atoms were made of yet smaller particles.
- The work of *Albert Einstein*, a German, revolutionized physics in his "miracle year" of 1905, in which he published four papers on the photoelectric effect, Brownian motion, special relativity, and the equivalence of mass and energy, which were to vault him to the center of the academic debates in physics.

  - Einstein further disrupted the comfortable assumptions of an orderly, rationally discoverable universe that Newton's 17th century physics had supported and encouraged relativism in ethics, politics, and world views. Thus, the new field of quantum physics emerged.

ART

- *Expressionism*, abstract and nonrepresentational, replaced *impressionism* and was pioneered by *Vincent van Gogh* (1853–1890), *Paul Cézanne* (1839–1906), and *Paul Gauguin* (1848–1903), who painted with bold colors and images to focus on emotions and imagination.

- *Pablo Picasso* (1881–1973), a Spaniard, invented *cubism,* the depiction of mood through the use of geometric angles, planes, and clashing lines.
- Architecture exemplified functionalism, buildings designed with practicality and clean lines instead of ornamentation.

LITERATURE

- Joseph Conrad's *Heart of Darkness* portrayed Africa as a dark continent made darker by the imperialism of Europeans and the horrors brought with it.
- *Vladimir Lenin* wrote strongly against imperialism in his *Imperialism, the Highest Stage of Capitalism,* as did J. A. Hobson in *Imperialism: A Study.*
- British writer Rudyard Kipling wrote *The White Man's Burden,* and *The Jungle Book,* to portray the superiority of Western thought over that of the "less civilized" peoples of the world.

TIMELINE OF IMPERIALISM

Year	Event
1839–1842 1856–1860	First and Second *Opium Wars* in China in which the British gained the rights of extraterritoriality, to sell opium, to stay in China all year, and to trade without the Cohong.
1854	Commodore Matthew Perry used "gunboat diplomacy" to open Japan up for trade with the Western world.
1854–1856	Crimean War: Russia lost to the Western nations and Turkey, ending its imperialist aims.
1857–1858	■ *Sepoy Mutiny* in India was led by Hindu and Muslim soldiers who believed that their ammunition was exposing them to pig and cow fat, contrary to their religions. ■ Sepoys were the 300,000 South Asian soldiers in the British East India Company army.
1869	Suez Canal completed with French investment.
1871	Diamonds were discovered near Cape Town, South Africa in what became the Kimberley diamond mines.
1871	Germany united into one nation.
1872	Henry Stanley met David Livingstone in the African jungle.
1873	Three Emperors' League formed: Germany, Austria-Hungary, Russia.
1877	Queen Victoria crowned "Empress of India."
1877–1878	■ Russo-Turkish War over Romania and Bulgaria in which Russia defeated the Ottoman Empire and gained access to warm water ports in Bulgaria and elsewhere on the Balkan Peninsula. ■ The *Congress of Berlin of 1878* was held by Bismarck to host the great powers and avoid problems in the Balkan region after the Russo-Turkish War of 1878 and to establish peace between all powers regarding that region, which was divided between Austria-Hungary, the Ottoman Empire, and the four Balkan states (Greece, Serbia, Romania, and Montenegro).
1879	British defeated by the Zulus at the Battle of Isandlwana.
1879	Dual Alliance between Austria-Hungary and Germany.
1881	Italy joined Dual Alliance forming the Triple Alliance.

Year	Event
1884–1885	Egypt declared a British Protectorate.
1885	■ The *Berlin Conference* divided Africa between the European nations, but this division is on a map only. ■ The nations did not hold the land they claimed at this point, and there were Africans there who believe that they ruled themselves.
1888–1895	Britain and Germany created East, Central, and South African trading companies.
1896–1897	Sino-Japanese War in which Japan went from being imperialized in 1854 to being imperialist just 42 years later.
1898	Battle of Omdurman in which the British led by General Kitchener killed 10,000 Ansar warriors and injured 13,000 more while losing only 48 men.
1898	Ethiopia repelled an attempted Italian invasion.
1898	*Fashoda Incident* in which Kitchener went south "up the Nile," defeated the Muslims, and met the French at *Fashoda*. ■ The French backed down and recalled their general, Marchand. ■ Crisis averted.
1899	Rudyard Kipling wrote "The White Man's Burden" to encourage the United States to get into the imperialism business.
1899–1902	■ Spanish-American War in which the Americans helped win independence for Cuba. ■ Also gained control of Puerto Rico and the Philippines. ■ Spain ended as a colonial power. ■ The Filipinos revolted against the Americans, resulting in a brutal suppression that killed between 100,000 and 500,000 natives.
1901	■ Boer War in South Africa, in which the British signed up in large numbers to fight for the right to "civilize" the people of Africa. ■ This was a turning point in world opinion toward imperialism as the brutal tactics used to suppress the Afrikaners were reported, and Europeans lost some of their zeal for imperialism. ■ This was also the first war of the new century as the 1900s began with war and saw the most brutal wars ever fought.
1904–1905	Russo-Japanese War in which Japan defeated the Russian navy completely and demonstrated that an Asian nation could defeat a European one.
1905	*Moroccan Crisis* in which Germany attempted to prevent France from attaining the colony of Morocco. ■ Was settled by the Algeciras Conference in 1906 in which the Germans tried to bully France into again turning against Britain. This brought Britain and France closer together, and the conference resulted in hostile attention from Britain, France, Russia, and the United States toward Germany. This was Wilhelm II getting a wake-up call that he ignored.
1911	Serbian "Black Hand" nationalist group formed that assassinated Archduke Ferdinand in 1914.
1911	The *Moroccan Crisis of 1911* saw a German gunboat sent to Morocco to protest French occupation of the city of Fez. Britain supported France again, and Germany backed down in return for minor concessions in equatorial Africa.
1914	Panama Canal opened, reducing the shipping miles from Asia to Europe.
1916	**Mohandas K. Gandhi** returned from South Africa to India, where he would fight tirelessly for Indian independence, through *passive resistance* and the *Indian Congress Party* until independence in 1947.

LONG-TERM CAUSES OF THE FIRST WORLD WAR

There were *four* "MAIN" causes of the First World War: *Militarism, Alliances, Imperialism,* and *Nationalism.* These four forces converged at a time and place that could only result in war and revolution across Europe.

It is also important to look at two factors NOT covered by the acronym MAIN: *socialism* and *industrialization.* The rise of socialism can be seen as a factor because governments in Europe were being led by conservative leaders who wanted to use the war to distract the frustrated working classes (who wanted social changes) by patriotic calls for unity against their enemies. Further, the *industrialization* of Europe gave countries the ability to conduct massive military buildups as never before. Overconfident military leaders were eager to use their new weapons and tactics and wage war on an industrial scale. Additionally, this war was fought over natural resources needed for industry for the combatant nations.

Militarism

Militarism also emerged as a powerful force at the beginning of the twentieth century. A warship-building race emerged between Great Britain and Germany, with Germany constructing a navy intended to rival the British navy. A massive buildup of arms and weapons—including modern artillery and explosives, machine guns, and rifles—increased pressure for war in Europe.

Alliances

Alliances had held Europe in a balance of power from the time of Charlemagne through Machiavelli and onward, and the complex alliances in place during this period constitute what is referred to as the *Bismarckian Alliance System.* In this system no one declared war because they knew the alliances would make war too costly.

- The Three Emperors League of 1873 failed when Russia and the Ottomans battled over the Balkans, and Russia was too near to Austria for their liking. Bismarck alienated Russia at the Congress of Vienna (Austria acquired Bosnia-Herzegovina), but he wanted peace and unity in Eastern Europe.
- The *Congress of Berlin of 1878* was held by Bismarck to host the great powers and avoid problems in the Balkan Peninsula after the Russo-Turkish War of 1878. Bismarck intended to establish peace between all powers regarding that region, which was divided between Austria, the Ottoman Empire, and the four Balkan states (Greece, Serbia, Romania, and Montenegro).
- He then created the *Dual Alliance* between Germany and Austria-Hungary, which would last from 1879 to 1918.
- He pressed Russia and Austria-Hungary into the Alliance of the Three Emperors in 1881.

  - Mutual defense pact against the Ottomans in the Balkans and France in the west.
  - Russia refused to renew in 1887.

- In the Triple Alliance (1882–1915) Bismarck tried to tilt the balance of power in his favor at the Congress of Berlin.

  - Arranged a defensive alliance between Italy, Austria-Hungary, and Germany.
  - Italy withdrew in 1915, because Germany and Austria-Hungary had gone on the offensive.

- Russia exited the Three Emperors League in 1887.

  - Germany, in an attempt to keep peace with Russia, arranged the *Russian German Reinsurance Treaty* in which both promised neutrality if the other was attacked.
  - Kaiser William II did not like this friendly attitude toward Russia and dismissed Bismarck as a result.
  - Refused to renew the policy.
  - France and Russia then became allies.

In 1902, the two imperialist island nations that industrialized first on their respective continents formed an alliance:

- Britain and Japan were firmly committed in the Anglo-Japanese Alliance (1902–1915).

  - United States was its usual noncommittal self, but followed loyally at Britain's side.

- Anglo-French Entente seemed like a good idea to both sides by 1904.
- Britain was the only great power (Splendid Isolation) that had remained uncommitted to any other country during this time.
- After the *Boer War*, some countries began to feel threatened and considered an alliance between Austria-Hungary, France, Germany, and Russia against Britain.

  - Britain tried to resolve this problem and remain on good terms with the other countries.
  - France's prime minister, Theophile Déclassé, also wanted better relations with Britain and France and arranged the Anglo-French Entente.

- Settled any outstanding disputes between Britain and France.
- Gave support to Britain if the other countries decided to form an alliance against it.
- At the *Algeciras Conference* in 1906, the Germans tried to persuade France to turn against Britain.

  - This brought Britain and France closer together and the conference resulted in hostile attention from Britain, France, Russia, and the United States toward Germany.
  - This was Wilhelm II getting a wake-up call that he ignored.

- In 1907, the Russians, who recently had lost a fleet, destroyed in battle by the Japanese, asked the British to join an alliance.

  - Anglo-Russo Alliance began.
  - The *Triple Entente* would finally emerge with Russia, Britain, and France in 1914.
  - They, along with the United States, would be known as the *Allied Powers* during the First World War.

Imperialism

Imperialism was also a major factor. Throughout the nineteenth century, each major European country's population pressure, desire for wealth, and pride urged it to gain overseas possessions regardless of its population's desires. Imperialism was also vital to a capitalist economy to expand.

Some examples of how imperialism increased international tensions follow:

- The *Berlin Conference* in 1885 marked Germany's late coming to imperialism, which led Bismarck to spearhead the movement to establish rules for carving up Africa.

- The *Kruger Telegram* in 1902 roused British ire at Germany for congratulating the Boers on their victories over British troops in South Africa.
- The *Moroccan Crisis* of 1911 saw a German gunboat sent to Morocco to protest French occupation of the city of Fez.

  - Britain supported France, and Germany backed down in return for minor concessions in equatorial Africa.

Nationalism

Nationalism caused leaders and countries to do strange things for national pride. Wilhelm II of Germany was building up his navy to attempt to rival the British navy. This forced Britain to build its navy rather than focus on David Lloyd George's "People's Budget."

- German nationalism was looking for another great military victory to bring glory and colonies to Germany.
- Nationalism was tearing the dual monarchy of Austria-Hungary apart.
- A good example of this is the Balkan Wars.

  - In the *First Balkan Crisis* (1874–1878), Bosnia and Herzegovina rebelled against Ottoman rule, leading to Serbia declaring war on the Ottoman Empire in June 1876.
  - Russia, a largely Slavic country, like Serbia, had a policy of *pan-Slavism*, or protecting all Slavic people, and declared war on the Ottoman Empire.
  - Britain, concerned with protecting its Mediterranean interests against Russian movements, supported the Turkish sultan, Hamid I.
  - In 1878, Turkey sought peace.

- Greece and Bulgaria took Macedonia, leading to the *Second Balkan Crisis* (1885), a conflict between Bulgaria and Serbia over territory.

  - Russia warned it was ready to occupy Bulgaria if it did not yield to Serbian demands over Macedonia.
  - Austria-Hungary supported Bulgaria, and Germany supported Austria-Hungary.
  - This nationalist pressure ended the Alliance of the Three Emperors.

- In the *Third Balkan Crisis* (1912–1913), Italy was in conflict with the Ottoman Empire over holdings along the Adriatic Sea.
- In the *First Balkan War*, Serbia took Macedonia in 1912.
- In the *Second Balkan War* (1913), Serbia attacked Bulgaria in hopes of gaining a seaport.

  - Russia, with its policy of pan-Slavism, supported Serbia, while Austria-Hungary still supported Bulgaria.
  - Britain and Germany urged peace.
  - Serbs were enraged at Austria-Hungary for its support of Bulgaria and its occupation of Bosnia-Herzegovina.
  - In the end, nationalism directly led to the **Third Balkan War**, which turned into the First World War.

PRACTICE LONG-ESSAY QUESTIONS

The questions that follow are samples of the various types of thematic essays that appear on the AP exam. (See pages 30–31 for a detailed explanation of each type.) Check over the **generic rubric** (see pages 32–33) before you begin any of these essays and use that rubric to score your essay if you write one.

Question 1

Compare the European colonial policies before 1815 with those of the later nineteenth and early twentieth centuries.

COMMENTS ON QUESTION 1

This is a COMPARE skill question, so be sure to describe similarities and differences between the "European colonial policies before 1815" and the "European colonial policies of the later nineteenth and early twentieth centuries" as well as account for, or explain, them by providing specific examples of how they are similar and different and tying those similarities and differences to historical developments such as the growth of technology, economic ambitions, nationalistic tensions, and political ideas. Sometimes called colonialism, the European colonial policies before 1815 followed the Age of Exploration of the mid-fifteenth to the early nineteenth centuries. It was characterized by commercial ventures, control of seaports for the seagoing trade, and trade with the local peoples. There was little attempt, except in the New World, to encourage immigration to the colonies; there was very little attempt to impose the European social, political, or economic structures on the local population.

In contrast, the "New Imperialism" of the late-nineteenth century took over the governing of its colonies; it exploited native labor and natural resources; it judged local behavior according to European mores; and it forced religious conversion.

The two forms of imperialism were similar in that the Europeans rarely attempted to absorb the culture of their colonies, nor did they encourage colonial immigration to the mother country.

Question 2

By the end of the nineteenth century, to what extent had European nations divided the rest of the world among themselves?

COMMENTS ON QUESTION 2

This question tests the CHANGE AND CONTINUITY OVER TIME skill. Be sure to describe the level of historical continuity and change, and to analyze specific examples of what changed, what parts of the world had been divided by Europe, and what remained the same such as religions, traditions, and class structure, and why things changed or stayed the same as European imperialism evolved. The essay must explain how Europe conquered most of the world during the nineteenth century, and must support assertions with specific evidence.

Consider the various regions that were targets of imperialism in the nineteenth century. The scramble for Africa left only two independent nations: Liberia and Ethiopia. In Asia, coastal China and some inland regions were divided into spheres of influence that left a disintegrating monarchy, but one that was Chinese. Japan maintained its independence, and when it was forced to open up to Western trade, rapidly industrialized; within 50 years, Japan defeated Russia in a land and naval conflict to become the only Asian nation to win a war over a European power. In the Western Hemisphere, the United States regarded Latin America as its sphere of influence.

Question 3

Compare the responses of China and Japan to Western encroachment.

COMMENTS ON QUESTION 3

This is a COMPARE skill question, so be sure to describe similarities and differences between the Japanese and Chinese reactions to European imperialism, as well as to account for or explain them by providing specific examples of how they are similar and different, and tie those similarities and differences to historical developments such as the use of Western ideas and technology.

The contrast was glaring: China resisted Westernization, and parts of the country became regions dominated by foreign influence, while Japan modernized and kept its autonomy. Why and how? Detail the Chinese response to Western imperialism from the Earl of McCartney to the Opium Wars to the Boxer Rebellion to the establishment of Sun Yat-sen's republic. Trace the Japanese response from the "opening" by Commodore Perry to the Russo-Japanese War. The comparison of similarities can be made by explaining that both nations managed to hold onto their rich and ancient cultures: one did so by stubbornly sticking to tradition, the other by blending the best of the West with its own unique ways.

PRACTICE SHORT-ANSWER QUESTIONS

1. Please use the excerpt below and your knowledge of European History to answer all parts of the question that follows it.

Imperialism, the Highest Stage of Capitalism

Precisely the parasitism and decay of capitalism, which are characteristic of its highest historical stage of development, i.e., imperialism. As is proved in this pamphlet, capitalism has now singled out a handful (less than one-tenth of the inhabitants of the globe; less than one-fifth at a most "generous" and liberal calculation) of exceptionally rich and powerful states which plunder the whole world simply by "clipping coupons." Capital exports yield an income of eight to ten billion francs per annum, at prewar prices and according to prewar bourgeois statistics. Now, of course, they yield much more.

Obviously, out of such enormous superprofits (since they are obtained over and above the profits which capitalists squeeze out of the workers of their "own" country) it is possible to bribe the labor leaders and the upper stratum of the labor aristocracy. And the capitalists of the "advanced" countries are bribing them; they bribe them in a thousand different ways, direct and indirect, overt and covert.

—Vladimir Ilyich Lenin 1916

(A) Briefly explain why the author of the document above would believe and assert that imperialism is "the highest stage of capitalism."

(B) Cite one piece of evidence that supports Lenin's assertion and explain why it supports the assertion.

(C) Cite one piece of evidence that refutes Lenin's claim and explain why it refutes that claim.

2. Please use the excerpt of the treaty below and your knowledge of European History to completely answer all parts of the question that follows.

The Dual Alliance Between Austria-Hungary and Germany—October 7, 1879

ARTICLE 1.

Should, contrary to their hope, and against the loyal desire of the two High Contracting Parties, one of the two Empires be attacked by Russia the High Contracting Parties are bound to come to the assistance the other with the whole war strength of their Empires, and accordingly only to conclude peace together and upon mutual agreement.

ARTICLE 2.

Should one of the High Contracting Parties be attacked by another Power, the other High Contracting Party binds itself hereby, not only not to support the aggressor against its High Ally, but to observe at least a benevolent neutral attitude towards its fellow Contracting Party.

ARTICLE 4.

This Treaty shall, in conformity with its peaceful character, and to avoid any misinterpretation, be kept secret by the two High Contracting Parties, and only communicated to a third Power upon a joint understanding between the two Parties, and according to the terms of a special Agreement.

(A) How did the treaty above help to cause the First World War to emerge?

(B) Briefly explain each of the four main causes of the First World War that historians usually cite.

(C) Briefly explain how many historians do not see the First World War as the first truly global conflict.

Short-Answer Explanations

1. (A) You should explain that Lenin, as the founder of the USSR, is pointing out the evils and oppression caused by capitalism as part of his communist viewpoint in order to gain support for his communist ideas and to get the Russians to reject capitalism in favor of communism. You should further explain that communists call for all workers to seize power together to wrest it from the hands of the elite wealthy classes so that there can be a more equitable distribution of wealth and output. You should also explain that the evils done in the name of imperialism, from the genocide of the Native Americans to the destruction of the Congo, gave him a platform from which he could claim that communism had the higher moral ground.

   (B) You could note any of the following and explain why they support Lenin's assertion: vast wealth going from the rest of the world to Europe, military and political dominance of most of the world enriched Europe, Europeans' concept of the "White Man's Burden," and the few Europeans who gained wealth from imperialism while the costs were spread among all taxpayers, and exporting capitalism to imperialized nations.

   (C) To refute the claim, you should note and explain why any ONE of the following refutes the claim that imperialism is the highest level of capitalism: government involvement in imperialism; some foreigners becoming wealthy, too; improvements to infrastructure in imperialized nations; the Japanese reaction to imperialism, going from isolation to imperial power in 50 years; or the improved standard of living for most citizens of imperialized nations due to European intervention.

2. (A) You should explain that the secret treaty between Austria and Germany forced both to go to war if either were attacked or if either got into a conflict with Russia. You could also explain that the overall system of alliances turned a local conflict into a European war with all powers getting involved, and that imperialism also brought the distant regions Europeans had colonized into the conflict as well. You may include that Russia did not have a plan to mobilize troops against either Germany or Austria, only for both.

   (B) You should cite Militarism, Alliances, Imperialism (or Industrialization), and Nationalism—the "MAIN" causes of the First World War—and briefly explain how they each led to war. Militarism could simply be the military buildup of the European powers at the start of the twentieth century, or the competition between Germany and the United Kingdom for naval dominance. Imperialism could point to the competition for the best colonies as a cause of the war, but some may cite the Fashoda Incident or other actions taken by the Germans and the British and French leading up to the war. Alliances should be blamed for igniting a local conflict in the Balkans into a full-fledged world war because of nations' obligations to each other.

   (C) You should cite other conflicts that were fought on multiple continents. The one most often cited is the Seven Years' War, which was fought in Asia, the Americas (called the French and Indian War by the British colonists in North America), Europe, and the coast of Africa. Another possible example would be the Crimean War, if all combatants are accounted for.

PRACTICE MULTIPLE-CHOICE QUESTIONS

Questions 1 to 3 refer to the image below.

The Sepoy Mutiny, 1857–58: contemporary illustration by an unknown native artist. The Granger Collection.

1. The picture above is of a rebellion against the British in 1857 by which of the following areas in which the British had gained dominance?

   (A) Egypt
   (B) China
   (C) India
   (D) Ceylon

2. Which of the following reasons is the most likely reason that the British were successful in putting down the rebellion depicted above?

   (A) The natives were poorly trained fighters.
   (B) The British had superior weapons.
   (C) The British outnumbered the natives.
   (D) The natives were not dedicated to their rebellion.

3. Which of the following was a contributing cause in the rebellion depicted above?

   (A) The Sepoys were fierce warriors who could not be trusted by the British.
   (B) The Sepoys were tired of long hours and low pay.
   (C) The British belief in their superiority led them to ignore native traditions.
   (D) The British banned all native people from first-class travel within the empire.

The White Man's Burden
Take up the White Man's burden—
Send forth the best ye breed—
Go, bind your sons to exile
To serve your captives' need;
To wait, in heavy harness,
On fluttered folk and wild—
Your new-caught sullen peoples,
Half devil and half child.

Take up the White Man's burden—
In patience to abide,
To veil the threat of terror
And check the show of pride;
By open speech and simple,
An hundred times made plain,
To seek another's profit
And work another's gain.

Take up the White Man's burden—
The savage wars of peace—
Fill full the mouth of Famine,
And bid the sickness cease;
And when your goal is nearest
(The end for others sought)
Watch sloth and heathen folly
Bring all your hope to naught.

4. This poem is associated with which of the following concepts that shaped Europe's interaction with the rest of the world in the late nineteenth century?

   (A) Ethnic Self-determination
   (B) Social Darwinism
   (C) Cultural Nihilism
   (D) The Golden Rule

5. Which of the following is the best description of the impact of this poem and the philosophy it represents?

   (A) It created a mass political movement that shook monarchies.
   (B) It was used to discourage nations from engaging in imperialist actions.
   (C) It was used to encourage native populations who had been imperialized to revolt.
   (D) It was used to justify European conquest of overseas territories.

6. Which of the following countries had reaped the greatest benefits from adopting and exporting the philosophy supported by the poem by 1914?

(A) Japan

(B) China

(C) India

(D) Egypt

7. Which of the following is the best description of European overseas empires from 1750 to 1914?

(A) European empires were steadily growing in a consistent manner throughout the period cited.

(B) The same nations that started with large colonial empires continued to be the largest empires as they all built on their strong starts.

(C) The focus of European empires shifted from Asia to the Americas due to rising profits there as the period progressed.

(D) The colonies in the Americas broke free from Europe, and Europe began to colonize Africa and Asia as the period progressed.

Multiple-Choice Explanations

1. **C** 3. **C** 5. **D** 7. **D**
2. **B** 4. **B** 6. **A**

1. **(C)**

(A) is wrong because the Sepoy Mutiny was in India.

(B) is wrong because the Sepoy Mutiny was in India.

(C) is CORRECT because the Sepoy Mutiny was in India.

(D) is wrong because the Sepoy Mutiny was in India.

2. **(B)**

(A) is wrong because the Sepoys were soldiers trained by the British.

(B) is CORRECT because the British (and all European imperialists) relied heavily on the superiority of their weapons to control native populations many times larger than the British occupying force.

(C) is wrong because the natives were far more numerous than the British.

(D) is wrong because natives were dedicated, but could not defeat the superior weapons and technology of the British.

3. **(C)**

(A) is wrong because the British used the Sepoys as their soldiers before the rebellion.

(B) is wrong because the Sepoys got better pay and hours from the British than they did working for Indian rulers.

(C) is CORRECT because the British forced the Sepoys to use bullets coated with cow and pig fat, which was against their religious beliefs, and this was a cause of the rebellion.

(D) is wrong because the British did not ban all natives from first class travel.

4. **(B)**

(A) is wrong because the poem supports Western domination, not ethnic self-determination.

(B) is CORRECT because the idea of Social Darwinism is associated with the poem and the concept of "The White Man's Burden."

(C) is wrong because cultural nihilism means a lack of culture, which is not evident here.

(D) is wrong because the Golden Rule is a biblical concept of "treat others how one wishes to be treated," which is certainly not evident here.

5. **(D)**

(A) is wrong because the poem and Social Darwinism did not lead to massive social movement in Europe.

(B) is wrong because it encouraged, not discouraged, imperialism.

(C) is wrong because it was in favor of the conquest, not the revolt of the natives in Africa and Asia.

(D) is CORRECT because "The White Man's Burden" was used as a support for Social Darwinism, which was a justification for the European conquest of natives around the world.

6. **(A)**

(A) is CORRECT because Japan used the help of the West to modernize and, by 1905, defeated Russia, a European power, in war.

(B) is wrong because China's best coastal cities were controlled by foreign powers at the end of the Qing dynasty, and the country is just now recovering from the nineteenth century.

(C) is wrong because India was controlled by the British until after the Second World War.

(D) is wrong because Egypt was mostly controlled by the British after 1882.

7. **(D)**

(A) is wrong because Spain lost its empire, and the British lost the United States during this period.

(B) is wrong because Spain was in full decline by 1914.

(C) is wrong because the Europeans were focused on building colonies in Africa and Asia, not on trade with the Americas.

(D) is CORRECT because, as the American colonies broke free, European countries turned to Asia and Africa for new sources of markets and raw materials.

Time Period Three (1815–1914): Practice Assessment

KEY CONCEPTS AND OVERVIEW

KEY CONCEPT 3.1 The Industrial Revolution spread from Great Britain to the Continent, where the state played a greater role in promoting industry.

KEY CONCEPT 3.2 The experiences of everyday life were shaped by industrialization, depending on the level of industrial development in a particular location.

KEY CONCEPT 3.3 Political revolutions and the complications resulting from industrialization triggered a range of ideological, governmental, and collective responses.

KEY CONCEPT 3.4 European states struggled to maintain international stability in an age of nationalism and revolutions.

KEY CONCEPT 3.5 A variety of motives and methods led to the intensification of European global control and increased tensions among the Great Powers.

KEY CONCEPT 3.6 European ideas and culture expressed a tension between objectivity and scientific realism on one hand, and subjectivity and individual expression on the other.

PRACTICE ASSESSMENT

Each time period concludes with a mini-test consisting of some multiple-choice questions, two short-answer questions, and two essay choices, of which you should choose to answer at least one. This is not so much to simulate an exam, which will have more questions and a DBQ, but to help you prepare for the types of questions seen on the exam and to allow you time to practice those skills. The document-based questions (DBQs) can be found in the Introduction to this book, in the two sample exams at the end of this book, and in the online version of the exams that accompany this book, which can be found at: *http://barronsbooks.com/AP/ap-european-hist/*. This assessment should take you about two hours. Detailed explanations of all questions follow the assessment.

TIME PERIOD THREE (1815–1914): PRACTICE ASSESSMENT

Section I, Part A

Multiple-Choice Questions (15 Questions)

> **Directions:** Please read the passages and then choose the most correct answer choice for each of the following questions.

Questions 1 to 3 refer to the following excerpt written by Lenin.

We have to begin with as precise and full a definition of imperialism as possible. Imperialism is a specific historical stage of capitalism. Its specific character is threefold: imperialism is monopoly capitalism; parasitic, or decaying capitalism; moribund capitalism. The supplanting of free competition by monopoly is the fundamental economic feature, the quintessence of imperialism. Monopoly manifests itself in five principal forms: (1) cartels, syndicates and trusts—the concentration of production has reached a degree which gives rise to these monopolistic associations of capitalists; (2) the monopolistic position of the big banks—three, four or five giant banks manipulate the whole economic life of America, France, Germany; (3) seizure of the sources of raw material by the trusts and the financial oligarchy; (4) the (economic) partition of the world by the international cartels has begun. There are already over one hundred such international cartels, which command the entire world market and divide it "amicably" among themselves—until war re-divides it. The export of capital, as distinct from the export of commodities under non-monopoly capitalism, is a highly characteristic phenomenon and is closely linked with the economic and territorial-political partition of the world; (5) the territorial partition of the world (colonies) is completed.

—*Imperialism and the Split in Socialism* by Vladimir I. Lenin, 1916

1. Which of the following is the best description of Lenin's opinions of imperialism?

   (A) It is a reflection of the evil of capitalism.
   (B) It is being done incorrectly and needs to be reformed.
   (C) It is the most important way for socialists to dominate the world.
   (D) It is an idea that has no place in a capitalist economy.

2. Which of the following occurred as a result of the conflict between Enlightenment ideals and the profit motive in regard to imperialism?

   (A) All European governments nakedly pursued imperialist gains.
   (B) A robust debate broke out in Europe about the morality, costs, and benefits of imperialism.
   (C) European artists influenced artists all over the world without being influenced themselves.
   (D) Europeans began to be controlled by non-Europeans within Europe.

3. Which of the following people would be most likely to disagree with Lenin's views on imperialism?

(A) Mohandas K. Gandhi
(B) Otto von Bismarck
(C) Sun Yat-sen
(D) Cecil Rhodes

Questions 4 to 6 refer to the following excerpt from British governmental archives.

"Girls," says the Sub-Commissioner [J. C. Symons], "regularly perform all the various offices of trapping, hurrying" [Yorkshire terms for drawing the loaded coal corves], "filling, riddling, tipping, and occasionally getting, just as they are performed by boys. One of the most disgusting sights I have ever seen was that of young females, dressed like boys in trousers, crawling on all fours, with belts round their waists and chains passing between their legs."

"When I arrived at the board or workings of the pit I found at one of the sideboards down a narrow passage a girl of fourteen years of age in boy's clothes, picking down the coal with the regular pick used by the men. She was half sitting half lying at her work, and said she found it tired her very much, and 'of course she didn't like it.' The place where she was at work was not 2 feet high. No less than six girls out of eighteen men and children are employed in this pit."

—From *Parliamentary Papers*, 1842, Vol. XVI

4. Which of the following implications of the report above was the most significant change brought on by industrialization?

(A) Hard work for long hours
(B) Workers set their own hours
(C) Gender roles changed
(D) Children began to work for profit

5. Which of the following best explains a middle class attitude that helped lead to reports like the one above?

(A) Bourgeois families became focused on the nuclear family, with distinct gender roles for men and women.
(B) Bourgeois families were very concerned with the education of their children.
(C) Bourgeois families spent huge amounts of money on servants and entertaining.
(D) Bourgeois families were dedicated to Victorian ideals that eschewed sexuality of all types.

6. Which of the following laws created by Parliament did the LEAST to improve the lives of the workers cited above?

(A) Mines Act of 1842
(B) Factory Act of 1833
(C) Combination Acts
(D) Ten Hours Act

Questions 7 to 11 refer to the following sonnet by Wordsworth.

Earth has not anything to show more fair:
Dull would he be of soul who could pass by
A sight so touching in its majesty:
This City now doth, like a garment, wear
The beauty of the morning; silent, bare,
Ships, towers, domes, theatres, and temples lie
Open unto the fields, and to the sky;
All bright and glittering in the smokeless air.
Never did sun more beautifully steep
In his first splendour, valley, rock, or hill;
Ne'er saw I, never felt, a calm so deep!
The river glideth at his own sweet will:
Dear God! the very houses seem asleep;
And all that mighty heart is lying still!

— "Composed upon Westminster Bridge, September 3, 1802," by William Wordsworth

7. Which of the following artistic movements does the poem above seem most associated with?

   (A) Romanticism
   (B) Impressionism
   (C) Realism
   (D) Neoclassicism

8. Which of the following themes of the nineteenth century seems to be voiced most loudly in the poem above?

   (A) Awe at the power of the supernatural
   (B) Reverence for the beauty and power of nature
   (C) Nationalistic yearnings
   (D) The achievements of the individual

9. Which of the following was NOT a problem faced by the cities of England during the first half of the nineteenth century?

   (A) Overcrowding due to increased urbanization
   (B) Increasing pollution
   (C) A lack of public space to exercise and recreate
   (D) Massive unemployment

10. Which of the following factors was unique to Britain, allowing it to have an industrial revolution?

(A) Coal deposits
(B) Entrepreneurial class
(C) Available capital
(D) Stable government

11. At the time the poem was written the author most likely referred to the absence of which of the following by the words "in the smokeless air"?

(A) Steel mills
(B) Railroads
(C) Coal fires
(D) Steamships

Questions 12 to 15 refer to the following writing by Giuseppe Mazzini.

In principle, as in the ideas formerly laid down by the men influencing every national party, nationality ought only to be to humanity that which the division of labor is in a workshop—the recognized symbol of association; the assertion of the individuality of a human group called by its geographical position, its traditions, and its language, to fulfil a special function in the European work of civilization.

The map of Europe has to be remade. This is the key to the present movement; herein lies the initiative. Before acting, the instrument for action must be organized; before building, the ground must be one's own. The social idea cannot be realized under any form whatsoever before this reorganization of Europe is effected; before the peoples are free to interrogate themselves; to express their vocation, and to assure its accomplishment by an alliance capable of substituting itself for the absolutist league which now reigns supreme.

—Giuseppe Mazzini, "Europe: Its Condition and Prospects," 1852

12. At the time this was written which of the following would have been the best category for the concept of nationalism?

(A) It was a liberal idea calling for change.
(B) It was a conservative idea calling for patriotism.
(C) It was a reactionary idea calling for change.
(D) It was a radical idea espoused only by criminals.

13. The author of the piece above is often referred to as the "heart" of Italian unification, in large part because of the nationalism he fostered whose effects throughout history can best be described as which of the following?

   (A) It has been a unifying force throughout time.
   (B) It was first used to unify nations, then to destroy empires.
   (C) It was strongest in France and the Netherlands.
   (D) It was always a force that destroyed people.

14. Which of the following political groups had claimed nationalism as a reason worthy of war just as those who had traditionally supported it rejected it in 1913?

   (A) Liberals
   (B) Conservatives
   (C) Marxists
   (D) Chartists

15. Who of the following was the Italian nationalist who was inspired multiple times by Mazzini's words to take military action?

   (A) Camillo Benso di Cavour
   (B) Vincento Gioberti
   (C) Benito Mussolini
   (D) Giuseppe Garibaldi

Section I

Part B: Short-Answer Questions

Directions: Answer both questions completely.

1. Answer ALL parts of the question. Historians have argued that industrialization allowed Europe to dominate the rest of the world for over a century (1830s to 1970s).

   (A) Identify TWO pieces of evidence that SUPPORT this argument and explain HOW each supports the argument.

   (B) Identify ONE piece of evidence that UNDERMINES this argument and explain HOW the evidence undermines the argument.

2. Use the excerpt and the image as well as your knowledge of European history to answer all parts of the question that follows.

Source 1

Among them are mills on the river, in short, the method of construction is as crowded and disorderly here as in the lower part of Long Millgate. Right and left a multitude of covered passages lead from the main street into numerous courts, and he who turns in thither gets into a filth and disgusting grime, the equal of which is not to be found—especially in the courts which lead down to the Irk, and which contain unqualifiedly the most horrible dwellings which I have yet beheld. In one of these courts there stands directly at the entrance, at the end of the covered passage, a privy without a door, so dirty that the inhabitants can pass into and out of the court only by passing through foul pools of stagnant urine and excrement.

—*The Condition of the Working-Class in England,* by Friedrich Engels, 1844.

Source 2

Child Labor, 1871. Paying children for their labor
in the brickyards. English wood engraving.

(A) Briefly explain ONE economic development that led to the conditions seen in the two sources.

(B) Briefly explain ONE governmental response to the conditions seen in the two sources.

(C) Briefly explain ONE social change brought on by urbanization.

Section II: Long-Essay Question

Directions: In this section, you will choose between one of two long-essay questions. The following questions are meant to illustrate an example of a question pairing that might appear in this section of the exam, in which both questions focus on the same historical thinking skill (in this case, Comparison) but apply it to different time periods and/or topics.

LONG-ESSAY CHOICES

1. Compare the methods used by Cavour and Bismarck in unifying their respective nations.

2. Assess the quote below. What ideas did both Adam Smith and Karl Marx draw upon in order to formulate their ideas? What were their conclusions and why were they so different?

Adam Smith's enormous authority resides, in the end, in the same property that we discover in Marx: not in any ideology, but in an effort to see the bottom of things. In both cases their greatness rests on an unflinching confrontation with the human condition as they could best make out.

—Robert Heilbroner, American economist and historian

ANSWER EXPLANATIONS

Multiple-Choice Explanations

1. **A**	5. **A**	9. **D**	13. **B**
2. **B**	6. **C**	10. **D**	14. **B**
3. **D**	7. **A**	11. **C**	15. **D**
4. **C**	8. **C**	12. **A**	

1. **(A)**

   (A) is CORRECT because Lenin as a Marxist saw imperialism as the last stage of capitalism and used imperialism to prove the evils of capitalism.

   (B) is wrong because Lenin wanted to abolish, not reform, imperialism.

   (C) is wrong because Lenin did not believe socialists would need imperialism at all.

   (D) is wrong because Lenin tied capitalism to imperialism inextricably.

2. **(B)**

   (A) is wrong because although some governments engaged in imperialism, some did not pursue such gains, e.g., Switzerland.

   (B) is CORRECT because a debate between all thinkers, artists, and politicians of the era emerged as to what the correct approach should be.

   (C) is wrong because European artists were influenced by the world as much as they influenced it.

   (D) is wrong because non-Europeans did not control Europeans within Europe as a form of imperialism.

3. **(D)**

   (A) is wrong because Gandhi as an Indian nationalist agreed with Lenin that imperialism was evil.

   (B) is wrong because Bismarck saw imperialism as a distraction from nation building.

   (C) is wrong because Sun Yat-sen as a Chinese nationalist, agreed with Lenin that imperialism was evil.

   (D) is CORRECT because Cecil Rhodes was a British imperialist financier who dominated Africa at the end of the nineteenth century with his dream of a Cairo-to-Cape Town railroad.

4. **(C)**

   (A) is wrong because the people had always worked long hours at a tempo set by nature.

   (B) is wrong because workers' hours were set by the factory after the Industrial Revolution.

   (C) is CORRECT because the changing gender roles and division of labor by gender changed European social life the most of those offered.

   (D) is wrong because children had worked for profit under the putting-out system before industrialization.

5. **(A)**

(A) is CORRECT because the bourgeois prejudices in favor of the nuclear family that they could afford to rely upon was a major factor in making laws affecting women in the workplace, such as the Mines Act of 1842.

(B) is wrong because the report does not address education.

(C) is wrong because the expenditure on servants and parties did not affect legislation on gender roles.

(D) is wrong because the focus on the nuclear family was more impactful in this situation than were Victorian ideals.

6. **(C)**

(A) is wrong because the Mines Act of 1842 benefited working miners by raising their wages and protecting their children.

(B) is wrong because the Factory Act of 1833 benefited workers and their children.

(C) is CORRECT because the Combination Acts were anti-union laws that hurt workers.

(D) is wrong because the Ten Hours Act benefited workers and their children by limiting their hours.

7. **(A)**

(A) is CORRECT because Wordsworth was a Romantic poet and this poem typifies that through its nationalist and nature-loving themes.

(B) is wrong because the poem is not impressionist, which is usually associated with oil paintings instead of poetry.

(C) is wrong because the poem is not realist, which is usually associated with harsh depictions of reality from which overly emotional reactions are omitted.

(D) is wrong because the poem is not neoclassical, which is usually associated with emotional, nationalistic glory in the tradition of ancient Rome.

8. **(C)**

(A) is wrong because the poem does not focus at all on the supernatural.

(B) is wrong because the poem focuses more on the beauty and grandeur of London than that of nature, stating that the sun never saw anything more beautiful in nature than London.

(C) is CORRECT because the poem glorifies Britain, stating that the sun never saw anything more beautiful in nature than the sights of the city, clearly displaying British nationalism.

(D) is wrong because the poem does not glorify any individual.

9. **(D)**

(A) is wrong because cities did face a lot of overcrowding in Britain during the first half of the nineteenth century.

(B) is wrong because cities in Britain did have major pollution during the first half of the nineteenth century.

(C) is wrong because cities in Britain did not have areas to recreate or parks during the first half of the nineteenth century.

(D) is CORRECT because cities did not face massive unemployment, but rather a labor shortage during the first half of the nineteenth century.

10. **(D)**

(A) is wrong because many nations in Europe had coal deposits, but did not have an industrial revolution until Britain led the way.

(B) is wrong because many nations in Europe had entrepreneurs, but did not have an industrial revolution until Britain led the way.

(C) is wrong because many nations in Europe had plenty of capital, whether held by nobles or others, but did not have an industrial revolution until Britain led the way.

(D) is CORRECT because Britain was the only country with the above factors and a stable government to boot.

11. **(C)**

(A) is wrong because steel mills did not exist in London in 1802.

(B) is wrong because railroads did not exist in London in 1802.

(C) is CORRECT because coal fires were the only choice that existed in London in 1802.

(D) is wrong because steamships did not exist in London in 1802.

12. **(A)**

(A) is CORRECT because nationalism began as a liberal idea that would dissolve empires in favor of nations.

(B) is wrong because conservatives did not try to co-opt nationalism until after 1848.

(C) is wrong because reactionaries could not support nationalism until the mid-1900s, when it had become an old idea again.

(D) is wrong because many middle class liberals (people not engaged in crime) supported it.

13. **(B)**

(A) is wrong because it has been used to cause war and destroy nations such as Poland during World War II.

(B) is CORRECT because when it was first conceived as a liberal idea, it unified Germany and Italy, but later it was used to destroy the Austrian Empire and parts of Russia.

(C) is wrong because the Netherlands was not at all a hotbed of nationalism.

(D) is wrong because it was used to create unity in Germany and Italy.

14. **(B)**

(A) is wrong because the liberals were no longer supporting nationalism as a reason for war; that was at first a radical idea, then a conservative one.

(B) is CORRECT because nationalism was co-opted by conservatives like Bismarck and Cavour to create nations and eventually it would be used as an excuse for the First World War by conservatives such as Nicholas II, Wilhelm II, Franz Joseph, and Napoleon III.

(C) is wrong because Marxists saw nationalism as a repugnant result of capitalism that would disappear when the revolution occurred.

(D) is wrong because the Chartists were mostly British, but were not nationalist in character, but more classist.

15. **(D)**

(A) is wrong because Cavour was a planner and the "brains" of Italian unification, but Giuseppe Garibaldi was the "sword" who brought the armed forces of his Red Shirts with him.

(B) is wrong because Gioberti was a priest who wanted the pope to lead Italian unification, but Giuseppe Garibaldi was the "sword" who brought the armed forces of his Red Shirts with him.

(C) is wrong because Mussolini was a post–First World War Italian dictator.

(D) is CORRECT because Giuseppe Garibaldi was the "sword" who brought the armed forces of his Red Shirts with him.

Short-Answer Explanations

1. (A) A good answer will give two pieces of evidence to support the assertion that industrialization enabled Europe to dominate the world from the 1830s through the 1970s, such as, but not limited to: imperialistic gains, the carving up of Africa, British Empire and trade dominance, Boxer and Taiping Rebellions, Sepoy Mutiny, tracking GDP or standard of living during this time in each region, Belgian Congo, Ethiopia and Italy, Berlin Conference, Open Door Policy in China, Opium Wars, Opening of Japan, "White Man's Burden"/ Social Darwinism/paternalism, African Zulu wars, and the battle of Omdurman.

(B) A good answer will give one piece of evidence to refute the assertion that industrialization enabled Europe to dominate the world from the 1830s through the 1970s, such as, but not limited to: Russo-Japanese War of 1905, Japanese after the First World War, American dominance after the Second World War, the Cold War, Chinese Communist Revolution, French colonial losses after the Second World War, the strength of Asian and African cultures that persevered, and the rise of the American economy.

2. (A) A good answer will explain how factors led to the crowded cities that were cesspools of filth and disease, such as, but not limited to, the following: the emergence of the factory system, the poverty of landless cottagers, the loss of the putting-out system, the loss of farmland and common land, the exploitation of a proletariat by the bourgeoisie, immense wealth being created for a very few, and a truly free market with no safety nets.

(B) A good answer will briefly explain how one of the following improved the conditions of the majority of the people during the era, such as, but not limited to: the Factory Act of 1833, the Mines Act of 1842, the Chadwick Commission that led to running water, Factory Act Extensions and Agricultural Gangs Acts of 1867, the reorganization of Paris and other cities, streetcars and other public transportation, zoning, the Ten Hours Act, German/Prussian child labor laws under Bismarck, reforms of Napoleon III, and the emergence of germ theory and modern medicine.

(C) A good answer will explain the impact of one of the following social developments, or one very much like them: increased class consciousness, increased gender divide, many children being raised without parents around, aid societies and poor houses, charities like soup kitchens, poverty cycles created, start of homelessness, temperance movement, increased betting and emphasis on sports, increased education, public schools, night classes for adults, increased socialization, and the emergence of romantic love as a justification for marriage.

Long-Essay Question Sample Answers and Explanations

QUESTION 1

Compare the methods used by Cavour and Bismarck in unifying their respective nations.

COMMENTS ON QUESTION 1

- Follow the "Simple Procedures" for writing an essay. (See page 35.)
- First, you must decide: *Which skill is being tested?* This is a COMPARE skill question, so be sure to describe similarities and differences between the paths and methods used by Bismarck and Cavour in uniting their respective nations, as well as explain them by providing specific examples of how they are similar and different at each phase of unification, and tying those differences to other historical developments such as the growing European feeling of nationalism, or the failure of the Concert of Europe after 1848.
- Second: *What does the question want to know?* The "compare" part of this question is relatively easy; the "contrast" part is more subtle.
- Third: *What do you know about it?* Both men headed the dominant states of the respective unions; both men used "power politics," realpolitik, diplomacy, perfected Machiavellian manipulations, and war—to gain their ends. Both viewed their roles with the kind of hardheaded realism that avoided romantic illusions about the processes and results of unification. Their contrasts: their domestic policies differed and their methods of "power politics" differed because of the different degrees of independent strength of their states. Bismarck could rely on "Blood and Iron" from his dominant army, while Cavour maneuvered among the giants, pitting one power against the other. Bismarck led his nation to become an international power to be reckoned with, while Cavour built Italy into a unified state that was still left as a minor power player in Europe.
- Finally: *How would you put it into words?* Use the question's basic structure of "contrast" and "compare" to develop your essay. Be sure to offer specifics to back up your generalizations.

SAMPLE ANSWER

The failure of the Revolutions of 1848 utilized a new diplomacy, "Power Politics," a very ungentlemanly and often ruthless application of the Machiavellian credo that "the end justifies the means." Camillo di Cavour and Otto von Bismarck became masters of the game and won the unification of two of Europe's regions that had not been unified autonomously for centuries. The methods in achieving unification that both Cavour of Italy and Bismarck of Germany used can be contrasted: One built up democracy at home, while the other suppressed it; one relied on the help of stronger nation-states, while the other conquered all opposition without outside help. Their methods can be compared in that they used deceit and war to achieve their ends.

Before 1861, Italy had been a well-defined geographic area due to its geographic nature as a peninsula, shaped like a boot, was made up of separate political entities, one of which was independent, most of which were dominated by the Austrian Empire, and all of which had long been battlegrounds in the struggle for hegemony by the larger nation-states of Europe. Before 1871, Germany was a conglomeration of nearly 40 fiercely independent states, and Prussia and Austria competed for economic and political dominance within that conglomeration.

Napoleon's battlefield successes in the early 1800s, and his consolidation in both regions, passed on the passion of nationalism to both the Italians and the Germans. It took the right timing, the gifted leadership of the heads of the two outstanding states of each region, and war to achieve national unification in both cases.

In the decade before unification, the Kingdom of Piedmont-Sardinia was the only independent state of Italy. Under Cavour, its prime minister, the state became a constitutional monarchy. It was modernized by a system of roads and railroads; it was industrialized; it was reformed by the abolition of all forms of manorialism, by the reduction of the influence of the Roman Catholic Church, and by the establishment of a strong parliament. It served as a model for liberal reform and was a leader in the movement for unification.

After joining in the Crimean War, mostly to gain the favor of Napoleon III, Cavour negotiated an alliance with him to act as the protector of Piedmont Sardinia against Austrian invasion in exchange for Nice and Savoy. Cavour then tricked Austria into declaring war: Austria was provoked into a declaration of war in 1859; Napoleon III kept his promise; the Austrians were defeated. This was "power politics" at its most ruthless and effective.

Then the bottom dropped out of the plan. Napoleon III made a separate peace with the Austrians because of opposition to the war in France and because of fear of the Prussians, who opposed French dominance in Italy. But revolutions in a number of other northern Italian states created governments whose electorates voted for union with Piedmont. Despite opposition from the Austrians and the pope, who lost territory in those revolutions, the Kingdom of Piedmont was recognized by a number of powerful European states.

Unification was completed when Giuseppe Garibaldi's Red Shirts conquered Sicily from its Bourbon rulers and then Naples. The former Kingdom of the Two Sicilies was joined with the expanded Kingdom of Piedmont-Sardinia, and in March 1861 Victor Emmanuel II became King of Italy. Venice joined after the Seven Weeks' War led to Austrian defeat in 1866, and Rome was the last piece to create a united modern Italy in 1871.

Prussia was the most modern and powerful of the German states. Referred to as "an army before it was a state," its efficient and fast-growing industry supported its influential military establishment. In 1862, the parliament voted down military appropriations, and King Wilhelm I appointed the tough-minded Junker, Otto von Bismarck, to deal with the crisis. Over the next several years, Bismarck's gap theory virtually wiped out parliamentary democracy in the country. He collected taxes over the protests of parliament, enlarged the army, and ignored the opposition. He and Prussia were ready to lead the battle for Germanic unification.

His "realpolitik" was similar to Cavour's power politics: He used deceit, intimidation, and insult to precipitate war with national unification the goal. First Bismarck gave his army a test run allied with Austria against Denmark in the Prussian-Danish War of 1863, which set up a doomed joint Austrian/Prussian administration of the conquered region. Bismarck nurtured a dispute between Prussia and Austria over the administration of this region and then tried to isolate Austria from potential allies, promising them territory. Austria managed to get the support of the German Confederation (most of the other independent states of the region), and in 1866 they went to war against Prussia, who was without allies.

In seven weeks, the well-led, well-equipped and well-trained Prussian army (the first army to use breech-loading rifles), defeated Austria and her allies. Deliberately moderating the terms of the peace treaty to gain German support for his next venture, Bismarck dissolved the old German Confederation (originally set up by Napoleon) and replaced it with the North German Confederation, a watered-down constitutional monarchy, made up of the bulk of the Germanic states and ruled by the Prussian King, but without the southern independent states of Bavaria, Saxony, and Wurttemberg.

Bismarck used the issue of the succession of a German to the Spanish throne to incite France into a war he could use to unite Germany. He even manipulated his own King by altering the Ems Telegram to enrage Napoleon III. Bismarck stirred up popular opinion in both Germany and France. In July 1870, France declared war on Prussia, meaning Bismarck had perfectly manipulated the politics to allow Prussia to seem to be attacked and thus prevented the intervention of other European powers while encouraging German sympathy for the cause.

Less than six months later, France was defeated, Napoleon was humiliated, and the remaining German states had joined the North German Confederation to form the German Empire. Both men used political genius and the manipulation of their own citizens and foreign powers to exploit the growing nationalism in Europe at the time as a method of unifying their nations. Both men knew that war must be employed to unite their people, and both were powerful ministers of monarchs who chose them to make better decisions than the monarchs could. Bismarck utilized much more force, both militarily and politically, than Cavour did, and created a nation that was a greater force in the world than Cavour's Italy. Cavour's and Bismarck's methods in unifying their countries can be contrasted with those of Hitler and Stalin, who used terror and mass murder as tools of the state to increase their power over their people and those of other nations and to extinguish all freedoms, including freedom of thought.

EVALUATE THE SAMPLE ANSWER

Now go back and look at the rubric. It is clear that this essay fulfills all of the requirements for a score 6 on the rubric. The essay answers all parts of the question thoroughly with concrete evidence, at length, with a well-balanced essay. The thesis is appropriate and gets the thesis point. The essay describes the similarities and differences and explains the historical significance of these developments through specific evidence, which means that it uses historical reasoning to explain relationships among the evidence presented. It also utilizes evidence to corroborate the argument, gaining both Evidence and both Analysis and Reasoning points. The essay explains how the unification of Germany and Italy fits into the context of Europe after the Revolutions of 1848 and the Napoleonic Wars, with specific examples of relevant evidence, and it utilizes those specific pieces of evidence to fully and effectively substantiate the thesis and other arguments, gaining the Contextualization point.

RATER'S COMMENTS ON THE SAMPLE ANSWER

6—Extremely Well Qualified

Not only does this essay contrast the methods of Cavour and Bismarck in unifying Italy and Germany by "showing differences," but it clearly compares their styles and means by "examining similarities." The introductory paragraphs lay out the structure of the argument. The essay then provides relevant historical background. The body of the essay demonstrates a scholarly, fact-based account of the methods of each man in operation. The conclusion sums up admirably.

Question 2

Assess the quote below. What ideas did both Adam Smith and Karl Marx draw upon in order to formulate their ideas? What were their conclusions and why were they so different?

COMMENTS ON QUESTION 2

- Follow the "Simple Procedures" for writing an essay. (See page 35.)
- First, you must decide: *Which skill is being tested?* This is a COMPARE skill question, so be sure to describe similarities and differences between the ideas of Adam Smith and Karl Marx and where each man's ideas came from, as well as explain them by providing specific examples of how they are similar and different and what each man saw that led to his conclusions, and tie those differences to other historical developments, such as the growing class consciousness, gaps in income, industrialization, urbanization, and consolidation.
- Second: *What does the question want to know?* This multifaceted question has many tasks. It may be good to list the tasks first. Who were Smith and Marx? What were their ideas? What were their similarities and differences? How did they form them? Does the quote apply? Why or why not? What were their conclusions and why were they so different?
- Third: *What do you know about it?* You need to know that these two men are the economic philosophers upon whom the economies of the nineteenth and twentieth centuries were based, capitalism and communism. You also need to know that they both based their ideas upon what they observed, and that the differences in what they concluded was in large part because of the different conditions that they observed, supporting the quote. While in these situations it is sometimes good to go against the direction that the test leads you, and try to disprove the quote, it is not recommended in this situation.
- Finally: *How would you put it into words?* One way to structure this essay is with thesis paragraphs: one paragraph on what Smith saw and read, one on what Marx saw and read, and one on why their conclusions were so different, followed by a concluding paragraph. It can also be done with a thesis, followed by one paragraph on the quote, one on both men's influences, and a third one on what their conclusions were and why those conclusions were so different, followed by a conclusion. That is the format used in the sample answer.

SAMPLE ANSWER

Adam Smith and Karl Marx are two men who changed the world immensely. Both were brilliant historians and philosophers due to their ability to synthesize the situations of their times, and both provided conclusions to help change society. The quote is clearly spot on because their conclusions differ greatly, due to the different times in which they lived, and their other different influences, such as the people they consorted with and the books that they read, yet have both changed the world immensely.

Both Smith and Marx were products of their time. Much of the reason that Smith and Marx were so influential was that both men were looking to assess the conditions that really existed and to discover what needed to be done in order to improve these conditions, thus proving the quote. Because of this, the people of their contemporary societies could relate to their ideals and beliefs. Smith arose as a wealthy Scotsman during the prime of the Commercial Revolution. The processes of proto-industrialization and land enclosure were reaping fine rewards for the entrepreneurs of the day. Smith observed this at the same time as the system of mercantilism and joint-stock companies rose. The ideas he was confronted with were those of early British entrepreneurship and rising wealth. Smith was influenced by principles of fair competition that were becoming popular during his time. François Quesnay, who opposed mercantilism and supported laissez-faire economics, was a particularly strong influence on Smith. These observations and ideas, along with the fact that he lived in the wealthiest nation in the world, Great Britain, shaped his conclusions that an invisible hand of self-interest controlled prices and wages as well as what was produced, and did so very well as long as the government did not interfere.

Marx, on the other hand, lived long enough after Smith to see the developing system of capitalism rear the ugly head of industrialization. He was a student of the French socialists, whose writings were popular in his time, and he was also strongly influenced by social science. The exploitation of the proletariat worker, and the trend of urbanization and industrialization, had led to the stratification of society and the gap between classes, which left Marx screaming for a revolution. In essence, Smith's and Marx's conclusions that capitalism was rapacious and would be replaced by a revolution of the abused working class, which would grow, were based upon what they observed and what they thought was the most efficient means of managing society, yet the varying historical perspectives and experiences of these men caused their conclusions to be so different.

The conclusions of Marx and Smith, while so different, both changed the world greatly. A major difference between the two men is that Smith saw self-interest as a positive thing, while Marx saw it as the downfall of society. Another major difference was that, due to history, Marx was more politically radical than Smith. While Smith institutionalized the idea of entrepreneurship, which had only been recently realized through the Protestant idea of the work ethic to that point, he never creamed his ideas of laissez-faire would be used to rebel against economic control and taxation, or be part of the causes of the American and French Revolutions. The first movements toward representative governments and political freedom also sprang from the ideas of laissez-faire. Smith gave the entrepreneur a voice in a time when international trade was growing and economies were developing. On the other hand, Marx fomented revolution in the name of the worker, justice, and efficiency.

Although both men came to vastly different conclusions, they transformed industrial and postindustrial society. In the end, Smith and Marx were both great thinkers, who based their ideas on what they saw around them, and due to their difference in experiences, their ideas clashed greatly. While currently, no part of the world uses Smith's style of capitalism, and no country uses Marxist communism, the ideas and worldviews of both men have been highly influential in the establishment of economic systems and social movements. They were both extremely successful at "getting to the bottom" of the societies that created them and analyzing the human condition as best they could.

EVALUATE THE SAMPLE ANSWER

Now go back and look at the rubric. It is clear that this essay fulfills all of the requirements for a score 6 on the rubric. The essay answers all parts of the question thoroughly with concrete evidence, at length, with a well-balanced essay. The thesis is appropriate and gets the thesis point. The essay clearly describes the similarities and differences and explains the reasons for these similarities and differences with specific evidence utilizing historical reasoning to explain the relationships among evidence provided. It also corroborates and modifies an argument that addresses the entirety of the question by explaining how both men changed the world. Together, these qualities earn both Evidence and both Analysis and Reasoning points. The argument addresses the similarities and differences between Smith's and Marx's views, citing specific, relevant evidence and utilizing those specific pieces of evidence to substantiate the thesis and other arguments fully and effectively. The extra concrete support draws on appropriate ideas and methods from different fields of inquiry and the political and social implications as well as the economic ones.

RATER'S COMMENTS ON THE SAMPLE ANSWER

6—Highly Qualified

This is a strong essay with a strong thesis. This essay answers all parts of the question with historic insight and support. It is well-crafted and explores qualities of each man in many paragraphs rather than in the simpler format of one paragraph per man and a third about their differences and why. All topics were covered thoroughly, and the explanation was strong.

The essay would have been stronger if it had mentioned Hegel, Proudhon, and other writers who had a strong influence on Marx. The eras of Enlightenment versus Romanticism could also have been examined as a way to tie to other historical periods and be certain of a 6.

Time Period Four: c. 1914 to Present

KEY CONCEPTS AND OVERVIEW

KEY CONCEPT 4.1 Total war and political instability in the first half of the twentieth century gave way to a polarized state order during the Cold War and eventually to efforts at transnational union.

KEY CONCEPT 4.2 The stresses of economic collapse and total war engendered internal conflicts within European states and created conflicting conceptions of the relationship between the individual and the state, as demonstrated in the ideological battle between liberal democracy, communism, and Fascism.

KEY CONCEPT 4.3 During the twentieth century, diverse intellectual and cultural movements questioned the existence of objective knowledge, the ability of reason to arrive at truth, and the role of religion in determining moral standards.

KEY CONCEPT 4.4 Demographic changes, economic growth, total war, disruptions of traditional social patterns, and competing definitions of freedom and justice altered the experiences of everyday life.

TIME PERIOD OVERVIEW

This time period is the twentieth century and the early twenty-first century. It was defined by the total-war military policy of the First and Second World Wars, as well as by the efforts toward diplomacy and European unity that followed the Cold War. The twentieth century was characterized by large-scale suffering brought on by warfare and genocide, but there also were tremendous improvements in the standard of living. The rise and fall of communism in Europe is examined in this unit, from the Russian Revolution through the fall of the Berlin Wall and until the conflicts in Ukraine in 2014 and 2015, including the effects of the rise and fall of the Soviet Union, which weigh heavily on European history. Likewise, the rise and fall of other ideologies of the twentieth century, such as of Fascism, must be examined to understand the era. The primacy of economic life in Europe becomes apparent in this time period, with the Great Depression and many European responses to it, creating the true modern welfare state. The peak of imperialism in the years just before the First World War and then its decline after the Second World War are also important forces to be examined. The marginalization of minorities and then their recognition after the Second World War is also of note. The ideological conflict known as the Cold War was a central theme of this period and must be examined in detail. Crucial to understanding this time period are the movements both toward and away from unity within Europe, culminating in the creation of the Eurozone. This time period includes the traditional delineations of the following:

The First World War
The Russian Revolution
The Age of Anxiety, or Interwar Years
The Second World War
Decolonization, Recovery, and Cold War
Modern Europe

These traditional delineations do overlap in many ways, and the themes within them, as stated above in the key concepts, can be seen woven through the next three chapters of this book.

The First World War, and the Russian Revolution and the USSR Until 1939

10

KEY TERMS/PEOPLE

- → FIRST WORLD WAR
- → SCHLIEFFEN PLAN
- → GALLIPOLI CAMPAIGN
- → *LUSITANIA*
- → THE FOURTEEN POINTS
- → TREATY OF VERSAILLES
- → COMMAND ECONOMY
- → WALTER RATHENAU
- → RUSSIAN REVOLUTION AND USSR
- → ALEXANDER III
- → CONSTITUTIONAL DEMOCRATS (KADET)
- → VLADIMIR LENIN

- → REVOLUTION OF 1905
- → CZAR NICHOLAS II
- → OCTOBER MANIFESTO
- → BLOODY SUNDAY
- → ALEXANDER KERENSKY
- → RASPUTIN
- → MARCH REVOLUTION
- → DICTATORSHIP OF THE PROLETARIAT
- → FIVE-YEAR PLANS
- → FARM COLLECTIVIZATION
- → COMMUNES
- → THE PURGE TRIALS

OVERVIEW

The beginning of the First World War marked the height of European power on this planet; its ending marked the beginning of the decline. Great empires fell in this war: the Russian, Austro-Hungarian, German, and Ottoman. Others (Britain and France), which had reached the zenith of imperialist expansion by 1914, saw their economies all but extinguished by 1918. A generation of young European men was decimated in the trenches of France, on the plains of Eastern Europe, and on other global battlefronts.

It was the first "total war," involving mass civilian populations in a war effort that required rationing, employed both sexes in war plants, and pumped up popular fervor with distorted propaganda.

Narrow nationalism flourished with the fall of the old ethnically diverse empires when dominant ethnic groups formed the basis for smaller nation-states such as Yugoslavia, Czechoslovakia, Austria, and Hungary. The triumph of communism in Russia was a direct result of the war; Fascism in Italy and Nazism in Germany were indirect results. The drain of Europe's resources made the United States the world's leading creditor and greatest producer, and the unresolved issues of the vindictive and haphazard peace process led inevitably to the Second World War.

Meanwhile, Czarist Russia had been in decline for some time. Defeats in foreign wars tended to lead to domestic reform in Russia, and the losses in Crimea in 1856 and against Japan in 1905 led to massive change, such as the slow emancipation of the serfs and the creation of the Duma, a Russian legislature. The brutal exploitation of rural peasants under feudal serfdom changed to oppression of industrial workers in factories, which led many to call for another way.

The Revolution of 1917 began as an attempt at reform by the middle class and some enlightened nobles. When the moderates maintained Russia's unpopular involvement in the war, the radical Marxist Bolsheviks seized power and established the communist regime that would change the politics of the twentieth century.

EVENTS LEADING TO THE FIRST WORLD WAR

June 28, 1914: Archduke Francis Ferdinand, heir to the Austrian throne, was assassinated along with his wife in Sarajevo, capital of the Austrian province of Bosnia and Herzogovina.

- When evidence was uncovered that high Serbian officials had plotted the murder, Austria sought German support to crush Serbia.
- Kaiser Wilhelm issued the infamous *blank check*, promising backing for any action Austria might take.
- Serbia turned to "big brother" Slav, Russia, which in turn got a guarantee of French support against Germany and Austria in a similar *blank check*.

July 23, 1914: Austria presented an ultimatum to Serbia that would make Serbia a virtual protectorate of Austria.

July 28, 1914: Austria declared war on Serbia after pronouncing the Serbian response inadequate. Russia mobilized.

August 1, 1914: Germany declared war on Russia.

August 3, 1914: France declared war on Germany.

August 4, 1914: Britain declared war on Germany after German forces violated Belgium's neutrality in their campaign to invade France.

THE FIRST WORLD WAR

The Combatants

> *The Allies:* Britain, France, and Russia (1914), formerly the Triple Entente.
> > Italy (1915)
> > United States (1917)
> > Russia out (1917)
> *The Central Powers:* Germany, Austria-Hungary, and the Ottoman Empire.
> > Bulgaria

The Western Front

August–September 1914: Germany's *Schlieffen Plan* for a rapid invasion of France failed. Since a *war of attrition* (wearing down of the resources and morale of the enemy) was to Germany's disadvantage because of the superior land mass, resources, and population of its enemies, Germany aimed for a quick victory.

THE STRATEGY OF THE SCHLIEFFEN PLAN

1. Defeat France in six weeks, as in the Franco-Prussian War.
2. Hold off Russia, which the German high command estimated would take six months to fully mobilize.
3. Invade France through neutral Belgium, by being granted access, in order to outflank the French armies and seize Paris.

WHY THE SCHLIEFFEN PLAN FAILED

1. The Belgians protested and put up unexpectedly stiff resistance.
2. The Russians mobilized with great speed, drawing German forces to the Eastern Front to bolster the Austrians in the field.
3. The French counterattacked heroically at the *Battle of the Marne* River (September 5, 1914) to stop the German drive to Paris.

THE WESTERN FRONT STALEMATED INTO TRENCH WARFARE

1. The trench lines extended from the North Sea coast to the border of Switzerland in the South.
2. The bloody, costly fighting, after the Battle of the Marne, achieved no significant breakthrough for either side.
3. Technological developments in weaponry were far in advance of the infantry tactics:

   - Machine guns
   - Poison gas
   - Submarines
   - Barbed wire
   - Mass artillery
   - Tanks
   - Aerial strafing
   - Bombing from aircraft

4. The result was the slaughter of a generation of young Western Europeans in the trenches of France and Flanders (region of Northern France and parts of Belgium).
5. The *Battle of the Somme*, July–November 1916, typified this stalemate and was one of the bloodiest battles in world history, with over 1,200,000 soldiers killed or wounded; the *Battle of Verdun* lasted through most of 1916 and is another example where fixed fortifications failed at a cost of 700,000 casualties. The fortifications at Verdun were supposedly impenetrable, but the Germans annihilated the fortress and the surrounding area, proving the futility of fixed fortifications in the modern era.

   - The Battle of the Somme lasted from July until November 1916 and saw changes of territory amounting to only 125 square miles.

The Eastern Front Remained a Mobile War

1914: German forces, under *Paul von Hindenburg* (1847–1934) (later a president of the postwar Weimar Republic) and Erich Ludendorff won important victories over the Russians.

- The Russians pushed the Austrians out of Galicia (Western Poland).

1915: A year of Central Powers' successes.

- Combined German-Austrian forces pushed the Russian forces out of Poland and inflicted awesome casualties.

- Bulgaria entered the war on Germany's side (Germany and its allies became known as the Central Powers).
- The Germans overran the Balkans.
- The British launched the *Gallipoli Campaign* to knock the Ottoman Empire (Turkey), which had joined the Central Powers, out of the war by landing at the Dardanelles, a vital control point for access between the Aegean and Black Seas.

  - This campaign failed as the Ottomans drove back the combined British, Indian, and Australian troops and held the straits.

1916: The Germans pushed deep into Russian territory.

- Czar Nicholas II went to the front to take personal command of the troops in a conflict in which Russia was being outfought and outproduced.

  - The Russians were still using single-shot rifles that had to be reloaded after each shot while the Germans used machine guns.
  - Millions of Russians—soldiers and civilians—were slaughtered or starved in this war.
  - Nicholas was no help, and he was now personally responsible for the ongoing defeat of his army by the Germans, who continued to advance.
  - The people of Russia wanted peace and food.

- The Gallipoli Campaign failed, and its planner, future British prime minister Winston Churchill (1874–1965), resigned his post as First Lord of the Admiralty, in charge of the navy.

1917: The Russians retreated and the war spread.

- The Russian czar abdicated in March; the provincial government under Alexander Kerensky (1881–1970) continued the war.
- The Bolsheviks seized power in November and eventually pulled Russia out of the war.
- The Russian withdrawal from the war was exactly what the Allies did not want.
- This left Germany with only one front on which to fight, but the United States had joined the Allies just before Russia pulled out of the war, somewhat balancing the loss of Russia as an ally.
- If Russia had stayed in the war, the Central Powers could have been defeated sooner.
- The Japanese, who had joined the Allies, attacked parts of China in a bid for colonial territory and natural resources.
- Near the end of the war Turkish forces slaughtered around a million Armenian civilians in what is becoming widely termed the *Armenian Genocide.*

  - Difficult to rule a multi-ethnic empire.
  - Accusations of disloyalty during the First World War added to this slaughter.

Waging the War

The First World War was the twentieth century's first *Total War*, whereby the entire civilian populations of the belligerent nations were mobilized for winning the war.

- Propaganda lionized the men at the front and dehumanized the enemy.
- News was censored.

- Economic production was focused on the war effort:

  - Women replaced male factory workers who now were in uniform.
  - Rationing of food and scarce commodities was instituted.
  - People financed the war by buying bonds.
  - Each side aimed at "starving out" the enemy by cutting off vital supplies to the civilian population.

- The war in Europe quickly spread to non-European theaters, transforming the war into a global conflict.

  - The *Arab Revolt* against the Turks in 1916 was exploited by the British, specifically by their agent, T. E. Lawrence, who fought with the Arabs against the Turks from within the Ottoman Empire, eventually leading to British claims on the mandate of Palestine.
  - The Japanese used the war as an excuse for imperialism on the Chinese mainland and elsewhere in the Pacific.
  - Hundreds of thousands of colonial soldiers from Africa and Asia were used by both sides during this war.

Naval Blockades

1. Britain used its superior fleet and sea mines to cut off the Central Powers from overseas trade.
2. Germany employed *unrestricted submarine warfare* to prevent the British from getting vital materials from their colonies and war supplies from the United States.

   - The sinking of the British passenger ship *Lusitania* in May 1915, with many American passengers, helped turn U.S. public opinion against Germany.
   - (Note: There is strong evidence to suggest that the *Lusitania* was carrying contraband munitions, as the Germans claimed.)

Diplomacy

1915: Neutral Italy entered the war against the Central Powers (its former allies) with the promise of being given *Italia Irredenta* (unredeemed Italy) and some German colonies and Ottoman territories.

1917: The infamous *Zimmermann Note* promised Mexico some of its former American holdings if it entered the war on Germany's side against the United States.

- Arabs and Jews in Palestine were promised autonomy if they joined the Allies.
- Eastern Europeans were promised ethnic control in return for support of the Allies.

The End of the War

Although the United States had only a small standing army when the war began, it was able to field nine divisions in France by the summer of 1918, in time to help halt the last major offensive of the exhausted German army. The effects of military stalemate and Total War induced the citizens, both military and civilian, to protest and turn to insurrection in the belligerent nations eventually leading to revolutions that changed the international balance of power.

By the fall of 1918, Bulgaria and Turkey had sued for peace, Austria-Hungary had collapsed, and Germany was wracked with revolution. The Kaiser abdicated and fled to neutral Holland, and a provisional German government requested negotiations on the basis of U.S. President Wilson's *Fourteen Point peace plan*.

On the eleventh hour of the eleventh day of the eleventh month of 1918, an *armistice* ended the First World War.

> **NOTE**
>
> More people died in the influenza epidemic, called the Spanish Flu, that followed the war than died in the war itself—10 million died in combat and nearly 20 million from the disease, yet it was still the bloodiest war the world had ever seen.

THE PEACE SETTLEMENTS

The Fourteen Points: Wilson's peace plan, which was never implemented because of the secret treaties and diplomatic maneuvering that had taken place among the Allies before the entrance of the United States in the war.

1. End to secret treaties
2. Freedom of the seas
3. Free trade
4. Arms reduction
5. Just settlement of colonial claims
6-13. Evacuation of occupied territories *and* national self-determination
14. Establishment of a League of Nations: an international political organization to settle disputes

> **NOTE**
>
> Ironically, even though it was Wilson's creation, the United States never joined the League. It was largely ineffectual, for this and other reasons, in dealing with the aggressive dictatorships of the 1930s.

The Paris Peace Conference, January 1919

The Big Three—Woodrow *Wilson* of the United States, David Lloyd *George* (1863–1945) of Britain, and Georges *Clemenceau* (1841–1929) of France made all the decisions. Italian Vittorio *Orlando* was also a leader of the conference at its beginning. But he left, upset that Italy was not getting the gains he had hoped for when his country joined the war on the Allied side.

- The Central Powers were excluded.
- The Fourteen Points were compromised.
- Nationality lines in Central and Eastern Europe were blurred.

The *Treaty of Versailles* ended the war with Germany but **never settled** the explosive issues that had led to war in the first place. *Many of its provisions provided grist for Nazi propaganda mills in the 1920s and 1930s.*

PROVISIONS OF THE TREATY OF VERSAILLES

1. Certain German territories were ceded to the Allies (such as Alsace to France, Schleswig to Denmark, West Prussia to Poland, control of the mineral-rich Saar region to France), and German overseas colonies were distributed among the Allies.
2. Germany was blamed for starting the war in the infamous "war guilt" clause, article 231.
3. The German army and navy were severely cut back to 100,000 servicemen.
4. The Rhineland (the vital strip between France and Germany) was to be demilitarized and occupied by Allied troops.
5. The *League of Nations* was created to intervene in international disputes and prevent future wars. It was a weak organization, and the United States never joined.
6. Germany had to pay *indemnities* for the civilian damage done in the war, totaling $33 billion. That is over $500 billion when adjusted for inflation to 2014 dollars.

THE CAUSES, EVENTS, AND RESULTS OF THE FIRST WORLD WAR

Causes of the First World War

- Historians generally agree that the German military buildup and the personal will of Kaiser Wilhelm II to use his new military, especially his navy, helped cause this war.

  - His offer to Austria to pay any war reparations if they were defeated also helps historians perceive the immediate causes of the war in this light.

- Events leading to the war include the Balkan Wars, the assassination of Archduke Franz Ferdinand and his wife, and increased conflict and bickering over colonial holdings, such as the *Fashoda Incident* and the *Boer War*.
- Sidney Bradshaw Fay and Henry Elmer Barnes stated that the First World War was inevitable, and blame rested on all the nations equally.
- They blamed Austria-Hungary and Serbian nationalism (Gavrilo Princip's assassination of Archduke Franz Ferdinand and his wife) as short-term causes.
- They saw the long-term causes as militarism (arms race and economic rivalry), the alliance system, imperialism, and nationalism (*MAIN*).
- This view was accepted and led to the Treaty of Versailles not being fully enforced against Germany, which may have helped lead to the Second World War.
- German historian *Franz Fischer* refuted the now classic view stated above, using German secret documents as evidence in 1961. "He believed that Germany did not will and covet the Austro-Serbian war."
- Fischer said Germany was worried about Russia; Germany's growing ambitions for colonies and more territory in Europe, and its attempt to distract the socialist menace at home, all led to the First World War.

Events of the First World War

- The war quickly became a global conflict, with the colonial empires of all belligerent nations becoming involved to some degree or another.
- This war was fought by people who lived on six continents.
- The Germans quickly advanced on Paris, but the *Battle of the Marne* stopped them before they could take the French capital.

- Both sides built miles of parallel trenches, leading to a stalemate in which battle after battle saw each side attempt to break through the enemies' lines.
- At the *Battle of Verdun*, the Germans again tried to break through, leading to over 700,000 killed and wounded.
- The *Battle of the Somme* was the Allied counterattack, costing over 1,200,000 casualties (killed, wounded, and missing) for no clear gain.
- The Eastern Front saw Germany destroy the Russian army and that loss led to the abdication of the czar and the eventual Russian Revolution.
- Led to the Russian Revolution.
- In the only major naval engagement, the *Battle of Jutland*, the German navy failed to break through the British naval blockade and from then on resorted to submarine warfare, which drew in the United States.
- American involvement decided the outcome of the war due to the productive capacity of the United States, which escaped warfare at home.
- Revolutions overthrew monarchies in Russia, Germany, Austria, and the Ottoman Empire, resulting in each one pulling out of the war or calling for an armistice.

Results of the War

- The war cost over $300 billion. That is over $4.5 trillion in 2014 dollars when adjusted for inflation.
- The Russian, German, Austrian, and Ottoman Empires ended.
- The war strained the resources of all the belligerents as they experimented with command economies.
- National unity was reinforced for a time, but also caused great hardship due to lack of supplies, to disruption and dislocation.
- The war contributed greatly to the increased involvement of the government in society, leading to increased propaganda.
- The war also contributed to women's suffrage.
- Many social customs faded out, and society became more open (at least for a time).
- There was also a rapid development of new technology.
- The economy was greatly hurt by the war, as world trade had been totally disrupted, changed to a wartime economy, and then had to transition back.
- The Russian Revolution put the world's first communist country on the map.
- A patchwork of weak, ethnically mixed states was created for political conveniences in Central and Eastern Europe.

  - New nations such as *Poland*, *Czechoslovakia*, *Hungary*, and *Yugoslavia* were created in Europe as a result of the *Treaty of Versailles*.

- The German and Ottoman colonial possessions were divided up between France and Great Britain, and the *British mandate system* was imposed in the areas Britain controlled.

  - This mandate system disturbed the balance of power.
  - Remains a factor today in the unrest in the Middle East, where the bulk of these territories were located.
  - Made worse by the presence of oil there and by historical Western support for dictatorial regimes there.

- Turkey modernized, and Kamal Ataturk created a secular democracy in Turkey that endured for over a century; Turkey has been literally and figuratively a bridge between Europe and Asia.

  - In the 1990s a suspension bridge between the continents was built in Istanbul, and one can travel from Asia to Europe and back without leaving Turkey.

- Over 25 million people died as a result of the war, and another 21 million soldiers were wounded, leaving a generation grieving after losing many of their best leaders.

The Second World War broke out in Europe 20 years after the signing of the Treaty of Versailles.

THE RUSSIAN REVOLUTION AND THE SOVIET UNION UNTIL 1939

Chronology

1881–1894

Czar Alexander III (r. 1881–1894), reacting to the assassination of his predecessor by radical socialists, instituted a reactionary policy of "Russification, orthodoxy, and autocracy."

1890s

Russia industrialized, but the great mass of its population was still made up of rural peasants whose quality of life was comparable to that of farmers in the West during the Middle Ages.

- Since the French were eager for Russian support against the Germans, they granted loans and credits that enabled the Russians to build factories, import Western technology, and expand the railroad system.
- The *Trans-Siberian Railroad* linked European and Asiatic Russia.
- A commercial middle class grew in influence.
- A proletariat of exploited workers also grew.
- Political parties were formed to meet the demands of these new elements.

  - *Constitutional Democrats (Kadets)* reflected the aims of the new middle class and some liberal landowners for parliamentary government and gradual reform.
  - Social Revolutionaries (Narodniks) stressed the glories of Slav culture (Slavophiles) and sought to keep Russia agrarian.
  - *Marxists* urged radical revolution.

1903

A meeting of the Russian Marxist Congress resulted in a split in the party when *Vladimir I. Lenin* (1870–1924) favored a party of elite revolutionaries instead of an open democratic organization.

- When most of the attendees walked out in protest, Lenin convinced those remaining to endorse his ideas.
- Although his supporters made up a minority of the party, he called them *Bolsheviks* (majority) and referred to the actual party majority as Mensheviks (minority).

1904–1905

The Russo-Japanese War: Competing over Manchuria (a mineral rich province of China), Russia and newly modernized Japan came to blows.

- What the czar hoped would be a "short, glorious war" to divert unrest in his realm was a devastating defeat, the first in modern times of a European power by a nation outside of Europe.

  - A surprise attack on the Russian fleet at Port Arthur in Manchuria, a defeat at the Battle of Mukden on Manchurian soil, and the sinking of the Russian European fleet in Tsushima Straits brought a peace mediated by President *Theodore Roosevelt*.
  - The Treaty of Portsmouth granted Japan Russia's railroad rights in Manchuria, half of the Sakhalin Islands off Russia's Pacific coast, and a guarantee of Japan's protectorate in Korea.
  - Humiliated, Russia suffered from the Revolution of 1905 before the war was even over.

- *The Revolution of 1905:* Faced with the growing unrest of the working class, *Czar Nicholas II* (r. 1894–1918) commissioned a Russian Orthodox priest, *Father Gapon*, to organize a conservative union to counteract the radical Marxists.

  - Gapon, horrified by the conditions in St. Petersburg (the czarist capital), led a peaceful protest march of tens of thousands of workers and their families on Sunday, January 22, 1905.
  - Troops fired on the crowd, killing hundreds. This "Bloody Sunday" provoked general strikes, peasant uprisings, and the formation of workers' revolutionary councils, *soviets*.
  - In the *Zemstvos* (the provincial councils elected by landowners and peasants and set up in 1864 by Czar Alexander II (1818–1881) as part of his great reforms), the liberals demanded reforms.
  - The *October Manifesto*: After a general strike was called by the Soviet of Petersburg, Nicholas II issued a promise for reform.

- Its major provisions were a constitution, civil liberties, and a Duma (legislature) to represent all classes.

1906

A Duma was elected, but did not include the Marxists, who boycotted the elections because they mistrusted the czar's motives.

- Nicholas dissolved the Duma anyway because it demanded that his ministers be answerable to it.
- Reforms were instituted, including the strengthening of the Zemstvos, abolishing the peasant debt for the emancipation of serfs in the 1860s, and thereby creating a wealthy peasant class, the *kulaks*, who farmed large tracts of land and hired workers.

1914

With the outbreak of the First World War, the government suspended the Duma so that political bickering would not compromise the war effort.

- A national union of *Zemstvos*, made up of the various local elective districts, was organized to increase productivity
- *Rasputin* (1869–1916), "the mad monk," began to influence *Czarina Alexandra* after he claimed to have cured the czar's only son of hemophilic episodes.

1915

Horrific losses at the front provoked the national union of Zemstvos and the middle class to demand that the Duma be reconvened to initiate reforms.

1916

The Duma met for the first time since its disbanding and, with support of its dominant conservatives, criticized the czar's government.

- Rasputin, whose sway over Alexandra had poisoned her advice to her easily influenced husband, was murdered by a band of young noblemen.
- The czar attempted to suppress any reform.

1917

The March Revolution: Food riots broke out in Petrograd (St. Petersburg), and when the czar ordered the Duma to dissolve and troops to suppress the disorder, neither obeyed.

- Workers and soldiers in Petrograd organized the radical legislative bodies called soviets.

  - Rebellion spread throughout the country and to the troops at the front.
  - Soldiers deserted by tens of thousands.

- On March 14, the Duma formed a provisional government under *Prince Georgii Lvov* (1861–1925).
- *Alexander Kerensky* (1881–1970), a moderate member of the soviet, played a major role in running the *Provisional Government.*
- On March 15, the czar abdicated.
- On March 17, Russia was proclaimed a republic.
- *Lenin* and other *Bolshevik* leaders came back from exile to Petrograd in April.

  - Their demands to the provisional government:

    1. Russia withdraw from the war.
    2. The Petrograd Soviet runs the government.
    3. Land was to be distributed to the peasants, and factories were to be controlled by the workers' committees (soviets).

- After an abortive coup in July, Lenin and the Bolshevik leaders fled to Finland.
- Prince Lvov turned over the provisional government to Kerensky.

The October Revolution (November 1917 by the Western calendar).

- Kerensky's government failed to win the support of the people because of continued shortages and because it stayed in the war against the Central Powers.
- Lenin returned to Petrograd with the rallying cry of "Peace, Land, Bread."
- *Leninist Doctrine:* According to orthodox Marxism, a social revolution is possible only in highly developed capitalist countries, such as those in the West during this period.

  - Since Russia was virtually a feudal society and primarily agrarian, some Bolsheviks argued for a coalition with the middle classes until Russia had developed sufficiently.
  - Lenin argued that since Western Europe was ripe for revolution, a Marxist seizure of Russia would precipitate such takeovers elsewhere, and these in turn would help Russia to bypass the capitalist stage.
  - Lenin won the support of Leon Trotsky (1870–1940), Joseph Stalin (1878–1953), and most of the Bolshevik leaders.

- *October 6–7:* The Bolsheviks stormed the *Winter Palace*, headquarters of Kerensky's government, and seized other key centers in Petrograd.

  - Kerensky's provisional government fled.
  - The Congress of Soviets, representing the local soviets, formed all over Russia.
  - Established a Council of People's Commissars.

- Lenin as head, Trotsky as foreign minister, and Stalin as nationalities minister.

  - Within months, the government abolished the freely elected legislative assembly and established a secret police organization, the Cheka, also variously known later as the OGPU, NKVD, MVD, and KGB.

1918

The Dictatorship of the Proletariat was proclaimed, in tune with Leninist doctrine; the Bolsheviks renamed their party "Communist."

- Important industries were nationalized.
- Russian Orthodox Church lands were seized.
- Russia pulled out of World War I, surrendering Latvia, Lithuania, Estonia, Poland, and the Ukraine to Germany in the *Treaty of Brest-Litovsk*.

1918–1922

The *Russian Civil War* was fought for control of the remainder of the Russian Empire.

- Opposed by czarists, the middle class, many peasants, and socialist factions, the communists were able to win because their enemies could not unite.
- Despite the intervention of many Allied nations, including the United States, which feared the spread of communism, the Red Army under Trotsky conquered European Russia by the end of 1920 and Siberia and central Asia by 1922.
- The Communist International (Comintern), to organize Communism worldwide, was organized in 1919.

- Lenin also began to institute policies designed to improve economic conditions in the new Soviet Union and rebuild the damage caused by the First World War and the Russian Civil War.

  - Plan was called Lenin's *New Economic Policy* (NEP).

- Allowed peasants some autonomy in selling their own goods.
- State controlled all banks, foreign trade, and large industrial projects.
- Private ownership of some small enterprises allowed.

1922

Nationalities Reform: What remained of the Russian Empire was reorganized into the Union of Soviet Socialist Republics (USSR), uniting the various nation groups into a federal entity of major republics and smaller autonomous regions. Cultural identity was encouraged and toleration of various ethnic groups became official policy.

1924

The Constitution:

1. Only workers and peasants are allowed to vote for local soviets.
2. Local soviets elect provincial or district soviets that, in turn, choose a republic soviet for each autonomous republic.
3. The *Congress of Soviets* represents all the republics and elects a *Council of People's Commissars* (similar to a government cabinet).

Lenin died at the age of fifty-four, never fully recovering from an assassination attempt in 1920.

- Trotsky was at a disadvantage in becoming Lenin's successor both because he was a Jew in an anti-Semitic society, and because he was considered an intellectual by the rank and file.
- As secretary of the Communist Party, Stalin garnered loyalty within the party by making many key appointments.
- Their policy differences further alienated the men from each other.

  - Trotsky pushed for a worldwide revolution.
  - Stalin argued for a strengthening of Russia by industrialization before it undertook the promotion of worldwide revolution.

    - "Building socialism in one country."

1927

- Stalin won the support of the party.
- Trotsky fled the country.

  - Murdered in 1940 by a Stalinist agent.

1928

The first *Five-Year Plan* promoted rapid industrialization by centralized planning.

- Coal and steel production were accelerated, and a modern transportation system was developed, using the domestic resources of the USSR, since foreign nations were hostile to the new government.

EARLY 1930s

- *Farm collectivization* consolidated small farms into *communes*, modernizing agriculture but displacing many peasants, some of whom resisted the process.
- The *kulaks*, who had been the most successful peasant farmers, were destroyed as a class.

  - Between 5 and 12 million people perished by murder and famine.
  - Most deaths were in the Ukraine.

1933

A second Five-Year Plan was begun that increased production of steel and heavy industry, modernized Soviet factories, created a boom when the West was in the depths of the *Great Depression*, and made Russia a leading industrial power.

1936–1937

The purge trials: Stalin's paranoid tendencies convinced him of plots within the party and the government to unseat him. Many original Bolsheviks, instrumental in carrying out the revolution, as well as high military officers (some of the most competent), were tried on trumped-up charges.

- As many as 1 million were executed.
- 5 to 7 million were sent to the gulags (Siberian labor camps), where many died.
- Stalin strengthened his hold over the party, the government, and the nation.
- Became one of the century's most powerful dictators.

FIGURES AND EVENTS OF THE RUSSIAN REVOLUTION

Figure	When	Important Facts

Czar Alexander II	1861	■ He emancipated the serfs because:
		  – He felt pressure from below.
		  – It was his personal will.
		  – He needed to react to the loss of the Crimean War.
		■ He began the process of emancipation in 1861.
		■ His assassination in 1881 moved Russia to the right.

Czar Nicholas II	1894–1917	■ The last czar of Russia, he was a better family man than he was a ruler.
		■ Major weaknesses:
		  – His devotion to his German wife, Alexandra, and their children.
		  – His lack of interest in affairs of state from an early age.
		  – His familial responsibilities to his cousins, George V, ruling England, and Wilhelm II, ruling Germany.

Russo-Japanese War	1904–1905	■ Russia was humiliated when its attempt to take parts of China was foiled by Japan, which defeated the Russian navy twice, leaving her without a functioning fleet. ■ This led to the Revolution of 1905 and the creation of the Duma, Russia's legislative body.
Father Gapon/ *Bloody Sunday*	1905	■ A priest, who was state-appointed to help emancipated serfs adjust to their new lives; he circulated a workers' petition to the czar that was considered revolutionary. ■ Over 200,000 people marched on the Winter Palace in St. Petersburg to present the petition to the czar, but troops opened fire, killing many.
Peter Stolypin	1905–1911	■ He oversaw the creation of the Duma as prime minister to Nicholas II. ■ His agrarian reforms were very unpopular, and he was assassinated in 1911.
Gregori Rasputin	1905–1916	■ He was a peasant-born mystic healer whom Alexandra believed helped keep the sickly Alexei alive. ■ His debauchery was legendary and rumors of his influence on the Romanov family helped lead to their downfall.
First World War	1914–1918	■ Russia entered the First World War in 1914 to play its traditional role as protector of the Eastern Orthodox faith, this time in defense of Serbia. ■ Russia was not industrialized enough to be prepared for this war, for which Germany and England had been arming. ■ Russia was decimated by the Germans, and even though Nicholas II took personal control of the army, they still lost, leading to his abdication in 1917. ■ The Provisional Government was committed to staying in the war, and Lenin used that to help overthrow it in the October Revolution.

Figure	When	Important Facts
Alexander Kerensky	1917	■ He was the leader of the Provisional Government formed in March 1917, when Nicholas II abdicated. ■ He and his popular Kadet (Social Democrat) Party fought for land reform while he kept the war going as a middle ground in contrast to the Bolsheviks, who wanted to end the war immediately.
General Kornilov	1914–1918	■ He was an important First World War general who stayed loyal to Kerensky as his commander in chief. ■ Described as having the "heart of a lion and the brains of a sheep." ■ He led the White Army during the Russian Civil War in which he was captured and killed.
Vladimir Ilyich Lenin	1917–1924	■ Father of the Russian Revolution. ■ He was the Russian Bolshevik leader who was banished in 1903 and convinced the Germans to allow him back into the country in 1917. ■ He promised the people "Peace, land, and bread," and won them over to his side. ■ He used the Soviets in each town and the educated elite to foment revolution among the masses. ■ This new take on Marxism led to a successful revolution placing him in power of the world's first communist nation, the Union of Soviet Socialist Republics (USSR), after a brutal civil war.
Leon Trotsky	1917–1924	■ He was Lenin's co-conspirator in the Revolution. ■ He helped issue **Army Order Number 1** in which companies voted whether or not to follow commands. ■ He also took over the military and the train stations during the October Revolution that placed Lenin in power. ■ He was pushed out by Joseph Stalin, who created a completely totalitarian regime in Russia and eventually had Trotsky killed in Mexico.
Joseph Stalin	1924–1953	■ He ruled the USSR with an iron fist. ■ He instituted **five-year plans** to modernize and industrialize while purging his nation of supposed enemies. ■ Between ruining the agricultural output, causing starvation, and authorizing political imprisonment and killings, it is estimated that Stalin killed more than 50 million of his citizens. ■ He did, however, rally his people to defeat the German invasion during the Second World War. ■ His actions and lack of trust with Franklin Roosevelt and Winston Churchill led directly to the Cold War.

PRACTICE LONG-ESSAY QUESTIONS

These questions are samples of the various types of thematic essays on the exam. (See pages 30–31 for a detailed explanation of each type.) Check over the **generic rubric** (see pages 32–33) before you begin any of these essays and use that rubric to score your essay if you write one.

Question 1

To what extent was each of the belligerents in Europe responsible for the outbreak of the First World War?

COMMENTS ON QUESTION 1

This one is a CAUSATION question because it requires you to explain how each of the belligerent nations caused a specific outcome: the outbreak of the First World War. Remember to describe causes of the First World War, indicating which was caused by which belligerent nation and support your analysis of the causes and effects of that war with specific facts. The essay must also explain how each nation was or was not responsible, citing specific evidence. Many Americans, influenced to this day by creative Allied propaganda and by German aggression in the Second World War, believe that Germany, alone, was responsible for starting the First World War. Certainly the Kaiser's prewar arrogance was one of the friction points, but England, France, and Russia each carried out policies that aggravated the tension. In framing your answer, consider: the network of alliances that France and Germany engineered after the Franco-Prussian War; economic rivalry between Germany and Britain; the roles of Britain as well as Germany in the naval arms race; the mentalities of both "have" and "have-not" nations in the race for colonies; Russian support for Pan-Slavism in Austria-Hungary, and the volatile Balkan situation.

Question 2

Explain why the war ended the Russian, Austro-Hungarian, Ottoman, and German empires.

COMMENTS ON QUESTION 2

This one is another CAUSATION question because it requires you to explain how the collapse of each of the empires—Russian, German, Austro-Hungarian, and Ottoman—was caused by a specific stimulus, the First World War. Remember to describe causes of the decline of each empire, indicating the degree to which each one's downfall was caused by the First World War, using specific evidence to prove the cause of the decline of these empires. "Explain" in this context means to "offer the causes and reasons for" the collapse of those great empires. The scope of the issue is very broad, so a detailed accounting of each issue is not practical. Look for causes common to all three: the strains of a war of attrition, shortages, casualties, political instabilities, nationalist pressures, weakness of colonial holdings, defeats in battle. Emphasize the different characters of their problems: the Bolshevik movement in Russia; ethnic rivalries in Austria-Hungary; Arab nationalism within the Ottoman Empire; democratic and socialist opposition movements in Germany.

Question 3

Compare the Fourteen Points with the peace settlements in Paris.

COMMENTS ON QUESTION 3

This is clearly a COMPARE skill question, so be sure to describe similarities and differences between Woodrow Wilson's Fourteen Point Peace Plan and the reality of the Versailles Peace Settlement, as well as account for or explain why they were so different by providing specific examples of how the plans for peace went awry. It is also important to tie the events of the peace conference to other historical trends politically, militarily, socially, economically, or scientifically.

Had President Woodrow Wilson's idealistic plan for peace been implemented, the grievances that led to the Second World War might have been settled. The main provisions of the Fourteen Points were: no secret treaties; freedom of the seas; free trade; arms reduction; settlement of colonial claims; national autonomy and adjustment of borders; and establishment of a League of Nations. The Big Four Allied leaders met in Paris and drew up three treaties to end the war, without the involvement of representatives from any of the Central Powers. It is not necessary to show the differences or to ascertain similarities between the Fourteen Points and each of these treaties. In general terms, show what Wilson gave up during the negotiations in order to attain his prime goal, the League of Nations.

Question 4

To what extent and in what ways did the failure of reform and abortive revolution of 1905 lead to the Revolution of 1917?

COMMENTS ON QUESTION 4

This is another CAUSATION question because it requires you to explain to what extent and how the failure of reforms in Russia and the weak Revolution of 1905 CAUSED the Russian Revolution of 1917—support your analysis by citing specific evidence. Remember to describe causes and effects of the Russian Revolution, indicating the degree to which it was caused by failed reforms and the abortive Revolution of 1905; support your explanation of the causes and effects of the revolutions with specific facts. "How and to what extent" did attempts to make the government better, improve the economy, and modernize the institutions of Russia cause the open rebellion of the people against the government and the social structure? "How and to what extent" did the failed Revolution of 1905 contribute? What were the attempts at reform? When did Russia modernize its economy, and how did this lead to greater discontent among the people? Why was the Duma reconvened, and how did it precipitate events? How did the Russo-Japanese War cause discontent? What was "Bloody Sunday?" What reforms were aimed at by the marchers? What was the October Manifesto? What were Stolypin's reforms? What were the implications of his death?

Question 5

Evaluate the modernization of the Soviet Union under Lenin and Stalin.

COMMENTS ON QUESTION 5

This one tests the CHANGE AND CONTINUITY OVER TIME skill. Be sure to describe the level of historical continuity (as in what did not change and how the Soviet Union did not progress) and change (as in how the Soviet Union increased industrial production and urbanization), and analyze specific examples of what changed and what parts of Soviet society advanced compared to the parts that did not, such as the agricultural disaster created by collectivization, and the gulags. The use of the Cheka and other secret police after them can be seen as one part of continuity, while victory in the Second World War must be seen as evidence of huge industrial advancement. The impulse, if you know the cost of Soviet totalitarianism, 30-million-plus lives to start, is to claim that it was not worth the cost. It is easy to overlook the modernization and industrialization of a feudal society on the face of the facts alone, without reverting to ideological biases. The first step in this question is to define "progress." Is it economic? Social? Some indefinable movement forward? One can get lost in trying to measure the improvement of the human condition from one age to another. Do the drudgery and social stagnancy of feudalism compare to the alienation and confusion of modernity?

Stick to the tangible. The New Economic Policy and the five-year plans: Did they improve life for the Soviet people, and at what cost? Was the better standard of living for the Russian people under communism or under the czar? Was communist tyranny worse than czarist despotism?

Remember, whether you defend or refute, it is the case you make that counts.

Question 6

Compare the methods of governing the Soviet Union under Lenin and Stalin.

COMMENTS ON QUESTION 6

This is clearly a COMPARE skill question, so be sure to describe similarities and differences between Lenin's methods of governing the Soviet Union and the way Stalin did it, as well as to account for or explain why they were so different by providing specific examples of how the two men differed in experiences, style, outlook, and mental health. It is also important to tie the events of their lives to other historical trends politically, militarily, socially, economically, or scientifically.

The contrast is glaring: Lenin established the basic institutions of Soviet communism; Stalin evolved them into a grotesque parody of their original aims. Lenin ruled for about seven years; Stalin for over thirty. Lenin believed that the end justified the means; Stalin's paranoia distorted even this precept. Lenin designed the blueprint for modernization and reform; Stalin built the edifice into one of the world's worst totalitarian regimes.

The similarities are in their usurpation of power to gain their ends, their use of dictatorship, their methods of suppressing dissent.

This is a difficult question that requires broad statements backed by selective facts.

An examination of both of their relationships with Trotsky may add light to this subject as well.

PRACTICE SHORT-ANSWER QUESTIONS

1. Please use the diary excerpt and your knowledge of European history to answer all parts of the question that follows.

Selections from My Daily Journal, 1915–1916

We notice our rations are increased but there is no variety—tea, bread, hard biscuits, butter, jam, bacon, bully-beef, maconochie, fresh meat, cheese, rice, dried vegetables. These are the supplies but they are not of daily occurrence. It may be tinned food one day and fresh meat the next and so on. It is general knowledge that rations are increased when we go into the line. The rum we heard so much about came up tonight. We are given a tot—a few teaspoons full either at night or early morning. It is much appreciated as it helps the circulation which gets very slow these cold nights for want of movement . . . . The way our old soldiers, physical drill instructors, bayonet fighting instructors disappeared under the stress of battle to realms of easier work was a great disappointment to us . . . .

Before being relieved the enemy had taken its toll. Tom Smith going to the assistance of a wounded man was sniped at receiving an explosive bullet in the arm and shattering it completely, returning to Calgary several months later, an amputation case. Blackie Sayce had his arm almost torn off and is disabled for life. Hannan was also wounded and both bombing officers were casualties. L/Cpl. Dalziel, 6 ft. 2 ins. of humanity, finally came out of the shambles, leading the remaining bombers with an enhanced reputation.

—Private Donald Fraser, Canadian Expeditionary Force

(A) Briefly explain ONE economic change that the Allied powers implemented to ensure that the troops received the food and other materials they needed to fight the Central Powers during the First World War.

(B) Briefly explain ONE way that the social structure in Europe was changed after the First World War as a reaction to life in the trenches described in the excerpt above.

(C) Briefly explain how the technology from the Industrial Revolution impacted the way that the First World War was fought.

2. Please use the image and the excerpt below and your knowledge of European history to answer all parts of the following question.

Source 1

Soviet Poster 1922

Caption reads: "We Don't Want to Fight, but We'll Defend the Soviets."

Source 2

DECLARATION OF THE RIGHTS OF THE TOILING
AND EXPLOITED PEOPLES, 1918

The Constituent Assembly sets for itself as a fundamental task the suppression of all forms of exploitation of man by man and the complete abolition of class distinctions in society. It aims to crush unmercifully the exploiter, to reorganize society on a socialistic basis, and to bring about the triumph of Socialism throughout the world. It further resolves:

1. In order to bring about the socialization of land, private ownership of land is abolished. The entire land fund is declared the property of the nation and turned over free of cost to the toilers on the basis of equal right to its use. All forests, subsoil resources, and waters of national importance as well as all live stock and machinery, model farms, and agricultural enterprises are declared to be national property.
2. As a first step to the complete transfer of the factories, shops, mines, railways, and other means of production and transportation to the Soviet Republic of Workers and Peasants, and in order to ensure the supremacy of the toiling masses over the exploiters, the Constituent Assembly ratifies the Soviet law on workers' control and that on the Supreme Council of National Economy.

3. The Constituent Assembly ratifies the transfer of all banks to the ownership of the workers' and peasants' government as one of the conditions for the emancipation of the toiling masses from the yoke of capitalism.

4. In order to do away with the parasitic classes of society and organize the economic life of the country, universal labor duty is introduced.

(A) Please explain ONE way in which the messages of **Source 1** and **Source 2** are consistent with each other.

(B) Please explain TWO ways that **Source 2** changed Russian (Soviet) society.

Short-Answer Explanations

1. (A) You should identify either the rationing on the home front or the government agencies such as the War Raw Materials Board in Germany that took control of the economy as a part of the Total War effort. You should go on to explain how the transition to a mostly command economy was a huge and temporary change to the mostly market economies seen in Europe before the First World War.

(B) You should explain the growing equity in society after the First World War that resulted from the indiscriminate way that enlisted men and officers died without regard to their positions in civilian life. You should cite more equal voting rights, more government programs to promote equity and alleviate poverty, and the rise of social welfare and employment programs.

(C) You should explain how war became much more mechanized and much more deadly as a result of the Industrial Revolution. You should cite support among the following facts: artillery became much more prevalent and larger; trains were used to move troops, weapons, and supplies; poison gas was used; Total War meant that all of industry supported the war efforts in Europe, machines were used to build trenches, and there were new weapons such as machine guns, grenades, tanks, airplanes, submarines.

2. (A) You should note that the most prevalent consistency between the sources is that people must sacrifice and give up what they have (peace in **Source 1** and possessions in **Source 2**) to support the Soviet government. For this point, you should further explain that both sources are uses of propaganda for credit.

(B) You must explain TWO of the following to receive credit: The class structure was completely turned asunder: private property was abolished, which changed the distribution of wealth: the idea of class was abolished: banks were abolished, which destroyed the entire upper class; all Soviet citizens were required to work for the state; workers gained power over their former masters; the peasant classes were more equalized; mismanagement of the resources of the state led to famine; increased militarism made military service among the best jobs in the nation; collectivization of agriculture changed the social structure of peasants; the capitalist and entrepreneurial class was abolished; and many wealthy and noble Russians emigrated to save their lives and/or what wealth that they could take with them.

Questions 1 to 3 refer to the propaganda poster from the First World War below.

1. This poster depicts the sinking of the ocean liner *Lusitania*, which the poster seems to use to encourage which of the following?

    (A) Putting women on the front lines
    (B) Men joining the war effort
    (C) Submarine warfare
    (D) Women's suffrage

2. Which of the following nations gained the most power and international influence as a result of the First World War?

    (A) Great Britain
    (B) France
    (C) Germany
    (D) The United States

3. Which of the following artistic styles should the poster above be considered an example of?

    (A) Art Deco
    (B) Impressionism
    (C) Art Nouveau
    (D) Surrealism

Questions 4 to 7 refer to the photograph below of the Russian soldiers taking the oath of allegiance to the October Revolution in 1917.

Source: Russian army officers take the oath of allegiance to the October Revolution. 1917. Soldiers gathered in the square of the Winter Palace.

4. To which of the following Russian governments were the soldiers loyal immediately before the October Revolution in 1917?

   (A) The royal government of Czar Nicholas II
   (B) The Provisional Government led by General Kornilov
   (C) The Provisional Government led by Kerensky
   (D) The Bolshevik government under Trotsky

5. Which of the following was something like a shadow government in Russia from February 1917 until October 1917 and helped plan the October Revolution and win workers' support for governmental actions?

   (A) The Petrograd Soviet
   (B) The Provisional Government
   (C) The Bolshevik Party
   (D) The Menshevik Party

6. Which of the following was V. I. Lenin's plan to improve the Soviet Union's production and distribution of goods and services?

   (A) The five-year plans
   (B) The New Economic Policy
   (C) The New Deal
   (D) The Act of Collectivization

7. Lenin and Trotsky needed the allegiance of the army, seen above, for which of the following?

(A) To defeat Germany in the First World War
(B) To defeat the invading capitalist corporations who wanted to stop the Russian Revolution
(C) To win a territorial war with Poland
(D) To win the Russian Civil War

Multiple-Choice Explanations

1. **B**	3. **C**	5. **A**	7. **D**
2. **D**	4. **C**	6. **B**	

1. **(B)**
   (A) is wrong because women were not allowed on the front lines in the United Kingdom until the twenty-first century.
   (B) is CORRECT because the *Lusitania*'s sinking was used to get men (and the United States) to join the war effort.
   (C) is wrong because it is actually against unrestricted submarine warfare.
   (D) is wrong because this poster does not support women's suffrage in any way.

2. **(D)**
   (A) is wrong because Great Britain did gain power after winning the First World War, but not nearly as much as the United States did.
   (B) is wrong because, although France did gain power after winning the First World War, it was not nearly as much as the United States won.
   (C) is wrong because Germany lost power and prestige after losing the First World War.
   (D) is CORRECT because the United States went from being a non-factor in world issues to becoming the only undamaged economy in the Western world and gained financial and military respect as a result of the war and the Young and Dawes plans after the war.

3. **(C)**
   (A) is wrong because this poster is too flowing and decorated to be Art Deco, which is very geometric and clean.
   (B) is wrong because the image is far too clear to be an impressionist piece.
   (C) is CORRECT because the emotionality of the subject, the flowing, curvilinear designs, and the propagandist message all point to the Art Nouveau period.
   (D) is wrong because the image is too realistic to be surrealist.

4. **(C)**

(A) is wrong because the czar had abdicated in the February Revolution, months earlier, and the Provisional Government and the Petrograd Soviet ran the country until the October Revolution.

(B) is wrong because General Kornilov was not the ruler of the Provisional Government; Kerensky was.

(C) is CORRECT because the government overthrown in the October Revolution was the Provisional Government of Kerensky.

(D) is wrong because the Bolshevik government is who they are swearing allegiance to in the photo above.

5. **(A)**

(A) is CORRECT because the Petrograd Soviet was a workers' council that met in St. Petersburg right next to the Duma, and this soviet would approve the decisions of the Duma for the workers.

(B) is wrong because the Provisional Government of Kerensky was the one being overthrown in the photo above.

(C) is wrong because the Bolshevik Party, although powerful, did not have full control of the Petrograd Soviet and used the Mensheviks to help them plan.

(D) is wrong because the Menshevik Party did not have control of the Soviet and shared power in the Petrograd Soviet with the Bolsheviks.

6. **(B)**

(A) is wrong because the five-year plans were Stalin's plans for economic progress after Lenin died.

(B) is CORRECT because Lenin's plan for economic growth in the USSR was called his New Economic Policy.

(C) is wrong because the New Deal was Roosevelt's plan to help the American economy recover.

(D) is wrong because "collectivization" was done by Stalin rather than Lenin.

7. **(D)**

(A) is wrong because Russia surrendered to Germany with the treaty of Brest-Litovsk as soon as Lenin took power.

(B) is wrong because capitalist corporations did not invade the Soviet Union.

(C) is wrong because there was no war with Poland, as Poland did not exist as a separate nation until after the First World War.

(D) is CORRECT because the Soviets needed to defeat the Whites in the Russian Civil War and required the army to succeed.

Democracy, Depression, Dictatorship, World War and Its Aftermath (1919–1945)

11

KEY TERMS/PEOPLE

- → ISOLATIONISM
- → GREAT DEPRESSION
- → AGE OF ANXIETY
- → STREAM OF CONSCIOUSNESS
- → TARIFF POLICIES
- → JAMES JOYCE
- → FRANZ KAFKA
- → JEAN PAUL SARTRE
- → KEYNESIANISM
- → ERICH REMARQUE
- → VIRGINIA WOOLF
- → WERNER HEISENBERG
- → SURREALISM
- → STOCK MARKET CRASH
- → BENITO MUSSOLINI
- → GERMAN WEIMAR REPUBLIC
- → FASCIST
- → WEIMAR CONSTITUTION
- → ADOLF HITLER

- → NATIONAL SOCIALIST GERMAN WORKERS' PARTY (NAZIS)
- → *MEIN KAMPF*
- → NUREMBERG LAWS
- → HOLOCAUST
- → LEAGUE OF NATIONS
- → AXIS POWERS
- → BLITZKRIEG
- → BRITISH MANDATE SYSTEM
- → NONAGGRESSION PACT
- → ATLANTIC CHARTER
- → JOSEPH STALIN
- → UNITED NATIONS
- → ARMENIAN GENOCIDE
- → NEW TECHNOLOGY OF WARFARE
- → SUPERPOWERS
- → IRON CURTAIN
- → COLD WAR
- → MARSHALL PLAN

OVERVIEW

The First World War saw states increase the degree and scope of their authority over their economies, societies, and cultures. "Total War" had required the centralization of power and the regimentation of the lives of citizens. During the war, governments sought to control information and used propaganda to create stronger emotional ties to the nation and its war effort. Ironically, these measures also produced distrust of traditional authorities. The fall of four great empires after the First World War—Russian, German, Ottoman, and Austro-Hungarian—not only created a central Europe comprised of smaller nations but left a political vacuum among peoples without a tradition of democracy. Their weak economies and ethnic tensions compounded the problem of a lack of democratic traditions, making progress in these newly created nations difficult and pushing citizens to accept more extreme viewpoints and solutions to perceived national problems. In the two decades between the world wars, totalitarian dictatorships were established in Russia (the Stalinist regime in the USSR), Italy, Spain, and Germany. For the first time in history, governments of great nations were dedicated to the total control of every area of human life, and individuals were expected to subordinate themselves to the needs of the state as defined by the single party in control. Soviet communism, despite its idealistic goal of the withering away of the state, imposed brutal repression to enforce the "dictatorship of the proletariat." Italian Fascism and German Nazism shared a common ideology of racist nationalism and the glorification of war. Fascism promised to solve economic problems through state direction, although not ownership, of production. These movements also promised to counteract the provisions of the Treaty of Versailles by rearming and by territorial expansion. The efforts of Fascist governments to revise the Treaty of Versailles led to the most violent and destructive conflict in human history (the Second World War), a clash between liberal democracies, temporarily allied with communist Russia, and Fascist states.

The Western democracies of England, France, and the United States came out of the First World War with their heritage of democracy intact. In the 1930s, their tradition of dissent and their democratic institutions were sorely tested both by economic collapse and by the aggressions of the dictatorships. Ten years after the end of the First World War, the worst depression in modern history began and lasted for over a decade. The human misery brought each of these nations close to the point of collapse and encouraged extremist movements, both on the left and the right, to offer simple solutions that would have destroyed democracy.

Wracked by weakness and dissent, the democracies were unwilling to respond to the aggressions of the European dictators and the Japanese militarists. The policy of appeasement, which sought to placate the aggressors with concessions, only whetted the dictators' appetites and led eventually to worldwide war.

During the twentieth century, European thought and culture generally moved from an optimistic view that modern science and technology could solve the problems of humankind to the formation of eclectic and sometimes skeptical movements that doubted the possibility of objective knowledge and of progress. Existentialism, postmodernism, and renewed religiosity challenged the supremacy of science as an epistemological method. While European society became increasingly secular, religion continued to play a role in the lives of many Europeans.

As many as 70 million people perished in the Second World War, and for the first time in history, tens of millions of the casualties were noncombatants. Saturation bombing of cities, widespread starvation caused by war damage and displacement of people, and state-sponsored murder to exterminate a people (genocide) contributed to the terrible losses.

The war was fought on three continents by combatants from six continents; it was global in scale; it was made up of separate conflicts, each with an identifiable beginning and end; it was a series of strategic improvisations rather than the result of carefully laid plans; it began at various times, as early as 1931 for the Manchurians and Japanese, as late as 1941 for the Americans.

It began over issues never resolved after the First World War: the failure of the Versailles Treaty to settle the problems of nationalistic yearnings for autonomy, of economic security, of blame for the First World War. The nations without large colonial holdings (Germany, Italy, and Japan) fell under the rule of repressive dictatorships and sought to redress what they saw as the inequities of the peace settlements after the First World War. The imperialist nations, the United States, France, and England, were absorbed in dealing with economic depression and with avoiding another costly war. When the Western democracies' policy of appeasement failed to stop the aggressions of the formative Axis powers, war resulted. It was officially declared in Europe in September 1939, after Germany's invasion of Poland. It ended with the unconditional surrender of Nazi Germany to the Russians, British, Americans, and French in May of 1945 and with the surrender of Japan in September 1945.

It not only changed the balance of power in Europe with an international "balance of terror" created by nuclear weapons, but it gave rise to a nonmilitary conflict between the world's two new superpowers: the Cold War.

THE WESTERN DEMOCRACIES AFTER THE FIRST WORLD WAR

The conflicting goals of the First World War peace negotiators in Paris pitted diplomatic idealism against the desire to punish Germany, producing a settlement that satisfied few. The war created a "*lost generation*," fostered disillusionment and cynicism, transformed the lives of women, and democratized societies. Wilsonian idealism clashed with postwar realities in both the victorious and the defeated states. Democratic successor states, such as Poland, Czechoslovakia, Hungary, and Yugoslavia, emerged from former empires and eventually succumbed to significant political, economic, and diplomatic crises. The *League of Nations*, created to prevent future wars, was weakened from the outset by the nonparticipation of major powers, including the United States, Germany, and the Soviet Union. The Versailles settlement, particularly its provisions on the assignment of guilt and reparations for the war, hindered the *German Weimar Republic's* ability to establish a stable and legitimate political and economic system.

1920s in England

The nation did not recover, during the 1920s, from the economic losses suffered during the war. Its merchant fleet had been decimated by German submarines and its foreign trade had declined disastrously. International competition from worldwide industrialization; the proliferation of tariffs; rival shipping nations; defaulted loans by investors, by business owners, and homeowners; and war relief programs further eroded a British economy already saddled by war debts.

POLITICS

- The Liberal Party, headed by David Lloyd George, fell into decline.
- Replaced by the Conservatives (Tory Party), who favored high tariffs and welfare payments to the growing numbers of unemployed.
- The Labour party, whose program included a gradual nationalization of major industries, took power briefly.
- By 1929 and the start of the Depression, an alliance of Labourites and Conservatives led by *Ramsay MacDonald* (1866–1937), then *Stanley Baldwin* (1867–1947), and finally *Neville Chamberlain* (1869–1940) ran the government until the start of the Second World War.

  – Chamberlain's black umbrella became a symbol for the policy of *appeasement* (the willingness to give in to the demands of the aggressive dictatorships).

FOREIGN POLICY

- The League of Nations distributed former German and Ottoman possessions to France and Great Britain through the mandate system, thereby altering the imperial balance of power and creating strategic interest in the Middle East states and their oil.

  – Middle East mandates included *Lebanon, Syria, Iraq*, and *Palestine*.

- British foreign policy during this period was consumed by the *Irish Question*, the granting of eventual independence to Southern Ireland after failure to suppress rebellion.
- The ending of the *British protectorate* in *Egypt*, although control of the Suez Canal was continued, was another major issue.
- The Statute of Westminster formally recognized the equality of the British dominions such as Canada and Australia.
  - Set up a Commonwealth of Nations, which enjoyed special trading privileges.

1920s in France

The death, devastation, and debt of the First World War created economic chaos and political unrest. When the Germans defaulted on their reparation payments to France (which was to get 52 percent of the German reparations of $33 billion [valued at $510 billion in 2014 dollars]), the French economy nearly collapsed.

POLITICS

- Through the 1920s, the government (a multiparty system requiring coalitions to function) was dominated by the parties on the right—which supported the status quo and had the backing of business, the military, the Church, and the wealthy upper classes.

GERMANY AND REPARATIONS

- In 1922, when Germany managed to pay only part of that year's reparation bill, Raymond Poincaré (1860–1934), prime minister, sent French troops to occupy the mineral-rich Ruhr Valley in western Germany.
- The Dawes Plan, the Young Plan, and the Lausanne Settlement each, in turn, pared down German payments and diminished the ability of the French to collect.
- Tax and spending reforms by Poincaré's government, though, led to a temporary resurgence of prosperity until the worldwide depression hit.

FRENCH FOREIGN POLICY

- Aimed at neutralizing Germany in the event of a resurgence of militarism there.
- A series of alliances with buffer states such as Belgium and Poland surrounded Germany with French allies.
- The *Locarno Pact* of 1925 attempted to settle French-German border disputes.
- The *Kellogg-Briand Pact* of 1928 aimed at outlawing war and was championed as the high point of post–First World War diplomacy, despite its futility in reality.

1920s in the United States

FOREIGN POLICY

- Disillusionment with the *Versailles Treaty* resulted in the Senate's rejection of U.S. membership in the League of Nations.
- Despite nostalgia for traditional *isolationism,* the United States participated in a series of naval disarmament conferences that agreed to limit the building of new battleships and fix the size of the major powers' navies.

- Despite an economic boom in the United States, international trade was thwarted by a series of shortsighted *tariffs* (taxes on imports) that contributed to the *Great Depression* by diminishing foreign markets and limiting the ability of the Europeans to pay off their war debts to the United States.
- Immigration quotas, which favored Northern Europeans over those from the south and east, ended the *age of immigration* that peaked at the turn of the century.

THE AGE OF ANXIETY

The carnage and disruption of the First World War and the collapse of the "old order" that had defined European politics and diplomacy for nearly a century resulted in what commentators have called an *age of anxiety*. The traditional assumption of the perfectibility of mankind through reason collapsed under the weight of events and new ideas.

Philosophy, science, the arts, and literature contributed to this crisis of confidence and conscience, but also offered new models to explain and portray humanity.

The Lost Generation

After the First World War, Ernest Hemingway popularized Gertrude Stein's term, the *Lost Generation*, to describe those who had come of age during the war. It included the thinkers below who showed a rejection of the belief in reason and technology to solve the problems of humanity.

PHILOSOPHY

Edmund Husserl and *Martin Heidegger* (1889–1976), both Germans, extended the work of Nietzsche and *Soren Kierkegaard* (1813–1855) to establish the foundations of *existentialism*, a philosophical school, popularized by *Jean-Paul Sartre* after the Second World War, that emphasized individual responsibility and capability for giving meaning to a meaningless universe.

PHYSICS

Werner Heisenberg (1901–1976) developed the *uncertainty principle* that stated that a particle's velocity or position (but not both) could be calculated.

- **This fundamental uncertainty about the nature of matter is endemic of the "Age of Anxiety."**
- The theories of *relativity* of *Albert Einstein* (1879–1955), another German, further disrupted the comfortable assumptions of an orderly, rationally discoverable universe that Newton's seventeenth-century physics had supported and encouraged: *relativism* in ethics, politics, and worldviews.
- *Neils Bohr* explained the fundamental ideas of chemistry and quantum physics by explaining the arrangement of the electron shells around atoms.
- *Enrico Fermi,* an Italian, worked on inducing radioactivity and eventually built the first nuclear reactor in Chicago.
- *Erwin Schrödinger* created a wave particle theory that shook up quantum physics.

LITERATURE

Throughout the century, a number of writers challenged traditional literary conventions, questioned Western values, and addressed controversial social and political issues. The aftermath of the war and intellectual trends, such as Freudianism, influenced writers to emphasize the irrational aspects of the human condition.

- *Stream of consciousness*, the portrayal of an individual's random thoughts and feelings, was a style perfected by *James Joyce* (1882–1941), an Irish novelist, and *Virginia Woolf* (1882–1941), an English fiction writer.

  - It reflected the prevailing view of human life as alienated, irrational, and chaotic.

- The horrors of the First World War were examined by *Erich Remarque* in *All Quiet on the Western Front*, which found meaninglessness in war and subsequently was banned by the Nazi government.
- *Franz Kafka* explored the overreaching power of the state in *The Trial* and *Metamorphosis*, which explored themes of alienation, brutality (both physical and psychological), bureaucratic labyrinths of futility, and parent–child conflicts.

VISUAL ART

Expressionism—abstract and nonrepresentational—replaced impressionism and was pioneered by Vincent van Gogh (1853–1890), Paul Cézanne (1839–1906), and Paul Gauguin (1848–1903), who painted with bold colors and images to focus on emotions and imagination.

- Pablo Picasso (1881–1973), a Spaniard, invented cubism, the depiction of mood through the use of geometric angles, planes, and clashing lines.
- Dadaism and surrealism were among the abstract styles created by artists of many nationalities, most of whom did their experimentation in postwar France.
- Architecture exemplified *functionalism*—buildings designed with practicality and clean lines instead of ornamentation.

ARCHITECTURE

The Bauhaus movement considered form and function to be united and saw over-ornamentation as a crime. Clean-lined steel and glass buildings were created as well as modernist furniture to go into these buildings.

- A house was seen as a machine for living in.
- Minimalist and Spartan in nature.
- Foundation of the modernist artistic movement.
- Walter Gropius was a leader of this movement.

MUSIC

Some music of the era challenged existing aesthetic standards, explored subconscious and subjective states, and satirized Western society and its values.

- Igor Stravinsky revolutionized classical music with his *Rites of Spring* and other works and eventually adopted the 12-tone technique of composition of Arnold Schoenberg, another revolutionary composer of the era.
- The tone poems of Richard Strauss were also a new way to look at music.

MEDICINE

Medical theories and technologies extended life but posed social and moral questions that eluded consensus and crossed religious, political, and philosophical perspectives. Some of the most controversial ones are seen below:

- *Eugenics:* The idea of breeding the best people and sterilizing or killing the undesirables; utilized by Hitler.
- *Birth control* revolutionized reproductive freedom but many religious and moral objections abounded.
- Abortion became legal throughout much of Europe and remains controversial to this day.
- Fertility treatments have been developed to allow those with conception problems to become parents but they are very expensive and the world is overpopulated.
- Genetic engineering is now approaching the point where we can clone and engineer humans: Should we?

MEDIA

Film and radio became major means for entertainment, information, and propaganda in the 1920s and 1930s. National broadcasting networks were set up by every major European power, and radio was employed by Adolf Hitler and other European dictators for propaganda and indoctrination.

- Movies became a prime medium for mass entertainment and also were employed to produce powerful propaganda.
- The modern cult of celebrity or the (ironic) glorification of the personalities who portrayed people other than themselves, was born with the advent of movies.

THE GREAT DEPRESSION (1929–1939)

The Great Depression, caused by weaknesses in international trade and monetary theories and practices, undermined Western European democracies and fomented radical political responses throughout the Continent.

- First World War debt, nationalistic tariff policies, overproduction, depreciated currencies, disrupted trade patterns, and speculation created weaknesses in economies worldwide.
- Dependence on post–First World War American investment capital led to financial collapse when, following the 1929 stock market crash, the United States cut off capital flows to Europe.
- Despite attempts to rethink economic theories and policies and forge political alliances, Western democracies failed to overcome the Great Depression and were weakened by extremist movements.

United States

The *economic boom* of the "Roaring Twenties" masked a deep-seated malaise. Farm prices had dropped disastrously after the selling peak during wartime; sizable segments of the population were poor; credit buying encouraged exorbitant personal debt; a dearth of new products (once the market for radios, autos, and refrigerators had been saturated) discouraged business investment.

- The *stock market crash* of October 1929 was more a symptom than a cause of the economic depression that seized America and most of the industrialized world for the next decade.
- There were many contributing factors to the Great Depression, including:

  - Buying stocks on large margins.
  - Stock bubble that was not sustainable.
  - Adjustment from a wartime economy to a peaceful one.
  - Increased mechanization creating structural unemployment.
  - Changes in international patterns of trade.
  - Declines in consumption caused by the aftermath of the First World War.

- The Federal Reserve also exacerbated a weak economy by tightening the money supply when it needed to be loosened.

  - Created deflation, which further devastated a weakened world economy.
  - World was using the dollar more than any other single currency.

- *American and European economies were interdependent through extensive investments and war debts owed to the United States.*
- Failure of the U.S. economy led to a global breakdown.

  - The *command economy* of the USSR managed to maintain, and even surpass, earlier productivity.
  - By 1932, nearly 15 million Americans were unemployed, about a quarter of the work force.
  - Herbert Hoover's stubborn insistence that the Depression was a normal fluctuation of the economy that would run its course brought the Roosevelt Democrats into the White House with a "New Deal."
  - Franklin Delano Roosevelt (FDR) (1882–1945) and the New Deal may not have ended the Depression in America, but they helped preserve capitalism and democracy in the United States.

    - Used the deficit-spending theories of economist *John Maynard Keynes* (1883–1946), who had predicted the Great Depression.

- Established a theory that justified profound involvement of the federal government in the economy.
- Created idea of economic stimulus and restraint.
- Although the Depression ended in the United States only when it began to rearm (1940–1941), the New Deal created a social *welfare state* with the obligation to relieve economic hardship, while it preserved a modified and revitalized American capitalism.

Great Britain

During the 1930s, under the *National Party* (the coalition of Labourites and Conservatives) the British tried to alleviate the Depression by reorganizing industry, abandoning free trade, reforming finances, and cutting government spending.

- Also utilized the ideas of Keynes to help alleviate the worst parts of the Depression.

  - Great Britain was able to create a strong recovery and by 1937 advance output to 20 percent above 1929.
  - Conservative governments paid generous unemployment benefits.
  - They focused more on the domestic market than exports.
  - Low interest rates brought on a housing boom.
  - New industries like appliances and automobiles helped spur consumption.
  - The North stayed depressed while the South expanded and renovated.
  - Like the United States, Britain came out of the Depression only through rearmament for the coming world war.

France

The Depression increased class tensions and gave birth to a radical right that supported government reorganization along Fascist lines.

- After a financial scandal that involved high government officials in 1934, pro-Fascist riots broke out all over France
- A coalition of socialists, republicans, labor unionists, and communists responded by organizing the **Popular Front**, which opposed Fascism, supported reform, and upheld the republic.

  - In 1936, socialist *Leon Blum* (1872–1950) became prime minister under the **Popular Front** banner.
  - He instituted a "French New Deal," which offered labor and agricultural reforms similar to those in the United States except that his measures were ineffective in ending the Depression.
  - Opposed by the conservative bloc in the Senate, the program failed to hold together the Popular Front coalition, and Blum resigned in 1937 to be replaced by conservative Edouard Daladier (1884–1970), who overturned the Blum reforms and practiced a policy of *appeasement* of Hitler's aggressions.

Scandinavia

The Scandinavian answer to the Great Depression: The Social Democrat Party in Norway and Sweden developed a unique brand of socialism.

- Strong worker and peasant reforms.
- Used Scandinavian tradition of cooperative community action to create a flexible non-revolutionary socialism.
- Agricultural cooperatives joined together to form organizations that benefited all.
- Labor leaders and capitalists worked together.
- Deficit spending to stimulate the economy.
- Higher taxes.

- Like New Deal but more intense with greater spending and taxation of the wealthy.
- This worked and was seen as a middle way between capitalism and communism.
- Created the model for the *modern welfare state*.
- Still in practice in most of Europe today.

DICTATORSHIP

What Is Fascism: A Brief on Fascist Ideology

Fascism is the belief in a strong state allied with corporations to organize and control a "willing" population and glorify the state. It is one-party **totalitarianism** that limits the political power of the individual and sees people as mere cells in the organism of the state. It is extremely nationalist in nature and is led by a charismatic dictator with unlimited power, usually a military leader. Fascists favor private ownership of property and Fascist governments ally with big businesses to weaken or eliminate labor unions and communists. It is important to note that Fascism was a negative response to communism, and that the two ideologies were opposed to each other. However, BOTH Fascism and communism were created in this era as **totalitarian** systems of rule by only one party. The unique aspect of totalitarian regimes is that they make total claims on the actions and thoughts of the populations ruled by them. The following Venn diagram shows the similarities and differences between the two ideologies as they existed in Europe during the first half of the twentieth century.

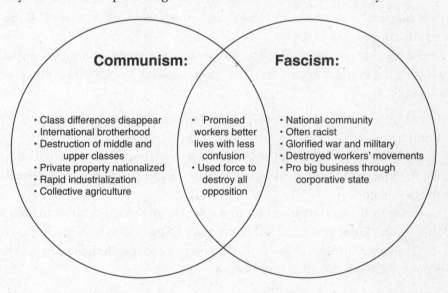

Communism:
- Class differences disappear
- International brotherhood
- Destruction of middle and upper classes
- Private property nationalized
- Rapid industrialization
- Collective agriculture

- Promised workers better lives with less confusion
- Used force to destroy all opposition

Fascism:
- National community
- Often racist
- Glorified war and military
- Destroyed workers' movements
- Pro big business through corporative state

Nazism was a special case of Fascism in which race was the primary factor for determining one's role in the state in Germany. Germans were the "master race," meant to be served by the Slavic peoples of Europe, who would be slaves and workers. Other ethnic groups, such as Jews and the Roma, were to be eliminated to make more room for the "superior" Germanic people.

Fascism in Italy

The peace settlements that ended the First World War were extremely disappointing to Italian nationalists. None of the Austrian and Ottoman territories and German colonies in Africa that had been promised were received. To add to Italian discontent, a depression hit in 1919 and provoked nationwide strikes and class antagonisms. Terrified of a communist revolution, the propertied classes looked hopefully for a strong leader to restore order.

Benito Mussolini (1883–1945), editor of a socialist newspaper and paradoxically an ardent nationalist, organized the Fascist Party, a combination of socialism and nationalism, named after fasces (the rods carried by Imperial Roman officials as symbols of power).

- His *squadristi*, paramilitary *blackshirts*, attacked communists, socialists, and other enemies of his program.
- Promising to protect private property, Mussolini won the support of the conservative classes and quickly abandoned his socialist programs.
- The Fascist *March on Rome*, October 1922, caused the government to collapse and won Mussolini the right to organize a new government. King Victor Emmanuel III granted him dictatorial powers for one year to end the nation's social unrest.
- The *corporate state* was the economic core of Italian Fascism: "Labor unions" run by the Fascist Party managed and controlled industry.

  - Those unions then set the national political agenda.
  - Unlike socialist corporate states, where workers make decisions, authority flowed from the top.

- The Fascists consolidated power through the 1920s by rigging elections and intimidating and terrorizing opponents.

  - By 1928, all independent labor unions had been organized into government-controlled syndicates, the right to vote had been severely limited, and all candidates for the Italian parliament were selected by the Fascist Party.
  - Through the 1930s, an organization of corporations, headed by Mussolini, effectively replaced parliamentary government.
  - Democracy was suppressed; the totalitarian state was created in Italy.

FASCIST ACCOMPLISHMENTS IN ITALY

- Internal improvements such as electrification and roadbuilding.
- More efficient municipal governing.
- Suppression of the Mafia.
- Improvement of the justice system (except for "enemies of the state").
- Reconciliation with the papacy through the *Lateran Pact* of 1929, which gave the papacy $92 million for seized church lands in return for Pope Pius XII's recognition of the legitimacy of the Italian state.
- The notoriously undependable trains in Italy finally ran on schedule.

FASCIST FAILINGS

- Italian democracy destroyed.
- Press censorship.
- No right to strike.
- Denial of all dissent.
- Destruction of suffrage.
- Terrorism became a state policy.
- Poor industrial growth was seen due to militarism and colonialism.
- Attempt to recapture the imperialistic glories of ancient Rome led to disastrous involvements in war.

The Rise of Nazism in Germany

THE WEIMAR REPUBLIC

In November 1918, a provisional government, both socialist and democratic, was organized to negotiate a peace with the Allies. Although this government had very little input to the decisions made at the Paris Peace Conference, it did sign the Versailles Treaty and would be held responsible by conservative factions for the pact's inequities.

- The *Weimar Constitution*, drafted in July 1919, set up Germany's first modern democracy.
  - Provided for a directly elected president.
  - Provided for a directly elected parliament (the *Reichstag*).
  - A senate (the *Reichsrat*) would represent the German states.
  - Provided for a chancellor (prime minister), who represented the majority party of the Reichstag, and a cabinet to run the government.

- After the *inflation of 1923*, Germany defaulted on its reparations to France, the French seized the Ruhr Valley, and German workers there went on a general strike.
- To pay these workers, the Weimar government printed paper currency and the prevalent inflation in the country became runaway.
- When debtors rushed to pay off their creditors with this worthless currency, the middle class was financially wiped out.

THE MUNICH BEER HALL PUTSCH

The Weimar government's economic disasters in 1923 encouraged *Adolf Hitler* (1889–1945) and his Nazi *Brownshirts* to attempt to seize power from the government of Bavaria, a state of southern Germany. Hitler, Austrian by birth, had fled poverty in his native land and joined the German army at the start of the First World War. He helped organize the *National Socialist German Workers' Party (Nazis)* after the war.

- Racist, paranoid, sociopathic, and megalomaniacal, Hitler was a brilliant orator and political strategist who played on popular discontent with the Weimar government.
  - Blamed democracy, communism, and the Jewish people for Germany's ills.

- He and *Erich Ludendorff* (1865–1937), a distinguished general who had led German troops to victory on the Eastern Front during the First World War, led an attempted coup in Munich at the end of 1923.

  - It was suppressed, and Hitler was sentenced to five years in jail.
  - He served only about a year of his already-lenient term.
  - Many higher-ups in the justice system sympathized with his narrow nationalistic goals.
  - While in prison, he wrote his blueprint for domination of Germany and eventually Europe, *Mein Kampf (My Struggle)*.

    - A rambling, irrational, but convincing work.
    - Argued that Germany was never defeated in the First World War but was betrayed from within by Jews and socialists.
    - Claimed the Treaty of Versailles was a humiliation.
    - Propagated the idea that Germans were a master race destined to expand into Eastern Europe to obtain *lebensraum* (living space) and to rule or exterminate inferior races, such as Jews and Slavs.

Germany 1923–1933

After the *Dawes Plan* stabilized Germany's economy in 1924, the Nazi party's membership fell off so that by 1928 the Nazis won only 12 seats in the Reichstag.

- For a short while after the Beer Hall Putsch, conditions were hopeful in Germany and in Europe as a whole.
- Gustav Stresemann, the chancellor and then foreign minister of the Weimar Republic, oversaw a short period of prosperity from 1925–1929, known as the Weimar Golden Age.

  - Part of the *Locarno* treaties of 1925 in which all European nations agreed to respect the borders drawn after the First World War.
  - Also a signatory to the 1928 *Kellogg-Briand Pact*, condemning warfare.
  - The Weimar Golden Age was a culturally vibrant and politically idealistic brief flicker in the otherwise dismal Germany of the early twentieth century.
  - This can be used to contrast the political and cultural conservatism that dominated the rest of the period.

- When the Depression hit Germany in 1930, the Nazis won 107 seats and the communists 77.

  - Center parties, the socialists and Christian Democrats, were unable to maintain a ruling coalition.
  - Many conservatives, including large landowners, industrialists, and army officers, threw their support to Hitler to avoid a communist takeover.

- In January, 1933, after a series of machinations, Hitler was invited by the aging president of the Weimar Republic, *Paul von Hindenburg* (1847–1934), another renowned general of the First World War, to form a government as chancellor.
- Hitler entered government legally, according to the constitution that he was publicly dedicated to destroy.

The Nazi Revolution

The week before the elections of March 1933, which Hitler ordered to obtain a clear majority in the Reichstag, the *Reichstag building was destroyed by arson*.

- Although Nazis are believed to have started the fire, Hitler used it as a pretext to declare emergency powers for the government.
- The election that followed was influenced by suspension of freedom of the press and of speech, and by outright terrorizing of political opponents.
- After gaining a majority coalition in the Reichstag, the Nazis granted dictatorial powers to Hitler for four years with the *Enabling Act*.
- Within six months, all political parties but the Nazis were outlawed.
- When President Hindenburg died in 1934, Hitler merged his office of chancellor with that of president with 90 percent of the German voters approving.

The Nazis Consolidated Power

- *Dachau*, the first concentration camp, was opened in March 1933.

  - Although the camps did not become death factories for mass extermination until 1941, they were brutal centers for punishing political opponents of the Nazis.

- During the *Night of the Long Knives*, in June 1934, Hitler purged the party by executing left-wing Nazis who had pushed for the socialist programs that Hitler had promised, and also leaders of the Brownshirts who had maintained autonomy within the party.

  - The black-uniformed elite guard, the infamous *SS* (Schutzstaffel, or "Protection Squadron") became the party's and the nation's enforcers.
  - The *Gestapo* was the secret police force of the SS.

    - A rigorous selection and training process was set up for the SS.
    - Became the overseers of the death camps.

- Labor unions were replaced, as in Fascist Italy, by a Nazi-led labor organization.

  - Strikes were outlawed.
  - Factories put under the management of local Nazi officials who had dictatorial powers over the workers.

- Full employment resumed with military production that thrived despite its prohibition under the terms of the Versailles Treaty.
- A policy of *autarchy*, economic self-sufficiency, was developed to make Germany independent of imports and foreign markets.
- The *Nuremberg Laws* of 1935 stripped Germany's half-million Jews of their rights as citizens.

  - When Nazi mobs wrecked Jewish shops and synagogues throughout Germany during *Kristallnacht* ("Night of the Broken Glass") in 1938, it was the beginning of the *Holocaust*—the systematic extermination of Jews in Germany and eventually throughout Europe.
  - About 200,000 German Jews managed to escape from Germany.
  - Of those that remained, over 90 percent were murdered.
  - The Holocaust was used to eliminate all of Hitler's enemies:

    - Many ethnic groups.
    - Those politically opposed to him.
    - Those whom his theories stated were weakening the German state.
    - Communists, Catholics, Jewish people, Roma, homosexuals, and the handicapped were systematically imprisoned, enslaved, and eliminated.
    - In the end over 6 million Jews and 7 million others were killed, with millions more enslaved or imprisoned.

Authoritarian Dictatorships in Central and Eastern Europe

After failures to establish functioning democracies, authoritarian dictatorships took power in Central and Eastern Europe during the interwar period. Poland, Hungary, and Romania all established authoritarian dictatorships that functioned poorly.

- In Poland, Jozef Piłsudski never claimed personal power, although he exercised extensive influence over Polish politics after the Sanation coup d'état in 1926 promised a restoration of political life.
- In Romania the Iron Guard led by Ion Antonescu forced King Carol II to abdicate in 1940, allowing their pro-Nazi regime to take power.
- In Hungary a Fascist prime minister was appointed by 1932 and the arrow cross movement of Fascists there gained power.

PRELUDE TO WAR

The rise of nationalist, industrialist, and imperialist single-party states was a significant factor contributing to the outbreak of the Second World War. One political factor was the personal will of Adolf Hitler, which many historians credit with being a major cause of the war. Another was the weakness of the Treaty of Versailles, which did not fix the underlying economic and social pressures in Western Europe, leaving the Continent ripe for another war. The failure of the League of Nations to intervene in many instances when Hitler or Hideki Tojo (r. 1941–1945) broke the Treaty of Versailles made the dictators more brazen. Finally, the policy of appeasement, as outlined below, led to more and more aggression from the Axis Powers of Germany, Italy, and Japan.

> ## SPECIAL NOTE
>
> The Second World War is examined in chronological order, broken into different periods of the war from aggression and appeasement to the aftermath.

AGGRESSION AND APPEASEMENT

1931

- Japan invaded Manchuria and the League of Nations did not intervene in any meaningful way.
- Japan began to imperialize China.
- The Japanese occupation of Manchuria lasted until the end of the war.

1933

- Hitler pulled Germany out of the League of Nations.

1935

- Hitler began rebuilding the German armed forces in open violation of the Treaty of Versailles.
- The Western powers, immersed in the Great Depression, objected but did not act.
- The Saar Plebiscite returned the Saar Valley to Germany.
- Mussolini attacked the independent kingdom of Ethiopia in East Africa.
- The League ordered *sanctions* (an embargo on trade in arms and raw materials) against Italy, but the sanctions were not enforced.

1936

- Hitler's troops occupied the *Rhineland*, which the Treaty of Versailles had made into a demilitarized zone between France and Germany.
- France and England failed to act, giving birth to the policy of *appeasement*.

- General *Francisco Franco* and his Spanish Falangists (Fascists) began an insurrection against the democratically chosen republican government of Spain.

    - The Fascist dictators, Mussolini and Hitler, supported Franco with men, arms, and money.
    - Stalin backed the Republicans, a significant number of whom were Communists.
    - The brutal and destructive *Spanish Civil War*, which lasted for over three years and claimed the lives of 600,000, became a testing ground for the war machines of the dictatorships.
    - The Fascists won, and Franco remained as the longest-reigning Fascist dictator, his regime ending only when he died in 1975.

1937

- The second Sino-Japanese War began in earnest as the Japanese launched a full-scale attack, made significant territorial gains, and committed atrocities on the Chinese people, such as the Rape of Nanking.

    - The League of Nations again did not respond.

- Germany, Italy, and Japan signed the *Anti-Comintern Pact* to oppose international communism.

    - Marked the beginning of their alliance, the *Axis*.

- Japan invaded mainland China, quickly conquering the seacoast and driving *Chiang Kai-shek's Nationalists* deep into the interior, where they, along with their political opposition led by Mao Tse-tung, waged a guerrilla war that proved costly to the Japanese.

1938

- Hitler engineered the *Anschluss* (the forced union of Germany and Austria), again in violation of the Versailles Treaty.
- Once again the Western powers failed to act.
- Hitler prepared to annex the *Sudetenland* (a part of Czechoslovakia that before the First World War had been German territory).

    - France and England, at the urging of the USSR, issued warnings.
    - After tensions and talks, a conference was called, at Mussolini's suggestion, in which *Neville Chamberlain*, prime minister of Britain, and Édouard *Daladier*, prime minister of France, met with Hitler and Mussolini.
    - The infamous *Munich Conference* ceded the Sudetenland to Germany and marked the pinnacle of appeasement.

1939

- Hitler seized the rest of Czechoslovakia, abandoned by the West, and the western part of Lithuania.
- Mussolini invaded Albania.
- Hitler and Stalin signed a *Nonaggression Pact*, which cleared the way for Hitler's *invasion of Poland*.

TRIUMPH OF THE AXIS POWERS (1939–1942)

Although Germany, Italy, and Japan were often referred to as Fascists, their dictatorships were significantly different.

- The German Nazis and, to a lesser degree, the Italian Fascists imposed totalitarian systems upon their people.
- The Japanese, whose constitutional government was loyal to the emperor (who was seen as a "living god"), had a military dictatorship imposed in the 1930s.
- The term "Axis" came from the Rome, Berlin, Tokyo Axis, a pledge of mutual cooperation between the three nations that in the end led to virtually no combined military ventures involving the two European powers and Japan.

The War Against the Minorities

In addition to the military attacks on nations, wars against ethnic and other minorities, waged more by Germany and Japan than by Italy, were a separate front.

- The Japanese economically and militarily dominated the areas they conquered.

  - The Japanese turned the civilians into a slave-labor force, including hundreds of thousands of women forced into prostitution for Japanese soldiers, commonly referred to as "comfort women."
  - It is believed that almost 20 million Chinese were killed in the course of the Second World War.
  - The Japanese performed medical experimentation on the Chinese civilians with biological agents.

- The Nazis created a systematic method for enslaving the peoples they conquered.

  - They had a system for deciding a civilian's fate by ethnicity.

    - Germanic people held all positions of importance or power.
    - Slavs and Russians were sent to forced work camps and factories.
    - Jews, the Roma, homosexuals, handicapped people, known communists, and dissidents were sent to concentration camps to be exterminated.

  - The Jews were a special target for genocide.

    - Jews were first ostracized and forced from positions of authority by the racist Nuremberg Laws.
    - Then, all Jewish people in Nazi occupied territories were sent from their homes without their possessions to ghettoes to live in squalid conditions.
    - After the secret Wannsee Conference of 1942, the Germans decided on a *Final Solution* in which the ghettoes would be liquidated and all the Jews would be sent to death camps, such as Auschwitz and Majdanek.
    - Many Jewish people were saved by Christians and humanitarian networks.

- The stories of *Anne Frank* and *Elie Wiesel* testify to the brutality of the Nazi regime.
- One Christian response was to try to protect Jewish people and others as seen in the famous poem and actions of the Protestant minister, *Martin Niemoller*.

1939

September 1: Hitler invaded Poland, ostensibly to get back the part of East Prussia that the Versailles Treaty had ceded to Poland for access to the Baltic Sea, the *Polish Corridor.*

- The Germans used the *blitzkrieg* technique for this invasion: a massive air strike at a specific area of the enemy lines, followed by a reinforced, rapid, and massive mechanized attack at the point of the air strike.

  - The Germans penetrated Polish lines and divided the enemy troops, who could then be eliminated in sections by the superior firepower of the German war machine.
  - Tanks and mechanized infantry swept in at lightning speed, giving the *blitzkrieg* its name, "lightning war."
  - The Germans also used their *Einsatzgruppen*, a special military force dedicated to killing leaders of Jews, communists, and the Roma during the invasion.

September 3: England and France declared war against Germany to honor their treaty with Poland.

October: Poland fell, occupied by the Germans in the West and the Russians in the East as part of the 1938 *Nonaggression Pact* between the two dictatorships.

- Russia also annexed the Baltic states of *Latvia*, *Lithuania*, and *Estonia*, which had been granted autonomy by the Versailles Treaty.

1940

The time period from the fall of Poland to April 1940 was called the "sitzkrieg" because the French sat behind their supposedly impregnable *Maginot Line*, a series of fortresses on the German border, and the *British Expeditionary Force* in France made no moves. Meanwhile, the Germans prepared for a spring offensive.

- In this time, German forces overran and occupied Denmark and Norway in a matter of days.
- In May 1940, the German army cut through neutral Belgium and Luxembourg to outflank the Maginot Line.
- Within six weeks, the Nazi tactics of *blitzkreig* caused France to fall.
- Isolated and surrounded, the 250,000-man British Expeditionary Force retreated to *Dunkirk* in Belgium, most of them to be evacuated to England along with about 100,000 French troops. The Allies lost their heavy equipment.
- Mussolini invaded southern France, an invasion that was ineffectual militarily but symbolic of Nazi-Fascist solidarity.
- France surrendered on June 22. Germany occupied the north and west, and there, as in all the Nazi-occupied lands, terror and repression reigned.

  - A puppet French government, known as the Vichy Regime, led by First World War hero *Marshal Philippe Petain*, controlled the south and the North African possessions.
  - General Charles de Gaulle (1880–1970), however, escaped to Britain, where he took command of the "Free French":

    - Continued to fight the Nazis.
    - Claimed the role of the Provisional Government of France.
    - The French Resistance undermined the Nazis from inside France.

- The *Battle of Britain*, an air war for supremacy of the skies over Britain.

  - Began in August 1940.
  - Targeted industrial cities of southern England, including London.
  - Subjected to nightly bombings called "the Blitz," harking back to the "lighting" or *blitz*, in *blitzkrieg*.

1941

This was a pivotal year for the war. It looked like Great Britain was the last holdout at the beginning of the war when the war moved to Africa, but that fall Germany invaded the USSR and in December the Japanese attacked the United States at Pearl Harbor and in the Philippines. The USSR and the United States joined the British as enemies of the Axis.

- The United States had been supporting the British through a "lend-lease" program that allowed the British to have the use of American-built ships and to purchase war materials.
- After Russia was invaded, it looked like it too might fall quickly, but the Germans soon were caught in the Russian winter just as the Americans declared war on the Axis powers.
- President *Franklin D. Roosevelt*, Prime Minister *Winston Churchill*, and Soviet Premier *Joseph Stalin* became the **"Big Three,"** who made Allied policy.

1942

By June, the Axis powers in Europe controlled virtually the entire continent from the Atlantic in the West to the gates of Moscow in the East, from Scandinavia in the North to a good part of North Africa in the South.

- The Nazis set up extermination camps in Poland, Austria, and Germany:

  - Transported millions of Jews, other minorities, Soviet prisoners of war, and political enemies there for systematic murder.
  - *Auschwitz:* the most infamous of these new extermination camps.
  - Almost 12 million people were slaughtered inside concentration camps in accord with Nazi racist doctrine; 6 million were European Jews (about 60 percent of the pre-war Jewish population).

- The Asian Axis partner, Japan, had seized the cities of coastal China and taken Indochina from the French, Indonesia from the Dutch, Malaya and Burma from the British, and the Philippines from the United States.
- General *Erwin Rommel*, the "Desert Fox," had managed to push back the British in North Africa deep into Egypt, threatening the Suez Canal, a lifeline of the British Empire.

THE TIDE OF WAR TURNS (MID-1942–1943)

1942

- *June–November:* Rommel's Afrika Corps, the elite mechanized force that spearheaded the advance of Axis troops in this theater of war, was defeated at El Alamein in Egypt by the British under Field Marshall Bernard Montgomery.
- *June:* American aircraft carriers and their fighter planes won a stunning victory against a superior Japanese naval force at the *Battle of Midway* in the Pacific.

- *Summer to winter:* The Russian city of *Stalingrad* stood against German invaders and counterattacked.

  - The fierce battle there marked the end of Nazi advances in the Soviet Union and the eventual destruction of the German Sixth Army, with a loss of 600,000 troops.

- *November:* A joint Anglo-American force landed on the shores of Axis-held territory in North Africa.

1943

The Axis was cleared from North Africa.

- The Russians began the advance that would lead them ultimately into Germany itself.

  - About 80 percent of German casualties in the Second World War were inflicted by the Soviets.
  - Between 25 and 30 million Russians, combatants and civilians, died during the war.

- Allied leaders Roosevelt and Churchill and representatives of Stalin met at *Casablanca* in North Africa and agreed to settle on a strategy of only stopping the war when they had achieved the *unconditional surrender* of the Axis powers.

ALLIED VICTORIES (1943–1945)

1943

- American, British, and Canadian forces invaded the island of Sicily off the boot of Italy.
- Mussolini overthrown.
- Allies landed in Italy proper and fought against determined German resistance.
- At the *Tehran Conference* the Big Three agreed that they would accept only unconditional surrender from all three of the Axis powers, and that after the war was won, Germany would be occupied by the Allied powers and demilitarized.

1944

The *D-Day Invasion* of the French coast at *Normandy* marked the beginning of the end of Nazi domination of the Continent.

- Paris was liberated by August.
- The last German offensive took place at the *Battle of the Bulge* in Belgium that December.
- From that point on, the Germans were in retreat on all fronts.

1945

In February a huge Allied air attack dropped 3,900 tons of high explosives and incendiary bombs on the old German city of Dresden, a cultural landmark, setting it ablaze, and killing 25,000 civilians.

Meanwhile, the Soviet Army smashed into East Prussia, Hungary, and Czechoslovakia while the Americans crossed the Rhine River. Hitler committed suicide; encircled Berlin was seized by the Russians; Germany surrendered, unconditionally, on May 8.

- *August 6:* The United States dropped the *first atomic bomb* on the Japanese city of *Hiroshima.*

  – 70,000 people died immediately; tens of thousands suffered after-effects.

- *August 9:* A second atomic bomb was dropped on the city of *Nagasaki,* and Japan surrendered.
- *September:* Japan signed an official surrender and agreed to occupation by U.S. forces.

  – Under the supervision of the commander of Allied forces in the Pacific theater, *General Douglas MacArthur,* the emperor denied his own divinity.
  – An antiwar constitution was imposed on Japan.
  – With American financial aid, Japan's wartime destruction was repaired.
  – Technical and financial assistance was given for further industrialization and modernization.
  – A democratic government was set up that still thrives today.

AFTERMATH OF THE WAR

Crucial Conferences for Postwar Europe

The *Yalta Conference,* among the Big Three in February of 1945, drew up a plan for the postwar settlement in Europe. Its main provisions:

- Eastern Europe (Bulgaria, Czechoslovakia, Hungary, Poland, and Romania) would be set up with coalition governments of communists and non-communists until free elections could be held.
- Germany would be partitioned into four zones of occupation: American, British, French, and Soviet.
- The Soviet Union would enter the war against Japan in return for territories in Asia and islands north of Japan.
- The *United Nations* was set up as a successor to the defunct League of Nations, with a *General Assembly* to represent all member nations in deliberations.

  – A separate *Security Council* of 15 members dominated by five permanent members: the "Great Powers," (the United States, the USSR, Britain, France, and China), each of which was given veto rights over any proposal for involving the organization in preserving international peace.

The *Potsdam Conference,* July 1945, was attended by Churchill, Stalin, and Harry S. Truman, who had become president after Roosevelt's sudden death in April. Already, cracks showed in the alliance between the Western democracies and communist Russia when Truman and Churchill criticized Stalin for not allowing free elections in Soviet-occupied Eastern Europe.

- Millions of refugees from concentration camps and from the war itself attempted to return home or to make new lives for themselves.

  – Many tried to reconnect with families and friends with varying degrees of success.
  – Thousands of refugees from the Soviet Union and Yugoslavia were returned to those nations by the Western powers.

- The Marshall Plan offered U.S. financial aid to the European countries devastated by the Second World War.

  - The money came in the form of loans that had to be spent on American goods, helping to transition economies from wartime to peacetime.
  - The Marshall Plan also helped draw the lines between the capitalist countries that were tied together through the financial web of trade, symbolized by the Marshall Plan, and the communist nations that rejected Marshall Plan aid.
  - Led to greater interconnectedness between the economies of Western Europe and the dissolution of trade barriers that had plagued prewar Europe.

The Conflict for Control of Europe

At the end of the Second World War, only two great powers remained with the resources, land mass, population, industrial capacity, and military strength to affect world events. The United States, physically undamaged by the war, and the USSR, devastated but industrially and militarily powerful, became *superpowers*.

- Since the seventeenth century, there had been powerful single nations in Europe (Spain, France, England, Austria) but six or seven other great states had managed, through alliances, to maintain a balance of power.
- Soon after the war, two competing blocs would emerge: the *Soviet Bloc* with its *satellites* of puppet governments in Eastern and Central Europe and the *Western Bloc* or "Free World" made up, primarily, of the democracies.
- With the collapse of the colonial empires (see Chapter 9, "Imperialism"), a third bloc would emerge: the *Developing World*, consisting of newly independent nations.
- In a speech in Fulton, Missouri, in 1946, former prime minister Winston Churchill described Stalin's expansion of Communist totalitarianism as bringing down an *Iron Curtain* separating the captive peoples of Eastern and Central Europe from the rest of the world.
- A competition developed between the *superpowers* to win Europe, its cities in ruins, its population decimated and displaced, but still a great industrial and population center of the world.

The *Cold War* had begun.

Casualties of the Second World War by Nation

Country	1939 Population	Military Death Totals	Civilian Death Totals	Total Jewish Holocaust Deaths	Death Totals	Deaths as Percentage of 1939 Population
Albania	1,073,000	30,000		200	30,200	2.63%
Australia	6,998,000	40,500	700		41,200	0.57%
Austria	6,653,000		40,500	65,000	105,500	5.5%
Belgium	8,387,000	12,100	49,600	24,400	86,100	1.02%
Bulgaria	6,458,000	22,000	3,000		25,000	0.38%
China	517,568,000	3,800,000	16,200,000		20,000,000	3.86%
Czechoslovakia	15,300,000	25,000	43,000	277,000	345,000	2.25%
Denmark	3,795,000	2,100	1,000	100	3,200	0.08%
Dutch East Indies	69,435,000	11,350	2,500,000–4,000,000		2,511,350–4,011,350	3.75%–5.75%
Estonia	1,134,000		50,000	1,000	51,000	4.50%
Finland	3,700,000	95,000	2,000		97,000	2.62%
France	41,700,000	217,600	267,000	83,000	567,600	1.35%
Germany	69,623,000	5,533,000	1,540,000	160,000	7,233,000	8.6%
Greece	7,222,000	20,000	220,000	71,300	311,300	4.31%
Hungary	9,129,000	300,000	80,000	200,000	580,000	6.35%
Iceland	119,000		200		200	0.17%
Italy	44,394,000	301,400	145,100	8,000	454,500	1.02%
Japan	71,380,000	2,120,000	580,000		2,700,000	3.78%
Latvia	1,995,000		147,000	80,000	227,000	11.38%
Lithuania	2,575,000		212,000	141,000	353,000	13.71%
Luxembourg	295,000		1,300	700	2,000	0.68%
Netherlands	8,729,000	21,000	176,000	104,000	301,000	3.44%
Norway	2,945,000	3,000	5,800	700	9,500	0.32%
Poland	34,849,000	240,000	2,760,000	3,000,000	6,000,000	17.2%
Romania	19,934,000	300,000	64,000	469,000	833,000	4.22%
(Soviet Union) USSR	168,500,000	10,700,000	11,400,000	1,000,000	23,100,000	13.71%
United Kingdom	47,760,000	382,700	67,100		449,800	0.94%
United States	131,028,000	416,800	1,700		418,500	0.32%
Yugoslavia	15,400,000	446,000	514,000	67,000	1,027,000	6.67%
World Totals	1,963,205,000	25,282,100	42,168,400	5,752,400	73,169,900	3.71%

PRACTICE LONG-ESSAY QUESTIONS

These questions are samples of the various types of thematic essays on the exam. (See pages 30–31 for a detailed explanation of each type.) Check over the **generic rubric** (see pages 32–33) before you begin any of these essays and use that rubric to score your essay if you write one.

Question 1

To what extent was Nazi totalitarianism a different breed from ordinary dictatorship?

COMMENTS ON QUESTION 1

This is a COMPARE skill question, so be sure to describe similarities and differences between Nazi totalitarianism and other forms of totalitarian dictatorship, as well as account for or explain them by providing specific examples of Nazi totalitarianism and other dictators such as Stalin, Mussolini, or Franco. You must consider the phrase "different breed." It implies that the Third Reich was far more encompassing and repressive than the usual military dictatorship. The task is to explain how. How did the Nazis use state-sponsored terrorism to gain and hold power? How did their racist theories lead to genocide? What was the structure of their police state? How did they use propaganda and education to inculcate their program? How was war an integral part of their ideology? This essay cannot be complete without comparing and contrasting Hitler's regime with that of Stalin, Mussolini, Franco, or other totalitarian rulers.

Question 2

Explain how the Versailles Treaty gave birth to the Nazis while the Great Depression gave them power.

COMMENTS ON QUESTION 2

This one is a CAUSATION question because it requires you to either support or refute the idea that two events, the Treaty of Versailles and the Great Depression, resulted in specific outcomes: the birth of the Nazi Party, and its rise to power. Remember to describe causes AND/OR effects of the Nazi party growth and rise to power, and support your analysis of those causes and effects through citing specific evidence. The essay must explain reasons that the Treaty of Versailles helped the Nazis be created while they increased their power through the Great Depression, and must utilize specific evidence as a relevant support. A few crucial questions point the way when answered. How did the Nazis and other right-wing extremists grow in membership after Germany's defeat in the First World War? What part did the war guilt clause of the treaty play in their propaganda? How did the indemnity payments destabilize the German economy? How was racism involved? Why were the Nazis different from each other? What was happening to Nazi party membership during the late 1920s, and how did the emergence of the Great Depression affect that trend?

Question 3

Compare German Nazism with Italian Fascism.

COMMENTS ON QUESTION 3

This is a COMPARE skill question, so be sure to describe similarities and differences between Nazism and Italian Fascism, as well as account for or explain them by providing specific examples of the similarities and differences between Nazism and Italian Fascism. The similarities are easier to lay out: the means by which Hitler and Mussolini got into office, gained control of the state, and used propaganda, education, and force to subdue internal enemies; the ideology of war for the glorification of the state; the subversion of the institutions of society to serve the state.

The differences are of kind and degree: the Fascists in Italy never preached or practiced the poisonous racism that led to genocide; their military never achieved the kind of power that enabled the Nazis to impose their murderous policies all over the Continent; their program and ideology were never digested by the Italian people with the relish with which many Germans swallowed Nazism.

Question 4

Assess the extent to which the Allied decision to demand "unconditional surrender" of the Axis powers lengthened the war needlessly.

COMMENTS ON QUESTION 4

This one is a CAUSATION question because it requires you to explain how much the policy of "unconditional surrender" of the Axis powers resulted in a specific outcome, the lengthening of the Second World War. Remember to describe causes AND/OR effects of the lengthening of the Second World War, and to support your analysis of those causes and effects through citing specific evidence. The essay must also EXPLAIN how the need for unconditional surrender did or did not lengthen the war needlessly citing specific relevant evidence as support. This has been an issue much argued, "a hypothesis contrary to fact." Would the war have ended sooner if the Allies had negotiated with the Axis governments or even with antigovernment military factions? In framing your answer, consider that despite the saturation bombing of Germany's cities, the Nazis maintained an iron grip until the end; despite assassination attempts, Hitler ruled until his suicide when the Russians were at the gates of Berlin; despite firebombing and the dropping of the first A-bomb, and running out of soldiers, the Japanese refused to surrender.

Question 5

Compare the results of the Second World War on both the United States and the USSR.

COMMENTS ON QUESTION 5

This is a COMPARE skill question, so be sure to describe similarities and differences between the results of the Second World War on the Soviet Union and the United States, as well as account for or explain them by providing specific examples of how the United States and the USSR experienced similar and different results from the war. Show differences: What was the destruction to the homelands of each? What political, social, or economic changes took place for each? What were the human losses? What were the war gains? Examine similarities: They were the only two powers, *superpowers*, with the strength left to influence European and world events; they had established parallel spheres of influence; both were brought into the war through sneak attack; they had simultaneously solidified their competing ideologies and launched the Cold War. This is an abstract question that requires crisp organization and thoughtful presentation.

Question 6

Why did the wartime cooperation of the United States and the Soviet Union degenerate, within a few years after the end of the Second World War, into the Cold War?

COMMENTS ON QUESTION 6

This one is a CAUSATION question because it requires you to explain what caused the degeneration of the alliance that had won the largest war in history into a virtual stalemate referred to as the Cold War. Remember to describe causes AND/OR effects of the Cold War, and to support your analysis of those causes and effects through citing specific evidence. The essay must also explain specific causes for the disintegration of the relationship between the United States and the Soviet Union, such as the Soviet actions in Eastern Europe and the American capture of Nazi scientists as specific relevant support. The wartime alliance between the West and the Soviet Union was the cooperation of competing systems in order to defeat a common enemy. Strains showed early in the Russian push for opening a second front—strains seen in the tensions at Yalta and at Potsdam in the Russian refusal to allow free elections in Russian-occupied Eastern Europe. The distrust between American and Soviet generals added fuel to the fire. The geographic expansion of communism because of the war frightened the West. The presence of massive American forces in Europe, American possession of atomic weapons, and personal distrust between Stalin and the new leaders of the other powers frightened the Soviets. The importance of the military propaganda, ideological differences, and huge profits for the American "military industrial complex" (which Eisenhower warned of in his farewell address) should also be examined.

PRACTICE SHORT-ANSWER QUESTIONS

1. Please use the excerpt below and your knowledge of European History to answer all parts of the question that follows.

The Decline of the West

The idealist of the early democracy regarded popular education as enlightenment pure and simple—but it is precisely this that smooths the path for the coming Caesars of the world. The last century [the nineteenth] was the winter of the West, the victory of materialism and skepticism, of socialism, parliamentarianism, and money. But in this century blood and instinct will regain their rights against the power of money and intellect. The era of individualism, liberalism and democracy, of humanitarianism and freedom, is nearing its end. The masses will accept with resignation the victory of the Caesars, the strong men, and will obey them. Life will descend to a level of general uniformity, a new kind of primitivism, and the world will be better for it.

—Oswald Spengler, 1922

(A) Briefly identify and explain ONE way that this source expresses the prevalent mood of Europeans in the period between the First World War and the Second World War.

(B) Briefly explain ONE assertion of the source above that was proven to be correct over the last century.

(C) Briefly explain ONE assertion of the source above that was proven to be incorrect over the last century.

2. Please use the song below and your knowledge of European History to answer all parts of the question that follows.

From Finland to the Black Sea
(German Marching Song from the Second World War)

The march of Horst Wessel began
In the brown robe of the SA
End completely the gray columns:
The great hour is here!
From Finland to the Black Sea:
Forward, forward!
Forward to the east, you stinging army!
Freedom the goal,
Victory the banner!
Leader, commanded!
We follow you!

Now the armies roar into the
Russian country.
Comrades, now to the rifles!
The victory will be ours!
From Finland to the Black Sea:
Forward, forward!
Forward to the east, you stinging army!
Freedom the goal,
Victory the banner!
Leader, commanded!

(A) Briefly identify and describe how the source above supports the Nazi idea of *Lebensraum.*

(B) Briefly explain how the Soviet Union was brought into the Second World War.

(C) Briefly explain how the Nazi culture is expressed in the song above.

Short-Answer Explanations

1. (A) You should identify the period between the world wars as the Age of Anxiety and explain the anxiety about the future of Europe that is expressed in the source by citing specific facts from the source that express that anxiety, such as: the idea that Europe's dominance of the world was ending in 1922, the fear of the loss of individualism, the fear of losing democracy, the fear of losing freedom, the fear of losing humanitarianism, and the fear of the rise of strong leaders who would crush the will of the citizens.

   (B) You should explain the rise of dictators Lenin, Stalin, Hitler, and Mussolini as proof that strong men would rise and crush individual freedoms. An alternative is for you to cite the Second World War and the rise of blood and instinct regaining power.

   (C) You should explain that the West continued to gain power almost until the end of the century. Another option is for you to explain that individual rights and freedoms as well as humanitarianism have continued to grow in Europe throughout the twentieth century.

2. (A) You should explain that the idea of gaining land for the German people to expand into is the concept of *Lebensraum*, and that the song supports Germany expanding to reach from Finland to the Black Sea by conquering Soviet territory and annexing it into the German state.

   (B) You should start with the German-Soviet nonaggression pact of 1939, also known as the Molotov–Ribbentrop Pact. You should then explain Operation Barbarossa, the German invasion plan for the Soviet Union, which aimed to gain land and oil resources for the German people.

   (C) You should explain that the song supports the ideals of the German "master race" and the growing militarism of the Nazi regime. It should also explain German reverence for their Nazi leaders, the idea of the Third Reich, and the idea that Germans would always be victorious in war.

PRACTICE MULTIPLE-CHOICE QUESTIONS

Questions 1 to 4 refer to the following excerpt from the introduction of *Economic Consequences of the Peace* by John Maynard Keynes.

We assume some of the most peculiar and temporary of our late advantages as natural, permanent, and to be depended on, and we lay our plans accordingly. On this sandy and false foundation we scheme for social improvement and dress our political platforms, pursue our animosities and particular ambitions, and feel ourselves with enough margin in hand to foster, not assuage, civil conflict in the European family. Moved by insane delusion and reckless self-regard, the German people overturned the foundations on which we all lived and built. But the spokesmen of the French and British peoples have run the risk of completing the ruin, which Germany began, by a Peace which, if it is carried into effect, must impair yet further, when it might have restored, the delicate, complicated organization, already shaken and broken by war, through which alone the European peoples can employ themselves and live.

1. Which of the following peace settlements was Keynes criticizing in the passage above?

   (A) The Treaty of Amiens
   (B) The Peace of Paris
   (C) The Treaty of Maastricht
   (D) The Treaty of Versailles

2. Which of the following conflicts disturbed the creation of the treaty above by making the negotiations more drawn out and arduous?

   (A) The conflict between Wilsonian idealism and the desire to punish Germany
   (B) The conflict between Russia and Prussia over the fate of Poland
   (C) The conflict between Great Britain and France over colonial empires
   (D) The conflict between nationalism and socialism

3. Which of the following was NOT a new nation created as a result of the treaty mentioned above?

   (A) Czechoslovakia
   (B) Palestine
   (C) Hungary
   (D) Yugoslavia

4. Which of the following was correctly predicted by Keynes as a result of the peace treaty that he opposed?

   (A) Germany once again rose to be an economic powerhouse.
   (B) The Scandinavian economies did the best during this period.
   (C) A massive worldwide depression occurred as a long-term result of the treaty.
   (D) Great Britain rose to economic dominance of the world.

Questions 5 to 7 refer to the following chart about Soviet farming.

Year	No. of Collective Farms in 1,000s	Sown Area of Collective Farms in Millions of Hectares	% of Collective Sown Area Serviced by Machine Tractor Stations (MTS)
1929	57.0	4.2	—
1930	85.9	38.1	27.4
1931	211.1	79.0	37.1
1932	211.1	91.5	49.3
1933	224.6	93.6	58.7
1934	233.3	98.6	63.9
1935	245.4	104.5	72.4
1936	242.2	110.5	82.8
1937	243.7	116.0	91.2
1938	242.4	117.2	93.3
1939	241.1	114.9	94.0

5. Which of the following policies enacted by Stalin led to the growth in agriculture seen above?

   (A) Supporting the kulaks
   (B) Collectivization
   (C) Five-year plans
   (D) War communism

6. Which of the following is the best description of the major differences between the economic policies of Lenin and Stalin?

   (A) Lenin's five-year-plans moved the country forward during the 1930s while Stalin's New Economic Policy met mixed results.
   (B) Stalin exerted much more state control over the economy with his five-year-plans than Lenin did with his New Economic Policy.
   (C) Lenin exerted much more state control over the economy with his five-year-plans than Stalin did with his New Economic Policy.
   (D) Stalin had more favorable policies toward the better-off peasants, or kulaks, than Lenin did.

7. Which of the following was the most likely fate for comrades who did not meet their economic targets under Stalin during the years cited above?

   (A) They were reeducated in Moscow.
   (B) They were sent to live as they pleased in Siberia.
   (C) They were imprisoned in gulags.
   (D) They were deported to capitalist countries.

Questions 8 to 10 refer to the laws enacted in 1935 seen below.

Article 1

1. Marriages between Jews and subjects of the state of German or related blood are forbidden. Marriages nevertheless concluded are invalid, even if concluded abroad to circumvent this law.
2. Annulment proceedings can be initiated only by the state prosecutor.

Article 2

Extramarital relations between Jews and subjects of the state of German or related blood are forbidden.

Article 3

Jews may not employ in their households female subjects of the state of German or related blood who are under 45 years old.

8. The three articles above were a part of a series of laws that defined racial purity in Germany known as which of the following?

   (A) The Wannsee Laws
   (B) The Reichstag laws
   (C) The Nuremberg Laws
   (D) The Nazi code

9. Which of the following can be best supported by the actions of the Nazi government in Germany?

   (A) Germany wanted to establish hegemony over the entire world.
   (B) Germany wanted to create a new racial order in Europe.
   (C) Germany wanted to rid Asia of Asians to make room for more Europeans.
   (D) Germany wanted to destroy the national character of every European nationality.

10. Which of the following was the meeting at which the "final solution" was agreed upon by the Nazis?

   (A) Wannsee Conference
   (B) Berlin Conference
   (C) Tehran Conference
   (D) Potsdam Conference

Multiple-Choice Explanations

1. **D**	4. **C**	7. **C**	10. **A**
2. **A**	5. **C**	8. **C**	
3. **B**	6. **B**	9. **B**	

1. **(D)**

(A) is wrong because Keynes is famously criticizing the Treaty of Versailles that ended the First World War.

(B) is wrong because Keynes is famously criticizing the Treaty of Versailles that ended the First World War.

(C) is wrong because Keynes is famously criticizing the Treaty of Versailles that ended the First World War.

(D) is CORRECT because Keynes is famously criticizing the Treaty of Versailles that ended the First World War.

2. **(A)**

(A) is CORRECT because the major problem at the conference table creating the Treaty of Versailles was the conflict between Wilson's idealistic Fourteen Points and the others' desire to punish Germany.

(B) is wrong because Prussia ceased to exist in 1871.

(C) is wrong because France and the United Kingdom saw eye to eye at the conference table and did not squabble over possessions.

(D) is wrong because nationalism and socialism began to work together in the 1880s after Bismarck joined them inextricably in Germany.

3. **(B)**

(A) is wrong because the Treaty of Versailles did create the official nation of Czechoslovakia.

(B) is CORRECT because the League of Nations made Palestine a British protectorate, but did not create a separate nation.

(C) is wrong because the Treaty of Versailles did create the official nation of Hungary.

(D) is wrong because the Treaty of Versailles did create the official nation of Yugoslavia.

4. **(C)**

(A) is wrong because Keynes predicted a worldwide depression, not the rise of Germany; rather he predicted its fall.

(B) is wrong because Keynes predicted a worldwide depression, not the rise of Scandinavian economies that used his ideas.

(C) is CORRECT because Keynes predicted a worldwide depression.

(D) is wrong because Keynes predicted a worldwide depression, not the rise of Britain; rather he predicted its fall.

5. **(C)**

(A) is wrong because Stalin eliminated the kulaks, rather than supported them.

(B) is wrong because the collectivization was a serious failure, and the output in agriculture only increased due to the mechanization provided by the five-year plans.

(C) is CORRECT because the five-year-plans allowed the increase of industry and the mechanization of agriculture, leading to higher output.

(D) is wrong because war communism was used to fight the civil war, but did not improve agriculture.

6. **(B)**

(A) is wrong because Lenin had a New Economic Policy while Stalin had his five-year plans.

(B) is CORRECT because Stalin's five-year plans did exert much more state control than Lenin's New Economic Policy.

(C) is wrong because Lenin had a New Economic Policy, while Stalin had his five-year plans.

(D) is wrong because Stalin eliminated the better-off peasants as a class.

7. **(C)**

(A) is wrong because Moscow was the center of Soviet power, and dissidents were sent away from there.

(B) is wrong because if they were sent to Siberia, they worked in prison camps and did not live as they pleased.

(C) is CORRECT, as the gulags were the prison camps for dissidents in the Soviet Union.

(D) is wrong because the soviets wanted to punish their wrong-minded citizens rather than reward their disobedience.

8. **(C)**

(A) is wrong because the Wannsee Conference was held to determine the fate of all Jewish people by deciding to exterminate all of them, as opposed to the Nuremberg Laws, which were Germany's racial-purity laws and a step toward the dehumanization of Jewish people in Germany.

(B) is wrong because the Reichstag was the lower legislative branch in Germany, not a set of racist laws.

(C) is CORRECT because the Nuremberg Laws were Germany's racial-purity laws and a step toward the dehumanization of Jewish people in Germany.

(D) is wrong because there was no Nazi code relating to race called such.

9. **(B)**

(A) is wrong because Germany only wanted hegemony in Europe at first.

(B) is CORRECT because the Nazis tried to create a new racial order in which Slavs would be servants to the superior Germans and Anglo-Saxons, while Jews, the Roma, and others would be exterminated.

(C) is wrong because Germany was allied with Japan.

(D) is wrong because Germany was very nationalistic and wanted to preserve its own culture.

10. **(A)**

(A) is CORRECT because the Wannsee Conference was held to determine the "final solution" of exterminating the Jewish people from the world.

(B) is wrong because the Berlin Conference was held in 1885 to reorganize African colonies.

(C) is wrong because the Tehran Conference was among Allied leaders during the Second World War.

(D) is wrong because the Potsdam Conference was among Allied leaders during the Second World War.

Recovery, Cold War, and Contemporary Europe (1945 to Present)

12

KEY TERMS/PEOPLE

- → MORGENTHAU PLAN
- → BLOCKADE OF BERLIN
- → THE MARSHALL PLAN
- → BERLIN AIRLIFT
- → TREATY OF MAASTRICHT
- → BALKAN WARS OF 1990s
- → NORTH ATLANTIC TREATY ORGANIZATION (NATO)
- → KOREAN WAR
- → DOUGLAS MACARTHUR
- → BABY BOOM
- → MARGARET THATCHER
- → SCHUMAN AND MONNET PLAN
- → THE GENEVA SUMMIT
- → WARSAW PACT

- → PRAGUE SPRING
- → COMECON
- → FIDEL CASTRO
- → EUROPEAN ECONOMIC COMMUNITY
- → SIMONE DE BEAUVOIR
- → PARIS SUMMIT
- → COMMON MARKET
- → BAY OF PIGS
- → *SPUTNIK*
- → BERLIN WALL
- → BREZHNEV DOCTRINE
- → CUBAN MISSILE CRISIS
- → TRUMAN DOCTRINE
- → BRAIN DRAIN

OVERVIEW

The destruction of Europe after the Second World War was far more extensive than that at the end of the First World War. The technology and tactics of the First World War had limited the worst damage to specific regions of Europe: Flanders, which consists of northeastern France and parts of Belgium, and Poland and sections of European Russia, some provinces of northern Italy and southern Austria; some areas of the Balkans. During the Second World War, the mass bombing of industrial and population centers severely damaged virtually all the cities of the European belligerents and it left Germany in ruins. The German destruction and the scorched-earth policy of the Soviets leveled tens of thousands of villages, towns, and cities in the western Soviet Union. It ruined transport systems, factories, and housing and shattered the economies of Western and Eastern Europe.

The economic recovery of Western Europe was so amazing, it was referred to as "the miracle." Within a decade, productivity had reached prewar levels; within two decades, unparalleled prosperity prevailed. West Germany, so recently defeated, demoralized, and divided from East Germany, had been the key to recovery. The United States infused massive aid through the Marshall Plan to rebuild not only its former Allies but also its former enemies—West Germany and Italy. By the end of the 1950s, Western Europe had made the first moves toward economic and, eventually, political union. The United States also aided Japan and set up a viable democratic government.

The rebuilding of the USSR was no less spectacular. Under Stalin's five-year plans, most of the war damage had been repaired within a decade. A vastly expanded Soviet empire, established by the successes of the Red Army against the Nazis, included most of the countries of Eastern Europe, which became satellites of the brutally repressive Stalinist Soviet Union. After the death of Stalin in 1953, new leaders redefined the role of Soviet communism but kept an iron grip on the USSR and Eastern Europe. The emergence of the United States and the USSR as superpowers at the end of the war created a new balance of power in Europe and in the world. Europe quickly became divided into the West and the Communist bloc—the West dedicated to the containment of Soviet expansionism, the communists intent on both spreading their philosophy and defending their gains against the "capitalist conspiracy." The Cold War (the ideological, economic, and, at times, military rivalry between the two adversaries) was all the more dangerous for the development of nuclear weapons. Several hot spots in the Cold War—such as the Korean War, the Cuban Missile Crisis, the Vietnam War, the Yom Kippur War, and the Soviet invasion of Afghanistan—caused the world great concern. Peaks of tension, during which the superpower confrontations almost led to war or even nuclear holocaust, alternated with "thaws," until a policy of "peaceful coexistence" emerged.

In the 1970s, high energy prices resulting from instability in the Middle East and the disintegration of the American-dominated global monetary system brought about a worldwide recession. Western Europe suffered stagflation and huge government deficits.

During this decade, détente (a relaxation of tensions between East and West) was furthered by West Germany's attempts to reconcile with Eastern Europe and by the Helsinki Agreements, and it was strained by the U.S. involvement in Vietnam, the Soviet involvement in Afghanistan, and a massive American arms buildup.

The most important and dramatic developments of the 1980s and early 1990s were the largely peaceful anti-communist revolutions in Eastern Europe and the collapse of Soviet communism that led to the dismantling of the Soviet Union. The Solidarity movement in Poland, liberalization in Hungary and Czechoslovakia, and the unification of East and West Germany marked the end of Soviet domination of Eastern Europe. The gradual decline of Soviet economic strength under Brezhnev and Andropov led Gorbachev to initiate profound political and social reform (*glasnost*) and economic restructuring (*perestroika*). In 1989, the first free elections were conducted since the 1917 Revolution. An attempted military coup against Gorbachev in the summer of 1991 faced popular opposition and failed. Many Soviet republics declared independence and, with the promise of reform, Boris Yeltsin was elected president of the Russian Republic. Vladimir Putin replaced Yeltsin in 2000, and oversaw the privatization of the Soviet state possessions such as oil companies and other industry. Dmitri Medvedev replaced Putin in 2008 as his handpicked successor, while Putin still held actual power as prime minister. Putin was reelected president in 2012 when he became constitutionally eligible to do so.

The entrance of great numbers of women into the workplace and the feminist movement altered the lives of women in Europe and the United States. The birth rate dropped, the divorce rate rose, and sexual and social attitudes toward women changed. At the beginning of the twentieth century, women could not vote, and at the time of publication of this book women have been elected as prime ministers in Great Britain, Germany, India, Portugal, Norway, Yugoslavia, Lithuania, Pakistan, France, Poland, Turkey, and many other nations. The twentieth century was the century of the woman in many ways. Women in many countries gained intellectual and professional freedom and increased earning power. Widespread use of contraception led to increased emancipation in industrialized nations, allowing women to participate more equally in society as their roles changed from caretakers to wage earners in many cases. By the 1990s, laws preventing wage and other forms of discrimination against women were prevalent in Western Europe as well as in the United States, Canada, and other industrially advanced countries. Women have risen to the highest positions of power in Europe and elsewhere as they have gained more legal, political, and economic freedom than at any time in European history.

Most recently, increasing nationalism in Europe has led to anti-immigration and right-wing parties gaining ground in elections. Financial crises, as well as increasing sentiment against Muslim immigrants and others who are changing the national cultures within Europe, threaten the once growing European unity.

WESTERN EUROPEAN RECOVERY (1945-1957)

The 1940s After the War: Setting the Stage for the Cold War

Since Germany's *Ruhr Basin* was the industrial center of a devastated Europe, the Western Allies decided that Germany would have to be rebuilt. The Soviets had hoped to use German reparations for reconstruction of their own massive war damage, and the *Morgenthau Plan* had been developed by the U.S. secretary of the treasury to transform Germany back into an exclusively agricultural society. Led by the Americans, the British and French agreed that in order for Western Europe to recover, Germany would have to be rebuilt.

- The United Nations (UN), which replaced the defunct League of Nations and began with just 50 nations, now includes 193 nations and many non-governmental organizations (NGOs) such as Amnesty International, which join in debate but do not vote.

  - The UN has a General Assembly and six main committees as well as a Human Rights Council and an Economic and Social Council; and its Security Council must approve any international military action.
  - The Security Council has five permanent members with vetoes: France, Russia, China, United Kingdom, and the United States.
  - The UN works to prevent human tragedy, preserve and promote human rights, improve health through the World Health Organization, improve education and economic development, and promote international peace and understanding.

- Joint administration of the *four occupation zones* in Germany broke down in 1946.

  - The American, British, and French sectors eventually became West Germany; the Russian sector, East Germany.

- Agitation by communist parties in France and Italy worsened relations between the democracies of Western Europe and the Soviet Union.
- In 1948 the Czech communists seized power in Prague and set up a government.
- *The Marshall Plan*, developed by Secretary of State *George Marshall* (1880–1959), former U.S. military chief of staff, was put into operation.

  - Billions of dollars in grants went to Western Europe to rebuild housing, transportation systems, and industrial plants.
  - The Western European nations created the Committee of European Economic Cooperation in 1948 as a result of the Marshall Plan as a way to coordinate economic efforts and get the most out of their aid dollars.

- This eventually led to the creation of the Organization for European Economic Cooperation (OEEC), which was a primary tool of European integration until it was replaced by the Organization for Economic Co-operation and Development (OECD), which helped usher in the European Union.

■ The Soviet response to the OEEC and the Marshall Plan was COMECON, the Council for Mutual Economic Assistance, set up in 1949 to facilitate and coordinate the economic activity of those countries in Eastern Europe in the Soviet sphere of influence known as the Eastern Bloc.

■ Western Europe created new benefit systems for its citizens to reduce the peaks and valleys that capitalism creates in the human condition and to support basic necessities for all citizens, known as the *modern welfare state.*

- Unemployment insurance became universal and lasted for long periods of time.
- Housing subsidies were provided to low-income families.
- Medical care is given to all for free, as a human right.
- Pensions were created for all citizens.
- Subsidies were given for large families.
- Child-care was provided in state-sponsored facilities.
- Higher taxes on the wealthy paid for these benefits for the neediest.

■ The rapid transformation of West Germany into an economic powerhouse that became the leading economy in Europe was labeled the *Wirtschaftswunder* or "West German miracle" due to the miraculous nature of economic growth there.

- The 1950s saw increasing standards of living with a 73 percent rise in purchasing power for the average West German.

■ The United States and 11 other nations formed the North Atlantic Treaty Organization (NATO) to rearm non-communist Europe and safeguard it against invasion.

- Soon after, West Germany (the Federal Republic of Germany), Greece, and Turkey joined.
- Eventually Germany was encouraged to organize a national army under NATO command.

■ The *Warsaw Pact* was formed as an alliance of the Soviet Union and its Eastern European satellite nations (East Germany, Poland, Czechoslovakia, Hungary, Rumania, Bulgaria, and Albania) as an answer to the formation of NATO by Western Europe

Western Europe Begins Economic Integration

Productivity in those countries that received *Marshall Plan* aid had exceeded prewar rates, and the United States urged the Europeans to develop a European free-trade zone similar to that among the various American states.

■ The *Marshall Plan* combined self-interest (communism in Europe would be contained and markets for U.S. goods opened) with altruism.

■ The *General Agreement on Tariffs and Trade (GATT)* was completed in 1948 in which signatories agreed to reduce tariffs and negotiated during the United Nations Conference on Trade and Employment.

- Resulted due to the failure of negotiating governments to create the International Trade Organization (ITO).
- GATT was signed by 23 nations in Geneva on October 30, 1947, and took effect on January 1, 1948.
- Lasted until the signature by 123 nations in *Marrakesh* on April 14, 1994, of the Uruguay Round Agreements, which established the *World Trade Organization (WTO)* on January 1, 1995.

■ Under the French-sponsored *Schuman and Monnet Plan*, six industrial countries on the Continent (Belgium, France, Holland, Italy, Luxembourg, and West Germany) formed the *European Coal and Steel Community* to pool their resources in 1952.

- The *European Economic Community*, the *Common Market*, was created by the same six nations that formed the European Coal and Steel Community.
- It aimed at an end to internal tariffs and for the free exchange of money and workers between members.
- By 1968, its plan would be in full effect.
- In 1973, Britain, previously denied membership by France, joined as a full partner along with Ireland and Denmark.

■ By 1960, many of the best scientists and engineers left Europe to go to the United States for higher salaries, creating the "brain drain."

DECOLONIZATION

France, Belgium, Great Britain, Italy, the Netherlands, and Portugal all gave up their colonial empires in the period after the Second World War. By 1975, most of Africa and Asia was back under African and Asian rule, with a few minor exceptions. The horrors of the world wars had destroyed much of the confidence the Western powers had that they were better than those they ruled and allowed Europeans to see that the rest of the world deserved self-rule.

■ Britain gave up India first in 1947; then much of Africa was relinquished after 1960.

- The British also gave up governing parts of the Middle East that now include Syria, Iraq, and Israel.
- A Jewish homeland was created in Israel in 1948.
- There was considerable bloodshed during British decolonization: For example, between 12,000–20,000 Mau Mau rebels are estimated to have died fighting for independence in Kenya; and Jewish rebels in Palestine fought fiercely against occupying British troops to force the United Kingdom to withdraw.

■ The French gave up Indochina after their resounding defeat at Dien Bien Phu in 1954 but fought very hard to keep Algeria.

- It was a long and brutal conflict that sapped France of resources and forced it to fight against guerilla tactics and a native nationalist movement.
- The conflict ended with a French Commonwealth that included most of the African area France had fought to keep.

■ Belgium had ruled a portion of Africa that was 75 times the size of Belgium.

- The Democratic Republic of the Congo was formed in 1960, ending more than a century of Belgian rule there.

- The Portuguese also decolonized slowly and reluctantly as their world power dissipated.

    - Angola was an example of their attempt to preserve rule that brutalized natives.

- Despite indigenous nationalist movements, independence for many African and Asian territories was delayed until the mid, and even late, twentieth century by the imperial powers' reluctance to relinquish control, threats of interference from other nations, unstable economic and political systems, and Cold War strategic alignments.

    - The *Indian National Congress* agitated for independence, for almost half a century, under the leadership of Mohandas K. Gandhi before the British simply walked out of India in 1948.
    - In Vietnam, *Ho Chi Minh* organized the Viet Minh to fight for independence, first from France and then from American control, as he worked to establish Vietnam as a communist state.
    - In Indonesia, Sukarno led his people to independence from the Netherlands, which had tried to restore its rule there after the Second World War.

- Some scholars argue that the proliferation of European languages in education and finance, as well as Cold War political pressures, led to an era of *neocolonialism* in which nations are still dominated financially and politically rather than militarily.

May 1968 in France

The economy of France was brought to a standstill, and President Charles de Gaulle was unable to solve the problems caused by a general strike and fled the country.

- The strikes began with student protests against the expulsion of a few students, the general poor quality of education in France, and the closure of major universities such as the Sorbonne.
- Workers joined the students, and a general strike brought the country to its knees. When de Gaulle returned in a landslide victory, and dissolved the National Assembly and promised to bring in the army, the strike lost momentum and the republic was saved.
- Questions plague historians as to whether or not these protests were part of a cultural diffusion from the United States, where riots over the shootings of Martin Luther King, Jr., and Bobby Kennedy led to general unrest and protests against the Vietnam War.

COMMUNISM: THE SOVIET UNION AND ITS SATELLITES (1945–1968)

Immediately After the Second World War

Backed by the USSR "Red" Army, local communist parties in Eastern Europe (Bulgaria, Czechoslovakia, Poland, and Romania) took over the coalition governments and fell under the Soviet orbit. East Germany, under Soviet occupation, also became a satellite.

Albania and *Yugoslavia*, under Communist Party rule, managed to maintain independence from Moscow since they had not been liberated from the Nazis by Soviet troops.

The Soviets Consolidate Power (1945–1953)

Communist governments in the satellite nations carried out land distribution reforms and nationalization of industry.

- Forced *collectivization* of agriculture was only moderately successful. Soviet-type five-year plans helped reconstruction and built up heavy industry at the expense of consumer goods.
- Police state methods were used (domestic spying, arbitrary imprisonment, censorship, torture) to silence opposition parties and to neutralize the influence of the Roman Catholic Church in newly communist nations such as Poland.
- Repression was tightened to the breaking point in the USSR itself during the last years of Stalin.

  - His achievements (industrialization of Europe's backward giant, victory in the *Great Patriotic War* against the Nazis, postwar reconstruction accomplished in a decade, and the spread of a Soviet communist empire to Eastern Europe) has to be measured against the brutal repression he imposed on the Russian people.
  - Over the course of his totalitarian regime he was responsible for the slaughter of perhaps 30 million of his citizens, for denying basic civil rights, for establishing forced labor camps (gulags), and for repressing any and every form of free expression.

- Stalin died in 1953, and there was a power struggle in the Soviet Union.

  - The party leadership executed Lavrenti Beria, head of the secret police, to prevent a coup, and it set up a figurehead premier.
  - Riots against Soviet domination broke out in East Berlin, a precursor of greater resistance from the satellites.

The Era of Khrushchev (1956–1964)

Nikita S. Khrushchev (1894–1971), a former deputy of Stalin and by 1954 head of the Soviet Communist Party, gave a speech to the Central Committee on the *crimes of Stalin*. Stalin, he said, had built a *cult of personality*, created terror among citizens and party leaders alike, and had even been responsible for the dismal failure of Soviet troops to stop the initial advances of the Nazi invaders in 1941.

- Khrushchev tried to find a middle road between the Western democracies and the old party hard liners who had thrived under Stalin by defending communism while trying to fix the excesses of Stalin.

  - Khrushchev liberalized the arts, as typified by his allowing the publication of Soviet dissident Alexander Solzhenitsyn's *One Day in the Life of Ivan Denisovich*.
  - In a speech at the United Nations, he threatened to destroy the United States.
  - In 1962, in response to U.S. missiles being placed within range of Moscow, he attempted to site nuclear missiles on the newly communist Cuba and had a famous face-off with John F. Kennedy in the *Cuban Missile Crisis*.
  - He also blockaded Berlin, which caused the United States under Kennedy to respond with a massive airlift to West Berlin in order to keep them living the Western capitalist lifestyle.

- After the Cuban Missile Crisis, he softened his tone toward the United States; he signed a nuclear test-ban treaty in late 1963.
  - By backing down against Kennedy, he sealed his fate and lost power in the USSR.

- *De-Stalinization* encouraged resistance in the satellites; *revolts* broke out *in Poland and Hungary.*

  - In Poland, *Wladysaw Gomulka* (1905–1982) managed to win concessions from Soviet leaders to liberalize the government.
  - In Hungary, armed revolt in Budapest and other cities threatened the communist regime, and the Soviets brutally crushed all resistance.

- The launching of the first artificial earth satellite, *Sputnik*, in 1957, pointed out the considerable technological achievements of the Soviets.
- In 1949, they had tested *their first atomic bomb.*
- In 1953, they had developed their first *hydrogen bomb.*
- Their work on rocketry, aided by German scientists captured after the war, enabled them to eventually develop *intercontinental missiles* capable of striking the United States.
- *Centralized economic planning (Gosplan)* had developed the five-year plans that reconstructed the USSR after the Second World War and had raised the Soviet gross national product from 30 percent of the American in 1950 to about 50 percent in the mid-1960s.
- Agriculture performed badly, though, partly because of the failure of collectivized farms to provide incentives for production and partly because of bad decisions by Khrushchev.
- Khrushchev was ousted in 1964: party rivals resented his personal power, and they found an excuse to oust him in his alleged weakness with American presidents Kennedy and Johnson.

The Conflicts of 1968

In August, Soviet leaders sent a massive military force to end the *liberalization of Czechoslovakia*, a threat to both the Warsaw Pact and Soviet domination.

- The *Brezhnev Doctrine*, formulated by head of the Soviet Communist Party and future premier Leonid Brezhnev (1906–1982), stated that the *USSR had the right to intervene* in the internal affairs of any satellite nation if communism was threatened.
- This doctrine and the intervention in Czechoslovakia discredited Soviet leadership of the communist world and its role as a model for communist governments in the coming years of the Cold War.

RECENT EUROPEAN ECONOMIC HISTORY

Through the 1960s, Europe, led by the *Common Market*, accounted for a quarter of the world's industrial output. West Germany was third behind the United States and Japan in gross national product. In 1970, 25 years after the Second World War had ended, prosperity and democracy in Western Europe submerged centuries of national rivalry and promised peace and even greater economic progress and political cooperation.

- The United States exerted financial dominance in the capitalist Western democracies after the Second World War through the Marshall Plan and through control of vast amounts of gold.

- The Bretton-Woods Agreement set up rules for international financial exchange rates based upon a set rate of gold for the dollar.

    - Other currencies could exchange for dollars or gold at a set exchange rate.
    - The International Monetary Fund (IMF) and the World Bank were also created to finance nations in times of crisis.
    - The IMF and the World Bank became tools in the Cold War and afterward for imposing austerity measures on nations, which almost always meant a loss of benefits to their citizens by promising loans to debtor nations only by supporting such austerity measures.

        - Many liberal people across Europe and the United States protested against the intervention by the World Bank and the IMF in global economies because they thought that the policies of the IMF and World Bank would further impoverish those on the bottom rungs of the socioeconomic ladder.

- The United States was providing the capital that kick-started German, Japanese, and Western European economies as a way to create prosperity to fight communism.
- The *oil embargo of 1973* helped change this rosy picture.

    - The *Arab-Israeli War of 1973* incited Arab oil-producing nations to stop the flow of oil to those nations that had supported Israel.
    - This stance was encouraged by the Soviet Union, which provided weapons and support to the Arab nations.
    - Since over 70 percent of Western Europe's petroleum came from the Middle East, the embargo and the resulting price rise threatened to destroy not only Europe's economy but the world's economy.
    - *Stagflation*, a combination of slowdown and inflation that developed into a worldwide recession, had already been a problem that the oil embargo only aggravated.
    - Western Europe's unparalleled economic growth and prosperity in the postwar period was threatened, as was that of the United States and the rest of the industrialized world.
    - Although the recession, the most severe since the Great Depression of the 1930s, improved by early 1976, and while unionism and welfare benefits enabled working people to cope with it more easily, economic growth rates slowed.

- The 1980s saw Great Britain and the United States reduce spending on social programs under conservatives *Margaret Thatcher* and Ronald Reagan, respectively, which contrasted with the strong social programs in the rest of Europe.

    - Thatcher also led Britain during the last clear war for imperialism, when she had the British Navy defend the Falklands Islands off Argentina when the Argentines invaded.
    - Her brand of conservatism conflicted with the fact that she was a woman who led society forward on one social issue as she was cutting benefits to the poor in the UK on another social issue.

- By late 1991, the 12 members of the *European Community*, the Common Market, had completed a plan to integrate economically and to consolidate politically. The *Maastricht Treaty* that went into force in November 1993 was the first major step toward European unification into the *European Union* (EU), which now shares a common currency, a central bank, and a set of trade regulations.

- There are no tariffs or restrictions between the 28 member states that comprise the economic entity, which has one of the largest GDPs in the world, at over $14 trillion.
- The European Union has become a leading political as well as economic force on the world stage.
- 18 of these nations use the *euro* (€) as their currency, but all of them participate in a mixture of supranational and intergovernmental cooperation that holds this confederation of European states together.
- The member states are: Austria, Belgium, Bulgaria, Croatia, Cyprus, the Czech Republic, Denmark, Estonia, Finland, France, Germany, Greece, Hungary, Ireland, Italy, Latvia, Lithuania, Luxembourg, Malta, the Netherlands, Poland, Portugal, Romania, Slovakia, Slovenia, Spain, Sweden, and the United Kingdom.
- Member states are responsible for their own defense, but many belong to NATO.
- The presidency of the European Union currently rotates, but there is some discussion about an elected president for the European Union.
- This union has allowed cooperation on many fronts, from the financial sector to the law enforcement sector, to planning common infrastructure and energy policy, to cooperation in engineering and science.

  - The European Space Agency and Airbus, the world's second largest airplane manufacturer, are joint European projects demonstrating that the European Union is a study in international cooperation.

- The expansion of the European Union into Eastern Europe and the Baltic states has caused tensions with Russia, but has also modernized the economies of those areas.

  - The Russian incursion into Ukraine in 2014 was caused in part by the citizens there protesting in favor of joining NATO.

- Turkey has made gestures at joining the European Union, but so far that has not come to fruition.
- This economic and political union has helped revive Europe as an economic powerhouse during the transition from the twentieth to the twenty-first century.
- In less than a decade, the euro became one of the most important currencies in the world, gaining value against other world currencies, such as the dollar.
- Since 2013, the euro has been falling in value in large part due to the *Greek debt crisis*, which has threatened the strength of the European Union by testing the economic integration as well as the true independent sovereignty of member nations.

■ In 1994 the *World Trade Organization (WTO)* was created by the Marrakech Agreement, signed by 123 nations on 15 April 1994.

- The WTO is an international trade regulating body that enforces agreements on international trade, and it includes a judicial body that has the power to impose penalties on member nations. By providing a framework for negotiating trade agreements and a dispute-resolution process aimed at enforcing participants' adherence to WTO agreements, which are signed by representatives of member governments, the WTO has become a powerful non-governmental organization (NGO) globally.

COLD WAR

The *Cold War* was the economic, cultural, ideological, political, diplomatic, and, under certain circumstances, military struggle between the Western nations and the Communist bloc. This conflict took place over decades, in varying degrees of severity, after the end of the Second World War. The two superpowers (the United States and the USSR) that led the opposing alliances allocated great portions of their productive output to increasing their military might for the aim of defeating the other in a projected war, but they never did *directly* confront each other in a direct military clash. The Cold War shaped the economic and political history of the second half of the twentieth century in many ways, from the ideological conflict to exacerbating problems in the Middle East and Africa, using these regions in proxy battles in the Cold War.

- The initial phase of the Cold War involved a struggle for control of war-devastated Europe.

  - By the late 1940s, U.S. aid had shored up the exhausted democracies of Western Europe against Soviet encroachment.
  - The Soviets had installed communist governments in Eastern Europe under Moscow's domination.

- The next phase involved the **containment** of communism by the West in the "Less Economically Developed Countries" (LEDCs), those regions that had emerged from colonialism after the Second World War.

  - In 1946, former prime minister Winston Churchill helped to define the Cold War (after he was dismissed by voters from office), when he spoke at Westminster College in Fulton, Missouri, and stated that "an iron curtain has descended upon the continent," describing the nations in the Soviet sphere of influence as prisoners in totalitarian regimes.
  - Wars involving the European democracies or the United States against Marxist nationalists broke out in Asia, Africa, and Latin America.

    - When China's communist revolution led by Mao Zedong (Mao Tse-tung) was triumphant in 1949, the United Nations refused to recognize the government of Mao and, instead, recognized the Nationalist Chinese government of Chiang Kai-shek in Taiwan.
    - The Soviet Union boycotted the United Nations as a result of the decision.
    - At this time, North Korea invaded South Korea with Soviet aid in 1950, attacking a United Nations force. Since the Soviets were boycotting the UN, they could not prevent the body voting to oppose the North Koreans.

- The UN declared a police action to stop the North Korean invasion, and the Soviet Union was not in the Security Council to veto the action.
- Eventually the fighting was stopped at the 38th parallel, and a demilitarized zone was created between North and South Korea.
- With no official truce ever signed, this remains a military hotspot that instills fear around the world.

  - Foreign aid and regional alliances, primarily provided and engineered by the United States, countered the influence of Moscow.
  - A nuclear arms race created a "balance of terror" between the two superpowers, while cracks in their systems of alliances aggravated the overall conflict.

- The world was saved from nuclear holocaust only by the fact that both sides knew that either side could literally destroy all human life on Earth, and, therefore, they could not afford to come into open conflict.
- This balance of power, dubbed *Mutually Assured Destruction*, is credited by many historians for preventing a nuclear conflict between the superpowers.
- The role of the United Nations expanded as more newly independent nations joined, and the superpowers realized the limitations of their might.

- The first substantive reduction in Cold War tensions was realized in the *Helsinki Accords*, which were the final act of the Conference on Security and Cooperation held in 1975 in Helsinki, Finland.

  - Most of the European nations on both sides of the *Iron Curtain* signed these agreements.

    - Codified respect for national sovereignty.
    - Acknowledged the national borders.
    - Promised to not use force against other nation signatories.
    - Promised non-intervention in internal affairs of other nations.
    - Respect for human rights.

- Détente prevailed in the years that followed.

  - Splits in the ranks of both the Western alliance and Communist bloc had changed relations between the two superpowers, which through the late 1940s and the 1970s had faced off with the support of allies or satellite nations.
  - De Gaulle's France had questioned the leadership of the United States in European affairs, just as Mao's China had questioned that of the Soviet Union in the communist world.
  - The military suppression of Czechoslovakia tarnished the Soviet image just as the Vietnam War had tarnished the American image.

- A prosperous and independent Western Europe took more and more charge of its own affairs.
- Nationalist resistance in Eastern Europe diminished Soviet influence.
- The Cold War began to "thaw."

The Special Case of Turkey

Turkey poses a special problem as the twenty-first century begins in that it lies partially in Europe, but mostly in Asia. It has been the traditional and literal crossroads between Asia and Europe for millennia and has had both Asian and European identities. It must be examined as a political entity for this course because of its impact on the rest of Europe, but is Turkey a part of Europe? That is for the reader to decide as it is a current political question that the Turks themselves have not fully answered, although it appears that as their global trade increases, they may be attempting to create their own identity separate from Asia and Europe. The chart of ideas that follows may help you decide where to put Turkey in the camps of civilizations.

Is Turkey Part of Europe?

Part of Europe	Not Part of Europe
Center of Christianity for a thousand years	Majority Muslim
Partially in Europe	Many tribal and rural people
Some welfare systems	Majority of nation in Asia
Modern economy	Crusades separated cultures
Industrialized	Ottoman Empire
Secular state	Muslim banking system
50% of trade is with Europe	In 1999 72% of trade was with Europe
Democracy	Current leadership most Islamic ever
Many centuries of trade with Europe	Thus far prevented from joining European Union

THE COLLAPSE OF COMMUNISM AND THE END OF THE COLD WAR

In 1985, the election of *Mikhail Gorbachev* (1931–) by the Soviet Communist Party leadership to serve as party general secretary promised fresh blood to reform the ailing economy and to invigorate the party after the stagnation of the Brezhnev era. His policies of *glasnost*, or openness, and *perestroika*, or restructuring, gave the peoples of Eastern Europe hope for a better life, and the façade of Soviet power crumbled, leaving the people ready for bigger changes. An intended reformer, Gorbachev became the agent of an unintended and unexpected revolution that led to the collapse of communism and the dissolution of the world order that had reigned since the end of the Second World War.

- In 1987, two years after he took office, Chairman Gorbachev and President Ronald Reagan signed the *INF Treaty*, which began the delicate and dangerous process of nuclear disarmament with the destruction of all short- and intermediate-range nuclear missiles.
- Two years after that, the USSR withdrew from the *War in Afghanistan*.
- The Soviets were defeated by the local militias, the mujahidin, who were funded and armed by the American government through agents such as Osama bin Laden.
- Gorbachev's *perestroika*, or restructuring of the economy, and his policy of *glasnost* seemed to be moving Soviet communism toward reform.
- The NATO nations engaged in a military buildup in the 1980s, along with massive television broadcasts across the Iron Curtain countries, implying American capitalist life was like *Dallas* and the *Jeffersons*, effective propaganda that destroyed the social belief in the communist system.

  - Systemic corruption and party privilege also played huge roles in destroying faith in the communist system.
  - Even the brutal suppression by the state police, such as the Stasi in East Germany or the KGB in the USSR, could not prevent the people in Warsaw Pact nations from revolting.

- The *collapse of the Soviet Union* in 1989 marked a very important change in the European balance of power.

  - With the collapse of the Eastern Bloc in the 1990s, the Cold War is said to have ended.

- The Soviet regime was overturned throughout Eastern Europe in mostly bloodless revolutions.
- The Supreme Soviet lost power to the *Congress of People's Deputies.*

  - The new body demanded greater reforms.
  - Soviet Union was dissolved.
  - May have seen a bloody coup if Moscow mayor, *Boris Yeltsin* (1931–2007), had not intervened to ease tensions.
  - Many nations were formed from the former Soviet Union:

- Turkmenistan
- Ukraine
- Georgia

  - Communism was rejected as a failure throughout the Continent.
  - China was left as the only major communist power.
  - The United States, after the dissolution of the Soviet Union, became the sole superpower.

    - The Cold War gave a focus to the amorphous conflict and competition among Earth's peoples, and decades of waging this conflict seemed to establish some rational limitations to winning it.
    - The two main protagonists managed to keep the peace between themselves for nearly a half century.
    - Despite its repressiveness and creaky inefficiencies, Soviet communism helped to restrain the uglier expressions of narrow nationalism and ethnic rivalry.

  - *Solidarity*, the Polish trade-union movement, led by Lech Walesa (1943–), who opposed the rigid communist government.

    - Had been suppressed under martial law.
    - Swept into office by the first free elections since before the Second World War.

  - Changes in the communist governments of Hungary, Bulgaria, and Czechoslovakia took place over the next several months.

    - In November of 1989, the *Berlin Wall*, symbol of communist oppression, was breached.

- Marked the beginning of the downfall of the communist East-German government.

  - Violent revolution in Romania overthrew the longtime communist dictatorship.
  - Free elections established non-communist governments in many of the old East European satellites.

- In October of 1990, *Germany reunited*. Despite fears of a resurgent and aggressive united Germany, Gorbachev had allowed the union of West and East Germany without the promise of its neutrality.

  - Germany joined NATO, and less than a year later the Warsaw Pact, its communist counterpart, was dissolved.

The *Cold War officially ended* in November, when Soviet, U.S., and Western European leaders signed the *Charter for a New Europe.*

TIMELINE FOR THE START OF THE COLD WAR

What follows is a detailed timeline of the Cold War that covers the era with more than enough information to answer any questions that may appear on the AP exam.

Year	Event
1945–1947	■ Communist-agitated strikes in Western Europe and takeovers of governments in Eastern Europe, contrary to Stalin's previous promises, worsened relations between the former Second World War Allies, the United States, and the USSR.
1947	■ The *Truman Doctrine* was announced, pledging military aid to Greece, Turkey, and any other nation threatened with communist aggression and expansion.
1948	■ A Soviet *blockade of Berlin*—the former capital city administered by the four occupying powers, but deep within the Russian zone—was countered by the *Berlin Airlift.* ■ The Soviets had initiated the blockade to retaliate for the unification of the American, British, and French zones into West Germany.
1948	■ The *European Recovery Plan* (Marshall Plan) went into effect, and the Soviets, although invited, declined to participate and forbade their satellites to do so.
1949	■ *NATO* was established along with regional military alliances in the Middle East, Southeast Asia, and the Southwest Pacific. ■ After nearly two decades of civil war, the Chinese Communists led by *Mao Zedong* (1893–1976) and aided by the USSR, defeated the corrupt regime of *Chiang Kai-shek's Nationalists*, despite massive U.S. military aid. ■ Drove them from the Chinese mainland to the island of *Formosa (Taiwan)*. ■ The United States opposed the recognition of the communist government of Mao and, instead, recognized the Nationalist Chinese government of Chiang Kai-shek in Taiwan.
1950	■ The Korean War (1950–1953) was the first major military conflict between the West and the communists. After the Japanese withdrew from the peninsula, Korea was governed in the north by a government backed by the Soviets and Communist Chinese and, south of the 38th parallel, by a government backed by the United States and the United Nations. ■ The Soviets rejected free elections for a unified Korea and, instead, supported a satellite regime under Kim Il Sung. ■ In June 1950, a powerful North Korean army, supported by Soviet aid, invaded south of the 38th parallel and appeared to have won a quick victory. ■ President Truman, determined not to repeat the pre–Second World War policy of appeasement, convinced the United Nations Security Council to condemn North Korean aggression and oppose it militarily. ■ Since the Russians were boycotting the United Nations for failing to recognize Communist China, they could not veto the proposal. A UN force led by General Douglas MacArthur (1880–1964) made up of mostly U.S. troops landed in South Korea. Fifteen other nations provided mostly token contingents. ■ The UN force advanced northward until hundreds of thousands of Chinese Communist troops counterattacked in November 1950, driving them back to the 38th parallel. ■ General MacArthur insisted on attacking China itself. ■ President Truman, fearful of involving the United States in an Asian land war, removed MacArthur from command.

Year	Event
1951	■ A cease-fire ended serious fighting in July 1951.
1953	■ The war pitted United States forces against a communist foe supported and aided by the Soviet Union, and despite the losses: (36,574) U.S. dead, and almost 3 million Koreans and Chinese), it convinced the United States that military might could contain the spread of communism. ■ Neither the European democracies, preoccupied with rebuilding their shattered nations, nor the large, non-communist Asian nations of India, Burma, and Indonesia, mistrustful of a new kind of Western imperialism, shared the U.S. enthusiasm. ■ The death of Stalin thawed the Cold War. ■ Tensions rose and relaxed and then returned again, but peaceful coexistence seemed possible. ■ An armistice, returning the Koreas to the situation before the war, was signed in 1953.
1955	■ The Geneva Summit between President Dwight Eisenhower, the British and French prime ministers, and Soviet leaders led to a conciliatory atmosphere.
1956	■ War in the Middle East, between Israel and its Arab neighbors, renewed tensions between the Soviets, who aided the Arab states, and the West, who supported Israel (France, Britain, and Israel invaded Egypt for its nationalizing of the Suez Canal and captured the canal). ■ The Geneva Accords divided Vietnam into the communist North and the non-communist South.
1959	■ U.S. and Soviet relations soured further when Fidel Castro, an avowed Marxist, was openly aided by Soviet and Chinese Communists in his overthrow of Cuban dictator Fulgencio Batista.
1960	■ The Paris Summit ended when Khrushchev proved that the United States had been making spy flights over the USSR after a U-2 high-altitude reconnaissance plane had been shot down over Soviet territory. ■ The USSR became capable of launching nuclear ICBM missiles.
1961	■ The Bay of Pigs invasion of Cuba by anti-Castro Cuban refugees was a total disaster and a humiliation for newly elected president John F. Kennedy, whose administration had supported it. ■ The infamous Berlin Wall, as powerful a symbol of Soviet tyranny as the Bastille had been of royal abuses, was erected.
1962	■ The first U.S. troops, "military advisers," arrived in South Vietnam to shore up its anti-communist government against attacks by Communist North Vietnamese infiltrators and South Vietnamese Vietcong guerrillas. ■ The Cuban Missile Crisis brought the world to the brink of nuclear war when President Kennedy demanded that Premier Khrushchev remove nuclear missiles the Soviets had installed in Cuba. ■ The "eyeball-to-eyeball" confrontation ended when the Russian bases were dismantled.
1963	■ A nuclear test ban treaty to stop atmospheric explosions was signed by three of the world's four nuclear powers: the United States, the USSR, and Britain. France refused. ■ A hotline or direct communication phone was installed between the Kremlin and the White House to prevent accidental nuclear war. ■ A rift between the Soviets and Chinese Communists led to growing tensions and a parting of the ways between the two giants.

Year	Event
1964	■ Communist China became the fifth member of the "nuclear bomb club."
1965	■ Lyndon Johnson, who succeeded to the presidency after the assassination of Kennedy, bolstered American involvement in the Vietnam conflict by continuing bombing raids against North Vietnam and by sending in a massive ground force. ■ The Soviets and Chinese Communists supplied great quantities of arms and other aid to help the North Vietnamese and Vietcong maintain the fight against an eventual U.S. force of well over 500,000 troops.
1968	■ *Prague Spring* in Czechoslovakia occurred when the reformist Alexander Dubcek was elected and tried to give his people more civil and economic rights. ■ The other Warsaw Pact nations, led by the USSR, invaded with tanks and occupied the country until 1990.
1969	■ During the administration of President Richard Nixon, an avowed anti-communist in his early political career, he and his secretary of state, Henry Kissinger, pursued a policy of détente, peaceful coexistence between the West and the Communist bloc, although they widened the Vietnam War throughout Southeast Asia. Leaders exchanged visits, and the SALT negotiations (Strategic Arms Limitations Talks) began. ■ The United States landed a manned expedition on the moon.
1970	■ A nonproliferation treaty to limit the spread of nuclear weapons was signed by the United States and the USSR. ■ Unfortunately, nations with nuclear power plants proved it was possible to reprocess spent fuel in order to make nuclear bombs. ■ India became the sixth member of the "nuclear bomb club" in this way in 1974.
1972	■ Nixon's dramatic visit to Communist China, followed by scientific and cultural exchanges, established relations between the two former enemies.

ART

The period after the Second World War is often referred to as the post-modern period. *Postmodernist* ideas in philosophy and the analysis of culture have drastically influenced works of literature, architecture, and design, as well as reverberating in marketing/business and the interpretation of history, law, and culture. Postmodernism is typified by a re-evaluation of the entire Western value system (love, marriage, popular culture, shift from industrial to service economy)—a re-evaluation that began in the 1950s and 1960s and is reflected in the movement. Although the term was popularized by Arnold Toynbee in the 1930s, it is a good way to define the reaction against the functionalism of the "Age of Anxiety." Many new artistic forms have emerged.

- *Modernism* eliminated ornamentation and attempted to create clean, uncluttered lines for easy living as typified by the Bauhaus movement.
- *Postmodernism* revived ornamentation, and a personal relationship with art and life.
- *Pop art* emerged to poke fun at the art industry and to make art available and accessible to the common masses as typified by the soup cans of Andy Warhol.
- *Abstract expressionism* typified by the works of Jackson Pollock moved the center of the art world from Paris to New York City in the 1950s. It was a successor to surrealism and focused on spontaneous or subconscious creation.

SCIENCE

The Second World War changed the way scientists did their work, how they were funded, and where their research was directed. Scientists the world over were employed by their various governments to aid the war effort, and their work led to technological advances, such as the use of atomic energy, the development of radar and jet aircraft, and the advent of computers. New discoveries, inventions, and industries spurred research after the war in both *pure and applied science*.

- New means of funding and organization of the increasingly specialized fields of research led to the advent of *big science*, which stressed teamwork, the combining of theoretical research with engineering techniques, and complex research facilities with professional managers and expensive, sophisticated equipment.

    - The United States took the lead in this area after the Second World War, and by the mid-1960s most scientific research (which doubled the sum of human knowledge every decade) was funded by the U.S. federal government, whose principal aim was defense.

- Many of the best scientists from Europe went to the United States for better wages and budgets in a phenomenon known as the *brain drain*.
- A "space race" between the United States and the USSR led to Russia's development in 1957 of the first artificial satellite, *Sputnik*, and to a manned moon landing in 1969 by the United States.
- To stem the *brain drain* of their best scientists to the United States, European nations began funding their own research programs. The European Union, gaining prominence and focusing on cooperation, did much to stem the *brain drain*.

    - Cooperative endeavors such as the international laboratory at CERN, creator of the world's largest particle collider, the Large Hadron Collider, drew scientists back to Europe in order to use the most advanced tools in the trade.

        • Other international projects have led to retention of the best minds in science.
        • Many scientists came from America and Asia to work on government-supported projects in Europe thanks in large part to the European Union.

- Advances in genetics and medicine have raised many ethical questions in the last half century.

    - Fertility treatments have allowed couples who could not conceive to do so.
    - Scientific means of fertilization have led to people gaining much more control of when and how they will bear children.
    - Genetic engineering can already detect and sometimes alter genetic maladies in utero.
    - Parents may soon be able to genetically alter their offspring.
    - How will we use genetic information?

POPULATION AND POVERTY

Industrialization, urbanization, attitude changes, and modern contraception had lowered the birthrate during this century in Europe and other areas with developed economies. In the Less Economically Developed Countries (LEDCs), including newly independent nations that had been colonial possessions (mostly in Asia and Africa), the population exploded in the second half of the twentieth century. Cultural and religious attitudes and economic dependence on large families maintained a high birth rate. Better food production and distribution, and modern medical and sanitation practices led to a decline in the death rate. Investments that could have been made to improve the standard of living in these areas were used instead to support the burgeoning population. Even with population-control programs and a growing women's movement, the problem continued to get worse.

- The gap between the rich industrialized nations and the less economically developed countries widened.
- When the worldwide recession of the early 1970s caused the West to reduce its aid to the LEDCs, the less developed nations became more militant in demanding a more equitable share of the world's resources and industrial production.
- This was exploited by the Soviet Union, and many communist movements gained strength and even power in former colonial possessions in Latin America, Africa, and especially in Asia.

    - Women in the Soviet Union had a much bigger burden than the men because they were expected to be equal professionally, but still had to do all of the traditional women's work at home, such as cooking, child care, elder care, and cleaning.
    - Asian nations China, Vietnam, North Korea, Cambodia, and to some extent Burma (Myanmar) all had or still have some form of "communist" leadership.

- The result is a revolution of rising expectations that helps create worldwide political instability.

    - This can be seen in even the nations that still claim to be communist such as China and Vietnam.
    - The period after the Cold War would see rising incomes occur globally.

After the Cold War

- In mid-1991, *Boris Yeltsin*, an outspoken and charismatic political rival of Gorbachev, was elected as president of the Soviet Republic of Russia.

    - He ran as an independent candidate on a platform of drastic economic and political reform.

- During that same month, June, *Croatia and Slovenia declared their independence from Yugoslavia*, and a civil war, made more brutal by ancient ethnic rivalries, broke out.
- *START,* the Strategic Arms Reduction Treaty, was signed in July of 1991 by Gorbachev and President George H. W. Bush to reduce the number of long-range nuclear missiles of both nations.

    - One month later, old-line party and military leaders launched a coup against the vacationing Gorbachev by sending military units toward Moscow.

- Within days, the coup collapsed in the face of massive public demonstrations against its leaders.
- *Latvia, Lithuania, and Estonia* declared their independence from the Soviet Union.
- By late 1991, Russia, Ukraine, and Belarus had formed the *Commonwealth of Independent States* and the Soviet Union effectively ceased to exist.

■ By 1993, ethnic rivalries among the former Soviet controlled republics resulted in a bloody war pitting Serbia and Croatia against their former Yugoslavian brothers Bosnia and Herzegovina.

- Despite initial reluctance to get involved in the Balkan crisis, the United States and Western European nations have imposed a settlement on the warring factions and have prosecuted war criminals in the World Court.

■ The nations that comprise NATO all agreed to intervene, and Serbian aggression was halted in Bosnia-Herzegovina and Kosovo, Europe's newest country.

■ Former Yugoslavia was reorganized into several countries: Serbia, Bosnia-Herzegovina, Croatia, Macedonia, Slovenia, Montenegro, and Kosovo.

■ The Yugoslav Wars can be divided into four smaller wars:

- The Ten-Day War (1991)
- The Croatian War of Independence (1991–1995)
- The Bosnian War (1992–1995)
- The Kosovar War (1998–1999)

■ NATO was instrumental in preventing ethnic cleansing during the Yugoslav Wars of the 1990s as Croats, Muslims, and Serbs all tried to eliminate each other in these countries, although over 140,000 people were still killed.

■ The collapse of communism in Europe created a *fluid* political situation globally that is similar to the disruptions of the old orders after the First and Second World Wars.

- Power shifted; the rules changed, and Asia is rising in importance in the twenty-first century. How will Europe meet that challenge?

■ The end of the Cold War diminished the prospects of nuclear war but has created new rivalries and unleashed bloody ethnic conflicts to test the resolve of NATO.

■ Increasing nationalism combined with old conflicts, and new wealth and power made for disruptive situations.

■ The allies of the Gulf War Coalition adopted varying policies in the Middle East that often reflect their own economic interests. At the same time, Russia gave tacit support to Iran as the rest of the world attempted to prevent them from attaining a nuclear weapon.

■ The birth of a new international order also took into account the rising wealth in Asia and growing military power there.

EUROPEAN SOCIETY AT THE END OF THE TWENTIETH CENTURY

After the Second World War, European class distinctions blurred due to unprecedented economic growth in the West and the accompanying opportunities in jobs and in higher education. Western Europeans enjoyed a new social mobility and a greater democratization of their governments. Powerful social changes occurred after the Second World War.

- Education and ability outweighed family connections in reality for the first time ever.
- Health care and other social security programs alleviated traditional class conflicts and promoted greater economic equality.
- General prosperity promoted a *consumer culture*, making big businesses out of such products and services as food, leisure, entertainment, and travel.
- Prosperity and increased educational opportunities swelled the middle classes in both Europe and the United States.
- Government policies, such as subsidies for large families and government-run and funded child care facilities, encouraged population growth after the Second World War, resulting in a *baby boom*.
- With science and technology wedded by war, *big science*, which was funded by government and industry, created new products and new career opportunities.

  - With greater educational opportunities available to women, more females sought careers outside the home.
  - Cities grew as more agricultural workers left the farms in search of new, more lucrative, and exciting vocations.

- In the 1960s, a youth culture, which grew first in the United States from the great numbers of *baby boomers*, the unparalleled prosperity, and the increased enrollment in higher education, spread globally.

  - Rebellion against the status quo manifested itself in rock music, widespread use of illegal drugs, and less rigid sexual attitudes.
  - The materialism of the West encouraged a revolutionary idealism among young people, who participated in the antiwar movement in the United States and in the student radicalism of Europe.
  - Student revolts against rigid educational practices in universities broke out in France (1968) and in other European countries.

- Economic setbacks in the 1970s and 1980s spurred changes in family life.

  - In order to maintain the family's standard of living, many women in Europe and the United States went into the work force.
  - Income independence enabled more women to get divorces.

- Birth control allowed people to plan their families and resulted in a decreased birthrate.

  - *Margaret Sanger*, an American who worked with poor immigrant women as a nurse and writer, championed the development and dissemination of birth control.

- This newfound independence and a number of gifted female writers, such as *Simone de Beauvoir* in France and *Betty Friedan* in the United States, helped launch a new feminism or a *second wave* of feminism, that attacked gender inequalities in all aspects of society and used political action and attitude alteration.

  - The dissolution of the Soviet Union and its communist satellites also led many women, who had lived in those more gender emancipated cultures, to encourage further emancipation of Western European women.
  - The increasing prevalence of scientific, business, and political leaders who are women, from Rosalind Franklin to Oprah Winfrey to *Margaret Thatcher*, has also done much for the feminist cause.

    - *Margaret Thatcher* was prime minister of the United Kingdom from 1979–1990.
    - *Mary Robinson* was president of Ireland from 1990 to 1997.
    - *Edith Cresson* was prime minister of France for less than a year in 1991.

  - Moral questions arose about abortion, fertility treatments, and birth control—questions stimulated by the rise of feminism—and Europeans generally answered that women should decide for themselves without government interference and, thus, it has become a more divisive issue in America than in Europe.
  - Europeans are more concerned about issues of genetic engineering than Americans are in general.
  - Women still face many social and professional inequalities such as lower pay for the same work and underrepresentation in management.
  - The twenty-first century is witness to common bumper stickers that state that feminism is the radical notion that women are people.

- At the dawn of the 21st century, political parties such as the *Green Party* and the Pirate Party advocate for the desires of new generations of Europeans, who want a sustainable system and increased freedoms and social responsibility.
- Organized religion continued to play a role in European social and cultural life regardless of the challenges resulting from world war and ideological conflict, modern secularism, and rapid social changes.

  - Reform in the Catholic Church found expression in the *Second Vatican Council*, which redefined the Church's dogma and practices and started to redefine its relations with other religious communities.

    - It reshaped the Roman Catholic Church to the church it is today.
    - Engaged in modern dialogue.
    - Pardoned Galileo.
    - Made attempts at reconciliation with other world religions.

  - Pope John Paul II was originally from Poland, and his support for the Solidarity movement helped to topple communism.
  - Increased immigration into Europe altered Europe's religious makeup, causing debate and conflict over the role of religion in social and political life particularly in regard to Islam as more Muslim immigrants arrived on the continent.

    - Many non-Europeans came as *guest workers* after the Second World War and began to create ethnic enclaves in European countries.

- These workers and their children were not citizens.
- The Turks in Germany are one example.
- Many immigrants now come from Africa and the Middle East.

  - Increasing xenophobia in Europe has resulted in the emergence of modern nationalist parties in many European nations, such as France and Austria, in the French National Front and the Austrian Freedom Party.

- Nationalism has remained a potent force in Europe, and there has been a continuation and even an increase in the strength of various *separatist movements* in Europe, which have continued to exert pressure for independence or have increased such pressures.

  - Ireland has finally become a complete separate nation from the United Kingdom.
  - The Basque in the Pyrenees Mountains between Spain and France have continued to campaign for independence, both violently and peacefully.
  - The Chechen rebels in Chechnya have been trying to gain independence from Russia for almost two decades.
  - The Scottish held a referendum on separation from the United Kingdom in 2015 but decided to stay.
  - Some Flemish have been agitating for independence from Belgium as well.

RECENT DEVELOPMENTS

The 1990s marked powerful political and economic changes in Europe, comparable in magnitude to those at the end of the two world wars. After the collapse of communist governments in the former Soviet Union and its Cold War satellites, a new order emerged. The modern era saw a growth of European unity after the Second World War, to include the creation of a common market and the European Union.

- Much of Western Europe, with the exception of Britain, Switzerland, and most Scandinavian nations, instituted a *monetary union*, a natural evolution from the political and economic ties of the European Union, creating the **euro**, one of the most powerful and stable currencies in the world.
- Germany, completely and peacefully united (although with unforeseen complications that came from the need to absorb the formerly communist East Germany), set up its capital in Berlin once again, and became the most powerful economy in Europe, a status it had not held since the end of the Second World War.

  - There was some inequality between the former East Germany and West Germany, as it took a long time to reindustrialize the antiquated systems and training of the former East Germans.
  - With Berlin once again named national capital, the houses of the Reichstag and the Bundesrat were moved there.

- Poland, Hungary, and the Czech Republic established democratic governments, instituted capitalist reforms of their economies, and joined NATO.
- Independence movements from the Serb-dominated Yugoslavian government in Belgrade degenerated into bitter and bloody struggles between various ethnic groups (Serbs, Croats, Bosnians, Kosovars, Montenegrins, Albanians) and revived the specter of *genocide* in the form of "*ethnic cleansing.*"

- The intervention of NATO resulted in a precarious peace and in the prosecution of Slobodan Milosevic, Serbian president, and other Serbian leaders for war crimes.

■ Russia, the largest, richest, and most populous republic of the former Soviet Union, grappled with a faltering economy, a fitful start to democratization (widespread corruption during Boris Yeltsin's presidency tainted the effort), and a bloody ethnic war with Chechnya.

- The replacement of Yeltsin by Vladimir Putin as president promised reform, a renewed *détente* with the West, and a more enlightened role for Russia in regional and world affairs.
- Promise not kept.

  • Putin used power as a tool to enrich himself and his cronies.
  • *Oligarchs* became immensely rich businessmen with ties to the former Communist Party.

- Widely regarded as decreasing freedom and opportunity in Russia.

  • Putin and his former KGB connections enriched themselves through corruption.

- Temporarily replaced as president in 2008 by Dmitri Medvedev, but remained as a key power holder.
- Was re-elected president in 2012.

■ The *9/11 Terrorist Attacks* against the United States in 2001 marked the beginning of a new international era more dangerous to world peace and stability than at any time since the height of the Cold War.

- Widespread poverty in the LEDCs and ethnic rivalry all over the globe have fostered religious fanaticism and conflict, such as that in the Middle East between Israelis and Palestinians.
- Anti-Muslim xenophobia in Europe has resulted in laws like those that ban female face coverings in French public space.

■ There was a huge financial crisis in 2007–2008.

- A housing bubble in the United States that imploded in 2006 caused a large global financial crisis.
- Brought on by high-risk lending, the securitization of mortgages, and the irresponsibility of banks, this economic failure in the United States soon spread to Europe where banks were heavily invested in the U.S. housing market through mortgages and securities.
- Banks in many European nations failed. Iceland, Ireland, Spain, Portugal, Greece, and Cyprus experienced deep economic crises in large part to these bank failures, high national debt, and deficit spending.
- As credit became more expensive after the financial crisis, these national economies, the European Union, and the euro were vulnerable.
- In June of 2016, the United Kingdom voted to leave the European Union in an event commonly referred to as *Brexit*. This change in the ongoing trend toward European Unity marks a drastic change in the political and financial momentum of unity that had been observed in Europe from the 1980s until 2016. Further reductions in

unity have been seen in the interactions between current EU member states and the United Kingdom and in the exit terms being negotiated. This could be a turning point in European history to keep an eye on.

Up to this point, the European landscape was changed a number of times. Wars were fought and accords signed. Here is a quick summary of important treaties and agreements that molded the European continent.

IMPORTANT TREATIES AND AGREEMENTS IN EUROPEAN HISTORY

The Peace of Augsburg (1555)

This treaty ended the religious wars in the Holy Roman Empire and the surrounding area, including the Habsburg–Valois Wars. The Holy Roman Emperor (Charles V), lost the power of choosing the religion of the Germanic peoples, as he allowed each German Prince to choose the religion of his people (Catholicism or Lutheranism). It was a major victory for Lutherans, but Calvinism and other forms of Protestantism were not tolerated.

The Peace of Westphalia (1648)

Treaty ended the Thirty Years' War, which began with the Defenestration of Prague in 1618. It was a treaty made between France, the Holy Roman Emperor (HRE), miscellaneous German principalities, Sweden, and Holland. France emerged as a powerful force in Germanic politics and took another step toward its longtime policy of keeping Germany divided. Ironically, the French regent, Cardinal Richelieu, had France fight with Protestant forces against Catholic Austria in the war, and the treaty gave freedom to more Protestants. In many ways it was an extension of the Peace of Augsburg, but allowed Calvinism in Germanic states. It was a checkmate to the Counter Reformation. The HRE lost the Swiss cantons and the Dutch. France gained parts of Alsace and Lorraine. Over 300 German states attained the right to conduct their own diplomacy and make treaties with foreign powers. The Holy Roman Empire was badly weakened and was forbidden from making laws, levying taxes, and recruiting soldiers without consent of the imperial estates. Sweden got the bishoprics of Bremen and Verden and the west half of Pomerania, including Stettin. THE TREATY WEAKENED THE HRE TO THE POINT THAT IT BECAME ALMOST INCONSEQUENTIAL.

The Peace (Treaty) of Utrecht (1714)

This treaty, which ended the War of Spanish Succession, was made between France on one side and Britain, Austria, miscellaneous German principalities, Sweden, and Holland on the other. Spain's colonial holdings were divided amongst the victors, and the thrones of Spain and France were never to be united. This treaty was a final loss for Louis XIV as his wars came to an end. The British got Gibraltar and Minorca as well as the right of the assiento (exclusive right to sell slaves to Spanish colonies in the New World). The Duke of Savoy (aka Piedmont) attained Sardinia, and it became the KINGDOM of Sardinia (around which Italy would eventually unite); Austria got Milan, Naples, Sicily, and the Spanish Netherlands (soon to be Belgium). Louis XIV's grandson was crowned Philip V of Spain (but had to promise never to unite the kingdoms of Spain and France). Britain gained Newfoundland, Nova Scotia, and the

Hudson's Bay Territory from France. France kept Louis's gains in Franche-Comte and Alsace-Lorraine. The Grand Duchy of Brandenburg became the KINGDOM OF PRUSSIA.

Treaty of Aix-La-Chapelle (1748)

This treaty ended the eight-year-long War of the Austrian Succession and was made between France, Austria, and Prussia. It recognized Frederick the Great's annexation of Silesia.

Austria kept Belgium for a buffer zone to protect the Dutch from the French. The treaty demonstrated the weakness of France under Louis XV.

Peace of Paris (1763)

It ended the Seven Years' War involving Britain, Spain, and France, and which began in 1756 (the French and Indian War to the provincial Americans). This treaty ended the first war to be fought on three continents, and it has been termed the first truly global war. France gave all French territory in North America EAST of the Mississippi to Britain. Canada became BRITISH. France gave all holdings WEST of the Mississippi to SPAIN. France was prohibited from building forts or negotiating with Princes in India but could still trade there. France kept Guadeloupe and Martinique but did not want competition there anyway. This treaty resulted in British domination of international trade and at this point they were undisputedly the most important naval power in the world. France realized that it could not simultaneously fight in Europe and overseas due to lack of resources and naval power.

The Congress of Vienna (1815)

This treaty completely overhauled European borders and involved Castlereagh for Great Britain, Metternich for Austria, and Talleyrand for France. The Congress of Vienna ended the Napoleonic Wars and affected every nation in Europe. France, the belligerent power, was divided and penalized after European conquest. The Congress of Vienna occurred in three stages.

The First Peace of Paris: The Allies were lenient to France because they wanted to restore the Bourbons. France kept the borders of 1792, much of which had not been part of France in 1789. The Allies abandoned claims for indemnity

The Second: The Congress of Vienna was a meeting of the victors after the Battle of Nations, when Napoleon was exiled to Elba. The principles of settlement were: Legitimacy, Compensation, Balance of Power.

1. "Hundred Days" (March 20–June 22, 1815): Napoleon returned from exile and organized a new army.
2. Congress capitalized on stalled talks at Congress of Vienna.
3. Congress established German Confederation: 38 German provinces with Austria and Prussia.
4. Italy was reorganized.
5. Prussia and Russia were compensated. Alexander I wanted to restore the old kingdom of Poland; Prussia agreed if it could have a large German territory.
6. On January 3, 1815, Britain, Austria, and France made a secret alliance against Russia and Prussia to preserve the balance of power. Russia got a small part of Poland, and Prussia got a small part of the German province.

7. Battle of Waterloo, June 1815: Napoleon defeated by an Anglo-Allied army led by Duke of Wellington, and Prussians led by von Blücher.
8. Napoleon exiled to St. Helena.

The Third: The "Second" Treaty of Paris: dealt more harshly with France; large indemnity, some minor territories.

1. France had to cede lots of land back to the Netherlands, Sardinia, Prussia, and the Germanic Confederation.
2. France was restricted to the boundaries of 1790.
3. Seventeen fortresses on the north and east frontiers were to be garrisoned for not more than five years by Allied troops. France had to pay their expenses.
4. France had to pay 700,000,000 francs for the cost of the war.
5. Art treasures that France had taken from all over Europe had to be returned to their rightful owners.

Treaty of Frankfurt (1871)

This treaty ended the Franco-Prussian War. Alsace and Lorraine were ceded to Germany. German nationalism had grown and prevailed just as Bismarck had predicted. Germany became united as a result of this war, and Kaiser Wilhelm I was crowned emperor in the Hall of Mirrors at Versailles.

Treaty of Nanking (1842)

It was a very unequal treaty upon China after the First Opium War. It was the treaty that introduced China to the concept of "most favored nation status," because they were forced to grant that status to Great Britain.

1. Abolished trade system carried out in Canton.
2. Five ports were opened to the British (Nanking, Ningbo, Shanghai, Xiamen, and Fuzhou).
3. Chinese paid $21 million in indemnities to the British.
4. British received Hong Kong until 1997, when it was given back to China.

Treaty of Brest-Litovsk (1917)

Lenin took Russia out of the war but was forced to give up a quarter of Russian territory and a third of its population in exchange for immediate peace in order to fulfill his promises to the Russian people and organize his new socialist state.

Treaty of Versailles (1919)

- The Paris Peace Conference of 1919 was set up to create a lasting peace.
- The Big Three plus Italy's Vittorio Orlando, who was the president of the conference: David Lloyd George (Britain), George Clemenceau (France), Woodrow Wilson (United States).

  1. Central powers were excluded from negotiations.
  2. France was concerned mainly with its future security and reparations.

3. Wilson gave up his other famous 14 Points for self-determination and the League of Nations.
4. The United States refused to ratify the treaty and avoided the League of Nations.
5. The Versailles Treaty of 1919 mandated for former colonies and territories of the Central Powers to go to Allied countries.
6. Article 231 placed sole blame for war on Germany. Germany would be severely punished:
    a. Germany forced to pay huge reparations to Britain and France ($33 billion, which is over $500 billion in 2014 dollars).
    b. German army and navy were severely reduced.
    c. The Rhineland would be demilitarized.
    d. The Saar coal mines were taken over by France.
    e. Germany lost all its colonies.

Nazi-Soviet Nonagression Pact (August 1939)

The world was shocked that these two natural enemies agreed to not attack each other. They agreed to a plan to divide Poland.

Atlantic Charter (1941)

An agreement between FDR and Winston Churchill that an eventual peace to World War Two would be based on sovereign rights and self-government for countries deprived of them by Nazis. Equal access to world trade and resources was guaranteed.

United Nations Created (1945)

All anti-Axis powers meet in San Francisco to establish the United Nations, an international organization to promote peace and global well-being, and prevent another world war. The United States joined along with most countries in the world. The five most powerful nations (United States, United Kingdom, France, China, and the USSR) were made permanent members of the UN security council with veto powers on all security decisions.

General Agreement on Tariffs and Trade (1948)

The United States convinced other countries to reduce trade restrictions on a bilateral basis, forming the General Agreement on Tariffs and Trade (GATT) in 1948. It began with 23 nations and expanded to 100 in the 1990s.

North Atlantic Treaty Organization (1949)

The North Atlantic Treaty Organization was created by the former Allies that were capitalist countries as a way to deter threats from the Soviet Union and her satellite states. It was a part of the Cold War and helped draw the lines between communist and democratic nations. Some former communist nations joined after the fall of the Berlin Wall in 1989.

Warsaw Pact (1955)

This was a Soviet alliance created to counter NATO. It helped to continue the Cold War, included all Soviet satellite states, and saw a further ideological split between Eastern and Western Europe.

Treaty of Rome (1957)

In 1957 this treaty created the European Economic Community (EEC), an international organization dedicated to create a common market and integration of European economies. The founding members were Belgium, France, Italy, Luxembourg, the Netherlands, and West Germany. Later, Spain, Denmark, Ireland, Greece, Portugal, and the United Kingdom joined. The admission of the United Kingdom was at first opposed by French president, Charles de Gaulle, so the United Kingdom did not join the European Economic Community until 1973.

Merger Treaty (1965)

The Merger Treaty (also known as the Brussels Treaty) combined the European Coal and Steel Community, the European Economic Community, and the European Atomic Energy Commission into a single institution called the European Economic Community. Some regard this as the beginning of the European Union that was formally created in 1993 after the Treaty of Maastricht came into effect.

Treaty of Maastricht (1991)

This treaty created the European Union (EU) and established the rules for a single currency, the euro. A single currency (monetary union) was seen as a step toward political unity to come. Some Europeans opposed a monetary union, partly because of fears of a centralized bureaucracy and fears of cuts in social benefits.

PRACTICE LONG-ESSAY QUESTIONS

These questions are samples of the various types of thematic essays on the exam. (See pages 30–31 for a detailed explanation of each type.) Check over the **generic rubric** (see pages 32–33) before you begin any of these essays and use that rubric to score your essay if you write one.

Question 1

Evaluate the changing role of NATO in the defense of Western Europe from 1949–2010.

COMMENTS ON QUESTION 1

This question tests the CHANGE AND CONTINUITY OVER TIME skill. Be sure to describe the level of historical continuity (as in how did the role of NATO stay the same from its creation until the present?) and change (as in how has the role of NATO changed over that time?), and to explain the reasons for the continuity and change by giving specific examples of what changed and what NATO did after the Cold War ended compared to NATO's role during the Cold War.

    NATO seems to have averted an invasion of Western Europe after its inception. The stationing of hundreds of thousands of American troops as well as bases and nuclear weapons on European soil not only aided the Western Europeans in their defense, but it enabled them to invest in their economies the huge sums otherwise needed for defense. The United States also gave billions of dollars to other NATO powers to build up their military forces, and U.S. bases boosted their local economies. It needs to be evaluated not just for its success but for the threat of nuclear war that the ideological conflict between the United States and the Soviet Union held over the world. The changing role of NATO as the Cold War ended must be evaluated. The actions in former Yugoslavia as well as the changing political role of NATO should be assessed. Finally, the expansion of NATO to countries formerly in the Soviet sphere, such as Poland, should be examined for costs and benefits.

Question 2

Analyze the movement toward economic union in Western Europe.

COMMENTS ON QUESTION 2

This question tests the CHANGE AND CONTINUITY OVER TIME skill. Be sure to describe the level of historical continuity (as in how did the level of European unity stay the same from 1945 until the present?) and change (as in how has Europe become more unified?), and to explain the continuity and change through specific examples of what changed from a time when Europe was united into two separate camps, the Warsaw Pact and NATO, and how the end of the Cold War and the creation of the European Union has affected European unity for the entire continent. Be sure to include a discussion of those states not included in the European Union.

    Recall that the Marshall Plan inspired the Organization for European Economic Cooperation. Did this set the tone for the Schumann and Monnet Plan? What was the European Coal and Steel Community? How did it evolve into the Common Market? Who were the Common Market's first members? What was the role of the French in delaying British membership? How has European consolidation gone beyond the economic sphere? How did all of this lead to the creation of the European Union and the euro? How did the Treaty of Maastricht come about? How has the development of the euro strengthened the European Union? How has the EU hurt unity? Who has been excluded? How has NATO been affected?

Question 3

Compare the status of the Eastern European satellites before and in the two decades after the death of Stalin.

COMMENTS ON QUESTION 3

This is clearly a COMPARE skill question, so be sure to describe similarities and differences between the Eastern European satellites both under Stalin and in the 20 years after his death, 1953–1974, as well as account for or explain why they were so different by providing specific examples of how the nations were ruled differently. It is also important to evaluate the significance of these changes. This question could also be handled as a CHANGE AND CONTINUITY OVER TIME question, in which case you should describe what in the satellite states remained the same, and what changed after Stalin died as well as account for why these changes occurred, with reasons other than the death of Stalin.

Either way, you must explain that Eastern Europe before the Soviet takeover after the Second World War was an agricultural, not an industrial, region. How did land redistribution and Soviet-type five-year plans change this? What was the political situation for the satellites? How did the East Berlin riots of 1953 set a new precedent in the relations between the Soviets and their satellites?

How did "de-Stalinization" help precipitate revolts in Poland and Hungary in 1956? How did these revolts affect the political and economic reform of Eastern Europe? How did the suppression of Czechoslovakia in 1968 diminish the Third World's opinion of the Soviet reputation as anti-imperialistic? What changed, what remained the same after Stalin's death?

Question 4

Analyze how and why the Cold War gradually thawed.

COMMENTS ON QUESTION 4

This is another CAUSATION question because it requires you to explain HOW and WHY the Cold War generally thawed, or asks what CAUSED it to thaw. Remember to describe causes and effects of the thawing of the Cold War, indicating the degree to which it was caused by each factor by citing specific evidence. Remember to explain the reasons WHY the Cold War thawed over time.

The death of Stalin cannot be underestimated as an influence. Be aware, though, that while the "cult of personality" diminished in Soviet political life, the edifices of the totalitarian state remained. The so-called thaw involved a number of "quick-freeze" crises. The realization that any nuclear confrontation would destroy humanity (or at least reduce the global standard of living), and the Mutually Assured Destruction (MAD) theory, led both powers to be more conciliatory.

The summit meetings played an invaluable role in decreasing superpower tensions. The Cuban Missile Crisis may have alerted the United States and the USSR to the ultimate disaster that "brinksmanship" could lead to. The year 1963 was significant in that the Test Ban Treaty was signed and the monolithic Communist bloc cracked with the Soviet-Chinese rift. Nixon's policy of détente, despite the Vietnam War, was a giant step. The Nonproliferation Treaty and the SALT treaties were also significant.

The growing gap between the standard of living enjoyed by citizens of Western capitalist countries, compared to the standard of living endured by citizens of communist nations, should be assessed as another cause of the thaw in the Cold War. The broadcast of the capitalist standard of living on television and radio around the world also helped persuade those living in communist nations that capitalism was a better system of production.

Question 5

To what extent and in what ways did Gorbachev's reforms bring about the dissolution of the USSR?

COMMENTS ON QUESTION 5

This is another CAUSATION question because it requires you to decide to what extent Gorbachev's reforms CAUSED the dissolution of the Soviet Union. Remember to describe causes and effects of the thawing of the dissolution of the Soviet Union and, by citing specific evidence to support your claims, indicate the degree to which it was caused by Gorbachev's reforms. Explain reasons why these changes took place. How important were his reforms in the process? Which ones affected it? Consider both *perestroika* and *glasnost*. Be sure to show how their degree of success or failure brought about the final breakdown. Consider his repudiation of the Brezhnev Doctrine. Would the USSR have dissolved without Gorbachev's reforms?

Question 6

Assess the causes of the economic crisis of the 1970s.

COMMENTS ON QUESTION 6

This is another CAUSATION question because it requires you to assess what CAUSED the economic crisis of the 1970s. Remember to describe causes and effects of the thawing of the crisis, and indicate the degree to which it was caused by each factor identified, citing specific evidence to support your claims. Explain the reasons why these changes took place or why they caused certain other effects. Trace the causes and determine the relationships of the world monetary crisis and the OPEC oil embargoes in bringing about the regional stagflation of the 1970s. The reasons for the embargoes, such as Western support for Israel, should be examined. This essay must examine the changing structures of the world economy and financial system seen in the 1970s—from Bretton-Woods to the end of the gold standard and the results of those changes.

Question 7

How did the entrance of great numbers of women into the workplace alter European society?

COMMENTS ON QUESTION 7

This question tests the CHANGE AND CONTINUITY OVER TIME skill. Be sure to describe the level of historical continuity (as in what did not change in society when women entered the workforce?) and change (as in what was different after women entered the workforce?), and analyze specific examples of what changed from a time (1850 until 1950) when Europe saw women work mostly in the home, and how the entry of women into the workforce has affected European society. Be sure to include a discussion of how women were integrated into the workforce, and of the movement for women's rights. *Relate the "big picture" and offer specific effects of this powerful trend.* How has life changed for the mass of European women? How has this affected the expectations placed on a modern woman? How has the trend affected family, birth rate, divorce, and marriage? How have wages and leisure time been affected?

PRACTICE SHORT-ANSWER QUESTIONS

1. Please use the excerpt from the speech below and your knowledge of European History to answer all parts of the question that follows.

Speech by Secretary of State George Marshall, 1947

The truth of the matter is that Europe's requirements for the next three or four years of foreign food and other essential products—principally from America—are so much greater than her present ability to pay that she must have substantial additional help or face economic, social, and political deterioration of a very grave character.

The remedy lies in breaking the vicious circle and restoring the confidence of the European people in the economic future of their own countries and of Europe as a whole. The manufacturer and the farmer throughout wide areas must be able and willing to exchange their products for currencies the continuing value of which is not open to question.

Aside from the demoralizing effect on the world at large and the possibilities of disturbances arising as a result of the desperation of the people concerned, the consequences to the economy of the United States should be apparent to all. It is logical that the United States should do whatever it is able to do to assist in the return of normal economic health in the world, without which there can be no political stability and no assured peace. Our policy is directed not against any country or doctrine but against hunger, poverty, desperation, and chaos.

—George Marshall

(A) Briefly explain the plan authored by George Marshall to maintain peace and prosperity after the Second World War.

(B) Briefly Explain TWO effects of the Marshall Plan discussed above.

2. Please use your knowledge of European History to fully answer all parts of the following question. Many historians believe that the second half of the twentieth century saw increasing liberalism in much of Europe.

(A) Identify TWO pieces of evidence that support this assertion.

(B) Identify ONE piece of evidence to refute this assertion.

Short-Answer Explanations

1. (A) You should explain that the United States created the Marshall Plan to offer funds to all participants in the Second World War, funds those nations could use to buy American goods ranging from agricultural products to heavy equipment, and to the machines that run factories in order to prevent further economic turmoil as the world transitioned from a wartime economy to a consumer economy. The offer of funds to nations on both sides of the Iron Curtain should be mentioned. The answer should mention that the nations under the influence of the Soviet Union rejected this offer of funds from the United States.

   (B) You must fully explain TWO of the following: the divide between Eastern (communist) and Western (free market) Europe after the plan; the rebuilding of Western Europe; the economic miracle in West Germany and/or Japan; the rise of American global power; the elevation of the dollar as the international currency of exchange; the Cold War; the creation of NATO and the Warsaw Pact; the rise of the European Union; and the continuation of democracy and the market system in Western Europe.

2. (A) You should identify TWO of the following: the rise of feminism, the end of the death penalty in much of Europe, the rise of socialized medicine, the growing welfare systems in Europe, the fall of the Berlin Wall and the Soviet Union, the spread of democracy, the rise of the Green party, the rise of environmentalism, the growing acceptance of homosexuality, decolonization, the rise of more protests by citizens of all beliefs being allowed by the rise of the European Union, reducing the criminalization of drug use, changing gender roles, and increased worker rights.

   (B) You should identify ONE of the following: growing nationalism at the end of the century, the rise of Vladimir Putin, the reduction of benefits in the United Kingdom under Margaret Thatcher, French actions in Algeria, Charles de Gaulle's putting down of the 1968 protests, neo-Nazis' rise, the ethnic wars in the former Yugoslavia, and decreasing contributions as a percentage of GDP from European nations to the United Nations.

PRACTICE MULTIPLE-CHOICE QUESTIONS

Questions 1 to 3 refer to the following excerpt from *The Second Sex* by Simone de Beauvoir.

But first we must ask: what is a woman? 'Tota mulier in utero', says one, 'woman is a womb.' But in speaking of certain women, connoisseurs declare that they are not women, although they are equipped with a uterus like the rest. All agree in recognizing the fact that females exist in the human species; today as always they make up about one half of humanity. And yet we are told that femininity is in danger; we are exhorted to be women, remain women, become women. It would appear, then, that every female human being is not necessarily a woman; to be so considered she must share in that mysterious and threatened reality known as femininity. Is this attribute something secreted by the ovaries? Or is it a Platonic essence, a product of the philosophic imagination? Is a rustling petticoat enough to bring it down to earth? Although some women try zealously to incarnate this essence, it is hardly patentable.

Source: *The Second Sex* by Simone de Beauvoir, 1949

1. Which of the following movements of the twentieth century is being examined in the passage above?

   (A) Totalitarianism
   (B) Nihilism
   (C) Syllogism
   (D) Feminism

2. Which of the following was NOT a goal achieved by women in the twentieth century in Europe?

   (A) Women earned equal pay for equal work.
   (B) Women gained suffrage rights.
   (C) Women gained access to higher education.
   (D) Women gained access to new professions.

3. Which of the following innovations was most liberating for women?

   (A) Electrical household appliances
   (B) Women gaining the right to own property
   (C) The example of Soviet women changed Western European women
   (D) The birth-control pill was developed

Questions 4 to 7 refer to the passage below by British novelist John le Carré.

It was man who ended the Cold War in case you didn't notice. It wasn't weaponry, or technology, or armies or campaigns. It was just man. Not even Western man either, as it happened, but our sworn enemy in the East, who went into the streets, faced the bullets and the batons and said: we've had enough. It was their emperor, not ours, who had the nerve to mount the rostrum and declare he had no clothes. And the ideologies trailed after these impossible events like condemned prisoners, as ideologies do when they've had their day.

—John le Carré, British novelist, *The Secret Pilgrim*, 1990

4. Which of the following is the best explanation of what the passage above has in common with other twentieth century Western European literature like that of Erich Remarque and Franz Kafka?

   (A) It is dark and foreboding, instilling fear.
   (B) It points out the strengths of Western society.
   (C) It questions the values of Western society.
   (D) It attacks the communists as morally weaker than capitalists.

5. The nations of Eastern Europe referred to in the passage above were said to lie behind what imaginary structure during the Cold War?

   (A) The fortress of solitude
   (B) The Iron Curtain
   (C) The Berlin wall
   (D) The red curtain

6. Which of the following is the best description of the end of the Cold War in Eastern Europe?

   (A) The transition from communist to democratic rule was mostly peaceful, but saw ethnic conflict in the Balkans and was violent in Rumania.
   (B) The transition from communist to democratic rule was brutally oppressive with the former Soviets being slaughtered by their new masters almost everywhere.
   (C) The transition from communist to democratic rule was fought by the leadership of the Soviet Union and all other communist nations.
   (D) The transition from communist to democratic rule was never accomplished in much of Eastern Europe.

7. Which of the following policies by Mikhail Gorbachev encouraged public openness and accountability of the government to the people, helping to bring about the changes noted in the quote above?

   (A) *Perestroika*
   (B) War communism
   (C) *Do svidaniya*
   (D) *Glasnost*

Questions 8 to 10 refer to the following speech given by Fidel Castro.

With what moral authority can [the U.S.] speak of human rights[,] . . . the rulers of a nation in which the millionaire and beggar coexist; where the Indian is exterminated; the black man is discriminated against; the woman is prostituted; and the great masses of Chicanos, Puerto Ricans, and Latin Americans are scorned, exploited, and humiliated. . . . Where the CIA organizes plans of global subversion and espionage, and the Pentagon creates neutron bombs capable of preserving material assets and wiping out human beings.

—Fidel Castro, Speech, 1978

8. Which of the following nations would be most likely to support the views of Castro at the time he gave this speech?

   (A) Poland
   (B) France
   (C) Chile
   (D) Belgium

9. The Cuban Crisis that occurred 16 years before this speech heightened which of the following effects of the Cold War?

   (A) Economic competition between developed and developing nations increased.
   (B) The entire world became increasingly afraid of nuclear conflict.
   (C) The Soviets fomented revolutions in many Caribbean nations.
   (D) The race to put a man on the moon.

10. If true, which of the following political parties would agree with the American stance toward racial minorities as Castro describes it?

   (A) The French National Front
   (B) The Bolshevik Party
   (C) The Austrian Green Party
   (D) The French Popular Front

Multiple-Choice Explanations

1. **D**	4. **C**	7. **D**	10. **A**
2. **A**	5. **B**	8. **A**	
3. **D**	6. **A**	9. **B**	

1. **(D)**

(A) is wrong because the passage is about feminism as evidenced by the author and statements about femininity and women, not totalitarianism.

(B) is wrong because the passage is about feminism as evidenced by the author and statements about femininity and women, not nihilism.

(C) is wrong because the passage is about feminism as evidenced by the author and statements about femininity and women, not syllogism.

(D) is CORRECT because the passage is about feminism as evidenced by the author and statements about femininity and women.

2. **(A)**

(A) is CORRECT because women have achieved all other goals, but still did not attain equal pay for equal work.

(B) is wrong because women won the right to vote after the First World War.

(C) is wrong because women were accepted equally at most universities in Europe after the Second World War.

(D) is wrong because women did gain access to new professions, such as government, after the Second World War.

3. **(D)**

(A) is wrong because while household appliances did liberate them from some work, they did not change their biology to give them the greater freedom over their reproductive systems that the pill gave them.

(B) is wrong because women gained the right to own property throughout most of Europe during the nineteenth century.

(C) is wrong because Western European women were not strongly affected by Soviet women for the most part.

(D) is CORRECT because the birth-control pill gave women greater freedom over their reproductive systems.

4. **(C)**

(A) is wrong because the excerpt is hopeful rather than dark and foreboding.

(B) is wrong because the excerpt points out a failure of Western society to meet the challenge of the Cold War, while the Soviets are depicted as meeting that challenge.

(C) is CORRECT because it challenges Western superiority and praises the communist leader for his courage to speak out against the conflict.

(D) is wrong because the excerpt praises the communists.

5. **(B)**

(A) is wrong because the fortress of solitude exists only in Superman's world.

(B) is CORRECT because the Iron Curtain was the metaphorical divider between the communist and capitalist regions of Europe.

(C) is wrong because the Berlin Wall was a real barrier constructed by the Soviets and East Germans to surround West Berlin.

(D) is wrong because the red curtain was made up for this question.

6. **(A)**

(A) is CORRECT because transition from communist to democratic rule was mostly peaceful but saw ethnic massive conflict in the Balkans and was violent in Rumania.

(B) is wrong because there was no massive slaughter of communists.

(C) is wrong because many communist nations like Poland welcomed the fall of communism.

(D) is wrong because all of Europe transitioned out of Soviet capitalism.

7. **(D)**

(A) is wrong because *perestroika*, while a policy of Gorbachev, was not the openness of *glasnost*.

(B) is wrong because war communism played no role in the fall of communism in the Soviet Union.

(C) is wrong because *do svidaniya* is goodbye or farewell in Russian, and it was not a reform plan of Gorbachev.

(D) is CORRECT because *glasnost* is a Russian word that means openness and Gorbachev's *glasnost* policy opened up the workings of the Soviet government to its people and made them aware of problems within their society and of ways to fix them.

8. **(A)**

(A) is CORRECT because Poland was in the Soviet sphere of influence behind the Iron Curtain and thus would support any criticism of the United States.

(B) is wrong because France would not have openly criticized so much about America, whom it valued as an ally.

(C) is wrong because Argentina was ruled by an arch-capitalist dictator, Augusto Pinochet, who was receiving CIA support and was thus in debt to the United States, and in political conflict with Castro.

(D) is wrong because the Belgians are close NATO allies and would not publicly criticize the United States like that.

9. **(B)**

(A) is wrong because the Cuban Missile Crisis was about nuclear weapons in Cuba, not about economic conflict.

(B) is CORRECT because the Cuban Missile Crisis was about nuclear weapons in Cuba, and frightened the entire world as the brink of nuclear war.

(C) is wrong because the only successful Soviet-style revolution in the Caribbean was in Cuba.

(D) is wrong because the Cuban Missile Crisis was about nuclear weapons in Cuba, not about putting a man on the moon.

10. **(A)**

(A) is CORRECT because the French Nationalist Front is against immigrants and is widely seen as racist toward Muslims in France.

(B) is wrong because although the Bolsheviks did liquidate minorities under Stalin, it was never party policy to put any nationality above another.

(C) is wrong because the Green Party is anti-discriminatory.

(D) is wrong because the French Popular Front, a political party led by Leon Blum during the Depression, was socialist in nature, but not discriminatory.

Time Period Four (1914 to Present): Practice Assessment

KEY CONCEPTS AND OVERVIEW

KEY CONCEPT 4.1 Total war and political instability in the first half of the twentieth century gave way to a polarized state order during the Cold War and eventually to efforts at transnational union.

KEY CONCEPT 4.2 The stresses of economic collapse and total war engendered internal conflicts within European states and created conflicting conceptions of the relationship between the individual and the state, as demonstrated in the ideological battle between liberal democracy, communism, and Fascism.

KEY CONCEPT 4.3 During the twentieth century, diverse intellectual and cultural movements questioned the existence of objective knowledge, the ability of reason to arrive at truth, and the role of religion in determining moral standards.

KEY CONCEPT 4.4 Demographic changes, economic growth, total war, disruptions of traditional social patterns, and competing definitions of freedom and justice altered the experiences of everyday life.

PRACTICE ASSESSMENT

Each time period concludes with a mini-test consisting of some multiple-choice questions, two short-answer questions, and two essay choices for which you should choose to write at least one answer. This is not so much to simulate an exam, which will have more questions and a document-based question (DBQ), but to help you prepare for the types of questions seen on the exam and to allow you time to practice those skills. DBQs can be found in the Introduction to this book, in the two sample exams at the end of this book, and in the online version of the exams that accompany this book, which can be found at: *http://barronsbooks.com/AP/ap-european-hist/*. This assessment should take you about two hours. Detailed explanations of all questions follow the assessment.

Section I, Part A

Multiple Choice

> **Directions:** Please read the passages and then choose the most correct answer choice for each of the following questions.

Questions 1 to 3 refer to the painting depicted below.

—*Lenin on the first day of Soviet Power.* The Granger Collection

1. What was the most important reason that Lenin was depicted in the painting above with this group of people?

    (A) It was good propaganda to depict Lenin with common men.
    (B) These are the men Lenin took the palace with.
    (C) It was a revolution and they are military men.
    (D) It makes him look more important to be the only one wearing a tie.

2. Which of the following leaders was replaced by Lenin?

    (A) Joseph Stalin
    (B) Czar Nicholas II
    (C) Czar Nicholas I
    (D) Alexander Kerensky

3. During the Russian Civil War, 1918–1921, which of the following was in favor of Bolshevik rule?

   (A) The middle class
   (B) Peasants
   (C) Urban workers
   (D) The Allied powers of the First World War

Questions 4 to 6 refer to the excerpt from a telegram by German foreign minister Bethmann-Hollweg to Austrian emperor, Franz Joseph, on July 6, 1914.

In the meantime His Majesty desires to say that he is not blind to the danger which threatens Austria-Hungary and thus the Triple Alliance as a result of the Russian and Serbian Pan-Slavic agitation. . . . [He] is anxious to bring about an understanding between Bulgaria and the Triple Alliance.

His Majesty will, furthermore, make an effort at Bucharest, according to the wishes of the Emperor Francis Joseph, to influence King Carol to the fulfilment of the duties of his alliance, to the renunciation of Serbia, and to the suppression of the Rumanian agitations directed against Austria-Hungary.

Finally, as far as concerns Serbia, His Majesty, of course, cannot interfere in the dispute now going on between Austria-Hungary and that country, as it is a matter not within his competence.

The Emperor Francis Joseph may, however, rest assured that His Majesty will faithfully stand by Austria-Hungary, as is required by the obligations of his alliance and of his ancient friendship.

—Bethmann-Hollweg

4. Which of the following is the most commonly accepted historical interpretation of the telegram quoted above?

   (A) It promised German support in whatever action Austria took against Britain.
   (B) Germany promised a "blank check" from Russia to Serbia.
   (C) Germany encouraged the Austrian military against Serbia and Russia.
   (D) It created a rift between Russia and France.

5. Which of the following factors was most responsible for expanding the "Third Balkan War" into the First World War?

   (A) A military modernization in Russia
   (B) The alliance system conceived by Otto von Bismarck
   (C) The British naval dominance of the entire globe
   (D) The desire of the French and Russians to increase colonial holdings

6. Once the war began, which of the following is the best characterization of the offensives on the Western Front?

(A) Armies made significant territorial gains.

(B) Offensives were minor skirmishes.

(C) Offensives saw the slaughter of massed infantry units.

(D) Offensives were won by the attacking army.

Questions 7 to 10 refer to the image below of German road construction workers in the 1930s.

German Road Construction Workers, 1930s.

7. Government workers build roads in Germany as a result of government stimulus spending that was proposed by which of the following economists?

(A) Milton Friedman

(B) Karl Marx

(C) Adam Smith

(D) John Keynes

8. The Scandinavian response to the Great Depression represented which of the following?

(A) Fascist response

(B) Capitalist response

(C) Communist response

(D) Middle path between capitalist and communist responses

9. The Weimar Republic (1919–1933), despite a valiant attempt to introduce democracy to Germany, failed to gain support of the German people mostly due to which of the following?

   (A) The Nazis maintained a wide following throughout the 1920s and 1930s.
   (B) Von Hindenburg's presidency was marred by his personal corruption.
   (C) Monarchists, supporters of the abdicated Kaiser, and militarists, humiliated by defeat in the First World War, opposed it from the start.
   (D) The government was unable to stabilize the economy or maintain law and order.

10. As a result of the destruction of the economy, the aftermath of the Great War, and the general feeling of anxiety seen during this era, European thought in the early twentieth century was LEAST influenced by which of the following?

    (A) The concept of existentialism proffered by Nietzsche
    (B) The Darwinist concept of evolution
    (C) The Enlightenment works of Voltaire and Montesquieu
    (D) The uncertainty principle of Heisenberg

Questions 11 to 13 refer to a 1947 speech given by U.S. Secretary of State George Marshall about his plan to rebuild Europe.

Aside from the demoralizing effect on the world at large and the possibilities of disturbances arising as a result of the desperation of the people concerned, the consequences to the economy of the United States should be apparent to all. It is logical that the United States should do whatever it is able to do to assist in the return of normal economic health in the world, without which there can be no political stability and no assured peace. Our policy is directed not against any country or doctrine but against hunger, poverty, desperation, and chaos. Its purpose should be the revival of a working economy in the world so as to permit the emergence of political and social conditions in which free institutions can exist. Such assistance, I am convinced, must not be on a piecemeal basis as various crises develop. Any assistance that this Government may render in the future should provide a cure rather than a mere palliative. Any government that is willing to assist in the task of recovery will find full cooperation.

—George C. Marshall, at Harvard University, June 5, 1947.

11. Which of the following was the overall result of the plan created by the speaker above?

    (A) Europe was divided into spheres of influence based upon who had been offered funds and who had not.
    (B) European reconstruction after the Second World War was slow and sporadic, especially in West Germany.
    (C) Western and Central Europe underwent an extended period of growth often referred to as an economic miracle.
    (D) Eastern Europe saw a period of massive economic growth known as the economic miracle while Western Europe's economy stagnated.

12. After the implementation of the plan associated with the author of the speech above, which of the following best characterizes the role of the United States in Europe?

(A) The United States exerted a strong military, political, and economic influence in Western Europe.

(B) The United States exerted a strong military, political, and economic influence in Eastern Europe.

(C) The United States adopted an isolationist policy and removed itself from the affairs of Europe, Africa, and Asia.

(D) The United States embarked on a plan for world domination, and now controls most of Europe, Asia, and Africa as well as the Americas.

13. In addition to the plan implemented above, most European nations adopted which of the following reforms designed to ensure that there would never be such a deep economic depression again?

(A) Welfare systems including national medical systems, pensions systems, and unemployment systems were implementing the creation of modern welfare states.

(B) All factories were nationalized and all unemployed people were put to work in them across Europe.

(C) Strong international banking and investing laws were created to prevent future speculation from destroying markets and real businesses.

(D) All aid to workers and the poor was abolished and a pure capitalist system emerged, creating an economic miracle that is still going strong today.

Questions 14 to 16 refer to the following map.

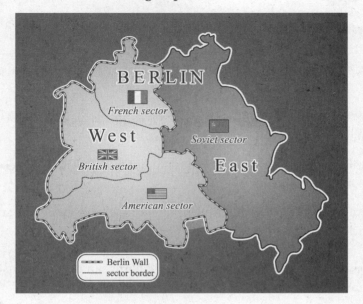

—Map of Berlin during the Cold War, including the Berlin Wall. Infographics map.

14. The wall shown on the map above was created by the East Germans for which of the following reasons?

    (A) It was built to prevent West Berliners from coming to East Berlin to buy the less-expensive goods there.
    (B) It was built to prevent the West Berliners from coming to East Berlin to take advantage of the free medical care there.
    (C) It was built to prevent the East Berliners from coming to West Berlin to escape the communism of East Germany.
    (D) It was built to prevent the East Berliners from coming to West Berlin to purchase the cheaper goods available there.

15. From the late 1940s into the 1970s the concept of encircling each other was which of the following major strategies of the Cold War?

    (A) *Perestroika*
    (B) *Glasnost*
    (C) Domino Theory
    (D) Containment

16. Historians often argue over the importance of the Berlin Wall's construction and symbolism, but most agree that which of the following had significant importance symbolically, socially, and politically?

    (A) The East German political demonstrations that occurred as a result of the construction of the Berlin Wall
    (B) The beginning of the destruction of the Berlin Wall in November of 1989
    (C) The art and graffiti that adorned only the West German side of the wall
    (D) The combination of the French, American, and British sectors into the nation of West Germany

Section I Part B

Short-Answer Questions

> **Directions:** Answer both questions completely: answer ALL parts of the question.

1. Historians have argued that Germany deserves to be blamed for starting the First World War.

   (A) Identify TWO pieces of evidence that <u>support</u> this argument and explain how each supports the argument.

   (B) Identify ONE piece of evidence that <u>undermines</u> this argument and explain how the evidence undermines it.

2. Use the passage below and your knowledge of European history to answer all parts of the question that follows.

   The Government of the German Reich and the Government of the Union of Soviet Socialist Republics desirous of strengthening the cause of peace between Germany and the USSR and proceeding from the fundamental provisions of the Neutrality Agreement concluded in April 1926, 1939 between Germany and the USSR, have reached the following agreement:

   ARTICLE I
   Both High Contracting Parties obligate themselves to desist from any act of violence, any aggressive action, and any attack on each other, either individually or jointly with other powers.

   ARTICLE II
   Should one of the High Contracting Parties become the object of belligerent action by a third power, the other High Contracting Party shall in no manner lend its support to this third power. . . .

   ARTICLE IV
   Neither of the two High Contracting Parties shall participate in any grouping of powers whatsoever that is directly or indirectly aimed at the other party.

   ARTICLE V
   Should disputes or conflicts arise between the High Contracting Parties over problems of one kind or another, both parties shall settle these disputes or conflicts exclusively through friendly exchange of opinion or, if necessary, through the establishment of arbitration commissions.

   (A) Briefly identify and describe one benefit of the treaty for EACH nation involved: Germany and the USSR.

   (B) Briefly explain the impact of this treaty on Poland and analyze the extent to which it ushered in the start of the Second World War.

Section II: Long-Essay Question

ESSAY CHOICES

1. *"Every successful revolution puts on in time the robes of the tyrant it has deposed."*

   Evaluate this statement with regard to the English Civil War (1640–1660), the French Revolution (1789–1815), and the Russian Revolution (1917–1930).

2. Explain how, during the Great Depression, traditionally democratic European governments maintained their democracy while some of the newer European democracies fell under dictatorship.

ANSWER EXPLANATIONS

Multiple-Choice Questions

1. **A**	5. **B**	9. **C**	13. **A**
2. **D**	6. **C**	10 **C**	14. **C**
3. **C**	7. **D**	11. **C**	15. **D**
4. **C**	8. **D**	12. **A**	16. **B**

1. **(A)**

(A) is CORRECT because the most important reason that Lenin is pictured with this group of people, who he certainly was not with on the first day of the revolution, is to show him as a man of the people for propaganda purposes.

(B) is wrong because Lenin did not take the palace and was not with these men in reality on the day of the revolution.

(C) is wrong because the image was painted for propaganda purposes and even though these were military men, the propaganda was the best reason.

(D) is wrong because the clothes have nothing to do with why he is depicted with those other figures, which was purely propagandistic.

2. **(D)**

(A) is wrong because Joseph Stalin ruled the Soviet Union after Lenin, not before him.

(B) is wrong because Czar Nicholas II abdicated to the provisional government run by Alexander Kerensky.

(C) is wrong because Czar Nicholas I ruled from 1825–1855.

(D) is CORRECT because, like the French Revolution before it, the Russian Revolution was largely supported by the urban workers, the vaunted *proletariat*.

3. **(C)**

(A) is wrong because the middle class supported the czar and then the Whites during the civil war.

(B) is wrong because the peasants were traditional and mostly favored the Whites.

(C) is CORRECT because, like the French Revolution before it, the Russian Revolution was largely supported by the urban workers, the vaunted proletariat.

(D) is wrong because the Allied Powers were wary of the communists and had made deals with the provisional government of Kerensky.

4. **(C)**

(A) is wrong because although it did promise support to Austria, it was only against Serbia and Russia, not Britain that that support was promised for.

(B) is wrong because Germany made a promise of a blank check from Germany to Austria, not from Russia to Serbia.

(C) is CORRECT because it did support Austrian aggression and promised German support against Russia and Serbia if pursued.

(D) is wrong because the telegram did not affect Russian/French relations.

5. **(B)**

(A) is wrong because although Russia was trying to modernize, that modernization was slow and far behind her neighbors, and was not a major factor in expanding the conflict; rather if Russia had been more modern, its mobilization may have waited, and the war could have been smaller in scope.

(B) is CORRECT because the Bismarckian Alliance system required many nations to come to the defense of their treaty partners and expanded a local conflict into a global one.

(C) is wrong because the alliance system was a larger factor than British naval dominance in expanding the conflict, although the Germans were aggressive, in part as a desire to reduce British naval dominance.

(D) is wrong because the French and Russians did not desire colonial expansion in 1914.

6. **(C)**

(A) is wrong because armies dug in, and trench warfare was the rule with little gain and terrible losses.

(B) is wrong because offensives were huge battles, like the Somme, in which over 1.1 million people were casualties—dead, wounded, and missing.

(C) is CORRECT because massive infantry assaults charging "over the top" of their trenches, were the main type of fighting on the Western Front, and many infantrymen died in those massive assaults.

(D) is wrong because armies usually held their own trenches, and the attacking force was repelled.

7. **(D)**

(A) is wrong because Milton Friedman was against stimulus spending, which Keynes proposed.

(B) is wrong because Marx would have the government run the entire economy, which differed greatly from Keynesian stimulus.

(C) is wrong because Smith, as the father of economics, advocated little government involvement in the economy.

(D) is CORRECT because Keynes in his *General Theory of Employment, Interest, and Money,* explained fiscal and monetary stimulus as tools to fight recession.

8. **(D)**

(A) is wrong because Scandinavians rejected Fascism and decided to cooperate more.

(B) is wrong because Scandinavians rejected pure capitalism and decided to cooperate more.

(C) Scandinavians rejected pure capitalism and decided to cooperate more, but preserve property rights and free enterprise.

(D) is CORRECT because Scandinavians found a middle road and pioneered modern socialism that is so prevalent in Europe today.

9. **(C)**

(A) is wrong because the Nazi Party had a small following until there was a burst of support at the end of that period.

(B) is wrong; Hindenburg was not corrupt in any way.

(C) is CORRECT because those most conservative and most militaristic Germans never accepted their loss or their part in it.

(D) is wrong because the Weimar Republic did preserve law and order, and it finally did stabilize the economy for a bit.

10. **(C)**

(A) is wrong because the existentialism of Nietzsche and Camus was very prominent among intellectuals during this time.

(B) is wrong because the ideas of Darwin were also being used and misused to encourage examination of the world and racism.

(C) is CORRECT because the Age of Reason had been overtaken by the curtailing of individual rights by totalitarian regimes of the Fascist and communist varieties.

(D) is wrong because the uncertainty principle of Heisenberg typified the era of anxiety as most people lost faith on reason and knowledge.

11. **(C)**

(A) is wrong because all nations in Europe were offered funds, but those already under the Soviet sphere of influence declined aid.

(B) is wrong because the recovery of Western and Central Europe was steady, strong, and referred to as a miracle, while Eastern Europe stagnated.

(C) is CORRECT because the recovery of Western and Central Europe was steady, strong, and referred to as a miracle, while Eastern Europe stagnated.

(D) is wrong because the recovery of Western and Central Europe was steady, strong, and referred to as a miracle, while Eastern Europe stagnated.

12. **(A)**

(A) is CORRECT because the United States became the leader of a North Atlantic and Western European nations coalition, NATO, and was a world leader in all areas, in no small part due to economic aid such as the Marshall Plan.

(B) is wrong because Eastern Europe was under the Soviet sphere of influence and was not overly affected by the United States.

(C) is wrong because the United States was engaged in the Cold War and rejected isolationism for good after the Second World War.

(D) is wrong because the United States had not gained control of those areas and was, in fact, feared but not in control in world foreign policy circles.

13. **(A)**

(A) is CORRECT because cradle-to-grave welfare systems proliferated after the Second World War.

(B) is wrong because most factories that were nationalized were in communist nations, but some were nationalized in NATO countries, too, but not nearly all were.

(C) is wrong because there have never been strong limitations on international investing and banking designed to prevent over-speculation.

(D) is wrong because just the opposite happened with the creation of the welfare state.

14. **(C)**

(A) is wrong because it was not built to prevent West Berliners from coming to East Berlin, but the other way around.

(B) is wrong because it was not built to prevent West Berliners from coming to East Berlin, but the other way around.

(C) is CORRECT because the East Germans and Soviets built it to keep the East Germans from escaping communist rule by using West Berlin as an access route to the West.

(D) is wrong because the goods in West Germany were more expensive than those in East Germany.

15. **(D)**

(A) is wrong because it was a Soviet reform policy of "restructuring," which Mikhail Gorbachev began.

(B) is wrong because it was a Soviet reform policy of "openness," which Mikhail Gorbachev began.

(C) is wrong because the "Domino Theory" was about the spread of communism, not stopping the spread.

(D) is CORRECT because the containment policy or the Truman Doctrine was the idea of stopping the spread of communism everywhere by containing it.

16. **(B)**

(A) is wrong because the East Germans certainly did not protest the construction of the Berlin Wall.

(B) is CORRECT because the fall of the Berlin Wall came to symbolize the end of Soviet dominance of Eastern Europe and of the Cold War itself.

(C) is wrong because although the art and graffiti on the wall have become well known, they are not nearly *as* important symbolically, socially, and politically as the fall of the wall.

(D) is wrong because the creation of West Germany, although important, was not *as* important symbolically, socially, and politically as the fall of the wall.

Short-Answer Explanations

1. (A) A good answer will give two pieces of evidence to support the assertion that Germany deserves to be blamed for starting the First World War, such as but not limited to: imperialistic gains, the Berlin Conference, German naval development, arms race, blank check, declarations of war, invasion of Belgium, German telegrams, *Lusitania*, any propaganda mentioned specifically, and ambassadorial reports.

   (B) A good answer will give one piece of evidence to refute the assertion that Germany deserves to be blamed for starting the First World War, such as but not limited to: Austrian warmongering, Serbian assassination, Russian blundering and mobilization, Belgian resistance, victors writing history, incompetence rather than bloodthirsty, and nationalism in other countries.

2. (A) A good answer will explain how each nation got to be free from fear of each other and how they decided on the partition of Poland between the powers. It was also good for Stalin and Hitler to take measure of each other as totalitarian leaders and opponents. It also postponed what each saw as an inevitable conflict and enabled them both to pre-pare more for it whilst the other was preoccupied with other matters.

(B) A good answer will include that Poland was at first divided between Germany and Russia, then the Nazis captured the entire country. They used Polish people as slave labor throughout the war and constructed some of the worst death camps of the Holocaust in Poland. When the Soviets liberated Poland from the Nazis, they then imposed Soviet-style communist rule there that lasted from 1945 to 1991.

You must also explain, for the second point, that the German invasion of Poland was the start of the Second World War in Europe. This was when Great Britain and France declared war on Germany and prepared in earnest for the coming storm of 1940.

Long-Essay Question Sample Answers and Explanations

Question 1

1. *"Every successful revolution puts on in time the robes of the tyrant it has deposed."*

Evaluate this statement with regard to the English Civil War (1640–1660), the French Revolution (1789–1815), and the Russian Revolution (1917–1930).

COMMENTS ON QUESTION 1

- Follow the "Simple Procedures" for writing an essay. (See page 35.)
- First, you must decide: *Which skill is being tested?* This is a CHANGE AND CONTINU-ITY OVER TIME skill question, so be sure to describe the level of historical continuity (as in what did not change in Britain, France, and Russia when they had revolutions) and change (as in how did each set of revolutionaries gain and utilize power?), and to utilize specific examples of what changed in each country when revolutionaries took power. Explain the reasons for, and to what extent, each revolutionary became a dictator like the one he replaced.
- Second: *What does the question want to know?* Did the protagonists of the revolu-tions mentioned—Cromwell, Robespierre, Danton, Marat, Lenin, Trotsky, and Stalin— become tyrants as much as were the men/regimes they deposed? This question allows you to review the three most important political revolutions covered in the course, and compare the results of these revolutions.
- Third: *What do you know about it?* Examine the leaders who took power after the revolu-tions. In the case of England, that would be Cromwell. In France the leaders covered can range from Robespierre, Danton, and Marat to Napoleon and Louis XVIII, depending upon how you want to argue it. The Russian Revolution should compare the Romanov reign to the rule of the Bolsheviks under Lenin and Stalin. Sophisticated essays may postulate how Trotsky could have ruled differently.
- Finally: *How would you put it into words?* This essay lends itself to easy paragraphs for each of the revolutions examined. If the writer writes a thesis explaining that each revo-lution did indeed don the robes of the tyrant to some degree and then examines in the

body the degree to which each revolution did that, then the essay will be strong. It is often a good idea to contradict the proposition given on a question to distinguish the essay from others. A way to do that here is to be clear about the different degrees to which each revolution did indeed become tyrannical.

SAMPLE ANSWER

These three revolutions are pivotal points in the political history of Europe and have been much studied by historians. Crane Brinton proposed a cycle of revolutions based upon all three revolutions, that does indeed suggest that each of these revolutions did become tyrannical to some degree. The leaders of all three revolutions or their successors became more tyrannical than those they replaced to different degrees and in different arenas in each case.

Oliver Cromwell became the leader of the Puritans during the English Civil War of the mid-seventeenth century. He led a revolt against King Charles I because he felt that the King was forcing religious changes upon the people and was not recognizing the legal power of Parliament. He advocated with other members for open insurrection against the King. He molded the New Model Army into an efficient fighting machine that fought in the name of the Lord and British common law. He was able to take over Parliament after using his army to defeat the King. He orchestrated a trial of the King and had him beheaded in the name of Parliament and England. Parliament became the first supreme legislature in Europe. Eventually, Cromwell became the de facto ruler of England. He controlled Parliament and eventually dismissed the members with armed force. He closed the theaters and houses of ill repute and enforced strict observation of religious practices that he favored. He also instituted taxes on the people without the consent of Parliament. In the end, Cromwell died a worse tyrant than the man he deposed.

John Locke wrote about the second English political revolution in 1689 in which England gained a Bill of Rights and began the application of scientific thought to politics. His work was built upon by the French philosophes such as Montesquieu and Condorcet, work which, along with a revolution in America, led to a revolution in France based upon Enlightenment ideals. The leaders of the French Revolution also came to a radical phase in which one, Marat, was assassinated, and another, Danton, was repudiated by the third, Robespierre, and guillotined. These leaders perpetrated the Reign of Terror upon France in which tens of thousands were killed as supposed enemies of the revolution. Eventually the Directory took over in 1795, but only for four years. Then, Napoleon took power and began his own censorship, militarism, and autocratic rule. The reign of Louis XVI had been feudal, but the revolutionaries were much more tyrannical because they did not follow their own laws and rewrote the constitution whenever it suited the government. At least the French had known what to expect before the tyrannical revolutionaries took power.

The Russians were perhaps the most oppressed Europeans in 1914. Serfdom still existed and each person was in fact the personal servant of the czar if asked to serve. Czar Nicholas II and his family lived a life of luxury, while the peasants starved or eked out a living. Industrialization was slow and controlled by the nobility. The revolution, led first by common soldiers and Kerensky and then by the Bolsheviks, ended up being more brutal and tyrannical than anyone could have imagined. Lenin came to power offering land, peace, and bread. When Stalin took over in 1924, he instituted a brutal regime that forced massive change on the nation resulting in loss and starvation. He then "purged" the country of people perceived as classist or against the revolution, causing the deaths of tens of millions of his own fellow citizens. The Russian Revolution did indeed become more tyrannical than the regime it deposed.

In all three cases, the revolutions produced governments that at least for a period were more tyrannical than those they deposed. Even though they were tyrannical in different ways, with the English more concerned about religion and the Russians more concerned about class, the truth is that all three revolutions did not relieve tyranny, but increased it.

EVALUATE THE SAMPLE ANSWER

Now go back and look at the rubric. It is clear that this essay fulfills all of the requirements for a score 6 on the rubric. The essay answers all parts of the question thoroughly, with concrete evidence, at length, with a well-balanced essay. The thesis is appropriate and gets the thesis point. The essay definitely uses historical reasoning and evidence to explain how the revolutions mentioned are interrelated and corroborates an argument that addresses the entirety of the question and utilizes specific examples attaining all Evidence points. The argument clearly addresses the topic with specific relevant examples of evidence and utilizes that evidence to fully and effectively substantiate the stated thesis. The Analysis and Reasoning is strong and demonstrates a complex understanding of the prompt and use of evidence gaining both points. The Contextualization point is given because, while the essay does describe the historical contexts of each revolution somewhat, it does not show how that context influenced the topic of the question.

RATERS COMMENTS ON THE SAMPLE ANSWER

5—Highly Qualified

This essay clearly and completely answers the question. There are some details such as the "rump parliament" or the "long parliament" missing, but the essay is strong, clear, and comprehensive. The structure makes it clear to the reader that the writer knows the events of the three revolutions and the major players in each.

The details about the closure of theaters in England were great, but the omission of censorship and the absence of an examination of how Cromwell took power, take away from this essay. The examination of the French Revolution provides enough support to make the point, but could build much more upon the importance of the tyranny of both Robespierre and Napoleon. The examination of Stalin as more tyrannical than the most tyrannical absolutist power was a powerful contrast. More detail on Stalin could have been given as support. The big problem with this essay is a lack of the explanation of the reasons for continuity and change, just evidence to support that it occurred.

Question 2

2. Explain how, during the Great Depression, traditionally democratic European governments maintained their democracy while some of the newer European democracies fell under dictatorship.

COMMENTS ON QUESTION 2

- Follow the "Simple Procedures" for writing an essay. (See page 35.)
- First, you must decide: *Which skill is being tested?* This is a CHANGE AND CONTINUITY OVER TIME skill question, so be sure to describe the level of historical continuity (as in what did not change in England, France, and other nations that retained democracy?) and change (as in how did totalitarian regimes gain and utilize power?), and to utilize specific examples of what changed in each totalitarian regime from the USSR to Spain to Germany when each totalitarian took power, and cite reasons for either the continuity or change. Remember to analyze why the nations that had newer democracies fell to totalitarian rule while older democracies, such as Great Britain and the Netherlands did not.
- Second: *What does the question want to know?* You must "offer the reasons for" and "detail" why democracy survived in some European nations and failed in others.
- Third: *What do you know about it?* In Britain, the Netherlands, and France, the institutions and impulses of democracy prevailed over the crisis. In Britain, a coalition reformed the economic system. In France, the socialist "French New Deal" matched Roosevelt's policies in the United States. In Germany, the weak Weimar Republic crumbled with the election of a plurality of Nazis. In Spain, the Republican government, lacking popular support, was crushed by Franco's Falange. In Italy, Mussolini's Fascists completed the "corporate state" in response to the depression.
- Finally: *How would you put it into words?* This essay lends itself to easy paragraphs for each of the nations examined. If the writer writes a thesis explaining that totalitarianism gained in nations with less experience with democracy, then you can order the essay according to nation. Be sure to explain why democracy prevailed or failed in each nation.

The economic disaster of the Great Depression shattered international trade, resulted in unemployment rates as high as 30 percent in the capitalist world, and tested the political systems of the traditional democracies and those created after the First World War. Britain, the Netherlands, and France relied on their "habits" of democratic problem-solving to deal with the crisis. Germany, the Soviet Union, Spain and, to some degree, Italy fell under the yoke of dictatorship during the depression.

Britain's well-established parliamentary system came to the fore during the Depression, when a coalition of the Labour and Conservative parties developed a program to regulate commerce and industry and to extend the social welfare system that had its foundations in the pre-First World War period. A responsiveness to the electorate had been achieved gradually through the course of British history, and it prevailed over the extremist promises of the right and left. The same could be said of the Dutch.

The strong socialist segment in France's political life came through with a "French New Deal" patterned after the programs of America's Franklin Delano Roosevelt. Labor legislation and farm subsidies, put through the assembly by a coalition led by the Socialists, offered hope to the electorate. Although the program was largely unsuccessful, rather than falling under the sway of the growing Communist Party or French Fascists, the people returned the government to conservative factions. The hard-won republican democracy of the French seemed to have ingrained a sense of moderation and mistrust of extremism. Additionally, the social movements in France led to the Art Deco movement that preceded the functional modernism that would come from the German experience at the time.

In the new Soviet Union when the Constituent Assembly was dismissed by the navy under orders of Lenin, it became clear that democracy would not be attempted after the second revolution as it had been after the first. The increasing power and tyranny of the state—including forced collectivization resulting in the deaths of millions, horrific purges, the use of secret police and the gulags—led to a dictatorship worse than that of any czar, and a short-lived democracy in Russia failed as the Bolsheviks eliminated all opposition due in no small part to the Russians' very short experience of less than 13 years of any democracy and only six months of democracy for most.

The Weimar Republic was a creation of the peace conferences at the end of the First World War. Resented by the conservatives for its part in accepting the harsh Versailles Treaty, mistrusted by the masses for its haphazard responses to the runaway inflation of the mid-1920s and to the hardships of the depression, it was destroyed from within. When his Nazis won a plurality of Reichstag seats in 1932, Hitler was appointed chancellor and within less than two years had laid the foundations for one of the world's most terrible totalitarian regimes. Democracy had been imposed on the Germans by their enemies; their history had not developed democratic institutions. The monarchies of the separate states, the despotism of Bismarck's new empire, and the virtual absolutism of Kaiser Wilhelm II's aggressive "fatherland" were only the prelude to the messy and inefficient coalition governments of the Weimar Republic. Hard times nurtured extremists, like the Nazis, who promised simplistic solutions. The Nazis were elected by the very democracy they then destroyed.

Since its unification in the late fifteenth century, Spain has been the bulwark of Catholic, monarchical conservatism. When a republic was set up in 1931, after the king was ousted, leftists tried to diminish the influence of the Roman Catholic Church by secularizing the schools, seizing church lands, and abolishing the Jesuits. This attempt, along with their land redistribution program, alienated the conservative faction, (the military, the church, the monarchists), and Spanish Fascists organized a government. When the popular election in 1936 put a coalition of leftists back in power, General Francisco Franco started a civil war against the republican government. Backed by a sizable segment of the populace and by the arms and men of the Italian Fascists and the German Nazis (the Republicans were backed by the Soviet communists), Franco won the bloody and costly civil war and seized power in 1939. He ruled Spain as the world's longest-reigning Fascist dictator until his death in 1975.

Mussolini used the Great Depression as an excuse to impose his plan for the "corporate state" on Italy. He and his party had been in power since 1922, and he completed his restructuring of the government by about 1934. In essence, labor unions managed industry and set the national political agenda. The unions were unrepresentative of the workers' real needs, however, and they were dominated by the Fascists.

The failure of democracy during the Great Depression in Germany, Italy, and Spain resulted from the lack of adaptable democratic institutions and from the peoples' general mistrust of an unaccustomed form of government. Its success in Britain, the Netherlands, France, and the United States came from their well-established constitutional systems.

EVALUATE THE SAMPLE ANSWER

Now go back and look at the rubric. It is clear that this essay fulfills all of the requirements for a score 6 on the rubric. The essay answers all parts of the question thoroughly with concrete evidence, at length, with a well-balanced essay. The thesis is appropriate and gets the thesis point. The essay clearly uses historical reasoning and evidence to explain the relationships between the successful and failed democracies after the First World War and corroborates the argument with strong evidence, gaining both Evidence points and both Analysis and Reasoning points. The argument certainly addresses the topic of the question with specific examples of relevant evidence. It goes on to utilize those examples to fully and effectively substantiate this strong thesis. The artistic analysis of France and Germany further shows the historical reasoning skills of the author. The essay explains multiple contexts of the threats to democracy in multiple nations and explains how the context of each country affected the stability of democracy in each nation. This is particularly true of the part about Italy.

RATER'S COMMENTS ON THE SAMPLE ANSWER

6—Extremely Well Qualified

The essay more than fulfills the requirements of the question. It offers the two most important examples of European democracy's resilience during the depression and three of the most important instances of its failure. The essay is supported by accurate information, although its tone is generalized. Specific mention might have been made of the personalities and parties that led the British and French governments during this crisis: Labourite Ramsey MacDonald, Conservatives Stanley Baldwin and Neville Chamberlain for Britain; rightist Raymond Poincaré, socialist Leon Blum, conservative Edouard Daladier, the Fascist-type party, Action Francaise, and the pro-republican coalition, Popular Front for France. The Fascist movements in Eastern Europe, Latin America, and Asia could also have been mentioned, including Ioannis Metaxas in Greece, the Arrow Cross in Hungary, the Green Shirts in Ireland, Brazil's Vargas, Hideko Tojo and his Imperial Way faction in Japan, Novo and Ante Paveli of Croatia, the Iron Guard of Romania, or the Slovak People's Party in Slovakia.

PART THREE
Model Exams

ANSWER SHEET
Model Test 1

SECTION I

1. Ⓐ Ⓑ Ⓒ Ⓓ
2. Ⓐ Ⓑ Ⓒ Ⓓ
3. Ⓐ Ⓑ Ⓒ Ⓓ
4. Ⓐ Ⓑ Ⓒ Ⓓ
5. Ⓐ Ⓑ Ⓒ Ⓓ
6. Ⓐ Ⓑ Ⓒ Ⓓ
7. Ⓐ Ⓑ Ⓒ Ⓓ
8. Ⓐ Ⓑ Ⓒ Ⓓ
9. Ⓐ Ⓑ Ⓒ Ⓓ
10. Ⓐ Ⓑ Ⓒ Ⓓ
11. Ⓐ Ⓑ Ⓒ Ⓓ
12. Ⓐ Ⓑ Ⓒ Ⓓ
13. Ⓐ Ⓑ Ⓒ Ⓓ
14. Ⓐ Ⓑ Ⓒ Ⓓ
15. Ⓐ Ⓑ Ⓒ Ⓓ
16. Ⓐ Ⓑ Ⓒ Ⓓ
17. Ⓐ Ⓑ Ⓒ Ⓓ
18. Ⓐ Ⓑ Ⓒ Ⓓ
19. Ⓐ Ⓑ Ⓒ Ⓓ
20. Ⓐ Ⓑ Ⓒ Ⓓ

21. Ⓐ Ⓑ Ⓒ Ⓓ
22. Ⓐ Ⓑ Ⓒ Ⓓ
23. Ⓐ Ⓑ Ⓒ Ⓓ
24. Ⓐ Ⓑ Ⓒ Ⓓ
25. Ⓐ Ⓑ Ⓒ Ⓓ
26. Ⓐ Ⓑ Ⓒ Ⓓ
27. Ⓐ Ⓑ Ⓒ Ⓓ
28. Ⓐ Ⓑ Ⓒ Ⓓ
29. Ⓐ Ⓑ Ⓒ Ⓓ
30. Ⓐ Ⓑ Ⓒ Ⓓ
31. Ⓐ Ⓑ Ⓒ Ⓓ
32. Ⓐ Ⓑ Ⓒ Ⓓ
33. Ⓐ Ⓑ Ⓒ Ⓓ
34. Ⓐ Ⓑ Ⓒ Ⓓ
35. Ⓐ Ⓑ Ⓒ Ⓓ
36. Ⓐ Ⓑ Ⓒ Ⓓ
37. Ⓐ Ⓑ Ⓒ Ⓓ
38. Ⓐ Ⓑ Ⓒ Ⓓ
39. Ⓐ Ⓑ Ⓒ Ⓓ
40. Ⓐ Ⓑ Ⓒ Ⓓ

41. Ⓐ Ⓑ Ⓒ Ⓓ
42. Ⓐ Ⓑ Ⓒ Ⓓ
43. Ⓐ Ⓑ Ⓒ Ⓓ
44. Ⓐ Ⓑ Ⓒ Ⓓ
45. Ⓐ Ⓑ Ⓒ Ⓓ
46. Ⓐ Ⓑ Ⓒ Ⓓ
47. Ⓐ Ⓑ Ⓒ Ⓓ
48. Ⓐ Ⓑ Ⓒ Ⓓ
49. Ⓐ Ⓑ Ⓒ Ⓓ
50. Ⓐ Ⓑ Ⓒ Ⓓ
51. Ⓐ Ⓑ Ⓒ Ⓓ
52. Ⓐ Ⓑ Ⓒ Ⓓ
53. Ⓐ Ⓑ Ⓒ Ⓓ
54. Ⓐ Ⓑ Ⓒ Ⓓ
55. Ⓐ Ⓑ Ⓒ Ⓓ

SHORT ANSWER: Use dark blue or black ink only for the short-answer questions. Do not write outside of the box.

Question 1

SHORT ANSWER: Use dark blue or black ink only for the short-answer questions. Do not write outside of the box.

Question 2

SHORT ANSWER: Use dark blue or black ink only for the short-answer questions. Do not write outside of the box.

Question 3 or Question 4 (Please indicate which question you answered.)

SECTION II

Circle the number of the Essay that you are answering on this page.	Mandatory: 1	Circle one: 2, 3, or 4

SECTION II

Circle the number of the Essay that you are answering on this page.	Mandatory: 1	Circle one: 2, 3, or 4

SECTION II

Circle the number of the Essay that you are answering on this page.	Mandatory: 1	Circle one: 2, 3, or 4

SECTION II

Circle the number of the Essay that you are answering on this page.	Mandatory: 1	Circle one: 2, 3, or 4

Model Test 1

SECTION I

Part A: Multiple-Choice Questions

TIME: 55 MINUTES
NUMBER OF QUESTIONS: 55
PERCENTAGE OF TOTAL AP EXAM SCORE: 40%
WRITING INSTRUMENT: PENCIL REQUIRED

Directions: Section I, Part A of this exam contains 55 multiple-choice questions. Indicate all of your answers to the multiple-choice questions on the multiple-choice answer sheet. No credit will be given for anything written in the exam booklet, but you may write on the exam booklet to take notes and do scratch work.

Use your time efficiently, working as quickly as possible without losing accuracy. Do not spend too much time on any one question. Go on to other questions and come back to the ones that you have not answered if you have time. It is not expected that you will know the answers to all of the multiple-choice questions.

Your total score on the multiple-choice section is based only on the number of questions answered correctly. Points are not deducted for incorrect answers or unanswered questions.

Questions 1 to 3 refer to the image below.

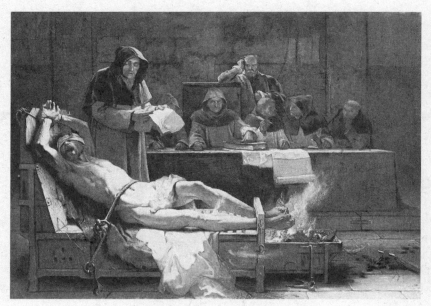

Source: Clergy torturing a layman.

1. The illustration above illustrates the draconian tactics at times used during which of the following state actions used to control religion and morality?

   (A) The Ecclesiastical reforms of the Russian Church in the mid-seventeenth century at the behest of the Patriarch Nikon and the tsar

   (B) Persecution of the French Huguenots during the late seventeenth century after Louis XIV issued his Edict of Revocation

   (C) The initiation of Ferdinand and Isabella's Inquisition in 1478 to test the faith of those non-Catholics whom had converted to Catholicism

   (D) Religious turmoil in England, during the Tudor dynasty, between Catholics and Protestants

2. Religious trials, such as the one above, usually focused on the persecution of which of the following?

   (A) Recent converts to Christianity

   (B) Those accused of witchcraft

   (C) Christians in the Ottoman Empire

   (D) Calvinists found to have sinned

3. Which of the following is the best characterization of how much control the state has had over the religion and morality of its citizens in Europe from 1450 to the present?

   (A) There has been a steady gain in personal choice in morality and religion.

   (B) There was generally a rise in freedom of choice from 1517 until 1648 but, after that, freedom of choice declined for two centuries until it rose recently.

   (C) There has been a general rise in personal freedom of religion and morality free of state control across Europe since the end of the Second World War.

   (D) Degrees of personal choice in morality and religion have gone up and down but have been at an all-time high in Europe as the twenty-first century begins.

Questions 4 to 7 refer to the excerpt below.

I am of opinion that the principal and true profession of the Courtier ought to be that of arms; which I would have him follow actively above all else, and be known among others as bold and strong, and loyal to whomsoever he serves. . . .

I would have him well built and shapely of limb, and would have him show strength and lightness and suppleness, and know all bodily exercises that befit a man of war; whereof I think the first should be to handle every sort of weapon well on foot and on horse, to understand the advantages of each, and especially to be familiar with those weapons that are ordinarily used among gentlemen. . . .

Our Courtier then will be esteemed excellent and will attain grace in everything, particularly in speaking. . . .

I would have him more than passably accomplished in letters, at least in those studies that are called the humanities, and conversant not only with the Latin language but with the Greek, for the sake of the many different things that have been admirably written therein. Let him be well versed in the poets, and not less in the orators and historians, and also proficient in writing verse and prose, especially in this vulgar [vernacular] tongue of ours. . . .

You must know that I am not content with the Courtier unless he be also a musician and unless, besides understanding and being able to read notes, he can play upon divers instruments. . . .

I wish our Courtier to guard against getting the name of a liar or a boaster, which sometimes befalls even those who do not deserve it.

—From Baldassare Castiglione's *Book of the Courtier*, 1528

4. The text above was most likely seen as which of the following at the time it was written?

    (A) A guide for educating and training a "Universal Man"
    (B) A guide for how to be a good absolute ruler
    (C) A guide for how to meet a wife
    (D) A guide for how to be a troubadour

5. Which of the following themes of the Renaissance era is the above writing most connected to?

    (A) Secularism
    (B) Individualism
    (C) Humanism
    (D) Perspective

6. Which of the following reforms would Castiglione most likely want to institute?

    (A) The creation of coeducational public high schools paid for by the state
    (B) The creation of male-only public high schools paid for by the state
    (C) The creation of public universities without tuition where all students of both genders could learn
    (D) The creation of private high schools for elite young men with many extracurricular activities

7. Which of the following skills that Castiglione recommends for a courtier would be valued LEAST by a European gentleman at the end of the twentieth century?

(A) Expertise with multiple languages
(B) Being strong and attractive
(C) Expertise with many kinds of weapons
(D) Ability to write poetry and prose

Questions 8 to 12 refer to the pair of excerpts below, written by explorer Christopher Columbus and the Dominican Bishop of Chiapas, Mexico, Bartholomew de las Casas.

Source 1

Indians would give whatever the seller required. . . . Thus they bartered, like idiots, cotton and gold for fragments of bows, glasses, bottles, and jars; which I forbad as being unjust, and myself gave them many beautiful and acceptable articles which I had brought with me, taking nothing from them in return; I did this in order that I might the more easily conciliate them, that they might be led to become Christians, and be inclined to entertain a regard for the King and Queen, our Princes and all Spaniards, and that I might induce them to take an interest in seeking out, and collecting and delivering to us such things as they possessed in abundance, but which we greatly needed.

—Christopher Columbus: letter to Raphael Sanchez, 1493

Source 2

It was upon these gentle lambs . . . that from the very first day they clapped eyes on them the Spanish fell like ravening wolves upon the fold, or like tigers and savage lions who have not eaten meat for days. The pattern established at the outset has remained unchanged to this day, and the Spaniards still do nothing save tear the natives to shreds, murder them and inflict upon them untold misery, suffering and distress, tormenting, harrying and persecuting them mercilessly. We shall in due course describe some of the many ingenious methods of torture they have invented and refined for this purpose, but one can get some idea of the effectiveness of their methods from the figures alone. When the Spanish first journeyed there, the indigenous population of the island of Hispaniola stood at some three million; today only two hundred survive. Their reason for killing and destroying such an infinite number of souls is that the Christians have an ultimate aim, which is to acquire gold, and to swell themselves with riches in a very brief time and thus rise to a high estate disproportionate to their merits.

—Bartholomew de las Casas: *A Short Account of the Destruction of the Indies,* 1542

8. Which of the following motives for exploration does de las Casas seem to be criticizing in **Source 2**?

(A) Converting the natives to Christianity
(B) Financial gain
(C) Personal glory
(D) Finding new mates

9. The free flow of plants and animals, as well as trade goods, between Europe and the Americas is referred to by historians as the Columbian Exchange, and affected the natives in which of the following ways?

(A) Economic opportunities were reduced.
(B) They were subjugated and destroyed.
(C) Economic opportunities were created.
(D) They were enriched through trade in agricultural goods.

10. The free flow of plants and animals, as well as trade goods, between Europe and the Americas is referred to by historians as the Columbian Exchange, and affected the Europeans in which of the following ways?

(A) Economic opportunities were reduced.
(B) They were subjugated and destroyed.
(C) Economic opportunities were created.
(D) They were enriched through trade in Native American slaves.

11. Which of the following motives for exploration is de las Casas most likely to think is most important in **Source 2**?

(A) Converting the natives to Christianity
(B) Financial gain
(C) Personal glory
(D) Finding new mates

12. Which of the following would best account for the differences between the interactions of the Spaniards and the natives as described in the two accounts?

(A) De las Casas was exaggerating to support the start of African slavery.
(B) Columbus was biased in favor of himself in his writings.
(C) Columbus's men were nicer to the natives than were later expeditions.
(D) De las Casas wanted the Spanish to leave the Americas.

Questions 13 and 14 refer to the sketch below of the circulatory and skeletal systems by Andreas Vesalius, c. 1546.

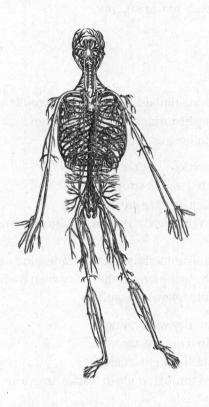

13. This print clearly illustrates which of the following truths about scientific advances in this era?

    (A) They led to significant declines in mortality rates from disease during the sixteenth and seventeenth centuries.

    (B) They created the experimental proof for the theories of ancient Greeks such as Aristotle and Galen.

    (C) They occurred as a result of the rediscovery of ancient Greek and Roman texts.

    (D) They occurred as a result of the accumulation of information from dissection and led to conceptualizing the human being as a set of integrated systems.

14. The understanding of the human body that Vesalius displays is most similar to which of the following?

    (A) The mechanical universe explained by Sir Isaac Newton

    (B) The notion, espoused by astrology, that celestial bodies could affect events on Earth

    (C) The Enlightenment view that all problems can be solved through reason

    (D) The idea of subatomic quanta explained by Max Planck

Questions 15 to 17 refer to the passage below by John Calvin.

If we need to be recalled to the origin of election, to prove that we obtain salvation from no other source than the mere goodness of God, they who desire to extinguish this principle, do all they can to obscure what ought to be magnificently and loudly celebrated, and to pluck up humility by the roots. In ascribing the salvation of the remnant of the people to the election of grace, Paul clearly testifies, that it is then only known that God saves whom upon which there can be no claim. They who shut the gates to prevent anyone from presuming to approach and taste this doctrine, do no less injury to man than to God; for nothing else will be sufficient to produce in us suitable humility, or to impress us with a due sense of our great obligations to God. Nor is there any other basis for solid confidence, even according to the authority of Christ, who, to deliver us from all fear, and render us invincible amidst so many dangers, snares, and deadly conflicts, promises to preserve in safety all whom the Father has committed to His care.

—John Calvin, *Institutes of the Christian Religion*, 1559

15. Which of the following beliefs, supported first by Calvin, does this passage seem to best support?

    (A) Salvation
    (B) Predestination
    (C) Divinity of Jesus
    (D) Simony

16. Which of the following religions that started around the same time as Calvinism was destroyed for supporting adult baptism and pacifism?

    (A) Huguenots
    (B) Lutherans
    (C) Presbyterians
    (D) Anabaptists

17. Which of the following was NOT an abuse of the Catholic Church that Calvin and other religious leaders criticized?

    (A) Papal wealth
    (B) Pluralism
    (C) Nepotism
    (D) Indulgences

Questions 18 to 20 refer to the excerpts below from the Navigation Acts of 1651.

[A]fter the first day of December, one thousand six hundred fifty and one, and from thence forwards, no goods or commodities whatsoever of the growth, production or manufacture of Asia, Africa or America, or of any part thereof; or of any islands belonging to them, or which are described or laid down in the usual maps or cards of those places, as well of the English plantations as others, shall be imported or brought into this Commonwealth of England, or into Ireland, or any other lands, islands, plantations, or territories to this Commonwealth belonging, or in their possession, in any other ship or ships, vessel or vessels whatsoever, but only in such as do truly and without fraud belong only to the people of this Commonwealth, or the plantations thereof, as the proprietors or right owners thereof; and whereof the master and mariners are also of the people of this Commonwealth, under the penalty of the forfeiture and loss of all the goods that shall be imported contrary to this act, , , ,

[N]o goods or commodities of the growth, production, or manufacture of Europe, or of any part thereof, shall after the first day of December, one thousand six hundred fifty and one, be imported or brought into this Commonwealth of England, or any other lands or territories to this Commonwealth belonging, or in their possession, in any ship or ships, vessel or vessels whatsoever, but in such as do truly and without fraud belong only to the people of this Commonwealth, and in no other, except only such foreign ships and vessels as do truly and properly belong to the people of that country or place, of which the said goods are the growth, production or manufacture.

18. Which of the following was the desired outcome of the above legislation by the Rump Parliament of England in 1651?

    (A) To prevent England's colonies from being bombarded with cheap goods manufactured by their mainland European competitors
    (B) To reclaim domination of the slave trade from Portugal in order to meet the growing need for slaves for sugar plantations in the English Caribbean colonies
    (C) To end Dutch domination of maritime trade by limiting their ability to move goods between England and her colonies as well as goods to and from England from other countries
    (D) To extricate the French from the Atlantic sea trade as well as the cod and whaling industries which at this time were dominated by the French

19. The aforementioned 1651 Navigation Acts above conflict with which of the following economic philosopher's theories and beliefs?

    (A) Thomas Malthus
    (B) Josiah Child
    (C) Adam Smith
    (D) Jean-Baptiste Colbert

20. Which of the following best describes the outcome of the Navigation Acts of 1651?

(A) They served as a catalyst for the growth of English shipping and overseas trade, but did little to limit the prospects of the Dutch in the seventeenth century.

(B) They brought about almost immediate hardships for the Dutch economy as their dominance of overseas trade quickly ended.

(C) They were rescinded during the restoration of the Stuarts as they sought normal diplomatic relations with the Dutch so as not to need Parliament's financial support for war.

(D) They led to nearly a century of recurrent war between England and the Netherlands, which would not end until after American independence.

Questions 21 to 23 refer to the map below.

21. Which of the following is the best characterization of the impact of the land acquisitions of Peter I of Russia from 1682–1715?

(A) They were of great strategic importance because Russia gained the ability to spy better on Prussia.

(B) They were of great economic importance due to the vast mineral resources there.

(C) They included many large cities and generally had a high population density.

(D) They allowed Peter the Great to build a port and a new capital city.

22. Which of the following events allowed continued Russian territorial expansion after Peter left the throne?

   (A) The Ottoman Empire was weakened after the loss of the Battle of Vienna, leaving territory open to Russian expansion.

   (B) The Austrian Empire was weakened after the Napoleonic Wars, leaving territory open to Russian expansion.

   (C) The Spanish monarchy was weakened after the defeat of the Spanish Armada, leaving territory open to Russian expansion.

   (D) Poland and Russia made an alliance to divide the Germanic states.

23. Which of the following was a goal of Peter the Great that was continued by Catherine the Great but never realized under Romanov rule?

   (A) The complete subjugation of the boyar nobility through their taxation and service to the czar

   (B) The westernization of Russia as it embraced the culture and traditions of Western Europe

   (C) The creation of a strong navy that could fight against the other great navies of the world

   (D) The emancipation of the serfs in an equitable fashion in order to modernize Russia

Questions 24 to 27 refer to the following quote from Voltaire in response to the 1755 Lisbon earthquake.

My dear sir, nature is very cruel. One would find it hard to imagine how the laws of movement cause such frightful disasters in the best of possible worlds. A hundred thousand ants, our fellows, crushed all at once in our ant-hill, and half of them perishing, no doubt in unspeakable agony, beneath the wreckage from which they cannot be drawn. Families ruined all over Europe, the fortune of a hundred businessmen, your compatriots, swallowed up in the ruins of Lisbon. What a wretched gamble is the game of human life! What will the preachers say, especially if the palace of the Inquisition is still standing? I flatter myself that at least the reverend father inquisitors have been crushed like others. That ought to teach men not to persecute each other, for while a few holy scoundrels burn a few fanatics, the earth swallows up one and all.

—Voltaire, in a letter, 1755

24. Voltaire is best known for supporting which of the following demands of the Enlightenment *philosophes*?

(A) Deism should be adopted by all as the only logical religion.
(B) Religious toleration leads to the destruction of social unity.
(C) Skepticism is not a reliable way of examining information.
(D) Religious toleration should be given to all people of all religions.

25. Voltaire's statement in the last sentence, criticizing persecution, is most likely influenced by which of the following?

(A) New concepts of legal equity and individual rights expressed by Locke and Rousseau
(B) Europeans gaining a more thorough understanding of the rich cultural diversity to be found through trade and travel
(C) New concepts of a deterministic mechanical universe based upon the discovery of Newton's mathematical laws
(D) Challenges on multiple fronts to the monopoly on truth held by the Roman Catholic Church

26. Which of the following Enlightenment *philosophes* questioned reliance on reason and began the Romantic movement for the rationale given?

(A) Jean-Jacques Rousseau because he thought society corrupted noble souls.
(B) Baron Montesquieu because he thought that governments were not capable of being fair.
(C) Mary Wollstonecraft because she railed against the subjugation of women emotionally.
(D) Adam Smith because he stated that reason could not be used to understand how another feels.

27. The ideas expressed by Voltaire, above, best illustrate which of the following characteristics of Enlightenment intellectuals?

(A) Many were accomplished scientists, who added important pieces to human understanding of the universe.
(B) They utilized new methods of communicating their ideas, such as salons and inexpensive printed pamphlets.
(C) Most rejected religion altogether and adopted atheism as the only credo of a rational man.
(D) Many believed that the new scientific discoveries justified a more tolerant and objective approach to social and cultural issues.

Paris has a short memory. If I remain longer doing nothing, I am lost. In this great Babylon one reputation quickly succeeds another. After I have been seen three times at the theatre, I shall not be looked at again. I shall therefore not go very frequently. (diary, 1798)

If the press is not bridled, I shall not remain three days in power. (diary, 1799)

The presence of a general is necessary; he is the head, he is the all in all of an army. It was not the Roman army that conquered Gaul, it was Caesar, it was not the Carthaginians that made the armies of the Roman republic tremble at the very gates of Rome, it was Hannibal. (diary, 1801)

My power proceeds from my reputation, and my reputation from the victories I have won. My power would fall if I were not to support it with more glory and more victories. Conquest has made me what I am; only conquest can maintain me. (diary, 1802)

The revolution in France is over and now there is only one party in France and I shall never allow the newspapers to say anything contrary to my interests. They may publish a few little articles with just a bit of poison in them, but one fine day I shall shut their mouths forever. (diary, 1805)

28. Napoleon's entry from 1802 indicates that his conquest of most of Europe was due in part to which of the following?

    (A) Napoleon's fear that if he did not continue to win military victories, he would lose power.
    (B) Napoleon's belief that he must conquer all of Europe to conquer the press.
    (C) Napoleon's confidence that he will be the greatest leader Europe has ever seen.
    (D) Napoleon's appreciation of his soldiers and their collective efforts.

29. While Napoleon was often praised for implementing his Napoleonic Code and a meritocracy in the army, the domestic issue that he was most often criticized for was which of the following?

    (A) Placing his relatives on foreign thrones
    (B) Changing the criminal code of France
    (C) Financial mismanagement
    (D) Curtailment of citizens' rights

30. Napoleon instituted the Continental System to accomplish which of the following?

    (A) Unify Italy with his brother as king
    (B) Punish Russia for his ill-fated invasion
    (C) Defeat England through economic war
    (D) Create a united Europe under the leadership of France

Press Law

So long as this decree shall remain in force no publication which appears in the form of daily issues, or as a serial not exceeding twenty sheets of printed matter, shall go to press in any state of the union without the previous knowledge and approval of the state officials. Writings which do not belong to one of the above-mentioned classes shall be treated according to the laws now in force, or which may be enacted, in the individual states of the union. . . . Each state of the union is responsible, not only to the state against which the offense is directly committed, but to the whole Confederation, for every publication appearing under its supervision in which the honor or security of other states is infringed or their constitution or administration attacked. . . .

—*Carlsbad Resolutions* adopted by the Germanic States, 1819

31. According to the above-mentioned decrees, the German confederated states most feared which of the following?

   (A) The effect liberal, young students would have on an impressionable faculty and the surrounding communities, where they would surely spread their message.
   (B) The dissemination of liberal ideas by the media and the sharing of nationalist or liberal ideas at the university in the classroom or in secret.
   (C) The dissolution of the union of German states that they had just created.
   (D) Support of Bonapartism, which was growing in strength prior to the passage of these *Carlsbad Resolutions* and preceeding Napoleon's invasion.

32. The *Carlsbad Resolutions* were another of Metternich's schemes, like the Concert of Europe, which aimed to accomplish which of the following?

   (A) Establish control of European states by democracy in the tradition of the Enlightenment.
   (B) Suppress all voices in government other than his own and control all aspects of his citizens' lives.
   (C) Suppress all nationalist revolutions across the continent.
   (D) Suppress all speech but that of monarchs and the churches that they approve of.

33. Which of the following nineteenth-century figures would have been the LEAST likely to oppose those liberals described in the above decrees?

   (A) Pope Pius IX
   (B) Klemens Von Metternich
   (C) Giuseppe Mazzini
   (D) William Frederick I

Under the name of Chartist well-meaning inconsiderate men and other misled men have in very many cases, all over the country from the extreme west to the extreme east and from Brighton in the south to nearly the extreme north of Scotland, denounced every man who is not a working man, applied to him, the grossest epithets and most atrocious intentions and conduct, have threatened them with vengeance and in some places, have proposed plans for the seizure and division of their property—numbers of misled men and others of bad character, under the self-denomination of Chartists have gone from place to place and in the most violent manner disturbed and dispersed meetings of various kinds. Your Committee object to the words Household Suffrage since under any honest definition of the words—they would exclude a large majority of the men of these kingdoms—and because they have become reasonably obnoxious to the political portion of the working people.

—Excerpt of a letter from British social reformer Francis Place, written in 1842

34. Which of the following best characterizes the historical point of view of the document above?

(A) The author must not be a radical reformer because he criticizes the Chartists.
(B) The author must be a radical reformer because he criticizes the Chartists.
(C) The author believes in universal male suffrage.
(D) The author thinks the Chartists are the best part of the reform movement.

35. The primary goal of the Chartist movement was which of the following?

(A) Universal suffrage
(B) Universal male suffrage
(C) Universal health care
(D) Social security and unemployment insurance

36. Which of the following is the political reaction led by Klemens von Metternich that occurred as a result of the Chartists, the French Revolution, and other liberal movements?

(A) Liberalism
(B) Radicalism
(C) Nationalism
(D) Conservatism

—*Scene at the Barricade*, Paris, June 1848.

37. The above image suggests which of the following about the French Revolution of June 1848?

    (A) It was a multi-ethnic revolution in which many people of multiple races rose up in rebellion.
    (B) It was only a minor conflict when compared with the February Revolution of 1848.
    (C) It involved many Parisians, who had to be extricated from the narrow streets and barricades, resulting in high casualties.
    (D) It was particularly troublesome for Parisians, who had to battle the Prussians and then their own National Assembly's military force.

38. In which of the following ways was the experience of the Polish revolutionaries different from that of the French as seen above?

    (A) The Polish were successful in their revolt and a constitutional government was formed.
    (B) The Polish were first encouraged by the Prussians, who had their own revolution going on, but then their statehood aspirations were also crushed by the Prussians, resulting in a foreign military controlling them.
    (C) The military intervention of a coalition force of reactionary states Austria, Prussia, and Russia to quell the radical revolution occurred in Poland.
    (D) The Polish citizens in the cities took much heavier losses than the French citizens because more of them joined the revolution.

39. When compared to the other revolutions in the rest of Europe in 1848, the revolution in France can be characterized as which of the following?

(A) They involved far more bloodshed but brought about many more positive, long-term changes for those involved.

(B) They brought about change too swiftly, leading to an equally conservative backlash cancelling out any gains.

(C) They mirrored the others where the revolutionaries failed to unite and were, therefore, played against one another, undermining the movement.

(D) They were limited due to the threat of intervention by the old Congress System countries to the East.

Questions 40 to 42 refer to the painting below.

—Jean Francois Millet, *Gleaners*, 1857.

40. Which of the following would be a suitable depiction of the above image?

(A) Women of Western Europe during the height of the open-field system in Europe

(B) Peasant farmers in France during the poor grain years immediately before the 1789 Revolution

(C) Prussian serf women of the mid-nineteenth century serving in the fields of Catholic Center Party members

(D) British peasant farmers of the early Hanoverian years engaging in gleaning during lean farming years

41. Which of the following would have likely been the fate of women, such as these above, in England as the Enclosure Movement moved forward?

   (A) The women would have likely been compelled to work on a communal farm, which they detested.
   (B) These women were likely destined to work in cottage industries, furthering proto industrialization.
   (C) The corvée would have required that these women continued service at the behest of the state each year.
   (D) Emigration was likely, as the Encomienda system was in a strong need of female workers in the New World.

42. Whose theories on population and inadequate food supply would the above image best support?

   (A) David Ricardo
   (B) Thomas Malthus
   (C) Karl Marx
   (D) Cornelius Vermuyden

Questions 43 to 46 refer to the following excerpt from a speech by Vladimir I. Lenin.

The independence of our country cannot be upheld unless we have an adequate industrial basis for defense. And such an industrial basis cannot be created if our industry is not more highly developed technically. That is why a fast rate of development of our industry is necessary and imperative. We cannot go on indefinitely, that is, for too long a period, basing the Soviet regime and socialist construction on two different foundations, the foundation of the most large-scale and united socialist industry and the foundation of the most scattered and backward, small commodity economy of the peasants. We must gradually, but systematically and persistently, place our agriculture on a new technical basis, the basis of large-scale production, and bring it up to the level of socialist industry. Either we accomplish this task—in which case the final victory of socialism in our country will be assured, or we turn away from it and do not accomplish it—in which case a return to capitalism may become inevitable.

—Vladimir I. Lenin *Industrialization of the Country and the Right Deviation in the C.P.S.U.*, November 19, 1928

43. Which of the following compromises of his New Economic Policy is Lenin saying needs to be fixed in the speech above?

(A) Compromising with free markets in rural areas after the civil war
(B) Sharing power with the provisional government
(C) Giving the government too much power to further communism
(D) Freeing the peasants from their landlords in exchange for their support

44. Which of the following policies of Joseph Stalin was NOT used to correct the problem cited by Lenin above?

(A) Collectivization
(B) Persecution of the better-off peasants
(C) The Berlin blockade
(D) The five-year plans

45. What was the result of Stalin's attempt to fix this problem?

(A) The Soviet Union saw steady growth in both industry and agriculture.
(B) The Soviet Union saw steady growth in industry and a decline in agriculture.
(C) The Soviet Union saw steady growth in agriculture but industrial production fell behind.
(D) The Soviet Union saw steady decline in both industry and agriculture.

46. Which of the following events was most likely the greatest influence on Lenin in his desire to industrialize his new nation?

(A) His exile in Switzerland and other places led him to see how the industrialization of the West was needed in the Soviet Union.
(B) Russia had a large percentage of its population working in factories before the revolution occurred, and he wanted to build on that.
(C) Trotsky was able to lead the Bolshevik revolt in 1917 because he had control of the rail and telegraph stations.
(D) The humiliating defeat of Russia during the First World War had led to his rise to power and he knew another defeat would spell his doom.

Questions 47 to 48 refer to the following text.

Addison's Act had been conceived in the belief that, unless working-class aspirations were quickly met after the war, Britain might experience a revolution similar to that in Russia. By 1920 that fear was beginning to recede and Addison's policy was being regarded as extravagant. An immediate victim of the new attitude was the Borough's Kingfield Street scheme, provisional plans for which were approved in September 1920. Much to the Council's surprise, the Government's Housing Board deferred the scheme, "having regard to the Council's present commitments and the money available at the present time, and in May 1921 the Government announced a drastic curtailment of the housing programme, cutting the housing target by half.

> —Excerpt from a work by English historian Hermione Hobhouse,
> *Public Housing in Poplar: The Inter-war Years*, 1994

47. Which of the following attitudes prevalent after the First World War is evident in the passage above?

    (A) Women's suffrage should increase
    (B) Democratization of society
    (C) Increased disillusionment and cynicism
    (D) The rise of communism as a world power

48. Which of the following is the best description of the plans being changed above?

    (A) Welfare programs were questioned after the First World War.
    (B) Housing was a large part of the British budget.
    (C) Workers were threatening communist revolution.
    (D) The government Housing Board wanted to build more houses.

Questions 49 to 51 refer to the charts below.

Table 1: Troops and Weapons Lost in the Battle of Stalingrad, August 1942 to February 1943

Nation	Casualties	Lost Tanks	Lost Artillery	Lost Planes
USSR	1,129,619	4,341	15,728	2,769
Axis Total	850,000	500	6,000	900
Germany	400,000			
Romania	200,000			
Italy	130,000			
Hungary	120,000			

Table 2: Total Casualties from the Second World War in Selected Nations

Country	Total Population as of 1/1/1939	Military Deaths	Civilian deaths due to military activity and crimes against humanity	Total Deaths	Deaths by percentage of population
Soviet Union	168,524,000	8,800,000 to 10,700,000	12,700,000 to 14,600,000	23,400,000	14.2%
Germany	69,850,000	5,530,000	1,100,000 to 3,150,000	6,630,000 to 8,680,000	7.8% to 10%
Poland	34,849,000	240,000	5,380,000 to 5,580,000	5,620,000 to 5,820,000	17.2%
United Kingdom	47,760,000	383,800 including overseas possessions	67,100	450,900	0.94%
Belgium	8,387,000	12,100	75,900	88,000	1.05%
Global Totals	1,995,537,400	22,426,600 to 25,487,500	37,585,300 to 54,594,000	62,171,600 to 78,041,700	3% to 4%

49. Which of the following was the clearest result of the Battle of Stalingrad according to the data in Table 1 above?

(A) The Axis powers saved their soldiers for future conquests while the Soviets did everything they could to defend their city.

(B) The Axis powers suffered greater losses on the Western front than they did on the Eastern Front during 1943.

(C) An entire generation of men was decimated.

(D) The Germans won the battle and drove the Russians out of the territory surrounding Stalingrad.

50. Which of the following contributed most to the overall pattern shown in Table 2?

    (A) Greater populations in Russia and Poland were causing hunger problems there.

    (B) The German army was better trained, equipped, and fed than any other army.

    (C) The new Nazi racial order eliminated millions of people in Eastern Europe.

    (D) The Allies were unprepared for the Axis onslaught, and took high casualties.

51. The data in both tables indicate which of the following about how Total War affected the citizens' loyalty and respect for their nation-states?

    (A) Citizens lost all respect for their nation-states in many places during the Second World War.

    (B) The nation state gained power over the people to the point where it could get them to treat other humans in ways that was previously inconceivable to most Europeans.

    (C) The citizens displayed greater respect for their nation-states and loyalty to them after the Second World War than they did during the war.

    (D) Nation-states found that they had lost the respect and loyalty of their citizens after the war.

Questions 52 to 55 refer to the political platform below.

To help heal the planet we will:

- Make achieving international agreement and action to limit climate change to below 2 degrees C of warming the major foreign policy priority.
- Invest in an £85 billion public programme of renewable electricity generation, flood defenses and building insulation.
- Support local sustainable agriculture, with respect for animals and wild places.

To become more equal and support our public services[,] we will:

- End privatization in the National Health Service
- End tuition fees and cancel student debt.
- Provide 500,000 social homes for rent over the five-year Parliament
- Control excessive rents and achieve house price stability.
- Increase public spending to almost half of national income.
- Make tax fair and crack down vigorously on tax avoidance and evasion.
- Ensure respect for everyone whatever their ethnicity, gender, age, religious belief or non-belief, sexual orientation, class, size, disability or other status.
- Make the highest wage in any organization no more than ten times the lowest wage.

To create a truly democratic central and local government and a common citizenship and to promote peace based on democratic principles[,] we will:

- Reform the benefits system. End workfare and sanctions. Double Child Benefit and pay a pension that people can live on in the longer term, unite tax and benefits in a Basic Income system covering everyone.

- Fund local government adequately and set democratically elected local authorities free to decide how to run education, public transport and other local services and to raise local taxes.
- Respect immigrants for the contribution they make and control immigration fairly.
- Decommission the Trident nuclear deterrent system and promote peacemaking.

—The 2015 Manifesto of the Green Party of England

52. Which of the following twentieth-century events was the political platform outlined in the passage reacting to most?

(A) The failure of the European welfare state
(B) The expansion of women's rights
(C) The increasing political and economic integration of Europe
(D) The growing influence of consumerism

53. Which of the following trends in late-twentieth-century Europe is reflected in the platform's references to minorities and multicultural communities?

(A) The collapse of communism in Eastern Europe
(B) The increasing reliance on immigrant labor
(C) The reaction against the influence of American pop culture
(D) The effects of the postwar baby boom

54. Education and public services as a central plank in their platform are most clearly evidence of which of the following?

(A) The emergence of nationalist political parties
(B) The requirements of membership in the European Union
(C) The influence of Catholic reforms after the Second Vatican Council
(D) The political debate over the cost of the welfare state

55. Based on its platform, the Green Party of England likely supported which of the following?

(A) Bans on immigration
(B) Expanded civil rights for gays and lesbians
(C) Free trade
(D) Expansionary foreign policy

If there is still time remaining, you may review your answers.

SECTION I

Part B: Short Answer

TIME: 40 MINUTES
NUMBER OF QUESTIONS: 4
PERCENTAGE OF TOTAL AP EXAM SCORE: 20%
WRITING INSTRUMENT: PEN WITH DARK BLUE OR BLACK INK

> **Directions:** Section I, Part B of this exam contains four short-answer questions. Write your responses in the corresponding boxes on the short-answer response sheets. You must answer Questions 1 and 2, but you choose to answer either Question 3 OR 4. Please indicate which question you answered on the answer sheet.
>
> Answer all parts of every question. Use complete sentences; an outline or bulleted list alone is not acceptable. You may plan your answers in your exam booklet, but no credit will be given for what is written there. Sources have been edited for the purposes of this exercise.

Answer all parts of the questions that follow.

1. Historians have sometimes referred to the Renaissance era as the start of modern history.

   (A) Provide TWO pieces of evidence to <u>support</u> this characterization of this period and explain how they support it.

   (B) Provide ONE specific piece of evidence that <u>undermines</u> this characterization of this time period, and explain how it undermines it.

Use the image below to answer both parts of the question that follows.

—*The Persistence of Memory*, by Spanish artist Salvador Dali, 1931.

2. (A) Briefly analyze how the artwork above reflects artistic trends in the first part of the twentieth century.

   (B) Based on the painting and your knowledge of European history, briefly analyze two aspects of change that affected Europeans' perceptions during the time between the First and Second World Wars.

Please choose to answer either #3 or #4 and indicate which question you answer.

Use the passages below to answer all parts of the question that follows.

Source 1

The Cold War was a tragic conflict that was unnecessary and detrimental to people living on both sides of the Iron Curtain. The personal conflicts between the allied leaders, Winston Churchill and Joseph Stalin[, led] to increasing distrust and eventual hostility between two factions that emerged from the allied powers that had been victorious in World War II, the Warsaw pact or COMINTERN, and NATO. The United States was strongly influenced by Churchill to oppose Soviet foreign policy goals and thus created NATO to oppose all communist expansion. The cost of the military spending by both NATO and the COMINTERN nations was a huge loss of consumer goods and services. The costs of trying to supply consumer goods and services while continuing a military build-up eventually brought the Soviet Union to the point of collapse as the incredible consumer economies of the United States and other NATO nations out-produced them in almost every area. In the end, the Soviet Union fell and the Cold War ended because the NATO nations produced more goods and services including military goods and services which led the people of the COMINTERŃ nations to want a better life through capitalism, resulting in the fall of communism there.

—Historian Henokh Sharon, 2013

Source 2

Communism was a corrupt system that was bound to fail before the revolution ever began in Russia in 1917. The Cold War was an ideological battle based upon the moral superiority of the freedom associated with capitalism. The leadership of the Soviet Union believed in a fantasy of a classless society that their people knew would never be created due to the failings of human nature. The alliance of convenience with Joseph Stalin against the Nazi aggression was a necessary evil, but Western Europe realized the [S]oviet threat after World War II and met the threat of communist expansion everywhere with military force and economic aid, bringing communism to an end by the choice of its own leaders who saw the flaws in their system and chose to reform it.

—Historian Ruben van der Straaten, 1992

3. (A) Explain ONE major difference between Sharon's and van der Straaten's interpretations of the Cold War.

   (B) Provide ONE piece of evidence from the Cold War that supports Sharon's interpretation (**Source 1**) and explain HOW it supports the interpretation.

   (C) Provide ONE piece of evidence from the Cold War that supports van der Straaten's interpretation (**Source 2**) and explain HOW it supports the interpretation.

4.

Source 1

Louis XIV was synonymous with the history of Europe for almost two decades. His influence on events was so immense that he was adored and feared by the people he ruled. He created the model for how to tame the nobility and become a true absolute monarch for all of Europe. France under Louis XIV was at its zenith of international power and has declined ever since his fall, with the exception of the Napoleonic Era. Louis XIV made the French court at Versailles the model of court life in Europe at the time. He influenced political and military events to make France the leading nation in Europe. He was a figure so grand and so spectacular that it was said that when Louis sneezed all of Europe caught cold.

—Historian Burke Arielle

Source 2

Louis XIV may have been one of the most influential rulers of the time, but he was resented and resisted by the nobility in his realm, and he mismanaged the finances of the state so badly that the final result of his rule was the French Revolution, which occurred as a result of failed French finances. He was obsessed with his image and believed that appearances were the substance of ruling a nation. He was devoutly observant, but never lived by religious virtues. He may have been good for France for a short while, but his actions led to the bankruptcy of the French state by Louis's waging costly wars and building the palace of Versailles. That bankruptcy, although he did not live to see it, eventually caused the end of the Bourbon reign and monarchy in France.

—Historian Jessica Gillespie

(A) Based on **Source 1**, briefly analyze the positive aspects of the reign of Louis XIV for the European continent.

(B) Based upon **Source 2**, briefly analyze the negative aspects of the reign of Louis XIV for the European continent.

(C) What role did war play in the legacy of Louis XIV?

STOP

If there is still time remaining, you may review your answers.

SECTION II: EUROPEAN HISTORY

TOTAL TIME: 100 MINUTES
NUMBER OF QUESTIONS: 2
PERCENTAGE OF TOTAL AP EXAM SCORE: 40%
QUESTION 1: 25%
QUESTION 2: 15%
WRITING INSTRUMENT: PEN WITH DARK BLUE OR BLACK INK

> **Directions:** Section II of this exam contains three essay questions. You must respond to Question 1, the document-based question, but you must CHOOSE to answer either Question 2 or 3 for your long-essay question. No credit is given for work written on the exam itself, all responses must be written in dark blue or black ink in essay format in the answer booklet. Be sure to indicate which long-essay question you are answering on each page of the answer booklet.

Question 1 (Document-Based Question—DBQ)

TIME: 60 MINUTES
SUGGESTED READING PERIOD: 15 MINUTES
SUGGESTED WRITING TIME: 45 MINUTES

> **Directions:** Question 1 is based on the accompanying documents. The documents have been edited for the purpose of the exercise.
>   In your response you should do the following:
>
>   - State a relevant thesis that directly addresses all parts of the question.
>   - Support the thesis or a relevant argument with evidence from all, or all but one, of the documents.
>   - Incorporate analysis of all, or all but one, of the documents into your argument.
>   - Focus your analysis of each document on at least one of the following: intended audience, purpose, historical context, and/or point of view.
>   - Support your argument with analysis of historical examples outside the documents.
>   - Connect historical phenomena relevant to your argument to broader events or processes.
>   - Synthesize the elements above into a persuasive essay that extends your argument, connects it to a different historical context, or accounts for contradictory evidence on the topic.

1. Analyze how changing reactions and responses to socialism reflected social, political, and economic changes in Europe from 1800 to 1949.

DOCUMENT 1

Source: *Letters from an Inhabitant of Geneva to His Contemporaries*, by Henri Saint-Simon, early French socialist, 1803.

Compared with those who own no property, you are not very many in number: how, then, does it come about that they consent to obey you? It is because the superiority of your intellect enables you to combine your forces (as they cannot), thus for the most part giving you an advantage over them in the struggle which, in the nature of things, must always exist between you and them.

Once this principle has been accepted, it is clearly in your interest to include those without property in your party; those who have proved the superiority of their intelligence with important discoveries; and it is equally clear that the interest being *general* for your class, *each* of the members who compose it should contribute.

Until you have adopted the measure which I propose to you, you will be exposed, each in your own country, to the sort of evils which some of your class have suffered in France. In order to convince yourselves of the truth of what I have said, you have only to think about the events that have occurred in that country since 1789. The first popular movement there was secretly fomented by scientists and artists. Once the success of the insurrection had lent it the appearance of legitimacy, they declared themselves its leaders. The resistance they encountered to the direction they gave to that insurrection's direction aimed at the destruction of all the institutions which had wounded their self-esteem, provoked them to inflame the passions of the ignorant and to burst all the bonds of subordination which, until then, had contained the rash passions of those without property. They succeeded in doing what they wanted. All the institutions which from the outset they had intended to overthrow were destroyed inevitably; in short, they won the battle and you lost it. This victory was to cost the victors dear; but you who were defeated have suffered even more.

Source: *The People's Petition of 1838*, a document of the Chartist movement.

It was the fond expectation of the people that a remedy for the greater part, if not for the whole, of their grievances, would be found in the Reform Act of 1832.

They were taught to regard that Act as a wise means to a worthy end; as the machinery of an improved legislation, when the will of the masses would be at length potential.

They have been bitterly and basely deceived.

The fruit which looked so fair to the eye has turned to dust and ashes when gathered.

The Reform Act has effected a transfer of power from one domineering faction to another, and left the people as helpless as before.

Our slavery has been exchanged for an apprenticeship to liberty, which has aggravated the painful feeling of our social degradation, by adding to it the sickening of still deferred hope.

We come before your Honourable House to tell you, with all humility, that this state of things must not be permitted to continue; that it cannot long continue without very seriously endangering the stability of the throne and the peace of the kingdom; and that if by God's help and all lawful and constitutional appliances, an end can be put to it, we are fully resolved that it shall speedily come to an end.

We tell your Honourable House that the capital of the master must no longer be deprived of its due reward; that the laws which make food dear, and those which by making money scarce, make labour cheap, must be abolished; that taxation must be made to fall on property, not on industry; that the good of the many, as it is the only legitimate end, so must it be the sole study of the Government.

Source: *Socialist Allegory*, an English illustration supporting the International Socialist and Trade Union Congress of 1896, showing the nations of Europe and America represented by workers.

—English illustration by Walter Crane. The Granger Collection.

Source: *The War and the Workers*, by Rosa Luxemburg, a German socialist in the working class, 1916.

The fall of the socialist proletariat in the present world war is unprecedented. It is a misfortune for humanity. But socialism will be lost only if the international proletariat fails to measure the depth of this fall, if it refuses to learn from it.

The last forty-five year period in the development of the modern labor movement now stands in doubt.

The [Franco-Prussian] War and the defeat of the Paris Commune had shifted the center of gravity for the European workers' movement to Germany. As France was the classic site of the first phase of proletarian class struggle and Paris the beating, bleeding heart of the European laboring classes of those times, so the German workers became the vanguard of the second phase. By means of countless sacrifices and tireless attention to detail, they have built the strongest organization, the one most worthy of emulation; they created the biggest press, called the most effective means of education and enlightenment into being, gathered the most powerful masses of voters and attained the greatest number of parliamentary mandates. German Social Democracy was considered the purest embodiment of Marxist socialism.

And what did we in Germany experience when the great historical test came? The most precipitous fall, the most violent collapse. Nowhere has the organization of the proletariat been yoked so completely to the service of imperialism. Nowhere is the state of siege borne so docilely. Nowhere is the press so hobbled, public opinion so stifled, the economic and political class struggle of the working class so totally surrendered as in Germany.

But German Social Democracy was not merely the strongest vanguard troop, it was the thinking head of the International. For this reason, we must begin the analysis, the self-examination process, with its fall. It has the duty to begin the salvation of international socialism, [and] that means unsparing criticism of itself.

Source: Nazi propaganda poster from 1944.

Nazi propaganda poster from the Second World War. This antisemitic and anti-Soviet German poster, written in the Polish language, says: "Death to Jewish-Bolshevik plague of murdering!" Posted on the streets of Kraków, which was under German occupation, c. 1944.

Source: *Conservative Party Principles*, by Winston Churchill, former British prime minister, 1946.

We oppose the establishment of a Socialist State, controlling the means of production, distribution and exchange. We are asked, "What is your alternative?" Our Conservative aim is to build a property-owning democracy, both independent and interdependent. In this I include profit-sharing schemes in suitable industries and intimate consultation between employers and wage-earners. In fact we seek so far as possible to make the status of the wage-earner that of a partner rather than of an irresponsible employee. It is in the interest of the wage-earner to have many other alternatives open to him than service under one all-powerful employer called the State. He will be in a better position to bargain collectively and production will be more abundant; there will be more for all and more freedom for all when the wage-earner is able, in the large majority of cases, to choose and change his work, and to deal with a private employer who, like himself, is subject to the ordinary pressures of life and, like himself, is dependent upon his personal thrift, ingenuity and good-house-keeping. In this way alone can the traditional virtues of the British character be preserved. We do not wish the people of this ancient island reduced to a mass of State-directed pro-letarians, thrown hither and thither, housed here and there, by an aristocracy of privileged officials or privileged Party, sectarian or Trade Union bosses. We are opposed to the tyranny and victimization of the closed shop [*Note: a unionized workplace where all workers must join the union*]. Our ideal is the consenting union of millions of free, independent families and homes to gain their livelihood and to serve true British glory and world peace.

Source: *Why Socialism*, by Albert Einstein, 1949.

The profit motive, in conjunction with competition among capitalists, is responsible for an instability in the accumulation and utilization of capital which leads to increasingly severe depressions. Unlimited competition leads to a huge waste of labor, and to that crippling of the social consciousness of individuals which I mentioned before.

This crippling of individuals I consider the worst evil of capitalism. Our whole educational system suffers from this evil. An exaggerated competitive attitude is inculcated into the student, who is trained to worship acquisitive success as a preparation for his future career.

I am convinced there is only one way to eliminate these grave evils, namely through the establishment of a socialist economy, accompanied by an educational system which would be oriented toward social goals. In such an economy, the means of production are owned by society itself and are utilized in a planned fashion. A planned economy, which adjusts production to the needs of the community, would distribute the work to be done among all those able to work and would guarantee a livelihood to every man, woman, and child. The education of the individual, in addition to promoting his own innate abilities, would attempt to develop in him a sense of responsibility for his fellow men in place of the glorification of power and success in our present society.

Nevertheless, it is necessary to remember that a planned economy is not yet socialism. A planned economy as such may be accompanied by the complete enslavement of the individual. The achievement of socialism requires the solution of some extremely difficult socio-political problems: how is it possible, in view of the far-reaching centralization of political and economic power, to prevent bureaucracy from becoming all-powerful and overweening? How can the rights of the individual be protected and therewith a democratic counterweight to the power of bureaucracy be assured?

Question 2, Question 3, or Question 4

SUGGESTED WRITING TIME: 35 MINUTES

Directions: Choose EITHER Question 2, Question 3, or Question 4.

In your response you should:

- State a relevant thesis that directly addresses all parts of the question;
- Support your argument with evidence, using specific examples;
- Synthesize the elements above into a persuasive essay that extends your argument, connects it to a different historical context, or connects it to a different category of analysis.

2. Compare the impact of the printing press on the daily life and culture of the European people with that of the Columbian Exchange on the daily lives and culture of the European people.

3. Compare the impact of the French Revolution of 1789 on the daily life and culture of the French people with that of the Russian Revolution of 1917 on the daily lives and culture of the Russian people.

4. Compare the impact of the Scientific Revolution (1540–1700) on the daily life and culture of the European people with that of the Industrial Revolution (1780–1914) on the daily life and culture of the nineteenth-century Europeans.

If there is still time remaining, you may review your answers.

SCORING AND ANSWER EXPLANATIONS

The AP European History exam is composed of four parts grouped into two sections. The multiple-choice test is scored with one point given for each correct answer.

- *There is no penalty for guessing,* so you should answer every question on the exam.
- Each of three short-answer questions is given a score of 0 to 3.
- The long essay is given a score from 0 to 6.
- The Document-Based Question (DBQ) is scored from 0 to 7.

To attain your final AP score on this exam, the following method should be used:

Multiple-Choice Score $\times$ 1.091 = _____

$+$

Short-Answer Score $\times$ 3.334 = _____

$+$

DBQ Score $\times$ 5.357 = _____

$+$

FRQ Score $\times$ 3.75 = _____

Total of all above scores is composite score = _____(round your score)

Score Range	AP Score
104–150	5
91–103	4
79–91	3
69–78	2
0–69	1

To get a final score for the exam, compare your composite score to the chart directly above.

Following are four separate guides to scoring each section of this exam. Once you have scored each piece of the exam, place the score on the appropriate line above. When you are done, do the computations to get your final score. Remember that this test is designed to mimic the AP exam, but you will not take it in the same conditions that you will during the real test, and it is not scored by professionals, who are reading 1,000 or more essays daily. While this test is a good predictor of success, it is only as good as the student using it, so do not stop studying just because you got a good score here.

Scoring Guide for the Multiple-Choice Section

> **Directions:** Use the guide below to check your answers to the multiple-choice questions. There is an answer key at the end of this section with all of the answers, but you are advised not to use it other than to score your exam.

> ### SPECIAL NOTE
>
> There is a lot of valuable information in the explanations for the multiple-choice questions, so make certain to read the explanations for ALL responses for every question that gave you any trouble!

1. **(C)**

   (A) is wrong because, despite roughshod treatment of non-conformists to Nikon's church by reformed church officials, most violence on Old Believers was self-inflicted.

   (B) is wrong because in France the Revocation of the Edict of Nantes mostly dealt with deportations, forced baptisms, and destruction of Huguenot churches.

   (C) is CORRECT because, even though the amount of torture was less than originally thought, it was a common practice to force confessions from recent converts.

   (D) is wrong because, although there were trials of non-conforming religious figures by Catholics and Protestants in England at this time, torture was mostly reserved for those accused of treason and other crimes.

2. **(A)**

   (A) is CORRECT because Jews (and some Muslims) not converting were deported, and as for those who did convert, the Spanish crown suspected they practiced their old religion in private.

   (B) is wrong because witch trials were intermittent, occurred in more isolated areas of Europe, and the accused tended to be women.

   (C) is wrong because the Ottomans, provided a tax was paid, were generally more tolerant of Christians than Christians were to Jews and Muslims.

   (D) is wrong because Calvinists often dealt out swift and harsh punishments, but not usually necessitating the use of torture.

3. **(D)**

   (A) is wrong because incidences such as the rise of the Nazis, and the communist ban on religion, made the rise of personal choice in religion and morality see sporadic growth.

   (B) is wrong because, after Napoleon spread his legal code across most of early nineteenth-century Europe, freedom of choice rose significantly throughout the Continent.

   (C) is wrong because, even though the amount of torture was less than originally thought, it was a common practice to force confessions from recent converts.

   (D) is CORRECT because personal freedom is at an apex, in large part because of the end of communism in Europe and also the growing cultural relativism that has been trending upward slowly since the Enlightenment.

4. **(A)**

(A) is CORRECT because Castiglione's *Book of the Courtier* is about how to become the ideal "Renaissance Man."

(B) is wrong because Castiglione's *Book of the Courtier* is not about how to become an ideal ruler, but how to serve one.

(C) is wrong because Castiglione's *Book of the Courtier* is not about how to find a wife, but about how to become a courtier.

(D) is wrong because Castiglione's *Book of the Courtier* is not about how to become trou-badour (although it encourages musicianship), but about how to become a courtier.

5. **(C)**

(A) is wrong because, although the reading explains many ways to improve as an individual, it is also focused on Greco-Roman texts and on perfection as an educational pursuit, making it more closely tied to humanism than to individualism.

(B) is wrong because although the reading does not mention any religious theme or goal, it is focused on Greco-Roman texts and on perfection as an educational pursuit, making it more closely tied to humanism than to secularism.

(C) is CORRECT because the reading is focused on Greco-Roman texts and on perfection as an educational pursuit, making it more closely tied to humanism than to individualism or secularism.

(D) is wrong because perspective was an artistic method not mentioned or alluded to in this reading.

6. **(D)**

(A) is wrong because the Renaissance was an elitist movement, and Castiglione was against the noisy public being educated, and the idea of boys and girls being educated together would have been unacceptable to him.

(B) is wrong because the Renaissance was an elitist movement, and Castiglione was against the noisy public being educated and would thus be against any kind of public schooling.

(C) is wrong because the Renaissance was an elitist movement, and Castiglione was against the noisy public being educated, and the idea of boys and girls being educated together would have been unacceptable to him.

(D) is CORRECT because the Renaissance was an elitist movement, and Castiglione wanted to get the best education in all pursuits for the young men of the upper classes only.

7. **(C)**

(A) is wrong because gentlemen at the end of the twentieth century in Europe were expected to know multiple languages, but not how to fight with many weapons.

(B) is wrong because gentlemen at the end of the twentieth century in Europe were still expected to be strong and attractive or "shapely of limb," as Castiglione puts it, but were not required to fight with multiple weapons.

(C) is CORRECT because gentlemen at the end of the twentieth century in Europe were no longer expected to know how to fight with multiple weapons.

(D) is wrong because gentlemen at the end of the twentieth century in Europe were expected to know how to write both prose and poetry, but not how to fight with multiple weapons.

8. **(B)**

(A) is wrong because, as a bishop, de las Casas would not criticize the converting of natives.

(B) is CORRECT because he is criticizing the greedy nature of the Europeans and how they have devastated the natives for profit.

(C) is wrong because personal glory is not mentioned.

(D) is wrong because they did not cross the ocean to find new mates.

9. **(B)**

(A) is wrong because, although opportunities were reduced, the subjugation and destruction of all natives was a greater and clearer impact.

(B) is CORRECT because the natives were wiped out by the Europeans.

(C) is wrong because economic opportunities were not created for these enslaved peoples.

(D) is wrong because their agricultural wealth and produce were stolen from them.

10. **(C)**

(A) is wrong because economic opportunities increased for them, as many came to the new world to get rich.

(B) is wrong because the natives were wiped out by the Europeans.

(C) is CORRECT because economic opportunities were created for the Europeans.

(D) is wrong because their slave trade was not in Native Americans.

11. **(A)**

(A) is CORRECT because, as a bishop, he would want to bring as many Christians into the faith as possible.

(B) is wrong because he is criticizing the greedy nature of the Europeans and how they have devastated the natives for profit.

(C) is wrong because personal glory is not mentioned.

(D) is wrong because they did not cross the ocean to find new mates.

12. **(B)**

(A) is wrong because there is no evidence of exaggeration.

(B) is CORRECT because he clearly wrote to make himself and his discovery look better.

(C) is wrong because de las Casas stated that they were cruel from the start.

(D) is wrong because there is no evidence of de las Casas wanting Spain to leave.

13. **(D)**

(A) is wrong because mortality rates did not decline as a result of science until the eighteenth century.

(B) is wrong because the ideas of Galen and Aristotle were discredited by experimental science.

(C) is wrong because these discoveries relied upon experimentation, not the revival of old ideas.

(D) is CORRECT because Vesalius's idea that the circulatory system carried blood as but one system in the human body was supported by his dissections of corpses.

14. **(A)**

(A) is CORRECT because the image displays the human body as a set of systems much as the universe was a system according to Newton.

(B) is wrong because astrology is based upon belief without proof, unlike Vesalius's work.

(C) is wrong because this image does not illustrate anything to support social problems being solved through reason.

(D) is wrong because those ideas are not related in any way, other than through this question, with one being about entropy and the other being about systems working—they could even be opposites.

15. **(B)**

(A) is wrong because while the passage does discuss salvation, it is clearly more about the elect and predestination than about salvation alone.

(B) is CORRECT because the passage describes the elect, who are predestined to go to heaven, according to Calvin.

(C) is wrong because the passage is not really about Jesus.

(D) is wrong because simony is paying someone else to perform one's church duties.

16. **(D)**

(A) is wrong because the Huguenots were French Calvinists, who did not believe in adult baptism.

(B) is wrong because Lutherans did not believe in adult baptism.

(C) is wrong because Presbyterians were Scottish Calvinists who did not believe in adult baptism.

(D) is CORRECT because the Anabaptists believed in adult baptism and pacifism and were virtually wiped out.

17. **(A)**

(A) is CORRECT because Calvin and other reformers did not focus on the wealth of the popes, but on their alleged immorality and ignorance.

(B) is wrong because reformers of the era did criticize pluralism.

(C) is wrong because reformers of the era did criticize nepotism.

(D) is wrong because reformers of the era did criticize indulgences.

18. **(C)**

(A) is wrong because, although many products did stream into the English colonies, much of the flow was not "cheap," but merely was done at a lower cost than the English could do it for and almost exclusively carried by the Dutch.

(B) is wrong because the Portuguese were not the intended targets of this legislation and also did not have a monopoly on the Atlantic slave trade at this time.

(C) is CORRECT because, after a failed attempt at an alliance, the British sought to simultaneously exert more financial control over their North American colonies as well as challenge Dutch maritime supremacy.

(D) is wrong because the French did not dominate the cod or whaling industry nor were they the main focus of this legislation.

19. **(C)**

(A) is wrong because Thomas Malthus did not specifically attribute inadequate food and capital to the acts of mercantilism.

(B) is wrong because Josiah Child was a major proponent of mercantilism and a supporter of the Navigation Acts.

(C) is CORRECT because Adam Smith deliberated at length in his works condemning mercantilist practices carried out by many of the world's leading economic superpowers.

(D) is wrong because Jean-Baptiste Colbert was a rigid proponent of mercantilist policies, many of which helped consolidate much wealth for Louis XIV to spend freely.

20. **(A)**

(A) is CORRECT because from the mid-seventeenth century onward the British overseas trade grew significantly, but the Dutch were negatively affected in the years immediately after its passage.

(B) is wrong because the Dutch continued their successful economic success well into the late seventeenth century, but wars and diplomacy led to their economic demise in the beginning of the eighteenth century.

(C) is wrong because the Navigation Acts were not rescinded by the Stuarts, and they in fact fought numerous times in the latter part of the seventeenth century.

(D) is wrong because, although the countries did engage in war several times, they did not continue to war late into the eighteenth century.

21. **(D)**

(A) is wrong because the lands gained were not of strategic importance other than gaining a port.

(B) is wrong because the territories gained had little economic importance.

(C) is wrong because the land was taken from Sweden and Poland.

(D) is CORRECT because the result of the land acquisition was Peter I gaining his "window to the West" in the new capital of St. Petersburg, which had a port in the summer.

22. **(A)**

(A) is CORRECT because the Russians expanded southward and eastward under Catherine the Great, taking the Crimean Peninsula and the surrounding area.

(B) is wrong because, after the Napoleonic Wars, Austria was the strongest empire in Europe, with its foreign minister, Klemens von Metternich, a central figure in the alliances of the time.

(C) is wrong because the Russians did not gain any meaningful territory from the decline of Spain.

(D) is wrong because Russia did not invade the German states, and did not have an alliance with Poland to do so.

23. **(B)**

(A) is wrong because the nobility was subjugated by Peter, and by Ivan IV before him, leaving them docile and never a real threat to Catherine II.

(B) is CORRECT because both Peter and Catherine were known for attempting to westernize Russia without really finding much success with the lower classes.

(C) is wrong because Catherine did not pursue Peter's obsession with creating a Russian navy and did not show the zest he had for it.

(D) is wrong because Alexander II emancipated the serfs, and Peter I never had any intention of doing so.

24. **(D)**

(A) is wrong because the *philosophes*, and Voltaire in particular, believed in religious toleration, not imposing any religion on anyone.

(B) is wrong because Voltaire was a proponent of religious toleration.

(C) is wrong because they did support skepticism and believed it was a good way to analyze data.

(D) is CORRECT because this passage clearly supports religious toleration.

25. **(B)**

(A) is wrong because, although those concepts did influence this era, they are not referenced in that sentence.

(B) is CORRECT because the concept that the Church should stop its discrimination against and conversion of peoples of different faiths around the world came from seeing the virtues of other cultures and methods of living and interpreting the world.

(C) is wrong because, although those concepts did influence this era, they are not referenced in that sentence.

(D) is wrong because, although those concepts did influence this era, they are not directly referenced in that sentence.

26. **(A)**

(A) is CORRECT because Rousseau did start the Romantic movement by questioning pure Reason.

(B) is wrong because Montesquieu wrote about the separation of powers in government.

(C) is wrong because Wollstonecraft was an early feminist who defended the French Revolution.

(D) is wrong because Adam Smith wrote about economics, not religion.

27. **(D)**

(A) is wrong because, while many were accomplished scientists, that idea is not being expressed here.

(B) is wrong because, while they did have new ways of communicating, that is not the thrust of this document.

(C) is wrong because only a very few thinkers of this era were atheists; most were deists.

(D) is CORRECT because, just as they were discovering the relative nature of the universe, they thought that humanity should also be viewed with a new sense of cultural relativism.

28. **(A)**

(A) is CORRECT because the passage makes clear that he believes his conquests keep him in power.

(B) is wrong because Napoleon does not need to conquer the Continent to destroy the press.

(C) is wrong because his diary shows more doubt than confidence.

(D) is wrong because Napoleon credits commanders rather than soldiers with success in this passage.

29. **(D)**

(A) is wrong because placing relatives on foreign thrones is foreign, not domestic, policy.

(B) is wrong because he was praised for his Napoleonic Code, which was both a criminal and civil code.

(C) is wrong because the finances of the empire were well managed.

(D) is CORRECT because Napoleon was criticized for his secret police and censorship of the press at home.

30. **(C)**

(A) is wrong because the Continental System was a form of economic warfare that banned British ships from continental trade and had nothing to do with Italian unification.

(B) is wrong because the Continental System was a form of economic warfare that banned British ships from continental trade and was implemented *before* Napoleon invaded Russia.

(C) is CORRECT because the Continental System was a form of economic warfare that banned British ships from continental trade.

(D) is wrong because the Continental System was a form of economic warfare that banned British ships from continental trade and had nothing to do with a unified Europe.

31. **(B)**

(A) is wrong because while they were concerned about liberal young men, the decrees control the press.

(B) is CORRECT because the decree is clearly concerned with the press and information disseminated.

(C) is wrong because the union of Germanic states was not strong, and Metternich wanted them weak so as to not threaten Austria.

(D) is wrong because Napoleon was already on St. Helena when this was written.

32. **(C)**

(A) is wrong because Metternich opposed the ideas of nationalism, democracy, and self-determination that came from the Enlightenment.

(B) is wrong because, while Metternich was oppressive, he did not have the tools to control his people as much as this answer would require.

(C) is CORRECT because Metternich, as Austria's foreign minister, was more concerned with nationalist revolts in his multi-ethnic empire than with any other threat to Austria.

(D) is wrong because he knew that such suppression would stagnate his society.

33. **(C)**

(A) is wrong because Pope Pius IX was very conservative and supported a Metternichian view.

(B) is wrong because Metternich helped to create the decrees.

(C) is CORRECT because Mazzini was a radical Italian nationalist republican.

(D) is wrong because the "Soldier King," as he was called, was very conservative and would support no changes.

34. **(A)**

(A) is CORRECT because the Chartists were the most radical of the reformers who called for universal male suffrage.

(B) is wrong because if he were more radical, he would support the Chartist movement.

(C) is wrong because the author makes it clear that he thinks some are not qualified to vote.

(D) is wrong because the author is criticizing the Chartists.

35. **(B)**

(A) is wrong because the Chartists did not fight for women's right to vote.

(B) is CORRECT as the Chartists fought for universal male suffrage among other reforms, such as the end to the Corn Laws.

(C) is wrong because the Chartists just wanted the vote; government-supported health care was not even thought of as yet.

(D) is wrong because they were focused on getting the right to vote first; the other reforms came much later in England.

36. **(D)**

(A) is wrong because liberalism was the movement that led to the Chartists.

(B) is wrong because radicalism was extreme liberalism, and that was the opposite of what Metternich wanted.

(C) is wrong because nationalism was a powerful force in the nineteenth century, but it was a part of liberalism and not supported by Metternich.

(D) is CORRECT because Metternich created conservatism in Europe.

37. **(C)**

(A) is wrong because the revolutions in Prague and Vienna were actually multi-ethnic, while France's was much more homogenous.

(B) is wrong, as a small number of fatalities occurred in the February revolution, but there were thousands in the June revolution.

(C) is CORRECT because General Cavaignac was forced to storm the barricades in the narrow Paris streets, and heavy casualties were the result.

(D) is wrong because the answer refers to events at the end of the Franco-Prussian War in 1871.

38. **(B)**

(A) is wrong because the Polish people were not successful in their revolt.

(B) is CORRECT because the Polish revolt began in Prussia and was ended by Prussia, resulting in animosity between the nations.

(C) is wrong because the coalition did not go into Poland.

(D) is wrong because the Polish citizens did not join up in higher numbers or die in higher numbers, as most of the Polish revolutionary force was made of released Polish prisoners from Prussian jails.

39. **(A)**

(A) is CORRECT because, although thousands died, an election for president immediately took place, and domestic reforms improved civilian life immensely.

(B) is wrong because, although Cavaignac crushed the June uprising, the elections held thereafter included universal male suffrage and brought about at least a temporary republic.

(C) is wrong because the violence and desperate economic situation and absence of overwhelming conservatism allowed the movement to succeed.

(D) is wrong because Austria and Hungary, not France, felt the pressure of foreign troops to thwart the gains of the revolutionaries.

40. **(A)**

(A) is CORRECT because women in Western Europe, prior to the Agricultural Revolution, practiced gleaning exclusively when the open-field system was popular.

(B) is wrong because France was utilizing crop rotation by the end of the eighteenth century, and rotation and the famine had little to do with one another.

(C) is wrong because serfdom was outlawed by 1807, during the wars of coalition against Napoleon, who enforced the emancipation of serfs.

(D) is wrong because the Hanoverian period in Britain did not begin until 1714, which was after crop rotation had been introduced and the open-field system had ended.

41. **(B)**

(A) is wrong because the answer here refers to the Russian Mir or, later, forced agriculture, which was compulsory in the Stalinist USSR.

(B) is CORRECT because many farmers became landless cottagers who made their living in the "putting out system," producing textiles for entrepreneurial businessmen.

(C) is wrong because the corvée had been around since antiquity and certainly did not arise due to the downfall of the open-field system.

(D) is wrong because the Encomienda was a system of agriculture in the New World specific to the Spanish Empire, using labor of indigenous people, at least a century before the end of the open-field system.

42. **(B)**

(A) is wrong because, although Ricardo did address food and labor with supply and demand, his studies did not focus specifically on population demographics and famine.

(B) is CORRECT because the Malthusian Dilemma addresses the likelihood that the world's food supply is not sufficient to keep up with population growth.

(C) is wrong because Marx's writings delve into feudalism and the rise of capitalism but he does not theorize specifically about population and food supply.

(D) is wrong because Cornelius Vermuyden was responsible for the reclamation of land from swamps and bogs, not for writing about population theories.

43. **(A)**

(A) is CORRECT because Lenin's New Economic Policy allowed the peasants to own their property, sell produce, and make profits, which led to the creation of the kulaks, or better-off peasant class.

(B) is wrong because Lenin did not share power with the Provisional Government.

(C) is wrong because the passage is not about that trade-off.

(D) is wrong because the passage is not about that trade-off.

44. **(C)**

(A) is wrong because collectivization was used by Stalin to end the kulak class, create huge farms, and increase agricultural production.

(B) is wrong because persecution of the better-off peasants, or kulaks, was a policy used to get the peasants to collectivize their farms and work together to feed the Soviet Union.

(C) is CORRECT because the Berlin blockade was after the Second World War, and was a part of the Cold War tensions in Germany, which have nothing to do with this passage.

(D) is wrong because the five-year plans included Stalin's plans to collectivize farms and have the government run them.

45. **(B)**

(A) is wrong because, while industrial production rose incredibly as a result of the five-year plans, collective agriculture was a failure that resulted in the starving of millions of Soviet citizens.

(B) is CORRECT because, while industrial production rose incredibly as a result of the five-year plans, collective agriculture was a failure that resulted in the starving of millions of Soviet citizens.

(C) is wrong because agriculture was destroyed as a result of collectivization, resulting in the starving of millions.

(D) is wrong because simony is paying someone else to perform one's church duties.

46. **(D)**

(A) is wrong because, while he was in Switzerland and did see technology there, Russia's experience of losing two wars within 12 years—the 1905 Russo-Japanese War and the First World War—was ever present in his mind.

(B) is wrong because there was a relatively small percentage of Russians working in factories before the Revolution.

(C) is wrong because while Trotsky did facilitate the Revolution through those means, Russia's experience with losing two wars within 12 years was ever present in his mind.

(D) is CORRECT because Russia's experience with losing two wars within 12 years was ever present in his mind.

47. **(C)**

(A) is wrong because there is nothing about women's suffrage in the passage.

(B) is wrong because the democratization of society is considered a good thing by the above author.

(C) is CORRECT because the passage indicates that the government is cynical about the creation of new housing and is disillusioned with the welfare system.

(D) is wrong because communism's rise is not the main thrust of this reading.

48. **(A)**

(A) is CORRECT because the public housing program, a form of welfare, is being questioned.

(B) is wrong because the British budget is not examined in this piece.

(C) is wrong because, although the threat of a revolution is mentioned, it is not the workers who are driving it.

(D) is wrong because the Housing Board wanted to cut down on building houses.

49. **(C)**

(A) is wrong because the data do not indicate what was done with reserves, and the fact that both sides took huge losses is more evident.

(B) is wrong because the data do not indicate what was happening on the Western Front, and the fact that both sides took huge losses is more evident.

(C) is CORRECT because such huge losses in one battle alone indicate much larger losses.

(D) is wrong because the data do not indicate that the Germans or Russians won, and the Russians in fact eventually won the battle.

50. **(C)**

(A) is wrong because there is no evidence of the hunger there causing the problems, and the pattern is that there were huge losses of civilian life in Eastern European countries conquered by the Nazis.

(B) is wrong because the better training does not explain lower Belgian and British casualties.

(C) is CORRECT because the pattern is that there were huge losses of civilian life in Eastern European countries conquered by the Nazis, where the death camps were, and the Jewish people and other minorities were exterminated to make room for more Germans.

(D) is wrong because the lack of preparation does not explain lower Belgian and British casualties.

51. **(B)**

(A) is wrong because fighting for your country, and perhaps killing or dying for it, are the ultimate signs of loyalty and respect for a government.

(B) is CORRECT because the Nazis had convinced their citizens to undertake a "holocaust" that included slavery, degradation of large populations, and genocide, which the German people enthusiastically carried out because of their loyalty to the state and respect for it.

(C) is wrong because fighting for your country and perhaps killing or dying for it are the ultimate signs of loyalty and respect for a government.

(D) is wrong because most veterans, meaning most men at the time, respected their nation and felt loyal to it.

52. **(D)**

(A) is wrong because the welfare state has not been deemed a failure or a success, and that point is a matter of political debate in England and in other countries, but the Green Party seems to support the welfare state.

(B) is wrong because the Green Party supports women's rights, which had ceased to become a major plank in their platform.

(C) is wrong because the Green Party does not generally oppose economic integration and, in fact, wants to use it as a tool of foreign policy to encourage more environmental responsibility internationally.

(D) is CORRECT because Green parties were created in many nations as a reaction to growing consumerism and its effects on the environment.

53. **(B)**

(A) is wrong because, although the Cold War ended with the collapse of the communist regimes, the platform does not reflect that.

(B) is CORRECT because many of the workers who came to Europe as invited guests in the 1950s and 1960s settled permanently but have been denied full citizenship rights, which the Green Party wants for them.

(C) is wrong because the Greens would react negatively to the consumerism of American pop culture.

(D) is wrong because the baby boom is no longer having a significant impact, and the European population is not growing rapidly, or may even be shrinking.

54. **(D)**

(A) is wrong because there is no evidence of nationalism in this platform nor in the Greens philosophy.

(B) is wrong because the EU does not make such requirements, and the Greens want to expand their movement internationally to include more services to increase equality.

(C) is wrong because the Greens are very secular and do not ally with any religion.

(D) is CORRECT because Greens support the welfare state that has come under increasing scrutiny as conservatives and liberals argue over its efficacy and function.

55. **(B)**

(A) is wrong because the Greens support immigrants.

(B) is CORRECT because the Greens support equal rights for all.

(C) is wrong because the Greens think that fair trade is not fair to workers and has led to globalization and thus the eradication of culture and the promotion of consumerism.

(D) is wrong because most Greens condemn the idea of nations trying to expand their reach as being an increase in consumerism and conquest.

Multiple-Choice Quick Scoring Guide

For your convenience, this chart was created to allow you to quickly score the multiple-choice section. Please read the explanations on the previous pages for any and all questions that confused you.

1.	**C**	21.	**D**	41.	**B**
2.	**A**	22.	**A**	42.	**B**
3.	**D**	23.	**B**	43.	**A**
4.	**A**	24.	**D**	44.	**C**
5.	**C**	25.	**B**	45.	**B**
6.	**D**	26.	**A**	46.	**D**
7.	**C**	27.	**D**	47.	**C**
8.	**B**	28.	**A**	48.	**A**
9.	**B**	29.	**D**	49.	**C**
10.	**C**	30.	**C**	50.	**C**
11.	**A**	31.	**B**	51.	**B**
12.	**B**	32.	**C**	52.	**D**
13.	**D**	33.	**C**	53.	**B**
14.	**A**	34.	**A**	54.	**D**
15.	**B**	35.	**B**	55.	**B**
16.	**D**	36.	**D**		
17.	**A**	37.	**C**		
18.	**C**	38.	**B**		
19.	**C**	39.	**A**		
20.	**A**	40.	**A**		

Scoring Guide for the Short-Answer Section

Short Answers are very straightforward. Either you did or did not get one point for each of the points available. Each question is worth up to 3 points for a total of 0–12 points available in this section, worth 20% of the exam score.

1. **0–3 points (2 points for A and 1 point for B)**

(A) ONE point will be given for EACH of TWO explanations of HOW pieces of evidence support the argument that the Italian Renaissance marked the start of modern history, such as: Italian Intellectual hallmarks (individualism, humanism, and secularism), new methods of gathering information, increased interaction with the rest of the world, artistic achievement, reorganization of society and governments such as oligarchies and republics, the rise of the merchant elite, the rising importance of wealth, increased emphasis on perfection, and a revival of Greco–Roman political ideas.

(B) ONE point will be given for an explanation of HOW one piece of evidence undermines the argument that the Italian Renaissance marked the start of the modern world, such as: Europe was already increasing trade during the Crusades, these were not new ideas but a revival of old ideas from Greece and Rome; the Renaissance was primarily an artistic movement; the Renaissance affected only the upper classes; the Renaissance was still a mostly Medieval time; religion was able to stop the advance of knowledge in Italy, such as with Galileo; and Italy became the center of the Counter-Reformation.

2. **0–3 points (1 point for A and 2 points for B)**

(A) ONE point will be given for an analysis of how Salvador Dali's image is typical of the trends of the early twentieth century such as, but not limited to: it questions perceptions of reality, it is typical of surrealism (with explanation of surrealism), it places traditional objects into nontraditional formats or representations, it is dark in mood, it pokes fun at established rules and perceptions, and it displays a certain anxiety, all of which are characteristics of the interwar period in which it was created.

(B) TWO points will be awarded, ONE EACH for analysis of change that affected European thought during the period between the world wars. A change must be more than mentioned, but explored for causes and effects to be awarded a point for this question. Some changes to analyze include, but are not limited to, loss of faith in reason and science or religion to solve problems, increasing scientific knowledge without increasing moral knowledge, economic problems (the great depression or German hyperinflation), the rise of dictators in most of Europe, the rise of relative morality and existentialism, pacifism increases, governments and people become increasingly radical on both conservative and liberal sides.

3. **0–3 points (1 point for each letter, A, B, and C)**

(A) ONE point will be given for pointing out a significant difference between the historians' interpretations of the Cold War. Some examples of evidence include: Sharon argues more about economics while van der Straaten argues more about ethics. Van der Straaten seems biased against communists—he and they have different causes for the start of the Cold War, have different causes for the end of the Cold War, and they were written almost a generation apart, and so forth.

(B) ONE point will be given for a good answer that explains HOW one piece of evidence to support Sharon's argument that the Cold War was a wasteful, unnecessary struggle caused by personalities, or his argument that the Cold War was an economic struggle of production won by the NATO nations because they could produce more and have a higher standard of living. Evidence to support the first claim includes Churchill's Iron Curtain speech, the Truman Doctrine, the Cuban Missile Crisis, the Korean War, missile tests, or peace dividend statistics. Evidence to support the second claim could include: the use of economic statistics, the Marshall Plan, the COMINTERN, the Common Market, the fall of the Soviet Union and the Berlin Wall, the rise of capitalism in Eastern Europe after 1990, the creation of the European Union, and the Americanization of Europe after 1990.

(C) ONE point will be given for an explanation of HOW one piece of evidence supports van der Straaten's argument that the Cold War was an ideological battle of freedom versus tyranny, or his second argument that the Cold War was ended by its own leaders. Evidence to support the first argument that it was an ideological battle can include: propaganda, the Red Scare, the Cuban Missile Crisis, the Prague Spring, the Afghan invasion of 1979, Soviet support of terrorism against NATO nations, the legacy of Cold War battles in Africa, Latin America, and the Middle East, or the brutal suppression of Soviet-style governments in all of Eastern Europe. Evidence to support the second claim—that communism was brought down by its own leaders—can include: Mikhail Gorbachev's *perestroika* and *glasnost*, the failed coup when Yeltsin was elected, Gorbachev's peaceful dissolution of the Soviet Union, the quick fall of the Berlin Wall, and communism all over Eastern Europe ended mostly bloodlessly.

4. **0–3 points (1 point for each letter, A, B, and C)**

(A) ONE point will be given for explaining the positive aspects of the rule of Louis XIV. The answer should explain how France rose to international esteem under the rule of Louis XIV. It should be pointed out that other rulers, such as Peter I of Russia and the Habsburgs, copied his model of how to run a royal court. Additionally, the response should point out Louis's military victories and how he used his military to increase the power of his nation. It should also explain how his reign unified the French people under his rule because they were proud to be led by him.

(B) ONE point will be given for a good answer that explains the negative aspects of Louis XIV and his rule of France. It should indicate that his nation was at war for more than half of his reign. It should explain how his overuse of the military and the opulence of Versailles were responsible for eventually bankrupting the nation, leaving it open to revolution. Additionally, the essay should point out how the nobility detested Louis XIV. His use of clothes and wigs and ceremonies without any substance but meant to enhance his image should be noted. His opulent lifestyle while his people suffered through war, enforced labor obligations, and turmoil should also be noted.

(C) ONE point will be given for an explanation of HOW war affected the legacy of Louis XIV, who said on his death bed that he had "gone to war too often and pursued it for vanity's sake." The resulting debts from those wars should be mentioned and placed into context. The might and reputation of the French military as a deterrent to any power attacking France should also be mentioned. The winning of the Thirty Years' War should also be mentioned as leaving Europe divided religiously, which allowed France to dominate the region for another century. The French role in the War of the Spanish Succession and how the rest of Europe mostly teamed up against Louis XIV to prevent his armies from leaving France in control of the entire Iberian Peninsula should also be mentioned.

Scoring Guide for the Essay Section

The Document-Based Question (DBQ)

The DBQ emphasizes your ability to analyze and synthesize historical evidence, including textual, quantitative, or visual materials. The question also requires you to formulate a thesis and support it with relevant evidence. The seven documents accompanying each DBQ may vary in length, type, and content, but they will allow you to illustrate complexities and interactions within the material and to utilize a broad spectrum of historical skills.

The document-based question will typically require you to relate the documents to a historical period or theme and, thus, to focus on major periods and issues, in this way assessing your ability to incorporate outside knowledge related to the question but beyond the specifics of the documents. This ability to place the documents in the historical context in which they were produced is essential for your success.

Scoring Your DBQ

Maximum Possible Points: 7

A. THESIS AND ARGUMENT DEVELOPMENT (0–1 total points)
Targeted Skill—Argumentation

1 point: Presents a thesis that makes a historically defensible claim and responds to all parts of the question. The thesis must consist of one or more sentences located in one place, either in the introduction or the conclusion.

You must present a thesis that directly addresses all parts of the question and makes a historically defensible claim. The thesis must do more than restate the question.

> **Superb Thesis:** "Socialism, which emerged as a response to the cruelties of pure capitalism, was at first an idea that was accepted only by radicals, but as the workers gained economic and political power, the ideas became mainstream and were even utilized by conservatives, but they then became an issue of debate between conservatives and liberals after World War II." This thesis is strong because it makes a historically defensible claim, responds to all parts of the question, and develops a cohesive argument that clearly recognizes historical complexity by explicitly illustrating relationships among historical evidence and includes qualification. Some evidence of this is that the thesis is specific in its assessment of both political viewpoints, (liberals, conservatives, and radicals), and political, social, or economic changes (workers gaining economic power, World War II, conservatives gaining power).

Acceptable Thesis: "From 1800 to 1949 views on socialism changed as the world changed and opinions became more enlightened and focused on the plight of the common man." (This gets one point for directly addressing the question but does not account for historical complexity by illustrating any relationships.)

Unacceptable Theses:

- "Those who were more radical or more liberal were always more in favor of socialism than those who were less radical as can be seen through changes over time." (This is unacceptable because even though it states views, it does not state specific social, political, or economic changes.)
- "From the emergence of capitalism through the Industrial Revolution and the rise of nation states, to the Great Depression, and through World War II, views on socialism have changed." (This is unacceptable because, although it mentions specific social, economic, and political events, it mentions no specific views on socialism.)

B. CONTEXTUALIZATION (0–1 total points)

1 point: The essay must describe a broader historical context immediately relevant to the question.

Acceptable Contextualization:

- "After distrust as partners during World War II, Churchill came out publicly against Stalin in his speech in America in order to try to get the United States to be more active in challenging the growing power of the Soviet Union."
- "As the Cold War began, the opinions on socialism changed to a harder line from conservatives and were looked at more critically for flaws by intellectuals like Albert Einstein."

Unacceptable Contextualization:

- "As the general who planned the Allied victory, Churchill was dedicated to keeping Europe free." (Churchill was not a general in World War II; he was the British political leader.)
- "As the inventor of the atomic bomb, Einstein was worried about a nuclear war." (There is no evidence to support that Einstein was worried in this document, and Einstein did not invent nuclear weapons.)

C. EVIDENCE (3 total points)

1 point: The essay must utilize the content of at least **THREE** documents to address the topic of the question. **Note** that this analysis may be in the topic sentence; the analysis must be connected to the argument.

OR

2 points: The essay must utilize the content of at least SIX documents to support an argument about the question. **Note** that this analysis may be in the topic sentence; the analysis must be connected to the argument.

AND

EVIDENCE BEYOND THE DOCUMENTS (0–1 total points)

1 point: The essay explains how at least one additional piece of specific evidence beyond those found in the documents relates to an argument about the question.

Note: This evidence must be DIFFERENT from the evidence used to earn the point for contextualization. This point is NOT awarded for a phrase or reference.

Acceptable Outside Historical Evidence:

- "Bismarck's welfare reforms in Germany created the first modern welfare state there as a way to undermine the liberals and co-opt socialism into the conservative platform and thus convince voters to choose conservative leaders."
- "As the Fascists had come to power spreading hatred of Communism across Europe, it made sense that one of the late propaganda posters in Germany would try to reignite that sentiment."

Unacceptable Outside Historical Evidence:

- "The Nazis didn't like communists so it makes sense that their poster was against the Bolsheviks." (Unacceptable because the evidence is pretty clear from the document and no true outside evidence was presented.)

D. ANALYSIS & REASONING (0–2 total points)

1 point: For at least THREE documents, the essay explains how each document's point of view, purpose, historical situation, and/or audience are relevant to the argument.

2 points: Demonstrates a complex understanding of the historical development that is the focus of the prompt, using evidence to corroborate, qualify, or modify an argument that addresses the question.

Guidance on awarding this point is below:

Example of acceptable analysis: "Winston Churchill, after having been voted out of office as prime minister of England after winning World War II with the Allies, was mistrustful of socialism in general and of Stalin and his expansionary plans in particular, which is why he is asking the Conservative party to condemn socialism." (This correctly places Churchill in place, time, and importance, and specifically explains point of view and purpose as well as giving some context.)

Example of unacceptable analysis: "The Nazi propaganda poster seems to be supporting socialism instead of Bolshevism." (This is incorrect because this poster condemns Bolshevism, which was a specific type of socialism.)

Intended Audience

Acceptable: "The People's Petition was written to present to members of Parliament, but also to convince workers and others to join the Chartist Movement."

Unacceptable: "The People's Charter was written for the people." (This is far too vague; specify which people in which place at which time.)

Purpose

Acceptable: "The Nazi propaganda poster was created and posted to encourage the German soldiers and citizens to continue to fight the advancing Soviet army."

Unacceptable: "Winston Churchill is writing to show how he supported socialism so everyone should." (This is a misinterpretation as Churchill is mostly writing against socialism.)

Historical Context

Acceptable: "As the recently dismissed prime minister, Winston Churchill may be attempting to help his party get reorganized."

Unacceptable: "Because the Cold War was over, Einstein was writing that socialism was better than capitalism." (This is wrong because the Cold War was just getting going when Einstein wrote this.)

Author's Point of View

Acceptable: "As an ardent communist, Rosa Luxemburg would of course be disappointed that socialism was losing power in Germany during the First World War."

Unacceptable: Because he was the king of England, Winston Churchill's statements should be considered as coming from the upper classes." (This is wrong because Churchill was prime minister rather than king, although he certainly was upper class as the Duke of Marlborough.)

Document 1

Key Points

- Pro-socialist.
- Calls for those without property to share in profits.
- Warns of revolution if things do not change.
- Believes scientists and artists are leaders of change.
- States proletariat won in France and the bourgeoisie lost.
- Asks scientists and artists.

Contextualization

- Napoleon ruling France in Empire period.
- Industrial Revolution in England only.
- French Revolution just ended.
- Concert of Europe and Metternich alliance system in place against radical change.

Document 2

Key Points

- Pro-socialist.
- Calls for universal male suffrage, property tax, and more equality.
- Part of political movement for suffrage and to repeal Corn Laws.
- Believes equality is coming.
- Pre-communist ideas.
- Asks scientists and artists.

Contextualization

- Part of political movement for suffrage and to repeal Corn Laws.
- Industrial Revolution in England has spread to the Continent.
- New class consciousness developing.
- Huge gaps in wealth.
- Urbanization.
- Just after failed revolutions of 1830, but before 1848.

Document 3

Key Points

- Pro-socialist.
- Indicates international community of workers.
- Appears peaceful and not radical through brotherhood.
- Romantic era artistic themes and techniques.
- Pre-communist ideas.
- Common man depicted.
- Trade unions legal and powerful across Europe in 1896.

Contextualization

- Part of political movement for suffrage and to repeal Corn Laws.
- Industrial Revolution in England has spread to the European Continent.
- New class consciousness developing.
- Huge gaps in wealth.
- Urbanization.
- Just after failed revolutions of 1830, but before 1848.

Document 4

Key Points

- Pro-socialist and written by a Jewish woman who was an immigrant and a communist.
- Indicates frustration at the setbacks socialism faced during the First World War.
- Wanted to find problems in Socialist Party and fix them and has a lamenting but angry and undeterred tone.
- Examines Germany's history as a strong socialist economy.

- Communist ideas and revolutionary outlook shared by communists at the time.
- Common man depicted.
- Trade unions legal and powerful across Europe in 1896.

Contextualization

- Rosa Luxemburg was murdered by the Freicorps in 1919.
- An ardent communist, Luxemburg was a Polish Jew who grew up in Germany.
- Era of self-criticism and of criticism of others, too, was to begin shortly.
- The First World War was going on with a "Total War" effort in all countries requiring rationing, price controls, and government institutions such as the German War Raw Materials Board and the British Ministry of Munitions.
- The war lasted much longer than anyone believed it would before it started.
- The First World War ended in 1918, and the "Age of Anxiety" began to question the belief that science and reason could create a better world.

Document 5

Key Points

- Anti-communist.
- Nazi propaganda poster indicating that Bolsheviks create pain and suffering.
- Meant to scare Polish citizens about what would happen if the Bolsheviks (Soviets) took over their region.
- Bolshevism is a specific type of socialism, and the Nazi Party had socialist in its name, but the Nazis hated communists and claimed the Fascist mantle.
- Shows German racial prejudices at the time.
- Just one of tens of thousands of pieces of German propaganda used on its people.

Contextualization

- Stalin and Hitler had created a "nonaggression pact" at the start of the Second World War in Europe in 1939, despite each hating the other's ideas and personality, but Germany invaded the USSR in 1941 and was not driven out until the end of 1944.
- The Soviets were very harsh on the people in the Polish and German areas they conquered at the end of the Second World War.
- Communism and Fascism were diametrically opposed ideas, but both systems ended up creating similar totalitarian dictatorships.
- The Second World War was going on with a "Total War" effort in all countries, requiring rationing, price controls, and government institutions comparable to the German War Raw Materials Board and the British Ministry of Munitions during the First World War.
- The Second World War ended leaving the Cold War in its wake.

Key Points

- Anti-socialist.
- Winston Churchill was a conservative leader of the United Kingdom during the Second World War, but was ejected from power and is explaining what his party must do to regain power and send his country in the right direction.
- He is known for distrusting Stalin, communism, children, and pets as well as for being pompous, egotistical and very conservative.
- He gave the speech that defined the Iron Curtain and helped get America more involved in the Cold War.
- Shows his frustration at losing power, his plan for his party to regain it, and that he thinks socialism has gone too far.
- He did support welfare and unemployment, just not the modern welfare state.
- Shows concern for a state that has grown too powerful and is too involved with the economic lives of its citizens.

Contextualization

- The Second World War has just ended, and the Cold War has not yet begun.
- The Soviets were taking over Eastern Europe and spreading their brand of communism.
- The United States was supporting much of the world through the Marshall Plan and the beauty of the plan was that it spread capitalism, reliance on American goods, and goodwill toward America all over the world.
- The Second World War had been a "Total War" effort for all countries, requiring rationing, price controls, and government institutions to run the economy, and the world was transitioning back to a peacetime consumer economy.

Document 7

Key Points

- Pro-socialist.
- Albert Einstein, one of the most brilliant theoretical physicists ever and of Jewish heritage, emigrated from Germany to the United States before the Second World War.
- Known for the theory of relativity and for urging Roosevelt to create an atom bomb before Hitler would do it.
- Explains why raw capitalism is not a fair system and why society would be better served through a socialist system.
- Shows his frustration at losing power, his plan for his party to regain it, and that he thinks socialism has gone too far.
- Calls capitalism evil and blames it for economic depressions, stating it must be fixed or replaced.
- Written to show Americans and others that although there was a lot of propaganda starting up against socialism, it was a really good system if done right.
- Shows concern for a state that has grown too powerful and is too involved with the lives of its citizens.

Contextualization

- With the Cold War starting, as was the development of atomic weapons, he felt guilty for suggesting the Allies build the bomb.
- The Soviets were taking over Eastern Europe and spreading their brand of communism.
- The United States was supporting much of the world through the Marshall Plan and the beauty of the plan was that it spread capitalism, reliance on American goods, and goodwill toward America all over the world.
- The Second World War had devastated the world, and he did not want another war over idealism.

Scoring Guidelines for Long-Essay Question 2

Compare the impact of the printing press on the daily life and culture of the European people with that of the Columbian Exchange on the daily lives and culture of the European people.

Maximum possible points: 6

COMMENTS ON QUESTION 2

This is clearly a COMPARE skill question, so be sure to describe similarities and differences between the ways that the daily lives and culture of people of all classes were affected by the advent of the printing press and the Columbian Exchange, as well as account for or explain why they were so different by providing specific examples of how the two changes differed in human experiences, duration, impact on learning and knowledge, and societal changes. It is also important to tie the events that resulted from both the spread of the printing press and the Columbian Exchange to other historical trends politically, militarily, socially, economically, or scientifically.

The contrast is glaring: The printing press spread knowledge that people of Europe had been compartmentalizing for centuries and increased literacy as well as access to knowledge, while the Columbian Exchange brought with it changes in the European balance of power, the foods people ate, the opportunities available to Europeans, and many other commodities and agricultural products.

A detailed rubric for this specific question follows to help you score your long-essay response.

A. THESIS (0–1 total points)

1 point: The essay presents a thesis that makes a historically defensible claim and responds to all parts of the question. The thesis must consist of one or more sentences located in one place, either in the introduction or the conclusion.

Special Note: The thesis MUST consist of one or more sentences located in the introduction or the conclusion of the essay. However, neither the introduction nor the conclusion is strictly limited to one paragraph.

Acceptable thesis statements create an argument that responds to the task: identifying relevant impacts upon the social life and culture of the citizens of each nation caused by each revolution AND explaining the similarities and differences between the ways each innovation changed the culture and lives of the people. For example, the printing press meant that killing a person with new ideas that challenged the status quo would no longer end those ideas and better spread knowledge to the lower classes as books became less expensive, while the Columbian Exchange opened new lands for Europeans to own and new people for them to exploit as well as much new wealth and many new products such as chocolate and vanilla.

You must present a thesis that directly addresses all parts of the question. Your thesis must do more than restate the question.

Acceptable Thesis: "While both the spread of the printing press from Asia to Europe and the Columbian Exchange affected the knowledge and lives of Europeans, they did so in different ways with the printing press making all information more accessible, easier to record and share, and spurring a reading revolution, while the Columbian Exchange brought in knowledge from previously unknown parts of the world, opened up economic opportunities to colonize, and opened up entire new fields of knowledge because it involved another continent." (This thesis is acceptable because it is specific in its assessment of both innovations, and it gives specific comparisons and accounts for the similarities and differences between them.)

Unacceptable Theses:

- "The printing press and Columbian Exchange had many effects on their peoples that were different and similar in a lot of ways." (This is unacceptable because it does not state any specific similarities or differences, much less account for them.)
- "Both the printing press and the Columbian exchange changed the lives and culture of European with the printing press allowing Europeans better access to information they already had, and the Columbian Exchange giving them access to new knowledge, organisms, and economic opportunities." (This is unacceptable because even though it compares and contrasts the Columbian Exchange with the printing press, there is nothing in the thesis about the daily lives of their citizens or their culture.)

B. CONTEXTUALIZATION (0–1 total points)

1 point: The essay describes a broader historical context immediately relevant to the question.

C. EVIDENCE (0–2 total points)

1 point: Develops and supports an argument that: Provides specific examples of evidence related to comparing the impact of the Columbian Exchange and the spread of the printing press.

OR

2 points: Adequately supports an argument about the comparison of the impact of the Columbian Exchange and the spread of the printing press.

D. ANALYSIS & REASONING (0–3 total points)

1 point: Uses historical reasoning (e.g., comparison, causation, CCOT) to frame or structure an argument that addresses the prompt.

OR

2 points: Demonstrates a complex understanding of the historical development that is the focus of the prompt, using evidence to corroborate, qualify, or modify an argument that addresses the question.

Acceptable Comparison: The essay compares and contrasts the social, economic, and political impacts of the Columbian Exchange with that of the spread of the printing press throughout Europe and accounts for the different impacts of the two innovations through historical reasoning and presentation of evidence of how each changed culture and daily life in different European nations.

Unacceptable Comparison:

- The essay is focused either solely on the printing press or the Columbian Exchange, but not both.
- The essay examines the events caused by each innovation, but not the effects on the culture and daily lives of the citizens.
- The essay looks at similarities and differences in the culture and daily lives of the citizens but fails to account for them and/or provide detailed evidence for support.

Scoring Guidelines for Long-Essay Question 3

Compare the impact of the French Revolution of 1789 on the daily lives and culture of the French people with the impact of the Russian Revolution of 1917 on the daily lives and culture of the Russian people.

Maximum possible points: 6

COMMENTS ON QUESTION 3

This is clearly a COMPARE skill question, so be sure to describe similarities and differences between the ways that the French and Russian people were affected by their respective revolutions through their daily lives and cultural changes, as well as account for or explain why they were so different by providing specific examples of how the two revolutions differed in human experiences, duration, control of the people, societal changes. It is also important to tie the events of the revolutions to other historical trends politically, militarily, socially, economically, or scientifically.

The contrast is glaring: While the French went through a relatively short period of terror and chaos, they ended up with a written constitution and a set of laws that created some degree of personal liberty while the Soviets traded all freedom for the illusion of equality and lived under totalitarian dictatorship for over 70 years.

A detailed rubric for this specific question follows to help you score your long-essay response.

A. THESIS (0–1 total points)

1 point: The essay presents a thesis that makes a historically defensible claim and responds to all parts of the question. The thesis must consist of one or more sentences located in one place, either in the introduction or the conclusion.

Special Note: The thesis MUST consist of one or more sentences located in the introduction or the conclusion of the essay. However, neither the introduction nor conclusion is strictly limited to one paragraph.

Acceptable thesis statements create an argument that responds to both tasks: identifying relevant impacts upon the social life and culture of Europeans during each era caused by each revolution <u>AND</u> explain the similarities and differences between the ways the people of all classes were affected by each revolution; for example, the Scientific Revolution was short-lived and resulted mostly in upper-class changes and new discoveries that reshaped thinking that would later affect the lives of most people, while the Industrial Revolution is an ongoing process of industrialization that reshaped almost every aspect of life for most people on Earth of all classes in different ways from changing the tempo of their work to their standard of living.

You must present a thesis that directly addresses all parts of the question. Your thesis must do more than restate the question.

Acceptable Thesis: "The French became more egalitarian and gained national pride as a result of their short-lived revolution, gaining many freedoms, while the Russian Revolution of 1917 left the Russian people as Soviet comrades who due to totalitarian rule had little freedom to make any important choices in their lives for over 70 years." (This thesis is acceptable because it is specific in its assessment of both revolutions, and it gives specific comparisons and accounts for the similarities and differences between the revolutions.)

Unacceptable Theses:

- "The French Revolution and Russian Revolution had many effects on their peoples that were different and similar in a lot of ways." (This is unacceptable because it does not state any specific similarities or differences, much less account for them.)
- "While both revolutions changed political beliefs, the French Revolution was much more about individual rights and political unity while the Russian Revolution was much more about economics and power." (This is unacceptable because even though it compares and contrasts the revolutions politically, there is nothing in the thesis about the daily lives of their citizens or their culture.)

B. CONTEXTUALIZATION (0–1 total points)

1 point: The essay describes a broader historical context immediately relevant to the question.

C. EVIDENCE (0–2 total points)

1 point: Provides specific examples of evidence related to comparing the French and Russian Revolutions.

OR

2 points: Adequately supports an argument about the comparison of the French and Russian Revolutions with specific and relevant evidence.

D. ANALYSIS & REASONING (0–3 total points)

1 point: Uses historical reasoning (e.g., comparison, causation, CCOT) to frame or structure an argument that addresses the prompt.

OR

2 points: Demonstrates a complex understanding of the historical development that is the focus of the prompt, using evidence to corroborate, qualify, or modify an argument that addresses the question.

Acceptable Comparison: The essay compares and contrasts the political changes in each country to the changes in daily life and culture in that country and compares and contrasts the similarities and differences between those changes citing specific facts to those arguments. The impact of one party rule in the Soviet Union compared to many changes in French leadership over the same period can also be examined as factors that affected the freedoms and experiences of the citizens of each nation.

Unacceptable Comparison:

- The essay is focused either solely on the French or Russian Revolutions, but not on both.
- The essay examines the events of each revolution, but not the effects on the culture and daily lives of the citizens.
- The essay looks at similarities and differences in the culture and daily lives of the citizens but fails to account for them and/or provide detailed evidence for support: (1 point only).

Scoring Guidelines for Long-Essay Question 4

Compare the impact of the Scientific Revolution (1540–1700), on the daily life and culture of the European people with that of the Industrial Revolution (1780s–1914) on the daily life and culture of the nineteenth-century Europeans.

Maximum possible points: 6

COMMENTS ON QUESTION 4

This is clearly a COMPARE skill question, so be sure to describe similarities and differences between the ways in which the European people were affected by their respective revolutions through their daily lives and cultural changes, as well as account for or explain why they were so different by providing specific examples of how the two revolutions differed in level of impact on the common man, duration, effect on the economy, societal changes, intellectual changes, and artistic changes. It is also important to tie the events of the revolutions to other historical trends politically, militarily, socially, economically, or scientifically.

The contrast is glaring: While the Scientific Revolution changed the upper-class conception of the universe and led to the Enlightenment, there was little effect on the common man, while the Industrial Revolution changed not just the way the universe was conceived, but the way man lived, worked, and learned.

A detailed rubric for this specific question follows to help you score your long-essay response.

A. THESIS (0–1 total points)

1 point: The essay presents a thesis that makes a historically defensible claim and responds to all parts of the question. The thesis must consist of one or more sentences located in one place, either in the introduction or the conclusion.

Special Note: The thesis MUST consist of one or more sentences located in the introduction or the conclusion of the essay. However, neither the introduction nor conclusion is strictly limited to one paragraph.

Acceptable thesis statements create an argument that responds to the task: identifying relevant impacts upon the social life and culture of the citizens of each nation caused by each revolution <u>AND</u> explaining the similarities and differences between the ways that each innovation changed the culture and lives of the people. For example, The printing press meant that killing a person with new ideas that challenged the status quo would no longer end those ideas, and spread knowledge better to the lower classes as books became less expensive, while the Columbian Exchange opened new lands for Europeans to own and new people for them to exploit as well as much new wealth and many new products such as chocolate and vanilla.

You must present a thesis that directly addresses all parts of the question. Your thesis must do more than restate the question.

> **Acceptable Thesis:** "The Scientific Revolution began to move Europeans toward new ways of thinking and investigating the universe by revealing truths about the way it worked that eventually led to the Enlightenment and political and economic freedoms increasing first for the bourgeoisie, then many others, but did not result in large cultural changes in the daily lives of most Europeans, while the Industrial Revolution drastically and rapidly changed the lives of all classes of society as soon as it reached their nation." (This thesis is acceptable because it is specific in its assessment of both revolutions, and it gives specific comparisons and accounts for the similarities and differences between the revolutions and their impacts on the culture and daily lives of those who lived through them.)

> **Unacceptable Theses:**
>
> - "The Scientific Revolution and Industrial Revolution had many effects on their peoples that were different and similar in a lot of ways." (This is unacceptable because it does not state any specific similarities or differences, much less account for them.)
> - "While both revolutions changed knowledge, the Industrial Revolution was much more about technology and profit, while the Scientific Revolution was much more about pure thought and learning." (This is unacceptable because even though it compares and contrasts the revolutions intellectually, there is nothing in the thesis about the daily lives of their people or their culture.)

B. CONTEXTUALIZATION (0–1 total points)

1 point: The essay describes a broader historical context immediately relevant to the question.

C. EVIDENCE (0–2 total points)

Develops and supports an argument that:

1 point: Provides specific examples of evidence related to comparing the Scientific Revolution and the Industrial Revolution.

OR

2 points: Adequately supports an argument about the comparison of the Scientific Revolution and the Industrial Revolution with specific and relevant evidence.

D. ANALYSIS & REASONING (0–3 total points)

1 point: Uses historical reasoning (e.g., comparison, causation, CCOT) to frame or structure an argument that addresses the prompt.

OR

2 points: Demonstrates a complex understanding of the historical development that is the focus of the prompt, using evidence to corroborate, qualify, or modify an argument that addresses the question.

Acceptable Comparison: The essay compares and contrasts how the intellectual and technological changes during each era led to different changes in daily life and culture and compares and contrasts the similarities and differences between those changes citing specific facts to support those arguments. The lesser impact of the Scientific Revolution on the daily lives of most Europeans should be compared to the vast plethora of many changes to every aspect of life such as electricity, running water, urbanization, and increased production brought on by the Industrial Revolution.

Unacceptable Comparison:

- The essay is focused either solely on the Industrial or Scientific Revolutions, but not both.
- The essay examines the events of each revolution, but not the effects on the culture and daily lives of the citizens.
- The essay looks at similarities and differences in the culture and daily lives of the citizens but fails to account for them and/or provide detailed evidence for support (1 point).

This is the end of the scoring section. Once you have scored your answers, go back to the section on scoring the exam and plug your scores into the chart and compute to get your score on your practice exam.

ANSWER SHEET
Model Test 2

SECTION I

1. Ⓐ Ⓑ Ⓒ Ⓓ
2. Ⓐ Ⓑ Ⓒ Ⓓ
3. Ⓐ Ⓑ Ⓒ Ⓓ
4. Ⓐ Ⓑ Ⓒ Ⓓ
5. Ⓐ Ⓑ Ⓒ Ⓓ
6. Ⓐ Ⓑ Ⓒ Ⓓ
7. Ⓐ Ⓑ Ⓒ Ⓓ
8. Ⓐ Ⓑ Ⓒ Ⓓ
9. Ⓐ Ⓑ Ⓒ Ⓓ
10. Ⓐ Ⓑ Ⓒ Ⓓ
11. Ⓐ Ⓑ Ⓒ Ⓓ
12. Ⓐ Ⓑ Ⓒ Ⓓ
13. Ⓐ Ⓑ Ⓒ Ⓓ
14. Ⓐ Ⓑ Ⓒ Ⓓ
15. Ⓐ Ⓑ Ⓒ Ⓓ
16. Ⓐ Ⓑ Ⓒ Ⓓ
17. Ⓐ Ⓑ Ⓒ Ⓓ
18. Ⓐ Ⓑ Ⓒ Ⓓ
19. Ⓐ Ⓑ Ⓒ Ⓓ
20. Ⓐ Ⓑ Ⓒ Ⓓ

21. Ⓐ Ⓑ Ⓒ Ⓓ
22. Ⓐ Ⓑ Ⓒ Ⓓ
23. Ⓐ Ⓑ Ⓒ Ⓓ
24. Ⓐ Ⓑ Ⓒ Ⓓ
25. Ⓐ Ⓑ Ⓒ Ⓓ
26. Ⓐ Ⓑ Ⓒ Ⓓ
27. Ⓐ Ⓑ Ⓒ Ⓓ
28. Ⓐ Ⓑ Ⓒ Ⓓ
29. Ⓐ Ⓑ Ⓒ Ⓓ
30. Ⓐ Ⓑ Ⓒ Ⓓ
31. Ⓐ Ⓑ Ⓒ Ⓓ
32. Ⓐ Ⓑ Ⓒ Ⓓ
33. Ⓐ Ⓑ Ⓒ Ⓓ
34. Ⓐ Ⓑ Ⓒ Ⓓ
35. Ⓐ Ⓑ Ⓒ Ⓓ
36. Ⓐ Ⓑ Ⓒ Ⓓ
37. Ⓐ Ⓑ Ⓒ Ⓓ
38. Ⓐ Ⓑ Ⓒ Ⓓ
39. Ⓐ Ⓑ Ⓒ Ⓓ
40. Ⓐ Ⓑ Ⓒ Ⓓ

41. Ⓐ Ⓑ Ⓒ Ⓓ
42. Ⓐ Ⓑ Ⓒ Ⓓ
43. Ⓐ Ⓑ Ⓒ Ⓓ
44. Ⓐ Ⓑ Ⓒ Ⓓ
45. Ⓐ Ⓑ Ⓒ Ⓓ
46. Ⓐ Ⓑ Ⓒ Ⓓ
47. Ⓐ Ⓑ Ⓒ Ⓓ
48. Ⓐ Ⓑ Ⓒ Ⓓ
49. Ⓐ Ⓑ Ⓒ Ⓓ
50. Ⓐ Ⓑ Ⓒ Ⓓ
51. Ⓐ Ⓑ Ⓒ Ⓓ
52. Ⓐ Ⓑ Ⓒ Ⓓ
53. Ⓐ Ⓑ Ⓒ Ⓓ
54. Ⓐ Ⓑ Ⓒ Ⓓ
55. Ⓐ Ⓑ Ⓒ Ⓓ

SHORT ANSWER: Use dark blue or black ink only for the short-answer questions. Do not write outside of the box.

Question 1

SHORT ANSWER: Use dark blue or black ink only for the short-answer questions. Do not write outside of the box.

Question 2

SHORT ANSWER: Use dark blue or black ink only for the short-answer questions. Do not write outside of the box.

Question 3 or Question 4 (Please indicate which question you answer.)

SECTION II

Circle the number of the Essay that you are answering on this page.	Mandatory: 1	Circle one: 2, 3, or 4

SECTION II

Circle the number of the Essay that you are answering on this page.	Mandatory: 1	Circle one: 2, 3, or 4

SECTION II

| Circle the number of the Essay that you are answering on this page. | Mandatory: 1 | Circle one: 2, 3, or 4 |

SECTION II

Circle the number of the Essay that you are answering on this page.	Mandatory: 1	Circle one: 2, 3, or 4

Model Test 2

SECTION I

Part A: Multiple-Choice Questions

TIME: 55 MINUTES
NUMBER OF QUESTIONS: 55
PERCENTAGE OF TOTAL AP EXAM SCORE: 40%
WRITING INSTRUMENT: PENCIL REQUIRED

Directions: Section I, Part A of this exam contains 55 multiple-choice questions. Indicate all of your answers to the multiple-choice questions on the multiple-choice answer sheet. No credit will be given for anything written in the exam booklet, but you may write on the exam booklet to take notes and do scratch work.

Use your time efficiently, working as quickly as possible without losing accuracy. Do not spend too much time on any one question. Go on to other questions and come back to the ones that you have not answered if you have time. It is not expected that you will know the answers to all of the multiple-choice questions.

Your total score on the multiple-choice section is based only on the number of questions answered correctly. Points are not deducted for incorrect answers or unanswered questions.

—*School of Athens* by Raphael (1509–1511). This painting depicting the most famous Greek philosophers, such as Plato, Aristotle, Pythagoras, Euclid, and many others, was commissioned as one of four great masterpieces for the Papal Palace in Rome.

1. The painting above is often described as a Renaissance masterpiece that typifies the humanism that was which of the following?

    (A) Just starting to emerge but will continue to spread uninterrupted throughout Europe over the course of the next 500 years as a central ideal

    (B) Just coming to an end as the interaction with the Ottoman Turks in 1453 closed off trade routes and shut down communication between East and West

    (C) In its prime, as the only major power in Europe that refused to employ humanist artists was the Catholic Church

    (D) In its prime, as humanists such as Petrarch in Italy and Erasmus in Rotterdam were already writing major humanist works by the time this painting was finished

2. What are three characteristics in the painting above that make it an Italian Renaissance painting?

    (A) Perspective, sfumato, and scale

    (B) Chiaroscuro, perspective, and the number of people depicted

    (C) Perspective, humanist subject matter, and attention to anatomical detail

    (D) Colors used, humanist subject matter, and the fact that it was a fresco

3. Why would the patrons of this painting and its three companion paintings wish to pay huge sums of money for these works of art?

(A) They and the other people in their region believed that great public works of art demonstrated power and prestige to the people.

(B) They believed that it was their civic duty to pay people to paint in order to reduce unemployment in their towns.

(C) They simply wanted to be surrounded by beautiful objects and paintings because they loved beauty.

(D) They believed that if they surrounded themselves with pictures from ancient Greece that they would be very wise and live for a long time, like Greek ideas did.

Questions 4 to 6 refer to the following letter.

It happened . . . that a Spaniard saw an Indian . . . eating a piece of flesh taken from the body of an Indian who had been killed. . . . I had the culprit burned, explaining that the cause was his having killed that Indian and eaten him[,] which was prohibited by Your Majesty, and by me in Your Royal name. I further made the chief understand that all the people . . . must abstain from this custom. . . . I came . . . to protect their lives as well as their property, and to teach them that they were to adore but one God[,] . . . that they must turn from their idols, and the rites they had practiced until then, for these were lies and deceptions which the devil . . . had invented. . . . I, likewise, had come to teach them that Your Majesty, by the will of Divine Providence, rules the universe, and that they also must submit themselves to the imperial yoke, and do all that we who are Your Majesty's ministers here might order them.

—Hernan Cortez, *Fifth Letter* to Holy Roman Emperor Charles V, 1521

4. Which of the following motivations for exploration is most evident from the document above?

(A) The rise of mercantilism gave the state a new role in promoting commercial development and the acquisition of colonies overseas.

(B) European states sought direct access to gold and spices and luxury goods as a means to enhance personal wealth and state power.

(C) Individual captains sought great glory and wealth.

(D) Christianity served as a stimulus for exploration as governments and religious authorities sought to spread the faith and counter Islam, and as a justification for the physical and cultural subjugation of indigenous civilizations.

5. Which of the following was NOT a result of the European conquest of the Americas realized by the end of the seventeenth century?

(A) Europeans established overseas colonies on the coasts of the Americas and throughout the continent of Africa.

(B) Europe's colonial expansion led to a global exchange of goods, flora, fauna, cultural practices, and diseases.

(C) Europeans created vast global trade networks that allowed them to gain large accumulations of wealth.

(D) Europeans expanded the African slave trade in response to the establishment of a plantation economy in the Americas and to demographic catastrophes among indigenous peoples.

6. Which of the following superior technologies was most crucial to the Europeans' success in the New World?

(A) New sailing technologies like the compass and the astrolabe

(B) New ships like the carrack and caravel

(C) Weapons like cannons and war horses

(D) Better educational systems that taught navigation and warfare

Questions 7 and 8 refer to the excerpts below.

This corruption is repeatedly designated by Paul by the term sin . . . such as adultery, fornication, theft, hatred, murder, revellings, he terms, in the same way, the fruits of sin, though in various passages of Scripture . . . we are, merely on account of such corruption, deservedly condemned by God, to whom nothing is acceptable but righteousness, innocence, and purity.

—John Calvin, from *The Institutes of Christian Religion*, Book 2: Chapter 1, 1545

The covenant of life is not preached equally to all, and among those to whom it is preached, does not always meet with the same reception. This diversity displays the unsearchable depth of the divine judgment, and is without doubt subordinate to God's purpose of eternal election. But if it is plainly owing to the mere pleasure of God that salvation is spontaneously offered to some, while others have no access to it, great and difficult questions immediately arise, questions which are inexplicable, when just views are not entertained concerning election and predestination[,] . . . the grace of God being illustrated by the contrast, viz., that he does not adopt all promiscuously to the hope of salvation, but gives to some what he denies to others.

—John Calvin, from *The Institutes of Christian Religion*, Book 3: Chapter 21, 1545

7. Which of the following justifications used by Protestant reformers such as Calvin is alluded to above?

(A) They believed that their church should not be subordinate to the state.
(B) The corruption of the Roman Catholic Church and its leaders meant that reform was needed.
(C) Religion was used to challenge the authority of earthly monarchs.
(D) The concept that salvation comes from faith alone rather than through good works is supported.

8. Which of the following is the biggest contrast between the ideas of Calvinists when compared to their fellow Protestant Lutherans?

(A) Calvinists believed that the state is absolutely subordinate to the religious organization.
(B) Calvinists believed in consubstantiation while Lutherans believed in transubstantiation.
(C) Lutherans used the reformed faith to their political advantage to break free from domination from the pope and the Holy Roman Empire.
(D) Lutherans insisted upon maintaining all of the seven sacraments while the Calvinists chose to honor only two of them.

Questions 9 to 11 refer to the map below.

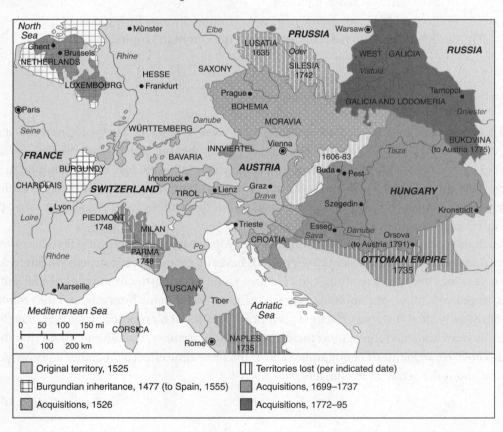

9. The shaded areas on the map above represent which of the following?

    (A) Dynastic lands of the Habsburgs in the sixteenth century
    (B) Participants in the Thirty Years' War in the seventeenth century
    (C) Protestant regions in the eighteenth century
    (D) Members of the Holy Alliance in the nineteenth century

10. The shaded areas additionally have in common which of the following during the sixteenth and seventeenth centuries?

    (A) They were regions that allowed religious pluralism during the sixteenth and seventeenth centuries.
    (B) They represent the areas that benefited most from transatlantic trade during the sixteenth and seventeenth centuries.
    (C) They represent areas where states took advantage of religious conflict to strengthen their own power during the sixteenth and seventeenth centuries.
    (D) They were areas that were mostly Roman Catholic by 1648.

11. Which of the following is the best description of how the map above would change were it drawn to represent the same area 100 years after the first acquisitions were made?

    (A) The diverse German and Italian states would be unified into nations.
    (B) The Ottoman Empire would be significantly reduced as Russia and Austria began to take control of Eastern Europe.
    (C) France would become smaller as wars continually took little pieces of it away.
    (D) Greece would gain independence from the Ottoman Empire.

Questions 12 to 15 refer to the following quote.

I had now decided beyond all question that there existed in the heavens three stars wandering about Jupiter as do Venus and Mercury about the sun, and this became plainer than daylight from observations on similar occasions which followed. Nor were there just three such stars; four wanderers complete their revolutions about Jupiter, and of their alterations as observed more precisely later on we shall give a description here. Also I measured the distances between them by means of the telescope. . . .

Such are the observations concerning the four Medicean planets recently first discovered by me, and although from this data their periods have not yet been reconstructed in numerical form, it is legitimate at least to put in evidence some facts worthy of note. Above all, since they sometimes follow and sometimes precede Jupiter by the same intervals, and they remain within very limited distances either to east or west of Jupiter, accompanying that planet in both its retrograde and direct movements in a constant manner, no one can doubt that they complete their revolutions about Jupiter and at the same time effect all together a twelve-year period about the center of the universe.

—Galileo Galilei, 1610

12. Which of the following Polish thinkers was most likely the person whose ideas convinced Galileo to have written the statement above?

(A) Nicolaus Copernicus
(B) Johannes Kepler
(C) Galileo Galilei
(D) Josef Pilsudski

13. Which of the following conclusions drawn in part from the observations above was the most revolutionary over time?

(A) There were four smaller stars that seemed to move around Jupiter.
(B) The Earth is not the center of the universe.
(C) The heavens are occupied by bodies revolving around each other rather than by God alone.
(D) The Earth is but one tiny planet in an infinite universe or even multiverse.

14. Which of the following intellectual hallmarks of the Renaissance seem most in conflict with the questioning of the ancient philosophers, such as Aristotle, through experimentation in *natural philosophy*?

(A) Humanism
(B) Secularism
(C) Individualism
(D) Arête

15. Which of the following is best demonstrated by the passage about intellectual thought at the time?

(A) It led to better scientific tools, which led to a rise in the standard of living during the seventeenth century across Europe.
(B) The ideas of the ancient Greeks guided all of their ideas.
(C) It used information obtained through experimentation to conceptualize the universe.
(D) It provided experimental proof of the theories of ancient thinkers, such as Aristotle, on how the universe worked.

Questions 16 to 18 refer to the following governmental report.

Of the 450 sick persons whom the inhabitants were unable to relieve, 200 were turned out, and these we saw die one by one as they lay on the roadside. A large number still remain, and to each of them it is only possible to dole out the least scrap of bread. We only give bread to those who would otherwise die. The staple dish here consists of mice, which the inhabitants hunt, so desperate are they from hunger. They devour roots which the animals cannot eat; one can, in fact, not put into words the things one sees. . . . This narrative, far from exaggerating, rather understates the horror of the case, for it does not record the hundredth part of the misery in this district. Those who have not witnessed it with their own eyes cannot imagine how great it is. Not a day passes but at least 200 people die of famine in the two provinces. We certify to having ourselves seen herds, not of cattle, but of men and women, wandering about the fields between Rheims and Rhétel, turning up the earth like pigs to find a few roots; and as they can only find rotten ones, and not half enough of them, they become so weak that they have not strength left to seek food. The parish priest at Boult, whose letter we enclose, tells us he has buried three of his parishioners who died of hunger. The rest subsisted on chopped straw mixed with earth, of which they composed a food which cannot be called bread. Other persons in the same place lived on the bodies of animals which had died of disease, and which the curé, otherwise unable to help his people, allowed them to roast at the presbytery fire.

—Report of the Estates of Normandy, 1651

16. Which of the following would be most responsible for ending the problems of hunger mentioned above?

    (A) The elimination of the Black Plague in Europe during the seventeenth century
    (B) The elimination of fallow fields through the Agricultural Revolution during the seventeenth century
    (C) The creation of a strong putting-out system that allowed people to be paid for their work
    (D) A declining population during the seventeenth century that led to better food yields and less hunger as Europe urbanized

17. Which of the following contributed the LEAST to the health and hunger problems faced by the French people in the seventeenth century?

    (A) Low-productivity agricultural practices
    (B) Adverse weather
    (C) Low taxes on the peasants and middle class
    (D) Poor transportation

18. Which of the following intellectual movements was occurring in Europe at the time this document was created and would help improve crop yields?

    (A) The Enlightenment
    (B) Divine right theory of rule
    (C) The rise of existentialism
    (D) The Scientific Revolution

Questions 19 to 21 refer to the following memoir.

Not only did he expect all persons of distinction to be in continual attendance at Court, but he was quick to notice the absence of those of inferior degree; at his lever, his couches, his meals, in the gardens of Versailles (the only place where the courtiers in general were allowed to follow him), he used to cast his eyes to right and left; nothing escaped him[;] he saw everybody. If anyone habitually living at Court absented himself he insisted on knowing the reason; those who came there only for flying visits had also to give a satisfactory explanation; anyone who seldom or never appeared there was certain to incur his displeasure. If asked to bestow a favor on such persons he would reply haughtily: "I do not know him"; of such as rarely presented themselves he would say, "He is a man I never see"; and from these judgments there was no appeal.

No one understood better than Louis XIV the art of enhancing the value of a favor by his manner of bestowing it; he knew how to make the most of a word, a smile, even of a glance.

He loved splendor, magnificence, and profusion in all things, and encouraged similar tastes in his Court; to spend money freely on equipages and buildings, on feasting and at cards, was a sure way to gain his favor, perhaps to obtain the honor of a word from him. Motives of policy had something to do with this; by making expensive habits the fashion, and, for people in a certain position, a necessity, he compelled his courtiers to live beyond their income, and gradually reduced them to depend on his bounty for the means of subsistence.

—Duke Saint-Simon, *Memoirs of Louis XIV and His Court and His Regency*, c. 1750

19. Which of the following is the best explanation of the bias found in the document above?

    (A) The duke, as a member of the French nobility, is sympathetic to King Louis.
    (B) The duke, as a member of the French nobility, is biased against the king because of his suppression of the nobility.
    (C) The duke, as a member of the French nobility, supported the extension of the administrative, financial, military, and religious control of the central state over the French population.
    (D) The duke, as a member of the French nobility, supported King Louis's preservation of the aristocracy's social position and legal privileges, while he removed their power.

20. Louis XIV was aided by many able advisors, but which of the following advisors helped him to reorganize France and make it into a world power?

    (A) Jean Martinet, his chief military advisor
    (B) Cardinal Mazarin, his regent and foreign policy advisor
    (C) Jean Baptiste Colbert, his finance minister
    (D) The Duke of Burgundy

21. Which of the following was the greatest weakness and regret of the rule of King Louis XIV?

(A) His domination of the nobility left him without friends and allies.
(B) He was so concerned with ceremonies and appearances that he did not rule his country well.
(C) He left the administration of his kingdom to professional bureaucrats known as intendants.
(D) He was at war for 2/3 of his reign and united the other major powers against him.

Questions 22 to 24 refer to the list of complaints below.

Article 3: Frenchmen should regard as laws of the kingdom those alone which have been prepared by the national assembly and sanctioned by the king.

Article 11: Personal liberty, proprietary rights and the security of citizens shall be established in a clear, precise and irrevocable manner. All *lettres de cachet* shall be abolished forever, subject to certain modifications which the States General may see fit to impose.

Article 12: And to remove forever the possibility of injury to the personal and proprietary rights of Frenchmen, the jury system shall be introduced in all criminal cases, and in civil cases for the determination of fact, in all the courts of the realm.

Article 17: All distinctions in penalties shall be abolished; and crimes committed by citizens of the different orders shall be punished irrespectively, according to the same forms of law and in the same manner. The States General shall seek to bring it about that the effects of transgression shall be confined to the individual and shall not be reflected upon the relatives of the transgressor, themselves innocent of all participation.
Article 21: No tax shall be legal unless accepted by the representatives of the people and sanctioned by the king.

—*Cahiers of the Third Estate of Versailles*, 1789

22. Which of the following was NOT one of the problems in France that caused the French Revolution referenced in the document above?

(A) Financial problems caused by debts and low revenues.
(B) The legal system of France was not equitable.
(C) The proliferation of Enlightenment ideals.
(D) There was a lot of social and political inequality in France in 1789.

23. Which of the following changes brought on by the French Revolution was most approved of by the peasants of France?

(A) Creation of a constitutional monarchy
(B) The abolition of feudal dues and rents
(C) Increased popular participation in politics
(D) Nationalization of religion

24. During the radical phase of the Revolution, which of the following changes instituted by Robespierre was LEAST beneficial to the defense of France?

    (A) The conscription of huge armies
    (B) Fixing prices and wages
    (C) Pursuing a policy of de-Christianization
    (D) Promoting soldiers based upon their merits in the field

Questions 25 to 28 refer to the following excerpt from a pamphlet.

You will do me the justice to remember, that I have always strenuously supported the Right of every man to his own opinion, however different that opinion might be to mine. He who denies to another this right, makes a slave of himself to his present opinion, because he precludes himself the right of changing it.

The most formidable weapon against errors of every kind is Reason. I have never used any other, and I trust I never shall.

The circumstance that has now taken place in France of the total abolition of the whole national order of priesthood, and of everything appertaining to compulsive systems of religion, and compulsive articles of faith, has not only precipitated my intention, but rendered a work of this kind exceedingly necessary, lest in the general wreck of superstition, of false systems of government, and false theology, we lose sight of morality, of humanity, and of the theology that is true.

I believe in one God, and no more; and I hope for happiness beyond this life.

I believe in the equality of man; and I believe that religious duties consist in doing justice, loving mercy, and endeavoring to make our fellow-creatures happy.

I do not believe in the creed professed by the Jewish church, by the Roman church, by the Greek church, by the Turkish church, by the Protestant church, nor by any church that I know of. My own mind is my own church.

All national institutions of churches, whether Jewish, Christian or Turkish, appear to me no other than human inventions, set up to terrify and enslave mankind, and monopolize power and profit.

I do not mean by this declaration to condemn those who believe otherwise; they have the same right to their belief as I have to mine.

—Thomas Paine, *The Age of Reason*, 1794–1795

25. The document above supports which of the following demands of the Enlightenment *philosophes*?

    (A) Deism should be adopted by all as the only logical religion.
    (B) Religious toleration leads to the destruction of social unity.
    (C) Skepticism is not a reliable way of examining information.
    (D) Religious toleration should be given to all people of all religions.

26. Paine's statement in the last sentence, criticizing persecution, was most likely influenced by which of the following?

(A) New concepts of legal equity and individual rights expressed by Locke and Rousseau

(B) Europeans gaining a more thorough understanding of the rich cultural diversity through trade and travel

(C) New concepts of a deterministic mechanical universe based upon the discovery of Newton's mathematical laws

(D) Challenges to the monopoly on truth held by the Roman Catholic Church on multiple fronts

27. Which of the following Enlightenment philosophes designed a system of checks and balances for government to avoid abuses of power?

(A) Jean Jacques Rousseau

(B) Baron Montesquieu

(C) Mary Wollstonecraft

(D) Adam Smith

28. The ideas expressed by Paine above best illustrate which of the following characteristics of Enlightenment intellectuals?

(A) Many were accomplished scientists who added important pieces to the human understanding of the universe.

(B) They utilized new methods of communicating their ideas, such as salons and inexpensive printed pamphlets.

(C) Most rejected religion altogether and adopted atheism as the only credo of a rational person.

(D) Many believed that the new scientific discoveries would allow humans to solve all problems.

Questions 29 to 32 refer to the documents below.

Source 1

If then by the Use of Machines, the Manufacture of Cotton, an Article which we import, and are supplied with from other Countries, and which can everywhere be procured on equal Terms, has met with such amazing Success, may not greater Advantages be reasonably expected from cultivating to the utmost the Manufacture of Wool, the Produce of our own Island, an Article in Demand in all Countries, almost the universal Clothing of Mankind?

In the Manufacture of Woollens, the Scribbling Mill, the Spinning Frame, and the Fly Shuttle, have reduced manual Labour nearly One third, and each of them at its first Introduction carried an Alarm to the Work People, yet each has contributed to advance the Wages and to increase the Trade, so that if an Attempt was now made to deprive us of the Use of them, there is no Doubt, but every Person engaged in the Business, would exert himself to defend them.

—*Statement by the Cloth Merchants of Leeds*, 1791

Source 2

Come, cropper lads of high renown,
Who love to drink good ale that's brown,
And strike each haughty tyrant down,
With hatchet, pike, and gun!

Oh, the cropper lads for me,
The gallant lads for me,
Who with lusty stroke,
The shear frames broke,
The cropper lads for me!

What though the specials still advance,
And soldiers nightly round us prance;
The cropper lads still lead the dance,
With hatchet, pike, and gun!

Oh, the cropper lads for me,
The gallant lads for me,
Who with lusty stroke
The shear frames broke,
The cropper lads for me!

—Luddite Song, *The Cropper's Song*, c. 1812

29. Which of the following economic theories is **Source 1** above referencing in support of the expansion and use of machines?

(A) Laissez-faire capitalism
(B) Mercantilism
(C) Industrialization
(D) Bullionism

30. **Source 2** was motivated most by which of the following changes brought on by industrialization?

(A) The movement of many agricultural workers to the new industrial cities increased urbanization.
(B) Industrialization was promoting significant population growth, as it was applied to many fields.
(C) Parliament supported industrialization for its own interests.
(D) Socioeconomic changes created divisions of labor that led to the development of self-conscious classes.

31. Which of the following best describes the governmental reactions to complaints such as those seen in **Source 2** before 1850?

(A) Governments did little to address problems of industrialization before 1850.
(B) Reform movements led to the creation of regulations on work hours and ages and gender of workers.
(C) The implementation of running water and sewers was begun in England.
(D) The government created a national health-care system.

32. Which of the following is NOT a result of the Industrial Revolution according to the documents and your knowledge of European history?

(A) In some of the less industrialized areas of Europe, the dominance of agricultural elites persisted into the twentieth century.
(B) Cities experienced overcrowding, while affected rural areas suffered declines in available labor as well as weakened communities.
(C) Class identity developed and was reinforced through daily life and participation in groups such as labor unions.
(D) Greater social and economic equity emerged as the workers and their bosses saw their incomes become more equal.

Questions 33 to 35 refer to the following excerpt.

Never were talents of the highest genius of the most exalted kind, more profusely bestowed upon a human being. The genius of Napoleon is astounding. All branches of human knowledge seemed alike familiar to his gigantic mind. His conversations at St. Helena, scattered through the numerous and voluminous memorials of those who gleaned them, are replete with intensest interest. During the long agony of his imprisonment and his death, he conversed with perfect freedom upon the events of his marvelous career, and upon all those subjects or morals, politics, and religion, which most deeply concern the welfare of our race. There is no mind which will not be invigorated by familiarity with these profound thoughts, expressed with so much glow of feeling and energy of diction.

—John S. C. Abbott, historian, *Napoleon at St. Helena*, 1855

33. Which of the following features of the French empire under Napoleon does Abbott seem most impressed with?

(A) Napoleon's secret police
(B) Napoleon's domestic reforms
(C) Napoleon's suppression of women's rights
(D) Napoleon's military tactics

34. Napoleon helped make the French Revolution an international movement in the areas he conquered

(A) by imposing a universal currency based on the French franc.
(B) by the brutal suppression of guerrilla resistance.
(C) by abolishing feudalism and manorialism.
(D) by encouraging the use of French as the universal language.

35. Which of the following actions of Napoleon does the author seem to be ignoring the hypocrisy of in his examination of the high mindedness and praiseworthiness of Napoleon?

(A) The invasion of Haiti to stop a slave revolt there
(B) The creation of the Napoleonic Code
(C) Promoting soldiers and government workers based upon their merits only
(D) His conquest of Europe and use of the Continental System

Questions 36 to 38 refer to the following excerpt.

The revolutionary seed had penetrated into every country and spread more or less. It was greatly developed under the régime of the military despotism of Bonaparte. His conquests displaced a number of laws, institutions, and customs; broke through bonds sacred among all nations, strong enough to resist time itself; which is more than can be said of certain benefits conferred by these innovators.

The monarchs will fulfil the duties imposed upon them by Him who, by entrusting them with power, has charged them to watch over the maintenance of justice, and the rights of all, to avoid the paths of error, and tread firmly in the way of truth. Placed beyond the passions which agitate society, it is in days of trial chiefly that they are called upon to despoil realities of their false appearances, and to show themselves as they are, fathers invested with the authority belonging by right to the heads of families, to prove that, in days of mourning, they know how to be just, wise, and therefore strong, and that they will not abandon the people whom they ought to govern to be the sport of factions, to error and its consequences, which must involve the loss of society.

Union between the monarchs is the basis of the policy which must now be followed to save society from total ruin. . . .

Let them not confound concessions made to parties with the good they ought to do for their people, in modifying, according to their recognized needs, such branches of the administration as require it.

Let them be just, but strong; beneficent, but strict.

Let them maintain religious principles in all their purity, and not allow the faith to be attacked and morality interpreted according to the social contract or the visions of foolish sectarians.

Let them suppress Secret Societies; that gangrene of society.

—Klemens von Metternich, *Political Confession of Faith*, 1820

36. Which of the following was the greatest cause of the fears expressed by Metternich in the document above?

(A) The ideas of personal liberty and nationalism conceived during the Enlightenment resulted in radical revolutions that could spread throughout Europe.

(B) The conquest of Europe by Napoleon led to the creation of new factions and shifted the European balance of power.

(C) The power of monarchs had grown to the point where it needed to be checked by other powers within each nation or domination of civilians would occur.

(D) The rising and falling economic cycle of the newly emerging capitalist economy could lead to civilian unrest that must be suppressed.

37. The final result of the negotiations led by Metternich during the Congress of Vienna is being referenced in the document above in which of the following ways?

(A) Metternich's statement about the military despotism of Bonaparte led to the elimination of all empires in Europe.

(B) Metternich's statement about fulfilling duties indicated his support for the Holy Alliance that controlled the fate of Europe.

(C) Metternich's statement about the unity of monarchs alludes to the creation of the Concert of Europe.

(D) Metternich's disgust for secret societies led to the creation of the Carlsbad Decrees.

38. Which of the following is the best description of the goals of the new ideology of conservatism as it was explained by Metternich?

(A) The suppression of all new ideas in every field to prevent any changes to society.

(B) The suppression of nationalist and liberal revolutions that called for democratic and economic reforms.

(C) The suppression of secret societies in hopes of spreading democracy to the masses.

(D) The suppression of political change only while allowing economic and social change.

Questions 39 to 41 refer to the following excerpt.

If civilized education developed in every child its natural inclinations, we should see nearly all rich children enamored of various very plebeian occupations, such as that of the mason, the carpenter, the smith, the saddler. I have instanced Louis the XVI, who loved the trade of locksmith; an Infanta of Spain preferred that of shoemaker; a certain king of Denmark gratified himself by manufacturing syringes; the former king of Naples loved to sell the fish he had caught in the market-place himself; the prince of Parma, whom Condillac had trained in metaphysical subtitles, in the understanding of intuition, of cognition, had no taste but for the occupation of church-warden and lay-brother.

The great majority of wealthy children would follow these plebeian tastes, if civilized education did not oppose the development of them; and if the filthiness of the workshops and the coarseness of the workmen did not arouse a repugnance stronger than the attraction. What child of a prince is there who has no taste for one of the four occupations I have just mentioned, that of mason, carpenter, smith, saddler, and who would not advance in them if he beheld from an early age the work carried on in blight workshops, by refined people, who would always arrange a miniature workshop for children, with little implements and light labor?

—Charles Fourier, *On Education*, 1838

39. Which of the following groups of intellectuals would Fourier belong to, according to the document above?

    (A) Utilitarians
    (B) Laissez-faire capitalists
    (C) Utopian socialists
    (D) Marxist communists

40. What nation experimented with utilizing the ideas of Fourier and others like him to create national workshops in 1848?

    (A) Germany
    (B) France
    (C) Great Britain
    (D) Austria

41. Many in Fourier's circles advocated for universal male suffrage, which was propagated most by which of the following groups?

    (A) Luddites
    (B) Liberals
    (C) Benthamites
    (D) Chartists

Questions 42 to 44 refer to the images below.

Image 1

—*Dance Song,* portrait of a family at home in Germany, by Hugo Bürkner, 1854.

Image 2

—*"Some foolish people imagine our ladies will neglect their family duties. Quite a mistake."* Cartoon from *Punch Magazine,* 1887.

42. To which of the following is the material prosperity evident in **Image 1** partially attributable?

   (A) The increasing standard of living of German industrial workers
   (B) The social welfare policies instituted by governments of the Germanic states
   (C) The adoption by the Frankfurt Parliament of a liberal constitution for Germany
   (D) The restoration of political stability in the aftermath of the Congress of Vienna

43. A historian of nineteenth-century European society is most likely to use **Image 2** as evidence that

   (A) many women used the Revolutions of 1848 as an opportunity to express their sexuality more freely.
   (B) many men were becoming more involved in child-rearing and household management.
   (C) many men feared that women's participation in the public sphere would undermine the established social order.
   (D) many women were increasingly taking on the role of decision-maker in their families.

44. Which of the following transformations in the ideals of family life and gender roles during the late 19th century is expressed in the images above?

   (A) The ideals were largely overcome by socialist notions of collective child rearing.
   (B) The ideals were increasingly adopted by working-class families.
   (C) The ideals were modified to accommodate the fact that most women had become part of the paid workforce.
   (D) The professional and academic journals of the time recommended fathers becoming less involved in child rearing.

Questions 45 to 47 will refer to the following government proclamation.

On the basis of the above-mentioned new arrangements, the serfs will receive in time the full rights of free rural inhabitants.

The nobles, while retaining their property rights to all the lands belonging to them, grant the peasants perpetual use of their household plots in return for a specified obligation[; . . . the nobles] grant them a portion of arable land fixed by the said arrangements as well as other property. . . . While enjoying these land allotments, the peasants are obliged, in return, to fulfill obligations to the noblemen fixed by the same arrangements. In this status, which is temporary, the peasants are temporarily bound. . . .

[T]hey are granted the right to purchase their household plots, and, with the consent of the nobles, they may acquire in full ownership the arable lands and other properties which are allotted them for permanent use. Following such acquisition of full ownership of land, the peasants will be freed from their obligations to the nobles for the land thus purchased and will become free peasant landowners.

WE have deemed it advisable:

3. To organize Peace Offices on the estates of the nobles, leaving the village communes as they are, and to open cantonal offices in the large villages and unite small village communes.

4. To formulate, verify, and confirm in each village commune or estate a charter which will specify, on the basis of local conditions, the amount of land allotted to the peasants for permanent use, and the scope of their obligations to the nobleman for the land.

6. Until that time, peasants and household serfs must be obedient towards their nobles, and scrupulously fulfill their former obligations.

7. The nobles will continue to keep order on their estates, with the right of jurisdiction and of police, until the organization of cantons and of cantonal courts.

> —Alexander II, "The Abolition of Serfdom in Russia," Manifesto of February 19, 1861

45. Which of the following best articulates the new conditions for the recently emancipated serfs of Russia as stated in the above passage?

   (A) The czar's manifesto allowed for a heterogeneous class of farmers to emerge, with many former serfs becoming quite prosperous while others struggled.
   (B) The manifesto was mostly ineffective in improving the economic condition of former serfs, but paved the way for local self-rule and, soon after, a national legislature.
   (C) The czar's insistence on cooperation between the nobility and recently emancipated people limited the financial potential of all impacted by the manifesto.
   (D) The manifesto, although emancipating the serfs, saddled them with financial responsibilities and other restrictions, while the aristocracy retained too many of their former rights.

46. Which of the following was a major impetus in convincing Czar Alexander II of the necessity of freeing the serfs?

   (A) Recent defeat in the Crimean War convinced the czar some domestic reforms were necessary.
   (B) Enlightened rulers in Prussia and Austria had recently done the same, which pressured Alexander II to act.
   (C) The Decembrist Revolt and its aftermath had convinced the young czar to make reforms.
   (D) A labor force to complete the Trans-Siberian Railroad was needed as well as military recruits.

47. Which of the following best describes the long-term effects of Czar Alexander II's emancipation?

   (A) Food production soared, which allowed Russians to export agricultural goods while investing the profits into their industrial sector.
   (B) The program was a complete disaster as agricultural output plummeted until Pyotr Stolypin's reforms made privatized Russian farming profitable.
   (C) The emancipation terms relegated former serfs to communal farming, thus keeping them in perpetual poverty, and made wealthy conservatives nervous.
   (D) No longer tied to the land, former serfs moved to the cities, thus spurning the commencement of an industrial revolution in Russia.

Questions 48 and 49 refer to the treaty below.

   The leaders of Europe, deeply sensible of their solemn duty to promote the welfare of mankind;

   Persuaded that the time has come when a frank renunciation of war as an instrument of national policy should be made to the end that the peaceful and friendly relations now existing between their peoples may be perpetuated;

ARTICLE I
The High Contracting Parties solemnly declare in the names of their respective peoples that they condemn recourse to war for the solution of international controversies, and renounce it, as an instrument of national policy in their relations with one another.

ARTICLE II
The High Contracting Parties agree that the settlement or solution of all disputes or conflicts of whatever nature or of whatever origin they may be, which may arise among them, shall never be sought except by pacific means.

—Kellogg-Briand Pact, 1928

48. Which of the following factors LEAST influenced the signatory nations to agree to this treaty?

(A) The effects of military stalemate and total war had led to protest and insurrection in belligerent nations during the First World War.

(B) Wilsonian idealism had not been adhered to in the Treaty of Versailles that created the weak League of Nations, and leaders were trying to create another tool to help prevent war.

(C) The leadership of Germany was threatening expansion again and the other nations wanted to be ready to meet the German threat.

(D) The ideas of John Maynard Keynes in *Economic Consequences of the Peace* said that the Treaty of Versailles was too harsh on Germany.

49. Which of the following is the best characterization of the international movement to prevent war from 1928 through the modern era?

(A) The movement has steadily gained speed as more and more nations in Europe have condemned war and refused to support military action.

(B) There was a period of pacifism until 1939, and since then there has been steadily increasing support for national military action.

(C) The idea of pacifism has been adopted when threats to national sovereignty and personal liberty are less apparent, but Europeans choose violent options whenever they are threatened.

(D) The concept of Europeans fighting wars has all but disappeared since the Second World War.

Questions 50 and 51 are based upon the following tables.

Source 1

The Movement toward European Union: The table below lists the years that each nation joined together with the first three forming a customs union in 1944 to be replaced by the European Economic Community (EEC) or Common Market then, finally, the European Union (EU).

Nation	Year Joined	Organization
Belgium	1944	BENELUX
Netherlands	1944	BENELUX
Luxembourg	1944	BENELUX
France	1951	EEC
West Germany	1951	EEC
Italy	1951	EEC
Denmark	1973	EU
Ireland	1973	EU
United Kingdom	1973	EU
Greece	1981	EU
Spain	1986	EU
Portugal	1986	EU
Sweden	1995	EU
Finland	1995	EU
Austria	1995	EU
Czech Republic	2004	EU
Estonia	2004	EU
Latvia	2004	EU
Lithuania	2004	EU
Cyprus	2004	EU
Hungary	2004	EU
Poland	2004	EU
Slovakia	2004	EU
Slovenia	2004	EU
Malta	2004	EU
Romania	2007	EU
Bulgaria	2007	EU
Croatia	2013	EU

Source 2

Historic Real GDP Measured in $Billions (Dollar Value for Base Year 2010)

Country	1969	1974	1979	1984	1989	1994	1999	2004	2009	2014	% Growth 1969–2014
Belgium	183.00	234.16	258.53	278.51	319.57	348.38	396.07	436.78	460.78	485.08	165%
France	985.10	1,280.00	1,470.67	1,588.30	1,842.63	1,969.14	2,216.00	2,443.33	2,523.49	2,635.73	168%
Greece	105.38	136.68	177.13	175.15	190.95	198.98	230.38	286.84	309.77	248.29	136%
Luxembourg	11.61	14.60	15.13	16.78	23.49	29.60	37.28	45.78	50.52	55.64	379%
Netherlands	278.29	346.93	387.30	412.19	478.51	541.50	655.03	712.40	766.05	774.06	178%
Poland	119.79	139.50	162.45	189.17	220.29	229.95	307.03	359.59	452.29	523.83	337%
Russia	823.71	959.21	1,117.01	1,300.76	1,457.58	916.23	865.03	1,204.49	1,459.27	1,670.38	103%
Ukraine	116.58	135.75	158.09	184.09	219.83	112.56	84.47	126.02	130.60	137.37	18%
United Kingdom	887.94	1,017.76	1,128.25	1,183.83	1,432.93	1,568.30	1,869.42	2,187.16	2,258.05	2,437.65	175%

—All data from World Bank

50. Using the information in <u>both sources</u>, which of the following best characterizes the economic achievement of the nations listed in **Source 2**?

(A) A nation's level of economic success can be tied directly to when it joined forces with other European nations economically.

(B) Those nations that did join together to eventually form the European Union in general did better than those that did not join.

(C) Those nations that joined together to eventually form the European Union all did better than those that did not join.

(D) The nations that had been part of COMECON did more poorly than those that had not.

51. Which of the following has been the greatest effect of the overall economic growth that Europe has experienced over the past half century?

(A) The welfare state has increasingly cared for the people of Europe, giving greater and greater amounts of aid to the poor across the Continent.

(B) The society has become generally wealthier, which has resulted in decreased national identities and tensions.

(C) Rising wages have allowed the vast majority of Europeans to become property owners as the class structures have generally eroded.

(D) Rising consumerism has caused many to purchase goods from all over the world, leading to environmental issues.

Questions 52 to 55 refer to the document below.

The Universal Declaration of Human Rights

Whereas the peoples of the United Nations have in the Charter reaffirmed their faith in fundamental human rights, in the dignity and worth of the human person and in the equal rights of men and women and have determined to promote social progress and better standards of life in larger freedom,

Now, Therefore THE GENERAL ASSEMBLY proclaims THIS UNIVERSAL DECLARATION OF HUMAN RIGHTS as a common standard of achievement for all peoples and all nations, to the end that every individual and every organ of society. . . .

Article 1
All human beings are born free and equal in dignity and rights. They are endowed with reason and conscience and should act towards one another in a spirit of brotherhood.

Article 2
Everyone is entitled to all the rights and freedoms set forth in this Declaration, without distinction of any kind, such as race, colour, sex, language, religion, political or other opinion, national or social origin, property, birth or other status.

Article 3
Everyone has the right to life, liberty and security of person.

Article 6
Everyone has the right to recognition everywhere as a person before the law.

Article 7
All are equal before the law and are entitled without any discrimination to equal protection of the law. All are entitled to equal protection against any discrimination in violation of this Declaration and against any incitement to such discrimination.

Article 18
Everyone has the right to freedom of thought, conscience and religion; this right includes freedom to change his religion or belief, and freedom, either alone or in community with others and in public or private, to manifest his religion or belief in teaching, practice, worship and observance.

Article 26
Everyone has the right to education. Education shall be free, at least in the elementary and fundamental stages. Elementary education shall be compulsory. Technical and professional education shall be made generally available and higher education shall be equally accessible to all on the basis of merit.

52. Which of the following is the best characterization of how the *Universal Declaration of Human Rights* was used by the different factions during the Cold War?

(A) It was used by the NATO nations to illustrate the lack of rights for those living in the Warsaw Pact nations.

(B) It was used by the Warsaw Pact nations to illustrate the lack of rights for those living in the NATO nations.

(C) It was used by both sides during the Cold War to prove that their side was more ethical than the other.

(D) Neither side used the Universal Declaration of Human Rights for propaganda purposes.

53. Which of the following trends in late twentieth-century Europe was affected most by the Declaration's references to minorities and multicultural acceptance?

(A) The collapse of communism in Eastern Europe

(B) The increasing reliance on immigrant labor

(C) The implementation of benefits in the growing welfare states

(D) Growing consumerism

54. Which of the following is the best description of how education and public services described as a right in the Declaration are treated politically in Europe at the start of the twenty-first century?

(A) The emergence of nationalist political parties has increased spending on these programs.

(B) The requirements of membership in the European Union compel higher spending on these programs.

(C) The influence of Catholic reforms after the Second Vatican Council have reduced spending on these programs.

(D) The political debate over the cost of the welfare state has threatened these programs in much of Europe.

55. Based on the Universal Declaration of Human Rights, the United Nations likely supports which of the following?

(A) Bans on immigration to Europe

(B) Expanded civil rights for gays and lesbians

(C) Barriers to trade

(D) Expanding European global power

STOP

If there is still time remaining, you may review your answers.

SECTION I

Part B: Short Answer

TIME: 40 MINUTES
NUMBER OF QUESTIONS: 3 OUT OF 4 CHOICES
PERCENTAGE OF TOTAL AP EXAM SCORE: 20%
WRITING INSTRUMENT: PEN WITH DARK BLUE OR BLACK INK

> **Directions:** Section I, Part B of this exam contains four short-answer questions. Write your responses in the corresponding boxes on the short-answer response sheets. You must answer Questions 1 and 2, but you choose to answer either Question 3 OR 4. Please indicate which question you answered on the answer sheet.
>
> Answer all parts of every question. Use complete sentences; an outline or bulleted list alone is not acceptable. You may plan your answers in your exam booklet, but no credit will be given for what is written there. Sources have been edited for the purposes of this exercise.

Use the passages below to answer all parts of the question that follows.

Source 1

Petrarch does not deserve to be praised for simply reviving the ideas of Greeks and Romans who were dead for centuries if not millennia. His idea of humanism was not his idea, but that of Socrates, Plato, and Aristotle, whose ideas were never lost, just ignored as they are in twenty-first century America. The only truly great humanist thinker of the Renaissance era was Erasmus. His Christian Humanism was a truly elegant new idea formed by combining the beauty of traditional Greco-Roman thought with Christian moral values. It this way, Erasmus was the greatest thinker of the Renaissance.

—Historian Jaw Switlick, 2008

Source 2

The Northern Renaissance was a third-rate copy of the Italian Renaissance with few new ideas and no new artistic methods, just less grand subject matter. All of the great thinkers of the Renaissance were Italians. Rafael, Donatello, Masaccio, Da Vinci, Michelangelo, etc. were all the first great thinkers to achieve new ideas in centuries of European intellectual stagnation known and the Dark Ages. The Renaissance was perhaps the greatest blossoming of thought that has ever occurred in Europe, and it was due to the genius of the Italian individual. Another Italian genius would also begin the field of modern science through his experimentation and willingness to record his observations and share them: Galileo Galilei, who ushered in the modern world, is but one example of the superior nature of the Italian Renaissance.

—Historian Eugene Cho, 1992

1. (A) Explain ONE major difference between Cho's and Switlick's interpretations of the Renaissance.

   (B) Provide ONE piece of evidence from the Renaissance that supports Switlick's interpretation (**Source 1**) and explain HOW it supports the interpretation.

   (C) Provide ONE piece of evidence from the Renaissance that supports Cho's interpretation (**Source 2**) and explain HOW it supports the interpretation.

Answer all parts of the question that follows.

2. Historians have often depicted the Cold War as a conflict between communism on one side, opposed by capitalism on the other side.

   (A) Provide TWO pieces of evidence to SUPPORT this characterization of this period and explain how they support it.

   (B) Provide ONE specific piece of evidence that UNDERMINES this characterization of this time period and explain how it undermines it.

Use the image below to answer all parts of the question that follows.

A late seventeenth-century engraving of the old observing room at the Greenwich Observatory, England. The Granger Collection, New York.

MODEL TEST 2

3. (A) Briefly explain ONE effect on the Protestant European economies during the seventeenth and eighteenth centuries due to their attitudes towards science and experimentation.

   (B) Briefly explain ONE effect on the Roman Catholic European economies during the seventeenth and eighteenth centuries due to their attitudes towards science and experimentation.

   (C) Briefly explain ONE effect on the ways approaches to knowledge in subjects outside of science changed as a result of the type of work done in the picture above.

Use the document and image given below to answer all parts of the question that follows.

Source 1

The City of Mexico is luxuriously provided with fruit, both of Spanish and native varieties: they all yield abundantly. There are excellent olive groves from which they gather quantities of eating olives. Grapes are brought in from Queretaro, and there are a few vines in the city, as well as peaches, large and small, pippins, quinces, pomegranates, oranges, limes, grapefruit, citrons, and lemons; the gardens produce in abundance all varieties of Spanish garden stuff and vegetables; the lake provides delicious fish of different sorts. [In the surrounding countryside] there are fertile fields which yield an abundance of corn, wheat, and other cereals, both native and Spanish; there is plenty of pastureland, and in consequence large cattle ranches of sheep and cows.

   —Antonio Vazquez, Carmelite Friar, *The Spread of European Plants and Animals*, 1620

Source 2

—Vincent van Gogh, Oil on Canvas, *The Potato Eaters*, 1885.

4. (A) Briefly analyze how the artwork above in Source 2 reflects artistic trends at the end of the nineteenth century.

   (B) Based on Source 1, and your knowledge of European history, briefly analyze ONE aspect of how interaction between Europe and the Americas changed the economic lives of Native Americans.

   (C) Based on Source 2 and your knowledge of European history, briefly analyze ONE aspect of how interaction between Europe and the Americas changed the economic lives of Europeans.

STOP

If there is still time remaining, you may review your answers.

SECTION II: EUROPEAN HISTORY

TOTAL TIME: 100 MINUTES
NUMBER OF QUESTIONS: 2
PERCENTAGE OF TOTAL AP EXAM SCORE: 40%
QUESTION 1: 25%
QUESTION 2: 15%
WRITING INSTRUMENT: PEN WITH DARK BLUE OR BLACK INK

> **Directions:** Section II of this exam contains three essay questions. You must respond to Question 1, the document-based question, but you must CHOOSE to answer either Questions 2, 3, or 4 for your long-essay question. No credit is given for work written on the exam itself, all responses must be written in dark blue or black ink in essay format in the answer booklet. Be sure to indicate which long-essay question you are answering on each page of the answer booklet.

Question 1 (Document–Based Question—DBQ)

TIME: 60 MINUTES
SUGGESTED READING PERIOD: 15 MINUTES
SUGGESTED WRITING TIME: 45 MINUTES

> **Directions:** Question 1 is based on the accompanying documents. The documents have been edited for the purpose of the exercise.
>   In your response you should do the following:
>
> - State a relevant thesis that directly addresses all parts of the question.
> - Support the thesis or a relevant argument with evidence from all, or all but one, of the documents.
> - Incorporate analysis of all, or all but one, of the documents into your argument.
> - Focus your analysis of each document on at least one of the following: intended audience, purpose, historical context, and/or point of view.
> - Support your argument with analysis of historical examples outside the documents.
> - Connect historical phenomena relevant to your argument to broader events or processes.
> - Synthesize the elements above into a persuasive essay that extends your argument, connects it to a different historical context, or accounts for contradictory evidence on the topic.

1. Analyze how changing reactions and responses to "Total War" reflected social, political, and economic changes in Europe during the first half of the twentieth century.

DOCUMENT 1

Source: V. Bourtzeff, Russian Socialist leader Letter to the Editor of the *London Times*, 1914.

Sir—May I be allowed to say a few words in connection with the excellent letter by my compatriot, Professor Vinogradov, which appeared in your paper today (September 14)? Professor Vinogradov is absolutely right when he says that not only is it desirable that complete unity of feeling should exist in Russian political circles, but that this unity is already an accomplished fact.

The representatives of all political parties and of all nationalities in Russia are now at one with the Government, and this war with Germany and Austria, both guided by the Kaiser, has already become a national war for Russia.

Even we, the adherents of the parties of the Extreme Left, and hitherto ardent anti militarists and pacifists, even we believe in the necessity of this war. This war is a war to protect justice and civilization. It will, we hope, be a decisive factor in our united war against war, and we hope that after it, it will at last be possible to consider seriously the question of disarmament and universal peace. There can be no doubt that victory, and decisive victory at that (personally I await this in the immediate future), will be on the side of the Allied nations—England, France, Belgium, Servia, and Russia.

The German peril, the curse which has hung over the whole world for so many decades, will be crushed, and crushed so that it will never again become a danger to the peace of the world. The peoples of the world desire peace.

To Russia this war will bring regeneration.

We are convinced that after this war there will no longer be any room for political reaction, and Russia will be associated with the existing group of cultured and civilized countries.

Source: Official Statement by French Prime Minister Aristide Briand on *Deportations from Lille*, June 30, 1916.

Not content with subjecting our people in the North to every kind of oppression, the Germans have recently treated them in the most iniquitous way.

In contempt of rules universally recognized and of their own express promises not to molest the civil population, they have taken women and girls away from their families; they have sent them off, mixed up with men, to destinations unknown, to work unknown.

The Germans decided to have recourse to compulsion. A General and a large force arrived at Lille, among others the 64th Regiment from Verdun.

On April 19th and 20th, the public were warned by proclamation to be prepared for a compulsory evacuation.

About three in the morning, troops, with fixed bayonets, barred the streets, machine guns commanded the road, against unarmed people.

Soldiers made their way into the houses. The officer pointed out the people who were to go, and, half an hour later, everybody was marched pell-mell into an adjacent factory, and from there to the station, whence the departure took place.

The victims of this brutal act displayed the greatest courage. They were heard crying 'Vive la France', and singing the Marseillaise in the cattle-trucks in which they were carried off.

It is said that the men are employed in agriculture, road-mending, the making of munitions and trench digging.

The women are employed in cooking and laundry-work for the soldiers and as substitutes for officers' servants.

For this severe work, housemaids, domestic servants and factory women have been taken by preference.

The unfortunate people, thus requisitioned, have been scattered from Seclin and Templeuve, as far as the Ardennes.

Their number is estimated at about 25,000, from the towns of Lille, Roubaix, and Tourcoing.

Source: Middle-class factory worker, Naomi Loughnan, *Munitions Work*, 1918.

We little thought when we first put on our overalls and caps and enlisted in the Munitions Army how much more inspiring our life was to be than we had dared to hope. Though we munitions workers sacrifice our ease we gain a life worth living. Our long days are filled with interest, and with the zest of doing work for our country in the grand cause of Freedom. As we handle the weapons of war we are learning great lessons of life. In the busy, noisy workshops we come face to face with every kind of class, and each one of these classes has something to learn from the others. Our muscles may be aching, and the brightness fading a little from our eyes, but our minds are expanding, our very souls are growing stronger. And excellent, too, is the discipline for our bodies, though we do not always recognize this. . . .

The day is long, the atmosphere is breathed and rebreathed, and the oil smells. Our hands are black with warm, thick oozings from the machines, which coat the work and, incidentally, the workers. We regard our horrible, be-grimed members [limbs] with disgust and secret pride.

Whatever sacrifice we make of wearied bodies, brains dulled by interminable night-shifts, of roughened hands, and faces robbed of their soft curves, it is, after all, so small a thing. We live in safety, we have shelter, and food whenever necessary, and we are even earning quite a lot of money. What is ours beside the great sacrifice? Men in their prime, on the verge of ambition realized, surrounded by the benefits won by their earlier struggles, are offering up their very lives. And those boys with Life, all glorious and untried, spread before them at their feet, are turning a smiling face to Death.

Source: Winston Churchill, British Prime Minister, *Letter to the Minister of Food*, July 4, 1941.

It is always difficult to hold the balance between the need for increasing total food supplies and the need to maintain a fair distribution. We should not be too hard on the private individual who increases his supplies by his own productive efforts.

It is satisfactory that the meat prospects are improving, and I hope that pressure on the United States to increase her pork output will soon enable us to raise the ration without risk of having subsequently to reduce it.

We do not wish to create a grievance among farmers by compelling them to slaughter beasts which they can fatten without imported feeding stuffs; on the other hand of course the country cannot go hungry because farmers do not choose to bring their beasts to market.

It will no doubt be possible to arrange with the Minister of Agriculture, perhaps by a carefully worked out price policy, a scheme which will keep the meat supply as constant as possible having regard to seasonal factors.

Source: Soviet propaganda poster from 1942.

"Follow This Worker's Example Produce More for the Front."

Second World War: Russian Poster, 1942.

Source: Joseph Stalin, Soviet Leader, *Order of the Day Number 55*, February 1942.

The enemy is still strong. He will exert his last forces in order to attain success. And the more he suffers defeat, the more brutal he will become. Therefore it is essential that in our country the training of reserves in aid of the front should not be relaxed for a moment. It is essential that ever-new military units should go to the front to forge victory over the bestial enemy. It is essential that our industry, particularly our war industry, should work with redoubled energy. It is essential that with every day the front should receive ever more tanks, planes, guns, mortars, machine-guns, rifles, automatic rifles, and ammunition.

Herein lies one of the basic sources of the strength and power of the Red Army.

But the strength of the Red Army does not consist only in this. The strength of the Red Army rests, above all, in the fact that it is waging, not a predatory, not an imperialist war, but a patriotic war, a war of liberation, a just war. The Red Army's task is to liberate our Soviet territory from the German invaders; to liberate from the yoke of the German invaders the citizens of our villages and towns who were free and lived like human beings before the war, but are now oppressed and suffer pillage, ruin and famine; and finally, to liberate our women from that disgrace and outrage to which they are subjected by the German-fascist monsters. What could be more noble, more lofty, than such a task? Not one German soldier can say that he is waging a just war, because he cannot fail to see that he is forced to fight for the despoliation and oppression of other peoples. The German soldier has no such lofty and noble aim in the war which could inspire him and of which he could be proud. But, in contrast, any Red Army man can say with pride that he is waging a just war, a war for liberation, a war for the freedom and independence of his Motherland. The Red Army does have a noble and lofty aim in the war which inspires it to great exploits. It is precisely this that explains why the patriotic war brings forth among us thousands of heroes and heroines ready to go to their death for the sake of the liberty of their Motherland.

Source: Charter of the United Nations, 1945.

WE THE PEOPLES OF THE UNITED NATIONS DETERMINED

- to save succeeding generations from the scourge of war, which twice in our lifetime has brought untold sorrow to mankind, and
- to reaffirm faith in fundamental human rights, in the dignity and worth of the human person, in the equal rights of men and women and of nations large and small, and
- to establish conditions under which justice and respect for the obligations arising from treaties and other sources of international law can be maintained, and
- to promote social progress and better standards of life in larger freedom,

AND FOR THESE ENDS

- to practice tolerance and live together in peace with one another as good neighbors, and
- to unite our strength to maintain international peace and security, and
- to ensure, by the acceptance of principles and the institution of methods, that armed force shall not be used, save in the common interest, and
- to employ international machinery for the promotion of the economic and social advancement of all peoples,

HAVE RESOLVED TO COMBINE OUR EFFORTS TO ACCOMPLISH THESE AIMS:

- to maintain international peace and security, and to that end: to take effective collective measures for the prevention and removal of threats to the peace, . . .
- to develop friendly relations among nations based upon respect,
- to achieve international co-operation in solving international problems of an economic, social, cultural, or humanitarian character, and in promoting and encouraging respect for human rights and for fundamental freedoms for all without distinction as to race, sex, language, or religion; and
- to be a center for harmonizing the actions of nations in the attainment of these common ends.

Question 2, Question 3, or Question 4

SUGGESTED WRITING TIME: 35 MINUTES

Directions: Choose EITHER Question 2, Question 3, or Question 4.

In your response you should:

- State a relevant thesis that directly addresses all parts of the question;
- Support your argument with evidence, using specific examples;
- Synthesize the elements above into a persuasive essay that extends your argument, connects it to a different historical context, or connects it to a different category of analysis.

---

2. Analyze the ways in which the opening of Atlantic trade led to or resulted from a shift in social, economic, and political power from the Mediterranean Basin to Western Europe.

3. Analyze the ways in which the public-health movement and urban planning led to or resulted from a shift in social, political, and economic power at the end of the nineteenth century.

4. Analyze the causes of the changing roles and rights of European women from 1900–2000.

ONLINE

Want more test-taking practice?

Visit *barronsbooks.com/AP/ap-european-hist/* to access three additional practice tests or scan the QR code below.

*Be sure to have your copy of *AP European History*, 9th edition on hand to complete the registration process.

STOP

If there is still time remaining, you may review your answers.

SCORING AND ANSWER EXPLANATIONS

The AP European History exam is composed of four parts grouped into two sections. The multiple-choice test is scored with one point given for each correct answer.

- *There is no penalty for guessing*, so you should answer every question on the exam.
- The long essay is given a score from 0 to 6.
- The Document-Based Question (DBQ) is scored from 0 to 7.

To attain your final AP score on this exam, the following method should be used:

Multiple-Choice Score $\times$ 1.091 = _____

$+$

Short-Answer Score $\times$ 3.334 = _____

$+$

DBQ Score $\times$ 5.357 = _____

$+$

FRQ Score $\times$ 3.75 = _____

Total of all above scores is composite score = _____(round your score)

Score Range	AP Score
104–150	5
91–103	4
79–91	3
69–78	2
0–69	1

To get a final score for the exam, compare your composite score to the chart directly above.

Following are four separate guides to scoring each section of this exam. Once you have scored each piece of the exam, place the score on the appropriate line above. When you are done, do the computations to get your final score. Remember that this test is designed to mimic the AP exam, but you will not take it in the same conditions that you will during the real test, and it is not scored by professionals, who are reading 1,000 or more essays daily. While this test is a good predictor of success, it is only as good as the student using it, so do not stop studying just because you got a good score here.

Scoring Guide for the Multiple-Choice Section

Directions: Use the guide below to check your answers to the multiple-choice questions. There is an answer key at the end of this section with all of the answers, but you are advised not to use it other than to score your exam.

SPECIAL NOTE

There is a lot of valuable information in the explanations for the multiple-choice questions, so make certain to read the explanations for ALL responses for every question that gave you any trouble!

1. **(D)**

   (A) is wrong because the spread of humanist ideas happened in bursts and stops throughout European history.

   (B) is wrong because humanism was at its height in the early 1500s with Erasmus just reaching his most productive period.

   (C) is wrong because the Roman Catholic Church's leaders embraced humanism, as this painting in the papal residences illustrates.

   (D) is CORRECT because humanists, such as Petrarch in Italy and Erasmus in Rotterdam, were already writing major humanist works by the time this painting was finished.

2. **(C)**

   (A) is wrong because sfumato cannot be used on frescos and is not present.

   (B) is wrong because chiaroscuro cannot be used on frescos and is not present.

   (C) is CORRECT because perspective, humanist subject matter, and attention to anatomical detail are all present characteristics of Renaissance Art.

   (D) is wrong because frescos have been used in European art since the Greek era.

3. **(A)**

   (A) is CORRECT because the Renaissance saw people believe that great public works of art demonstrated power and prestige.

   (B) is wrong because reducing unemployment was NOT seen as a civic duty at the time.

   (C) is wrong because they had other motives concerned with power and prestige that overrode the desire for beauty.

   (D) is wrong because the idea of getting wisdom from the Greeks was but a small part of what was going on, and misses the bigger picture.

4. **(D)**

   (A) is wrong because the document is more about religion than about mercantilism or profit.

   (B) is wrong because the document is more about religion than about gold and profit.

   (C) is wrong because the personal glory of captains is not mentioned in the document.

   (D) is CORRECT because the document clearly displays religious motivations for exploration.

5. **(A)**

(A) is CORRECT because the Europeans did not create colonies in the interior of Africa until the nineteenth century.

(B) is wrong because the Columbian exchange was a result of European overseas exploration.

(C) is wrong because vast trade networks were created as a result of European overseas exploration.

(D) is wrong because the slave trade with Africa resulted from European overseas exploration.

6. **(C)**

(A) is wrong because those technologies got them to the New World, but did not help them once there.

(B) is wrong because those technologies got them to the New World, but did not help them once there.

(C) is CORRECT because gunpowder and horses allowed the Europeans to conquer the natives with relative ease.

(D) is wrong because those technologies got them to the New World, but did not help them once there.

7. **(B)**

(A) is wrong because while Calvin and some other Protestants believed this, the document states nothing to support that idea.

(B) is CORRECT because the part about corruption at the start of this excerpt alludes to the corruption of the Roman Catholic Church.

(C) is wrong because while Luther and some other Protestants practiced this, the document states nothing to support that idea.

(D) is wrong because the idea of salvation through faith alone belongs to Martin Luther and is contradicted by the writings of Calvin supplied.

8. **(A)**

(A) is CORRECT because Calvinists indeed felt the religious organization supersedes all authority of the state.

(B) is wrong because Lutherans believed in consubstantiation while Calvinists believed the Eucharist was celebrated only to symbolize, not emulate, Christ.

(C) is wrong because Calvinists, or Huguenots, in France also used the Reformation for their political advantage to gain power and influence in France.

(D) is wrong because Lutherans chose to keep only communion, baptism, and absolution as the sacraments.

9. **(A)**

(A) is CORRECT because the shaded areas do represent the Habsburg lands during the sixteenth century, including Spain, Austria, the 17 provinces of the Netherlands as one nation, and parts of Italy.

(B) is wrong because the Germanic states would all be included, as would all of northern Italy if the map displayed the combatants of the Thirty Years' War.

(C) is wrong because most of the shaded area was Roman Catholic and still is.

(D) is wrong because Russia, Austria, and France would be shaded along with Prussia if this were a map of the Holy Alliance.

10. **(D)**

(A) is wrong because most of the areas shaded were Roman Catholic under the Habsburgs, who fought wars to preserve the religion there, such as the invasion of the Dutch and the Spanish Armada campaign.

(B) is wrong because Austria, Milan, and southern Italy would definitely not be shaded, as they lost significant power as a result of transatlantic trade.

(C) is wrong because most of the areas shaded remained Catholic as Habsburg lands, with only the Dutch taking advantage of this religious conflict.

(D) is CORRECT because most of the areas shaded remained Catholic as Habsburg lands and the Habsburgs fought numerous wars to ensure this including the Thirty Years' War that re-Catholicized the Bohemians and other areas such as modern Belgium.

11. **(B)**

THE KEY TO THIS QUESTION is the size of the huge Ottoman Empire and the unified Provinces of the Netherlands that tell you the place in time.

(A) is wrong because this map depicts the mid- to late sixteenth century, and a century later Germany and Italy would still not be unified until 1871.

(B) is CORRECT because this map depicts the mid- to late sixteenth century and during the late seventeenth century the Ottoman Empire began to decline as first the Austrians, then the Russians began to gain control in Eastern Europe.

(C) is wrong because France would begin to expand under Louis XIII and Richelieu and expand further under Louis XIV by the time a century had passed from the time depicted above.

(D) is wrong because Greece would remain under Ottoman control until the start of the nineteenth century more than a century after the time depicted on this map.

12. **(A)**

(A) is CORRECT because Copernicus wrote his *On the Revolutions of the Heavenly Spheres*, which opened up Europe to considering a heliocentric universe.

(B) is wrong because Kepler wrote the laws of planetary motion, but these writings seem more a reaction to Copernicus.

(C) is wrong because Galileo supported the Copernican theory in his *Dialogue Concerning the Two Chief World Systems*.

(D) is wrong because Pilsudski was important in Poland after the First World War.

13. **(D)**

(A) is wrong because the revolutions of Jupiter's moons was world-view changing, but not nearly as much as its implication that Earth is but one tiny planet in an infinite universe or even multiverse.

(B) is wrong because Earth's removal from the center of the universe was world-view changing, but not nearly as much as its implication that Earth is but one tiny planet in an infinite universe or even multiverse.

(C) is wrong because God's removal from the physical heavens above our heads to a metaphysical space did change Europe's world view, but not nearly as much as the fact that Earth is but one tiny planet in an infinite universe or even multiverse.

(D) is CORRECT because that realization is still affecting the development of all human society today.

14. **(A)**

(A) is CORRECT because humanism was an educational program based upon the ancient Greeks and Romans, such as Aristotle, and Galileo's observations and conclusions contradicted those of Aristotle and other Greeks.

(B) is wrong because the idea of removing Earth from the center of the universe did not conflict with the movement away from religion.

(C) is wrong because the idea of individualism and uniqueness and pursuit of excellence did not conflict with the movement away from religion.

(D) is wrong because the idea of arête or pursuit of excellence did not conflict with the movement away from religion.

15. **(C)**

(A) is wrong because the standard of living did not rise across Europe at that time, and their thought affected very few people for a long time.

(B) is wrong because Galileo actually went against ancient Greek thought in many areas in this writing.

(C) is CORRECT because Galileo is clearly using experimentation to help shift the European world view from the Aristotelian to the Copernican one.

(D) is wrong because it refuted Aristotle.

16. **(B)**

(A) is wrong because the Black Plague's elimination would lead to greater famine because there would be more mouths to feed.

(B) is CORRECT because the Agricultural Revolution increased food production, decreased hunger, and increased health.

(C) is wrong because the putting out system did not improve agricultural production in and of itself.

(D) is wrong because populations rose during the eighteenth century.

17. **(C)**

(A) is wrong because low agricultural production added to the problems with hunger.

(B) is wrong because adverse weather hurt crop production during this era, contributing to hunger problems.

(C) is CORRECT because low taxes would have stimulated the economy and increased food production, yet they paid relatively high taxes.

(D) is wrong because poor transportation led to poor harvests and distributions of those harvests further leading to hunger problems.

18. **(D)**

(A) is wrong because the Enlightenment occurred during the eighteenth century.

(B) is wrong because the divine right theory did not immediately improve crop yields.

(C) is wrong because existentialism is not conceived of until the late nineteenth century.

(D) is CORRECT because the Scientific Revolution led to scientific experimentation in farming that let to crop rotation, advanced breeding, fertilization of crops, and other innovations that improved agricultural production by the end of the seventeenth century.

19. **(B)**

(A) is wrong because the tone of this writing is critical of the king and, as a noble, he resents the subjugation of the nobility.

(B) is CORRECT because the duke is displaying his bias against the king for subjugating the nobility.

(C) is wrong because the duke clearly thinks that the king is overreaching his power.

(D) is wrong because the duke seems to be criticizing the nobility's subjugation through diversion.

20. **(C)**

(A) is wrong because, although Martinet trained the military well, Colbert, the finance minister, redesigned the finances of France based upon mercantilist theories.

(B) is wrong because, although Mazarin was his regent, Louis XIV dismissed him after the Fronde, and Colbert, the finance minister, redesigned the finances of France based upon mercantilist theories.

(C) is CORRECT because Colbert, the finance minister, redesigned the finances of France based upon mercantilist theories.

(D) is wrong because the Duke of Burgundy was not a major advisor to the king.

21. **(D)**

(A) is wrong because Louis XIV did not regret the subjugation of the nobility and, in fact, it made him a model for other monarchs.

(B) is wrong because although he delighted in ceremony, he was a strong leader who led France into an era of prestige.

(C) is wrong because the use of bureaucrats to perform the duties of state was beneficial to Louis XIV and France.

(D) is CORRECT because his wars were very costly, leaving the country in debt and detracting from his other successes.

22. **(A)**

(A) is CORRECT because the document does not address the debts of France.

(B) is wrong because the document explains the problems with the legal system.

(C) is wrong because the document refers to the ideals of the Enlightenment as the basis for what laws should be.

(D) is wrong because the document refers to problems with the equity.

23. **(B)**

(A) is wrong because the peasants cared more about their rents and dues than about the constitutional monarchy.

(B) is CORRECT because the peasants cared more about their rents and dues than about anything else.

(C) is wrong because the peasants cared more about their rents and dues than about their level of political participation.

(D) is wrong because the peasants did not really approve of the change in religion.

24. **(C)**

(A) is wrong because huge armies were needed to fight against the monarchies of Europe.

(B) is wrong because fixing wages and prices made it easier to plan for the defense of France.

(C) is CORRECT because this distracted many from their support of the revolution, as they were torn between their faith and their nation.

(D) is wrong because the promotion of soldiers based upon merit supported revolutionary ideals.

25. **(D)**

(A) is wrong because the *philosophes*, and Voltaire in particular, believed in religious toleration, not imposing any religion on anyone.

(B) is wrong because Voltaire was a proponent of religious toleration.

(C) is wrong because they did support skepticism and believed it was a good way to analyze data.

(D) is CORRECT because this passage clearly supports religious toleration.

26. **(B)**

(A) is wrong because although those concepts did influence this era, they are not referenced in that sentence.

(B) is CORRECT because the concept that the Church should stop its discrimination against, and conversion of, peoples of different faiths around the world came from seeing the virtues of other cultures and methods of living and interpreting the world.

(C) is wrong because although those concepts did influence this era, they are not referenced in that sentence.

(D) is wrong because, although those concepts did influence this era, they are not directly referenced in that sentence.

27. **(B)**

(A) is wrong because Rousseau wrote about *The Social Contract* and began the Romantic movement by questioning pure Reason.

(B) is CORRECT because Montesquieu wrote about the separation of powers in government.

(C) is wrong because Wollstonecraft was an early feminist who defended the French Revolution.

(D) is wrong because Adam Smith wrote about economics, not government.

28. **(B)**

(A) is wrong because, while many were accomplished scientists, that idea is not being expressed here.

(B) is CORRECT because this excerpt is from a pamphlet.

(C) is wrong because only a very few thinkers of this era were atheists; Paine clearly is not.

(D) is wrong because, while many did believe this at the time, that idea is not being expressed here.

29. **(B)**

(A) is wrong because the document cites the idea of building the national economy by reducing imports, which is mercantilism, while pursuit of capitalism would mean that they were not concerned with the government.

(B) is CORRECT because the document cites the idea of building the national economy by reducing imports, which is mercantilism.

(C) is wrong because industrialization is not an economic theory.

(D) is wrong because bullionism was a form of mercantilism.

30. **(D)**

(A) is wrong because urbanization was an issue, but not as much so as the growing class consciousness and changing way of life.

(B) is wrong because population growth is not discussed in this document and was not a part of the problems cited within it.

(C) is wrong because Parliament's support of industrialization was not as much a motivator for the lower classes as was their growing class consciousness brought on by socio-economic changes.

(D) is CORRECT because their growing class consciousness was brought on by socio-economic changes that are evident in the document.

31. **(B)**

(A) is wrong because the governments did pass reform bills like the Factory Act of 1833 and the Mines Act of 1842.

(B) is CORRECT because most of the reforms made before 1850 focused on work hours and separating genders at work.

(C) is wrong because the song does not mention or allude to Parliament.

(D) is wrong because the national health systems were not created until the end of the nineteenth century, or later in some places.

32. **(D)**

(A) is wrong because there was a domination of industry in Eastern Europe by nobility and aristocrats.

(B) is wrong because urbanization of society was one of the most important results of the Industrial Revolution.

(C) is wrong because class identity emerged and was supported by societal experiences.

(D) is CORRECT because social inequality emerged with wealthy factory owners contrasted with impoverished workers.

33. **(B)**

(A) is wrong because Abbott is praising Napoleon for being a cultured genius, and secret police are not very enlightened.

(B) is CORRECT because he is impressed with Napoleon's intelligence and worldliness, which were most evident in his domestic reforms such as the Napoleonic Code.

(C) is wrong because someone impressed by enlightened thinking would not be impressed by suppressing the rights of women.

(D) is wrong because although there is much to praise in the genius of his military tactics, Abbott is more impressed by the wide breadth of Napoleon's knowledge, which is most evident in his domestic reforms.

34. **(C)**

(A) is wrong because a universal currency was not imposed.

(B) is wrong because the suppression of guerrilla factions hurt the reputation of Napoleon internationally.

(C) is CORRECT because the Old Order (feudalism and manorialism) was dismantled by decree in all areas he conquered, inspiring a shift of power from the landowning aristocracy to the middle classes and promising all classes social and economic justice, which appealed to all Europeans.

(D) is wrong because French was in decline as an international language because of the rise of English.

35. **(A)**

(A) is CORRECT because the failed conquest of Haiti was in no way enlightened.

(B) is wrong because the Code Napoleon was indeed an enlightened action.

(C) is wrong because promoting soldiers and government workers based upon their merits only, was indeed an enlightened action.

(D) is wrong because although they were not great ideas, they did show the particular genius of Napoleon, and the invasion of Haiti is much more hypocritical for someone spreading freedom in Europe.

36. **(A)**

(A) is CORRECT because Metternich was displaying fears about the impact of spreading liberalism and revolution caused by those ideas, and he expresses plans to suppress them.

(B) is wrong because Metternich had already addressed this issue at the Congress of Vienna five years earlier and was no longer in fear of Napoleon or his impact.

(C) is wrong because Metternich is in favor of increasing monarchical power and preserving it.

(D) is wrong because the economic cycle is not addressed in this document, and fear of economic cycles was not a major issue in Europe until later in the nineteenth century.

37. **(C)**

(A) is wrong because empires were strong in Europe until after the First World War, 1914–1918.

(B) is wrong because the Holy Alliance was more of a formality than a real alliance, and it had very little power over European affairs.

(C) is CORRECT because the Concert of Europe was created as a way to promote unity and was the most important result of the Congress of Vienna.

(D) is wrong because the Congress of Vienna did nothing to address secret societies.

38. **(B)**

(A) is wrong because he did not want to stop all knowledge, just political and economic change.

(B) is CORRECT because the overall goal of conservatism at that time was to prevent the political and economic revolutions from occurring on the Continent the way they had in England.

(C) is wrong because suppressing secret societies harmed democracy rather than helped it.

(D) is wrong because at the time both political and economic change were considered by conservatives as worth stopping.

39. **(C)**

(A) is wrong because Fourier was not advocating the greatest good for the greatest number, but for a perfect society, which makes him an utopian socialist.

(B) is wrong because Fourier was not advocating for the government to leave business alone, but for a perfect society, which makes him a utopian socialist.

(C) is CORRECT because he argued in favor of creating a perfect society.

(D) is wrong because Fourier did not wish to eliminate or nationalize all private property.

40. **(B)**

(A) is wrong because Germany did not get far in creating a government in 1848 before the revolution ended.

(B) is CORRECT because France was led for a short while by Louis Blanc, who created national workshops according to Fourier's ideas.

(C) is wrong because 1848 did not affect Great Britain as it was already an industrialized democracy.

(D) is wrong because, from 1815 to 1848, Austria was run by Metternich, the prototype conservative, and he detested socialism in all forms.

41. **(D)**

(A) is wrong because Luddites wanted to smash machines and destroy the order, not join it by voting.

(B) is wrong because liberals were more moderate at this time and did not believe in universal male suffrage.

(C) is wrong because Benthamites wanted the greatest good for the greatest number while Chartists wanted universal male suffrage according to their Charter.

(D) is CORRECT because Benthamites wanted the greatest good for the greatest number.

42. **(D)**

(A) is wrong because, as industrialization began in Germany, many skilled workers lost their positions as a result of mechanization and because the illustration depicts a middle-class family.

(B) is wrong because states did not implement social welfare policies until the late nineteenth and early twentieth centuries.

(C) is wrong because in the years 1848 to 1849 the deputies in the Frankfurt Parliament failed to create a constitution for a united Germany.

(D) is CORRECT because the quarter century of revolutionary and Napoleonic wars in central Europe gave economic development a setback, which was only reversed by the return of stability after the Congress of Vienna.

43. **(C)**

(A) is wrong because the Revolutions of 1848 focused primarily on liberal and national political change; women participated, often on behalf of their class, but did not organize specifically for the gender freedom warned against in the cartoon.

(B) This option is incorrect. The cartoon satirizes the notion that the proper place of men is a domestic one, suggesting that his role reversal leads to social chaos.

(C) is CORRECT because, through its caption, the cartoon demonstrates a female reaction to male anxieties over the prospect of women becoming more engaged in political life.

(D) is wrong because, though companionate marriage patterns were developing in the nineteenth century, the primary decision-making role in families remained male-dominated.

44. **(B)**

(A) is wrong because socialist notions of family and child rearing did not take strong hold in Europe, despite being briefly embraced by leaders of the Russian Revolution.

(B) is CORRECT because as working-class families gained higher wages and had access to more leisure opportunities because of government reforms, they began to adopt similar child-rearing patterns and a more gendered division of labor.

(C) is wrong because women's entrance into the paid workforce in large numbers would not occur until the First World War.

(D) is wrong because the professional and academic journals of the time recommended fathers becoming more involved in child rearing.

45. **(D)**

(A) is wrong because, although there were still prosperous farmers, the majority of those were the previously wealthy landowners, and nearly all former serfs struggled working the new communal system.

(B) is wrong because the Zemstvovs' power was short-lived, and a national legislature did not come about until 1906, after the 1905 Revolution had forced the hand of Czar Nicholas II.

(C) is wrong because the wealthy landowning elite, although suspicious of the recent liberal reforms, were left in an economic condition vastly superior to that of former serfs.

(D) is CORRECT because the least-desired land was parceled to the serfs, and they owed large financial obligations, crippling them and often their children with debt.

46. **(A)**

(A) is CORRECT because Russian military and domestic ineptitude were exposed in this inglorious defeat, which convinced the new czar and his advisors that immediate, major reforms were needed.

(B) is wrong because serfdom was abolished by Napoleon in Prussia in 1807 and then in Austria as a result of the 1848 revolution.

(C) is wrong because the Decembrist Revolt occurred in 1825 and inaugurated the tenure of Nicholas I, one of Russia's most conservative czars.

(D) is wrong because the Trans-Siberian Railroad would not commence until thirty years later, in 1891, ten years after the czar's assassination.

47. **(C)**

(A) is wrong because food production increased but was offset by population increase, while the agricultural sacrifice for industrial glory was part of Stalin's five-year plan in the 1930s.

(B) is wrong because agricultural output did not plummet, and Stolypin's reforms improved the economic viability of only a fraction of peasant farmers.

(C) is CORRECT because the financial burden owed by former serfs limited their mobility and mostly kept them in debt, while conservative landowner elites felt the czar's administration had become overly radical.

(D) is wrong because many former serfs were financially limited, and their debts kept them from being able to seek employment in cities, thus preventing large numbers of them from relocating from their farms.

48. **(C)**

(A) is wrong because the fear of revolt encouraged leaders across the world to agree to this treaty.

(B) is wrong because the other tool was sorely needed to prevent war, as Germany rearmed and the rest of Europe practiced appeasement.

(C) is CORRECT because German leadership was not trying to expand Germany until after Adolf Hitler took office in 1933.

(D) is wrong because Keynes's work influenced many leaders and citizens to want to be easier on Germany and, thus, appeasement was put into effect.

49. **(C)**

(A) is wrong because the Second World War made this choice impossible.

(B) is wrong because this response ignores issues like Yugoslavia in the 1990s and Ukraine today.

(C) is CORRECT because whenever "civilized" Europeans are threatened, they seem to turn quickly to violence, as happened recently in Ukraine.

(D) is wrong because there is still fighting in Europe, right now, in Ukraine.

50. **(B)**

(A) is wrong because Belgium did more poorly than Poland or the United Kingdom, while Poland did better than any other nation and joined later than most.

(B) is CORRECT because that trend is true, with Russia and Ukraine doing worse than the EU nations.

(C) is wrong because Greece did worse than Russia or the Ukraine.

(D) is wrong because Poland did the second best of all and it was a COMECON nation.

51. **(D)**

(A) is wrong because with the fall of communism and the rise of conservatism in more recent years, the welfare state has been reduced across Europe, leading to a greater gap between the rich and poor, especially in Eastern Europe.

(B) is wrong because nationalism and national tensions have grown in Europe at the end of the twentieth century and into the twenty-first, as evidenced by the breakup of the former Yugoslavia and the issues in Ukraine in 2014–2015.

(C) is wrong because most Europeans do not own property, but rent their homes and always have done so.

(D) is CORRECT because rising GDP is a clear indicator of higher consumption, which has occurred mostly as a result of the rising consumerism at the end of the twentieth century.

52. **(C)**

(A) is wrong because it was used by both sides to make their side look better during the Cold War.

(B) is wrong because it was used by both sides to make their side look better during the Cold War.

(C) is CORRECT because it was used by both sides to make their side look better during the Cold War.

(D) is wrong because it was used by both sides to make their side look better during the Cold War.

53. **(B)**

(A) is wrong because the fall of communism did not really affect the racial composition of the Continent.

(B) is CORRECT because many of the guest workers who came to Europe as invited guests in the 1950s and 1960s settled permanently, but have been denied full citizenship rights, which the Green Party wants for them.

(C) is wrong because the benefits of the welfare state are not truly affected by racial discrimination.

(D) is wrong because while the economic miracle shook Europe and consumerism rose, none of this was based upon race or immigrant status.

54. **(D)**

(A) is wrong because nationalist parties throughout Europe at the start of the twenty-first century were against education as a right.

(B) is wrong because the EU does not have such requirements.

(C) is wrong because the Declaration was secular and did not ally with any religion, and the Catholic Church supported spending on such programs.

(D) is CORRECT because the political debate over the welfare state is tearing Europe apart as disagreement over austerity measures for Greece and the proper level of welfare spending are dominated by a rising conflict between liberals and conservatives in the modern sense of the terms.

55. **(B)**

(A) is wrong because the Declaration supports rights of immigrants.

(B) is CORRECT because the Declaration supports equal rights for all.

(C) is wrong because the Declaration of Human Rights was issued by the United Nations, which supports free trade.

(D) is wrong because the Declaration of Human Rights is against any nation dominating another.

Multiple-Choice Quick Scoring Guide

For your convenience, this chart was created to allow you to quickly score the multiple-choice section. Please read the explanations on the previous pages for any and all questions that confused you.

1.	**D**	21.	**D**	41.	**D**
2.	**C**	22.	**A**	42.	**D**
3.	**A**	23.	**B**	43.	**C**
4.	**D**	24.	**C**	44.	**B**
5.	**A**	25.	**D**	45.	**D**
6.	**C**	26.	**B**	46.	**A**
7.	**B**	27.	**B**	47.	**C**
8.	**A**	28.	**B**	48.	**C**
9.	**A**	29.	**B**	49.	**C**
10.	**D**	30.	**D**	50.	**B**
11.	**B**	31.	**B**	51.	**D**
12.	**A**	32.	**D**	52.	**C**
13.	**D**	33.	**B**	53.	**B**
14.	**A**	34.	**C**	54.	**D**
15.	**C**	35.	**A**	55.	**B**
16.	**B**	36.	**A**		
17.	**C**	37.	**C**		
18.	**D**	38.	**B**		
19.	**B**	39.	**C**		
20.	**C**	40.	**B**		

Scoring Guide for the Short-Answer Section

Short Answers are very straightforward. Either you did or did not get one point for each of the points available. Each question is worth up to 3 points for a total of 0–9 points available in this section worth 20% of the exam score.

1. **0–3 points (1 point for each letter, A, B, and C)**

    (A) ONE point will be given for pointing out a significant difference between the historians' interpretations of the Renaissance. Some examples of evidence include: Cho is more impressed by the Italians and Switlick by the Northern Europeans; Switlick criticizes Petrarch and praises Erasmus; Cho praises the artists more; Cho brings in science, etc.

    (B) ONE point will be given for a good answer that explains HOW one piece of evidence to support Switlick's argument that the Northern Renaissance is superior to that of the Italian Renaissance. Evidence to support the claim include: the Dutch Golden Age, Dürer, Shakespeare, Vermeer, Rembrandt, Brueghel, van Eyck, and the rise in Western European economic and political dominance.

    (C) ONE point will be given for an explanation of HOW one piece of evidence supports Cho's argument that the Italian Renaissance was the height of the Renaissance. Evidence to support this can include: mastery of Italian artists in memory of the world (Mona Lisa, etc.), the spread of Italian Renaissance ideas all over the world, the success of humanism and secularism absent from the Northern Renaissance, the importance of Galileo to Newton and others since.

2. **0–3 points (2 points for A and 1 point for B)**

    (A) ONE point will be given for EACH of TWO explanations of HOW pieces of evidence support the argument that the Cold War was a conflict between communism and capitalism, such as: Marxist propaganda from the soviets and capitalist propaganda from NATO nations; examination of property in both systems or nations; a look at who was aided by which side around the world during the Cold War; Mao's Little Red Book; Brezhnev Doctrine; Truman Doctrine; Iron Curtain speech; Marshall Plan funds use; IMF and World Bank rules, etc.

    (B) ONE point will be given for an explanation of HOW one piece of evidence undermines the argument that the Cold War was a conflict between communism and capitalism, such as: It was a power struggle; NATO is not capitalist, and the U.S.S.R. is not really communist; Scandinavian Compromise; still chilly relations 25 years after Cold War ended, etc.

3. **0–3 points (2 points for A and 1 point for B)**

    (A) ONE point will be given for explaining that the growth of science led to better machines and technology particularly for exploration, but eventually for weaponry and everything else, which was utilized by Protestant nations, giving them an advantage over the Catholic nations, such as Spain, that stayed away from science due to the Roman Catholic Church's conflict with Galileo and Copernicus.

(B) ONE point will be given for explaining that the growth of science led to better machines and technology, particularly for exploration for Protestants ONLY, giving them an advantage over the Catholic nations, such as Spain, that stayed away from science due to the Roman Catholic Church's conflict with Galileo and Copernicus; thus the Spanish and other Catholic nations, such as Austria, saw an economic decline.

(C) ONE point will be given for explaining that discoveries like those seen in the picture led to Newton's view of the universe changing how all knowledge was approached to allow Europeans to believe they could solve all social and legal problems through the use of reason and experimentation.

4. **0–3 points (1 point for each letter, A, B, and C)**

(A) ONE point will be given for an analysis of how Vincent van Gogh's image is typical of the trends of the late nineteenth century such as, but not limited to: it shows common people in daily pursuits, typifying realism; it shows the sympathy for the common man for the plight of the poor typical of the time; the artwork was a mass-produced lithograph indicating that more people consumed art at the time; it has a somber mood that fits the time.

(B) ONE point will be awarded for identifying one way natives were affected by transatlantic trade including, but not limited to: enslaved; depopulated; land stolen; Christianized; got horses, cows, goats, and many vegetables, epidemics, too; lost wealth and power.

(C) ONE point will be awarded for explaining impact on Europeans including, but not limited to: new foods like the potato and corn, new place to emigrate to, vast income comes to Europe, inflation, new immigrants to and from Europe, tobacco, racism, ability to own land in the New World, and reinforcement of their racism.

Scoring Guide for the Essay Section

The Document-Based Question (DBQ)

The DBQ emphasizes your ability to analyze and synthesize historical evidence, including textual, quantitative, or visual materials. The question also requires you to formulate a thesis and support it with relevant evidence. The seven documents accompanying each DBQ may vary in length, type, and content, but they will allow you to illustrate complexities and interactions within the material and to utilize a broad spectrum of historical skills.

The document-based question will typically require you to relate the documents to a historical period or theme and, thus, to focus on major periods and issues, in this way assessing your ability to incorporate outside knowledge related to the question but beyond the specifics of the documents. This ability to place the documents in the historical context in which they were produced is essential for your success.

Scoring Your DBQ

Maximum Possible Points: 7

A. THESIS AND ARGUMENT DEVELOPMENT (0–1 total points)

TARGETED SKILL—Argumentation

1 point: Presents a thesis that makes a historically defensible claim and responds to all parts of the question. The thesis must consist of one or more sentences located in one place, either in the introduction or the conclusion.

Student presents a thesis that directly addresses all parts of the question and makes a historically defensible claim. The thesis must do more than restate the question.

> **Acceptable Thesis:** "As the First World War began, rampant nationalism led many to embrace total war as the best means to forward their national agendas, yet some saw the dangers to civilians posed by total war as the concept gained governmental support through its success in both world wars, yet when the United Nations was formed in 1945, the international conflict over appropriate levels of governmental involvement in the economic lives of their citizens emerged into the Cold War." (This thesis is acceptable because it is specific in its assessment of how the concept of total war was viewed and it puts it into historical perspective with some qualification and contradiction.)

> **Unacceptable Theses:**

- "During the first half of the twentieth century views on total war changed as the world changed and people became more controlled by their governments." (This is unacceptable because it does not state any specific changes or any specific views on total war.)

- "Those who were more conservative or radical were always more in favor of total war than those who were less extreme as can be seen through changes over time." (This is unacceptable because even though it states views, it does not state specific social, political, or economic changes.)

B. CONTEXTUALIZATION (0–1 total points)

1 point: The essay must describe a broader historical context immediately relevant to the question.

> **Acceptable Contextualization:** "As the Cold War began, the concept of total war gave way to the use of more limited forms of war after nuclear weapons had been used in World War II."

> **Unacceptable Contextualization:** "Because so many women continued in the workforce as full time workers after the First World War, Lougnan should be seen as defending their new jobs." (Women did not remain in the workforce in large numbers until after WORLD WAR II, so the context here is incorrect.)

C. EVIDENCE (0–3 total points)

1 point: The essay MUST utilize the content of at least **THREE** documents to address the topic of the question. <u>Note</u> that this analysis may be in the topic sentence; the analysis must be connected to the argument.

OR

2 points: The essay must utilize the content of at least SIX documents to support an argument about the question. <u>Note</u> that this analysis may be in the topic sentence; the analysis must be connected to the argument.

AND

EVIDENCE BEYOND THE DOCUMENTS (0–1 total points)

The essay explains how at least one additional piece of specific evidence beyond those found in the documents relates to an argument about the question.

Note: This evidence must be DIFFERENT from the evidence used to earn the point for contextualization. This point is NOT awarded for a phrase or reference.

Acceptable Outside Historical Evidence:

- "The Scandinavian model of a strong social welfare system combined with high taxation and cooperation while allowing free markets between the wars left them more ready for the total war market reforms than other nations."

- "While total war allowed the European nations to meet the challenges of world wars, the economic boom of Western Europe during the 1950s and 1960s illustrates how free markets generate better standards of living."

Unacceptable Outside Historical Evidence: "Total war was supported by governments." (Unacceptable because the evidence is pretty clear from the document and no true outside evidence was presented.)

D. ANALYSIS & REASONING (0–2 total points)

1 point: For at least THREE documents, the essay explains how each document's point of view, purpose, historical situation, and/or audience is relevant to the argument.

2 points: Demonstrates a complex understanding of the historical development that is the focus of the prompt, using evidence to corroborate, qualify, or modify an argument that addresses the question.

Guidance on awarding this point is below.

1 point: For at least FOUR documents, explains how each document's point of view, purpose, historical situation, and/or audience is relevant to the argument

Example of acceptable analysis: "Joseph Stalin, the General Secretary of the Soviet Union, just as the Soviets are starting to push the Germans out after brutal sieges was urging his people to engage in total war in order to ensure victory and uses propaganda to motivate them." (This correctly places Stalin in place, time, and importance, and specifically explains point of view and purpose as well as giving some context.)

Example of unacceptable analysis: "United Nations Charter seems to be supporting total war." (This is incorrect because the charter explains that its goal is to prevent war.)

Intended Audience

Acceptable: "Churchill is very specific with the minister of food to whom he is writing because he wants his intentions to be followed." (This is clear that the letter was written to the minister of food, and even connects tone to audience.)

Unacceptable: "Loughnan was writing for anyone who cared about World War I women." (This is far too vague; specify which people in which place at which time.)

Purpose

Acceptable: "The Soviet propaganda poster was created and posted to encourage people on the home front to support the soldiers by working harder."

Unacceptable: "Winston Churchill is writing to show how he believed that the government should control every decision." (This is a misinterpretation as Churchill seems to be trying to limit the reach of the minister of food by asking to give farmers more control.)

Historical Context

Acceptable: "The Soviets were just beginning to push the Germans back from the sieges of their major cities."

Unacceptable: "Because the First World War was over, Aristide was making the Germans out to be evil to get France more in the peace treaty." (This is wrong because the First World War was in full force when Aristide wrote this.)

Author's Point of View

Acceptable: "The Soviet leader, Stalin, wanted to uplift his people and praise them for what they had done, but encourage them to keep working to defeat Germany completely."

Unacceptable: Because he was the king of England, Winston Churchill's statements should be considered as coming from the upper classes." (This is wrong because Churchill was prime minister rather than king, although he certainly was upper class as the Duke of Marlborough.)

Special Note: This evidence must be DIFFERENT from the evidence used to earn the point for contextualization. This point is NOT awarded for a phrase or reference.

Document Summaries: Each document's key points will be listed along with some information on how it may relate to concepts and themes or processes relevant to the document and the course.

Document 1

Key Points

- Pro Total War.
- Propagandistic.
- Anti-German but anti-nationalistic.
- From a socialist leader.
- Calls for support of the war from all fronts.

- Believes Allies will win war.
- Predicts Russian Revolution.
- States proletariat won in France and bourgeoisie lost.
- Asks scientists and artists.

Contextualization

- The First World War has just begun.
- Allies are Russia, France, Belgium, Serbia, and the United Kingdom.
- First time Total War was employed in full.
- Still very hopeful in tone, so definitely belongs to pre-war intellectual period.

Document 2

Key Points

- Against Total War.
- Complains of German abuses of French and Belgian citizens being used for Total War effort.
- Shows brutality of enemy in Germans.
- Official report so needs to be evaluated for validity because of diplomatic effect and propaganda.
- Illustrates German use of Total War during the First World War and its efficiency.

Contextualization

- Germany was starting to be outproduced by Allies.
- Both sides were dug in for trench warfare on the Western Front.
- First World War became a war of attrition.
- French and German enmity going back centuries and more recently to the Franco-Prussian War.

Document 3

Key Points

- Pro Total War.
- Indicates value and pride of female workers.
- Demonstrates efforts at total war on the home front.
- Written by a woman in favor of women working.
- Illustrates understanding of the loss felt by all who know/knew soldiers.
- Middle-class perspective supplied.

Contextualization

- Written in last year of war.
- Most of Europe won women's suffrage after the First World War.
- Displays very early inklings of modern feminism and links to later rights to work at all jobs for equal pay.

Document 4

Key Points

- Supports Total War, but wants some reasonable exceptions.
- Indicates frustration at the lack of available food for his nation.
- Alludes to rationing of food used by all nations during total war.
- Illustrates alliance with the United States in trade before the United States joined the war.
- Examines the best way to distribute and grow food.
- Common man depicted.
- Trade Unions legal and powerful across Europe in 1896.

Contextualization

- Churchill was prime minister of the United Kingdom at the time.
- He was a descendant of the Duke of Marlborough, and dedicated his life to serving his country regardless of his wealth.
- The United Kingdom was the last major power in Europe not to either fall to or make a nonaggression agreement with the Nazis who seemed to be winning the Second World War.
- Most nations involved in the war were attempting some form of Total War.
- The war lasted much longer than anyone believed it would before it started.

Document 5

Key Points

- Pro Total War.
- Soviet propaganda poster indicating that working in a factory helps the military win the war.
- Meant to encourage workers to work their hardest; even if they are not soldiers, they are still helping win the war.
- Propagandistic, and displays Soviet airplanes and factory as images of power and modernity.
- Has Lenin and Stalin together on the flag.
- Just one of tens of thousands of pieces of Soviet propaganda used on its people.

Contextualization

- Stalin and Hitler created a nonaggression pact in 1939, at the start of Second World War fighting in Europe, despite each hating the other's ideas and personality, but Germany invaded the USSR in 1941 and was not driven out until 1944.
- The Soviets were trying to catch up to the Germans industrially.
- Communism was trying to show the world that it would not be defeated by fascism.
- The Second World War was going on with a "Total War" effort in all countries, requiring rationing, price controls, and government institutions, comparable to the German War Raw Materials Board and the British Ministry of Munitions during the First World War.

- Communism used the tactics of Total War as far as government management of the economy went, so those countries that became the Warsaw Pact were more prepared for life under such conditions than they would have been without needing world wars and Total War to be employed.

Document 6

Key Points

- Pro Total War.
- Soviet propaganda, telling his people what needs to be done to defeat the Germans and why.
- Meant to encourage workers to work their hardest; even if they were not soldiers, they are still helping win the war.
- Stalin uses ideology, morality, fear, and praise together.
- Mentions heroines and also German abuse of women.

Contextualization

- The Second World War was going on with a Total War effort on in all countries, requiring rationing, price controls, and government control of all aspects of society.
- The Germans invaded the Soviet Union, violating their nonaggression pact, and the Soviets were just starting to break free of a German siege.
- The Soviets were trying to catch up to the Germans industrially.
- Communism was trying to show the world that it would not be defeated by Fascism.
- Communism used the tactics of Total War as far as government management of the economy went, so those countries that became the Warsaw Pact were more prepared for life under such conditions than they would have been without needing world wars and Total War to be employed.

Document 7

Key Points

- Against Total War and all war if possible.
- Created after the Second World War and very hopeful in tone, as it created the United Nations.
- Preserves human rights and Enlightenment ideals of justice and tolerance.
- Wants to improve the economic and social lives of ALL people.
- All nations were to become members.
- Tries to solve problems without war, but can declare international "police actions" by limited military force.
- Includes World Health Organization and UNESCO.
- Shows concern for any state that has grown too powerful and is too involved with the lives of its citizens.

Contextualization

- The League of Nations had failed to prevent the Second World War, and it needed to be replaced and strengthened.

- The Cold War was emerging, a contest between two superpowers armed with many nuclear weapons.
- The world economy needed to be rebuilt after years of warfare tore it apart.
- World war had devastated the world and most people did not want another war that many feared could eliminate humanity.

Scoring Guidelines for Long-Essay Question 2

Question 2

Analyze the ways in which the opening of Atlantic trade led to or resulted from a shift in social, economic, and political power from the Mediterranean Basin to Western Europe.

Maximum possible points: 6

COMMENTS ON QUESTION 2

This one is a CAUSATION question because it requires you to explain how one event, the opening of transatlantic trade, resulted in or CAUSED a specific outcome, the shift in social, political, and economic power from the Mediterranean Basin to Western Europe. Remember to describe causes of the shifts, indicating which shift was caused by each factor cited as a result of the Columbian Exchange, and to explain the reasons for the causes and effects of those shifts with specific facts.

Your essay should explain how and why exploration and colonization in the fifteenth and sixteenth centuries enabled the countries that bordered the Atlantic Ocean to achieve economic, social, political, and military dominance in Europe. For centuries, Italy dominated European trade with the Far East due to its strategic location on the Mediterranean. New trade routes with Asia established by Portuguese explorers and the discovery of the New World by Spanish and other explorers whose nations had Atlantic access offered new routes and new products. Explain how the Columbian Exchange gave Spain, and eventually England and the Netherlands, huge economic power. The importance of Northern European advances in naval technology and knowledge as factors in shifting power further north can also be examined.

A detailed rubric for this specific question follows to help you score your long-essay response.

A. THESIS (0–1 total points)

1 point: The essay presents a thesis that makes a historically defensible claim and responds to all parts of the question. The thesis must consist of one or more sentences located in one place, either in the introduction or the conclusion.

Special Note: The thesis MUST consist of one or more sentences located in the introduction or the conclusion of the essay. However, neither the introduction nor the conclusion is strictly limited to one paragraph.

Acceptable thesis statements create an argument that responds to the task: describing the causes <u>and/or</u> explaining effects of the opening of transatlantic trade on the shift in political, social, and economic power from the Mediterranean Basin (Italy), to Western Europe AND explaining specific examples that illustrate those causes and effects.

You must present a thesis that directly addresses all parts of the question. The thesis must do more than restate the question.

Acceptable Thesis: "When Western Europeans began to open transatlantic trade, vast wealth and resources poured into that region, and created the best opportunities to improve one's station in life that Europeans had had in centuries, drawing the best and brightest to Western Europe and shifting the social, political, and economic power center from Italy to first Spain, then to the rest of Western Europe." (This thesis is acceptable because it is specific in its assessment of the impact of the opening of trade across the Atlantic and provides specific reasons for the shifts in economic and political power.)

Unacceptable Theses:

- "The beginning of the Columbian Exchange had many effects on Europe and shifted political, economic, and social power from the Mediterranean Basin to Western Europe." (This is unacceptable because it does not state any specific ways that the opening of transatlantic trade caused those shifts.)
- "The opening of transatlantic trade made those in Western Europe rich and opened opportunities for trade, shifting the center of Europe's trade economy from Italy to Western Europe." (This is unacceptable because even though it explains causes for economic change, there is no cause for political or social change stated.)

B. CONTEXTUALIZATION (0–1 total points)

1 point: The essay describes a broader historical context immediately relevant to the question.

C. EVIDENCE (0–2 total points)

Develops and supports an argument that:

1 point: Provides specific examples of evidence related to how the opening of Atlantic Trade affected Mediterranean trade.

OR

2 points: Adequately supports an argument about how the opening of Atlantic Trade affected the Mediterranean basin.

D. ANALYSIS & REASONING (0–3 total points)

1 point: Uses historical reasoning (e.g., comparison, causation, CCOT) to frame or structure an argument that addresses the prompt.

OR

2 points: Demonstrates a complex understanding of the historical development that is the focus of the prompt, using evidence to corroborate, qualify, or modify an argument that addresses the question.

Special Note: Responses can only receive the second point if they also meet the criteria for the first contextualization point.

Scoring Guidelines for Long-Essay Question 3

Analyze the ways in which the public health movement and urban planning led to or resulted from a shift in social, political, and economic power at the end of the nineteenth century.

Maximum possible points: 6

COMMENTS ON QUESTION 3

This one is a CAUSATION question because it requires you to explain how two events, the start of urban planning and the public health movement, resulted in or CAUSED a specific outcome, the shift in social, political, and economic power at the end of the nineteenth century. Remember to describe causes of the shifts, indicating which was caused by each factor cited as a result of urban planning and the public health movement, and to support your explanation of the reasons for the causes and effects of those shifts with specific supporting evidence.

Your essay must first explain that the first half of the century had resulted in overcrowded cities full of people who for the most part lacked any political power. The conditions that led Marx and Engels to conceive of communism were rampant, with the workers oppressed and their conditions deplorable. From there you should explain how the implementation of public health laws and urban planning reduced overcrowding and unsanitary conditions, but also helped the working classes develop a class consciousness as they lived and commuted together, leading them to gain political power through the rise of republican forms of government, constitutional monarchies, and labor unions as a result of the urban planning and public health movements that made increased urbanization not only possible but desirable.

A detailed rubric for this specific question follows to help you score your long-essay response.

A. THESIS (0–1 total points)

1 point: The essay presents a thesis that makes a historically defensible claim and responds to all parts of the question. The thesis must consist of one or more sentences located in one place, either in the introduction or the conclusion.

Special Note: The thesis MUST consist of one or more sentences located in the introduction or the conclusion of the essay. However, neither the introduction nor conclusion is strictly limited to one paragraph.

Acceptable thesis statements create an argument that responds to the task: describing the causes and/or explaining effects of the implementation of urban planning and the public health movement on the shift in political, social, and economic power during the second half of the nineteenth century AND explaining specific examples that illustrate reasons for those causes and effects.

Student presents a thesis that directly addresses all parts of the question. The thesis must do more than restate the question.

> **Acceptable Thesis:** "While most urban workers lived in filth and despair in 1850 Europe, the rise of the public health movement and the beginning of urban planning in Europe eventually resulted in increased sanitation and convenience of city life, a growing understanding of the plight of Europe's poor among other classes, as well as time spent in con-

versation during commutes on newly created public transportation led to drastic changes in the social, political, and economic power structure of Europe by the end of the century including moderate constitutional monarchies in Germany and Italy, a republic or two in France, a generally growing standard of living, and a growing social welfare system across the continent." (This thesis is acceptable because it is specific in its assessment of both causes, and it gives specific effects of the causes supported by specific evidence.)

Unacceptable Theses:

- "The implementation of urban planning and public health movements resulted in many changes in the social, political, and economic structure of Europe by the end of the nineteenth century." (This is unacceptable because it does not state any specific social, political, or economic impacts.)
- "The implementation of public health laws and urban planning improved the lives of city dwellers in Europe by the end of the nineteenth century by giving them more sanitary lives, greater freedom of travel, and better incomes." (This is unacceptable because even though it gives specific social and possibly economic impacts, the political impacts are forgotten.)

B. CONTEXTUALIZATION (0–1 total points)

1 point: The essay describes a broader historical context immediately relevant to the question.

C. EVIDENCE (0–2 total points)

Develops and supports an argument that:

1 point: The essay provides specific examples of evidence related to the topic of the question.

OR

2 points: The essay adequately supports an argument about the question with specific and relevant evidence.

D. ANALYSIS & REASONING (0–3 total points)

1 point: Uses historical reasoning (e.g., comparison, causation, CCOT) to frame or structure an argument that addresses the prompt.

OR

2 points: Demonstrates a complex understanding of the historical development that is the focus of the prompt, using evidence to corroborate, qualify, or modify an argument that addresses the question.

Acceptable Causation:

- The essay explains how the public health movement led to more sanitary cities that drew more people to them.
- The essay explains how urban planning led to public transportation to relieve crowding, which then supported political movements and unionization as workers traveled together outside of work.
- The essay explains how better organized workers organized to gain political and economic power such as higher wages and voting rights.

Unacceptable Causation:

- The essay is focused either solely on the public health movement or urban planning, but not both.
- The essay is focused on a narrative and does not provide causation.
- The essay looks at causation of the changes to the social, political, and economic power structure of Europe during the second half of the nineteenth century, but fails to account for them and/or provide detailed evidence for support.

Essays can earn the point(s) here without a stated thesis if a relevant argument that completes both tasks effectively emerges in the body of the essay; for example, if an essay is able to develop an argument that draws on the changes in the social, political, and economic power of Europeans, such as: growth of democratic power, rise of constitutions, national unifications, rising standards of living, rising public education, healthier cities with low mortality rates, rising wages, etc., and tie them to how they were caused by the implementation of urban planning and public health laws.

Acceptable Arguments: The essay links the changes in social, political, and economic power in Europe at the end of the nineteenth century to the implementation of urban planning and public health laws, citing specific facts to support those arguments. The essay should tie these specific facts such as those stated above to the implementation of urban planning and public health laws.

Unacceptable Arguments:

- The essay is focused either solely on the urban planning or public health laws, but not on both.
- The essay examines the events of the end of the nineteenth century, but does not specifically cite causation of evidence.

Scoring Guidelines for Long-Essay Question 4

Analyze the causes of the changing roles and rights of European women from 1900–2000.

Maximum possible points: 6

COMMENTS ON QUESTION 4

This one is a CAUSATION question because it requires you to explain how changing gender perceptions, industrialization, the increase in individual rights, the world wars, and other factors, resulted in or CAUSED a specific outcome, the increased rights of women and a change in their roles in the family, the work world, the economy, and politics. Remember to describe causes of the shifts, indicating which was caused by each factor, and to support your explanation of the reasons for the causes and effects of those shifts with specific supporting evidence.

The essay must first explain that women, who for the most part lacked any political and economic power at the start of the twentieth century, gained power and individual rights. The causes of the increase in rights and the bending of gender roles must be examined. From there you should explain how those women of the nineteenth century who were just starting to advocate for their rights and changing roles as suffragettes, later became feminists who advocated for rights and responsibilities equal to those of men; account for how and why society and governments granted them those rights. The impact of industrialization, the rise of communism, the efforts of women, the increase in individual rights in general, the world wars and women's role in them, the reduction of religiosity, the economic realities of the twentieth century and global geopolitics—these all helped women gain rights and equality. The strongest essays will also point out that women have not yet achieved full equality in the realms of pay and household responsibility in much of Europe today.

A detailed rubric for this specific question follows to help you score your long-essay response.

A. THESIS (0–1 total points)

1 point: The essay presents a thesis that makes a historically defensible claim and responds to all parts of the question. The thesis must consist of one or more sentences located in one place, either in the introduction or the conclusion.

Special Note: The thesis MUST consist of one or more sentences located in the introduction or the conclusion of the essay. However, neither the introduction nor conclusion is strictly limited to one paragraph.

Acceptable thesis statements create an argument that responds to the task: describing the causes and/or explaining effects of changing gender roles and increased equality and rights for European women AND explaining specific examples that illustrate reasons for those causes and effects.

You must present a thesis that directly addresses all parts of the question. The thesis must do more than restate the question.

> **Acceptable Thesis:** "During the twentieth century women in Europe gained significant rights and were welcomed into spheres of influence that had eluded them for centuries such as the armed forces, the working world, politics, and business drastically changing how females functioned in society, politics, and the economy, in large part due to the impact of industrialization, the rise of Communism, the increase in individual rights in general, the world wars and women's role in them, the efforts of women, the reduction of religiosity, the economic realities of the twentieth century, and global geopolitics, which all helped women gain rights and equality." (This thesis is acceptable because it is specific in its assessment of both causes, and it gives specific effects of the causes supported by specific evidence.)

> **Unacceptable Thesis:** "Women gained more rights and changed their gender roles during the twentieth century because people became more open-minded." (This is unacceptable because it does not state any specific social, political, or economic causes of that change.)

B. CONTEXTUALIZATION (0–1 total points)

1 point: The essay describes a broader historical context immediately relevant to the question.

C. EVIDENCE (0–2 total points)

Develops and supports an argument that:

1 point: The essay provides specific examples of evidence related to the topic of the question.

OR

2 points: The essay adequately supports an argument about the question with specific and relevant evidence.

D. ANALYSIS & REASONING (0–3 total points)

1 point: Uses historical reasoning (e.g., comparison, causation, CCOT) to frame or structure an argument that addresses the prompt.

OR

2 points: Demonstrates a complex understanding of the historical development that is the focus of the prompt, using evidence to corroborate, qualify, or modify an argument that addresses the question.

Acceptable Causation:

- The essay explains how the First and Second World Wars required women to enter professions previously exclusive to men due to total war efforts on both sides.
- The essay explains how industrialization meant that most workers no longer needed brute strength, which left women on an equal basis with men in most professions.
- The essay explains how women organized themselves and their male allies to attain greater opportunities and voting rights.

Unacceptable Causation:

- The essay is focused either solely on the public women's rights or women's roles, but not on both.
- The essay is focused on a narrative and does not provide causation.
- The essay looks at causation of the changes to the social, political, and economic power structure of Europe during the twentieth century, but fails to account for them and/or to provide detailed evidence for support.

Acceptable Arguments: The essay links the changes in social, political, and economic rights and power of women in Europe during the twentieth century to the impact of industrialization, the rise of communism, the increase in individual rights in general, the world wars and women's role in them, the efforts of women, the reduction of religiosity, the economic realities of the twentieth century, and/or global geopolitics

Unacceptable Arguments:

- The essay is focused either solely on the women's rights or women's roles, but not both.
- The essay examines the events during the twentieth century, but does not specifically cite causation of evidence.

This is the end of the scoring section. Once you have scored your answers, go back to the section on scoring the exam and plug your scores into the chart and compute to get your score on your practice exam.

Index

BARRON'S

AP*

EUROPEAN HISTORY

9TH EDITION

Seth A. Roberts
AP and IB European History Teacher
Fredrick County Public Schools
Director of Teaching and Learning
International Bilingual School of Hsinchu

BARRON'S

DEDICATION

To those from whom I have learned the most, my students, my colleagues, my children, and my wife, Michelle.

—Seth A. Roberts

ONLINE

Want more test-taking practice?

Visit *barronsbooks.com/AP/ap-european-hist/* to access three additional practice tests or scan the QR code below.

*Be sure to have your copy of *AP European History*, 9th edition on hand to complete the registration process.

All inquiries should be addressed to:
Barron's Educational Series, Inc.
250 Wireless Boulevard
Hauppauge, NY 11788
www.barronseduc.com

ISBN: 978-1-4380-1067-0

ISSN: 2164-4519

PRINTED IN THE UNITED STATES OF AMERICA
9 8 7 6 5 4 3

10%
POST-CONSUMER WASTE
Paper contains a minimum of 10% post-consumer waste (PCW). Paper used in this book was derived from certified, sustainable forestlands.